RED BULL

A History of the 34th Infantry Division
in World War II

Volume I: From Mobilization to Victory in Tunisia

ROBERT NOEL STOKES, JR

CASEMATE
Oxford & Philadelphia

Published in Great Britain and the United States of America in 2022 by
CASEMATE PUBLISHERS
The Old Music Hall, 106–108 Cowley Road, Oxford OX4 1JE, UK
and
1950 Lawrence Road, Havertown, PA 19083, USA

Hardback Edition: ISBN 978-1-63624-046-6
Digital Edition: ISBN 978-1-63624-047-3

A CIP record for this book is available from the British Library

Printed and bound in the United Kingdom by TJ Books

Typeset in India by Lapiz Digital Services, Chennai.

For a complete list of Casemate titles, please contact:

CASEMATE PUBLISHERS (US)
Telephone (610) 853-9131
Fax (610) 853-9146
Email: casemate@casematepublishers.com
www.casematepublishers.com

CASEMATE PUBLISHERS (UK)
Telephone (01865) 241249
Email: casemate-uk@casematepublishers.co.uk
www.casematepublishers.co.uk

To my wife, Renée Meyer, with all my love forever.

Contents

PART IV: "SOME FLAMING, FATAL CLIMAX":
THE FINAL BATTLES IN TUNISIA

Preface

My father, Robert Noel Stokes, Sr., was for a time in late 1943 and early 1944 a platoon leader in Company C, and then commander of Company A, 1st Battalion, 135th Infantry Regiment, 34th ("Red Bull") Infantry Division, then fighting in the Italian mountains near Monte Cassino. It is a sad thing, which my siblings and I share with other children of veterans of World War II, that though I lived with my father for more than 22 years before his death in 1972, I did not learn from him very much of substance about his experience of war. That failure is a product in part of what we have since come to recognize as one of the harmful long-term psychological effects of the prolonged exposure of a person to the stresses and terrors of combat. Veterans often do not, or cannot, talk to others about their experiences, perhaps because there are no common terms of reference with which to articulate those experiences. Trained counselors and face-to-face mental health supports are needed. These facts are not yet fully impressed into the national consciousness. We have sent men and women back into the fights in Afghanistan and Iraq for multiple combat tours, and still seem not to make the connection with the consequences: frightening flashbacks; depression; irritability; aggressive, even violent behavior; substance abuse; and suicide.

Robert was somewhat older and better educated than most of the draftees who became private soldiers, because he was 26 years old and had attended the University of Indiana for a year. Nonetheless, he was fairly typical of the young men who were conscripted into the U.S. Army's expansion in 1940 and thereafter. He graduated from Broad Ripple High School in Indianapolis in 1934 as the Depression began to plumb its depths. Like most young men in America in those lean years, Robert struggled to find and keep a job. After living and working for a time in Chicago, he went to work for his maternal uncle, my great-uncle Noel Lee, near Richmond, Virginia. He was drafted in Chesterfield County, Virginia. Robert was inducted into the Army of the United States as a private on May 5, 1941, and assigned to the National Guard 29th ("Blue and Gray") Infantry Division, which consisted of regiments from Maryland and Virginia. The 29th Division trained at Fort A. P. Hill in Virginia and at Fort George G. Meade in Maryland. My father briefly recalled to me stories about training marches ("20-mile hikes") and bivouacs ("camps in farmers' fields") up and down U.S. Route 301, crossing the Potomac River between the two posts.

Private Stokes was assigned to Company A, 116th Infantry Regiment, 29ID, a unit which would achieve immortality: the 116th was in the first wave of troops to come ashore in front of the Vierville draw on Omaha Beach on June 6, 1944, where it suffered catastrophic casualties. Thirty-five soldiers of Company A, out of about 193, came from the small town of Bedford, Virginia. Nineteen of those 35 men are buried in the American cemetery above the bluffs at Vierville, Normandy. But my father's path through the War Department's Army Ground Forces training and unit assignment bureaucracy would lead him, with many tens of thousands of other soldiers, away from his first assignment to further training and assignment to other divisions in process of formation, before he joined the 34th Infantry Division in Oran after the North African campaign had concluded.

Private Stokes completed basic and some advanced infantry training while he was assigned to the 116th Infantry Regiment. Probably because he had been an Indiana All-State running back, he was the Browning Automatic Rifle (BAR) man in his rifle squad. He was promoted to the rank of corporal, making him the junior leader in his squad. He described his fellow inductees as "skinny young guys," who after 18 months of training and Army chow were transformed into "a bunch of gorillas." In the summer of 1942, the Army selected him and hundreds of other soldiers who had high school diplomas or more advanced education, or who had demonstrated leadership qualities, for Infantry Officers Candidate School. The other officer candidates in his class were at roughly the same point in the training cycle when they were selected; they had had the benefit of a full year or more of infantry training. The significance of that year, or rather of the 34th Infantry Division's lack of that year of military training, will become clear from this history.

Corporal Stokes was assigned to Officer Candidate School (OCS) at Fort Benning, Georgia on July 6, 1942, arriving July 11 when he was assigned to the 27th Company, 2nd Student Training Battalion. He told me that his first days at Benning were spent with axes, rifles, and flamethrowers, cleaning the rattlesnakes and overgrowth out of the trenches and bunkers of the World War I-era training areas and obstacle courses. Upon completion of the OCS course, there followed a typical War Department bureaucratic step: Corporal Stokes was honorably discharged for the convenience of the government on October 5, 1942. He was then commissioned as a second lieutenant in the Army of the United States on October 6, 1942, and given a new serial number.

The newly minted Second Lieutenant Stokes was assigned not back to the 29th Division, which was by then training in the United Kingdom, but as a platoon leader in Company I, 3rd Battalion, 395th Infantry Regiment, 99th Infantry Division at Camp van Dorn, Mississippi. Second Lieutenant Stokes was now one of the cadre of officers who were to stand up and train the brand new 99th ("Checkmate") Infantry Division upon its organization on November 16, 1942. 99ID would go on to Europe, become part of Lieutenant General Courtney Hodges's U.S. First

Army and play a stalwart role in defeating the German winter offensive famous as the Battle of the Bulge, before marching into Germany.

But not my father. Second Lieutenant Stokes and many thousands of other officer and enlisted replacements were reassigned to the now veteran combat units in North Africa in the late spring of 1943. He departed the continental United States on April 29, 1943, while the Battle of Hill 609 was still raging, and arrived at Oran in Algiers on May 10, 1943, several days before the surrender of all Axis forces in Africa to the Allies. He would return to the United States in June 1945. After a 30-day training course at the Fifth Army Leadership and Battle Training Center near Slissen, Algeria, he joined the 34th Infantry Division on August 1, 1943, as a platoon leader in Company C, 1st Battalion, 135IR, while 34ID and United States Fifth Army were preparing for the invasion of Italy.

While with the 99th Infantry Division in Mississippi, my father met Army Medical Corps Captain Elva Catherine George, of Leeds, Alabama. Elva was a nurse whom he would marry in 1945 and who became my mother. Captain Elva George, with her sister Captain Mary George, served with the U.S. Army's 8th General Hospital on New Caledonia and other bases in the South and Southwest Pacific Theaters.

A volume to follow this one will describe the 34th Infantry Division's battles in Italy. Had Second Lieutenant Stokes remained with the 116th Infantry, it is possible that I would not have been around to write this book. But Italy was no less dangerous than France or Germany. The average useful life expectancy of a platoon leader in Italy was about 40 days. The average for a company commander was not much more. Second Lieutenant Stokes was wounded in action in Italy on May 25, 1944. He was awarded the Purple Heart and his first Bronze Star for valor. During his time with the 34th Infantry Division, he was several times hospitalized with dysentery, pneumonia and, perhaps most seriously, what was then called combat related anxiety disorder.

After the end of World War II, and after he married Elva in Alabama on November 2, 1945, First Lieutenant Stokes chose to make the Army a career. He and my mother, who remained in the service until she became pregnant with me in 1949, were assigned to the American military assistance group in devastated South Korea from 1946 to 1948. Robert was then transferred to what was then the U.S. Second Army Headquarters at Fort George G. Meade, Maryland in 1948. He and Elva set about establishing a family in Laurel, Maryland. He was promoted to captain on March 1, 1949, just before his 34th birthday on March 11. My siblings and I were all born in the post hospital at Fort Meade. My father met me on the day of my birth thanks to a grant of emergency leave from an Information School course at the War College at Carlisle Barracks,[i] Pennsylvania.

---

i   Carlisle Barracks is a United States Army facility located in Carlisle, Pennsylvania. It is now operated by the United States Army Training and Doctrine Command (TRADOC) and is the site of the U.S. Army War College. It is the nation's second-oldest active military base.

In no small part because he had already served in Korea, Captain Stokes was assigned to the 25th ("Tropic Lightning") Infantry Division in Korea during 1951–2, chiefly performing internal security and civil administration duties. He was awarded his second Bronze Star with oak leaf cluster for valor in combat in Korea. He was reassigned to 2nd Army Headquarters in 1952. After assignments in the Panama Canal Zone and at Fifth Army Headquarters in Chicago in the late 1950s, he retired in 1961 with the rank of major, U.S. Army Reserve. Major Stokes died in February 1972 and was buried with full military honors in Arlington National Cemetery. My mother did not remarry and died 23 years later in July 2005. Elva received full military honors in her own right and was interred with my father at Arlington.

It has been only long after his death and even longer after the battle experiences of the men of the 34th Infantry Division that I realized that my father certainly, and many of his fellow Red Bull soldiers most probably, came home as unresolved cases of what we now call post-traumatic stress disorder. I do not say "untreated," because the U.S. Army medical system during World War II was acutely aware of the neuro-psychiatric trauma inflicted by exposure to combat and developed what were for the time advanced methods for diagnosing and treating the resulting disorders. My father's nightmares caught up with him in 1960, when he suffered what was then called a "nervous breakdown" while the family was living near Chicago. He was treated as an inpatient in the psychiatric ward at Great Lakes Naval Hospital. His premature death in 1972 was ruled to be service connected by the then Veterans' Administration.

My siblings and I believe that our father was never entirely free of the terror and shocking violence of "death's grey land"[ii] through which all the fighting men of the Red Bull had to pass during the Division's more than 500 days in combat. The 34th Infantry Division's story deserves to be told fully to honor him and the thousands of his fellow soldiers who fought through to victory for their fellow citizen soldiers, their homes and their families who loved them, and for civilization.

---

ii Siegfried Sassoon. "Dreamers", from *Counter-Attack and Other Poems*, E. P. Dutton & Company, New York (1918).

Acknowledgments

Great authors and scholars, far better writers than I, have written many excellent works on the North African and Italian campaigns, including the works of the leading military and political participants. I am entirely in their collective debt and have cited many of those books in the notes and listed them in the bibliography. The Rt. Hon. Sir Winston S. Churchill's majestic memoir *The Second World War* is a rich source of material on the strategic arguments and decisions, for better or worse, which led to the 34th Division's shipment in increments to Northern Ireland in early 1942 and to its later participation in Operation *Torch* and the Italian campaign. The first two books of Rick Atkinson's "Liberation Trilogy," *An Army at Dawn* and *The Day of Battle*, are works of compassionate insight, splendid narrative, and unmatched scholarship. They greatly assisted me in my own research, and I have quoted and cited widely from Atkinson's work. Numerous other works of history and original sources that I have read or consulted are listed in the Bibliography.

I am particularly indebted to the late Paul Fussell, Ph.D., and his bitingly discerning work *Wartime: Understanding and Behavior in the Second World War*. Fussell was a lieutenant leading a rifle platoon of the 103rd ("Cactus") Infantry Division in France and Germany. He was severely wounded in the spring of 1945. His military experiences provided the impetus for his war volumes, which reveal how commonly held romantic and euphemistic notions of war and heroism were actually methods of psychological self-defense from the unacceptable conditions of war. Fussell's teaching is that the self-delusions of individual civilians and soldiers, and the tendentious, even mendacious content of official and press statements and publications, have little relation to and cannot fully mask or dispel the actualities of the mind-numbing regimentation of Army life, the suffocation of all basic human desires, and the horrifically violent realities of combat. Our attempts to euphemize or hide the appalling gruesomeness of war are injurious to civilized culture, cheapening, and degrading every aspect of life and denigrating the experience of the combat soldier.

I have relied heavily on the Army's monumental official history, entitled *The United States Army in World War II*, the many volumes of which are often referred to as the "Green Books." The Green Books were republished by the United States Army Center for Military History beginning in the early 1990s as part of the

50th anniversary commemoration of World War II. For the purposes of this book and its future companion volume, I have chiefly used the works under the title *Mediterranean Theater of Operations*, which includes the following books of relevance to the history of the 34th Infantry Division:

Northwest Africa: Regaining the Initiative in the West by George F. Howe
Salerno to Cassino by Martin Blumenson
Cassino to the Alps by Ernest F. Fisher

"The United States Army in World War II Series" is available to the public online in both HTML and downloadable PDF. A Reader's Guide and introduction may be found at https://history.army.mil/html/bookshelves/collect/usaww2.html.

The 34th Infantry Division Association maintains a robust website that contains important original documents about the history of the division in World War II. I have used or cited some of those documents throughout this book. I have also sought out and used primary source records and materials and important historical works from the Library of Congress; the Eisenhower Presidential Library, Abilene, Kansas; the National Archives and Records Administration, College Park, Maryland; the United States Army Center for Military History; the United States Army Military History Institute, Carlisle Barracks, Pennsylvania; the Combined Arms Research Library at the U.S. Army Command and General Staff College, Fort Leavenworth, Kansas; the Donovan Research Library at Fort Benning, Georgia; the McKeldin Graduate Library at the University of Maryland, College Park; the Enoch Pratt Free Library, Baltimore, Maryland; the Iowa Gold Star Military Museum; and other libraries and institutions. I want to express my special thanks to Ms. Valoise Armstrong, an archivist at the Eisenhower Presidential Library, for her generous professional assistance and guidance.

The Charles W. Ryder Papers collection and the World War II Unit Information collections in the Eisenhower Presidential Library are rich troves of original documents about the 34th Infantry Division. I have referred to some of those documents in this volume, including orders, G-2 Intelligence and G-3 Operations reports, secret communications, and personal accounts. I have included in the appendix of documents the full text of Colonel Drake's account of the valorous three-day stand of the 168th Infantry Regiment at Djebel Ksaïra and Djebel Garet Hadid. Drake's account has been cited and published elsewhere, but I felt that a comprehensive history of the Division would be incomplete without it.

The Iowa Gold Star Military Museum and the 34th Infantry Division Association websites both contain important materials about 34ID and its component units. These are collections and compilations of contemporaneous and after-action reports including partial regimental histories of the 135th, 133rd and 168th Infantry Regiments, and the artillery battalions supporting each regiment, prepared by officers and enlisted clerks of those regiments during and immediately after their deployments with 34ID during World War II.

I have studied records and papers written by officers and enlisted men describing the battle experiences of the 34th Infantry Division infantry regiments and works about the field artillery battalions and other specialized units that fought with and supported 34ID. These materials include monographs written by men in advanced courses of the Infantry Training School at Fort Benning, Georgia, after their service with the 34ID in Africa and Italy. Those monographs offer rare and unique first-person perspectives on the fights in which 34ID units were engaged.

I owe an immense debt of gratitude and love to my wife Renée Meyer, most of all for her loving patience and encouragement, but also for her assistance in my research, and for untold hours of careful reading and editing of, and many brilliant comments on, the text.

I am completely and entirely responsible for the text. Any errors of fact or omission, and all commentary on the subject matter, are my sole responsibility. I beg pardon in advance of anyone whom I may inadvertently offend.

Introduction

In the campaigns in North Africa and in Italy during World War II, the soldiers of the 34th "Red Bull" Infantry Division endured the stresses and terrors of combat to an extreme. The Division was one of the last National Guard divisions called to the colors. As the reader will see, its early training was incomplete, haphazard, and deficient. It was still only partially trained and equipped when, for reasons that remain obscure to this day, it was chosen to be the first American combat division to be deployed to Europe and sent to Northern Ireland over a period of several months through mid-1942. In late October 1942 units of the Red Bull boarded transport ships and sailed directly into battle in North Africa. They landed near Algiers on November 8, 1942, not as an entire division but separately or as attachments to other units. From their brutal baptisms of fire and early defeats in late 1942 and early 1943—through horribly difficult fights against weather, terrain, and a skilled and remorseless enemy—to their victories in Tunisia in the spring of 1943, and during the Italian campaign until the capitulation of the German armies in May 1945, the 34th Infantry Division was in combat for more than 500 days. Some elements accrued almost 600 days in the combat zones. Not every soldier of the division was in combat for all those 500 days. Only a miserable few, growing ever fewer every day of the war, suffered that fate. As the reader will discover, the useful life of an infantry rifleman or other front fighter in continuous combat was perishingly short, between, at most, 180 and 200 days.

It is a reality of war that army commanders at every level must make cold professional calculations of the estimated casualties—dead, wounded and captured—and of the expenditure of ammunition and supplies necessary to achieve battle objectives and ultimate victory. When citizens decide to send soldiers to war, they have a responsibility to know how professional soldiers perform the calculus of battle. The commanders will, because they must, spend lives to defeat the enemy, to take objectives, to win a victory. Every attack, by a platoon or a regiment, is launched with a conscious realization that a proportion of the soldiers sent forward will die, and an even greater proportion will be wounded. During World War II, every United States front-line soldier required a ton of supplies every month. And every 200 days, perhaps less, the fighter himself would have to be replaced by another, because of death, wounds, disease, or mental breakdown. War is always about death and ugly waste, and this is the price of victory as it is of defeat. That their country was willing to pay that price made the inevitable grief and anguish no easier to bear for the GIs or for their loved ones.

The 34th Infantry Division was both the object of the highest strategic considerations by World War I leaders of the Western Allies and the subject of scathing criticism of its fighting ability by other Americans as well as by the British. Rick Atkinson, in his Pulitzer Prize-winning book *An Army at Dawn*, writes:

> Hamilton H. Howze, the 1st Armored [Division] operations officer and a future four-star general, later asserted [of the 1st Armored Division at the time of the *Torch* landings in North Africa], "*None of the division was worth a damn.*"

Atkinson continues:

> This harsh secret, suspected by few and believed by fewer, was equally true of other units. The 34th Infantry merits particular scrutiny because it had been the first American division dispatched to the European theater and because the division's saga, in North Africa and beyond, would embody the tribulations and triumphs of the U.S. Army as fully as any of the eighty-nine divisions ultimately mustered in World War II.[1]

The Red Bull Division participated in some of the most savage and justly famous, or in other instances notorious, engagements of World War II. This book describes 34ID's mobilization and early training, its experiences in Northern Ireland, and its battles in North Africa: the confused landings near Algiers, and the bold but flawed attempt by the 3rd Battalion, 135th Infantry Regiment, to seize the harbor at Algiers; the bravely fought but losing battle at Sidi Bou Zid in Tunisia, where two battalions of the 168th Infantry Regiment were practically destroyed and the survivors left aghast but wiser; the cotemporaneous defense at Sbiba, where the balance of the Division began the process of learning the operational art of war in earnest; the costly and unsuccessful first battle at Fondouk Pass (Fondouk el Okbi[iii]); the fumbling but ultimately victorious seizure of Fondouk Gap (Djebel Haouareb) on the second attempt; the great firefight and hard-won victory in the area of Hill 609 (Djebel Tahent[iv]) where sound tactical dispositions and combined arms synchronization prevailed over an entrenched and determined foe; and the final advance to the Chouïgui[v] Pass, followed by the destruction or wholesale capture of all Axis forces in North Africa.

Then came Italy, which will be treated in the second volume: the capture of Naples; the crossings of the serpentine Volturno River; the disastrous Rapido River crossing; the hideous early battles of Monte Cassino; the horrible First Winter Campaign of 1943–4; the amphibious move to the Anzio beachhead, and the stalemate before the

---

iii   Modern Funduq al 'Uqbi, Tunisia.
iv   Modern Jabal Tahint, Tunisia.
v   In GI jargon, the "Chewy-Gooey" Pass.

fight to break out of Anzio and capture Rome; the pursuit toward the Po; the Second Winter Campaign of 1944–5; and the final Allied spring offensive and pursuit to the Alps resulting in the total destruction of the German armies in Italy in May 1945.

There were genuine heroes among the fighting men of the 34th Infantry Division. But the Red Bull soldiers were human beings, mere mortals, representative of the whole of American society with all its flaws. They found themselves in bad country exposed to terrible danger while engaged in organized killing. During their prolonged experiences of war, homesickness, irremediable exhaustion, cold, wet, illness, the ever-present fear of death or maiming, and the recurring deaths of comrades, some soldiers of the 34th Infantry Division, especially those who had been in the division the longest and had accumulated the most service time, developed a heartfelt resentment against further service and a deeply held belief that they had done their part and should have been sent home. However unrealistic these feelings were in the larger context of a global war, their desperation was reflected in statistics that demonstrated a trend among some of them of indiscipline, misconduct, self-injury, desertion, and other crimes.

To establish the historical and organizational context for the story of the 34th Infantry Division, I have included materials concerning American politics and defense policy in the pre-war era and the wartime considerations of the United States government which bear directly on the fate of the Red Bull Division. I have described some of the history of the thoughtful but short-sighted federal legislation that established during the inter-war period the basis for the immense expansion of both the armed forces and their industrial base. Americans of the first half of the 20th century abhorred the idea of a large and expensive standing army. The Congresses of the inter-War period simply refused to appropriate sufficient funds to support the full Army establishment that their own statutes authorized. While that was a mistake in hindsight, they were wise enough to provide a mechanism by which the nation maintained a military organization and professional staff supported by advanced training schools that could be expanded when needed. That organization was enough, just barely, when conjoined with the fully mobilized industrial capacity of the United States, to win the global conflict with the Axis powers. The United States was still not fully prepared for war in June 1942. Two years later the nation had military power enough to capture Rome, invade France, and seize the Marianas while annihilating the naval airpower of Japan, all in the same month.

It is not my purpose to rehearse the debates on the merits of the grand strategy that led to Operation *Torch*, the North African campaign, and the Italian campaign. I do want to suggest, to the extent possible from such a distance in time and perspective, a little of the humanity and something of the nature of the battle experience of the citizen soldiers of 34ID, as well as the larger strategic context that placed those Red Bull soldiers, at first half trained and partly equipped, at the point of the Allied spear. My object is a clear description of where and when they fought, and how well they did in those fights. My intention is to do so in the voices of the soldiers of the 34th Infantry Division to the extent that is possible. I do not presume to clearly see the events of those 500 and more days of battle or to convey more than dimly the content of the hearts and minds of the Red Bull soldiers. They only truly know the war who fought it.

Battles are won by the actions of individual soldiers, in the smallest units led by the lowest ranking leaders, closing with and destroying the enemy. A division of the United States Army is an organization for directing and supporting the conduct of battle by its subordinate fighting and supporting units. A division is itself a part of larger military organizations. Two or more divisions may be organized under a corps, e.g. II Corps in North Africa. Two or more corps may be subordinate to an army, such as Fifth Army in Italy. Two or more armies may be coordinated by an army group, as British First and Eighth Armies and U.S. II Corps came under the control of 18 Army Group in North Africa. The higher organizations do not fight the battles. They are responsible for determining strategic priorities and tactical objectives and for providing the means for the combat units to achieve those objectives.

The 34th Infantry Division was one of 89 divisions of the Army of the United States mobilized for combat during World War II. In the years 1940–2, Army Chief of Staff General George C. Marshall's division building machine steadily increased the tempo of the expansion of the pitifully small pre-war army. The turbulence generated by the War Department's constant reassignment of soldiers, however, caused weaknesses in unit cohesion and morale that were difficult to repair. But some turmoil was necessary to grow the Army, as my father's early Army career illustrates.

The deservedly well-known 100th Infantry Battalion (Separate) was composed of U.S. citizens of Japanese descent and was attached to the 34th Infantry Division for much of the Italian Campaign, because the 2nd Battalion of the 133rd Infantry Regiment was detached from 34ID after the seizure of Algiers and assigned to guard duty at Allied Force Headquarters in Algiers. The 100th Battalion was the most highly decorated unit in the U.S. Army in World War II. After the liberation of Rome and the capture of Civitavecchia the 100th Battalion was assigned to (or rather, as the soldiers of the 100th might have preferred to say, was reinforced by) the equally famous 442nd Regimental Combat Team. Also composed of American soldiers of Japanese descent, the 442RCT was for a time attached to the 34th Infantry Division in Italy. The late Senator Daniel Inouye from Hawaii was an officer in the 442nd RCT. While serving with 34ID in Italy, he was severely injured in combat and lost his right arm. For his combat heroism, Captain Inouye was awarded the Congressional Medal of Honor, the Distinguished Service Cross, the Bronze Star, and the Purple Heart with Cluster.

The 34th Infantry Division as an organization was deactivated in November 1945. Of the several thousand National Guardsmen from the Upper Midwest who left for Louisiana during the frigid February of 1941, and who had been among the first

American troops to land in Europe and Africa, only a handful remained with the division when it was deactivated. Death, wounds, illness, transfers, and rotations had taken the rest. The division's combat record includes: 517 days of front-line combat in six major campaigns (more combat days that any other American division in any theater of the war, with some elements of the division credited with over 600 days); 21,362 casualties (3,737 killed, 14,165 wounded, 3,460 missing in action). Red Bull soldiers were awarded ten Congressional Medals of Honor (out of a total of 294 awarded to soldiers of the entire U.S. Army for valor above and beyond the call of duty during World War II), 98 Distinguished Service Crosses, and 1,072 Silver Stars. More than 4,000 Red Bull troops were awarded the Bronze Star for valor in battle and over 14,000 received the Purple Heart for wounds suffered in combat. The division garnered three Presidential Unit Citations, 15 Unit Commendations and 525 separate division citations. The French government awarded the 34th Infantry Division the Croix de Guerre with Palms for gallantry in action alongside its French soldiers.[2]

The division was reactivated and reorganized in 1991 as a National Guard Division with men and women soldiers from eight states. The Red Bull continues to this day to be an active fighting element of the Army National Guard. 34ID units have rotated through the fights in Kosovo, Iraq, and Afghanistan. The division has an active membership association.

Dreamers
By Siegfried Sassoon

Soldiers are citizens of death's grey land,
Drawing no dividend from time's to-morrows.
In the great hour of destiny they stand,
Each with his feuds, and jealousies, and sorrows.

Soldiers are sworn to action; they must win
Some flaming, fatal climax with their lives.
Soldiers are dreamers; when the guns begin
They think of firelit homes, clean beds and wives.

I see them in foul dug-outs, gnawed by rats,
And in the ruined trenches, lashed with rain,
Dreaming of things they did with balls and bats,
And mocked by hopeless longing to regain
Bank-holidays, and picture shows, and spats,
And going to the office in the train.

"Counter-Attack" and Other Poems, E. P. Dutton & Company, New York (1918)

Boxing
by Rudyard Kipling

Read here the Moral roundly writ
For him that into battle goes—
Each soul that, hitting hard and hit,
Encounters gross or ghostly foes:—
Prince, blown by many overthrows
Half blind with shame, half choked with dirt
Man cannot tell but Allah knows
How much the other side was hurt!

An Almanac of Twelve Sports by William Nicholson with words by
Rudyard Kipling, William Heinemann, London (1898)

PART I

"SOLDIERS ARE CITIZENS": PREPARING THE NATION FOR WAR

CHAPTER I

The Strategic and Political Situation

The United States had not yet become a formal belligerent in World War II in January 1941, when the 34th Infantry Division was called into federal service. There had been incidents in the North Atlantic involving United States Navy vessels and submarines of the German *Kriegsmarine*. Japan was engaged in its grinding conquest of China and preparing in great secrecy a sweeping aero-naval campaign to seize the resources of the East Indies and Southeast Asia but was not yet at open war with the Western powers. Britain and its Empire and Commonwealth were hard pressed by Axis forces both in the Home Islands and in North Africa. In the spring of 1941 German units had joined their Italian allies in Libya and the desert battles raged across the northern rim of Africa. In June 1941 Hitler launched the mighty German offensive against his archenemy the Soviet Union, under the name Operation *Barbarossa*. Russia staggered under the German blows and from Stalin's military incompetence.

A political debate among the American people about avoiding "foreign entanglements" and rejecting any involvement in another war in Europe had begun in the aftermath of World War I. It raged on still in 1941 even after the Axis Powers had conquered most of Europe. A war in the Pacific Ocean areas was unimagined by all Americans except the military planning staffs. At the time it was complete fantasy to think that the outcome of a new world war might transform the United States into a global economic and military superpower armed with weapons almost too terrible to contemplate. Not surprisingly, isolationist or non-interventionist factions in the United States, which tended to be center-right or conservative in political orientation, were concerned that American intervention against the Nazi regime would result in the expansion of the power and influence of the Union of Soviet Socialist Republics. Contrary to British "peripheralism," debates arose within American government and military circles over the far-reaching implications of potential American engagement with the Soviet Union and the British Empire for a post-war world order. Anglophobia and a well-founded distrust of the Stalinist tyranny underlay American defense posture. American government efforts to expand the Army, Air

Corps and Navy were in the early phases. The nation's actual construction of plants and production of military munitions and equipment had been driven more by requisitions and purchases by France, until that country surrendered to Germany, and by the United Kingdom, than its own defense requirements. Mobilization remained highly controversial. On August 12, 1941, as the 34th Infantry Division was about to participate in large-scale Army maneuvers in Louisiana, Congress passed by a margin of one vote (203–202 in the House) an extension of the Selective Service Act and the funding for continued mobilization for one year.

The United States and British governments, in deep secrecy, engaged in strategic discussions in the Washington Conference of January to March 1941, known as the American–British–Canadian Conference (ABC). The ABC-1 Staff Agreement called for the defeat of Germany first by a combined Anglo-American effort. There would be "unity of command in all theaters" but the integrity of the forces of each allied nation would be preserved. It called for the early defeat of Italy, for the eventual launch of an offensive to defeat Germany, and if Japan entered the war, for an initially defensive posture in the Pacific. The ABC-1 document, however, left many specifics unresolved and subject to misunderstanding, and there remained serious disputes of strategic priorities and direction.[1]

American governmental and military service internal policy debates in early 1941 had a distinctly nationalistic and conservative perspective not entirely aligned with British views but alert to the great danger the Axis and the Soviet Union posed to the United States.

The British government began to exercise its influence in American political and military circles, immediately upon the initiation of hostilities in 1939, to obtain American assistance and intervention in the European war. Settling the differences in policy and perspective between the British Empire and the United States, however, required time. British proposals in early 1941 for intermediate military steps in North Africa and the Middle East provoked latent Anglophobia and doubts about Britain's postwar aims within the highest levels of the U.S. military establishment. The senior leadership of the Army and Navy deprecated Britain's traditional policy of aligning the United Kingdom against the strongest continental power and the U.K.'s focus on its imperial commercial and military interests. The Joint Army–Navy planning committee in January 1941 warned against entrusting America's fortunes to British direction. The U.S. Navy advocated a Pacific First strategy, while some Army planners formulated the "Victory Program," under which the United States would mobilize a force of 210 Army divisions backed by huge fleets of ships and aircraft to defeat Germany almost alone. President Roosevelt, however, preferred a different and more moderate policy of dealing with the more dangerous German threat, first in close alliance with the British and later with the Soviet Union, to be carried out by a truly large but achievable and politically feasible American industrial and military mobilization.

Hitler's war against Russia impelled the United Kingdom to conclude an uneasy alliance with the Stalinist regime and presented the U.K. with options for peripheral military moves against Axis forces in Libya, Greece, and North Africa. In the United States, however, conservatives anguished over a policy of aiding Communist Russia against the Germans. The Nazi attack on Russia presented directly to the president and to Congress the question whether Nazi domination of Europe was such a threat to American security as to require the United States to ally itself not only with the British Empire but with the Soviet Union.

Roosevelt's sensitive political fingertips told him that he had to proceed deftly to obtain support for the Germany First policy. The fight in Congress over the extension of the draft law and its narrow passage cast doubt on American political support for an Operation Victory mobilization of the 200-plus U.S. divisions needed to fight the Germans without allies. Relationships with Britain and Russia, however fraught with tensions and competing global interests, would be necessary. Postwar relations with the USSR and future political and territorial issues had to be finessed until American forces were heavily engaged against the Germans and the necessity for U.S.–Soviet cooperation was clear to both Americans and Stalin. In the meantime, the Roosevelt administration had to procure Soviet moderation with respect to a postwar world order to quiet domestic conservative concerns about U.S. intervention in Europe. Roosevelt was determined to deal with Stalin on a friendly basis, and to keep Russia in the war against Germany. As a consequence, the president was also determined to open a military front against the Germans with American forces as soon as could be. The administration sought to build a basis of mutual trust with the Russians by establishing a military alliance with the Soviet Union on the basis of U.S. military and logistical support and eventual American engagement in combat against Nazi Germany. Roosevelt calculated that mutual confidence would smooth political relations with Stalin, mute congressional criticism, afford greater odds of military success and lay the foundations of postwar cooperation. Some of those goals were achieved. Other hopes came to grief in the Cold War.

> In military terms, these facts translated into an American strategy that placed a premium on quick, decisive victory, direct aid for the eastern [Russian] front and avoiding the diversion of precious American resources to remote theaters or to battlefields on the periphery of Europe… [T]he Russian "problem" injected a certain rigidity and lack of realism into American military planning, which meant problems with the British. But without the Russian problem, U.S. military intervention in Europe was impractical… Early on, the British would learn to live with American "rigidity" on strategic issues, but not without qualms.[2]

It is an exaggeration to say that concern about potential Soviet expansionism weighed on the general American public. Most Americans, however, peace loving and unwilling to go to war they might have been, correctly perceived the National Socialist regime and its associated powers and satellites (Italy, Hungary, Bulgaria, and Romania) to be a direct and present threat to the security of the United States.[3]

But most Americans were then unworried about the future fate of the Nazis' satellite countries. Informed Americans might have felt sympathy for the afflictions of Hungary which had been betrayed to the Nazis by traitors in its own military, and of Yugoslavia, where the Serbs had rejected the attempt to align Yugoslavia with the Axis and rebelled. Most Americans in the late 1930s and early 1940s reviled the Stalinist autocracy and saw through the mummery of Soviet show trials and purges to the morbid truth of the politics of murder and slave labor. Americans were revolted and disquieted by the cold-blooded *realpolitik* of the Nazi–Soviet non-aggression pact of August 1939. They were dismayed by the appeasement of Hitler by the Western powers at Munich and believed the Axis and its dictators when they promised war and conquest. The American in the street regarded the Axis as the primary threat. He or she had seen indicators of Axis intentions in America. The insidious German American *Bund*, which ironically prospered under American law and the right of free speech, was visibly working to undermine and destroy the Constitution and the American government. The words of the aviation hero and Hitler admirer Charles Lindbergh in testimony before Congress could not dissuade thinking Americans from the conclusion that the clear and present danger was Hitler's naked megalomania and aggression. President Roosevelt's political problem was how to guide the widely varying sentiments of the American public to the stage of determined confrontation of the threat. For the political reality was that despite their emotional attachments to the Allied cause, Americans overwhelmingly opposed entering the war or providing tangible support to combatant nations.[4]

> Public opinion hunched strongly toward greater aid to Britain. Poll after poll in the early weeks of 1941 showed that by roughly two-to-one margins people supported not only the Lend-Lease bill but also controversial specifics, such as use by British warships of American piers to repair, refuel, and refit; and the lending of warplanes and any other war supplies belonging to the United States services if the President judged that such aid would help the defense of the United States. A strong majority would help England win even at the risk of getting into war. Such opinions had a markedly geographical cast. Polls showed isolationist feeling to be strongest in the nation's broad hinterland, the Midwest and the Plains states. Generally, younger people were more isolationist than older; lower income than higher; less-informed than better-informed—differences that implied some weaknesses in the foundations of Roosevelt's three-party coalition…[5]

On the isolationist side of the argument were numerous groups and interests. Ethnic isolationists included the German–Americans and Italian–Americans, many of whom were angered by denigration of their homelands, and the Irish-Americans who harbored resentment over English domination. Many Americans believed that the United States had been seduced into the first war, had suffered excessive casualties, and then had been rejected as a grasping creditor of devastated nations. Left-wingers saw the wars in Europe and Asia as struggles among imperialist powers. The right-wing isolationists were afraid that American involvement in the war would mean more spending, heavier taxes, and bigger government; they were right but for the wrong reasons. The intellectual isolationists took various stances, including a not unwarranted fear of militarism, opposition to the seduction of innocent Americans by wily Europeans, and, like Paul Fussell, a sound view of war as corrosive of moral standards, stifling civil liberties, eroding social welfare, and generally destructive of civilized culture, cheapening and degrading every aspect of life.

The interventionists were divided, too, and in much the same way. No group was monolithic. The division over foreign policy within business, labor, and liberal groups seemed as sharp as the divisions between them. And bit by bit alignments were changing under the impact of events abroad. Underlying the cauldron of shifting attitudes was the general sentiment of the American voter expressed by the slogan "No Foreign Wars!" National defense was generally approved, arms and aid for the Allies were supported by a bare majority, but most citizens opposed the very idea of involving the country in another war overseas.

> Roosevelt had not only recognized this mood; he had helped create it. In speech after speech, he had made his obeisances to the God of No Foreign War. His protestations had reached a climax in the 1940 election campaign. Military action, he seemed to be saying, was no longer an alternative to be used prudently and sparingly as an instrument of foreign policy. It was flatly ruled out, except in case of outright invasion. But now this mood was confronting another mood, still of lesser sweep and intensity, but rising in the face of Nazi conquest, a mood resulting from indignation over fascist conquest and cruelty, hostility to Nazi racism, sympathy for afflicted peoples and occupied nations, concern for the Jews, admiration for the British.[6]

Congress, as befits a democracy, took up the debate under the influence of the many varieties of opinion. The Southern states tended to be more inclined to intervene. The Midwest and Mountain states were more isolationist. Both regions were overrepresented in the Senate and the debate often became an argument between committed extremists.

Roosevelt could not escape the hard policy choices. The time for decision, for policies and programs and for politicians who could work together, had come. The president had to make alliance with the moderate, interventionist Republicans. Wendell Willkie, the Republican candidate for president in 1940, had decided to visit embattled Britain. In mid-January 1941 he came to Washington to pick up his passport. Secretary of State Cordell Hull took him to see the president. The two men had a congenial conversation, and the president gave Willkie a letter addressed to "Dear Churchill."

> Wendell Willkie is taking this to you. He is being a true help in keeping politics out of things. I think this verse [of Longfellow] applies to you people as well as to us:
> "Sail on, O Ship of State!
> Sail on, O Union, strong and great!
> Humanity with all its fears,
> With all the hopes of future years,
> Is hanging breathless on thy fate!"

Churchill later recalled Willkie's visit:

> Later on in [January 1941] there arrived in England Mr. Wendell Willkie, the President's opponent in the recent election. He... brought recommendations of the highest character from the President, and as he was the accepted leader of the Republican Party every arrangement was made by us, with the assistance of the enemy, to let him see all he desired of London at bay.[7]

The fall of France brought home to Americans the fact that the Atlantic barrier to European conflicts had dramatically shrunk. With respect to rearmament and the defense of the Western hemisphere, both the public and Congress felt by June 1940 the need for action. They strongly supported the necessary expansion of the armed services, while giving less support to an increase and expansion of taxation to pay for it. By January 1941, American public opinion had in large part arrived at support of Lend-Lease and a great majority reluctantly felt that the United States would have to enter the war eventually. But the American people were still in no hurry to become a belligerent.[8]

But what action was America to take in early 1941 that would best meet its need to defend itself and to bolster the Allies whom so many believed were fighting America's fight? Mobilization was barely underway. Elements of the 34th Infantry Division had received federalization and mobilization orders only in the third week of January 1941.

> The President now faced a daunting political problem: how to gain congressional and popular support for a measure strong enough to give decisive aid to the democracies—but a measure that would be unfamiliar to most voters, expensive to the taxpayers, and obviously unneutral; a measure that would so entangle the nation's military and diplomatic affairs with Britain's—and with other nations'—as to arouse the isolationists; a measure that, above all, would challenge the popular mood of No Foreign Wars. The President's solution to this problem was simple. The Lend-Lease bill [serendipitously designated H. R. 1776] was to be presented as a step not toward war but away from war. Roosevelt would not challenge the mood-god of America.[9]

In an environment of loud public opposition by the isolationist press and representatives, H. R. 1776 was debated in the House under Roosevelt's shrewd political direction. The secretaries of State (Hull), Treasury (Morgenthau), War (Stimson), and Navy (Knox) testified before the House Foreign Affairs Committee. They warned that a German invasion of Britain then appeared to be likely within three months. They set before the committee the correlation of forces that would face the United States if the British Navy were beaten or taken, pointed out that in that case an invasion of the United States itself was possible, and asked for the widest executive discretion possible under the act. They were evasive on specifics, including the cost of Lend-Lease and what nations other than the U.K. might be included. The committee members asked two key questions: Would not Lend-Lease, to be effective, require United States naval help in convoying munitions across the Atlantic? And would not convoying mean war? All the secretaries dutifully kept to their chief's step-by-step tactics, asserting that Lend-Lease would be a way of reducing the chances of war.[10]

On February 8, 1941, as the regiments of the 34th Infantry Division were assembling for induction into federal service, the House passed the revised H. R. 1776, almost intact, 260 to 165. The battle for Lend-Lease then passed to the Senate:

> Argument resounded throughout the land… The America First Committee vied with the Committee to Defend America in disgorging pamphlets, broadsides, radio transcriptions, petitions, auto stickers, buttons, posters, news letters… These were the "respectable" adversaries; flanking them were a host of extremist, demagogic groups that had reduced the whole debate to a contest between "defeatists and fascists" on one side and "Commies and warmongers" on the other…[11]

The Secretaries of State, War and Treasury argued the administration's case, bolstered by the powerful support of Wendell Willkie, recently returned from his visit to bomb battered London. Willkie endorsed the bill. In mid-February the Committee on Foreign Relations sent the bill to the floor for a vote. The debate raged anew, but the amended bill passed both Houses with large majorities. The president signed HR 1776 into law on March 11 and the administration wasted no time offering available weapons and materials to the embattled Allies. Roosevelt asked Congress to appropriate seven billion dollars to fund Lend Lease:

> Roosevelt … moved quickly. Within a few hours of signing 1776 on March 11, he sent lists of available weapons to British and Greek officials and asked Congress for an appropriation of seven billion dollars to carry out the new law.
> Seven billion dollars—no one now could doubt the President's determination, or the nation's. After agonizing delays the United States had made a commitment to Atlantic unity and defense, a commitment that would hold for decades.[12]

Months later, on an afternoon in late July 1941, Harry Hopkins, secretary of Commerce and close confidant and personal advisor of President Roosevelt, appeared in the garden at 10 Downing Street to tell the prime minister that the president wished to meet Churchill "in some lonely bay or other."[13] Placentia Bay, in Newfoundland, near the then newly built U.S. Navy Operating Station Argentia, was chosen.[i] As Churchill recalled:

> I had the keenest desire to meet Mr. Roosevelt, with whom I had now corresponded with increasing intimacy for nearly two years…
> [A] conference between us would proclaim the ever closer association of Britain and the United States, would cause our enemies concern, make Japan ponder, and cheer our friends. There was also much business to be settled about American intervention in the Atlantic, aid to Russia, our own supplies, and above all the increasing menace of Japan.[14]

On August 9, 1941, while the 34th Infantry Division was participating in Third Army maneuvers in Louisiana, H.M.S. *Prince of Wales* hove into Placentia Bay with

---

i   Some American sources refer to the meeting place as Argentia Bay.

the prime minister on board, raw steel patches welded over her scars from the sea fight on May 24 with the German battleship *Bismarck* and heavy cruiser *Prinz Eugen*. The president was waiting for Churchill aboard the cruiser U.S.S. *Augusta*, and the conversations between the principals and their respective staffs began. Roosevelt proposed a joint declaration of war aims, which with amendments and additions, was destined to be known to history as the "Atlantic Charter." The principals also drew up and sent a joint message to Stalin concerning the future allocation of Anglo-American resources to aid Russia. They proposed a meeting to be held in Moscow to discuss those matters. Of the Joint Declaration,[15] Churchill observed:

> The profound and far-reaching importance of this Joint Declaration was apparent. The fact alone of the United States, still technically neutral, joining with a belligerent Power in making such a declaration was astonishing. The inclusion in it of a reference to "the final destruction of the Nazi tyranny" … amounted to a challenge which in ordinary times would have implied warlike action. Finally, not the least striking feature was the realism of the last paragraph, where there was a plain and bold intimation that after the war the United States would join with us in policing the world until the establishment of a better order.[16]

Insofar as the American people were seriously concerned before the attack on Pearl Harbor, Churchill overstated the case. But as to the significance of current and future United States participation, he was on target. Roosevelt wanted the United States to get involved in the fight to the maximum extent possible given American political and military constraints.

British policy was to prevent German entry into the Middle East, with its strategically important oil fields and production facilities, and at the same time to deliver munitions and supplies to the Soviet government through Iran. Prime Minister Churchill thought it was "eminently desirable to open the fullest communication with Russia through Persia."[17] The British in May 1941 had suppressed by military force a German- and Italian-supported revolt in Iraq and had joined with the French to occupy Syria. Those actions, "achieved as they were by narrow margins, blotted out Hitler's Oriental plan."[18] The British and Russians gave the government of Iran a joint ultimatum demanding the expulsion of German agents and residents and the cession of control of the oil fields and refineries to British and Russian control. "The joint Anglo-Soviet Note of August 17 met with an unsatisfactory reply, and the date for the entry of British and Russian forces into Persia was fixed for the 25th."[19] After two days' action, the Shah ordered a cease fire. Of this decidedly imperialist action "against a weak and ancient state," Churchill said: "Britain and Russia were fighting for their lives. *Inter arma silent leges*[ii]."[20] "The conditions imposed on the Persian government were, principally, the cessation of all resistance, the ejection of Germans, neutrality in the war, and the Allied use of Persian communications for the transit of war supplies to Russia."[21] The U.S. Army Transportation Corps

---

ii   *Inter arma silent leges* can be translated as "In time of war, the law is disregarded."

would later build and run railroads and port facilities from the Persian Gulf coast to the Russian border, over which millions of tons of Lend-Lease aid were shipped to the Soviets. The Iranian people noted this violation of their sovereignty and drew conclusions not necessarily in the long-term interests of the United States.

The Allied actions to secure the Middle East set the stage for developments in the Mediterranean Theater, regarded then by the British as the dominant theater. The British and the Axis powers used the summer of 1941 to reinforce their armies in the Libyan Desert. It is at this early point that grand strategic actions were taken that would affect the disposition and fortunes of the men of the 34th Infantry Division.

> [Churchill in late August 1941]… desired at this time to reinforce the East to the utmost shipping limit. I could not tell what would happen in the impending Desert battle, nor how the Russian front in the Caucasus would hold. There was always, besides, the menace of Japan… I wished to have two more British divisions moving eastward… [W]e should have something substantial in hand for unknowable contingencies. Here would be, in fact, that mobile reserve, that "mass of manoeuvre," which alone could give superior options in the hour of need. I had learnt about this in a hard school where lessons are often only given once.[22] [iii]

For this purpose, however, the British had no shipping. Churchill "felt sure, from the increasing cordiality of my correspondence with President Roosevelt, that he would lend me some fast American transports. Nor … was I wrong."[23] Churchill appealed to the president on September 1, 1941, for the loan of 12 United States liners and 12 United States cargo ships manned by American crews. The president sent on September 6 "a most helpful and generous response."[24] He wrote to Churchill: "I am sure …we can help with your project to reinforce the Middle East army. At any rate I can now assure you that we can provide transport for twenty thousand men."[25] The ships were to be U.S. naval transports manned by Navy crews. In addition, the U.S. would provide 10 or 12 ships to run between U.S. ports and Great Britain, so that Britain could release its own cargo ships for the voyage to the Middle East. This plan was implemented under Churchill's constant insistence on making the most of the precious new shipping.

> [The British had]… a plan for the rest of 1941 and for 1942… This plan was of course at this date based upon the United States still staying out of the war while giving [the British] all the aid that Congress would allow. [Churchill] had become aware through [his] correspondence with the President that [Roosevelt] was particularly alert about all naval affairs, and he regarded French North Africa, including Dakar, and the Atlantic islands of Spain and Portugal, with special interest not only from American but also from his personal ways of thought. These were also in harmony with [Churchill's] own views, and also… with a strategy which expressed the best [the British] could possibly do alone, and also the best that we and the United States, should they become a belligerent, could do together.[26]

---

iii The "hard school" was France in May 1940, when Churchill learned to his shock and dismay that the French Army had no mobile reserve, no "*masse de manoeuvre*," with which to check the German armored onrush.

After a pause of some four months from combat, a major British offensive in the Western Desert of Libya was scheduled to begin in mid-November 1941. Churchill sent to Roosevelt through Clement Attlee, then lord privy seal and deputy prime minister, and leader of the Labor Party, a personal letter dated October 20, 1941, for the president's eyes only, to be burnt or returned. The prime minister disclosed the fact of the offensive to come, told the president of British preparations to invade Northwest Africa by sea, and asked the president "to send three or four United States divisions to relieve our troops in Northern Ireland, as a greater safeguard against invasion in the spring [of 1942]."[27]

In his memoirs, in connection with accords reached between the United States and Britain at the First Washington Conference, code named "Arcadia," in late December 1941 and early January 1942, Churchill explained his reasons for his request.

> *I felt that the arrival of sixty or seventy thousand American troops in Ulster would be an assertion of the United States resolve to intervene directly in Europe. These newly raised troops could just as well complete their training in Ulster as at home, and would at the same time become a strategic factor.* The Germans would certainly consider the move as an additional deterrent against the invasion of the British Isles. I hoped they would exaggerate the numbers landed, and thus continue to pay attention to the West. Besides this, every American division which crossed the Atlantic gave us freedom to send one of our matured British divisions out of the country to the Middle East, or of course—and this was always in my mind—to North Africa. Though few, if any, saw it in this light, this was in fact the first step towards an Allied descent on Morocco, Algeria, or Tunis, on which my heart was set....
>
> Mr. Stimson, the War Secretary, and his professional advisers also found this move to Ireland in harmony with their inclination to invade Europe at the earliest moment. Thus all went forward smoothly. We were anxious that the enemy should be aware of this strategic movement, and made the fact public, without of course specifying numbers. We hoped also that this would detain German troops in the West and thus be not unhelpful to the Russian struggle...[28]

Churchill's memoirs shed light on the discussions and agreements underlying the decision to deploy American troops to Northern Ireland and how those troops might be transported.

> [President Roosevelt] had agreed to send nearly thirty thousand American soldiers to Northern Ireland. We had of course placed the two "Queens"—the only two 80,000-ton ships in the world—at his disposal for this purpose. General Marshall asked me how many men we ought to put on board, observing that boats, rafts, and other means of flotation could only be provided for about eight thousand. If this were disregarded, they could carry sixteen thousand men. I gave the following answer: "I can only tell you what we should do. You must judge for yourself the risks you will run. If it were a direct part of an actual operation, we should put all on board they could carry. If it were only a question of moving troops in a reasonable time, we should not go beyond the limits of lifeboats, rafts, etc. It is for you to decide." He received this in silence and our conversation turned to other matters. In their first voyages these ships carried only the lesser numbers, but later on they were filled to the brim. As it happened, Fortune stood our friend.[29]

The 34th Infantry Division, unready, untrained, and ill equipped as it was, was to be the first American Army unit sent to Europe in response to Churchill's request.

The 34th Division was rushed to Britain in January 1942 as a symbol of American commitment to the Allied cause. In Britain, the troops unloaded supplies and guarded various headquarters, with little opportunity for garrison soldiers to become combat killers. The division missed large-scale maneuvers in Louisiana[iv] and the Carolinas that benefited many other U.S. units. …[H]undreds of the division's best men left to form other units; the new 1st Ranger Battalion had been carved mostly from the 34th Division.[30]

By late 1941, the political mood of the American people had moved to a solid approval of measures to defend the Western hemisphere and the continental United States against the foreign threats. Most American political leaders saw the war coming. They enacted laws and made policy to vastly expand, redirect and apply the industrial might of the United States to support a great army and navy which, in conjunction with other allies, would defeat any combination of foes. The citizen soldiers of the 34th Infantry Division found themselves shipped to foreign shores, not fully trained, and only partially equipped, as a result of decisions by the president and the prime minister of which the troops were unaware. They were justifiably confused and uncertain about how they and their fellow millions of citizen soldiers came to be on the road to war.

---

iv   The 34th Infantry Division did participate in the earliest of the large-scale maneuvers in Louisiana, although, as we shall see, without great benefit to its soldiers.

CHAPTER 2

Congress and the Army of the United States

Before it was inducted into federal service in January 1941, the 34th Infantry Division existed "only in principle, as regiments of the Iowa National Guard and sister Guard units from Minnesota" and North Dakota.[1]

> Guardsmen in peacetime met once a week, usually on Monday evenings. For two hours of close order drill they earned a dollar. Training in the art of war was limited to bayonet assaults against a football goalpost and skirmishes across the town square, where platoons practiced outflanking the local Civil War monument. Training in more sophisticated martial skills was limited to a couple weeks of summer camp.[2]

The United States Army had nothing yet in 1941 and early 1942 remotely comparable to the vast National Training Center at Fort Irwin, California, and other modern bases with facilities to provide tough, realistic combined arms training for individual soldiers and both small and large units prior to their deployment into combat. Major General George S. Patton was developing a desert warfare and maneuver training area in the California desert in the summer of 1942 when he was summoned to command the forces sent to invade French Morocco at Casablanca. America's love of peace and neglect of the miserable necessities of war were to cost it dearly when American boys met Axis veterans in the battles in Tunisia.[3]

In the aftermath of World War I, Congress passed a sweeping amendment to the National Defense Act of 1916. The National Defense Act of June 4, 1920[4] (the NDA of 1920) governed the organization and regulation of the Army until 1950. Until the onset of the Cold War, it was the most comprehensive piece of defense legislation ever adopted by the United States. The NDA of 1920 established the "Army of the United States" as an organization with three components: the standing Regular Army, the National Guard, and the Organized Reserves.[5] The latter consisted of the Officers' Reserve Corps and the Enlisted Reserve Corps, two separate organizations. Each of the three Army components was to be regulated in peacetime so that it could contribute its share of troops in a war emergency. The NDA of 1920 continued the historical precedent for the defense policies of the United States: a standing peacetime Regular Army too small to be expanded to meet the needs of a large war, relying on an augmentation by citizen soldiers to be raised and trained when large-scale mobilizations were necessary. This policy was set out explicitly in the NDA of 1920.

> SEC. 3. ORGANIZATION OF THE ARMY. -The Organized peace establishment, including the Regular Army, the National Guard and the Organized Reserves, shall include all of those divisions and other military organizations necessary to form the basis for a complete and immediate mobilization for the national defense in the event of a national emergency declared by Congress.

These policies were to have deplorable consequences when real danger from foreign powers presented itself in the late 1930s. Legislators did not appreciate the rapidity and military significance of scientific and technological developments in the inter-war period, despite the advice of military authorities. Congress refused repeatedly to provide the funds requested by the Army and Navy for modernization of air and mechanized forces. It even exercised its power to reduce the size of the Regular Army several times in the inter-war period.

The NDA of 1920, in a reluctant nod to the new weapons introduced during World War I, added three new branches to the army (infantry, artillery, cavalry) and service branches. They were the Air Service, the Chemical Warfare Service, and the Finance Department.[6] "The Tank Corps that emerged during World War I, representing another new combat technique, was absorbed into the Infantry,"[7] an arrangement that fostered Army doctrine that the role of armor and the design of tanks was to support the infantry, not to be an independent mobile striking arm.[8] That doctrine was to prove troublesome for the U.S. Army in World War II. The Army had not fully conceptualized or given sufficient attention to the problem of defeating enemy armored fighting vehicles operating in large numbers in entirely mechanized units coordinated by radio. The Army bureaucracy was still committed in early 1942 to a doctrine of infantry fire and maneuver supported by artillery, tank destroyers and tanks. The Army relied heavily for reconnaissance and infantry support on light and medium tank designs which would be no match for the much more heavily armed and armored German fighting vehicles which had been rapidly improved upon after the armored engagements in France, North Africa, and Russia.

The establishment of a General Staff was the single most important provision of the NDA of 1920, providing the intellectual and professional basis for the Army to plan for future conflicts and to mobilize the nation's industrial power and manpower. The NDA of 1920 prescribed that "[t]he duties of the War Department General Staff shall be to prepare plans for national defense and the use of the military forces for that purpose, both separately and in conjunction with the naval forces, and for the mobilization of the manhood of the nation and its material resources in an emergency, to investigate and report upon all questions affecting the efficiency of the Army of the United States, and its state of preparation for military operations; and to render professional aid and assistance to the Secretary of War and the chief of staff."[9]

> [The NDA of 1920] specifically charged the War Department with mobilization planning and preparation for the event of war, assigning… the military aspects of that responsibility to the Chief of Staff and the General Staff. The World War I experience had greatly strengthened the position and authority of the General Staff in both Washington and Paris. When General John J. Pershing became Chief of Staff in 1921 he reorganized the War Department General Staff on the model of his wartime General Headquarters staff in France. The reorganized staff included five divisions: G–1, Personnel; G–2, Intelligence; G–3, Training and Operations; G–4, Supply; and a new War Plans Division that dealt with strategic planning and related preparations for war.[10]

The extent of the responsibility and influence conferred on the chief of staff and on the General Staff Corps by Congress was detailed in the Act.

> The Chief of Staff shall preside over the War Department General Staff and, under the direction of the President, shall cause to be made, by the War Department General Staff, the necessary plans for recruiting, organizing, supplying, equipping, mobilizing, training, and demobilizing the Army of the United States and for the use of the military forces for national defense. He shall transmit to the Secretary of War the plans and recommendations prepared for that purpose by the War Department General Staff and advise him in regard thereto; upon the approval of such plans and recommendations by the Secretary of War, he shall act as the agent of the Secretary of War in carrying the same into effect. Whenever any plan or recommendation involving legislation by Congress affecting national defense or the reorganization of the Army is presented by the Secretary of War to Congress, or to one of the committees of Congress, the same shall be accompanied, when not incompatible with the public interest, by a study prepared in the appropriate division of the War Department General Staff, including the comments and recommendations of said division for or against such plan, and such pertinent comments for or against the plan as may be made by the Secretary of War, the Chief of Staff, or individual officers of the division of the War Department General Staff in which the plan was prepared.[11]

Giving the General Staff the important responsibility of planning for both operations and mobilization was a significant improvement in American military organization and planning. The officers assigned to the General Staff undertook detailed analyses and planning efforts that would have beneficial consequences during World War II. The War Plans Division (WPD) became the intellect of the Army, drafting color-coded strategic plans for the event of war with individual nations, such as War Plan *Orange* for Japan. WPD also provided a cadre of highly skilled officers with the necessary breadth of vision and planning skills for a wartime General Headquarters to direct the Army's operations. The General Staff divisions assisted the chief of staff in his supervision of the military branches of the War Department and of the field forces. The only major change in this organizational framework during the 1920s came in 1926, when the U.S. Army Air Corps was established as an equal combat arm.[12]

Military training and education both within and outside the Army were given greater emphasis under the NDA of 1920. The policy of Congress was to provide for only limited peacetime preparation tempered by the grudging acknowledgment that the increasing complexity and raw destructive power of modern industrial warfare required the nation to have a cadre of highly educated and competent military staff officers. With recent memories of the slaughter in the trenches during World War I, every country's military investigated ways to achieve mobility and fluidity on the battlefield. Military professionals studied the potential of aircraft, armored fighting vehicles, and self-propelled artillery. For example, while over-investing in massive defensive fortifications, France also developed some of the best medium and heavy tanks of the 1930s. But only a few French officers gave thought to the exploitation of the mobility and striking power of armored formations. Further, France did not plan for or build sufficient factories to produce tanks or planes in large quantities when the need arose. Improved and structured training and education of American officers would provide the nation with people capable of conducting a total war and with the knowledge to mobilize the national economy to provide the requirements for fighting it.

> The U.S. Military Academy and the Reserve Officers' Training Corps (ROTC) program furnished most of the basic schooling for new officers. Thirty-one special service schools provided branch training. These branch schools trained officers and enlisted men of the National Guard and Organized Reserves in addition to the Regular Army, utilizing extension courses to supplement their residential programs. Three general service schools formed the capstone of the Army educational system. The oldest, located at Fort Leavenworth, Kansas, and known from 1922 to 1947 as the Command and General Staff School,[i] provided officers with the requisite training for divisional command and General Staff positions. In Washington, the Army War College and, after 1924, the Army Industrial College prepared senior officers with demonstrated ability for the most responsible command and staff positions and assisted in the development of war plans.[13]

By establishing the Industrial College, the Army recognized the high strategic value of industrial organization, mobilization, and logistics for the conduct of modern mechanized warfare. The General Staff's detailed knowledge of the structure of the American economy and the advanced industrial planning and management capability were to be decisive for the United States in World War II.

The importance of the Command and General Staff School to the professional and intellectual development of the Army as a whole was recognized by Congress in its provisions for the selection of officers for General Staff assignments.

> After the completion of the initial General Staff Corps eligible list, the name of no officer shall be added thereto unless upon graduation from the General Staff School he is specifically

---

i   Now known as the U.S. Army Command and General Staff College, still located at Fort Leavenworth, Kansas.

recommended as qualified for General Staff duty, and hereafter no officer of the General Staff Corps except the Chief of Staff shall be assigned as a member of the War Department General Staff unless he is a graduate of the General Staff College or his name is borne on the initial eligible list.[14]

General Staff officers were to perform only the duties assigned to the General Staff Corps. They were not to be administrators or to duplicate the work of other offices or divisions within the Army.

Hereafter, members of the General Staff Corps shall be confined strictly to the discharge of duties of the general nature of those specified for them in this section and in the Act of Congress approved February 14, 1903, and they shall not be permitted to assume or engage in work of an administrative nature that pertains to established bureaus or offices of the War Department, or that, being assumed or engaged in by members of the General Staff Corps, would involve impairment of the responsibility or initiative of such bureaus or offices, or would cause injurious or unnecessary duplication of or delay in the work thereof.[15]

The NDA of 1920 also provided, in a departure from past practice, for the training of the National Guard and of the Organized Reserves by the Regular Army during peacetime.

All policies and regulations affecting the organization, distribution and training of the National Guard and the Organized Reserves, and all policies and regulations affecting the appointment, assignment, promotion and discharge of reserve officers, shall be prepared by committees of appropriate branches or divisions of the War Department General Staff, to which shall be added an equal number of reserve officers, including reserve officers who hold or have held commissions in the National Guard, and whose names are borne on lists of officers suitable for such duty, submitted by the governors of the several States and Territories...[16]

Congress authorized a maximum Regular Army officer strength of 17,726 officers, more than three times the pre-First World War number, in part to provide enough Regular officers to train the Guard and Reserves. Not less than half the new career officers were required to be selected from the ranks of National Guard and Reserve officers who had served during World War I. To equalize opportunities for advancement, the NDA of 1920 required that officer promotions, except for doctors and chaplains, be made only from a single list.[17]

Congress authorized a maximum Regular Army enlisted strength of 280,000 men, but the actual enlisted and officer strengths would depend on the amount of annual Congressional appropriations.[18] In June 1920, the Regular Army numbered about 200,000 soldiers, roughly two-thirds the authorized maximum.[19] In February 1921, Congress directed a reduction in enlisted strength to 175,000 by instructing the Secretary of War to cease recruitments for the Regular Army until the Army reached that figure.[20] In June 1921, Congress again decreased the authorized strength to 150,000 to be achieved by liberalizing the grant of discharges from the Regular Army.[21] A year later Congress limited the Regular Army to 12,000 commissioned officers, 125,000 enlisted men, and the approximately 7,000 men in the Philippine

Scouts.[22] Army strength stayed at about that level until 1936. Military appropriations for the War Department also stabilized after the early 1920s at roughly $300 million per year.[ii] That amount was roughly half the estimated expenditure needed to implement fully the force structure authorized in the NDA of 1920.

During the inter-war period, the United States spent less on the Army than on the Navy, in accordance with Congressional policy of depending on the Navy as the first line of defense. War Department officials, especially in the early 1920s, repeatedly expressed alarm over Congress's failure to fully fund the force structure authorized by the NDA of 1920. Army planners, mindful of Congress's position that the Army was to defend only the territory of the United States and its possessions, argued for a minimum Regular Army enlisted strength of 150,000, a figure that grew to 165,000 after the Air Corps Act of 1926.[23] The Air Corps Act established an Assistant Secretary of War for Air Affairs, renamed the Air Service the Air Corps, and established representation of the Air Corps on the General Staff.[24]

The Air Corps Act of 1926 authorized the Air Corps to have a strength of 1,518 officers and 16,000 enlisted men. The Chief of the Air Corps, two of his three brigadier general assistants and 90 percent of all other Air Corps officers were to be qualified pilots, as soon as enough could be trained. The Air Act specified that a soldier could be rated as a pilot in peacetime only after he had 200 hours flying time in airplanes, 75 hours of which had to be solo. The pilot also had to complete the prescribed course of instruction. In wartime, one could qualify as a flying officer if he had received a rating as a pilot of service aircraft. Officers and enlisted men who regularly flew were authorized flight pay of an additional 50 percent over base pay. Provision was also made for rating enlisted men as air mechanics.[25]

The Air Corps's inventory of equipment was small but technologically current, in sharp contrast to the rest of the Army. The ground combat branches got along for almost two decades with World War I weapons. Army Chief of Staff General Douglas MacArthur noted in the War Department's annual report of 1933 that, despite the economic ravages of the Great Depression, the United States possessed in great abundance petroleum, iron, coal, minerals, and myriad other natural and agricultural resources. It had a large, under-employed workforce, and the largest industrial capacity on the planet, with substantial unused productive potential. Yet its army was puny.[26] MacArthur, who could be disappointingly arrogant and egotistic, was nonetheless brilliant and accomplished. After carefully analyzing the funds available to the Army and noting that Congress had steadily reduced those resources, he pulled no punches.

> In numerical strength our Army is so small that in this respect it does not constitute even a
> minor factor in the difficult problem facing the delegates at [the international conference at

---

ii   Approximately $4.13 billion in 2020 dollars. Compare the FY2021 DoD Appropriated Budget
      of $694.6 billion.

Geneva for the reduction and limitation of armaments]. The organized land forces of the United States still rank seventeenth in size among the world's armies, whereas if organized on the basis of population, total wealth, and length of frontier our Army would be second to none. No land disarmament program yet seriously proposed has contemplated such a sweeping and universal reduction of armies that world levels in military strength would descend to that already existing in this country. Even under the theory of maintaining only "police components" the United States would be entitled to increase, rather than be compelled to decrease, its permanent forces.[27]

The foreign dictator states no doubt took notice of the relative military weakness and the enormous undeveloped wealth of the United States. The Army was aware that the old weapons were becoming obsolete. In his 1933 annual report General MacArthur documented the obsolescence of both the Army's motor transportation and mechanized weapons.[28]

The great proportion of the motor equipment now in possession of the Army was built during the World War and is obsolete as well as largely worn out. The total needs of the Regular Army for general motorization purposes are 9,385 trucks and 279 tractors. For the National Guard, aggregate requirements are about 19,500. Ever since the World War the American Army has not only failed to keep pace with world trends toward increasing mobility in military forces but has actually retrogressed in this respect. Under the 1934 authorizations this deterioration will be accentuated. The situation with respect to fighting vehicles is similar. This subject, which was discussed at some length in my report last year, commands an increasingly intense interest throughout the Army. Except for about a dozen machines produced during the past few years, every tank in the Army today is of World-War manufacture. Their number is entirely inadequate. Even more serious than this is the fact that they are so obsolete in design as to be completely useless for employment against any modern unit on the battlefield. Their maximum cross-country speed is not over 4 to 5 miles an hour, whereas an ability to go 18 to 20 is mandatory, and a greater one is highly desirable.[29]

The Army used its limited funds to maintain its personnel strength, and to provide what training it could, rather than to buy new equipment. Army arsenals and labo-ratories were also restricted by small budgets. Army organizations worked to remain abreast of developments, to innovate new equipment and to improve old weapons, capitalizing on the rapid technological advances of the 1920s and 1930s. Service boards tested new prototypes and wrote doctrines for their use to be incorporated into training manuals. But no new arms or equipment for ground units were issued in quantity before 1936. One could argue that there was some benefit to Congressional parsimony. The emphasis on maintaining manpower meant that the acquisition of new equipment did not consume scarce funds in a period of rapid technological obsolescence.[30] This would be of no comfort to American soldiers who would have to fight the next war with 20-year-old weapons.

During most inter-war years only about a quarter of the officers and half of the enlisted men of the Regular Army were available for assignment to tactical units in the continental United States. Most were overseas in the Panama Canal Zone, Hawaii, and the Philippines. Many Army units existed only on paper and had only skeleton strength. The Regular Army's nine infantry divisions had an actual combined strength of three full divisions. In May 1927 one of those undermanned divisions, a cavalry brigade, and 200 aircraft participated in a combined arms maneuver in Texas. That event was unusual. The puny Regular Army was normally able to train only as battalions or companies.[31]

The NDA of 1920 authorized a National Guard of 436,000 men, but its actual inter-war strength was about 180,000. The Guard's chief duty was to deal with domestic disturbances within the states. It might have been available, but was in no sense ready or trained, for immediate induction into the active Army of the United States in the event of a national emergency. The War Department, in addition to supplying Regular Army training officers and surplus World War I matériel, allocated approximately one-tenth of its military budget to support the Guard between the wars. Guardsmen participated in 48 armory drills and 15 days of field training each year. This level of training was to prove wanting given the demands of a global war of expeditionary forces over vast distances and in every imaginable terrain. Though not comparable to Regular Army units in readiness for war, the increasingly federalized Guard was better trained in 1939 than it had been when mobilized for duty on the Mexican border in 1916. But that is not saying a great deal. Numerically, the National Guard was the largest component of the Army of the United States between 1922 and 1939. Militarily, however, the National Guard in the late 1930s was simply not ready for a real war against trained troops under professional officers organized as mechanized combined arms forces, equipped with continually improving tanks, long-range automatic weapons and mobile field artillery, and supported by tactical air forces.[32]

MacArthur dwelt at length upon the subject of training of both the Regular Army and of the National Guard in his annual report for 1933, again making his case in blunt terms.

> In no other profession are the penalties for employing untrained personnel so appalling and so irrevocable as in the military...
>
> The first essential of an efficient training system is a strong corps of highly qualified Regular officers...
>
> [T]he Regular officer corps must provide military instruction for all elements of the Army of the United States...
>
> Four times during the nineteenth century the United States went to war under conditions that forced us to incur needless sacrifices by committing units to action under the leadership of hastily and imperfectly trained commanders. In spite of those repeated lessons, the same error was committed in 1917... [While both allies and our opponents] were lost in admiration of the bravery of [American] troops that could sustain appalling numbers of casualties and still keep on attacking, they were aghast at the useless and costly sacrifices we made because of unskilled leadership in the smaller units. Training—professional training—and the skill and knowledge and morale resulting therefrom are the first indispensables to efficiency in combat.
>
> [T]he War Department has opposed... every attempt to diminish our already inadequate corps of Regular officers or to reduce its opportunities for training. [The same] considerations account also for the determined effort the Department has made to preserve the integrity of civilian component training. The value to national defense of the civilian forces is measured

by the extent to which they are equipped to perform the specific tasks allotted to them as emergency responsibilities.[33]

MacArthur recalled in his 1933 annual report that "this point was discussed at a hearing on April 26 [1933] by the Military Affairs Committee of the House of Representatives." He quoted part of his answer to "a question as to the possibility of employing in battle enlisted men with little or no training."[34]

> Of course, you can put an untrained person on the battle line just as you could put a novice in front of a typewriter in your office. In the latter case you would pay for inefficiency in multiplied costs... Although the salary you pay a good typist includes a factor that reimburses the worker for months of training spent in a secretarial school, increased efficiency nevertheless results in economy. Put a recruit in battle and the Nation pays in blood of its manhood and in multiplied risk of defeat. This country has time and again paid fearful prices for adhering to the doctrine that "a million men would spring to arms overnight." Men experienced in the actual business of fighting have learned this lesson, even if some of the theorists sitting far in the rear have failed to do so...
>
> With fine officers and noncommissioned officers in an established organization a recruit can take his place in ranks after a few short weeks of intensive training. But even under these ideal conditions a certain amount of time is necessary. [T]he important thing is that the training of the officers and noncommissioned officers capable of absorbing... recruits takes a much longer period... It is my professional opinion that far from overtraining any element of the Army of the United States we are not able under existing conditions to reach the standards that should prevail in the skeletonized nucleus that we maintain.[35]

From 1921 to 1936, American foreign and national defense policy was founded on the questionable premise that future wars with other major powers, except possibly Japan, could be avoided.[36] The efforts of the diplomats at the 1922 Washington Naval Conference produced treaties that for a time stopped the expensive race for naval supremacy. Construction of new capital ships was frozen in the United States, Great Britain, Japan, and other signatory nations for ten years. Limitations were set on individual capital-ship size and armament. A ratio of 5:5:3 for total permissible capital-ship tonnage of the United States, Great Britain, and Japan was established to assure none of the three great naval powers could successfully launch a Pacific offensive, provided each nation respected the treaty. Other provisions froze the construction of new fortifications or naval facilities in the western Pacific. The treaties made defense of the Philippines and other small island possessions by the United States against a Japanese attack nearly impossible. Guam, in the Marianas, near the Japanese held islands of Saipan and Tinian, became "a pillbox without guns," defended by a few U.S. Marines equipped with no defensive weapon larger than a .30 caliber machine gun. Still, the general agreement to maintain the status quo in the Pacific and in China provided some assurance at the time against a Japanese war of aggression if the Western powers did not themselves become embroiled in a major conflict in Europe and the Atlantic.[37]

Congress and several presidential administrations sought to keep the peace by maintaining minimal defensive military strength, avoiding commitments with European nations, and using American diplomacy and mediation to promote international peace and the limitation of armaments.[38] In 1928 the United States and France promulgated the Kellogg-Briand Treaty, also known as the Pact of Paris, through which signatory nations renounced war as an instrument of national policy.[39] The government of the United States declared that if other powers made the same commitment, it would restrict its armed forces to only those necessary to maintain internal order and to defend its national territory against aggression and invasion.[40] The American dream of global peace, however, has never been realized.

Deep and prolonged world economic depression from 1929 to 1933 caused panic among affected populations faced with hyperinflation, economic ruin, and starvation. When this was coupled with the rise of radical nationalist and authoritarian states, American hopes for international comity and peace were dashed. Although it was not generally recognized at the time, the conflicts that would become World War II began in 1931, when the Japanese army invaded Manchuria, established a puppet state, and ignored the diplomatic efforts of the League of Nations and the United States to end the occupation. Japan, hearing "ancestral voices prophesying war,"[iii][41] left the League in 1933. In 1934 the government of Japan formally announced that after the last of its obligations expired in 1936 it would not be bound by the postwar arms control treaties.

Adolf Hitler became chancellor of Germany in 1933, assuming dictatorial powers and ruling by force and terror. In rapid succession, the Nazi regime repudiated the Treaty of Versailles, embarked on rearmament forbidden by the treaty, and occupied the demilitarized Rhineland, all by 1936. Benito Mussolini, Fascist ruler of Italy since 1922, launched his own war of aggression by attacking Ethiopia in 1935. Spain's reactionary rebellion in 1936 under General Francisco Franco was supported by both Germany and Italy. The democratically elected leftist government of Spain was supported by the Soviet Union and by many non-governmental organizations in the West. The Spanish insurrection led to a protracted and savage civil war that provided a proving ground for the authoritarian powers' new weapons and tactics used later in World War II. The response of Congress to these violent developments was to pass a series of neutrality acts between 1935 and 1937, seeking to avoid involvement in European conflicts.[42] The United States also strengthened its international position during the first administration of Franklin Roosevelt by establishing diplomatic relations with the Soviet Union in 1933,[43] by promising eventual independence to the Philippines in 1934,[44] and

---

iii   Coleridge, Samuel Taylor, "Kubla Khan; or, A Vision in a Dream: A Fragment" (line 30), (London, 1816).

by liquidating its protectorates in the Caribbean area and generally pursuing the policy of the good neighbor toward Latin America.[45]

No changes in American military policy followed immediately upon the rise of Hitler to power or upon Japan's aggression in China. But American professional military men began warning the civilian leaders of danger ahead. Chief of Staff MacArthur used uncompromising language in his 1934 annual report on the state of the Army. After pointing out that the National Defense Act of 1920 provided for 17,728 officers and 280,000 enlisted men, MacArthur wrote:

> In spite of its moderate purposes, the National Defense Act has been given but little and decreasing support. Our military framework has become so attenuated that the ideal of reasonable security sought by the Congress which enacted it is far from attainment. Our Regular Army and National Guard are at considerably less than half the strength contemplated in the law. The Officers' Reserve Corps is inadequately supported in the essentials of training. We have no Enlisted Reserve. Stocks of matériel are in vital respects inadequate even for limited forces, and, such as they are, comprise principally World War equipment, manifestly obsolescent.
>
> The preparatory missions devolving upon the Military Establishment in time of peace cannot in some respects be efficiently performed; while the grave responsibilities that would fall to it in emergency would require frantic improvisations, and wasteful and possibly ineffective sacrifice of the Nation's manhood and material resources. These are facts—demonstrable both in the light of history's lessons and through logical analysis of existing conditions.
>
> This blunt expression of War Department conviction divulges the secrets of our weakness, which if known only to professional soldiers had probably best remain concealed. Unfortunately, they are secrets only to our own people in whom resides exclusively, in the last analysis, the power for correction. They are fully known to qualified military observers abroad and to all those governments that give more credence to the conclusions of the trained soldier than we do.[46]

Beginning in 1935 Congress made larger appropriations for the Army and Navy that allowed the armed forces to improve somewhat their readiness for war. Civilian recognition of the increasingly dangerous international situation and the prudent anticipatory planning of the War Department during General MacArthur's 1930–5 tenure as chief of staff resulted in changes in Army organization and administration from 1936 to 1938. The thrust of MacArthur's recommendations was American strategic and tactical mobility utilizing superior U.S. technology and industrial productivity. He observed that "[g]reater Infantry mobility on the march is certain to result from a maximum use of motors and of growing nets of good roads, both for transportation of supplies and equipment and, where possible, of personnel. Every great power recognizes the importance of this trend and is striving to provide appropriate transportation for its army. Animal transport will soon be found in Infantry formations only for very special uses, if at all."[47]

The chief of staff planned to use the Army's growing but still limited resources and America's motor vehicle industry to create a small, hard-hitting, and wholly motorized and mechanized Regular Army ready for emergency deployment. The Army prepared to mechanize and motorize its regular combat units as soon as possible and bring them to full strength for realistic and effective training.[48] It established new organizations to administer standardized training of larger ground and air units and combined-arms teams, and to exercise command and control in the event of war. Between 1932 and 1935 the War Department created four new regional army headquarters and a General Headquarters Air Force in the continental United States.

Beginning in the summer of 1935, the new General Headquarters conducted joint training exercises for select Regular Army and National Guard divisions and other units in summer maneuvers and other activities, including joint exercises with the Navy. In 1935 and again in 1936 Congress made appropriations that enabled the Regular Army to increase its enlisted strength to 165,000 by 1937.[49] Substantial increases in equipment and housing budgets followed, so that by 1938 the Regular Army had somewhat greater combat strength and improved readiness than five years earlier.[50]

The strength and readiness of foreign armies and air forces, however, had been increasing much faster. The 1938 annual report of General Malin Craig, chief of staff of the Army from October 1935 to August 1939, was included in an exhibit presented during hearings in April 1941 before a Senate Special Committee. Chaired by Senator Harry S. Truman, the committee was charged to investigate the progress and costs of the national defense program. Lieutenant General Malin Craig was obliged to state that the U.S. Army was still greatly inferior to its potential foes.

> It is a source of gratification to record that legislation enacted at the last session of Congress authorized the attainment of 165,000 enlisted men. Our Regular Army at this latter strength ranks only 18th among the standing armies of the world. This marked inferiority in strength suggests that it is all the more imperative that the armament of this force be equal to that it may be called upon to face. Here, too, we fell behind. We failed to keep pace with the development in defensive weapons that has occurred since the World War... Until the past year the limited amounts appropriated annually for armament were devoted largely to the procurement of aircraft. To a lesser extent they were applied to the procurement of tanks and similar combat vehicles. Substantially little was devoted to the new defensive weapons.[51]

The German annexation of Austria in March 1938 and the Czech crisis in September of the same year convinced some policy makers in the United States and the other democratic nations of the near certainty of another war. When Germany conquered Czechoslovakia in March 1939 and took over Czechoslovakia's advanced steel and weapons production plants and its first-rate arms and fortifications, war in Europe became inevitable. Most informed people discerned that Hitler intended to continue his policy of eastward expansion. The elected governments of Great Britain and France, although subject to continued opposition from both pro-fascist and appeasement factions, and from leftist and pacifist groups, decided that they must fight rather than yield to further German aggression.

In the summer of 1939, Soviet and Japanese armies clashed on the Manchurian-Mongolian frontier in a little-known conflict with far-reaching consequences both strategic and tactical. No mere border clash, this was an undeclared war that raged from May to September 1939. In a preview of the large-scale combined arms warfare that would characterize the North African and Eastern fronts, more than 100,000 troops and 1,000 tanks and aircraft were committed by the Soviets. The Red Army already then possessed the largest armored force on the planet, but it was equipped chiefly with obsolete models. The T26 light tank was vulnerable to the Japanese Type 95 tank and to infantry tank destroyer teams using Molotov cocktails. The better-designed BT-7 cruiser tank was fast but under gunned. The Russian tanks were brilliantly deployed, despite immense losses, in combined arms formations by the soon-to-be famous General Georgi Zhukov, who commanded with his characteristic indifference to casualties. Some 50,000 Russians were killed or wounded. In the climactic 12-day battle at Khalkhin Gol near the Mongolian-Manchurian border, from August 20 to 31, 1939, the Japanese were crushed although the Russians suffered more casualties.

The momentous result of this Central Eurasian conflict was the Soviet-Japanese Neutrality Pact. Soviet-Japanese détente coincided precisely with the conclusion of the German-Soviet Nonaggression Pact, under which Hitler made a deal with Stalin that provided for the extinguishment of the Polish state and nation and the partition of its territory between the dictatorial states. Hitler gave the Soviet Union a free hand in Finland and the northern Baltic states. On September 1, 1939, Germany invaded and in a matter of weeks conquered Poland. The Soviet Union invaded Poland from the east on September 17. The governments of France and Great Britain declared war on Germany but could provide no direct assistance to the Poles in time to save them from being crushed. The Western democracies now faced three radical authoritarian states or coalitions, free of constraints by the other dictatorships, possessing large modern armies and air forces, and supported by modern heavy industries.

In 1939, the majority of Americans still wanted to stay out of war. Franklin Roosevelt, the canniest politician since Lincoln, understood public opinion and took a step-by-step approach even as the aggressor nations attacked their neighbors. In the face of popular reluctance, American politicians adopted a cautious posture when remarking on the dangerous international situation. Roosevelt's "own leadership during these critical months responded far more to the isolationist pressures of the electorate than to his activist, worldly instincts... Any President during this period, given the confused state of public opinion and political combat, would have had to pick his way cautiously through the foreign policy maze of the mid-[nineteen] thirties."[52] President Roosevelt and his advisers nonetheless perceived the danger and responsibly directed a limited preparedness campaign at the beginning of 1939. Rapid improvements in aircraft technology and the unproven but intriguing theories of strategic bombing had introduced a new factor into the military calculations of the United States. The government recognized that soon a hostile European power might have the means to establish air bases in the Western hemisphere. Bombers on such bases could attack the Panama Canal, the vital strategic key to American continental and maritime defense strategy, or the continental United States itself. Foreign airfields in the western hemisphere would erase the oceanic security that the United States and the other American republics had long enjoyed. Increasing the power of the Army Air Corps to counter the air threat became a key goal of defense planners as Europe descended into war.[53]

Meanwhile, Army and Navy staff officers drafted a new series of war plans for facing a hostile coalition. Students at the Army War College researched coalition defense plans during 1934, working in close cooperation with the General Staff. The resulting *Rainbow* plans were the successors to the existing color-coded war plans against potential adversaries. The new plans incorporated aspects of both War College research and the older plans. In early October 1939, President Roosevelt formally approved the *Rainbow I* plan, changing the military policy of the United States from guarding only the United States and its possessions to *hemispheric defense*. That policy guided Army plans and actions until the end of 1940.[54]

The Army in the 1920s and 1930s was subject to the strategic requirements of and constrained by the resources allocated by the civilian political leadership. It was short on personnel, equipment, and funding. The Army had to focus on its primary assigned mission: the defense of the continental United States and its Territories. It was not prepared to fight the war that American civilian and military leadership expected it to fight. The goal of "Fortress America," a military and naval establishment large enough to wage a war to defend the Western hemisphere, was unreachable at the time. The Army was even less ready for the real war that erupted in late 1941. In the vastly different strategic world of 1941, France and Western Europe had fallen, both the USSR and the British Empire were close to collapse, and the Japanese Empire was the paramount military and naval power in the Pacific. The United States was compelled to prepare large mechanized expeditionary forces for overseas combat for a global, two-front war. None of this had been foreseen in the late 1930s, because the American people and their leaders were slow to recognize and appreciate how great the danger was. Advanced industrialized military technology was now in the hands of authoritarian governments led by ferocious racists and militarists. But Americans had been warned. Many, including Churchill himself, had been sounding the tocsin since before 1933 that the resurgent National Socialist German Reich and the Japanese militarists were real threats.[55]

The nation's military situation in 1940, however, was not hopeless. Under the NDA of 1920, the Army had in place the capability to plan for the complex mobilization of the country's resources for industrialized warfare on a global scale. The Army's Industrial Mobilization Plan of 1930, largely written by Eisenhower, established the basic principles for harnessing the nation's economic strength to war needs.[56] Continuous Army staff mobilization exercises and revisions of the plan through 1939 improved it.

Manpower planning followed a similar process that produced the Protective Mobilization Plan of 1937.[57] Under that plan, the first step in a general mobilization would be the induction of the National Guard into federal service, providing the Army of the United States with an initial protective force of about 400,000. The Navy and this defensive force would defend the country while the Army engaged in an orderly expansion to planned strengths of one, two, or four million, as necessary. The Army's manpower planning included, for the first time in peace, a definite training plan that specified the location, size, and construction schedules of replacement training centers, unit training centers, and schools. It specified the details of unit and individual training programs and provided for the printing of a variety of training manuals.[58]

While these plans helped to guide the mobilization that began in the summer of 1940, there were shortcomings. Military planners had assumed a maximum mobilization of World War I size, not the gigantic expansion for a planetary war that World War II would require. The planned training cycles overlooked the benefits of unit cohesion, and the resulting conflicts in training assignments and schedules impaired *esprit de corps* in new regiments and divisions. The soon-to-be vastly greater Army, Army Air Forces, Navy, and Marine Corps of the United States, and the forces of the Allied powers, required a commensurately larger domestic industrial production plant, not yet in existence, to supply their gigantic needs. The planners had assumed the Army would face an emergency without time to build up production or to select and produce the most modern weapon designs and would have to rely initially on matériel and equipment in inventory.

The 1939 Protective Mobilization Plan standardized many existing weapons to facilitate rapid procurement and stockpiling, an understandable decision considering the Army's poor equipment state and the international situation. But standardization, in combination with the Army's earlier emphasis on funding personnel strength at the expense of research and development, impeded weapons programs in an era that demanded the latest military technology. The Army entered World War II with weapons and vehicle designs from both World War I and from the mid-1930s, some of them already obsolete.[59] On the other hand, resources had not been wasted on obsolete equipment when it became possible to procure innovative designs, such as the M1 Garand rifle and the bazooka anti-tank rocket launcher. The War Department bureaucracy, however, lagged behind advances in the mobility and lethality of modern weapons, especially high-velocity artillery and ordnance, armored fighting vehicles, and tactical support aircraft.

When the Nazis invaded Poland on September 1, 1939, the president proclaimed a limited national emergency and authorized increases in Regular Army and National Guard enlisted strengths to 227,000 and 235,000, respectively.[60] He also proclaimed American neutrality, but at his urging Congress gave indirect support to the Western democracies by ending the prohibition on munitions sales to nations at war required by the Neutrality Act of 1937. British and French munitions orders had the immediate beneficial consequence of preparing American industry for the stupendously larger scale of war production that was to come.

The conquest of Poland was followed by an illusory lull in the war. The tempo of America's own defense preparations ebbed but did not stop. The Army concentrated on making its regular force ready for emergency action by supplying it with modern equipment as quickly as possible. The War Department conducted in April 1940 the first genuine corps and army training maneuvers in American military history. Those were followed in 1941 by the largest maneuvers in Army history up to that time, in Louisiana and North Carolina. The 1941 Louisiana maneuvers, in which the 34th Infantry Division participated to a limited extent, were an important testing ground for new doctrine and equipment as well as for the expanded officer corps. Armies, corps, and divisions conducted large motorized and armored movements in a series of "force on force" mock battles.

The adequacy of the Army's preparations depended greatly on the fate of France and Great Britain. Germany's April 1940 conquest of Denmark and Norway, the subsequent defeat of the Low Countries and France in May and June, and the grave threat which Great Britain faced by June forced the United States to adopt a new and vastly enlarged program for defense during that month. By the summer of 1940, it appeared that the United States might have to challenge the aggressors of the Old World and Asia almost alone.[61]

CHAPTER 3

National Pre-War Mobilization and Foreign Policy

In January 1940, when the European war was still in a lull called by the British *Sitzkrieg*,[i] President Roosevelt asked Congress for a national defense appropriation of $1.8 billion. By the middle of May, the Roosevelt administration began to advocate forcefully for the mobilization of America's industrial and military resources to oppose any further expansion of the European fascists and the Japanese. The destruction of Belgium and the Netherlands and the fall of France in the spring of 1940 greatly moved public opinion toward direct aid and support for the cause of the Western democracies. President Roosevelt felt he had strong support for his policy to sustain the British in their fight against the Axis and to request further appropriations for both national and expanded hemispheric defense.[1] In an address to Congress on May 16, 1940, as the German cataract sliced across France and the Low Lands, he said that the brutal force of modern offensive war had been loosed in all its horror by ruthless and daring men wielding new and deadly powers of destruction; that no defense was so strong that it did not require strengthening and that no attack was so unlikely that it could be ignored.

> Surely, [the President said] the developments of the past few weeks have made it clear to all of our citizens that the possibility of attack on vital American zones ought to make it essential that we have the physical, the ready ability to meet those attacks and to prevent them from reaching their objectives... This means military implements—not on paper—which are ready and available to meet any lightning offensive against our American interest. It means also that facilities for production must be ready to turn out munitions and equipment at top speed.

The president said that America had learned the lesson that unprepared nations found themselves overrun by the enemy. He emphasized that impregnable fortifications no longer existed and that an effective defense required the equipment to attack an aggressor "before he can establish strong bases within the territory of American vital interests."[2]

---

i   *Sitzkrieg* (n.) 1940, "static warfare" (such as prevailed in Europe in the winter of 1939–40), RAF coinage on analogy of blitzkrieg (q.v.), from German *sitz* "a sitting," from *sitzen* "to sit." Online Etymology Dictionary. https://www.etymonline.com/.

The president told Congress that he should like to see the United States "geared up to the ability to turn out at least 50,000 planes a year." He said, "that this Nation should plan at this time a program that would provide us with 50,000 military and naval planes." He requested $1 billion immediately to procure the essential equipment for a larger Army, to replace or modernize Army and Navy equipment, to increase production facilities for everything needed for the Army and Navy, and to accelerate all Army and Navy contracts to a 24-hour basis. The president reminded Congress that the nation's objective still was peace. Nevertheless, the people had to stand ready "not only to spend millions for defense but to give our service and even our lives for the maintenance of our American liberties."[3]

In another message to Congress on May 31[4] President Roosevelt made a request for over a billion dollars for national defense and for presidential authority to call the National Guard and the necessary Reserve personnel into active military service. He declared that "the almost incredible events of the past two weeks in the European conflict, particularly as a result of the use of aviation and mechanized equipment," required further increases in the military program. American defense had to be made robust while the possibility existed that all the continents might be involved in a global war. He again emphasized the necessity for expansion of facilities to produce munitions. His requests for appropriations were promptly met by Congress, as also was the president's request of July 10 for $5 billion more for the rearmament program. The president's request for authority to call the National Guard and Reserve personnel into active military service was granted in a resolution approved August 27, 1940. However, the legislation stipulated that the personnel ordered into active Federal service under this authority should "not be employed beyond the limits of the Western Hemisphere except in the territories and possessions of the United States, including the Philippine Islands."[5]

Secretary of State Cordell Hull gave an address on June 20, 1940, describing the danger to peaceful nations. He spoke of malignant forces in the world which sprang from "lust for power which seeks to hold men in physical slavery and spiritual degradation and to displace a system of peaceful and orderly relations among nations by the anarchy of wanton violence and brute force." Never before, Hull said, had there been so powerful a challenge to freedom and civilization, nor had there been a more desperate need for freedom-loving men and nations to unite their spiritual and material resources in their own defense. The secretary warned that there had never been a more vital test confronting the American people; that difficult and dangerous days were ahead; and that the national independence and democratic institutions of the United States were not immune from those malignant forces already plaguing the world. The United States could meet the challenge, he insisted, if Americans held on to their faith in the "everlasting worth of freedom and honor, of truth and justice, of intellectual and spiritual integrity, and an immutable determination to give their all, if necessary, for the preservation of the American way of life."[6]

The military catastrophes in Western Europe during May and June 1940 increased the real danger to the security not only of the United States but of all the American republics. This implicated the newly adopted policy of the president and of the Congress that the Army's mission was to be hemispheric defense. The Roosevelt administration used every available tool of diplomacy and economic influence to organize the other American republics to meet the Nazi threat. The foreign ministers of the American republics assembled at Havana, Cuba in late July 1940 to consider the danger posed by the aggressor states. They consulted on measures addressing three hemispheric security problems. The first was the possibility of the transfer of sovereignty of islands and regions in the Americas from one non-American state to another non-American state. The American republics had foremost in mind the French possessions in the Caribbean region and South America and the powerful elements of the French fleet at anchor in the harbors of the French West Indies and in French Guiana. The second threat was subversive activities in the American nations directed from outside the hemisphere. Axis subversion posed a real threat, especially in those countries with large populations of ethnic Germans and Italians and powerful right-wing elements in their national political cultures. Finally, and vitally important to the problem of supplying the Allied forces, the ministers considered the grave economic difficulties and dislocations resulting from the war.[7]

While the relations of the United States with its hemispheric neighbors proceeded under the cloud of previous United States interventions and economic imperialism, the Roosevelt administration's Good Neighbor policy had some practical benefits. The concerted American republics entered a formal accord known as the "Act of Havana." They formulated an arrangement for the provisional administration by an inter-American organization of any non-American possession in the Americas in case of a danger of change in its sovereignty. They agreed that each of the 21 republics would take cooperative measures to prevent subversive activities directed from abroad against the internal affairs of the American republics and would exchange information regarding the activities of foreign agents and sympathizers. The republics took steps to mitigate the inevitable economic disruptions of a protracted global war, including steps for increasing domestic consumption of exportable surpluses, to expand markets among the American nations for surpluses, and to create means for the temporary storing, financing, and handling of commodities and for their orderly marketing. The American republics declared "that any attempt on the part of a non-American State against the integrity or inviolability of the territory, the sovereignty or the political independence of an American State shall be considered as an act of aggression against the States which sign this declaration."[8] The natural resources and wealth of Central and South America would be marshalled for a cooperative defense of the hemisphere.

Shortly after the Havana Conference, on August 6, 1940, Secretary Hull said it was strongly believed at Havana that "the military and other sinister activities on the part of some nations in other large areas of the world present real possibilities of danger to the American republics." He said it was universally recognized that a threat to any part of the Americas meant a threat to each and all the American nations and that full and adequate preparations for hemispheric defense could not be taken too soon. He warned in magisterial language that "vast forces of lawlessness, conquest, and destruction were moving across the earth like a savage and dangerous animal at large" and that by their very nature those forces would not stop unless and until an unbreakable resistance opposed them. The secretary said that "the one and only sure way" for the United States to avoid being drawn into serious trouble or actual war and to command respect for its rights and interests abroad, was for Americans themselves to become thoroughly conscious of the danger. Americans had "to make up their minds that we must continue to arm, and to arm to such an extent that the forces of conquest and ruin will not dare make an attack on us or on any part of this hemisphere." Hull asserted that each citizen must be ready and willing for real sacrifice of time and of substance and personal service: "[W]e cannot pursue complacently the course of our customary normal life."[9] The American people knew very well the policy of the Roosevelt administration: to prepare defenses adequate to defeat any aggression against the Western hemisphere. The soldiers of the 34th "Red Bull" Infantry Division would become the embodiment of that policy.

Destroyers for Bases; Selective Service

Early in September 1940 an agreement between the United States and Great Britain was concluded whereby Great Britain received 50 old United States destroyers and the United States acquired the right to lease naval and air bases in Newfoundland, in British Guiana, and in the islands of Bermuda, the Bahamas, Jamaica, St. Lucia, Trinidad, and Antigua. In the background, Churchill had impressed upon Roosevelt Britain's immediate and vital need for more naval escort vessels. Roosevelt received advice that while he could not give the British the old destroyers, he might legally lease them for some sufficient consideration. The resulting deal well suited the interests of both soon-to-be allies. President Roosevelt reported to Congress that this agreement was not in any way inconsistent with the nation's status as a non-belligerent; that it was not a threat against any nation; that it was "an epochal and far-reaching act of preparation for continental defense in the face of grave danger." The president stressed that the value to the Western hemisphere "of these outposts of security is beyond calculation." He considered them essential to the protection of the Panama Canal, Central America, the northern portion of South America, the Antilles, Canada, Mexico, and [the U.S.] Eastern and Gulf seaboards. This was all quite true, as an examination of maps of the North Atlantic Ocean and the Caribbean Sea proves. It would also be proved that Allied bases on those islands were invaluable to defend the inter-American and trans-Atlantic sea lanes to Europe and Africa from both surface raiders and submarines. The United States government announced that bases would be made available to all American republics for the common defense of the hemisphere.[10]

Finally, the United States government took the essential step for national defense. On September 14, 1940, Congress enacted the Selective Service and Training Act.[11] The president signed the bill into law on September 16, 1940. For the first time in its history the United States adopted compulsory military training of manpower when the nation was not at war. The act included a provision that persons inducted into the land forces should not be employed beyond the Western hemisphere except in United States territories and possessions. A week later the president signed Executive Order No. 8545 prescribing selective service regulations governing the administration of the draft system.[12] The 34th Infantry Division would have to absorb many of the draftees, men with no military training whatsoever.

The Axis: Treaty of Alliance Between Germany, Italy, and Japan

In 1934 and 1935 reports had reached the United States government that Japan and Germany were contemplating or had consummated some sort of an agreement for joint action. In 1936 those powers joined publicly in the Anti-Comintern Pact. A year later Italy had become a party to that agreement. During the next three years it became clear that those three countries were pursuing a common pattern of aggression in both Europe and East Asia. On September 11, 1940, in a conversation with the newly arrived Vichy French Ambassador Gaston Henry-Haye, Secretary of State Hull directly declared to the envoy of the Nazi puppet government that for several years the United States had pursued the fixed policy of basing all statements and actions on the assumption that "Hitler was out to become the ruthless and utterly destructive conqueror of Europe, and that the Japanese military clique was bent on the same course in the Pacific area from Hawaii to Siam [Thailand]."[13]

American suspicions and expectations were confirmed when, on September 27, 1940, Germany, Italy, and Japan signed a treaty of alliance. That pact explicitly provided that Japan recognized and respected the leadership of Germany and Italy in the establishment of a new order in Europe; that Germany and Italy recognized and respected the leadership of Japan in the establishment of a new order in Greater East Asia; and that the three countries would assist one another with all political, economic, and military means when one of the powers was attacked by a power not then involved in the European war or in the Sino-Japanese conflict. The last item was aimed directly at the United States. Secretary Hull said that the tripartite pact did not substantially alter a situation which had existed for several years, and merely made clear a relationship which had long existed in practical effect.[14]

In a conversation on September 30, 1940, with the British ambassador, Philip Kerr, Marquess of Lothian, Secretary Hull said that the Axis alliance had come about because of "Hitler's effort to divert attention from his failure to invade Great Britain and to preserve his prestige by a sensational announcement of something that already existed." The secretary averred that Japan would assume that whether or not the United States and Great Britain had agreements to share naval and air bases in the Pacific including Singapore, the special relations between the U.S. and the U.K. assured that they would quickly make arrangements for the mutual use of their bases. The secretary emphasized to the ambassador that the United States government wanted Great Britain to prevail and that American actions and statements with respect to the Pacific region would be those which would most effectively aid Great Britain in winning the war.[15]

Secretary Hull's Address of October 26, 1940

As the European war entered its second year, the Roosevelt administration made its foreign and military policy clear both to citizens of the United States and to foreign powers. In his speech of October 26, 1940, Hull warned that all peaceful nations were "gravely menaced" because of the "plans and acts of a small group of national rulers who had succeeded in transforming their peoples into forceful instruments for wide-spread domination by conquest." Hull stated that Americans were living in the presence not of local or regional wars, but of an "organized and determined movement for steadily expanding conquest." The rulers of the aggressor nations, he said, had renounced and broken the long-accepted principles of peaceful and orderly international relations. They adhered to no geographic lines, and they fixed no time-limit on their program of invasion and destruction. The dictators cynically disregarded every right of neutral nations. They openly sought to wrest control of the high seas. They threatened peaceful nations with immediate dire consequences if these nations did not remain acquiescent while the conquerors seized the other continents. "Let no one comfort himself with the delusion that these are mere excesses or exigencies of war," the secretary continued, "to be voluntarily abandoned when fighting ceases."

The appalling global tragedy, the secretary said, was that peaceful nations had not recognized in time the true nature of the aims and ambitions of the rulers of the aggressor nations. Peace-loving people recoiled from the prospect of another wide-spread war and had permitted themselves to be lulled into a false sense of security by the lies of the dictators. The first need for free countries was to create for themselves, as quickly as possible, "impregnable means of defense." This was the "staggering lesson of mankind's recent experience."[16]

To strengthen its own defenses and to prevent attacks on any part of the Western hemisphere, Hull announced, the United States would lend all facilities possible to support nations which, while defending themselves against barbaric attack, were fighting the spread of tyranny and thus reducing the danger to the United States.

He was referring, of course, to the United Kingdom and to its Dominions. Under America's "inalienable right of self-defense," he said, the United States would provide aid to the non-aggressor states to the greatest possible extent. Hull admonished that nothing was more dangerous for the United States "than for us to assume that the avalanche of conquest could under no circumstances reach any vital portion of this hemisphere." He stated that oceans no longer gave the American republics any guaranty against the real possibility of economic, political, or military attack from abroad. If the Axis powers were to gain control of Eurasia, they would next concentrate on total control of the seas, of the air over the seas, and of the world's economy. They might then be able with sea and air power to strike at the communication lines, the commerce, and the life of the Western hemisphere, and "ultimately we might find ourselves compelled to fight on our own soil, under our own skies, in defense of our independence and our very lives."[17]

President Roosevelt's "Arsenal of Democracy" Address

In his famous radio broadcast speech of December 29, 1940, President Roosevelt told the American people that the National Socialist regime in Germany had made it clear that they would not only dominate all life and thought in their own country but intended to enslave the whole of Europe. With the resources of Europe, the Nazis would seek domination of the world. The United States, he said, could not talk of peace until the day that the aggressor nations abandoned all thought of conquering the world. He explained that although some Americans wanted to believe that wars in Europe and Asia were of no concern to them, it was in fact of vital concern to Americans that European and Asiatic aggressors not control the oceans which led to the Western hemisphere. If Great Britain were defeated, the Axis powers would control the continents of Europe, Asia, Africa, and Australia, and, with the British and French fleets, the high seas. They would then use those enormous military and naval resources against the American hemisphere, the peoples of which "would be living at the point of a gun—a gun loaded with explosive bullets, economic as well as military." This was a danger ahead against which the nation must prepare.

Roosevelt declared that America was strengthening its own defense with the utmost urgency and must now "integrate the war needs of Britain and the other free nations resisting aggression." American industrial genius, resources, and talents were to be converted from manufacturing peacetime products to making instruments of war. He warned that existing efforts were not enough. "We must have more ships, more guns, more planes; we must be the great 'arsenal of democracy.'"[18]

The fate of Poland in September 1939 and of the Netherlands, Belgium, and France in May and June 1940 had convinced Congress of the urgent need to prepare for the defense of the United States on a large scale. Under the leadership of Chief of Staff General George C. Marshall and, after July, of Secretary of War Henry L. Stimson, the Army initiated its planned expansion to protect the United States and the rest of the Western hemisphere from hostile forces from Europe and Asia. The Army expansion, including the rapid growth of the Army Air Forces, was matched by a naval program designed to give the United States a two-ocean Navy. The Navy was to be strong enough to deal simultaneously with the Japanese in the Pacific, and with Germany and Italy in the Atlantic, even if Great Britain were defeated. By the end of World War II, it would be not only the largest navy in the world, but the largest navy that had ever existed.[19] The expansion programs had the overwhelming support of the American people, who also were now convinced that the danger to the United States was real and imminent. Most Americans, however, remained opposed to entering the war.

Congressional appropriations between May and October 1940 reflected the threat and America's new defense posture. More than $8 billion was appropriated for the Army, a more than 70-fold increase in annual funding and a greater amount than the total appropriated over the preceding 20 years. The munitions program approved for the Army on June 30, 1940, called for the procurement of all items needed to equip and maintain a 1.2-million-man force by October 1941, including the greatly enlarged and modernized Army Air Corps. By September, the War Department was planning to increase the force to 1.5 million soldiers as soon as possible.[20]

Of immediate consequence to the men of the 34th Infantry Division, Congress on August 27, 1940, authorized the induction of the National Guard into federal service and the activation of the Organized Reserves to fill the ranks of the Army of the United States. Units of the National Guard, draftees, members of the Enlisted Reserve Corps, and the reserve officers required to train them all entered active service as fast as the Army could construct camps to house them. The active Army of the United States more than doubled in strength during the last six months of 1940. By mid-1941 it had achieved its planned strength of 1.5 million officers and men, including the Red Bull Division.

The new War Department General Headquarters took charge of training the Army in July 1940. The Army also established a separate Armored Force and subsequently the Antiaircraft and Tank Destroyer Commands. With the Infantry, Field Artillery, Coast Artillery, and Cavalry, the three new commands increased the number of ground combat arms to seven. The Infantry's tank units and the Cavalry's mechanized brigade combined to form the new Armored Force, despite the strenuous objections of the Infantry and Cavalry leaders. Chief of Staff Marshall mandated the Armored Force's creation to overcome the inertia of those traditionally conservative branches and to spur the transformation of the armor branch to a role broader than supporting the infantry and performing conventional cavalry missions.[21] He and other American officers had studied with horror the startling success of German *blitzkrieg* operations that used entire divisions of tanks supported by mobile infantry to pierce through opposing defenses, to disrupt the opponent's communications and lines of supply, and to isolate, surround, and destroy the enemy in detail.

During 1940 and 1941 the existing branch schools and a new Armored Force School focused on improving the fitness of National Guard and reserve officers for active duty. In early 1941 the War Department established officer candidate schools to train men selected from the ranks for junior leadership positions. In October 1940, the four continental armies assumed command of all ground units in the continental United States and thereafter trained them under the supervision of the General Headquarters. The former corps area commands became administrative and service organizations.[22]

American war planners expected and prepared for simultaneous operations in the Pacific and the European regions. Army and Navy senior leadership, despite grumbling from some in the Navy about giving priority to the Pacific threat, agreed with Roosevelt that Germany was the greater menace. If the United States did enter the war, its policy would be to concentrate first on defeating Germany. That principle became shared policy with the British and Canadians in the ABC[ii] staff conferences between American, Canadian, and British military representatives in Washington from January to March 1941. During and after those sessions, the Army and Navy began adjusting the most comprehensive of the existing war plans, *Rainbow 5*, to correspond with ongoing military preparations and actions. During the following months, the trend moved steadily toward actual American participation in the war against Germany. In April 1941, the president authorized an active naval patrol of the western half of the Atlantic Ocean in response to the predation of German submarines on convoys bound for the United Kingdom. In May the United States accepted responsibility for the development and operation of military air routes across the North Atlantic via Greenland to the United Kingdom and across the South Atlantic via Brazil to British and Free French controlled territories on the African continent. Also in May, it appeared to the president and his military advisers that a German attack through Spain and Portugal to northwestern Africa and its adjacent islands was possible. That prospect, and the havoc wreaked by the Germans in the North Atlantic, caused the president to proclaim an unlimited national emergency. He directed the Army and Navy to deploy an expeditionary force to the Portuguese Azores islands, strategically located in the eastern North Atlantic, as a step toward blocking any German advance toward the South Atlantic.[23]

In early June 1941, the president learned that Hitler was preparing to attack the Soviet Union. He informed the Russian government, Stalin ignored him, and the Germans invaded the Soviet Union on June 22, 1941. That offensive diverted German military power away from the Atlantic for some time.[24] Attacking Russia was Hitler's first and greatest strategic blunder. The Red Army was badly led with too

---

ii   American, British, and Canadian.

many static divisions, but the Soviet Union possessed tremendous strategic depth, enormous reserves of manpower and natural resources, a large military industrial plant, and massive armor and artillery arms. New Russian heavy and medium tanks that outclassed most of the existing German tanks were just then becoming available.

Denmark was already under the Nazi boot when the local government of Greenland asked the Allies for protection. U.S. Coast Guard cutters were dispatched to deliver arms and supplies and to establish a U.S. consular presence. The Greenland provisional government and the United States entered into an agreement for protectorate status in April, chiefly to secure the cryolite mine on the island. On June 25, U.S. Army troops landed in Greenland to protect the island from German attack and to build bases for the air ferry route across the North Atlantic. With the assistance of Greenland residents, the Army units and Coast Guard elements captured several German weather teams in the Greenland area providing information to the Nazi military, highlighting the strategic importance of the region and the urgency of its defense.

Earlier that month President Roosevelt had ordered a force of U.S. Marines to relieve British troops guarding another critical outpost in the North Atlantic, Iceland. The first contingent of U.S. forces reached Iceland in early July 1941. A sizable Army expeditionary force followed in September. By October, the U.S. Navy was fully engaged in convoy-escort duties in the western reaches of the North Atlantic. Navy ships, with assistance from Army aircraft, joined British and Canadian forces in the struggle against Nazi submarines. In November Congress repealed prohibitions against the arming of American merchant vessels and their entry into combat zones. The stage was set, as Churchill noted on November 9, for "constant fighting in the Atlantic between German and American ships."[25] American sailors were in the shooting war. The majority of Americans solidly supported these actions, although a small, vociferous minority criticized the president for departing from neutrality. But the American people were still not prepared for an open declaration of war against Germany.[26] Hitler with unaccustomed restraint bided his time. He was not ready for war with America.

American policy toward Japan toughened as the United States moved toward war in the Atlantic. Although the U.S. government hoped to avoid a two-ocean war, it was unwilling to do so by surrendering vital areas or interests to the Japanese as the price of peace. When the Japanese moved large forces into French Indochina (modern Laos and Vietnam) in late July 1941, the United States responded by cutting off oil shipments and freezing Japanese assets. At the same time the War Department recalled General MacArthur from his retirement and position as field marshal of the Philippine Army to serve as commander of both U.S. and Philippine Army forces in the Far East. Army reinforcements, including new B-17 heavy bombers, were deployed to the Philippines to dissuade the Japanese from making further southward moves. The Japanese government, under the sway of the fanatically nationalistic Imperial Japanese

Army, continued to negotiate with the United States, while making tentative plans in September to embark on a war of conquest in Southeast Asia and the Indies as soon as possible. The Imperial Japanese Navy developed a plan to immobilize the U.S. Pacific Fleet by a carrier-borne air strike against the naval base at Pearl Harbor on the island of Oahu in what was then the U.S. Territory of Hawaii. The Japanese would use novel aero-naval tactics and weapons, including armor piercing shells modified as gravity bombs and torpedoes altered to run shallow in Pearl Harbor's waters. When intensive last-minute negotiations in November failed to produce any accommodation, the Japanese made their decision for war irrevocable.[27]

CHAPTER 4

The 34ID Federalized: Prewar Mobilization and Early Training

On Tuesday, January 14, 1941, President Roosevelt issued Executive Order 8633 "Ordering Certain Units and Members of the National Guard of the United States into the Active Military Service of the United States."[1] Events then began to move quickly for the men of the soon-to-be assembled 34th Infantry Division. On February 6, 1941, Headquarters Iowa National Guard, Office of the Adjutant General, issued General Orders No. 3, pursuant to the Presidential Order, directing the Guard units to discharge remaining financial obligations with state funds and to be ready to enter federal service on February 10.[2] The War Department issued orders on Monday, February 10, 1941, federalizing the Iowa, Minnesota, and North Dakota regiments to form the 34th Infantry Division. The Red Bull was the 14th of the 18 National Guard divisions brought into the Army of the United States under the act of Congress which limited the Guard to 12 months of service in defense of the Western hemisphere. Regiments staged hasty recruiting drives to fill out their ranks before heading to Louisiana for training. The 151st Field Artillery Regiment, from Minneapolis, offered new recruits $21 a month and a chance to "go south with the Gopher Gunners…" Many of the recruits believed President Roosevelt, who had said in 1940 campaign speeches in Philadelphia and in Boston, "I have said this before but I shall say it again and again and again: Your boys are not going to be sent into foreign wars." Newspaper editorials across the Midwest expressed the same tone of denial. "World War II is a battle of airplanes and naval units," the *Daily Freeman Journal* of Webster City, Iowa, printed on February 27, 1941. "No one expects the United States Infantry to leave the borders of the United States, even if this country should get into war."[3]

The 34th Infantry Division—the "Red Bull"[4]—was, as Rick Atkinson points out, a typical National Guard division of the 1930s and early 1940s. It was a division in name only. The division's units were scattered throughout Iowa, Minnesota, and North Dakota, and truly came together as a division only in the summer of 1940 at Camp Ripley, Wisconsin. As in the case of Regular Army units, most Guard drills and maneuvers were conducted at the company and battalion level. The 34th Infantry

Division, created in 1917 for World War I, was a "square" division, as most divisions in the Army and all in the National Guard still were in 1940. Its structure comprised two brigades of two regiments each, totaling on paper 27,313 men. It had in fact only about 40 percent of its full complement. The Red Bull's major units were the 67th and 68th Infantry Brigades, consisting of the 135th Infantry Regiment from Minnesota, the 164th Infantry Regiment from North Dakota, and the 133rd and 168th Infantry Regiments from Iowa. It also had the 59th Field Artillery Brigade (consisting of three regiments), the 109th Medical Battalion, the 109th Engineer Battalion, and supporting divisional units of Military Police, Quartermaster, Chemical Corps and Signal Corps.[5]

The National Guard was an important element of social life in the farming communities of the Midwest in the 1920s and 1930s. Guardsmen were proud of their units' histories and had a sense of unit cohesion. The people of the towns bought shares to construct armories for the companies of the regiments, and the state government paid rent to the owners, bolstering local economies. Armories were also community centers. In additions to offices, a drill hall resembling a basketball court, an armory for small arms, and supply rooms, local armories had facilities for reunions, dances, banquets, and patriotic celebrations. Guardsmen received one dollar (in 1930s dollars) for attending a training session at a time when the average wage earner made about $850 per year. Their pay was an important source of supplemental income during the Depression and aided recruiting. Units met weekly to practice close-order drill and the manual of arms. At irregular intervals they performed small-unit maneuvers on a football field or in a city square. Summer training was conducted at state military camps, such as Camp Ripley, a 53,000-acre state military reservation in Minnesota established in 1930, and Camp Dodge, Iowa.

> The annual inspection in each armory was usually linked to a military ball, the highlight of the social season. Maj. Walter [Bedell] Smith[i] inspected the southwestern Iowa units in 1939 and called them a "very very fine organization." Other regiments in northern and northwestern Iowa, in Minnesota, and in North Dakota came together with the 168th to form the 34th Division, commanded in 1939 by Maj. Gen. E. A. Walsh of Minneapolis. In the summer of 1940, the division trained at Camp Ripley, Wisconsin (*sic*). Upon the troops' return to their armories, revised National Guard programs and schedules doubled their training time. The average guardsman in the 168th had eighteen months of service. Two-thirds were high school graduates; about one-third had some education beyond high school. Captains were between thirty-four and forty-five years of age, and many of them, and more senior officers, had served in World War I. Quite a few men joined the regiment in 1941 to avoid the draft.[6]

The 34th Infantry Division's training at Camp Ripley in the summer of 1940 was probably like that of any other National Guard division: small unit tactics, marksmanship, and close order drill. The only difference in the 1940 encampment

---

i   Major Smith was promoted quickly to Brigadier General, and later became Eisenhower's chief of staff and indispensable confidant.

from those of the inter-war period was a divisional headquarters and a three-week training session. They trained from August 4 to 24. After they returned from Camp Ripley in late August 1940, training time in local armories was doubled. Still, that armory training was severely limited; the units were too widely scattered to assemble for more complex instruction. By official Iowa Guard policy, so-called armory training consisted mainly of "discipline, use and care of arms, material and equipment, leadership, responsibilities of commanders, protection measures against chemical warfare, and target practice." In the physically constricted environment, little more could be done.[7] For the National Guard to become an effective fighting force, the federal government would have to provide the space and resources for far more comprehensive and realistic training.

Beginning in October 1940, units of the Red Bull began receiving alerts for imminent activation and induction into federal service. The units were alerted nine times, throwing personal lives into chaos and uncertainty. Division components were finally federalized in January and February 1941. The division headquarters and most of the major units were activated on February 10, 1941.[8] On Wednesday, January 22, 1941, the State of Minnesota, Department of Military and Naval Affairs, Adjutant General's Office issued Special Order 19, pursuant to Executive Order 8633, ordering the 135th Infantry Regiment and other units of the 34th Infantry Division in Minnesota into the active military service of the United States for a period of 12 months. The 135th Regiment had a glorious military history: its motto—"To the last man"—had been hard won and richly deserved at Gettysburg.[9] Similar orders were issued to the sister regiments from Iowa, the 133IR and the 168IR, related field artillery and supporting units in Iowa, and to the 164th Infantry Regiment and its supporting elements in North Dakota. On Friday, February 7, 1941, Headquarters, 135IR issued Special Order No. 7 containing instructions for the assembly and transport of the regiment to Camp Claiborne, Louisiana.[10]

On Saturday, February 8, 1941, the United States House of Representatives passed H. R. 1776, the Lend-Lease Bill, authorizing the president when he deemed it in the interest of national defense, to direct the Department of War, the Department of the Navy or any other agency of the government to manufacture or otherwise procure any defense article, and to sell, transfer title to, exchange, lease, lend, or otherwise dispose of any defense article to the government of any country whose defense the president deemed vital to the defense of the United States.[11] The passage of Lend-Lease established concretely the intention of the United States to be the "arsenal of democracy" against Axis aggression. Prewar foreign aid and arms sales had been largely a self-defense measure; France and Britain had been allowed to buy airplanes and munitions to help contain the military might of the Axis powers until the United States could complete its own protective mobilization. By supplying the Allies, the government incentivized American private industry to make the gigantic investments in new plant and equipment that would be necessary to support a global war effort.[12] In early 1941 the focus of American policy thus shifted overtly from hemispheric defense to limited participation in the war. It appeared to Army and Navy leaders and to President Roosevelt that the United States most certainly would be drawn into full participation in the not-too-distant future, which proved to be all too soon for the 34th Infantry Division. The export of new arms and equipment to allies overseas, however, would actually hamper the training and equipment of the 34th Infantry Division and its sister divisions.

On February 10, 1941, units of the 135th Infantry Regiment of the Minnesota National Guard assembled for induction into Federal service at points in Minnesota, pursuant to Special Order No. 19, Adjutant General, in compliance with Presidential Executive Order 8633, and Special Order 7, HQ, 135IR. The regiment assembled by elements in armories throughout the State of Minnesota.

Regimental Hq.	Minneapolis, Minn.
Hq. Company	Minneapolis, Minn.
Service Company	Minneapolis, Minn.
Anti-tank Company	Minneapolis, Minn.
Medical Det.	Minneapolis, Minn.
Band	Minneapolis, Minn.
Hq. Det. 1st Bn.	Minneapolis, Minn.
Company A	Stillwater, Minn.
Company B	Hutchinson, Minn.
Company C	Minneapolis, Minn.
Company D	Stillwater, Minn.
Hq. Det. 2nd Bn.	Owatonna, Minn.
Company E	Jackson, Minn.
Company F	Owatonna, Minn.
Company G	Albert Lea, Minn.
Company H	Austin, Minn.
Hq. Det. 3rd Bn.	Montevideo, Minn.
Company I	Madison, Minn.
Company K	Dawson, Minn.
Company L	Ortonville, Minn.
Company M	Appleton, Minn.

The 135th Infantry Regiment's manpower was 86 officers, 1 warrant officer (WO), and 1,489 enlisted men. [13]

An advance detail of 135IR departed by rail for Louisiana on Wednesday, February 19, 1941. On Friday, February 21, 1941, a motorized echelon of 135IR left for Louisiana. The main body of 135IR departed from their home stations by rail *en route* to Camp Claiborne on Tuesday, February 25, 1941. There were sorrowful farewells in homes, town squares, and on station platforms. "The 25th of February was a bitter cold day with the mercury hovering around 20 degrees below zero. Various local bands preceded the troops to their respective depots to board the special trains awaiting them. Crowds of local people, parents, and friends waited in the cold for the trains to be loaded and move away."[14] On that significant day, many guardsmen may have begun to realize the dark enormity of their fate as soldiers. Some of those leaving, like their Civil War predecessors, would not return after the victory was won.

The 135IR main body arrived at Camp Claiborne on Thursday, February 27, 1941. The Camp was incomplete with unpaved dirt roads. "The roads were a sea of mud. Much of the work required to complete the camp facilities, including graveling company streets and company areas, building sidewalks … and erecting the 16-foot by 16-foot pyramidal squad tents was done by personnel of the regiment."[15] Despite the rough conditions, the next day the 135IR and other 34ID units began a training program to improve the skill levels of all ranks in preparation for the incorporation of selective service draftees into the division. But after Lend-Lease was enacted, British needs for weapons and munitions were given priority over equipping U.S. Army units. The result was that units including the 34th Infantry Division began training either with World War I weapons or with makeshifts.[16] For the trainees, for example, none of the new light machine guns, .30 cal. M1 or 60mm light mortars M2, was available.

Meanwhile, in towns and villages across Iowa and North Dakota, 133IR, 164IR and 168IR had also assembled to leave for what the Guardsmen believed was to be a year's training.[17]

> For three weeks they … practiced the manual of arms in the same soup-bowl helmets their fathers had worn at the Meuse-Argonne, with the same Springfield bolt-action rifles… Then the time had come to leave, and in thirty-two Iowa towns during the first week of March 1941 the troops gathered at their armories while citizens lined the streets leading to the train depots… [In those] last days in Iowa, in February 1941… the [168th Infantry] regiment [and its sister regiments in 34th ID] had prepared for what everyone believed was a year's training. Those days were the benchmark against which all subsequent progress could be measured in the transmutation of ordinary American boys into troops capable of crushing the Third Reich."[18]

In late February and early March, all major units of the 34th Infantry Division were loaded on rail cars and trucks and moved to Camp Claiborne. In the hurriedly constructed and still incomplete camp, typical of those appearing around the country, the Red Bull men received an introduction to life in the "real" Army. But the "real Army" at Camp Claiborne was far different from the privation and dirt they would have to endure in Tunisia two years later. About 18 miles south of Alexandria, Louisiana, Camp Claiborne had rail facilities, quartermaster storage buildings, divisional and regimental headquarters buildings, post exchange buildings, mess halls and a recreation hall. Later construction added chapels, a "hostess house," two theaters, company day rooms, an officers' club, and a field house. The post had access to natural gas, which was piped to each tent and used generously during the damp and chilly spring months.[19] By March 5 the entire division had arrived.[20] On Sunday, March 9, 1941, the 34th Infantry Division as then constituted assembled in formation in front of division headquarters. On April 6, a Sunday, the division paraded in Alexandria, Louisiana for Army Day.[21] Assemblies, parades, and makeshift weapons, however, are not "real Army" combat readiness training.

The 34th Infantry Division had mobilized with 12,279 personnel.[22] The 13-week mobilization training program drawn up by the division staff was intended for all personnel notwithstanding prior service. This made good sense as any previous training level was generally poor to nonexistent. Most guardsmen had not had any standardized military training other than the rudiments of close-order drill and range firing. All enlisted men without exception were to cycle through basic training during the period March 10 – June 7. The staff's goal was to train, or retrain, individuals in their own small units (company level) for the first nine weeks, then move on to battalion and regimental training for the last four. Training areas were identified, classes assigned, and training schedules published.[23]

The comprehensive training of the individual combat soldier was vital to the success of the Army, from the squad to the division, in carrying out its missions. The infantryman, and particularly the rifleman, had to possess a wide range of skills and be capable of executing them quickly to survive and win in the deadly and unnervingly loud environment of the battlefield. It was critical to impart the necessary military skills.

> Ground combat in World War II required complex skills, which were in large part technical. Even in the Infantry, the ground arm requiring the least technical training, the private had to understand the use of a dozen weapons. He had to acquire at least an elementary knowledge of many things besides: camouflage and concealment; mine removal and the detection of booby traps; patrolling, map reading, and combat intelligence; recognition of American, Allied, and enemy aircraft, armored vehicles, and other equipment; the use and disposal of captured equipment; the processing of prisoners of war; first aid, field sanitation, and maintenance of life and health out of doors over long periods and under conditions of extreme difficulty. Thus the trained ground soldier was, on the basis of military instead of civilian skills, almost as much a specialist as anyone in the Army. Moreover, the knowledge and skills which the infantryman might need in battle were such that they could not be reduced to an anticipated routine. He had to know how to play his part under conditions of strain and confusion in the teamwork of squad and platoon, coordinating the various infantry weapons in a tactics of fire and movement. The mobile tactics and open formations of World War II demanded the greatest possible physical vigor and mental alertness in individual combat soldiers and required strong powers of leadership in commanders, even in units as small as the squad. The intelligence, skill, and stamina of semi-isolated riflemen and small-unit commanders were to determine not only individual survival on the battlefield but also in many cases the outcome of battle.[24]

The 34ID divisional training program looked good on paper. But it quickly became impossible to implement even by the best trainers. Many of the division's regimental officers charged with carrying out the divisional training program were transferred under orders from the War Department to the Infantry School at Fort Benning, Georgia to receive their own training at the same time they should have been training the enlisted men. As the experience of the 135th Infantry Regiment demonstrated, the goal of an orderly progression from individual training to collective training was drowned by floods of draftees arriving at Camp Claiborne. The 135th Infantry Regiment's strength was nominally almost 2,500 enlisted men and 86 officers. However, the initial physicals had disqualified several hundred guardsmen. On April 17, 650 new inductees reported from Fort Snelling, Minnesota with no military training whatsoever. Three days later 500 more draftees arrived. Therefore, five weeks into the company-level phase and just a few weeks away from the planned large unit training, almost half of 135IR's strength was men needing the most rudimentary military instruction. With so many training officers themselves away at Benning for their own instruction, and because the War Department had not thought to provide trained professional soldiers as adjunct temporary trainers for the draftees, there was no alternative but a wholesale restart of the basic training cycle.

The 13-week restart of basic training began on Monday, April 25, 1941. The cadres of the infantry regiments of 34ID, such as they were, trained the draftees. The 135th Infantry Regiment's regimental history baldly claims that its "training cadre... developed into a highly efficient group of instructors, and in a short time had the [draftees] going through close order drill like old soldiers..."[25] That may have been true as far as the manual of arms is concerned, but as to more complicated combat tasks, the reality was very much a case of the blind leading the blind. Lieutenant Colonel John Hougen's claim that as early as April 7, 1941, the "intensive training had resulted in a well-disciplined and high-spirited Division" is at best exaggerated.[26] The lack of battle experience and professional training among the officers and non-commissioned officers of the instructor cadres was typical of 34ID and of other National Guard divisions summoned to the colors.[ii]

By late July, after completion of the restarted basic training cycle, the infantry regiments of 34ID began training in small unit tactics, battalion and regiment tactical problems, and combat maneuver skills. "Maintenance of contact at night, scouting, patrolling and night operations were the main points stressed."[27] No matter what was stressed at Claiborne, the soldiers of 34ID would have to learn in North Africa how to march, fight, and retreat in the cold and dark where creature comforts like gas-heated barracks were only dreamed about.

The ages and less than ideal physical conditions of many officers and senior non-commissioned officers (NCOs) in the subordinate units of 34ID were a serious problem. The War Department estimated that more than 22 percent of National Guard first lieutenants were past age 40 in June 1941. Most of those men were unsuited for the strenuous physical and high-stress mental demands of leading soldiers in combat. The issue was soon addressed by the War Department by the adoption and ruthless enforcement of mandatory maximum age regulations. Significant

---

ii   On Thursday, May 1, 1941, Robert N. Stokes, Sr., the author's father, age 26 years, was inducted into the Army of the United States in Chesterfield County, Virginia as a private.

numbers of Army Reserve officers arrived to fill slots created by the attrition of older officers.[28] While the replacement of older leaders was necessary, the urgency imposed by impending war resulted in abrupt discharges or transfers which badly disrupted unit cohesion and would have far-reaching grave consequences later.

Even the division commander was not immune. The 34th Infantry Division was commanded by Major General Ellard A. Walsh from February to August 1941, while he continued to serve as Adjutant General of Minnesota. He was with his troops at Camp Claiborne when his chronic ulcers hemorrhaged, preventing him from participating in Corps training maneuvers. He returned to Minnesota for a six-week recuperation at the Mayo Clinic, but the Army's doctors were adamant that he should not return to field command. Walsh could transfer to a desk job in the Army—Marshall, the Army chief of staff, personally urged him to do so—but Walsh concluded that he could do more for the war effort and the country as Minnesota Adjutant General. Major General Walsh was relieved by Major General Russell P. Hartle on August 5.[29]

The 1941 Louisiana Maneuvers

Beginning Wednesday, August 6, 1941, the day after Major General Hartle succeeded Major General Walsh as Commanding General (CG) of the Division, 34ID participated in Corps exercises in preparation for U.S. Army General Headquarters (GHQ) maneuvers in Louisiana.[30] Meanwhile, in great secrecy, President Roosevelt and Prime Minister Churchill met at the Placentia Bay conference in Newfoundland on Saturday, August 9, 1941.

On Monday, August 11, 1941, 135th Infantry Regiment moved into a bivouac area near De Quincy, Louisiana in preparation for the upcoming maneuvers. The next day, the House of Representatives passed by one vote the extension of the Selective Service Act and of mobilization funding for one year.[31] By mid-1941, with no attack on the United States, National Guardsmen and draftees whose congressionally mandated 12 months of active service had begun in the fall of 1940 were growing restless and were eager to be discharged. A few threatened to desert. Although inadequate training facilities and equipment were gradually improving, GI morale dipped as political debate over an extension of service dragged on. In the camps, the hand-lettered acronym "O.H.I.O." (for Over the Hill in October, the end of the mandated year) appeared on walls, weapons, and vehicles. But Congress, by the one-vote margin in the House, precluded what American military leaders rightly feared would have been a disastrous disruption in the already problematic building of the Army. The period of service for all members of the military was extended for six months.[32]

The Louisiana maneuvers began in earnest on Saturday, August 16, 1941. The 135th Infantry Regiment and other 34ID units moved out of bivouac to participate.

34ID was continuously deployed in tactical formations and maneuvers for the following six weeks. This limited six-week experience was to be the division's only training in large-scale battle maneuvers before it deployed to Ireland. Some personnel of the 135th Infantry Regiment were granted furlough on Wednesday, October 1, 1941. Some men over the age of 28 were discharged from military service.[33]

According to their regimental histories, the men of the 34th Infantry Division thought they had performed well in the Louisiana maneuvers. The Red Bull Division was assigned to the V Corps of the Third Army, the Blue Force of Lieutenant General Walter B. Krueger. The maneuver area of the Blue Force was between the Red and the Sabine rivers in southwest Louisiana. The opposing force was called Red Force, under Major General George S. Patton. An umpire system, using designated officers who accompanied each unit, ruled on the outcome of simulated battles and engagements, and determined the number of casualties. The 34ID participants believed naively that the entire operation was as realistic as possible, including the use of blank small-arms ammunition.[34] The scribes of 135IR wrote:

> The maneuvers were divided into several phases, each lasting for a period of approximately one week, and each phase becoming more advanced in tactics, testing the endurance of the men… Offensive tactics were given the greatest amount of time and consideration. Night attacks, scouting and patrolling, terrain appreciation and selection of defensive positions were enforced for all units… Transportation elements gained valuable training of keeping supply and food up to the troops, while troops were constantly on the move… and a large number of deficiencies in supply which existed at the beginning of the maneuvers were ironed out… It also gave opportunities to develop the staff work. This was quite a problem at the time, as most members of the Regimental Staff had… never had the opportunity to work in coordination with such a large group in the field… The Regiment responded to this test and gave a good account of itself…[35]

Would that it had been so. The reality was that the individual soldiers of the 34th Infantry Division, and their squads, platoons, and companies, did not benefit greatly from the 1941 Louisiana maneuvers. Military historian Dr. Richard W. Stewart interviewed several participants in the maneuvers, including one officer who was a company commander at the time. Stewart's findings confirmed that the cumulative effect of the six-week maneuvers on the combat readiness of individual soldiers and small units of the 34th Infantry Division was marginal. No modern equipment, including machine guns and mortars, was available to the infantry troops and there was no live fire training except for an occasional visit to the rifle range. Most of the training time was devoted to close order drill in the Louisiana mud. One participant summed it up.

> There was no combined arms training integrated into daily training schedules. Artillery and mortar live fire exercises were yet to be introduced into training schedules. Training criteria issued to the National Guard did not provide for training in the installation and removal of land mines by the Rifle Companies, probably because it was anticipated engineers would do

this work. Even training in methods of evacuating the dead and wounded was antiquated and did not contemplate fast moving situations and was geared primarily to trench warfare or a more static situation.[36]

The level of military competence of the 34th Infantry Division should have improved dramatically in August 1941 during the Louisiana maneuvers. Sadly, it did not. The division was in V Corps reserve for almost the entire duration of the maneuvers. The officers and men remembered little more than repeated road marches and tactical foot marches with constant changing of orders, march, and countermarch. The soldiers of 34ID missed most of the simulated fighting that might have been useful to them. During Phase 2 of the maneuvers from September 24–29, 34ID crossed over the Red river at Alexandria under orders and spent the bulk of the maneuver period isolated on the east side of the river. Whatever the division staff may have learned about the movement of large bodies of men, the troops at the regimental level and below seem to have picked up only "additional calluses on their feet."[37] While the interviewees may not have represented the experience of every soldier in V Corps, the GIs of 34th Infantry Division missed an opportunity for realistic battlefield training.

There was an especially egregious omission from the training regime of the 34th Infantry Division. 34ID soldiers did not learn to maneuver with tanks in close support or how to fight them. Two Red Bull soldiers did not remember ever seeing a tank up close during the Louisiana maneuvers. One said that the first tank he ever saw at close range was a German *panzer*, after he was taken prisoner in North Africa, even though the Louisiana maneuvers massed the largest concentration of armored vehicles in U.S. history up to that time. The infantrymen who would have to fight both against and in coordination with tanks in North Africa did not see tanks in Louisiana because they were held in the Corps reserve in the rear, distant from the simulated battle. The critical lack of combined arms training would haunt and harm the Red Bull soldiers in battle against a real combined arms force in North Africa.[38]

The National Guard divisions involved in the Louisiana maneuvers experienced another blow to both training and morale in that fall of 1941. The War Department carried out what came to be known as the "October Purge" of National Guard officers. Lieutenant General Lesley J. McNair, chief of staff, General Headquarters (GHQ), had written during the critique of Phase 2 of the Louisiana maneuvers that "So far as I know, no drastic purge of weak leaders is contemplated, although the issue undoubtedly has been clarified in many cases by performance during these maneuvers." Notwithstanding McNair's bureaucratic language, just such an assessment was made by Marshall and the War Department. Clarification in the form of removals from duty soon followed. Within months of the end of the maneuvers at least six division commanders, all National Guard major generals who had participated in the maneuvers, were relieved, retired, or reassigned. In the case of other officer ranks, Lieutenant General McNair stated after the fact that, "It was found necessary to make almost 100 per cent replacements of the commissioned officers with troops from the grade of major general down through the grade of colonel and to replace an unusually high percentage of officers of lower rank."[39]

While the purge directly affected only 1 percent of the overall officer corps, the repercussions were felt throughout the National Guard divisions. The direct impact on the 34th Infantry Division was substantial. In addition to the replacement of Major General Walsh by Major General Hartle, more Army Reserve officers arrived to fill slots created by the removal or attrition of older field grade and junior officers. It was a hard necessity to weed out officers who were incompetent to command or simply too old or unfit to withstand the rigors of combat. The rapid turnover in the officer corps, however, greatly disturbed both enlisted men and officers. When floods of draftees with no hometown or other ties to the National Guard units arrived, the resulting personnel turmoil had a major negative impact on the division's training posture and unit cohesion. As one study of National Guard mobilization stated, "For divisions in training, personnel turbulence was unquestionably the leading obstacle to the development of proficient combat organizations."[40]

On Monday, October 20, 1941, the prime minister sent a personal and most secret letter to Roosevelt disclosing the British strategy for 1942: to invade and conquer French Morocco and Tunisia and to expel the Axis from North Africa. While the soldiers of 34ID were still struggling to learn the art of war with obsolete and insufficient equipment, constant unsettling change in leadership and grossly inadequate training regimes, their future was being shaped.

CHAPTER 5

The War Comes to America

On Sunday, December 7, 1941, Japanese naval aviation forces attacked the U.S. Pacific Fleet and its base at Pearl Harbor. The battleship force of the U.S. Pacific fleet was effectively rendered impotent for the near future. Two of the old battleships, USS *Arizona* and USS *Oklahoma*, were total losses and most of their 1,546 crew were killed. The other battleships were sunk on the shallow bottom. In a gargantuan salvage effort, those ships would be raised, repaired, and upgraded, and sent into future battles as floating bombardment and anti-aircraft platforms. USS *Nevada* became a flagship for the Normandy invasion. The surviving old battleships avenged the Fleet in the last battleship gunfight in history at Surigao Strait on October 25, 1944, against the Imperial Japanese Navy.

While the loss of the battle fleet was disastrous, the attack, presaged by the earlier British aerial attack on the Italian fleet base at Taranto, also rendered obsolete both heavily gunned and armored battleships and old battle line tactics. In future, the aircraft carrier was to be the sovereign capital ship and its aircraft the dominant weapon system on the oceans. It was of the utmost strategic importance, therefore, that the precious aircraft carriers based at Pearl Harbor had been at sea delivering planes to island outposts and had escaped damage. Further, the Japanese commander declined a third wave attack, leaving the aviation fuel storage tanks, naval fuel depots and graving docks intact. The United States Navy still had a striking force and a base in the Pacific.

When the news broke across the United States on that Sunday afternoon, the American people were galvanized to make war on Japan. Any remaining division of American opinion on participation in the war came to an end. The United States officially entered hostilities with a unanimity of popular support for war unprecedented and unreplicated in its history.

While shocked and genuinely resolved to prevail against the new enemy, America and Americans were militarily and psychologically unprepared for war. For the first time in its history, however, the United States entered a war with a relatively large force in existence and an industrial system partially retooled for large-scale production of arms and munitions. The Army was to defend the Western hemisphere against invasion with a force of 1,643,477 soldiers, albeit almost all lacking adequate training and wholly without battle experience. The American military establishment was not at all ready on December 7 to conduct this very different type of war, a war of large-scale expeditionary forces launched to conduct complex combined and joint operations across the expanses of three oceans. Even with the excellent planning that had been done, it would be many months before the United States could begin even limited offensives against the Axis powers.[1]

On Monday, December 8, 1941, President Roosevelt requested a joint session of an infuriated Congress to declare that a state of war existed between the United States and the Empire of Japan. Congress overwhelmingly proclaimed war on Japan on December 9. For a breathless moment, the Germany First strategy hung in the balance. The leaders of the United States were empowered only to direct U.S. military might against Japan. Then Hitler's hubris intervened. On Thursday, December 11, the German *chargé d'affaires* to the United States presented to the State Department a note over the signature of the Nazi foreign minister, von Ribbentrop.

> [T]he Government of the United States from initial violations of neutrality has finally proceeded to open acts of war against Germany… The German Government, consequently, discontinues diplomatic relations with the United States of America and declares that [it]…, as from today, considers itself as being in a state of war with the United States of America.[2]

American and British planning was vindicated. Germany, already committed against the Soviet colossus, was now also at war with the greatest industrial power on the planet. This was Hitler's second and fatal strategic blunder.

34th Infantry Division on Guard Duty

After the Pearl Harbor attack, the combat training of the 34th Infantry Division and other Army divisions was interrupted by the government's unease about internal security, homeland defense, and factory sabotage. Legitimate concerns for the protection of infrastructure metamorphosed into a near panic. The War Department implemented plans for continental defense. The president and the chief of staff deployed 19 of the 34 divisions then undergoing training all over the country to the Eastern and Western Defense Commands. Those commands dispersed units to patrol the coastline and guard key defense plants, bridges, and dams. These assignments to guard duty interrupted—sometimes for four to six months—the already deficient combat training of the inexperienced divisions and would prove to be a dangerously unwise decision in the long term.[3]

As the point defense assignments dragged on with no signs of invasion or sabotage, Lieutenant General McNair, now chief of Army Ground Forces, which had superseded the General Headquarters organization, argued for returning ground tactical units to their training cycles to prepare them for deployment overseas. General Marshall approved McNair's recommendation. He ordered most ground forces units to return to their training missions under the Army Ground Forces command.[4] But for the Red Bull Division, the War Department acted too late. 34ID would be sent to Northern Ireland. Ulster was to be its training ground.

While on guard duty, the regiments of the 34th Infantry Division were scattered about the southern United States from Texas to Florida guarding ports, oil refineries, communications centers, and rail junctions.[5] On December 8, 1941, 2nd Battalion, 135th Infantry Regiment (2/135) moved to coast defense facilities protecting New Orleans. On Tuesday, December 9, 1941, 3/135 was sent to Barrancas, Florida for coast defense duties. 1/135 was sent to Texas City, Texas to defend oil fields.[6]

Yet more personnel changes rattled the division. On Wednesday, December 10, 1941, the War Department applied the maximum age regulations to remove from the 135th Infantry Regiment and its sister regiments more of their field grade and junior officers. In the 135th Infantry Regiment, nine field grade officers and numerous junior officers were discharged or reassigned.[7] On the following Saturday, December 13, 1941, the 77th Congress passed Public Law 338,[8] applicable to all persons then in the armed forces of the United States, extending the term of federal service for the duration of the war plus six months. The United States and its soldiers were committed to a long war, to be fought until the dictator states were destroyed.

The urgent demands for American action to stem the tide of Axis victories forced Roosevelt and Marshall to act despite the unreadiness of American military forces. The United States government decided to send troops to the United Kingdom as Churchill had urged and the War Department selected the 34th Infantry Division to be one of the units to go to Ulster. On Thursday, January 1, 1942, 135IR and the other infantry regiments of 34th Infantry Division were relieved of defense duties and brought back to Camp Claiborne. They prepared for movement to what was rumored to be a port of embarkation. The 168th Infantry Regiment, which had been designated the first unit to move out, packed its equipment into boxes and loaded vehicles onto railcars. Suddenly, however, the 133rd Infantry Regiment was ordered to move out first. The men of 168IR hastily grabbed their belongings and equipment, while the 133rd hurriedly threw its equipment in disorder on railcars and departed.

The confusion, according to one officer of the division, was caused by Major General Hartle, then division commander. Hartle had been asked by Army Ground Forces which of his units was ready to depart first. He had mistakenly answered that it was the 133rd Infantry Regiment and changed the division plans to match his misstatement.[9]

At about the same time, eight officers and 378 enlisted men, or roughly two entire companies, were "taken" from the 1st Battalion of the 135th Infantry Regiment. It is not clear from the regimental narratives why those men were removed or where they went.[10] The rest of the 135th Infantry Regiment packed and prepared for transfer to Fort Dix, New Jersey. On Sunday, January 4, 1942, all furloughs were cancelled, furloughed personnel were recalled, and all 135IR personnel were restricted to post until Thursday, January 8, 1942, when the 135IR troops entrained. By Sunday, January 11, 1942, 135IR arrived at Fort Dix in anticipation of an overseas movement, but that did not occur until some months later.[11]

The 34th Infantry Division arrived at Fort Dix to find that the unit which had been at work constructing its new barracks had itself been shipped to Camp Claiborne. Many of the 34ID men had to move into tents, a drastic change from the warm climate and comfortable barracks in Louisiana. The tents at Fort Dix had inadequate stoves and poor lighting. There were insufficient quantities of both coal and winter clothing. The officers and men of the division now had some uncomfortable and foreboding insight into the nation's state of unpreparedness and their own.

> Dix was confusion worse confounded. In bitter, nine degrees below zero weather, men were assigned quarters, many in tattered tents with no lights or stoves, to say nothing of cots or other facilities. The 34th Division at Ft. Dix was the victim of a Nation, even at that late date, wholly unprepared for war. Ft. Dix [was]… a stark example of what unpreparedness can mean to a Nation suddenly confronted with war.[12]

Exacerbating the misery and confusion, the War Department directed the reorganization of 34ID into a triangular division just as the division was in the process of sending units overseas. The infantry brigades were disestablished. The 164th Infantry Regiment was reassigned to the 23rd "Americal" Infantry Division; it was to be among the Army units that would relieve the valiant 1st Marine Division on Guadalcanal.[i] 34ID exchanged its artillery brigade for four separate field artillery battalions.

The reorganization had a major negative impact on the division. Equipment was issued, reissued, lost, and scattered.[13] More seriously, what little division-level training there had been had focused on square division tactics with two brigades of two regiments each on the fighting line. Now an entirely new fighting doctrine of two regiments up and one back or three regiments on the line, with varying configurations of combat teams, mobile reserves, and task organizations, had to be absorbed and implemented by an already overtaxed divisional staff. Developments in weapons and technology required innovative tactics and new organizations to execute them. The division did not have either. Staff officers had little or no time to plan and wargame exercises in tactics and battle methods to reach the level of competence they needed to direct the new triangular division in battle. The 34th Infantry Division had made a mass cross-country movement followed by a tumultuous reorganization while preparing for an overseas deployment in a war situation that in January 1942

---

i   The 164th Infantry Regiment of the Americal Division went into action on Guadalcanal on October 13th, 1942, as the first United States Army unit to conduct an offensive operation against the enemy in any theater.

was decidedly bleak. The cumulative effect was further erosion of the confidence of the officers and men of the division in themselves and their division.[14]

On Monday, January 12, 1942, 135IR and other 34ID units began a period of the now-familiar close-order drills and road marches at Fort Dix while waiting for shipment to Ulster. In mid-March, with the coming of warmer weather, the division began live fire range training, including at last firing live rounds with newly issued 60mm mortars and 81mm mortars. Three mortars, 60mm, M2, weighing 42 pounds each, were allocated to the weapons platoons of each infantry company, for a total of 81 light mortars in the division. Six mortars, 81mm, M1, weighing 136 pounds each, were assigned to the weapons companies of each infantry battalion, for a total of 54 heavy mortars in the division. These crew-served weapons greatly augmented the combat power of the infantry units.

The ruthless culling of the older officers and NCOs continued. On April 19, 1942, Colonel Harold S. Nelson, CO of 135IR, was relieved and reassigned to II Corps HQ. Colonel Charles M. Parkin took over as CO. A week later Master Sergeant Galen W. Swank, Regimental Sergeant Major, 135IR, was commended for his 26 years of service and detached to the Post Complement, Fort Dix.[15]

CHAPTER 6

34th Infantry Division in Ireland

Why the 34th Infantry Division was selected to be the first American division to go to the European Theater of Operations is not clear to this day. "It is hard to imagine any rationale for the movement of a partially trained and poorly equipped National Guard division into a theater of war."[1] The division's destination was Northern Ireland. The shipment of 34ID and other American divisions to the United Kingdom was intended in part to establish "that mobile reserve, that 'mass of manoeuvre,' which alone could give superior options in the hour of need," and which Churchill always desired to have in hand.[2] Churchill believed that the green American troops could as well complete their training in the United Kingdom, while giving strategic pause to the enemy.[3]

The 34th Infantry Division was shipped to Britain in a series of convoys beginning in January 1942. Once in Ulster, the troops unloaded supplies and guarded various headquarters, with little opportunity for garrison soldiers to become the combat soldiers they would need to be. The division missed the standardized basic and advanced individual training cycles, and the later large-scale maneuvers in the continental United States, which benefited other divisions. Hundreds of the Red Bull's best men left to form other units. Most of the men in the new 1st Ranger Battalion were volunteers from the 34th Infantry Division. The success of the Rangers later in the war shows conclusively that the human material of 34ID was sound and quite capable of becoming competent soldiers, given the proper amount and type of training. Many men from Iowa and Minnesota still filled the enlisted ranks, but not the division's officer cadre. The general purge of older National Guard officers from the Army had left the 34th Division with few of the leaders who had led the men out of the Midwest. Once begun, personnel turnover accelerated. From January 1941 to January 1942, the officers of the division's 168th Infantry Regiment, for example, had been removed and replaced almost wholesale three times.[4]

The commanding general, Major General Hartle, with his chief of staff, Colonel (later Major General) Newman Hendrickson, a small staff group, and some elements of the division, travelled to Ulster in January 1942 to prepare for the main body.

It was during their absence, and on practically no notice, that the 34th Infantry Division reorganized from a square to a triangular division. Several units, including the 164th Infantry Regiment, were transferred from the division. Then in three increments between January 15, 1942, and May 13, 1942, the division went overseas, so that by the end of May all of 34ID was in Ulster. For some troops, the wait at Fort Dix was mercifully brief. The first elements of 34ID to leave for Ulster were the 1st Battalion, 133rd Infantry with its Service Company, Antitank Company and Headquarters and Headquarters Company, the 151st Field Artillery Battalion, Military Police and Medical detachments, and the Division Forward Echelon. The first group moved by truck and train to Brooklyn on January 14, 1942, boarded the British transport *Strathearn* and sailed on the morning of January 15. They docked in Belfast harbor on January 26. 1/133 and its supporting units were established in a camp near Limavady, about 61 miles northwest of Belfast. The 151st Field Artillery battalion was assigned to an area near Castlerock, a seaside village northeast of Limavady. Headquarters 34ID was established in the city of Ballymena, about 26 miles north of Belfast. Major General Hartle set up his headquarters at Wilmont House, an estate on the outskirts of Belfast.[5]

The division headquarters and headquarters units, the remainder of the 133rd Infantry Regiment, and the 168th Infantry Regiment moved on February 15 from Fort Dix to the Brooklyn Navy yard. This second contingent left Brooklyn on March 1, 1942. The troops were carried by ships in a convoy with a heavy escort including the battleship USS *New York*, an aircraft carrier, and destroyers. The Headquarters group boarded the U.S. transport *Barnett*. The 2nd and 3rd Battalions, 133rd Infantry Regiment and the 168th Infantry Regiment were carried on the British transport *Duchess of Athol*, with the 109th Ordnance Company and the 34th Quartermaster Company. The 109th Engineer Battalion boarded the U.S. transport SS *American Legion*. The 109th Medical Battalion were passengers on the U.S. transport *Fuller*. The transport SS *Betelgeuse* carried the 34th Reconnaissance Troop. The 34th Signal Company and the remainder of the 34th Military Police Company boarded the transport SS *Neville*. Upon arrival at Halifax, Nova Scotia, SS *American Legion* developed engine trouble and was forced to lay over. The 109th Engineers returned to Camp Edwards, Massachusetts until other shipping could be arranged. The convoy arrived at Belfast without further incident after a week at sea.[6]

The final increment of the division, the 135th Infantry and the 125th and 185th Artillery Battalions, sailed from New York on April 30, and arrived in the United Kingdom on May 11. It had taken almost four months to complete the movement of the division overseas.[7] 135IR's long anticipated overseas movement commenced on Monday April 27, 1942, when all personnel were restricted to post. 135IR was alerted on Tuesday, April 28, for movement per verbal orders of Rear Detachment, 34ID. The next day, April 29, at 12:32p.m., 135IR's Regimental Message Center closed and at 2:05p.m. 135IR "passed the initial point" at Fort

Dix and entrained for the Port of New York. The regiment arrived dockside at around 10:00p.m. and immediately began embarkation on SS *Aquitania*. By 2:30a.m. on April 30, 135IR had completed boarding and at 6:30 a.m. the ship cleared New York harbor and joined a convoy. On May 2, the convoy arrived in Halifax, Nova Scotia, where a soldier with a ruptured appendix and a medical officer were sent ashore. The convoy then departed for Northern Ireland. On Friday May 8, a battleship, a cruiser and three merchantmen left the convoy for Iceland, and on Monday, May 11 the convoy sighted land. SS *Aquitania* entered the Firth of Clyde and sailed up the Clyde River to Greenock, Scotland. At 10:00a.m. on May 12, the ship dropped anchor. At 7:00p.m. that day 135IR disembarked into three channel boats for transfer to Londonderry, Northern Ireland under cover of darkness. 135IR disembarked at Londonderry on the River Foyle. HQ and HQ Company, the Regimental Band, and 3/135 were transported to Camp Cromore, east of Castlerock. The Anti-Tank (AT) Company and the Service Company of 135IR were stationed at Portstewart, another seaside village northeast of Castlerock. 1/135 was stationed in Portrush, a small resort town northeast of Portstewart. 2/135 was sent to Ballycastle, about 18 miles east of Portrush, where some of the personnel were billeted in civilian homes.[8]

The countryside of Northern Ireland was rugged and wet. Jagged hills and bare moors were dotted with peat bogs and cut by brown mountain torrents. The Red Bull soldiers began work to accustom themselves to the difficulties of cross-country movement, which would comprise a large part of their daily existence in combat. The division at once began a training program for small units which, especially as it was being executed overseas in a country already under enemy fire, should have had greater real-time urgency than the Louisiana maneuvers.[9] But as they arrived in Ulster the units of the 34th Infantry Division were scattered in small battalion-size encampments miles away from one another. They occupied tents and steel Nissen huts recently vacated by British units. The training both of individual soldiers and of larger units suffered because of the dispersion. The major combat elements of the 34th Infantry Division would not be reunited to fight as a division under division command until after the Kasserine battles in southern Tunisia, about a year after the first convoy arrived in British waters.

Northern Ireland was not suited for large unit training. Even when 34ID battalions were brought together in regiments, the land did not allow large formation exercises. The intensely cultivated fields were divided up into small, picturesque plots separated by hedges and stone walls. The topography was, however, excellent training ground for what other units would face two years later in the *bocage* of Normandy.[10] In sum, as one infantry regiment executive officer observed: "During the nine months stay in [Ireland] the training of the division suffered greatly. This was due partly to the poor training facilities available and the [inadequate] supply of weapons and training materials from the United States."[11]

In the spring of 1942, Major General Hartle recommended that his aide-de-camp, artillery Captain William Darby, organize and train what would become the first modern American special forces unit. Soon after elements of 34ID had arrived in Ireland a call was made for volunteers to create the 1st Ranger Battalion.[12] Volunteer soldiers of both the U.K. and the U.S. participated in rugged joint exercises to assess the proposed project and to develop international team spirit and cooperation. Hartle's recommendation was approved by General Marshall in May 1942. 135IR sent two officers and a substantial number of volunteer enlisted men. The 1st Ranger Battalion became famous as tough and effective special forces troops later in the war.

On May 20, 1942, Hartle was transferred to become commanding general of U.S. Army V Corps under Major General James E. Chaney, commanding general, U.S. Army Forces (USFOR) in the British Isles.[i] Major General Charles W. Ryder[13] assumed command of the 34th Infantry Division on June 12, 1942.[14] Ryder was well known to the supreme commander, Allied Force, General Eisenhower. Ryder and Eisenhower, who held Ryder in esteem, were both Kansans and graduates of the United States Military Academy class of 1915, known as the class the stars fell on. "He had established a splendid record in the First World War, in which he won battlefield promotion to the grade of lieutenant colonel at an early age and had enjoyed a reputation as a sound soldier throughout the years intervening between the two wars. He was a man of sterling character and great gallantry in combat."[15] Ryder had served in occupation duty in Germany, four years in China, and in January 1941 he served as the U.S. IV Corps chief of staff during its organization. He also served as chief of staff, VI Corps during the 1941 Louisiana maneuvers. A year later, he became the assistant division commander for the Texas-Oklahoma 90th ("Tough 'Ombres") Infantry Division. He was certain that combat rather than garrisoning bases would be required of his poorly trained soldiers very soon. Training for combat was intensified.

A 21st-century reader can only vaguely appreciate the desperate situation of the United States and its fighting allies in mid-year 1942. The United States was taxed severely to assemble one combat-ready Marine division and adequate shipping to fend off the seemingly inexorable advance of Imperial Japan toward Australia. In Europe, the situation was even less encouraging.

> [C]onsider the picture in June 1942. The United States was just getting into its stride in the mobilization and training of its armies, navies and air forces. *Only the 34th Division, the*

---

i   Hartle continued to serve in that capacity under Eisenhower from June 15, 1942, to October 24, 1942. On November 2, 1942, Hartle became deputy commander of American troops in the European Theater of Operations United States Army (ETOUSA). Hartle commanded V Corps until his reassignment effective July 7, 1943, to Headquarters, Army Ground Forces, Washington D.C. and then was reassigned to Camp Fannin, Texas to train replacement troops.

1st Armored Division, and small detachments of the United States Air Forces had arrived in Northern Ireland. They were still only partially trained. The great bulk of the fighting equipment, naval, air and ground, needed for... invasion did not exist.[16]

But the exigencies of the war, and the urgent demand of the Soviet Union for the establishment of a new fighting front to draw away German forces from the sanguinary struggle in the East, would brook no delay.

Intensive training and long marches had commenced immediately for the infantry battalions of the 34th Infantry Division. By the end of May, it was apparent that the infantry regiments and artillery units of 34ID required more space for realistic combat training. On May 30, 1942, 135IR moved to new camps. Regimental Headquarters of the 135th Infantry Regiment was established in a castle known as Ecclesville House on the outskirts of the town of Fintona, County Tyrone, about 35 miles south of Londonderry. The Headquarters Company, Service Company, Medical Detachment, and Band were housed in Nissen huts in Fintona and the vicinity. 1/135 and 3/135 were stationed in Ashbrooke and Colebrooke, about 11 miles southwest of Fintona, in camps located on the estate of Sir Basil Brooke near Brookeborough. 2/135 was quartered in the city of Omagh, about eight miles northwest of Fintona. The Antitank Company was stationed in the village of Clogher, about eight miles southeast of Fintona.

Training took on what the Red Bull soldiers felt had the quality of battle school, with a ruggedly realistic, earnest flavor reflecting British experience.[17] It included instruction in firing rifles and machine guns on ranges with live ammunition. Heavy weapons training included mortars, anti-tank guns, and artillery, also with live ammunition where ranges were available, and sometimes firing on points off the coast. 135IR made two 25-mile marches and three 15-mile hikes every week in June in the soft clay Irish soil, a mild portent of the sticky mud of a Tunisian winter. There were obstacle courses to run, bayonet practice, and hand-to-hand and unarmed combat instruction. Major General Ryder enforced a "no such thing as a rainy day" training schedule. By late June, the troops were regularly put through exercises on live fire ranges, going through problems of fire and movement, with mortars and machine guns shooting overhead to accustom the troops to the use and effectiveness of heavy weapons in support and to the shocking noise of battle. For most Red Bull soldiers that was their first experience with firing live ammunition under anything approaching combat conditions. Safety precautions and lack of weapons had not previously permitted that type of training. There was no training, however, with incoming live fire and controlled explosions directed at or near the troops to simulate actual battle conditions.[18]

The troops of the 34th Infantry Division received no training in cooperating with armored forces, close support of ground troops by air forces, or the radio communications and inter-service liaison necessary to achieve that cooperation. Little was done to acclimatize soldiers and their leaders to the porosity of the fluid modern battlefield, where there often was no fixed front. There was no familiarization with the shock power and military momentum of armored forces with long-range weapons attacking from multiple directions, accompanied by mechanized infantry and self-propelled artillery, and supported by tactical aircraft. There was in short, as Lieutenant General Mark Clark might have put it, no "battle inoculation."[19]

In early June, the War Department's maximum age regulation resulted in the separation of yet more officers from the 135IR and other units of the 34th Infantry Division. Lieutenant Colonel Albert A. Svoboda, Lieutenant Colonel Jarrold A. Petraborg, Major Axel Jensen, Major William H. Williams, Captain Charles Snyder, and First Lieutenant William E. Musegades were discharged or transferred from the 135th Infantry Regiment. Subsequently, Lieutenant Colonel Myron P. Lund remained in command of 1st Battalion; Major (later Lieutenant Colonel) Edwin T. Swenson assumed command of the 2nd Battalion, and Lieutenant Colonel Robert P. Miller was assigned to command 3rd Battalion. Colonel Parkin was relieved of duty and assignment with the 34th Infantry Division as commanding officer (CO) of 135IR and assigned to V Army Corps as provost marshal on July 22, 1942. Lieutenant Colonel Lester A. Hancock took his place in command of the regiment and was promoted to the rank of colonel on July 23. In the last week of June 34ID combat engineers, who were then quaintly referred to in borrowed British parlance as "pioneer sections," were sent for training at Camp Killedeas, about 19 miles southwest of Omagh on the shores of Lower Lough Erne.[20]

Beginning on July 2, 1942, 34ID took part in a joint Anglo-American field exercise called "Scheme *Atlantic*." For the first time since World War I, British and American troops conducted joint operations with the aim of getting better acquainted with each other's methods and ironing out "certain little differences." *Atlantic* revealed American deficiencies in both combat skills and physical stamina. When the exercise ended on July 8, the immediate conclusion was that the GIs needed yet more conditioning.[21]

All 34th Infantry Division combat elements were then scheduled for further intensive combat and physical training. Ryder and his staff ordered a standardized plan of instruction to teach battlefield lessons and the Division G-3 [Operations] set up a Division Training Center to prepare and conduct the program. One can glean some idea of the 34th Infantry Division's training regime from the G-3 division's training memoranda, exercise plans, umpire checklists and records.

From August 8 to September 13, 1942, each battalion was moved to a division training area for three weeks. The units were given a series of problems, each intended to impart a different lesson in tactics and to develop battalion staff control of troops. One of the problems required each battalion to maneuver with close overhead artillery support as well as simultaneous supporting fire from infantry weapons. 2/135, for example, moved into Training Area No. 1, near Gorton in County Tyrone, for a week of field training that included a 24-hour problem with live overhead mortar and artillery fire.[22]

An exercise plan dated August 9, 1942 described a one-day exercise for 34ID battalions planned for August 11, 1942. The scenario was the approach of Red, an invading opposition force which included armored units. A Red infantry division had taken a ridge line in Tyrone (Blue) territory. 34ID units were to march from bivouac, under simulated air attack and artillery bombardment, to attack and take the ridge, and to prepare an all-round defense of the objective against both armor and infantry attacks.[23] One rifle company from each regiment would act as the opposition force to "outline" or delineate the Red forces. The exercise plan specified learning objectives to be performed and evaluated, as well as certain practical matters of the 24-hour simulated fire activity.

> Note a: Flash crackers to denote air bombing and artillery if available. If not available all umpires will indicate time of bombings and artillery fire and areas of impact to troops...
>
> Note b: Upon completion of attack and reaching first objective *time will be taken out to feed hot meal to troops in position by carrying parties. Balance of schedule will be adjusted as to time to allow for this.* [emphasis supplied]
>
> Among the criteria to be assessed by umpires were:
> ...
> 2.b. Did [a] reconnaissance patrol precede [the] battalion?
> 2.c. Was there flank protection?
> 2.d. Protection against air attack?
> 2.e. Protection against mechanized attack?
> ...
> 6. Were orders issued to all units?
> 7. Are heavy weapons so disposed as to support an attack launched from the line of departure?
> ...
> 16. Was resistance overcome by fire and movement?
> 17. All around defense:
> (a) Were tank traps, obstacles, etc. installed?
> (b) Were avenues of approach covered by fire?

The training records show that Ryder and his staff did what they could as professional soldiers to instill combat doctrine and skills, but they were constrained by inadequate training matériel and facilities. Ryder himself wrote and maintained the Training Manual for the 34th Infantry Division.[24] Training Memorandum (TM) No. 30, issued by Headquarters, 34th Infantry Division, Division Training Center on July 16, 1942, directed that concurrently with the battalion tactical training required by an earlier Training Memorandum No. 28, all infantry battalions were to conduct training under division control in accordance with a schedule and in areas shown on a map overlay attached to TM 30.[25]

Again, one rifle company from each regiment acted as the opposition force to "outline" the theoretical enemy forces. TM 30 provided that the 2,350 thunderflashes and 48 smoke generators issued to each regiment were to be divided and used by the chief umpires during the tactical training problems, but only the opposition forces were allowed to use those devices. The attacking forces were to simulate all fires, including artillery. All buildings and cultivated land containing crops in the maneuver area were declared "off limits" and all troops were enjoined not to damage hay and grain fields and growing crops. Detailed instructions were issued for field camp sanitation and disposal of waste.

TM 30 also specified tactical standards. The frontage of a battalion in the attack was normally to be 600 to 800 yards. In defense the battalion frontage might vary between 800 and 1,500 yards, the latter when broad flat fields of fire were available. TM 30 observed that "it should be kept in mind by all that the strength of attack and defense lies in depth" and that "attacking echelons should have wide intervals and use all available cover in moving forward. The successful soldier is the one that gets forward without being seen by the enemy... The goal to be sought in each phase of this training is perfection of the individual and unit in one method of execution." Yet there is no evidence in the records of 34ID that the training included incoming live machine-gun fire or artillery rounds in the field, or simulated attacks by actual tanks or airplanes.[26]

Leadership changes continued unabated in the 34th Infantry Division, as was the case throughout the Army. On July 30, Major Edwin T. Swenson was relieved as CO of 2/135; Captain William G. Kreger was assigned as executive officer of 2/135. Swenson was promoted to lieutenant colonel and assigned to command the 3rd Battalion, 135IR.

The future of the 34th Infantry Division was not to be in Northwestern Europe. The British pressed their proposal for an Allied invasion of Northwest Africa. That move, cast in persuasive Churchillian phrasing, was politically astute. Roosevelt was determined that American ground forces go into action somewhere in the European area before the end of 1942. The president had expressed a predilection for an undertaking against the Vichy French territories in Africa, so he hardly needed Churchill's eloquent rhetoric to win him over. When General Marshall and his colleagues in the Joint Chiefs of Staff suggested as an alternative that the United States should immediately go on the defensive in Europe and turn its main attention against Japan, Roosevelt brusquely rejected the idea. In mid-July the president's senior advisor Harry Hopkins, General George C. Marshall, chief of staff of the Army, and Admiral Ernest King, chief of Naval Operations, went to London under orders from the president himself to reach agreement with the British on a military operation involving American troops before the end of 1942. After a vain effort to persuade the British to reconsider an invasion of Europe in 1942, the Americans reluctantly agreed on July 24 to the North Africa operation to be launched before the end of October. The president, overruling Marshall's suggestion that a final decision be postponed until mid-September to permit a reappraisal of the Soviet situation, cabled Hopkins that he was "delighted" and that the orders were now "full speed ahead."[27]

Roosevelt and Churchill were agreed that only bold, decisive action could stem the Axis tide and bring relief to the Russians. American ground forces must be committed to engage Axis forces directly. Accordingly, on July 24, 1942, the Allied Combined Chiefs of Staff informed senior officers in secret that there was to be an invasion of Northwest Africa with an Allied force of all arms. The operation, code named *Torch*, was to be carried out under an American commander. Its execution was approved by the president on July 25. The British and American governments agreed that the whole venture should have initially a completely American complexion, so that the French authorities controlling Northwest Africa would receive the invading troops with no more than a nominal show of resistance to preserve French honor. The chances of favorable French reaction were much brighter if the operation were advertised as purely American. British standing among the French was at a low ebb in late 1942 because of aggressive and bloody British military and naval actions against Vichy military and naval facilities and personnel at Oran, at Dakar and in Syria. In those incidents, British forces had come into violent conflict with the French Army and Navy, sinking and damaging French ships, killing French soldiers and sailors, and occupying what had been French colonial territories. Those clashes had opened wounds of French national dishonor and loss of pride and had seriously impaired relations between the British and French. The matter of who among the French truly bore the honor of the French nation and its armed forces would complicate relations between the Free French and their comrades who had served the Vichy regime throughout the war.[28]

General Marshall informed Eisenhower on July 26 that Eisenhower was to be the Allied commander in chief of the North African expedition, and the appointment was made official in a directive from the Combined Chiefs of Staff in August.[29] Eisenhower was well aware of the military, logistical and international political risks of a military operation that with respect to shipping and manpower could generously be characterized as done on a shoestring. He had a little over 90 days to plan and execute the most ambitious transoceanic amphibious invasion ever attempted. Eisenhower keenly felt the burden.

> The decision to invade North Africa necessitated a complete reversal in our thinking and drastic revision in our planning and preparation. Where we had been counting on many months of orderly build-up, we now had only weeks. Instead of a massed attack across narrow waters, the proposed expedition would require movement across open ocean areas where enemy submarines would constitute a real menace. Our target was no longer a restricted front where we knew accurately terrain, facilities, and people as they affected military operations, but the rim of a continent where no major military campaign had been conducted for centuries. We were not to have the air power we had planned to use against Europe and what we did have would be largely concentrated at a single, highly vulnerable base—Gibraltar—and immediate substantial

success would have to be achieved in the first engagements... [A] beachhead on the African coast might be impossible to maintain...[30]

The initial selection of task force commanders was made with the expectation that there would be only two: one American and one British, Major General George S. Patton, Jr. and General Sir Harold R. L. G. Alexander. Events in the Libyan desert intervened, however, to change the command structure. The British, meaning Churchill in his role as minister of defense, were greatly displeased with the Axis forces' advance toward Suez, and found it necessary to make thorough high-level changes in the command of the Egyptian front. They substituted first Lieutenant General Sir Bernard Law Montgomery for General Alexander, and then Lieutenant General Kenneth A. N. Anderson for General Montgomery. Anderson had 31 years in the British Army, served through World War I, commanded the 11th Infantry Brigade in 1930, led British troops in Palestine in 1930–2, and commanded the 3rd Division in 1940 in France. When he assumed command of the Eastern Task Force, he was 50 years old. Major General Patton, 56 years old, had been a cavalryman prominent in the new armored force since his World War I service in France. At the time of his summons to Washington at the end of July 1942, he was commanding the I Armored Corps at his newly established Desert Training Center in California.[31]

Allied Force Headquarters (AFHQ), with Eisenhower in command, concluded that a third task force, the Eastern Task Force, would be needed for the assault on Algiers, to be drawn from both American and British resources. AFHQ assigned the U.S. II Army Corps, in the United Kingdom preparing for the cross-Channel invasion of France under the command of Lieutenant General Mark W. Clark, to provide and command the American parts of the assault forces at Oran and Algiers. Clark, who had commanded II Corps since June, objected that his responsibilities as deputy commander in chief, Allied Force, were incompatible with those of a task force commander and declined the post. General Marshall then proposed, on August 24, 1942, the appointment of Major General Lloyd R. Fredendall to command the Eastern Task Force. Fredendall, with much experience in Army training but no operational field experience, had succeeded Major General Joseph Stilwell as the prospective commander of an American force in Operation *Gymnast*, an early version of the plan to invade France. Fredendall had earlier commanded the II Corps. Lieutenant General Eisenhower requested Fredendall on October 1, 1942, and Fredendall arrived in London on October 9, mere weeks before the planned invasion.[32]

Eisenhower had known Fredendall only slightly before the beginning of the African operation "but his reputation as a fine trainer and organizer was unexcelled."[33] Eisenhower would have reasons to regret recommending and accepting Fredendall and others of the AFHQ staff and combat commanders who would disappoint him in the coming months. With the benefit of hindsight, he observed later that:

[T]he teams and staffs through which the modern commander absorbs information and exercises his authority must be a beautifully interlocked, smooth-working mechanism. Ideally, the whole should be practically a single mind; consequently misfits defeat the purpose of the command organization essential to the supply and control of vast land, air, sea, and logistical forces that must be brought to bear as a unit against the enemy. The personalities of senior commanders and staff officers are of special importance. Professional military ability and strength of character, always required in high military position, are often marred by unfortunate characteristics, the two most frequently encountered and hurtful ones being a too obvious avidity for public acclaim and the delusion that strength of purpose demands arrogant and even insufferable deportment.[34]

For the accomplishment of the primary Allied objective of seizing Tunis, the Eastern Task Force was to be commanded by Lieutenant General Anderson and was not expected to participate as such in the amphibious phase of the assault on Algiers. It was to be preceded by a smaller force, known as the Eastern Assault Force, with as high a proportion of U.S. troops as possible, under an American commanding general. That general was to be Major General Ryder, who since June had commanded the 34th Infantry Division.[35]

The four ground forces commanders—Patton, Fredendall, Ryder, and Anderson— were directly subordinate and answerable to Eisenhower at AFHQ. His control over British ground forces was defined in directives from the British War Office to General Anderson and other British Army officers.

The First Army has been placed under the Supreme Command of the Allied Commander-in-Chief, Lieutenant General Dwight D. Eisenhower, United States Army. In the exercise of his command, the national forces at his disposal will be used towards the benefit of the United Nations and in pursuit of the common object. You will carry out any orders issued by him.

In the unlikely event of your receiving an order which, in your view, will give rise to a grave and exceptional situation, you have the right to appeal to the War Office, provided that by so doing an opportunity is not lost, nor any part of the Allied Force endangered. You will, however, first inform the Allied Commander-in-Chief that you intend so to appeal, and you will give him your reasons.[36]

A naval task force was to land each of the three attacking forces at its objective and support it with naval gunfire and aviation. The Center and Eastern naval task forces were drawn chiefly from the resources of the Royal Navy. The Eastern Task Force bound for Algiers was under Rear Admiral Sir H. M. Burrough (British). Burrough, whose service in World War I included the battle of Jutland, had already seen bitter fighting off the Norwegian coast, on the hazardous Murmansk run, and in an August dash through the gantlet to Malta which persevered against Axis air bombardment.[37] Eisenhower exercised command over the naval portion of the Allied Force through Admiral Sir Andrew Browne Cunningham (Br.), naval commander in chief, Expeditionary Force. Admiral Cunningham became responsible for sea security and amphibious operations to the supreme commander, but for other wholly British naval operations in either the Mediterranean or the North Atlantic he reported directly to the British Admiralty.[38]

The 34th Infantry Division took part in a 36-hour training operation called *Pelican* on August 5 and 6. The opposition force was the Irish Home Guard, who bore little resemblance to German *Panzergrenadieren* (armored infantry). The exercise required motorized patrols to storm towns and reduce roadblocks while being harassed by guerilla warfare and snipers. Despite the imperfections, the Red Bull soldiers felt that many lessons were learned, especially the use of flank protection and of an active and aggressive vehicle-borne element on a unit's point.[39]

On August 7, Major Clarence Lee was assigned as the commanding officer of 2/135, just in time to oversee the relocation of 2/135 and its ammunition stores to higher ground to escape flooding in the River Mourne. On August 22, 2/135 moved over 30 miles from Omagh to Ely Lodge, located on an island in Lough Erne. The Ely Lodge camp had been built by the U.S. Army and had better facilities than Omagh. The kitchen had electric dough mixers, potato peeling machines, and even ice cream freezers. 2/135 began section training and conditioning marches immediately after moving in and policing the encampment. The troops were entertained by a show featuring Al Jolson, Merle Oberon, Al Jenkins, Frank McHugh, and Pat Morrison in the camp auditorium.[40]

In early August, the 34th Infantry Division received classified orders to move the 168th Regimental Combat Team from Ireland to Scotland in preparation for an undisclosed combat mission. In Scotland 168RCT underwent training for amphibious and mountain warfare. A hint of the nature of the operation came when a request was made for volunteers for No. 1 and No. 6 Commandos, British special forces units adept in amphibious raids, whose toughness was well known throughout the Allied services. As training progressed, further orders were received from AFHQ to form a planning group of staff officers to prepare a secret mission. In London, the 34ID officers learned that elements of the 34th Infantry Division had been selected for an important mission in North Africa. The force was to seize the port of Algiers and to keep it open for the supply of an Allied army which, moving rapidly eastward, was to occupy Tunisia, taking Rommel's Italo-German army from the rear.[41]

A highly compressed training schedule in the United Kingdom for the Center and Eastern Task Force assault units was arranged on August 25, 1942, at a meeting between Lieutenant General Mark Clark (U.S.), Lieutenant General Kenneth Anderson (Br.), Commodore John Hughes-Hallett (Br.), and Major General J. C. Haydon (Br.). The U.S. 1st Infantry Division, with all three of its infantry regiments, was assigned to the Center Assault Force to assault and seize the city and port of Oran. The 168th Infantry Regiment of 34ID and the 18th Infantry Regiment of 1ID trained at the British Combined Operations Training Center at Inveraray, Scotland from August 31 to September 12. They were followed by the 16th Infantry Regiment of 1ID from September 14 to September 26. From September 27 to October 7, the Allied invasion units loaded their equipment and supplies on ships.

From October 8 to 18, further rehearsals were staged, and the ships received the final combat loading. The Rosneath and Toward training area facilities were then used for simulated boat training of the 26th Infantry Regiment from 1ID because the landing craft were in dock to be conditioned for the operation itself and were not available for amphibious training. 18RCT and 168RCT left Inveraray during the week of September 21 and completed training in other areas. 16RCT, 1ID held landing exercises at Inverchaolain Peninsula (near Dunoon, Scotland) during the night of September 27–28, while 26RCT engaged in a second practice operation at Inveraray a day later. Combat Command B, 1st Armored Division, trained in Northern Ireland while the other amphibious elements were in Scotland and while many of 1AD's staff officers were in London to plan the division's role.[42]

The autumn 1942 training exercises of the Center and Eastern Assault Forces for debarkation and fighting ashore simulated as well as practically possible within the constraints of time and geography what awaited the assault troops on the Algerian beaches. But the haste demanded by the urgent circumstances necessarily meant that the training was incomplete. Once again, the program was hampered by the incessant withdrawal of men for assignment to officer candidate schools or to cadres of new U.S. Army units forming in the continental United States. Successive replacement waves filled out units with men whose training was at best uneven. The period of planning and preparations ended in late October in what the official Army history admits was "an atmosphere of unrelieved improvisation and haste, an unavoidable consequence of the determination to undertake an operation which stretched resources to the limit."[43] Eastern Assault Force troops were trained and rehearsed in ship-to-shore landings at various points in the United Kingdom, but the level of training for the amphibious operations in French North Africa, and for the subsequent ground combat phase of *Torch*, fell far below what would be needed to defeat determined resistance. "Whatever misgivings those preparing the expeditionary forces in the United States and the United Kingdom may have felt, they were attempting to do the best thing possible within the limitations imposed by inexperience, uncertainty, and shortness of time, rather than trying to turn out a force completely ready."[44] The commanding need for Roosevelt and Churchill to act decisively and immediately overbore all objections. Good enough would have to do and the only partially trained and equipped soldiers would have to learn their new art in combat, truly a trial by fire.

The 34th Infantry Division's Division Training School continued until September 13. Each battalion of the division was given a series of combat problems on offensive tactics and close artillery support. There was one fatal casualty in Company L, 3/135, when a round fell short. Again, there is no evidence of combined arms training or of training in fighting combined arms forces. After the Division Training School battalion exercises were concluded, the infantry units undertook long-distance conditioning marches. 2/135 went on a 40-mile foot march on September 15. The Rifle Team of 2/135 took first in a match with shooters from the RAF, Ulster Home Guard, and the Ulster Royal Constabulary on Thursday, September 17.[45]

From the moment that the political leaders decided upon *Torch*, Allied capacity for cooperation was tested. Planning for the operations at Algiers and for the subsequent offensive toward Tunis began with the assumption that the main operations would fall to British First Army, to be led by Lieutenant General Anderson. First Army planners had worked for a month on the project when the Allied high command announced their politically driven decision to have all three landing forces under American command. British and American intelligence reports had revealed that the Allies must put Americans in the vanguard of the invasion, to make the American character of the invading forces as conspicuous to the French as possible. Two American regimental combat teams would assault Algiers. The American forces were so small, however, that part of the assault elements and all of the reinforcements, two thirds of the combat troops assigned to the Algiers operation and the march to Tunis, were British.[46]

Major General Ryder left his headquarters in Northern Ireland as commanding general, 34th U.S. Infantry Division, to report on September 5 at Norfolk House as commanding general, Eastern Assault Force. AFHQ issued on September 16, 1942, its "Provisional Directive to Commanding General, Eastern Assault Force," addressed to Ryder. The directive, over the signature of Lieutenant General Clark, deputy commander in chief, Allied Force, by direction of Eisenhower, appointed Ryder to be military commander of the Eastern Assault Force operation against French North Africa. The object as a whole was stated to be the invasion and occupation of French North Africa, and the rapid buildup of land and air forces in Tunisia to reopen the Mediterranean and expel Axis forces from Libya. The tentative date of the assault was November 4, 1942.

The primary role allotted to Ryder's force was the assault and capture of the port of Algiers and the airdromes adjacent to it in order to facilitate the passage of Anderson's Eastern Task Force into Tunisia. The directive explicitly stated that "your attacks will be executed in such a manner as to present the overwhelming appearance of participation by American Forces."[47] Anderson's plans for the drive into Tunisia had to be adapted to the capabilities and requirements of an Allied task force serving at first and somewhat awkwardly under another commander. After Algiers had capitulated, Anderson would relieve Ryder. Then as commanding general, Eastern Task Force, Anderson was to lead the operations of First Army to seize Tunisia. The shift of command at Algiers was clarified in a conference of Generals Clark, Anderson, and Ryder on September 8. General Ryder was authorized to name Brigadier General Ray E. Porter (U.S.) as deputy commander, Eastern Assault Force.

Even Eisenhower felt that the "Eastern Task Force… had a somewhat curious organization."[48]

To preserve the American character of the assaulting forces they were placed under Major General Ryder, the commanding general of the U.S. 34th Division. Ryder was to lead the attack only until [Algiers] was captured. Once [the] Eastern Task Force was firmly established, command was to be taken over by Lieutenant General Sir Kenneth A. N. Anderson, commanding the British First Army. It was [Anderson's] mission to dash eastward as rapidly as the situation might permit... to secure Tunis.[49]

Ryder's two American regimental combat teams were the 168th Infantry Regiment from his own division, now commanded by Colonel John W. O'Daniel, and the 39th Infantry Regiment from the 9th Infantry Division, under Colonel Benjamin F. Caffey, Jr.[ii] 39IR had embarked from the United States in the same transports it was to use in the assault. It reached the United Kingdom on October 8. 39IR had received considerable battalion training and some regimental ship-to-shore training. Its transports were combat loaded, carried 60 days' supplies, ten units of fire for all weapons, and vehicles. The vehicles were waterproofed and restowed in the United Kingdom in the correct tactical order for a landing in darkness. In Ulster, 39IR troops spent a few days ashore stretching their legs, and then participated in a rehearsal exercise starting on October 17 from Tail of the Bank, River Clyde. The 168th Infantry Regiment had come overseas with regular equipment, except for artillery, and with maintenance support, but depended upon inventories in the United Kingdom for signal, engineer, ordnance, and quartermaster supplies and for ammunition.[50] All other troops for the invasion at Algiers were furnished from British First Army.[51]

The light artillery battalions of the 34th Infantry Division were issued the new and excellent British 25-pounder quick-firing gun/howitzers and received training in the operation of the weapon from British soldiers.

The GIs now wore the new M1 "pot" helmet system that became emblematic of the American soldier in World War II. The U.S. Army M1 steel helmet had been standardized and approved on June 9, 1941, for use in all the U.S. armed services, although it was not universally available for another year. The M1 weighed about three pounds and provided greatly improved protection compared to its M1917A1 "soup bowl" predecessor. The steel outer helmet had a chin strap made of cotton webbing attached to a metal loop, its only attachment. The chin strap was often left undone (or buckled on the back of the helmet). Although the interior suspension system of the liner was adjustable and would keep the helmet on the soldier's head even without the chin strap, there were times when an unstrapped soldier would have to hold his helmet on by hand. During the North African campaigns in 1943, however, the rigid hook fastener of the chin strap turned out to be a source of potential danger. Under the impact of a blast wave resulting from a nearby detonation, the

---

ii   By March 1943, Caffey was promoted to Brigadier General and was assigned as deputy commander, 34ID.

strap remained fastened, and the head jerked violently backwards, causing fractures or dislocations of the cervical vertebras. The helmet strap was redesigned with a clasp that remained closed during normal combat activities but allowed for a quick automatic release at pressures below the danger level.

The riflemen in the infantry platoons, and other soldiers not otherwise equipped, were armed with the Garand semiautomatic cal. 30.06 rifle, the world's first standard-issue semi-automatic military rifle.[52] The M1 rifle could be fired as fast as the soldier could pull the trigger. The semiautomatic operation allowed the soldier to keep his eyes and the muzzle on the target and maintain a greater volume of accurate fire on the enemy, giving the GI a marked advantage in combat. The excellent but elderly Springfield cal. 30.06 bolt-action rifle was retained in the infantry squad as a sniper weapon.

Upon General Anderson's relief of General Ryder as Commander, Eastern Task Force, Ryder's command was to be transformed. His American units would be redesignated the 34th Infantry Division and come under General Anderson's command as the Algiers garrison. His British units would revert to the British 78th Division. The Allied planners remained profoundly concerned about the prospects for the subsequent mission of the Eastern Task Force. General Anderson was responsible for establishing a base in Algiers and almost simultaneously moving east to speedily occupy eastern Algeria and then to charge into Tunisia with his objective Tunis itself.[53] The Allied military command knew that the march to capture Tunis was an exceedingly difficult enterprise, given the distances, the imminent onset of the winter rains, the small forces available, and, most critically, the small number of vehicles and the meager supplies immediately available to support an advance of 500 miles.

Ryder had already prepared and submitted to AFHQ his own plans for the operation against Algiers.[54] Ryder's "Outline Plan for Seizing and Occupying Algiers," dated September 8, 1942, provided that the "34th U.S. Division, supported by appropriate units of the Royal British Navy and Royal Air Force will seize and occupy ALGIERS and secure adjacent airfields..." The troops available, subject to later revision, were the Headquarters and Headquarters Detachment 34th Infantry Division (US), CT (combat team) 168 (US) with VI Commando attached, a provisional US regimental combat team, later determined to be the 39th Infantry Regiment, the 11th Infantry Brigade Group (British) and the 36th Infantry Brigade Group (British). The Outline Plan prescribed the landing beaches and assignments of the assault forces.

In Ryder's initial plan, 168RCT, with the British 6 Commando and a detachment of 1 Commando attached, was to make the main landing on the *Beer* beaches west of the city of Algiers. The commandos were to capture the fort and infrared detection installations at Sidi Ferruch and Rass Acrata, and to capture Fort Duperré and its detection station. 168RCT was to capture Fort L'Empereur and thereafter occupy the city of Algiers. 168RCT was to overrun the main government buildings and offices and the French Army headquarters, to seize the offices of the German and Italian Armistice Commissions and arrest their personnel, to take the radio station and the Post and Telegraph Office, to take control of the Admiralty office, the colonial governor's palace, and all military barracks. This provisional plan called for 168RCT to secure the port also, but that portion was later replaced by the British Operation *Terminal* which was to be carried out by the 3rd Battalion of the 135th Infantry Regiment. 39RCT with a detachment of 1 Commando attached was to land on the *Charlie* beaches east of Algiers and proceed inland to capture and secure from ground attack the important French airfield at Maison Blanche, capture the coast defense batteries and detection installations at Cap Matifou, and reduce the garrison at Maison Carré.

Ryder superseded his Outline Plan by his Field Order No. 1, dated October 4, 1942.[55] To the tasks assigned to the 168RCT and the attached Commando troops he added the capture of the fort and detection devices at Cap Caxine, the capture of Fort L'Anglais and Fort Independence, and the elimination of the coast defense observation post known as Point 270. In Annex #8 to Field Order #1, Ryder directed 168RCT to secure a number of important military, civil government, and infrastructure buildings and facilities, including all French Army branch headquarters, the residence of the governor general and the governor's palace, the police prefecture, the headquarters of the gendarmerie, and the pumps, cranes and machinery for the docks, the power station, the oil storage and pumping facilities, and the sea plane base.

Ryder's Annex #10 set out a plan for the supply and feeding of the landing forces. It prescribed that troops of 39RCT were to be supplied with U.S. standard rations, C, K, and D. But the men in 168RCT were to subsist on British Army 48 Hour Mess Tin Rations and British Emergency Rations. This British ration situation had been anticipated and discouraged by one thoughtful British officer, Brigadier F. W. Festing, commander of the 29th Independent Brigade Group. He had pointed out in a note dated June 26, 1942, that the British 48 Hour Ration was not advisable under all conditions. "This is too heavy and certainly, for hot climates, of an unsuitable type. Tins of bully beef and army biscuits are not encouraging during a long and thirsty march under a tropical sun… I understand that a really concentrated ration has existed for over a year; could it not be made available for combined operations?" Unfortunately, the GIs of 168RCT would have to live on the bully beef and crackers.

The troops of 34ID assigned to the assault forces began movements to assembly areas. Other Red Bull units prepared for embarkation in following convoys to land after Algeria had been secured. On Wednesday, September 23rd, 2/135 moved east about 24 miles from Ely Lodge to Camp Blessingbourne, near Fivemiletown. On Sunday, October 18th, 1942, Companies I, K, and L, and a platoon of Company M (Heavy Weapons), and one officer and sixteen enlisted men from the Medical Detachment, all from 3rd Battalion, 135IR, were placed on detached service to Sunnylands Camp, Carrickfergus, Northern Ireland, with LTC Edwin T. Swenson now in command. CPT William F. Snellman, executive officer, CPT Vilhelm Johnson (Surgeon, Medical Corps), 1LT Emory J. Trawick, 1LT Lieutenant Robert O. Foster, and 2LT George George also accompanied these units in addition to the full complement of company officers. At Sunnylands, 3/135 was equipped and organized for combat. The battalion had previously trained in boarding and disembarking from destroyers, including two practice landings on the docks of the harbor of Belfast, with the objective of securing the harbor installations. Preparations were made in deep secrecy for overseas movement. The 3rd Battalion soldiers did not know until they were at sea that they were to participate in a perilous amphibious attack on the harbor at Algiers.[56]

The 3rd Battalion of 135IR had been chosen for a particularly hazardous, and in fact harebrained, operation. The scheme, appropriately code named "TERMINAL," was concocted by the Royal Navy and was to be carried out on a pair of aged Royal Navy destroyers. Operation TERMINAL, a direct assault on the Algiers harbor by a special force combining British naval with American Army elements, was to be carried out simultaneously with the similar Operation RESERVIST at the Oran harbor. Both operations were included in Allied plans with a reckless disregard for the certainty of heavy casualties. 3/135 was to operate with and under the command of the Royal Navy and was known as the "TERMINAL Force." Its mission was to break the boom at the harbor of Algiers, land on the piers, fight its way to key port facilities, and secure the port and ships against sabotage. This operation was to be executed simultaneously and in conjunction with the main American and British landings of the Eastern Assault Force west and east of Algiers. Much depended on whether the French forces in Algiers would decide to fight or surrender.[57]

The War Department continued to remove and replace officers of the 34th Infantry Division, even on the eve of embarkation. Lieutenant Colonel John Hougen, a longtime and understandably parochial National Guardsman, later wrote about the replacements of Guard officers.

> Just before leaving Inveraray [Scotland for North Africa], things occurred [in] the Command [group] of the 168th Infantry Regiment which caused a rift of anger and despair to pass deep into the ranks. Officers of long standing with the Regiment, some of whom had been reared with it since boyhood, the services of others reaching back to World War I, were suddenly removed from Command, though they had carried the training of troops from the maneuvers of 1937 and 1940, through the year's training at Claiborne, including the great Louisiana maneuvers of 1941; through the many months of training in Ireland, and now, had completed the combat training in Scotland. And this was the third time within a year that officers of the Regiment had been removed and replaced.
>
> Colonel Folsom Everest was relieved of command of the Regiment shortly before departure from North Ireland for training in Scotland. This officer had come up through the ranks of the Regiment, had served in France in World War I, had been in command of the Regiment for several years before induction and shortly before being relieved of command, had received special commendation for the efficiency of the Regiment and, in particular, for its showing in field exercises in Ireland, witnessed by their Majesties, the King and Queen of England.

And now, in the concluding days of combat training in Scotland, Colonel (now Brigadier General) Philip Bettenburg, who succeeded Colonel Everest, was relieved as Regimental Commander. Major (now Colonel) Carl Goldbranson and Major John C. Petty were removed as battalion commanders, while Lt. Colonel Fred Oliphant was relieved as Executive Officer.

Replacement officers were sent over by Washington authorities. The strange thing about this policy was that the officers who took over remained with the Division just long enough to make the landing at Algiers. Not so strange, however, excepting for Major Petty who was killed in action at Sened Station, all replaced officers went on to higher responsibilities.[58]

The assault ships loading in the United Kingdom near Liverpool and Glasgow received their troop units late in September after most of the cargo had been stowed. Allied Force Headquarters decreed that the scarce shipping space should be used for troops rather than for vehicles, a directive that was to have unhappy consequences after Morocco and Algeria had been secured and the lack of wheeled transport slowed the advance of British First Army in Tunisia. The movement of troops to ports of embarkation was organized and controlled by a branch of the British War Office, aided by members of the U.S. Transportation Corps. American personnel tended to be overly secretive and reluctant to accept orders from a British agency, but the American ground and air units complied with the schedule. Equipment, supplies, vehicles, and troops moved into the ports according to a carefully prepared program and, once aboard ship, were taken to the Firth of Clyde.[59]

On October 17, the entire expedition, both Center and Eastern Task Forces, began to assemble in the Clyde. The assault transports proceeded north to the vicinity of Loch Linnhe to hold a final rehearsal just before daylight, October 19, then returned to the Clyde next day. Except for command post exercises ashore by small groups of officers and men, all waited aboard until time to depart. Then the great troop convoy sailed for Africa on October 26.[60]

An earlier convoy, of 46 slower cargo vessels with 18 escorting warships, had left port on October 22 on a schedule which would permit it to be overtaken by the troop convoy.[61] The troop convoy included 39 combat-loaded transports of the Center and Eastern Task Forces with 12 escorting warships. With the Eastern Task Force were Ryder's Eastern Assault Force. Commanding the consolidated armada was Rear Admiral Burrough (Br.), in the specially designed command ship H.M.S. *Bulolo*. With him were Major General Ryder, commander of the Eastern Assault Force in the Algiers operations, Major General Vyvyan Evelegh, CG, British 78th Division, and British Air Commodore G. M. Lawson.[62] Second in command of the convoy was Commodore Thomas H. Troubridge (Br.) in another headquarters ship, HMS *Largs*. Also, aboard *Largs* were Major General Fredendall, who would command U.S. II Corps after Oran and Algiers had been secured, Colonel Lauris Norstad (Assistant Commander, U.S. Twelfth Air Force), and Mr. Leland L. Rounds. Rounds had been brought out secretly from Oran, where he was an American vice-consul and an operative of the consular intelligence operation that had been created after the defeat of France.[63] His mission was to liaise with friendly French elements ashore and to provide political intelligence to Major General Fredendall. The escorts and most of the transports were British vessels, but the 39RCT continued to Algiers in the combat-loaded U.S. transports which had brought it across the North Atlantic. Some Polish and Dutch ships were in the Allied convoy.[64]

Eisenhower worried greatly about the small American force allocated to the Algiers operation, as the Americans were intended "to provide an entirely American façade to the attacking force."[65]

> Since lack of shipping did not permit us to bring more forces directly from the United States, the only American troops that could be committed to the Algiers attack were part of the 34th Division, then in Ireland, reinforced by a regiment of the U.S. 9th Division and a Ranger Battalion. This was not strong enough for the [military] task if any real resistance should be met, but British supporting units were so distributed in the landing forces that in only a few instances were they [the British] in the actual assault waves.[66]

The "part" of the 34th Infantry Division amounted to four infantry battalions: the 3rd Battalion of the 135th Infantry Regiment assigned to *Terminal* Force and the 168th Infantry Regiment assigned to land west of Algiers. From any perspective, even with the British brigades also landing, the landing force at Algiers was a very thin shoestring.

The men and matériel from the United Kingdom for the assaults at Oran and Algiers reached North Africa by voyages organized in a complicated but ingenious pattern. One problem of safe transit was solved by sending in advance as far as Gibraltar the first convoy of slow colliers, tankers, tugs, and other auxiliary craft, and three shallow draft oil tankers which the British, by clever means, had converted into the *Maracaibo* Class tank landing ships able to discharge tanks through bow doors and over steel ramps onto a beach.[67]

The Strait of Gibraltar was a bottleneck for the convoys. Any concentration of shipping that the enemy discovered was a target worth almost any risk to destroy. Transit into the Mediterranean during the darkness of two successive nights was scheduled for all except one small group of ships, which would enter in daylight. Before nearing the strait, both the slow convoy which had left the Clyde on October 22 and the fast convoy which departed on October 26 separated on November 4 into sections destined for Algiers and Oran, respectively. Preceded by a screen of warships of the formidable Force H, Royal Navy, the Algiers sections of the slow and fast convoys entered the Mediterranean Sea during the night of November 5–6. During daylight, November 6, the Oran section of the slow convoy followed, and in darkness, November 6–7, the Oran section of the fast convoy passed through the narrow waterway.

Inside the Mediterranean, the separate sections consolidated into the Eastern and Center Naval Task Forces. Some ships refueled in Gibraltar harbor. Other vessels refueled at sea from accompanying tankers at a position in the Mediterranean. By the time the assaulting forces arrived off the landing beaches, two sustainment convoys from the United Kingdom were well along the way to the Algiers and Oran areas.[68]

In late 1942, the Allies were still learning the complex art of large-scale transoceanic amphibious assault. The Allied movement of such large fleets of ships required masterly organization, and the joint naval plan for *Torch* was carried out with admirable competence. Between the Clyde and Gibraltar, no submarine sighted the ships although they passed through an area near which more than a score of Axis submarines operated. One German submarine, which was sighted by a Royal Navy air patrol, was kept submerged long enough to permit the ships to pass unsighted and unreported. In mid-afternoon of November 5, the Oran portion of the fast convoy steamed to the west while its destroyer screen made several aggressive attacks on submarines detected by the surface ships. No results were observed, but the Allied transports remained unscathed. After 21 and a half hours, the Oran-bound ships reversed course and approached Gibraltar after nightfall, November 6. But after passing through the Strait the landing assault flotillas had to proceed without the protection of antisubmarine air patrols. The seaplanes equipped for such missions had all become inoperable and the weather conditions at Gibraltar kept land-based aircraft on the ground. The Eastern Naval Task Force was unfortunate. The American attack transport USS *Thomas Stone* (APA-29), while steaming in the Mediterranean carrying troops of the 39th Infantry Regiment, was damaged by a torpedo from a German submarine 30 hours before the assault landings were to begin.[69]

The British First Army, with which the 34th Infantry Division would be intimately if not always cordially associated during the Tunisian campaign, had been activated on July 6, 1942, around the elements of an expeditionary force which had been training in western Scotland for several months. It consisted, at its inception, of V Corps (4th and 78th Divisions), 6th Armoured Division, and 22nd Antiaircraft Artillery Brigade. During the first week of August, the requirements for staging and executing a large-scale amphibious landing against opposition had been tested by the British First Army in Exercise *Dryshod*. The tests indicated that the 78th Division, from which troops for the Eastern Assault Force were to be drawn, was then capable of only the sort of weakly resisted operation anticipated near Algiers. To provide more combat power, if necessary, the British 11th and 36th Brigade Groups and 1 and 6 Commandos (partly manned by volunteers from the U.S. 34th Infantry Division) were also to engage in the amphibious assault.[70]

The remainder of the 34th Infantry Division stayed in Ireland, pending follow-on shipment to Algiers after the invasion. The units not participating in the invasion continued what the 135IR history characterized as "intense" training, including small unit tactics, long marches, and live fire practice. The division received many replacement junior officers, who were given a short course of instruction in the division's standard procedures and tactical doctrine.[71]

On October 21, 1942, three officers and 24 enlisted men of 3rd Battalion, 135th Infantry Regiment, embarked from Belfast on the old British destroyers HMS *Malcolm* and HMS *Broke*. Those men were personnel of the Heavy Weapons Company (M Company). On October 26, the balance of the 3/135 part of *Terminal* Force boarded the British cruiser HMS *Sheffield*. They put out to sea with the fast convoy bearing the Eastern Assault Force on October 26, 1942.[72] In addition to 74 Royal Naval personnel to board and seize ships in Algiers harbor and three British Army officers, the group included 24 American officers and 638 enlisted men.[iii] All personnel were in American Army uniform and under command of Lieutenant Colonel Swenson.[73] Commanding the entire *Terminal* Force was Captain Henry L. St. J. Fancourt (RN).[74] During the voyage to Gibraltar the plan of operation was detailed and refined by Fancourt, Lieutenant Commander Sears (RN), Lieutenant Colonel Swenson, Captain Snellman, the three company commanders, and the battalion communications officer. The plan was not disclosed to the troops until after HMS *Sheffield* cleared Gibraltar. Then maps and copies were distributed to all the officers and key non-commissioned officers. Everyone who was to lead men in the harbor assault was required to brief in classroom manner in front of the assembled officers and non-commissioned officers his exact role in the operation to thoroughly familiarize all the leaders with the plan and contingencies.[75]

The 34ID's 168th Infantry Regiment, reinforced, also sailed from British waters on October 26. 168IR was part of an Allied force of 10,421 officers and enlisted men assigned to land west of Algiers at the beaches code named *Beer* (rather than American *Baker*). 168IR and the British units of the *Beer* group were loaded on five troopships (*Keren, Winchester Castle, Otranto, Sobieski,* and *Awatea*) for the voyage to the Mediterranean. The objectives of the *Beer* group were to capture French forts and gun emplacements and to swiftly occupy and hold key points in the city of Algiers.[76]

PART II

"SOLDIERS ARE SWORN TO ACTION": OPERATION *TORCH*

CHAPTER 7

Algiers

Algiers was the most important military objective of Operation *Torch*. The ports critical to the Tunisian campaign that must follow *Torch* were fixed in Eisenhower's mind.

> Four important ports or port areas, within the extreme limits of our capabilities, were... desirable objectives. These were, from west to east, Casablanca on the Atlantic coast, and Oran, Algiers, and the Bône area on the Mediterranean. A successful direct landing in the Bizerte—Tunis area would have yielded great results, but that locality was far outside the range of fighter support, and since British experience in running convoys to Malta had been only little short of disastrous, this particular project was given up as beyond the bounds of justifiable risk.
>
> However, it was extremely desirable to capture the Bizerte—Tunis area at the earliest possible moment so that we could succor Malta and by land, sea, and air operate against Rommel's line of supply, thus assuring a victorious end to the war in Africa.[1]

The Allied Force was directed to establish lodgments elsewhere in French North Africa before seizing the easternmost of the French protectorates, Tunisia, and its ports, Bizerte and Tunis. Algiers was closest to Tunisia and the Combined Chiefs of Staff intended that the decisive attack of the *Torch* operation would set out from Algiers toward Tunis. Its port, the railroad terminal, the working space for a supply base, and its two all-weather airfields made Algiers a great prize. The facilities for housing and offices would support Allied Force Headquarters when it moved from London and Gibraltar. Allied control of the rear area during fighting in Tunisia or any subsequent operation in the Mediterranean theater would be based in Algiers.

Algiers was the crucial political location. It was the capital of Algeria and the seat of the French civil and military administration governing all the French North African colonies. The principal figures in the government of French North Africa were there, making Algiers the likely setting for the extraordinarily difficult French choice between neutrality and resumption of hostilities against the Axis countries. American diplomats and clandestine agents had contacted French officers and anti-Vichy patriots with whom arrangements were made to secure key places, to keep French Army units in barracks, and to win Algiers without bloodshed and without creating personal or national resentments.[2] Those American undertakings were well advanced on the ground in Algeria. The Allied leaders hoped that success in managing French intrigues and internecine hatreds might rally the French armed forces to the leadership of General Henri Giraud and return French forces to the war for the liberation of France, with or without the approval of the puppet government at Vichy.[3]

> The amphibious operations in the Mediterranean for the capture of Oran and Algiers united elements of the U.S. Army, the British Army, and the Royal Navy in two joint expeditionary forces, supported by units of the U.S. Army Air Forces and the British Royal Air Force. *The amount of training was generally below the requirements for success in operations against firmly defended shores.* Here, as on the western coast of Morocco, the Allied Force had stretched its capacities to the limit. There had been no time even for precise forging of the Allied military instrument, much less for polishing it. It was rough cast in the proper mold and used with that fact in mind. The complications of amphibious operations were many under the best of circumstances, but by using one country's army with another's navy the Allies unavoidably increased those complexities. The forthcoming operations in the Mediterranean were consequently expected to be unexampled in difficulty as well as in scale.[4]

Concerning the combat capacity of the 34th Infantry Division as its units approached the beaches, Atkinson writes:

> Eighty-seven weeks had passed since [the mobilization in February 1941], far short of the three years Sylvanus Thayer[i] deemed necessary to make a good army from the best men… [W]hether the [34th Infantry] division was worth a damn remained to be seen.[5]

The Plan of Attack

The Eastern Assault Force plan for capturing Algiers did not rely on any assistance from French forces. Ryder and the AFHQ planners had made a coldly objective military analysis of the terrain and the defenses. Eight thousand French ground troops were believed to be in the immediate vicinity of the city, 4,500 more west of it in the area Cherchel-Koléa-Blida-Miliana, and 3,500 east of it near Dellys-Tizi Ouzou-Fort National and Aumale. Far to the west near Orleansville and well to the east at Setif were additional potentially supporting French ground units. The French troops were well trained, long-term professional soldiers, but they were equipped with World War I weapons. The Algiers garrison included an armored unit of obsolete tanks and armored cars. From the Maison Blanche and Blida airdromes, 52 fighters and 39 bombers could contribute to the defense. At the coast were 12 or 13 fortified and protected batteries with infrared thermal detectors and range-finder stations, the predecessors of radar. The three principal batteries included one in the old fort

---

i   1785–1872. An American engineer and educator, Thayer served in the United States Army for 55 years. He is best known as the reforming superintendent of the United States Military Academy at West Point, New York, 1815–33, where he reorganized and improved the Academy, placing its curriculum and standards on a sound foundation.

at Cap Sidi Ferruch, one near Pointe Pescade at Fort Duperré, and the Batterie du Lazaret on Cap Matifou near Fort d'Estrees, but other powerful guns dominated the port and bay of Algiers and all sea approaches for miles on both sides of the city. The first mission for each of the large elements of the landing force was to gain possession of the coastal batteries near the beach at which it came ashore. The guns of Batterie du Lazaret, of Fort Duperré, and on the Jetée du Nord in the port, with their direction finders, searchlight installations, and other equipment, were to be captured intact and held for transfer to Allied coast artillery units. Other guns were either to be neutralized by removal of essential parts or to be demolished.[6]

Three zones of attack were selected for the landings and designated *Apples, Beer*, and *Charlie* Sectors. *Apples* Sector lay west of Algiers between Castiglione and a point about five miles southwest of Cap Sidi Ferruch. *Beer* Sector extended from Cap Sidi Ferruch to St. Eugene, a small village near the northwestern corner of Algiers bay. *Charlie* Sector was east of Algiers on the eastern side of Cap Matifou off Ain Taya and Surcouf. Eastern Assault Force could not use the best landing beach near Algiers on the eastern shore of Algiers bay because that area was well within range of the French coast defense guns.[7]

The *Apples* sector had two separated pairs of landing beaches designated *Green* and *White* located on either side of Cap Sidi Ferruch, along the seven miles nearest Castiglione. *Beer Green* and *Beer White* were just east of Cap Sidi Ferruch. *Beer Red* had four landing sites in coves and small bays along the rugged shore from three miles east of the projection of Rass Acrata to a point within the bay of Algiers almost a mile southeast of Pointe Pescade. *Charlie Green, Blue, Red 1*, and *Red 2* landing beaches were in the sector between Jean-Bart and the mouth of the Rerhaia river.[8]

Inland from the *Apples Sector* on the west was a narrow rolling coastal shelf rising to a set of parallel wooded ridges about three miles from the sea. Beyond the ridges lay the most intensively cultivated plain in Algeria. On the far side of the plain rose the foothills of the Atlas Tellian mountains that roughly paralleled the coast. The village of Castiglione on the southwest of *Apples Green* Beach had a population of less than 4,000. On the ridge south of *Apples White* was Koléa, a larger community with a substantial garrison. The ridges extended eastward as far as a river valley running northward to enter the ocean at the eastern end of *Apples White*. Beyond that stream, the hill mass shielding Algiers on the west widened out before descending to the bay.[9]

The *Beer* Sector fronted on that hill mass. Beach *Beer Green* on the west extended along the bay from the eastern side of Cap Sidi Ferruch headland. *Beer White* was near the center of the shore between Cap Sidi Ferruch and Rass Acrata point. The four landing sites at *Beer Red* were separated by points and bluffs, at Cap Caxine, Pointe Pescade, and near St. Eugene. Two good roads from the *Beer* Sector to Algiers crossed from west to east. There was a coastal road through small beach communities and along the cliffs, that ran about 16 miles from Cap Sidi Ferruch to Algiers. A second, shorter road ran through an abandoned Trappist agricultural community to the town of Cheragas, on a ridge about 600 feet above sea level, then through the suburb of Lambiridi to slope steeply downward to the city's western edge. Two secondary roads, one leading from *Beer White* to Bouzarea and the other from *Beer Green*, via Ouled Fayet, flanked the shorter route and could be reached over slopes partly covered with vineyards. *Beer Red's* four sections offered only small footholds at the base of high steep slopes and were chosen because they were near coastal batteries on the heights above them.[10]

The Eastern Naval Task Force provided escorts for three groups of troop and cargo transports. Antiaircraft protection was provided by heavily armed auxiliary anti-aircraft ships at each landing sector, and by fighters from the aircraft carrier HMS *Argus* and the auxiliary carrier HMS *Avenger*. Naval gunfire support was available on call. A forward observation officer (FOO) was assigned to move inland with each landing team, maintaining radio contact with a fire support ship assigned to the landing team's sector. If heavier fire than that available from a destroyer was needed, the units ashore could request heavy caliber from one of four Royal Navy cruisers, HMS *Sheffield*, HMS *Bermuda*, HMS *Scylla*, and HMS *Charybdis*, through combined support control aboard the headquarters ship HMS *Bulolo*. One FOO was with the force at *Apples* Sector, and four were with those landing at *Beer* Sector. In the case of calls for gunfire from the cruisers, a safety margin of 2,000 yards between the target and the nearest Allied troops was required.[11]

Naval aircraft were ready to assist the fire support ships in bombarding the coastal batteries with the aid of flares before daylight, and after daylight with dive-bombing, spotting, or smoke-laying, as requested. An interval of at least 30 minutes after a request was made was to be expected before bombers could reach a given target. Those aircraft furnished tactical reconnaissance and fighter patrols until Maison Blanche airdrome had been captured by 39RCT and occupied by Royal Air Force fighter squadrons of the Eastern Air Command. The land-based planes would provide air defense of the airfield, the port, and the convoys as well as reconnaissance and close support missions.[12]

The mostly British naval forces committed to the Allied attacks in Algeria entered the Mediterranean in a complex configuration which had been developed at the British Admiralty for Operation *Torch*. In the lead was the mighty Covering Force (Force H), containing Vice Admiral Sir Neville Syfret's flagship, HMS *Duke of York*, and two other battleships, HMS *Rodney* and HMS *Renown*, the aircraft carriers HMS *Victorious* and HMS *Formidable*, three cruisers, and 17 destroyers. The naval Covering Force had the mission of protecting the landing operations from interference by the Italian or Vichy French fleets. British submarines already in the Mediterranean took patrolling stations off Messina, off the northwestern corner of Sicily, and off Toulon. Allied warplanes from Gibraltar, Malta, and the United Kingdom began reconnaissance flights over the sea between Spain and Sardinia, between Sardinia and Sicily, and over southern French ports.[13]

Axis intelligence operatives and reconnaissance assets in Spain immediately spotted and reported the naval movements near Gibraltar. As early as November 4, the Germans were aware of a threat but did not yet recognize its import. "In Gibraltar, the Luftwaffe has ascertained up to now the presence of one battleship, two aircraft carriers, five cruisers, and 20 destroyers…" noted the keeper of the *Oberkommando der Wehrmacht/ Wehrmachtführungsstab* (*OKW/ WFSt:* High Command of the Armed Forces/Armed Forces Operations Staff) War Diary. "[T]he concentration of such important naval forces in the western Mediterranean seems to indicate an imminent operation, perhaps another convoy to Malta." The Italian Marshal Ugo Cavallero on the same day considered the possibility of an Allied landing on the coast of Africa. Before midnight, November 5–6, he was informed that Allied transports were entering the Mediterranean.

The Axis powers had expected Allied action on the Atlantic coast but had not anticipated an expedition passing Gibraltar into the Mediterranean. Their incorrect assumption, and the necessity of protecting the supply lines to their troops in Africa and the Balkans, had led the Germans and Italians to cluster their naval forces in the central and eastern Mediterranean instead of in the western Mediterranean where they might have been able to intercept the Allied invasion convoys. The enemy leaders well understood that the events of the next few days might determine Rommel's fate in Africa and cause a malign reversal of Axis fortunes in the Mediterranean basin. Hitler sent a special message to the crews of the submarines and the motor torpedo boats in the Mediterranean Sea: "The existence of the African Army depends on the destruction of the English convoys. I await a ruthless victorious attack."[14]

On November 7 and 8, Axis forces made only three contacts with the *Torch* convoys, resulting in some damage to vessels but no casualties. The enemy had 76 German planes flying over the western Mediterranean. Nine German and 26 Italian submarines were arranged in several lines to ambush Allied ships. Motor torpedo boat squadrons were ready for action if the weather permitted. A German submarine torpedoed the USS *Thomas Stone* at dawn on November 7, when it was almost 150 miles northwest of Algiers, bound for the *Charlie* beaches east of the city to deliver elements of 39RCT. The explosion broke off the ship's propeller and rudder. At sundown, another submarine struck HMS *Panther*, in the Covering Force, damaging but not sinking the ship. Force H repulsed an enemy air strike during the afternoon. The Allied ships heading for Algiers passed south of the westernmost group of Axis submarines and then swung toward the attack area. They did not encounter another line of enemy submarines further east.[15]

Hitler had recognized the danger of an Allied attack in the Mediterranean basin in 1942 and had ordered defensive measures that summer. He withdrew several armored divisions from the Eastern Front and deployed them to France, depriving

Nazi generals of the means to exploit their initial successes on the southern sector of the Russian front. Hitler had acknowledged his concern when *Grossadmiral* Erich Raeder in August warned that the Allies might be preparing to enter French North Africa with the connivance of the French and thus to inflict a serious blow to the Axis coalition. Hitler was alarmed, believing that the Allied convoys were tasked to recapture Crete rather than to attack Rommel's strong defensive position. He ordered the Crete garrison reinforced to repel seaborne and airborne attacks. In an attempt to provide a unified command against an amphibious attack, he assigned Field Marshal Albert Kesselring, directly under himself, as *Oberbefehlshaber Süd* (*OB Süd*: Supreme Commander South), responsible for the defense of all the coasts in the Mediterranean and Aegean Seas which were held by German troops, except those in Rommel's sector.[16]

Notwithstanding Hitler's bloodthirsty language about ruthless attacks, Nazi policy toward French North Africa was nuanced. The Axis partners operated under the fiction that the Mediterranean was Mussolini's theater of war, but the threat of an Allied invasion in the western Mediterranean was met in accord with German, not Italian, views of appropriate action. German policy from 1940 to 1942 was to allow the French State in unoccupied France to exist and thereby to forestall the creation of an alternate French government in North Africa that might renew the French fight against the Axis powers. Italian *Comando Supremo* was not at all concerned with unoccupied France. Mussolini and his generals were determinedly focused on measures to prevent or defend against an Allied invasion of French North Africa, especially Tunisia, which would threaten their army in Libya and Italy's hold on its colony. *Comando Supremo* held two Italian divisions in western Libya ready to enter French Tunisia quickly. The Italians thought rightly that Rommel's line of supply would be improved if the Axis made full use of Tunisia's ports and airfields.[17]

Both Axis partners recognized that an Axis incursion into Tunisia would arouse French hostility, but the Germans did not want to repeat the Greek fiasco of 1940, when the doughty Greeks had inflicted a disastrous defeat on the Italian invaders. Despite Italian urgings to seize Tunisia at once, Hitler insisted on maintaining friendly relations with the Vichy government. The Germans believed that any other course might precipitate a French turn to the Anglo-American Allies. Axis policy remained, by Hitler's fiat, to wait and not to send forces into Tunisia except in the role of friendly protectors and only on terms acceptable to the French government at Vichy. Rommel would have to get along without the Tunisian ports. The prickly Vichy question served Allied interests by keeping the Axis out of Tunisia before Operation *Torch* was launched.[18]

The Axis's lack of direct intelligence from the air and sea, conflicting interests and views, and hasty, misdirected countermeasures clouded the Germans' interpretation of the nature, strength, and destination of the Allied expedition. The ranking of possible targets by the German *Oberkommando der Kriegsmarine* (*OKM*: High Command of the Navy) was: "Tripoli-Bengasi, Sicily, Sardinia, the Italian mainland, and in the last place French North Africa." Kesselring, ever the practical airman, correctly foresaw that the landings, if any, would be made in the west out of the range of the Axis fighter-bombers and within range of Allied fighter cover. On the morning of November 7, Hitler still believed the Allies intended to stage a large-scale landing of four or five divisions at Tripoli or Benghazi from which to attack Rommel's army from the rear. He informed Mussolini of his analysis, but the Duce insisted that the Allies would land on the French North African coasts.[19]

The Italian assessment was prescient. The Allied Eastern Assault Force was to land near Algiers at precisely the same time as the two other Allied task forces came ashore near Oran and Casablanca. In the afternoon of November 6, 1942, Ryder received through secure Royal Navy channels a decrypted message from Eisenhower, marked at its head in large red letters HUSH—MOST SECRET and containing the typewritten word ULTRA set off by itself before the body text.[20] That message contained AFHQ's latest assessment of possible French resistance around Algiers. The information was based on human intelligence from Allied diplomats and agents in Algiers and the product of ULTRA, the highly classified British operation for intercepting and decrypting German radio transmissions encoded using the Enigma machine, which the Germans believed to be indecipherable. Flagpole (Allied Force Headquarters) provided specific information:

> [F]riendly reception expected at Sidi Ferruch and adjoining beaches. Defended positions and battery at that point with us. [The French officer in charge there] urges you not to start premature firing there. He wants you to send American Force to headquarters of his division by dawn on DOG-day. KNOX[ii] knows location. Major Dartois, commanding Maison Blanche airport, is reported friendly.

As to the French fleet, however, AFHQ advised Ryder that "French Navy expected to offer resistance but Kingpin [French Admiral Darlan] considers your plan for overcoming it sound. If Naval resistance offered it must be crushed immediately." Ryder instructed his subordinate commands, aboard their respective ships, directing them to proceed in the spirit of AFHQ's instructions.[21]

At 4:30p.m. on November 7, the destroyer *HMS Malcolm* came alongside *HMS Sheffield*, and the 3/135 *Terminal* Force elements detailed to *Malcolm* transferred at sea without incident. The force to board HMS *Broke* transferred immediately afterward. The ship-to-ship operations were completed at 5:30p.m. Lieutenant Colonel Swenson and Captain Fancourt joined the troops on HMS *Broke,* which was commanded by Commander Arthur F. C. Layard (RN). Morale and discipline were excellent. The night was very dark, the sky slightly overcast and visibility fair.[22]

---

ii   John Knox, American vice-consul in Algiers and one of the "Twelve Disciples" in Robert Murphy's covert intelligence operation in French North Africa. Knox or his agents were to meet the Americans on the beach.

Arrival at the Beaches

The headquarters ship HMS *Bulolo* and the 15 assault transports of the Eastern Naval Task Force sailed on an easterly course throughout daylight on Saturday, November 7, 1942. At 6:00p.m., as darkness was falling, the task force turned toward Algiers and divided into three columns, each on a heading for one of the landing beach sectors. The transports for the eastern landings, with escorts, headed for a rendezvous with a beacon submarine northeast of Cap Matifou; the other two groups formed a double column and continued together to a point northwest of Cap Sidi Ferruch. There they separated at about 9:30p.m., one section seeking rendezvous with its beacon submarine north of Cap Sidi Ferruch, and the other north of Castiglione. Admiral Burrough and General Ryder, the two commanders, were on the *Bulolo* with the center group nearest Cap Sidi Ferruch.[23]

Most of the opposing French troops and coastal guns lay in and behind *Beer* Sector. To attack and subdue those forces an Allied force of 10,421 officers and enlisted men, including the entire 168th Infantry Regiment, debarked from five troopships (*Keren, Winchester Castle, Otranto, Sobieski,* and *Awatea*) and ten cargo vessels. HMS *Palomares*[iii] furnished anti-aircraft protection. The monitor HMS *Roberts*[iv], the Polish destroyer ORP[v] *Blyskavica*, and the destroyer HMS *Wilton* provided fire support. The Commando troops attached to the 168th Regimental Combat Team were to move from *Beer Green* to seize Fort de Sidi Ferruch and capture its guns and infrared installations, from *Beer White* to gain control of a warning device on the projection of Rass Acrata, and from the separate sections of *Beer Red* to capture similar installations on Cap Caxine and the observation post at Point 270, and to occupy the battery at Fort Duperré. While the commando units were engaged in those missions, the American infantry troops were to press inland through Cheragas to the heights of La Bouzarea, almost 1,500 feet above sea level, and from there to advance down into Algiers.[24]

Later, the 34th Infantry Division's history, describing the *Torch* operations, concisely summarized the events of Sunday, November 8, 1942, at the harbor of Algiers and at the beaches to the west.

> [T]he Eastern Assault Force arrived off Algiers at the appointed time, 0100 hours on 8 November 1942. Due to certain errors, not all of the assault infantry waves were put ashore at the right places. In the case of the 168th Infantry a delay of several hours was caused by the landing of a battalion 17 miles away from its designated beach. Nevertheless, so thorough had been the briefing of all ranks on the situation and mission that the heights overlooking Algiers were under our control less than 12 hours after the first landing craft scraped upon the beach. The

---

iii   HMS *Palomares* was a former fruit carrier converted to an auxiliary anti-aircraft artillery ship.
iv   *Roberts* was a shallow draft, heavily armored gun platform; her main armament was a single turret mounting twin 15-inch guns. She was studded with numerous anti-aircraft weapons.
v   ORP, Okręt Rzeczypospolitej Polskiej [Warship of the Polish Republic].

3rd Battalion, 135th Infantry, had joined the expedition at almost the last minute, being given the task of landing from two [British] destroyers after they had smashed the boom guarding the entrance to the harbor. Although a gallant attempt was made to put this plan into execution the boom proved a more difficult proposition than was first thought and before the leading destroyer could bring up alongside the mole, French searchlights and guns had been alerted and severe damage was inflicted upon the two small ships. The infantry who managed to get ashore were opposed by Senegalese troops and French tanks—more than a match for the Americans who had only small arms. When our troops had fired all their ammunition their commander surrendered to prevent further bloodshed.[25]

The 168th Regimental Combat Team (reinforced, Colonel O'Daniel commanding) of 4,355 Americans and 1,065 British, to which part of 1 Commando and the entire 6 Commando (British and American) were attached, began landings west of Algiers at 1:00a.m. under control of Captain R. J. Shaw (RN), Senior Naval Officer Landings, on the *Keren*. Some 900 officers and enlisted men of the Commando units left the *Otranta* and the *Awatea* for their objectives along the coast from Cap Sidi Ferruch to the northwest corner of the bay of Algiers. Landing on *Beer Green*, five troops of 1 Commando attacked immediately to capture Fort de Sidi Ferruch and secure the defense installations there. Using the "scramble" beaches of *Beer Red*, places which were to be swiftly crossed and not organized for protracted use and defense, ten troops of 6 Commando assaulted first to seize Fort Anglais, Fort Independence, the infrared stations at Rass Acrata and Cap Caxine, and then attacked to take Fort Duperré and the observation station at Point 270. They were to capture intact the coastal batteries which threatened the Allied ships offshore. At the same time, the 168th Infantry was to land, assemble, reorganize, and advance inland.[26]

The 168th Infantry Regiment indeed landed at the *Apples* and *Beer* beaches west of Algiers. But the landings were made in substantial confusion. The 1st Battalion, 168th Infantry, was scheduled to land nearest Cap Sidi Ferruch on *Beer Green*, while the 2nd Battalion was to land at *Beer White*. The assault companies were to pass through the dunes and across gradually rising ground through vineyards and scrub-pine woods to two battalion assembly areas. They were to advance to reach the high ground dominating Algiers before sunrise and to be closely followed by a stream of reinforcements for the final operations to gain control of the city. The French Army barracks and defensive positions which lay in the path of advance were to be brought under control through surprise attacks. The French military's administrative headquarters in Fort l'Empereur, directly west of the port of Algiers, was to be occupied.[27] Those plans proved to be a good deal more difficult to execute in practice than to document.

The planned routes and schedule of advance of 168RCT were deranged almost from the moment the order was given to land the landing force. The procedures designed to guide the landing craft to assigned beaches failed from the outset. The motor launch which was to take aboard a pilot for *Beer White* from the beacon submarine first had to embark the principal beachmaster from one of the transports.

After that task had been accomplished, the crew of the motor launch could not find the submarine from which it was to pick up the pilot, so they went to the beach without him. The submarine waited until it was scheduled to move inshore, and then transferred the pilot to the nearest available landing craft. The pilot was able to guide formations from the transports *Winchester Castle* and the *Otranto* toward *Beer Green*. The motor launch, however, led the troops meant for *Beer White* toward what turned out instead to be a landfall in the *Apples* Sector 17 miles to the west, among troops of the 11th Infantry Brigade Group (Br.). Some of the landing craft guided by the pilot toward *Beer Green* were carried off course and reached the shore between *Beer Green* and *Beer White*. The first waves of the 168RCT were forced to improvise as soon as they touched the North African shore, with elements of each battalion scattered along 15 miles of coast.[28]

The small number of available vehicle landing craft and tank landing ships greatly slowed the arrival of vehicles to carry the heavy weapons, supplies, and equipment. From the beginning, machine guns, mortars, and boxes of ammunition had to be carried along the routes to Algiers by soldiers of the heavy weapons units, who were unable to keep pace with the less encumbered rifle companies. Heavy swells, the incomplete training of the landing craft crews, offshore obstacles, soft sand, and difficult beach exits forced the early closing of B*eer Green* and of all but 200 yards of *Beer White*. *Beer White* itself became seriously congested. Communication by radio among units ashore failed because of equipment damage and insufficient signal range now that the regiment's units were scattered so far from one another. The few jeeps and trucks that reached the beaches raced up and down the roads, carrying officers in search of missing elements of their commands or shuttling troops and weapons toward the front. Civilian transport was requisitioned. Officers were able to exercise only imperfect command and control. The march toward Algiers was finally organized and set off only after much delay.[29]

The 1st Battalion, 168th Infantry, was the most seriously scattered. Somewhat more than half its strength had arrived at beach *Beer Green* by 1:30a.m., but the remainder, including the commanding officer, Lieutenant Colonel Edward J. Doyle, was delivered at points southwest of Cap Sidi Ferruch on the wrong side of that headland, and as far southwest as the *Apples* beaches. The contingent at *Beer Green* made its way to the battalion assembly area near Sidi Ferruch and waited there while Captain Edward W. Bird of Company B rode forward on reconnaissance toward Lambiridi with two British officers. At the French barracks west of the town, they found the occupants to be hostile. They quickly withdrew, leaving one of the British officers a captive. In the absence of both the battalion commander and executive officer whose mission it was to organize beach defense, command of the battalion passed temporarily to Captain Bird. About 8:30a.m., 1/168 began its march along the southern route, via Ouled Fayet (La Trappe) to Lambiridi, with the mission of protecting the regiment's south flank.[30]

Lambiridi and Fort l'Empereur

Lieutenant Colonel Doyle at last overtook his battalion's column and led it aggressively through sporadic resistance as far as the outskirts of Lambiridi. From high ground on the western fringe of the town, a defending French force fired down upon the Americans. The advance halted while the 2nd Battalion came up on the left and the regiment planned a coordinated assault. The 2nd Battalion, 168IR, commanded by Lieutenant Colonel Dewey H. Baer, had been separated into numerous scattered parties during the landing phase. Nine boatloads from Companies E and F, commanded by Major Robert R. Moore, battalion executive officer, scheduled to land at 1:00a.m. from the transport *Keren* at Beach *Beer White*, were landed instead at *Beer Green*. They marched along the highway to rejoin the rest of the 2nd Battalion. The troops then advanced along the northern route to La Bouzarea, catching up with Lieutenant Colonel Baer during the final stage of the approach to Lambiridi. Still other elements of the 2nd Battalion, which had landed yet farther east, would not join up until later in the day.[31]

Colonel O'Daniel with a party from his regimental headquarters arrived at *Beer White* about 7:00a.m., after several hours on the water. They had first sailed to *Apples White* and then boated back along the coast to the correct destination. When the 3rd Battalion Landing Team (Lieutenant Colonel Stewart T. Vincent) began landing from the transport *Otranto* shortly after 7:30a.m., the rifle companies went forward to strengthen the impending attack on Lambiridi. The heavy weapons company, without motor transport and handicapped by its heavy equipment, soon fell behind the riflemen. At noon, the regimental command post moved to the vicinity of Chéragas, and Colonel O'Daniel went on toward Lambiridi to expedite the assault through the suburbs and into the city to capture Fort l'Empereur.[32]

Shortly after noon on November 8, Baer's 2nd Battalion, 168IR, on the left (north), Vincent's 3rd Battalion on the right of the most direct route, and Doyle's 1st Battalion working up from the south to the right rear, all started into Lambiridi. The 2nd Battalion had already forced back some outposts of resisting French troops. The 3rd Battalion was newly arrived and had not yet encountered resistance. The 1st Battalion, after a minor brush with French troops in barracks, was drawn to the northeast by the sound of firing. Some of the regiment's mortars were available for the attack, but the anti-tank guns had not arrived. The 3rd Battalion found Lambiridi's streets at first silent and empty. Company K approached the square in the center of the town by the main street. A French armored car halted the Americans with machine-gun fire in irregular bursts, driving Company K to cover. Concealed riflemen then began firing on the Americans, halting the advance. The fighting in Lambiridi continued throughout the afternoon, a French Red Cross ambulance driving about to collect the wounded of both sides.[33]

Lieutenant Colonel Doyle, Captain Bird, and a detachment of about 25 men left the 1st Battalion position, worked around the southern edge of Lambiridi, and continued into Algiers. Doyle's small party arrived about 3:00p.m., November 8, at the Palais d'Été and captured it, posting riflemen at its gate and in its vicinity. "[T]he intrepid group" with Doyle then set out to secure the Police Station, and to capture the German consul.[34]

> Doyle… [had grown] impatient with his unit's dawdling progress against French snipers… in Lambiridi… Ignoring orders to hold in place, Doyle flanked the skirmishers with two dozen men and sprinted through Algiers. Soon he was rattling the gates of the governor-general's Summer Palace. [The scene] was interrupted by the crack of a sniper's rifle. Doyle pitched to the pavement, mortally wounded… [Doyle] was the second American battalion commander to die that morning [in North Africa].[35]

The French snipers also wounded an enlisted man in Doyle's detachment.

The troops near the center of Lambiridi remained pinned down, but flanking parties overcame the armored resistance and pressed on to the vicinity of Fort l'Empereur. About 50 men from Company F and Company K took up positions northwest of the objective while, on the east and south, parts of Companies I and L arranged themselves with Browning automatic rifles and .30 caliber light machine guns in positions with good views of the enemy. The entrance could be approached only by crossing an open ravine. The Americans felt unequal to the task, and darkness fell as they waited for reinforcements and planned for action the next morning.[36]

The American and British forces landing west of Algiers in the *Apples* and *Beer* Sectors achieved on November 8 only some of their crucial objectives. Their progress was much slower than planned. They did not occupy the city of Algiers, which was the local strategic objective. But the Anglo-Americans had accomplished a great deal toward the goal of Allied control of Algeria and its ports, Algiers, Bône,[vi] and Philippeville.[vii] The coastal batteries were now in Allied possession. The road network was under Allied control. The airfield at Blida was in Allied hands and Allied aircraft would soon operate from there. The delayed execution of optimistic plans had, however, cost the Eastern Assault Force the benefits of friendly French action within Algiers during the early morning hours and any possible gains from the direct attack on the port by *Terminal* Force. Delay had resulted also in the temporary absence of all the *Terminal* Force troops landed on the harbor quays.[37]

Operation *Terminal*

The port of Algiers was attacked directly by the *Terminal* antisabotage force in the hope of preserving the harbor facilities for future Allied logistics and supply operations.

---

vi   Modern Annaba, Algeria.
vii   Modern Skikda, Algeria.

During the late afternoon of November 7, 24 American officers[38] and 638 enlisted men of 3rd Battalion, 135th Infantry Regiment, transferred while underway at sea from the cruiser HMS *Sheffield* to the two old British destroyers, HMS *Broke* and HMS *Malcolm*, Commander A. B. Russell, RN. In addition to the American infantrymen, *Terminal* Force included 74 Royal Naval personnel and three British Army officers to board and seize ships in Algiers harbor. All who were to go ashore were in U.S. Army uniforms. They had trained briefly for the mission in Belfast harbor and at a nearby camp but had learned *Terminal's* exact nature and objectives only during the final stage of the approach voyage from the United Kingdom.[39]

Terminal Force waited north of Pointe Pescade in the early hours of November 8 for the order to assault the harbor. Burrough, naval commander in chief, ordered the *Terminal* Force to attack and the two destroyers set course for the bay of Algiers at 1:40a.m. The lights of the city were visible as the ships slipped past the eastern shore. The harbor extended along the western edge of the bay more than one and one-half miles southward from the French naval base at Îlot de la Marine. A crescent-shaped sea wall, bowed toward the shore, protected the center of the harbor, while two jetties projecting from shore beyond the sea wall's extremities gave sheltered access to the open bay. Across these two entrances were barrier booms. Jutting out from the shore into the harbor were eight concrete moles of varying lengths and widths which in effect subdivided the entire area into four major basins. At the far north was the section controlled by the French Navy and protected by powerful fixed batteries mounted on the Jetée du Nord. Most of the other three sections were devoted to commercial shipping. On a flat shelf between the base of the moles and the steeply rising slopes of the city were paved streets and narrow lanes lined with warehouses and other port structures.[40]

The plan of attack called for HMS *Broke* to pierce the barrier, enter the southern basin, and discharge troops and naval boarding parties at the Quai de Dieppe. About 15 minutes later, HMS *Malcolm* was to follow a similar course to the Grand Mole. Infantry elements were to establish a defensive line to bar access by road from the south, while mixed teams of platoon strength secured an electric power station, a petroleum storage depot, and a seaplane base in the southwestern section of the harbor, in addition to the port offices, graving docks, and adjacent moles farther north. The assignment of missions was flexible, allowing for the possibility of failure by either ship to complete its approach or even for the necessity of withdrawing.[41]

Coastal batteries dominated the bay and harbor not only from the Jetée du Nord and Îlot de la Marine but also from high ground adjacent to the port. In a most advantageous position directly south of the port on the crest of a knoll about 300 feet high was the Batterie des Arcades with three medium guns. Machine-gun fire could be expected from other points as well as from these batteries. Against such strength and vigilance, *Terminal* Force could not expect to benefit from surprise.

The landings on the beaches near Algiers would have been in progress more than three hours before it reached the harbor.

The British plan, with evident misgivings about the high probability of heavy American losses, averred that it was just possible that, as an offset against the loss of surprise, some of the port's defenders might be drawn off to oppose the advance from the beaches. The coastal guns were the objective of Commando attacks which did in fact capture them before the harbor was approached. The Royal Navy planners also had thought it possible that the gun barrels of the harbor batteries could not be sufficiently depressed to strike targets within the harbor itself, but this was not certain. The planners had the destroyers fly large American flags in the hope of encouraging token resistance. The flags instead made excellent range markers for the shore batteries firing on the ships.[42]

The *Terminal* Force and its Royal Navy ships encountered fierce resistance by French forces at the entrance to Algiers harbor and on the quay. The destroyers made two unsuccessful attempts to find and break the boom across the harbor. The city's lights went out and searchlight beams swept across the bay that soon clearly illuminated the two vessels. Artillery fire from the harbor batteries followed immediately, particularly from the Batterie des Arcades. In the garish light and thundering noise, both ships circled for a third try. As the ships neared their objective, the order not to fire unless first fired upon of course became moot.[43] HMS *Malcolm* was hit by murderous fire from the French guns that killed many sailors and troops and badly damaged the ship. Just after 4:00a.m., *Malcolm* caught fire on deck and was forced to withdraw without landing its complement of American infantry. Casualties on *Malcolm* were ten killed and 25 wounded. The dead were buried at sea.[44]

> French gunners ranged *Malcolm*… [S]hells smacked through the hull, perforating the boilers and reducing the destroyer to four knots. Swathed in white steam, she made an easy target. Other shells hit the funnels. Fragments sprayed across the deck, where 300 infantrymen had flattened out behind the useless sniper shields… *Malcolm* managed to get under way again and limped seaward, where the crew spent the next several hours hosing blood and brains from the deck and heaving the dead overboard in weighted shrouds fashioned from mattress covers.[45]

The *Broke* persisted until a fourth try succeeded in taking her at top speed through the boom "like a knife through butter."[46] *Broke's* commander, Layard, had at last spotted a pair of dim green buoy lights marking the harbor entrance. He increased speed to 20 knots and sliced through the barrier of huge timber beams chained together. Despite the searchlights and flares, HMS *Broke* missed the designated point of mooring, either because some anchored vessels barred her path or because she mistook her objective in the darkness. She berthed instead along the Mole Louis Billiard.[47]

> We proceeded in the fourth time and the batteries began to pound [HMS *Broke*]. We returned fire from the destroyer. It looked like we were going to miss again and Captain Fancourt remarked

about it, however, Commander Layard, seeming not to hear anything, altered the course a little and ordered increased speed. We cut through the boom with hardly a sensation of hitting it and proceeded toward the quay. The quay we had planned on getting was filled by ships, so we berthed alongside the Quay de Falaise on Mole Louis Billiard. When we went through the boom we came under terrific machine gun fire from a small vessel in port and turned the Oerlikons[viii] on the vessel and shot it up considerably, silencing the fire. A number of naval personnel aboard the *Broke* were wounded by the machine gun fire, which seemed to be of a caliber comparable to our .50 caliber. There was some machine gun fire from the warehouses and ships in the harbor and the naval personnel returned with the Oerlikons, which seemed to silence the enemy guns. The troops aboard the *Broke* were quite shaken by the bombardment and were a little slow... to disembark. I went down on the deck as soon as we were getting into the quay and helped the officers get the men going...[48]

Half the *Terminal* Force, consisting of Company L, one section of Company M, and nine medics from the 135th Infantry, with some British naval personnel, came safely through the French fire, flattened on the deck of HMS *Broke*. Her armored rail offered but little protection. The destroyer's guns silenced sniper fire from the docks. Badly shaken, the 3rd Battalion troops were slow to rise from the deck, but eventually scurried across the extended brows to the quay. Swenson instructed his men to "light out like stripey-assed baboons up the wharf until you can get some cover, then fight like hell."[49] The 3rd Battalion's detachment debarked onto the quay at about 5:20a.m. and initially fought ardently against prepared defenses of artillery and machine guns.[50]

The American and British landing teams separated and proceeded to perform their respective missions. The troops took possession of the mole itself, the electric power station, and the petroleum tank farm, and began slowly extending a perimeter northward to the seaplane base and along the street paralleling the shore. Small arms and automatic weapon fire fell on the open intersections but did not stop the American advance. The resistance diminished first to occasional sniping and then to an ominous silence as the French officers appraised the situation. The naval boarding parties found no indications of scuttling or sabotage. The attack seemed to have succeeded even without HMS *Malcolm* and its portion of the *Terminal* Force. What remained was to establish contact with the American troops approaching the city, perhaps already entering its outskirts. But it was not to be. Instead, within a few minutes of each other, a delegation from the city consisting of two civilians and two police officers requested that arrangements be made for the formal surrender of Algiers to the Americans, and a sympathetic French officer appeared to warn that the Allied force was being surrounded by French troops with orders to attack them.[51]

At about 8:00a.m., French gunners opened an effective fire at the Allied troops on the docks. Rounds from the battery at Jetée du Nord a mile to the north began falling near HMS *Broke*. The third shell ricocheted off *Broke*'s bow and exploded

---

viii   20mm automatic anti-aircraft guns.

on the quay. Commander Layard parted all lines and moved the destroyer to a new position sheltered by a French freighter along the Quaie Dunkerque. Accurate fire from the Jetée du Nord drove the *Broke* to a third mooring and then forced yet another move to a spot which was better protected from the line of fire but which separated the ship from the American soldiers and the British naval party ashore. While waiting, pointed toward the entrance for quicker departure, *Broke* came under fire from an unseen weapon, probably a howitzer, which at 9:20a.m. made six near misses and then scored five hits in swift succession.[52] HMS *Broke* had to get out of the port. Fancourt sounded the recall siren, but with Swenson's troops scattered across the docks under sniper fire, only 60 men were able to reboard *Broke* before the destroyer again parted lines and moved out of the harbor.[53]

Most of the landed part of *Terminal* Force could not have reached *Broke* for several minutes, and even then, in Swenson's judgment, they would have been subject to greater danger from the French cannons and machine guns than if they remained ashore. Lieutenant Colonel Swenson believed at first that his force could hold out until the 168th Infantry Regiment arrived. He ordered his men to hold their positions. At 9:40a.m. the *Broke*, badly shot up and losing power, struggled out into the bay partially covered by her smoke. The escort destroyer HMS *Zetland*, after completing its bombardment of the Batterie du Lazaret on Cap Matifou, moved to cover HMS *Broke* and took her in tow. HMS *Broke* foundered from more than 20 holes in the hull and sank during the day, after *Zetland* took aboard all her crew.[54]

> Even with [*Broke*] gone, Swenson kept heart… He estimated that four French infantry companies surrounded Môle Louis Billiard—imposing numbers, but not overwhelming. But Royal Navy bombers pummeled the noisome battery on the Jetée du Nord, and Swenson continued to hope that the 168th Infantry would soon arrive as planned. Fashioning breastworks from hay bales and shipping crates, he organized an outer perimeter to keep French troops beyond hand grenade range and an inner defense to shield his wounded and heavy weapons.[55]

Royal Navy Albacore dive bombers silenced the coastal guns at the northern end of the harbor at about 11:00a.m. The firepower of the American troops temporarily overawed the Senegalese companies which hemmed them in. Lieutenant Colonel Swenson was out of touch with the troops in the vicinity of the power station and sea plane base, but from the sound of firing concluded that they were continuing the fight. He organized the immediate area south of a warehouse on Mole Louis Billiard for defense. Shortly after 11:00a.m. armored vehicles were reported to be approaching. Swenson positioned men to fire anti-tank grenades, but *Terminal* Force's ammunition was already low when several French light tanks and armored cars arrived about 11:30a.m. Three French tanks circled the area and subjected the Americans to fire from 37mm cannons and machine guns. Then two more tanks approached. It was apparent that the French were going to cover all openings with fire. The Americans' attempts to destroy the French armored vehicles with the grenades failed for lack of practice with the weapons. Swenson's men had no bazookas or anti-tank guns.

When Swenson saw the additional tanks approaching, he realized that the combined fire of the tanks could destroy his force and that his troops were in a hopeless situation. There was no sign from the city indicating the arrival of the 168th Infantry Regiment, which were in fact still several miles away, delayed by the misdirected landings and the mishandling of troops on the approach march.[56]

> Several Renault light tanks peppered the breastworks with machine-gun and 37mm cannon fire… Two more Renaults arrived to set up a crossfire, backing the Americans to the water's edge… With his riflemen low on cartridges, Swenson instructed his men to fix bayonets, then thought better of the order. Already, TERMINAL had cost 24 Allied dead and 55 wounded. Complete annihilation of the men on the dock would serve no cause.[57]

Lieutenant Colonel Swenson raised a white flag and surrendered his force to the French at about 12:30p.m. on November 8. The 3rd Battalion alone had suffered 48 casualties during the landing and the fight on the piers, with 15 killed and 33 wounded.[58] The French imprisoned the survivors of the landed part of *Terminal* Force for the next two days.[59] The U.S. Army's official history concluded that "Operation TERMINAL at Algiers, like Operation RESERVIST at Oran, had been undertaken in defiance of accepted principles of warfare and had failed, but the conduct of its participants had been gallant and the resistance which overcame them happily lacked the ruthlessness shown by the defenders at Oran."[60] Swenson, the mission's ground commander, candidly summarized the results.

> It was our mission to secure the port and prevent sabotage of the port and port facilities. It was good fortune to the allied cause, that the French decided not to sabotage the port or installation, and not the operation of the Terminal Force. We failed in our mission and at most merely caused a diversion.[61]

Meanwhile, the green troops of 168IR were still struggling to push through French resistance and were not yet in the city.

> The 168th Infantry of the U.S. 34th Infantry Division, which was supposed to hurry east to reinforce Swenson's beleaguered TERMINAL force at Algiers Harbor, was both late and lost. Four thousand Americans in the regiment were scattered along fifteen miles of coastline… The deficiencies of the past two years in preparing the 34th Division for war now began to tell. The amateurish football field maneuvers and town-square drilling by the Iowa National Guard seemed irrelevant in the scrub pines of eastern Algeria. The hurried dispatch of the 34th to Britain ten months earlier, the dispersal of regiments across Northern Ireland, the poor training facilities, the rapid turnover of mostly field grade commanders and the diversion of troops for use as laborers and headquarters guards meant that most of the infantry units arriving in Africa "were not prepared for combat service," as a division history acknowledged… [62]

In the afternoon of November 8, the survivors of *Terminal* Force on HMS *Malcolm* transferred to landing craft and reached the coast about 20 miles west of Algiers. At

4:00a.m. on Monday, November 9, the 3/135IR troops who had been returned to the beach received orders to march to Algiers and arrived in the city late that night. The next day, November 10, after a cease fire had been negotiated by Major General Ryder, the 3rd Battalion troops who had surrendered to the French were released. The elements of the battalion marching from the west rejoined their comrades. 3/135 remained in Algiers until January 2, 1943, engaged in garrison and police duty in the city. The battalion also acted as an honor guard for division events, which the soldiers believed was a reward for their brave conduct on the piers.[63]

The 39th Infantry Regiment (detached from the 9th Infantry Division) and the British 11th Brigade seized the vitally important airfields south of Algiers while the 168th Infantry sent patrols into the southwestern outskirts of the city. At the same time, negotiations were proceeding between Major General Ryder, as the Allied representative, and General Alphonse Juin, who was at the time the local French army commander. On the morning of November 9, a little more than 24 hours after the assault waves came ashore, a conference was held in Fort l'Empereur and an armistice was arranged which came into effect on November 11.[64]

Hostilities Cease in Algiers

In Vichy, the former resort and spa town in Central France that was now the capital of the rump *État Français*, just after 9:00a.m. on November 8, *Maréchal* Henri Philippe Pétain, head of state, received the American *chargé d'affaires*, Mr. S. Pinkney Tuck. Tuck delivered President Roosevelt's official message announcing the Allied invasion of French North Africa. The reply, already prepared by French diplomats for the marshal's use, was then signed by Pétain and handed to his visitor. France intended to resist the attack upon its empire. As the interview concluded, Marshal Pétain showed only amiability and good spirits. But later that day, the French informed Tuck that diplomatic relations with the United States were terminated.

The reactionary collaborator Admiral François Darlan was deputy prime minister of the French State, the senior French official in North Africa, outranking all other French civil and military figures. He was in Algiers by an unfortunate personal happenstance; he was attending the bedside of his son, gravely ill with polio.[65] When Darlan reported to Pétain on the Allied invasion, Pétain authorized him to act freely on the marshal's behalf, informing Vichy of what had been done.[66] Darlan's presence in Algiers also put him and most of the senior French North African government officials and military officers, of all political stripes, within Ryder's grasp.

Darlan was indecisive and procrastinated as the Eastern Assault Force closed in, surrounding Algiers. Major General Ryder left HMS *Bulolo* about 9:00a.m. on November 8 to join the advance echelon of his headquarters at Beach *Beer White*, operated by Brigadier General Ray E. Porter. Ryder's troops held the heights west of Algiers, the highways approaching the city from west and east, the airfields at

Blida and Maison Blanche, and the principal coastal batteries from Cap Sidi Ferruch to Ilôt de la Marine at Algiers harbor. Naval gunfire was falling on the Batterie du Lazaret on Cap Matifou. Allied artillery was shelling Fort l'Empereur. British dive bombers had already struck the Jetée du Nord, Fort Duperré, and Fort d'Estrees. Fort Duperré was ready to capitulate, but Fort d'Estrees was holding out. Darlan, Juin, and the other French leaders had the choice of waiting to be captured or marching out with their badly equipped forces into a futile battle with the Allies. The Eastern Assault Force had fallen behind schedule but the Allied presence, although not yet firmly established ashore with respect to resupply and reinforcement, was nonetheless there to stay in force.[67]

> Admiral Darlan recognized with the discernment of a professional survivor that the jig was nearly up. The Vichy commander-in-chief had only 7,000 badly armed troops in Algiers; both major airfields had been captured, his fleet was bottled up by British men-of-war, and the city was surrounded by 30,000 troops. At three p.m. on Sunday, Darlan appeared at the Villa des Oliviers, where the [American diplomats Robert Murphy and Kenneth Pendar] had been spared execution through the timely clemency of General Juin… Darlan announced that he was ready to parley. Would M. Murphy find the American commander, who was said to be on the beach ten miles west of Algiers?[68]

Shortly after 4:00p.m. on Sunday, General Ryder learned from one of Robert Murphy's staff that General Juin was ready to negotiate. Darlan had authorized Juin to arrange a settlement for Algiers but not for all French North Africa.[69]

> In Juin's limousine… the diplomats threaded their way through straggling columns of American soldiers west of Algiers. At Beach BEER White, they discovered Major General… Ryder… sitting on a large rock… Asked if he would discuss terms with the French, he replied evenly, "I will go anywhere to talk to anyone who wishes to surrender Algiers to me." Murphy… took the general by the arm and bundled him into the limousine.[70]

The arrangements for the cessation of hostilities in Algiers commenced with a brief face-to-face encounter between Ryder and Juin. They met at Juin's command post in Fort L'Empereur, the headquarters of the French Army in North Africa. Ryder was brought there with Murphy and two other American officers in Juin's own automobile, after passing through the lines in Lambiridi to the fort. Outside Fort l'Empereur, Juin's chief of staff, standing at attention in the street, extended his sword to Ryder, hilt first. Ryder, doing honor both to the man and to the French Army, indicated that he should retain the weapon, and the officer turned and went into the fort. Ryder and Murphy followed and entered a large hall where 50 French officers stood along the walls. Juin stood at the head of a conference table. Ryder and Juin concluded a simple oral agreement at 6:40p.m., November 8, to stop fighting at once. The French troops would return to their barracks, retaining their arms and colors. Americans would occupy key points in the city and rely on the aid of French police to maintain order. Allied units would enter the city at 8:00p.m. Prisoners were to be freed immediately, including the survivors from Operation *Terminal*. Detailed armistice terms would be discussed at a meeting next day. While these informal arrangements were implemented, Ryder returned to HMS *Bulolo* and reported to Eisenhower at Gibraltar, recommending an armistice on the mild terms prepared during Allied planning for a case of merely token resistance.[71]

Major General Ryder met the French chiefs once more in conference during the afternoon of Monday, November 9. Because he had not yet received from Allied Force Headquarters at Gibraltar a reply to his recommendation, Ryder decided to offer those easier terms on his own authority. The French accepted provisionally, subject to approval from Pétain, but the marshal's response could not be had for another day. Because the only safeguard for Allied forces was the promise of the French leaders that they would not resume hostilities without warning, Ryder insisted upon discreetly securing the French ammunition under American guards, pending a permanent agreement.

Political turmoil and new dangers intervened to upset Ryder's arrangements. The pacification of Algiers was subordinated to negotiations for a general cease fire covering Oran and Morocco, and the thorny question whether the French would resist the Axis forces that were at that moment moving into Tunisia from Libya and Italy. During the evening of November 9, Lieutenant General Anderson arrived by airplane at Blida, went to HMS *Bulolo*, and assumed command of the Eastern Task Force for the drive on Tunis. Lieutenant General Clark arrived to lead on behalf of Eisenhower the negotiations with Darlan, Juin, and others.[72] General Giraud also appeared at Algiers, with the assistance and approval of Roosevelt and Eisenhower, to rally French patriots who were prepared to resume hostilities against the Axis powers. While bitter fighting continued at Oran and in western Morocco, in Algiers a settlement between the French and the Allies seemed possible.[73]

Major General Clark arrived with orders from Eisenhower to help the French general Giraud take command of French forces and to secure a general armistice. But Giraud was in hiding in the home of the family of the sympathetic Vice Admiral Reynaud Fenard in Algiers and the collaborationist Admiral Darlan commanded the Vichy loyalist forces. Clark conferred with Major General Ryder, then accompanied the diplomat Murphy to the St. Georges hotel. In a small room where five French admirals and four generals awaited them, including Darlan. After an unproductive exchange of invective, threats, and banalities, General Juin held up his hand. "Give us five minutes." The Americans left the room. Murphy was deeply concerned that the French might choose not to back the Allies. If the Allies were to advance into Tunisia with secure lines of communication and supply, they needed French help. After a time, the French concluded their internal discussions and reached an arrangement. Darlan said to Murphy, "*J'accepte.*" Darlan laid paper before Clark announcing to all French troops that further battle was futile. Darlan took up a pen and scratched an order "in the name of the Marshal" ordering all land, sea, and air forces in North

Africa to cease fire, return to their bases, and observe a strict neutrality. "This will stand," Clark declared.[74] Clark immediately cabled Eisenhower at Gibraltar. "I deemed it of the utmost importance," he told Eisenhower, "to do anything to secure an order which would be obeyed to cease hostilities." General Giraud reappeared and announced that for the greater glory of France he would serve under Darlan in fighting the Germans.[75]

Then news arrived from Vichy that Marshal Pétain had removed Darlan as his military commander and repudiated any previous agreement with the Americans. The Americans had received reports that Darlan, under Vichy pressure, would reject the armistice signed only hours earlier. At 3:00p.m. on Tuesday, November 10, Clark and Murphy arrived at the Fenard family villa. Darlan was there conferring with Giraud. When Darlan threatened to revoke his order, Clark said: "Damned if you do!... You are now a prisoner." "Then I must be taken prisoner," rejoined Darlan. Clark ordered two infantry platoons to throw a cordon around Fenard's estate. An American colonel, Benjamin A. Dickson, II Corps G2 [Intelligence] chief, shoved past Darlan's aides to confront him directly. "*Mon Admiral*, by order of the supreme commander you are hereby under arrest in these quarters. Guards have been posted outside with orders to shoot if you attempt to escape." Dickson then went to the front gate of the villa and ordered the American riflemen to do exactly that.[76]

Darlan was then informed that during the evening of November 10, ten German and six Italian divisions had executed Hitler's Operation *Anton*, invading the *Zone Libre*, the theretofore unoccupied part of metropolitan France. Marshal Pétain no longer spoke for France. With two Allied armies in North Africa, Hitler could not risk an exposed flank on the French Mediterranean. Within hours the Axis forces overran southern France and *panzers* reached the Riviera.[77] On November 11, Darlan pledged once again his conversion to the Allied cause and his arrest was rescinded.

Clark was awakened at 5:00a.m. on November 12 to the news that Darlan had again changed his position. The armistice order to French commanders in North Africa had been suspended pending approval by General Charles Noguès, designated by Pétain as *le Maréchal's* plenipotentiary in North Africa. Another tumultuous meeting was convened in the St. Georges conference room. The issues were the structure of an interim French government in Northwest Africa and its status after the Nazi occupation of all of metropolitan France. At noon on November 13, Eisenhower arrived from Gibraltar to break the impasse.[78]

At the hotel, Clark and Murphy briefed Eisenhower. After hours of loud argument and posturing among the French senior officers, they had settled on an arrangement of French civil government and military affairs in North Africa that Clark thought was viable. Darlan was to become high commissioner of French North Africa, with Giraud as chief of the French armed forces, Juin as army commander, and Noguès remaining as governor-general of Morocco. At 2:00p.m. Eisenhower said to the assembled Frenchmen: "What you propose is completely acceptable to me. From this day on, Admiral Darlan heads the French North African state. In this attitude I am supported by President Roosevelt. We all must agree to put together all means to whip the Germans."[79]

Upon the Allied conquest of Algeria, Major General Ryder reverted to commander of the 34th Infantry Division under British First Army, led by Lieutenant General Anderson. Anderson charged Ryder with ensuring the security of the port of Algiers and of the airbases at Maison Blanche and at Blida. For this purpose, Ryder had under his control the four battalions of the 34th Infantry Division (168IR and 3/135) then present as well as the three battalions of 39IR (detached from the 9th Infantry Division). Anderson directed Ryder to neutralize enemy agents and saboteurs in the Algiers area, and placed all British field security personnel under Ryder's command, except those attached to the British 78th Division, then marching into Tunisia.[80]

Ryder wrote an initial short report of the Algiers operation.[81] He described the fate of the transport USS *Thomas Stone* (APA-29), damaged but not sunk by a torpedo. The rest of the task force left the *Thomas Stone* behind with the corvette HMS *Spey*. The troops of the 2nd Battalion, 39RCT, were loaded in 24 landing craft and left the ship escorted by HMS *Spey*. As the landing craft failed one by one in the rough seas, they were abandoned and scuttled. The troops were taken on board *Spey*, eventually landed in the corvette's boats, and rejoined 39RCT. Ryder wrote that the western landings were unopposed, but only the landing of the British 11th Brigade at *Apples* beaches had proceeded according to schedule. The first wave of the 168RCT's troops at *Beer* beaches landed as scheduled and advanced inland. But the follow-up waves of elements of 168RCT were landed approximately 18 miles from their proper landing sites, "due to the inexperience of the men handling the landing craft."[82] While the regiment's commander, Colonel O'Daniel, worked to concentrate his scattered troops, the leading wave moved rapidly. They had men in the city by 11:00a.m. but did not have the strength of numbers or arms to hold the city against spirited French resistance. Ryder noted the lack of vehicles which compelled the follow-up elements of 168RCT to march on foot 25 miles, carrying all their heavy weapons. Despite these obstacles, the regiment had attacked the high ground overlooking the city by the evening of November 8 and achieved full control of Algiers the next day.[83]

Eisenhower sent a cable to Marshall on November 11 extolling the performances of Clark, Ryder and Fredendall. Of the latter, Eisenhower told his chief: "Fredendall has done a fine job of leadership... I am confident that reports will show that he has fulfilled every condition of brilliant leadership in a difficult situation and will have deserved a prompt recommendation from me to you for his promotion."[84]

CHAPTER 8

The Early Tunisian Campaign, November 1942–February 1943

Eisenhower was a good bridge player, but poker was his favorite indoor sport. His gamble on rushing east to take Tunis, however, was lost to the unforgiving North African terrain and the cold winter rains. French support at last assured, the Royal Navy put British troops ashore close to the Tunisian border while an Allied column began the long overland trek. The Axis reacted swiftly. Tunisia was only "a panther's leap" from Axis bases in Italy, as the deputy Führer, Hermann Göring, had observed. The Germans demanded that the French State cede the use of airports in Tunisia and the department of Constantine in Algeria as bases for Axis aircraft. On November 9, the Vichy government informed the Germans that French air bases in these areas were available to the Luftwaffe. Despite the objections of the French governor-general of Tunisia, Admiral Jean Pierre Estéva, the first German planes began landing in Tunisia in mid-morning, and until darkness a steady stream of fighters, dive bombers, and air transports arrived at El Aouina airdrome, near Tunis. They brought German paratroopers and Kesselring's headquarters guard to protect the landing ground. By day's end, 90 aircraft had landed. On the morning of November 10, the Italian Air Force sent a flight of 22 *Macchi* 202 fighters.[1]

> The Wehrmacht's entrenchment in Tunis set the stage for confrontation between German and Anglo-American armies that was to scorch two continents over the next two and a half years and cost several million lives. Here began the struggle for the earth itself, or at least the western earth, an unremitting series of titanic land battles that would sweep across Salerno and Anzio, Normandy and the Bulge.[2]

Hitler was informed of the Allied invasion while stopped at a rail siding in Thuringia. He recognized that if the Allies seized North Africa, they could turn what had seemed a merely peripheral strike into a strategic springboard for the invasion of southern Europe. That would imperil Italy and Axis possessions from France to Greece. "To give up Africa means to give up the Mediterranean," the Führer declared. He refused to accept that Germany had lost the strategic initiative, insisting that Tunisia was to be the "cornerstone of our conduct of the war on the southern flank of Europe." By late November, the Führer's strategic vision would be articulated in a one-sentence order: "North Africa, being the approach to Europe, must be held at all costs." That proclamation condemned a million men on both sides to six months of misery in Tunisia.[3]

Kesselring became known to Allied soldiers as Smiling Albert for his toothy grin. He was an intelligent general, possessed of conviviality, personal confidence, unquenchable optimism, and a sound strategic vision. "One of the Reich's ablest commanders, he was both daring… and brutal."[4] On the morning after the Anglo-American invasion, Hitler told Kesselring by telephone that he had "a free hand" in Tunisia. That "free hand" would cause the Allies many misfortunes. Hitler appointed Kesselring as Mussolini's deputy on November 10, with authority over all Axis air and ground forces in the Mediterranean. Dismissing the warnings of subordinates, Kesselring had a keen sense of what was militarily feasible and dared to think it possible to regain the strategic initiative. On November 13, Kesselring ordered his staff to begin planning for an offensive. "The only way to forestall the loss of Africa was to counterattack across the Tunisian mountains into Algeria. Smiling Albert meant to chase the Anglo-Americans back to their ships."[5]

On November 24, Lieutenant General Anderson ordered Major General Evelegh to resume the advance on Tunis and Bizerte as swiftly as possible. On the Allied right flank, three British battalions in the 11th Brigade closed on Medjez el Bab in a two-pronged assault reinforced by American gunners. From the southwest, the 5th Battalion of the Northhamptonshire Regiment and the U.S. 175th Field Artillery Battalion, detached from the 34th Infantry Division, attacked before dawn on November 25. Three miles from Medjez, they killed a dozen Italians and seized the heights called Djebel [Arabic for "hill" or "mount"] Bou Mouss—soon renamed Grenadier Hill. A counterattack by German tanks from Medjez retook Djebel Bou Mouss within several hours, inflicting heavy casualties. Brits and Yanks together retreated.[6]

On November 26, the first tank battle between German and American forces was fought near Chouïgui pass. The Americans survived and held their ground only at great cost and by employing aggressive and evasive tactics. Early that day, Colonel Friedrich Freiherr von Broich sent a small force consisting of a company of the 11th Parachute Engineer Battalion, a company of the 3rd Tunis Field Battalion, and a company of the 190th Panzer Battalion from Mateur toward Tebourba. The German force drew near the pass, where the 1st Battalion, 1st Armored Regiment, 1st Armored Division, under command of Lieutenant Colonel John Knight Waters,[i] had taken up defensive positions. Waters's battalion had its Headquarters Company and three companies of M3 light tanks, an 81mm mortar platoon, and an assault gun platoon employing three 75mm pack howitzers on half-tracks, but it had no artillery, infantry, or engineers attached.[7]

---

i   The son-in-law of Major General George S. Patton.

The American battalion's Company C barred the southeastern entrance to the pass while the other three companies stood ready on high ground. Company B waited in hull-down positions parallel to the road approaching the northwestern entrance from the north. The other companies were dug in along the road from Sidi Nsir, extending as far west as St. Joseph's Farm near the Tine river. The enemy force, approaching from the north, included six new *PzKpfW Mark IV Ausführung F.* Those modern tanks, Lieutenant Colonel Waters soon realized, had a new, long-barreled 75mm gun, the LK 43, then unknown to Allied intelligence. The new gun's muzzle velocity of nearly 3,000 feet per second was twice that of American tank guns and had correspondingly greater penetrating power. The German force also had three or more upgraded *PzKpfW Mark III*s with new long-barreled 50mm main guns.[8]

The Germans continued southward past Major William Tuck's Company B, concealed in hull defilade on the reverse slope of a ridge on the enemy's left flank, to meet the challenge of Major Carl Siglin's Company A. After a bold preliminary skirmish by the assault gun platoon, firing its 75mm pack howitzers without armor piercing or anti-tank ammunition, Company A maneuvered to strike the enemy from the southwest. The M3 Stuarts of 1st Battalion's Company A were shredded by German main gun fire. They burst into flames, incinerating their crews. Only an attack by Company B into the flanks and rear of the enemy tanks resulted in the destruction of seven *panzers* and saved the remnants of Company A. While Major Siglin's men claimed the enemy's attention, Major Tuck's 37mm guns, firing at close range from the east flank and rear, knocked out the six new Mark IVs and one of the Mark IIIs before the enemy pulled back to the same walled farm it had occupied the previous day. The survivors of Company A and all of Company B aggressively pursued the withdrawing enemy to their farm complex stronghold, killing and wounding many *panzergrenadiers* and driving away the remaining *panzers*. The fight cost the Americans six M3s and most of their crews, including Major Siglin who was killed in the follow-up battle at the enemy farmhouse. Waters had essentially traded tank for tank and the first armored battle ended in a draw.[9]

The brilliant American writer and combat veteran Paul Fussell saw the M3 Stuart as a symptom of American fantasies about the nature of war.

> At the beginning of the war the little light tank, all bolted plane surfaces of one-inch armor plate with smiling men in football helmets looking out, was the standard equipment in the American army's four "mechanized cavalry" divisions. One model carried only machine guns, and the ordnance of the most heavily armed was the 37-mm gun. This light tank, the ten-ton "Stuart" or "Honey," was the one with which George Patton established his reputation as a genius with armor. Assistant Secretary of War John J. McCloy, speaking at the Amherst College commencement on June 14, 1941, recognized that many more such mechanized divisions were called for, but saw no need for heavier equipment. "More like Baby Austins than bloody tanks," commented an experienced British tanker as he watched a shipment of Honeys unloaded at a North African port.[10]

There were not enough British First Army troops to do more than secure two small Algerian ports. The ground column that marched into Tunisia was too late and lacked enough force to overcome both the Germans and the winter weather. Lieutenant General Anderson and his First Army made the effort but lacked the speed, mobility, and combat power to break the Axis forces continually reinforced through the formerly French Tunisian ports and airfields. Over the narrow body of water between Sicily and North Africa, and despite the early efforts of the Royal Navy and Allied air forces to interdict the Axis traffic, the Germans poured planes, men, and tanks. The Axis met no French resistance in Tunisia. Except for barren mountains in western Tunisia, Tunis and Tunisia were for the moment out of Allied reach.[11]

The Allies were compelled to revise their strategy and timing in North Africa when the last phase of Operation *Torch* failed to capture Tunis. To organize and sustain an offensive in the spring of 1943 required changes in the Allied chain of command and a massive buildup of both supplies and the means to transport them to the battlefield. By the middle of January 1943, decisions made at the Casablanca Conference had solidified the Allies' strategy for Africa and made the changes in Allied command structure, not all of them for the better. Eisenhower had broad experience in Army staff work and planning but was still learning the art of high-level military command and control, complicated by coalition politics.

The urgency for an early capture of Tunisia was intensified by the January 1943 decision to drive Italy out of the war by invading and conquering Sicily in mid-1943. To meet that timetable, the Allied Force would have to defeat the Axis armies in North Africa by early spring. AFHQ would have to prepare for the invasion of Sicily as it also ensured a steady growth in supplies and strength, improved the combat effectiveness of its troops, and drove into Tunisia to destroy the Axis forces. But a full-scale offensive restart in northern Tunisia was impossible until after the winter rains stopped, around the end of March. The original plan, to trap Rommel's army in Libya between the Eighth Army and a British force in Tunisia, had to be shelved. The Eighth Army would instead have to drive the Italo-German Army back into Tunisia. The final stage of operations in Tunisia would be a battle between two pairs of armies. Both coalitions would face difficult problems of command structure and control of tactical operations while struggling to meet the logistical requirements of their forces.[12]

After securing Algiers, most of the British units of the Eastern Assault Force had moved to Tunisia under First British Army. Some Red Bull soldiers went directly to the fighting front to join their allies. On November 15, 1942, the 175th Field Artillery Battalion was detached from the 168th Infantry Regiment, 34ID, and left Algiers for Medjez el Bab in northern Tunisia. The battalion, Lieutenant Colonel Joseph E. Kelly commanding, had 175 rounds of 25-pounder ammunition for each of its 12 British howitzers, six days' rations and .50 cal. machine guns mounted on its trucks. It was sent east at 8:00a.m. on November 16 with the British 78th Division. The battalion first went into action repelling an infantry-tank attack near Béja, Tunisia. Operating under the control of the 1st Parachute Battalion, 175FA was directed to reach Medjez el Bab by early morning, November 19, and there to assist French units in holding a bridge. French liaison officers guided the battalion to Medjez el Bab, where the battalion emplaced its batteries and was ready to fire before daylight.[13] Former Red Bull soldiers assigned to 1 and 6 Commandos also fought at the same time elsewhere on the Tunisian front. In an amphibious raid by 1 Commando on the coast west of Bizerte, British and American troops landed early on December 1, and cut the Bizerte–Mateur road for three days before retiring to Sedjenane on December 5, at a cost of 134 casualties, including 74 Americans.[14]

But other American units were not as well employed. On December 24, the 2nd Battalion, 168th Infantry, was attached to the 12th Air Force in Tébessa to guard airfields. On Saturday, January 2, 1943, AFHQ ordered the Anti-Tank (AT) Company of 168RCT to move to Biskra, Algeria, about 193 miles southeast of Algiers, to guard the airport. AFHQ directed that 3rd Battalion, 168RCT remain in Allied Force Reserve in Algiers to safeguard AFHQ. On Monday, January 4, 1943, 1st Battalion, 168RCT was placed under command of British First Army and ordered to guard the airfields near Youks Le Bain, Algeria, about 12 miles northwest of Tébessa. On January 11, 1943, 1/168 was ordered to Constantine, Algeria to guard lines of communication. The combat power of the 168RCT was scattered in widely separated packets along and behind the Allied front. Because of the dispersal of the units of the 168th Infantry Regiment, its new commanding officer, Colonel Thomas Drake, a tough and experienced soldier, had to travel 1,500 miles over ten days to inspect the elements of his command. On January 29, 1943, the 2nd and 3rd Battalions of the 168th Infantry Regiment were finally deployed to the Gafsa–Sbeïtla[ii] area for combat operations under command of the 1st Armored Division.[15]

The rest of 34th Infantry Division began moving to North Africa in December while the British First Army slogged into Tunisia and the 168th Infantry Regiment and the 3rd Battalion, 135th Infantry Regiment were garrisoning Algiers and doing guard duty in scattered posts. In Northern Ireland, the 2nd Battalion, 135th Infantry Regiment's Companies E, G, and H, and the bulk of 3rd Battalion's Company M, with attached communications and medical sections, were detached from 135IR to form part of the 34ID divisional advance party called Group II-A. On December 8, 1942, the 2nd Battalion elements left Camp Blessingbourne by truck to Fintons, where they entrained for Belfast, and there boarded ships to Liverpool, England. The next day, the 2nd Battalion less Company F, and with Company M (heavy weapons) and other 34ID troops in Group II-A, under command of Colonel Parkin, embarked at Liverpool en route to North Africa. On December 11, the remainder of

---

ii   Modern Subaytilah, Tunisia.

the 135th Infantry Regiment moved from stations in Northern Ireland to Liverpool in England and with other 34ID troops boarded ships on December 23 for their voyage to North Africa.

On December 21, 1942, Group II-A arrived at Oran and assembled in an area 18 miles from Oran. On December 30, the 34ID advance party and the 2nd Battalion, 135th Infantry Regiment moved by truck to Relizane, Algeria. They underwent training and performed operational duty guarding the lines of communication from Algiers to Tunisia until January 5, 1943.[16]

Central Tunisia: The Terrain

Terrain, the shape, dimensions, texture, and features of the land surface, is of paramount importance to the foot soldier. The battlefield experiences of the Red Bull soldiers in Tunisia can only be fully understood from a soldier's perspective on the ground. Every fold, valley, ridge, hill, mountain, and pass, every water course and depression, the condition of the soil in different seasons, and the vegetation or lack thereof, is of significance to the infantryman. He must know the roads and trails, the bridges and overpasses, the villages and towns, and the actual distances and the times required to get military forces and equipment from one place to another.

Central Tunisia lies between latitudes 36° north and 34° 30' north. Sousse on the east coast, about 90 miles south of Tunis, and Kairouan,[iii] about 36 miles inland from Sousse, are near its northeastern corner. A rough line from Mahares at the southeast to Gafsa at the southwest forms the border between central and southern Tunisia. Djebel Zarhouan (1,295m), at the yoke of the inverted Y from which the Eastern and Western (or Grand) Dorsal mountain ranges open out to the south and southwest, is within northern Tunisia, as is Le Kef near the Algerian border. The Eastern Dorsal and Western (or Grand) Dorsal mountain chains, the intermediate plateaus between them, and the lesser hills which divide these plateaus into a series of valleys, were to be the battle grounds for the 34th Infantry Division before the final and victorious offensive in northern Tunisia in late April 1943.[17]

On the coastal plain, the Muslim holy city of Kairouan, a road junction, and the port of Sfax, began serving the Axis powers as early as November 10, 1942, as bases for defense forces which operated toward the west. German and Italian detachments were installed at vantage points and around the Eastern Dorsal passes. In the interior plateaus to the west, there were roaming Axis patrols, and a few outposts that studded the sparsely settled, semiarid region. Because Kairouan was a destination for Islamic pilgrimages, it was the hub of many roads and tracks across the coastal plain. It was connected to the interior by two main roads, the more northerly of which was a

---

iii   Kairouan is now called al Qayrawan, Tunisia.

route over the saddle between Djebel Halfa (572m) and Djebel Ousselat (887m) to the valley and village of Ousseltia. The other road forked southwest of Kairouan, one branch climbing over Djebel ech Cherichera (462m) to Pichon,[iv] the other rising more gradually to penetrate the mountain chain through the Fondouk el Aouareb gap on the way to Hadjeb el Aïoun.[v]

Sfax was connected to the interior by a good road through Faïd pass, 75 miles inland. Faïd pass was a fateful two-way door through which mobile forces could easily pass, a fact fraught with peril for both sides. The road bifurcated after reaching the interior plain, one branch running northwesterly to connect with Sbeïtla and the other southwesterly through the village of Sidi Bou Zid, and then on through Bir el Hafey to Gafsa. Mahares, on the coast south of Sfax, was connected by both road and railroad with Maknassy and Gafsa. The towns in 1942 were very small: Sfax as the largest had a population of 45,000, with 22,000 in Kairouan and about 5,000 in Gafsa. All the other villages were even smaller.[18]

Five main roads of varying quality ran westerly or northwesterly through the Western Dorsal connecting the interior plateau areas with the mountainous area between the Western Dorsal and the Algerian border. (1) One route extended into northern Tunisia north of Djebel Bargou (1,266m) to the Rebaa Oulad Yahia valley and thence to Siliana and on to Le Kef. (2) A second went by way of Maktar, northwest of Pichon, across a high basin ringed by higher hills. (3) The third traversed through Sbiba and Ksour. (4) The fourth road followed the narrow, winding passage northwest of Kasserine into the Bahiret Foussana valley, and thence through the Monts de Tébessa to the village of Tébessa in eastern Algeria. An alternate road skirted the hills at the north through Thala and on to Ksour. (5) The fifth route ran through one of the gaps in Djebel Dernala (1,204m), northwest of Fériana, to Tébessa. Tébessa, near the center of a high plain at the eastern edge of Algeria, was linked with Souk Ahras, 75 miles north-northwest by road and railroad, which continued to the port of Bône on the coast, 65 miles farther.[19]

Central Tunisia's hills and mountains were more bare, with steeper contours, and displayed more variations in soil and rock colors, than those in northern Tunisia. The plateaus and valleys, like the high desert badlands of the American West, were greatly eroded and cut by water courses and dry arroyos or *wadis*. The land was sparsely covered with bunch grass, with cultivated cactus patches on which the Arabs fed their animals, and with scrub growth along some of the streams. From Roman times water draining from the higher slopes across the intermediate plateaus had been collected and drawn to the coastal towns by aqueducts. Farms were fewer in central Tunisia than farther north, for the rainfall through much of the year was light, except from December to March, when it was alarmingly plentiful. In the

---

iv   Pichon is now the modern Haffuz, Tunisia.
v   Now called Hajeb el Ayoun, Tunisia.

winter wet season, the powdery topsoil became deep sticky mud, and the many dry stream beds filled with water, justifying the bridges which might have seemed superfluous in the dry seasons. In this wide area of camel tracks, few hard surfaced roads, dry fords and steel bridges, scattered palm-fringed oases, and treeless plains, the first battles of the 34th Infantry Division's war in Tunisia were to be fought.[20]

CHAPTER 9

Allied Dispositions and Plans, January 1943

Operation *Satin*

AFHQ staff analyzed possible operations for January and February 1943 as the British First Army's winter drive down the Medjerda valley became a muddy stalemate. The recently activated German Fifth Panzer Army in northern Tunisia would be protected by the weather against a major Allied offensive for many weeks, but subsidiary attacks to pin down enemy forces and exploit local situations could be launched. If the British Eighth Army adhered to the schedule reported to Eisenhower by Alexander on December 27, 1942, Rommel's army might withdraw into southern Tunisia late in January. That consideration prioritized an Allied Force military operation to weaken or cut off and destroy the German-Italian Panzer Army as it retreated. Central Tunisia became the likely battlefield.[1]

Winter weather, steep hills, deep, sticky mud, and stubborn Germans had thwarted the Allied drive toward Tunis. Eisenhower expected First Army to remain stalled for at least two months. He thus shifted his attention farther south, considering an attack plan that would require the first big military operation launched in a Tunisian winter since the Punic Wars, 246–146 BCE. AFHQ weighed the hazards and risks of Central Tunisian operations. Should a mobile American armored force attempt to disrupt Rommel's line of supply? Success would yield a large reward but there were real dangers to be considered. Colonel General Hans-Jürgen von Arnim's Fifth Panzer Army's line in the north might be thinned, but not enough to enable British First Army to punch through to Tunis, or even to prevent an Axis armored attack southwestward through the French sector on the Americans' vulnerable northern flank. Whether the Fifth Panzer Army engaged the Americans or not, the German-Italian Panzer Army would without doubt move its powerful mobile armored forces quickly from Libya to protect its line of communications. What counterblows Rommel might make depended upon how much freedom of maneuver the British Eighth Army allowed. Allied planners understood that Rommel might concentrate a substantial mobile force, which could strike effectively either independently, or in conjunction with a force from General von Arnim's command. The Americans would then be opposed by experienced German armored units, whose military prestige at that stage of the war was enormous and well merited.

Allied concern about a joint attack by both Axis armies was to prove premonitory. AFHQ did not want the inexperienced Americans to find themselves engaged in a hard fight against battle-seasoned veterans instead of gradually supplementing their training by small and successful actions—a method the British believed to be better suited to increase American combat efficiency. Despite the risks, Operation *Satin*, an operation through Central Tunisia to disrupt the lines of communication between the Tunisian ports and Rommel's German-Italian Panzer Army, was favored by American staff officers both at AFHQ and II Corps. An outline for such an attack toward Sfax was approved at AFHQ on December 28, 1942.[2]

> Operation SATIN envisioned a quick thrust across southern Tunisia to the coastal town of Gabès, 260 miles south of Tunis. A rear guard laying minefields would then block any counterattack by Rommel's army driving from Libya into Tunisia, while the main force moved eighty miles up the coast to capture Sfax, a small port defended by 2,700 Axis troops with fifteen tanks. SATIN was to be an American production, undertaken by the U.S. II Corps.[3]

General Eisenhower believed that the British First Army had worked hard and "fought well," and he intended that it should eventually "deliver the decisive blow." Eighth Army was to continue pressing the German-Italian Panzer Army from the east in a renewed large-scale attack. In light of Eighth Army's timetable, Anderson curtailed First Army's local attacks for the next few weeks, enabling First Army to husband its resources rather than support the proposed American attack farther south. The question remained whether the eventual main effort would be aligned toward Sfax or toward Tunis. Some considered it prudent to abandon the American project altogether and to concentrate American armor in a mobile force-in-being on the southern flank of First Army, thus deterring possible German designs in that region.

Eisenhower astutely concluded that the immediate Allied objective was not the capture of Tunis and Bizerte, but the destruction of both German armies. He tentatively approved planning for Operation *Satin*, the risky thrust to the coast. Anderson then agreed to make subsidiary attacks intended to aid Operation *Satin* but proposed to retain the 18th Infantry Regiment of the U.S. 1st Infantry Division for First Army's operations until infantry of the British 46th Division (Major General H. A. Freeman-Attwood) arrived in the forward area to relieve the American regiment.[4]

On December 30, 1942, while the *Satin* plan was pending, Lieutenant General Clark and Major General Carl Spaatz (USAAF) surveyed the prospective battle area to formulate the steps necessary to achieve co-ordination between ground and air units. They decided, with General Marshall's approval, that the United States Army would not establish in Tunisia an American Army-level command controlling multiple corps. This was wise, given the scale of the forces involved in the North African contest and what was known about the combat power of the Axis foe, and the increasingly desperate state of the enemy's supply situation, which Allied naval and air forces were now interdicting with growing success. Lieutenant General Clark was ordered to Oujda, west of Oran, to activate the new American Fifth Army there for future purposes in Europe, while the American force in Tunisia was designated an army corps, the II Corps.[5]

> Eisenhower made several moves intended to exert tighter command over the newly configured front, none satisfactory and one ultimately disastrous. AFHQ needed a man to command II Corps. Eisenhower had just the man, and in him the makings of a debacle.[6]

General Marshall was prepared to promote either Major General Patton or Major General Fredendall to Lieutenant General for the command of the American ground forces in Tunisia. It was Fredendall, age 59, perceived to be "a Marshall man," who was chosen by the U.S. Army, that is, by Marshall and Eisenhower, to lead II Corps in combat against the Axis. In the pre-war Army he had earned a reputation as a capable trainer and skilled manager of troops. But a leader he was not.

Eisenhower approved Marshall's selection of Fredendall, but the appointment of Fredendall was a mistake by both leaders that each would rue bitterly.[7] Fredendall's elevation to command of a corps in combat was an unfortunate example of the "Peter Principle";[i] he had now reached his level of incompetence in the Army hierarchy during wartime. Curt, arrogant, and hot tempered, Fredendall had neither the tactical skills nor the personal confidence and fortitude to lead large formations in battle. His subordinate commanders would rapidly lose confidence in him as his poor command performance became more marked.[8]

The Allied right or southern flank in Tunisia from Tébessa southward to Gafsa was exposed to a sudden thrust by Axis forces. To counter that threat, Eisenhower at AFHQ directed the II Corps to move east from Oran to the Tébessa region of eastern Algeria near the Tunisian border. The 1st Armored Division, by this time largely brought back up to strength after its fight at Oran, *but with obsolete equipment types*,[9] was assigned to II Corps. Despite the difficult Axis logistical situation, Eisenhower was "convinced that the enemy would soon take advantage of our obvious weakness there... [and]... I nevertheless ordered the concentration of the corps of four divisions to begin and told the logistics people they would have to find a way to supply it."[10]

II Corps now had four United States Army divisions: (1) The 1st Infantry Division, ordered to move east to the II Corps sector as quickly as it could be assembled from its scattered positions in Algeria; (2) The 9th Infantry Division, less the 39th Regimental combat team which had participated in the Algiers assault and was detached to British First Army, gradually marching eastward over 1,000 miles from the Casablanca area to come under command of II Corps when that movement was completed; (3) The 34th Infantry Division, similarly ordered to begin moving

---

i   L. J. Peter and R. Hull, *The Peter Principle: Why Things Always Go Wrong*, William Morrow and Company, New York (1969).

from Oran and Algiers into the Central Tunisian area, its line of communications security duties to be taken over by the French; and (4) The 1st Armored Division, already in central Tunisia.[11]

On January 1, 1943, the Eastern Task Force was renamed First Army and came under Lieutenant General Anderson's command with Eisenhower assuming direct overall leadership of military operations on the entire front. Events quickly proved that the scope of that leadership was too broad even for Eisenhower. He attempted to exercise command and control through the advanced AFHQ command post Fairfield at Constantine, directed by Major General Lucian K. Truscott, Jr., deputy chief of staff, Allied Force. Between U.S. II Corps and British First Army, the detachment of the French Army was commanded from a forward post by General Juin. He controlled two zones, that of Major General Georges Barré's Tunisian Troop Command at the north and that of XIX Army Corps under Lieutenant General Louis-Marie Koeltz at the south.

AFHQ intended that at some point all units of the three nationalities then assigned to control by one of the other nationalities would be sorted out and integrated with their national contingents. But in January 1943 there were some Allied units attached to the major command of whatever zone they happened to be in. The XIX Army Corps detached to II Corps under Fredendall the Constantine Division (Brigadier General Marie-Joseph Edmond Welvert). The Tunisian Troop Command made five battalions of French infantry available to First Army and left one entire *groupement* (Colonel Paul-Jean Bergeron) in the British zone. French units under tactical command of an American or British commander remained in all other respects (supply, administration, discipline) under control of the headquarters of either Koeltz's XIX Corps or Barré's Tunisian Troop Command. All other French units positioned in the American or British zones remained entirely under the command of their French Generals Barré or Koeltz. AFHQ directed that in case of an attack by the enemy, the various French or Allied Force elements in any zone would obey the orders of the local headquarters regardless of nationality.[12]

Headquarters, U.S. II Corps, began moving to Constantine from Oran on January 4. One week later, its main section was operating there near Headquarters, First Army, while an advance corps command post under Brigadier General Porter opened in the town of Tébessa, near the eastern border of Algeria. Lieutenant General Fredendall placed II Corps's headquarters "[n]ine miles southeast of Tébessa, in a sunless gulch accessible only by a serpentine gravel road… Fredendall and sixty-eight staff officers… established residence in the ravine, officially called Speedy Valley…"[13] Eventually Fredendall's headquarters moved to the wooded hillside of that sunless gulch. Underground corridors were blasted out by II Corps engineers, while the advance command post under Brigadier General Porter went on to Gafsa. The construction of Fredendall's underground headquarters and the engineering unit time, manpower, and resources required for its construction were an unmitigated scandal in and of themselves. This was the first and not the least of Fredendall's shameful blunders.

> Fredendall had commanded the 19th Engineer Regiment to shelter his headquarters by boring a pair of immense, double-shafted tunnels in the ravine wall... Working from a blueprint labeled "II Corps Tunnel Job," engineers began excavating two complexes fifty yards apart, each with parallel shafts... Each complex was to be U-shaped, running 160 feet into the hillside with the parallel shafts joined at the rear by ample galleries designed for offices and a magazine [for the secure storage of ammunition]. Fredendall supervised the construction...[14]
>
> Some officers believed the tunnels a prudent precaution against enemy air attack. Others— noting that Speedy Valley was seventy miles from the front, well concealed, and protected by an anti-aircraft battalion—considered the project a ludicrous embarrassment. Some questioned Fredendall's personal courage...[15]

While plans for Operation *Satin* were evaluated and finalized, the troops to fall under Fredendall's command moved from northern Tunisia or came eastward from Morocco and Algeria.[16] Fredendall's II Corps Headquarters and elements of the several US divisions present in North Africa, including 1AD, 1ID, 9ID and 34ID, moved east toward central Tunisia. II Corps's general mission was to protect the right (or southern) flank of British First Army while First Army attacked toward Tunis.

On Sunday, January 3, 1943, the remainder of 135IR and some other 34th Infantry Division units debarked from transports at Mers-el-Kebir, the French naval base near Oran, Algeria. After a short stay in a muddy assembly area just south of the port, 135IR moved to Tlemcen, another ancient city 90 miles southwest of Oran. The 3rd Battalion, 135th Infantry, also moved from Algiers to rejoin 135IR at Tlemcen. 2nd Battalion, 133rd Infantry was assigned to Allied Force Headquarters in Algiers as guard troops and would remain attached to AFHQ until March 1944. That portion of the 34th Infantry Division in the Tlemcen area carried out what the regimental officers called "a rigorous training program." On January 4, 1943, C Company, 109th Medical Battalion and C Company, 109th Engineer Battalion were detached from 168IR and moved to Oran, Algiers to join the 34ID units then arriving in Algiers. The next day, Tuesday, January 5, 1943, 2/135 and the 34ID advance party concluded their brief training at Relizane, Algeria. 135IR assembled near Negier, Algeria on Monday, January 11, 1943, and began renewed training. It did not last long. The 34th Infantry Division, less the 168RCT and the 2nd Battalion of the 133RCT, received orders on January 30 to move to the Maktar, Tunisia area to relieve elements of the 1st Infantry Division and French units under command of the French XIX Corps.[17]

II Corps considered three alternative schemes for Operation *Satin*. Plan A boldly prescribed the seizure of the port of Sfax, with the subsequent possibility of a northward advance along the coast toward Sousse. Plan B called for an initial attack farther south, at Gabès, to be followed by a northward move against Sfax if conditions permitted. Plan C specified the capture of Kairouan, with a continuation to Sousse, doing enough damage to deny the port's usefulness to the Axis, and withdrawing when it became necessary. Eisenhower reserved to himself the choice of plan and the direction of the force to execute it. AFHQ set a tentative D Day of January 22.

Generals Eisenhower, Anderson, Juin, and Fredendall conferred on January 1 at Constantine. Without specifying which plan was to be implemented, the commander in chief defined the mission to be an attack against the enemy line of communications in the direction of Sfax, aggressively interrupting the port's use as much as possible. He assigned the undertaking to U.S. II Corps. The force was to include the 1st Armored Division, Major General Orlando Ward, commanding, to which were attached two battalions of 168RCT; the 26th Regimental Combat Team, detached from 1st Infantry Division, Colonel Alexander N. Stark, Jr., commanding; the British 1st Parachute Brigade, less one battalion, Brigadier J. W. C. Flavell commanding, for airborne missions; and the French Constantine Division, Major General Welvert, commanding. The British Middle East Command was to load ships which it would hold at Malta and send into Sfax when II Corps specified, supplementing the overburdened line of supply through Tébessa from Algiers.[18]

II Corps's detailed planning for the operation soon diverged wildly from AFHQ's outline of December 28. The required force rose from an estimated 20,000 men to 25,000 and then to more than 38,000. The axis of attack chosen by Fredendall would have lengthened the line of supply to such an extent and delayed the capture of Sfax for so long that a daily drawdown on reserves accumulated at Tébessa might be necessary. AFHQ did not supervise II Corps's planning closely and failed to discover Fredendall's changes. Predictable and severe logistical and tactical problems resulted and were discussed acrimoniously at a series of commanders' conferences in the second week of January, when the matter of overextended supply capacity was raised.[19]

> Eisenhower and his staff concocted SATIN, then paid it little attention as the impending Casablanca conference [between Roosevelt and Churchill and their senior advisors] and other diversions intruded. In the first two weeks of January, the proposed SATIN force grew... to 38,000; that meant pushing forward not 450 tons of provisions daily but 800 tons, a task beyond the frail Allied supply system. The plan had grown "logistically out of hand," a senior supply officer warned. Bickering persisted over the operation's ultimate objective, and whether swinging as far south as Gabès made sense. But Eisenhower was adamant that "it was fatal to do nothing." The attack was scheduled for the fourth week of January.[20]

On January 15, 1943, Eisenhower flew to Casablanca to report to the Allied Combined Chiefs of Staff at the second conference of Anglo-American military and political leaders, code named Symbol. The chief purpose of the Casablanca Conference was to determine the Allied strategic objectives for 1943 in all theaters, to establish priorities among them, and to reach decisions on the preparation and allocation of means to attain them. From January 13 to 23, 1943, the Combined Chiefs of Staff met formally at 15 meetings. President Roosevelt arrived on January 14, after a five-day voyage by train to Miami, and then by airplanes from the United

States to Africa, a first for any American president in wartime. On three occasions during the conference, the military chiefs met with the president and the prime minister to consider the agenda, to discuss the matters at issue, and to arrive at a final report of decisions taken. The sunny comfort and buoyant confidence surrounding the president and the prime minister contrasted sharply with the conditions endured by Allied troops in wet, muddy, and miserably cold Tunisia.[21] Aside from AFHQ's selection and preparation of the site in its gorgeous setting, including General Patton's security measures and housekeeping arrangements for the important personages, and briefings on operations in Northwest Africa, little of substance connected the discussions of Churchill and Roosevelt to the reality of the military situation.

The Symbol agenda of the Combined Chiefs of Staff did include operations in North Africa. To a meeting of the Combined Chiefs of Staff, and then at the first plenary session, Eisenhower briefed current and prospective operations in Tunisia.[22]

> At 2:30p.m. on January 15, a dozen of the most senior generals and admirals in the Anglo-American alliance strolled back from lunch to a high-ceilinged, semi-circular banquet room… of the Anfa Hotel [in Anfa, a suburb of Casablanca]… [T]he room was dominated by a large rectangular table. Sentries guarded the door, where a… placard read 'Business: Chiefs of Staff Conference.' This would be the third session of the combined chiefs in Casablanca, and… they were to hear from General Eisenhower… on the Tunisian campaign and his plan for Operation SATIN…. [Eisenhower] spoke without notes… The SATIN offensive, scheduled to begin in a week, looked promising. "At first, operations on the right flank were looked upon primarily as diversion," Eisenhower said. "But it now seems probable that it will be possible to advance on Sfax and hold it with infantry, while withdrawing the 1st Armored Division as a mobile reserve further to the rear." If successful, SATIN would cut the Axis forces in half.[23]

The reaction of the British generals to Operation *Satin* was unsparingly harsh. Field Marshal Alan F. Brooke, chief of the Imperial General Staff, scathingly questioned the justification for the risks of Operation *Satin* as proposed by Eisenhower:

> Brooke was disinclined to underestimate German ferocity, and he flatly disagreed with what he privately described as Eisenhower's "ridiculous plan" for SATIN… How, he asked, would the II Corps drive to the sea be coordinated with Anderson's First Army in the north and Montgomery's Eighth Army in Libya? If Anderson were bogged down for two more months, would not Arnim's forces "thin out in the north and defeat the Sfax forces in detail?" Montgomery was still a week from Tripoli… Rommel no doubt "would react like lightning" to any attack on Sfax that threatened his logistics lifeline. [Rommel]… had an estimated 80,000 German and Italian troops, Arnim 65,000. Would not II Corps risk being trapped between Arnim and Rommel, with little prospect of help from Anderson or Montgomery? In fact, an Ultra decrypt… had disclosed that Rommel's 21st Panzer Division had already begun moving north into Tunisia.[24]

Lieutenant General Alexander, just arrived from Cairo, reported that the British Eighth Army would reach Tripoli before the end of January, perhaps just as the scheduled attack on Sfax was starting. Alexander could give no assurance that Rommel's forces would be pinned down by the Eighth Army. The German-Italian Panzer Army's mobile forces might yet be able to intervene at Sfax or further inland.

General Montgomery's command might be temporarily immobilized. The Eighth Army's fuel and supplies would certainly be low while the port of Tripoli was being cleared and restored to service.[25]

Brooke went on forcefully to point out that if the attack on Sfax was begun by January 22, it might well provoke an Axis counterthrust which II Corps would have to withstand unassisted. That prognostication unfortunately turned out to be correct.[26] After a further conversation with Alexander, and considerably embarrassed at having AFHQ's plans for southern Tunisia so thoroughly and openly criticized by the chief of the Imperial General Staff in front of his American superiors, General Eisenhower agreed that *Satin* should be canceled for the time being. If the attack were to be undertaken later it would be coordinated with the operations of the British Eighth Army. "Eisenhower tried to regroup in the face of this onslaught, but he got no help from the American chiefs… [H]e looked forward to discussing the issue further and 'to make any necessary adjustments in the plan.' Eisenhower saluted and left the room with the grim look of a man in full retreat."[27] He returned to Algiers on January 16 with the intention of holding the American portion of his command on a short leash. On January 18 at a commanders' conference in Constantine, he directed that operations on the southern flank must be defensive and that as much as possible of II Corps, *particularly and emphatically the 1st Armored Division, was to be held in mobile reserve.* He issued a directive to this effect at noon, January 20.[28]

Headquarters, II Corps, had become operational in Constantine during the first week of January, then moved to the underground facility at Speedy Valley near Tébessa. Fredendall and the II Corps staff had then worked up plans for the seizure of Sfax pursuant to Operation *Satin*.

Brigadier General Paul M. Robinett was the commanding officer of Combat Command B (CCB), U.S. 1st Armored Division. CCB, first placed under British V Corps, reverted to control of 1st Armored Division on January 7. Beginning the next day CCB moved to Sbeïtla for participation in an impending Franco-American attack to regain Fondouk el Aouareb Gap and then to provide protection during Operation *Satin*. The remainder of 1st Armored Division came eastward from Oran to central Tunisia in early January, as did the 1st Infantry Division's 26th Regimental Combat Team (less its 3rd Battalion, which had already arrived in late November). Mobile anti-aircraft protection for the armored division was brought to Tunisia from Morocco.[29] Ten days' supplies of all types were accumulated at a new II Corps depot in Tébessa and at supply points extending eastward as far as Kasserine. A provisional ordnance group, assembled from northern Tunisia and Algeria, established its principal shops in Tébessa. An evacuation hospital and medical supply depot also opened in the town. The plans for the attack on Sfax via Gabès were well advanced when Eisenhower cancelled the undertaking on January 18 and directed II Corps to "act defensively."[30]

The abrupt scuttling of SATIN sent Allied planners back to the drawing board. There would be no drive to the sea, at least not until Eighth Army was in Tunisia to lend support. Instead, Fredendall's II Corps was to conduct raids and keep the enemy off balance until better weather allowed a coordinated offensive... At the commanders' meeting in the Constantine orphanage on January 18, Eisenhower laid out this strategy, calling it "offensively defensive." *[The French General] Juin listened closely, then warned "The Germans will not remain inactive."* Eisenhower replied with exasperation: "I don't want anything quiescent on this goddam front during the next two months."[31]

CHAPTER 10

The Enemy's Attack on the Eastern Dorsal Passes, January 18–28, 1943

Beginning that very day, January 18, German actions vindicated Juin, accommodated Eisenhower, and confirmed the wisdom of the Allies in abandoning the attack against Sfax. Axis troops already occupied the Eastern Dorsal mountain passes in the north, including the portals at Jeffna and Longstop Hill that opened on the east to Bizerte and Tunis. The British had been blocked at those places in bitter winter fighting. Now the Axis set out to capture the four main gaps through the Eastern Dorsal in central and southern Tunisia. Control of the passes would enlarge the Axis bridgehead and safeguard the coastal corridor linking Arnim's Fifth Panzer Army to Rommel's German-Italian Panzer Army, which was slowly closing into Tunisia from Libya.[1]

The immediate objective of the enemy was to gain control over Djebel Mansour (678m) and the main source of the water supply for Tunis, the great reservoir and dam on the Kebir river (Barrage de l'Oued Kebir) about 12 miles southwest of Pont-du-Fahs. The enemy also planned to drive the French from the Eastern Dorsal near Kairouan between the reservoir and Kairouan Pass.[2] For the attack against the French, Arnim put *Oberstleutnant* Friedrich Weber in command of a force temporarily organized for the attack designated *Kampfgruppe* [battle group] *Weber*. Colonel Weber organized his attacking force in three sections. The first consisted of the newly arrived 756th Mountain Regiment. This was reinforced by two armored sections, consisting of four Mark VI (Tiger) and four Mark III tanks, and engineer, artillery, and anti-aircraft elements. That force was ordered to open Kairouan Pass southeast of Pont-du-Fahs and to take Djebel Mansour. They were to support the movement of *Kampfgruppe Lueder* into the Ousseltia valley. *Kampfgruppe Lueder* comprised one company of tanks, partly Mark VI Tigers and partly Mark IVs, and a battalion of armored infantry, with a platoon of engineers and some anti-aircraft units. It was to push up the Kebir valley to the road fork at the southwest end of the reservoir, then swing south for about 12 miles to the Hir Moussa crossroads. After 756th Mountain Regiment had closed to the same area, *Kampfgruppe Lueder* was to turn east toward Karachoum Gap. The third part of *Kampfgruppe Weber*, Lieutenant Colonel Edwin Stolz, commanding, was designated

Kampfgruppe Stolz and comprised a composite German-Italian infantry regiment of the 1st (Superga) Infantry Division, consisting of four battalions, and was reinforced by a company of 190th Panzer Battalion. It was to exploit its success by advancing to the west perpendicular to Weber's main effort to complete the destruction of the French units on the Eastern Dorsal. Stolz would then build up a new line seven to nine miles farther west, extending from Djebel Mansour in the north to the heights just west of Hir Moussa.

Kesselring was keen to drive the Anglo-Americans back through Constantine and Bône, but first he needed firm possession of the Eastern Dorsal. To that end, the Axis attacks opened early in the morning of January 18 with diversionary thrusts by parachute infantry and by 50 *panzers* against the extreme south wing of British V Corps near the Bou Arada crossroads. Although the British parried these attacks successfully, fighting continued intermittently for a week without much change in position but with considerable losses on both sides. In the afternoon of January 18, German units charged toward British lines in the north in a feint to fix First Army in position and to screen the main Axis thrust, an assault by a heavy *panzer* battalion of new Mark VI *panzers* and 5,000 Axis infantrymen against the French positions around the reservoir 40 miles southeast of Medjez el Bab.[3] Strong enemy formations moved into the Ousseltia Valley, which controlled the critical pass to Kairouan. Within a day the equivalent of seven French infantry battalions had been cut off on the ridgelines. Juin reported to AFHQ that he was "not hopeful."[4] German troops broke through the French and opened the way into the Kebir valley for the Axis armored forces. After supporting the operation, *Kampfgruppe Lueder* regrouped, then pushed ahead to its objective, the road fork southwest of the reservoir. They reached it by midnight. *Kampfgruppe Stolz*, meanwhile, achieved what the Axis considered satisfactory progress in a subsidiary drive across the heights between the reservoir and Djebel Chirich (717m).[5]

On January 19, the Allies did not fully grasp the enemy's intentions. Some of the German armored forces passed the northern edge of Djebel Bargou (1,216m) into the Ousseltia valley but then Allied air reconnaissance reported movement from the reservoir area of an estimated 4,000 to 5,000 truckborne troops. This suggested a double thrust by Fifth Panzer Army to close the northern end of the Eastern Dorsal. By the end of the day the Axis forces had almost completed the first phase of their operation as planned. The small but powerful *Kampfgruppe Lueder* blocked the road to Rebaa Oulad Yahia near Sidi Said. The main force had advanced to the Hir Moussa crossroads. Stolz's battalions had continued to move west and relieved the 756th Mountain Regiment on Djebel Mansour which freed that unit to follow and reinforce Lueder.[6]

The French defenders were driven out all along the front. Once the enemy's hand had been more clearly shown, General Juin appealed for Allied reinforcements. British First Army requested II Corps to divert a suitable force northward to assist the

French.[7] Anderson immediately ordered a British infantry brigade to counterattack from the north, then asked Fredendall to dispatch Combat Command B from the 1st Armored Division to block further Axis advance in the south.[8] About 5:15p.m., January 19, Fredendall used a field telephone personally to call Major General Robinett, commanding Combat Command B, then in bivouac near Sbeïtla. He gave the following orders.

> Move your command, i.e., the walking boys, pop guns, Baker's outfit and the outfit which is the reverse of Baker's outfit and the big fellows to M, which is due north of where you are now, as soon as possible. Have your boss report to the French gentleman whose name begins with J at a place which begins with D which is five grid squares to the left of M. Further, CC/B will enter Corps Command net not later than 0900 hours, 20 January. CC/B will remain in contact with SATIN Force at Tebessa.[9]

The official historian recites Fredendall's message in full, but graciously refrains from further comment. Such informal communications practice, even to convey orders in rough code, was ludicrous. Fredendall had been a graduate of MIT and a distinguished graduate of the Command and General Staff School. He had been taught always to use standardized procedure and syntax to ensure clarity when transmitting orders to subordinate commanders, especially under the strain of combat. Fredendall's jargon, or efforts to conceal his orders from the enemy, on this and other occasions only confused his subordinates who lost precious time trying to discern his meaning.[10] The fatuous, almost indecipherable slang exhibits not only personal arrogance but also Fredendall's complete misunderstanding of and incompetence for combat leadership. Equally egregious, his message also demonstrates his habit of ignoring intermediate commands and commanders (in this case, Major General Ward, the commander of 1st Armored Division, Robinett's immediate superior officer) and of engaging in what today would be called flagrant micromanagement.

CCB's tanks (mostly M3 Grants), tank destroyers (M3 GMCs, half-tracks mounted with First World War 75mm guns), infantry and artillery, with engineer, medical, service, and maintenance companies, were on the road after dark on January 19. With over 3,400 troops, CCB reached a point near Kesra before morning the next day.

At AFHQ's advanced command post on January 20, Major General Truscott assessed the situation and coordinated resistance to the Axis attack by French, American, and British ground units, and by Allied air forces. Truscott's orders directed British First Army elements to move southeast and south toward the Rebaa Oulad Yahia valley to cut off and block the enemy's advance there, while Combat Command B, U.S. 1st Armored Division, was placed at Juin's disposition for operations as a unit in either the Rebaa Oulad Yahia or Ousseltia valleys as the situation demanded. Truscott also directed Fredendall to assemble in the Sbeïtla area another armored mobile force comparable to Combat Command B, to be used under II Corps command. That new force would join the French in an attack against Fondouk el Aouareb starting on January 23. Juin assigned CCB to Koeltz's XIX Corps to conduct combat operations in the Ousseltia valley. XIX Corps in turn ordered CCB to move into the valley during the night of January 20–21.[11] By 9:33a.m. on January 21, CCB had assembled its main body about five miles southwest of Ousseltia and was conducting active reconnaissance, with the 601st Tank Destroyer Battalion (less Company A) out ahead.[12]

The German and Italian forces met in the northern part of the Ousseltia valley on January 20 after converging from the northwest and northeast. They had accomplished most of their mission before CCB arrived. The Germans took the opportunity to try to clear the Eastern Dorsal completely as far as Djebel Ousselat, southeast of Ousseltia village, and to envelop French troops caught on the hills by pushing along the ridge and by attacking northwestward from the coastal plain. Only a shortage of infantry prevented the enemy from completely capturing the passes. By midnight, January 20–21, *Kampfgruppe Lueder* overran Allied roadblocks on the roads leading into Ousseltia village and reached the Ousseltia–Kairouan road about four miles northwest of Kairouan Pass. During the night only one battalion of the German 756th Mountain Regiment, using trucks borrowed from other units, was able to reinforce Lueder, but the enemy now blocked access to Kairouan from the west. The German force, assisted by Italian elements attacking from east of the pass, proceeded to destroy the French units, cut off on the ridge to the north of Djebel Bou Dabouss.[13]

At 12:45p.m., January 21, Koeltz ordered Robinett to counterattack eastward along the Ousseltia–Kairouan road. Robinett was determined to employ his entire force in a concentrated attack from Ousseltia toward the western entrance of Kairouan Pass. CCB's assault began about 3:00p.m., after an Allied air bombing and with strong artillery support in position. The onslaught progressed steadily against stiff resistance until nightfall but did not dislodge *Kampfgruppe Lueder* from its blocking position. At darkness, the enemy pulled back into a defensive laager, opening enough space to allow some trapped French troops on the heights near the pass to slip southward and escape.[14] At 6:30p.m., January 21, French XIX Corps put CCB under the control of Major General Agathon-Jules-Joseph Deligne of the Algiers Division, units of which had been holding the pass. In conformity with the Allied Force Headquarters directives of January 20, Deligne ordered Robinett at 4:35a.m., January 22, to abandon the counterattack, to adopt defensive measures toward the east, and to drive northward to meet the British forces at the northeastern end of Djebel Bargou.

Friction in war, the mundane but stubbornly recurring pitfalls of combat operations, affects both sides.[15] CCB was not ready to attack at dawn on January 22 because its ammunition and supply train failed to get through during the night. The enemy force, at the same time, had been weakened by a breakdown of radio communications and by interdicting fire from the 6th Battalion, Royal West Kents, on the direct road between *Kampfgruppe Lueder* and the 756th Mountain Regiment at Hir Moussa. The reinforced 2nd Battalion, 13th Armored Regiment, began a thrust northeastward up the Ousseltia valley at 2:30p.m., January 22, only to be stopped quickly by stiff Axis resistance.[16]

Late on January 22, II Corps asked Robinett what reinforcements, if any, he would need to carry out Major General Deligne's orders. In reply he included his estimate of the forces opposing his command: one battalion of infantry, two companies of tanks, four 88mm guns, and three or four batteries of howitzers of at least 105mm, against which he had one battalion of armored infantry, one battalion of 30 operational medium tanks [M3], nine self-propelled and six towed 105mm howitzers, 12 GMC M3 tank destroyers, and a battery of 40mm anti-aircraft weapons. Robinett reported that the enemy had placed artillery on high ground along the eastern edge of the valley and that an attack northward over the floor of the valley would be excessively risky until infantry could engage the enemy in the eastern hills and prevent the flanking fire which otherwise would ravage his force. To clear the valley, he estimated additional necessary reinforcements as two battalions of infantry, one battalion of field artillery, and one company of tank destroyers, as well as indirect assistance from the British units pushing strongly from the west into the valley.[17] The military dilemma posed by an entrenched enemy on high ground with hidden artillery covering the lower ground would continually challenge the Allies and 34th Infantry Division in Tunisia.

Units of the 1st Infantry Division were marching from Guelma in Algeria via Maktar to relieve French units in the Ousseltia valley. But Fredendall expected CCB to "restore" the situation. Based on his interpretation of decisions made at a command conference with Truscott at AFHQ Advance Command Post on January 21, Fredendall thought that the II Corps zone would be extended northward and that 1ID would be controlled by II Corps. He intended to command 1ID's subordinate units directly, rather than through 1ID or the French, and to have them operate under Colonel D'Alary Fechet, regimental commander of the 16th Infantry Regiment, 1ID. The infantry would coordinate with Robinett's forces rather than be directly under Robinett's command, while CCB withdrew. As a micromanager entirely focused on the movements of individual units, it is possible that Fredendall had missed and was unaware of AFHQ's attachment of CCB to XIX Corps. Alternatively, he may simply have ignored those orders. In any event, he now personally commanded Robinett to discontinue the CCB attack northward which Major General Deligne had ordered, and instead to hold CCB near Ousseltia village on the defensive. "Robinett's command was still attached to French XIX Corps and under orders by General Deligne to carry out the offensive, orders he was unable to execute without the reinforcements which, upon arrival would be operating… only in co-ordination with Combat Command B, rather than under attachment to it."[18]

Fredendall's orders to CCB contradicted AFHQ's assignment of CCB to French XIX Corps and directly countermanded Deligne's orders. Needless confusion and delay resulted, at great tactical and human cost to the Allies. It fell to Lieutenant Colonel Russell F. Akers, Jr., an Assistant G-3 of II Corps, to try to clean up the mess, while Robinett's force remained stationary. With its mission and command structure so uncertain, *CCB lost the opportunity to attack to the north in sufficient strength to force the enemy back and to rescue the French.*[19]

II Corps assigned elements of the 1st Infantry Division to reinforce CCB, and they began arriving before the end of the day on January 24. But they also were too late to save the French. The 26th Regimental Combat Team (less 3rd Battalion), 1ID, with the attached 7th and 33rd Field Artillery Battalions, was tasked by II Corps to attack toward Kairouan Pass but could not organize an attack before darkness fell. 26RCT, under command of Colonel Stark, instead began its strike at 9:00a.m. on January 25, supported by the artillery, but by that time the Axis forces had achieved their objectives and *Kampfgruppe Weber* was already withdrawing. The new Axis main line of resistance lay across the northern end of the Ousseltia valley and along the eastern edge to Djebel Ousselat and was now defended by an Italian force consisting of elements of the 1st (Superga) Infantry Division and Group Benigni. About noon, 26RCT engaged a battalion of Italian infantry, drove it back, and continued its charge through the night. By the next morning, January 26, 26RCT had gained the western end of the Ousseltia-Kairouan Pass but there came up against a German unit. Bloody but indecisive fighting followed during the next two days.[20]

Upon completing its mission to support the infantry operations that stopped the enemy at Ousseltia-Kairouan Pass, Combat Command B paused in place. Robinett was still uncertain about his mission until Lieutenant General Koeltz intervened in person and directly ordered CCB to move north on January 27 to clear the enemy from the Ousseltia valley. Robinett complied at once. At 3:30p.m. the attack began and advanced along the western edge of the valley at the base of Djebel Serdj (1,357m). During the night of January 27–28, the 1st Battalion, 26IR, 1ID, and 7th Field Artillery Battalion moved with armored escort to the northern end of Djebel Serdj. Enemy air attacks in the Ousseltia valley had increased beginning on January 25, but the Allies maintained their hold on the southern and western portions of the valley. At that point 26RCT's progress at Kairouan Pass, had it been supported by a unified and mutually supporting Allied attack, might have resulted in Allied control not only over its western exit but along its entire length.[21]

Combat Command B and 1st Battalion, 26th RCT were ordered to withdraw from the valley during the night of January 28–29 and returned to II Corps control. Their battle in the Ousseltia valley was ended. CCB made a long road march to Bou Chebka. 1/26 moved to the vicinity of Sbeïtla, where it was attached to Combat Command A, 1st Armored Division. With that disengagement, the official history admits that the Allies had missed the chance to regain the passes through the Eastern Dorsal before the enemy could become solidly established there. That lost opportunity was to have harsh consequences for the Americans, and for the 26th and 168th Infantry Regiments in particular, beginning in mid-February.[22]

The French had fought valiantly, but they had been left stranded on the hills by conflicting Allied commands and countermands. The French were also handicapped by inadequate supplies, and by the lack of modern weapons and means of communication. Eisenhower was chagrined by his overestimation of French capabilities and resolved to reinforce their sector with U.S. and British units until French weapons and equipment could be brought up to modern standards. Before CCB and 26IR withdrew from the Ousseltia valley, the U.S. 1st Infantry Division, with Major General Terry de la Mesa Allen commanding from its headquarters in Maktar, temporarily assumed defense of the Allied line running along the Ousseltia valley and southeast toward Pichon. Colonel Fechet's 16RCT was to be on the north and Brigadier General Theodore Roosevelt, Jr.'s mixed command of American and French units, on the south. The French units were to be relieved as rapidly as possible by the 18th Infantry Regiment, Colonel Frank U. Greer, commanding, and by Colonel Drake's 168th Infantry Regiment from the 34th Infantry Division, now attached to the 1st Infantry Division. 34th Infantry Division was later to relieve all 1st Infantry Division units and 1ID would join British First Army's reserve.[23]

CHAPTER II

Allied Expectations and Axis Intentions

With the Axis holding most of the passes through the Eastern Dorsal, Allied commanders were certain that the enemy would attack again in central Tunisia. The question was *where*. Intelligence was imperfect; even the super-secret ULTRA decrypts yielded only inconclusive evidence of the enemy's movements and intentions. The maneuvering of Axis armored formations was watched, like tea leaves, for indications of their intended points of attack. The 21st Panzer Division was known to be in the Faïd-Maknassy area. The battle-hardened 10th Panzer Division, then commanded by the highly competent General Wolfgang Fischer,[i] had shifted southeastward from the Medjerda valley so that most of it was near Kairouan, opposite the French XIX Corps. The Italian 131st (Centauro) Armored Division was northwest of Gabès in positions extending up toward El Guettar and Gafsa. The 15th Panzer Division was near the Mareth Position in southern Tunisia.

The enormous range and flexibility of mobile mechanized forces made forecasting difficult. Some of the signs could be interpreted to indicate an attack toward Pichon, either by way of the Fondouk el Aouareb Gap or by one of the routes north of it. Other indications pointed to enemy attacks along more than one axis. Astute analysis of the situation led Colonel Dickson, II Corps's Intelligence Officer (G-2), the same who had so boldly arrested Darlan in Algiers, to warn of a forthcoming primary strike on Gafsa from Gabès plus a major diversionary effort in the Pichon or Pont-du-Fahs areas. To the War Department's Military Intelligence Division (MID), the enemy's posture indicated a strong attack on the Sfax-Tébessa axis and an auxiliary assault from Kairouan moving west and northwest. Events would prove both "Monk" Dickson and MID to have been largely correct.[1]

Eisenhower had hoped that the Allies could stabilize the front, at the same time freeing a force large enough to retake Faïd Pass. But that simply could not be done with the Allied forces then in Tunisia considering the robust capabilities of the enemy. Nevertheless, the commander-in-chief's idea to have an armored fist in hand was sound. Lieutenant General Anderson abandoned a planned counteroffensive from Le Kef to Faïd to concentrate mobile armored forces at Fériana and Sbeïtla, with

---

i   Fischer was killed on February 1st by an unmarked Italian mine near Mareth. He was succeeded in command of *10th Pz. Division* by General Friedrich Freiherr von Broich.

forward elements near Gafsa and Faïd. Existing Allied positions from Medjez el Bab to Pichon would be held against all but the strongest enemy pressures. AFHQ alerted the Allied air forces to the possibility of a temporary switch of the bulk of available Allied tactical air support from the northern sectors to central Tunisia when necessary.[2]

The Axis Revises its Plans

The Axis powers also modified the operational objectives of their forces in Northwest Africa in January 1943. The high commands had earlier resolved to maintain two armies in the region by reinforcing Rommel's command while establishing in Tunisia the Fifth Panzer Army of four or more divisions. General von Arnim had assumed command of the new army on December 9, 1942, with a charge to launch an aggressive campaign. Now *Comando Supremo* authorized Rommel's German-Italian Panzer Army to retire from Marsa el Brega to Buerat el Hsun if it became necessary to avoid being cut off. *Comando Supremo* expected the German-Italian Panzer Army to hold at Buerat el Hsun indefinitely while its losses were made good, and the combat power of Rommel's army was restored.

The Axis commanders in the field understood the reality that Allied combat strength and resources were growing rapidly. Von Arnim and Rommel knew that the high command's plans could not be carried out without strong reinforcements, a radical improvement in transportation, and the provision of more equipment and supplies. Within a week of assuming command of Fifth Panzer Army, Arnim reported to *OB Süd* [Kesselring] that the current rate of supply was far below the basic requirements of Axis forces in Libya and Tunisia. He estimated the volume at 12,000 tons per month for his army and an equal amount for the German-Italian Panzer Army. Only half his army was then in Tunisia; the high command had to find a way to transport the remainder. The remaining six-to-eight-week window of opportunity for the buildup of the Fifth Panzer Army and to reach the 24,000-ton-per-month level of resupply for the two armies was closing. After that, the winter rains preventing the Allies from renewing their ground attack would end and the Axis armies would not be ready. At the existing rate of supply and manpower growth, the concentration of Axis forces scheduled to come under Arnim's command would take several months. In the meantime, Arnim knew that the Allies were already bringing enormous amounts of matériel and large numbers of fresh troops into Casablanca, Oran, and Algiers, and also building the means to get that power into Tunisia.

Rommel also faced a critical shortage of supply. On December 17, the day on which the German-Italian Panzer Army went into position at Buerat el Hsun, Rommel urgently reiterated his November 30, 1942, recommendation that he be authorized to pull back into Tunisia. His proposal was again rejected.[3]

Hitler had called a conference with Italian representatives at his Rastenburg[ii] headquarters on December18–22, 1942 to determine the scope and means of further operations in North Africa. Kesselring's headquarters presented a survey of Allied capabilities and a plan for providing the North African bridgehead with supplies and equipment. Hitler then reaffirmed his position that North Africa must be held at all costs to keep the inexorably growing power of the Allies as far as possible for as long as possible from the heartland of the Nazi Reich. Hitler also said, no doubt insincerely, that North Africa was an Italian theater which would remain under Italian command. He would send reinforcements into Tunisia, including some of his best troops, bringing the German strength there up to 130,000–140,000 men, and take measures that would ensure air superiority over the line of communications from Italy. He painted an optimistic picture of the logistical contest in North Africa.[4]

But by the end of 1942 Hitler could not follow through on his promises to his generals. He was forced to reduce supplies to North Africa to meet another, more pressing and more dangerous threat. The battle for Stalingrad had begun. It absorbed both Hitler's attention and the reserves at the disposal of the High Command of the Wehrmacht. That frozen slaughterhouse drained away the German and satellite divisions and supplies with which Hitler might have kept his earlier promises to Mussolini. The battle also, as the Russians intended, drew Hitler's focus away from the large new Russian forces assembling in great secrecy on the eastern bank of the Volga, north and south of the besieged city.

The only opportunity to gain the force necessary for aggressive Axis action in Tunisia was during the few weeks between the arrival of Rommel's army in Tunisia from Libya and that of the pursuing British Eighth Army. Mussolini therefore issued a directive, which the Italian Marshal Ettore Bastico delivered to Rommel on December 31, 1942, at Misurata, authorizing a conditional withdrawal into Tunisia. The German-Italian Panzer Army was to move to the Mareth Position south of Gabès in several stages and at a rate which would consume at least two months, the time required to repair and strengthen the old French fortifications at the Mareth Position. *Comando Supremo* stipulated that Rommel must have the approval of Marshal Bastico for the timing of each step in the withdrawal. This restraint was a precaution against the loss of immobile Italian foot soldiers to Allied motorized enveloping attacks. When Rommel protested that the duration and staging of his withdrawal would have to account for Allied maneuvering, *Comando Supremo*, with Hitler's concurrence, gave him freedom of action for six weeks, the time necessary for the German-Italian Panzer Army to reach a position just east of Tripoli.

---

ii　One of several *Führerhauptquartieren* (Führer Headquarters) built for Hitler, the Rastenburg complex was in the former East Prussia, now Ketrzyn, Poland. That was the site of the famous attempt by Colonel Claus Graf von Stauffenberg in July 1944, to assassinate Hitler by bomb. Stauffenberg was one of several officers who had served in 10th Panzer Division in North Africa who also participated in the July Plot.

The facts on the ground continued to put unexpected pressure on the Axis forces. On January 2, 1943, Rommel began sending back part of his nonmotorized force from Buerat el Hsun. By mid-January, the rest of Rommel's forces, less the 21st Panzer Division, had been forced back to the Tarhuna-Homs position. The rate of the German-Italian Panzer Army's retreat was suddenly accelerated by British Eighth Army movements which threatened Rommel with Allied envelopment at Tarhuna-Homs. On the night of January 19–20, he ordered his troops to start moving still farther west, beginning the last stage of withdrawal to the next defensible position, in southern Tunisia. Rommel sent his rear area commander to Sfax on January 19, 1943, to open a headquarters from which to regulate supply traffic southward through Gabès to the retreating army. The stage was set in Tunisia for the union and joint operations of all the Axis forces there.[5]

Comando Supremo rightly feared a vigorous Allied offensive from the Tébessa-Gafsa area intended to prevent the joining of the two Axis armies. Therefore, holding the entire Tunisian bridgehead and keeping open the connection to Rommel's army became the prime objectives of the Axis leaders. The German *OKW* concurred in a proposal by *Comando Supremo* to seize Gafsa to counter the Allied threat. To carry out this plan the depleted 21st Panzer Division was ordered to the Sfax area to be re-equipped and then to attack Gafsa. Kesselring, increasingly disturbed about the adequacy of the Axis forces in the African theater, pointed out the obvious: the mere shifting of units from one of the armies to the other could not be regarded as reinforcement. He requested two motorized divisions in addition to the units that had been promised him. Though he himself presented his rationale to Hitler on January 12, 1943, Hitler would only permit the Hermann Göring Division to move to Tunisia immediately. Kesselring also discussed the supply situation with Hitler and his staff. The combined armies in Tunisia would need 60,000 tons of supplies a month. *OB Süd* optimistically assured Hitler that with additional shipping, which was becoming available from ports in Southern France, those increased demands could be met, but he had well-founded misgivings about protecting the convoys from Allied predation.[6]

While Axis forces planned the seizure of Gafsa, the high command also considered more far-reaching operations. *OKW* ordered preparations for a bold attack north and northwest into Algeria to wrest control of the Tébessa area from the Allied force by an attack through Gafsa and Sbeïtla. The possibility of striking all the way to Bône and Constantine was considered, provided that enough forces would be available, concentrated, and adequately supplied. *OKW* recognized that such ambitious operations would require at least three mobile divisions, one of which would have to come from Rommel's army, and even so, only when the Fifth Panzer and German-Italian Panzer Armies had been combined and only if the improved Mareth Position was ready and able to protect the southern flank. The immediate decision, made in early February, was to break up the Allied concentrations at Sidi Bou Zid and Gafsa.[7]

Meanwhile a vicious large-scale struggle was being fought almost continuously in the skies and on the seas over and around Tunisia and across the Mediterranean to Italy. Allied preponderance in sea and air power in Northwest Africa was growing at an exponential rate, strangling the Axis armies and tactical air force of food, fuel, and ammunition supplies. By April 1943, almost half of all Axis shipments to Tunisia by sea would be destroyed en route. But even before then, it became clear to the Axis that sufficient sea transport was an unattainable goal. Ingenuity in devising stop-gap supply measures could not outstrip Allied air and sea power. Despite its losses and lack of shipping, however, the Axis managed to ship to North Africa substantial reinforcements and quantities of supplies. During the period from November 1942 through January 1943, 81,222 Germans and 30,735 Italians arrived in the Tunisian bridgehead, and 100,594 tons of supplies were brought in by air and sea.[8] The problem was that once in Tunisia, those troops could not be sustained indefinitely.

The Axis Forces: Strength and Disposition

The strength of Axis combat forces in Tunisia rose during January 1943 until it reached a total of about 100,000 troops, of which approximately 74,000 were German and 26,000 Italian.[9] The combat troops were supported, or rather perhaps encumbered, by even greater numbers of rear echelon troops. During January, Fifth Panzer Army defended the Tunisian front sector from the sea to the 34th parallel, the boundary with Rommel's forces. Early in February the boundary was shifted northward to run from a point on the coast ten miles northeast of Sfax through Mezzouna and Station de Sened to the Kbir river northwest of Gafsa. Initially Fifth Panzer Army's headquarters operated with minimum staff and without a German corps staff until Arnim organized a provisional Headquarters, *Korpsgruppe Fischer* on January 4 after the arrival, late in December, of elements of Weber's 334th Infantry Division. The 334th Infantry Division went into the Axis line between Division von Broich in the north and 10th Panzer Division (reinforced by the 5th Parachute Regiment) in the south. 10th Panzer Division covered the Medjerda Valley and the line south to Pont-du-Fahs. The Italian 1st (Superga) Division continued operating directly under Fifth Panzer Army in its sector which extended to Djebel Bou Dabouss (816m). On January 12, Headquarters, Italian XXX Corps took over the portion of the front south of the Superga Division, with Group Benigni, the 47th Grenadier Regiment, Lieutenant Colonel Ernst Buse, and 50th Special Brigade, Brigadier General Giovanni Imperiali. The 190th Panzer Battalion was held in reserve, to be committed only on Arnim's orders.[10]

When Rommel's German units arrived in southern Tunisia, they had been thoroughly battered and were at about half strength. They had approximately one third of their full tank strength (only 129 tanks, of which less than half were operational), one third of their complement of armored personnel carriers, about one fourth of their anti-tank guns, and one sixth of their artillery strength. Even towed vehicles were down to roughly one third of full strength, although the Germans had managed to preserve 60 per cent of their nominal complement of motor trucks. The combat effective manpower of Rommel's German units was about 30,000, including the 15th and 21st Panzer Divisions, 90th and 164th Light Africa Divisions, supplemented by the 1st Luftwaffe Jaeger Brigade, corps troops and reconnaissance units.[11]

The Italian divisions totaled about 48,000 troops: 131st (Centauro) Armored, 16th (Pistoia), 80th (La Spezia), 101st (Trieste), 13th (Young Fascists) Divisions, and the Saharan Group. Rommel temporarily lost the 131st (Centauro) Armored Division when it was reassigned to guard the El Guettar defile, and on January 20 the 21st Panzer Division, when it was placed under the direct control of Fifth Panzer Army to be refurbished near Sfax while simultaneously serving as Fifth Panzer Army reserve.[12] None of these divisions was anywhere near its full combat strength, so battle groups operated in configurations dictated by mission requirements rather than by traditional divisions or standard subdivisions of larger units. Allied sea and air interdiction became so effective that no new divisions could be sent to Tunisia from Europe after mid-January. It became impossible to continue the regular replacement process of filling up depleted units. Instead, it became the practice of German forces in North Africa to replace depleted battalions by assigning Tunis Field and Africa Replacement Battalions, units numbering about 900 men each, with a full complement of officers and light weapons.[13]

To implement the system of command in the Tunisian theater, Mussolini designated General Giovanni Messe to assume command of the new First Italian Army on January 23, and on January 26, Fifth Panzer Army was placed under direct operational control of *Comando Supremo*. Until the activation of Headquarters, Army Group Africa, all operations in Tunisia were "coordinated" by Arnim. Messe took up his new post with misgivings but immersed himself in his duties and the political complications of his command, while the Italian leaders waited with some impatience for Rommel's anticipated but delayed departure from North Africa.[14]

Axis air strength in Tunisia was consolidated into a single tactical air headquarters, *Fliegerkorps* Tunis, under Brigadier General Hans Seidemann, with headquarters at La Fauconnerie, northwest of Sfax, and with subordinate headquarters at Tunis and Gabès. Seven principal airfields, most with all-weather runways, from Bizerte to Kairouan, six fields near Gabès, and others at Mezzouna, Sfax, and La Fauconnerie were occupied by the 53rd and 77th Fighter Wings. The Axis had lost 201 aircrew and 340 of 877 aircraft in the early battles to halt the Allied advance toward Tunis. The Luftwaffe expected a period of temporary Axis preponderance in fighters and fighter-bombers in northern and central Tunisia while winter weather kept Allied planes on the ground and logistical difficulties impeded the buildup of the Allied air forces.[15]

CHAPTER 12

Changes in Allied Field Command: Eisenhower's Directives

The enemy's attack from Pont-du-Fahs to Ousseltia in the week following January 18, 1943 had resulted in important changes to the Allied Force. It brought an end to the brief period of national commands by the British First Army, American II Corps, and French XIX Corps, each directly under General Eisenhower. The enemy's attack had been well aimed; the spearpoint struck between British V Corps and the French. The Allied forces were compelled in the emergency to coordinate across their boundaries rather than respond under a unified command, and the inexperienced American II Corps was forced to undertake operations for which it was not ready. General Eisenhower belatedly discovered that control of the entire Allied line through his deputy General Truscott at the AFHQ advanced command post was impossible. On January 21, 1943, he flew with Major General Spaatz and Brigadier General Laurence S. Kuter to Constantine where he met Generals Anderson, Fredendall, Truscott, and Juin. In a renewed attempt to establish a working command structure Eisenhower did not really improve matters. He transferred to Anderson responsibility for "coordinating" operations in the three national sectors. General Juin accepted the new situation and General Giraud made no objection.[1]

It took only a short time to realize that Eisenhower's coordination approach to the Allied command and control problem simply did not work. After four days of chaos and defeat while the Axis attacks had secured the Eastern Dorsal passes, it was obvious that simple coordination of forces was not at all simple and was in fact unworkable. Anderson could not maintain the pace which had already taken him over more than 1,000 miles of bad Tunisian roads to confer with the independent Allied commanders and to negotiate decisions conforming to a general plan of action. The situation required a single authoritative command over the entire front.

Eisenhower and Anderson met at Telergma airfield, southwest of Constantine, on January 24.[2] Eisenhower made Anderson "responsible for the employment of American troops" in accordance with general directions from AFHQ. II Corps was attached to First Army. Eisenhower urged Juin to take similar action for French troops, whose sector was to be substantially narrowed. Following a long conference with Anderson that evening, Juin agreed, effective February 3, to subordinate all French Army formations to First Army, acting in this vital matter on his own authority because General Giraud was away at the Casablanca Conference. With the French concurrence, Eisenhower then gave Anderson overall command of the entire Tunisian front, including French and American units.[3] General Eisenhower's directive to General Anderson dated January 26, 1943, was comprehensive:

> The object of your current operations must be:
> a. To re-establish your central forces on the general line: FONDOUK [el Aouareb]—eastern exit of the pass east of OUSSELTIA—the terrain feature DJ BOU DABOUSS (0-85)—road junction 7 miles northeast of ROBAA [Rebaa Oulad Yahia]-BOU ARADA.
> b. As soon as you have accomplished a, to seize and hold the eastern exits of the passes along the general line: EL GUETTAR—MAKNASSY—FAID—FONDOUK.
> c. To protect your right (south) flank with particular attention to the air bases in the TEBESSA area. *In this connection, I deem it essential that you keep the bulk of the 1st Armored Division well concentrated*, so as to be prepared to take advantage of any opportunity the enemy may offer to act aggressively as well as to counter strongly any enemy thrust that may develop.
> The command arrangements arrived at by you in conferences with General Juin to meet the situation resulting from the enemy breakthrough in the area of the DORSALE ridge are confirmed. Under these arrangements you are given command of all Allied forces on the TUNISIAN front, including, in addition to the troops presently assigned to the First Army, the II Corps (U.S.), and a Composite Corps (French and U.S.). *The Composite Corps will consist ultimately of the 34th Division (less detachments) and certain French elements now in the OUSSELTIA area, all under a French corps commander.*
> I know that you will be fully sympathetic with the efforts of General Juin to conserve the French forces and uphold the honor of France, and that you will always welcome him at your headquarters and at the front, and afford him every facility which will contribute to that end.
> The regroupment of your forces incident to the above will envisage the relief of all elements of the 1st Division (U.S.) and their movement to an assembly area in the vicinity of GUELMA, where it will later pass to your control prior to the attack. *To this end, it is contemplated that the 168th CT (U.S.) will be made available to you for the relief of the 26th RCT (U.S.).*
> You are to bear in mind always that all operations now to be undertaken are for the purpose of facilitating the launching of a powerful coordinated attack as soon as the weather will permit and the necessary forces and supplies can be assembled in position. In this latter interest we must look well to the security of lines of communication and to increasing by every possible means the daily delivery of supplies in the forward area.
> For your information, the Allied Air Force is being directed to continue to pound Rommel's line of retreat including his critical ports so as to hamper to the utmost his withdrawal. General Giraud has been shown this directive and has concurred in it.[4]

Fredendall's 32,000 men in II Corps joined the 67,000 British and Americans, including the 34th Infantry Division, already in First Army, under Anderson's command and control, no longer reporting directly to Eisenhower through Truscott.[5] AFHQ directed that until dry weather arrived in the north, and the drive on Tunis resumed, II Corps was to act defensively in protecting the Allied right wing. Eisenhower had decreed on January 18—and he repeated the order on January 26 and February 1—that the 1st Armored Division was to remain concentrated in a tight fist as a mobile reserve capable of countering any Axis attack in lower Tunisia.

"[But Eisenhower] had no sooner issued these orders than he undercut them by authorizing the extended diversion of CCB to reinforce the Ousseltia Valley and by encouraging Fredendall to 'blood' the rest of Old Ironsides [1AD] in various raids... [1AD] was soon scattered across southern Tunisia."[6]

AFHQ transferred Combat Command B, 1st Armored Division to French command on January 20. AFHQ also ordered Fredendall to assemble in the Sbeïtla area an armored force of comparable strength. But plans for a French attack in the Pichon-Fondouk el Aouareb sector starting January 23, which CCB was to have reinforced, were now abandoned. First Army then directed General Fredendall to assume command of the ground troops of all three nationalities operating south of a line running through Morsott-Thala-Sbiba (excluding the towns), Djebel Trozza-Fondouk el Aouareb (including the mountain and the town), and north of a line from the salt marshes to Gabès. The mission of II Corps was limited to protecting the right flank of the Allied forces in Tunisia. The French were largely withdrawn for rest and rearming.[7]

The departure of the bulk of the French forces from the forward combat areas required amendment of the mission assigned to General Anderson in Eisenhower's directive of January 26. The modification read:

> a. To protect the airfields at SOUK EL KHEMIS, TEBESSA, and THELEPTE... so that our air forces may operate continuously from them; and to secure the defiles at MEDJEZ EL BAB and BOU ARADA which First Army will require when, in conjunction with Eighth Army, the offensive against the enemy in Tunisia begins.
>
> b. Without prejudice to the role in a above:
> (1) to secure the defiles at present held by the enemy which will improve our position when the offensive begins.
> (2) to interfere with the enemy's lines of communication in the coastal plain.
>
> In undertaking minor offensive operations, you are to consider the effect upon morale of costly failures. Sufficient means should be assembled to give reasonable assurances of success.

The revised directive continued with the following admonition:

> In the execution of the above mission, I deem it essential that your mobile striking forces in the south be held well concentrated so as to strike en masse when the need arises. I realize that it will not be possible for you to withdraw the 1st [Infantry] Division (U.S.) into reserve in the vicinity of GUELMA.[8]

Eisenhower wanted to keep the entire 1st Armored Division concentrated for the good reason that the Allies needed to cover the Allied south, or right, flank from incursions by powerful mobile German armored forces. Eisenhower wished the division concentrated as soon as possible, and repeatedly made his desires known to Anderson. Eisenhower's revised directive made it unambiguously clear that Anderson and his now subordinate II Corps were to assemble and maintain a large, armored reserve in the southern area. But he used words that did not express the firmness he intended. Phrases like "you are to consider the effect" and "I realize it will not be possible" do not articulate that the commander in chief commands that the thing be done. [9] And Eisenhower did not follow up to see that it was in fact done. [10]

By January 29, 1943, the Axis enemy had achieved local tactical success in northern Tunisia. Arnim's Fifth Panzer Army retained its positions guarding the routes eastward to Bizerte and Tunis. Farther south, the enemy controlled all the important passes giving eastward access to the coastal plain in the vicinity of Kairouan. The Italo-German thrust from the north into the Ousseltia valley had well and truly blocked Allied operations to recover the gap at Fondouk el Aouareb.

The Axis commanders also made good use of their knowledge of Allied dispositions and vulnerabilities. From hard-surfaced airfields in Tunis and Bizerte, Axis air forces could conduct reconnaissance missions during the rainy season while the Allied air forces generally could not. This intelligence led Fifth Panzer Army to predict that the British First Army's most likely course of action was for the U.S. II Corps to attack through Faïd Pass to seize Sfax. Another possibility was an attack further south from Gafsa to seize Gabès. If II Corps were to succeed in either mission, it would simultaneously isolate the Fifth Panzer Army and cut the recently redesignated German-Italian Panzer Army's line of communications. To prevent that disaster, preemptive action was urgently required. First Army was building up for an offensive on Fifth Panzer Army from the west and the British Eighth Army was pursuing the German-Italian Panzer Army from the east. The temporary advantage of the Axis forces was weakening with time and the offensive had to be carried out soon. [11]

The enemy had to protect its line of communications along the coast from Tunis toward Tripoli, which had become the sole supply route for Rommel's army, at that time falling back to the Mareth Position. The Allies in central Tunisia could attempt a disrupting attack toward the coast, so the enemy had to secure the routes from the interior. With the pending union of their two armies and a central position from which to operate, the Axis could achieve temporary local superiority against fragile French and dispersed American forces in central Tunisia, which made an operational offensive in late January possible.

The Axis also had to control the passes through the Eastern Dorsal as a prerequisite to the deeper offensive. The most important of these was Faïd, which was held by French troops and covered by II Corps. That done, the Axis force would advance to the west, destroy the American forces in the Tébessa area, and loot the vast supply depots there. Fifth Panzer Army ordered the 21st Panzer Division on January 24 to seize Faïd Pass and protect the Tunisian coastal roadway. *Comando Supremo* on January 28 ordered the Fifth Panzer Army to take offensive action at three points: the Rebaa Oulad Yahia valley, the pass through the Eastern Dorsal at Faïd, and the road center and oasis of Gafsa. Securing those points would largely forestall any Allied attempt to interdict the coast roads. Preparations for an Axis attack at Faïd Pass accelerated. [12]

II Corps's Plans

On January 18, II Corps adopted a plan to use American forces in accordance with AFHQ's directive to act defensively. The southern flank of British First Army had to be protected and the main II Corps supply base at Tébessa and the growing airbase at Thélepte were the two primary installations of consequence. Everything else supported the Allied forces still holding Faïd Pass and Gafsa, on the one hand, and covered the enemy-held pass at Fondouk el Aouareb on the other.

The possession of an Eastern Dorsal pass by either opposing force was a threat to the other. Now the Germans held more threats. The French were convinced that the Germans were coming and that both Faïd Pass and the oasis of Gafsa should be defended strongly. II Corps conceived three options: (i) use units of 1st Armored Division (reinforced) to strengthen the garrisons at those two points, or (ii) attempt to take Fondouk el Aouareb, Maknassy, or other places from the enemy, or (iii) concentrate the armored division in readiness to fend off any hostile intrusion and to threaten offensive action. Despite Eisenhower's directive to do the latter, Fredendall *postponed concentrating the U.S. 1st Armored Division* until all its elements had acquired battle experience.[13] If the official historian's characterization of Eisenhower's January 18 instruction as an order is to be accepted, then II Corps's failure to comply was insubordination. It was also a fundamental military error. II Corps now lacked a mobile armored reserve, what Churchill called a *masse de manoeuvre*, to oppose any sudden onset of concentrated Axis armor.

Fredendall and his II Corps staff had developed a plan of action before AFHQ sent Combat Command B, 1st Armored Division to the support of French XIX Corps in the Ousseltia valley. But II Corps's plan was hardly defensive; it provided for four simultaneous assaults against four different objectives, all to begin on January 22. It might have looked ingenious, even quite brilliant, on a map table deep inside a fortified bunker where one did not have to consider the terrain above. But on the actual ground, rugged mountains, valleys, and substantial distances would have separated each of the four forces and prevented any possibility of mutual support. Each force would have been exposed to destruction in detail by a local enemy concentration. Fortunately, that overly ambitious plan was shelved when AFHQ sent CCB to Ousseltia to help the French.[14]

While proposed attacks on the El Guettar defile and Bir Mrabott did not go forward, Combat Command A, 1st Armored Division, Brigadier General Raymond E. McQuillin, commanding, was sent to Sbeïtla to take over the mission of Combat Command B. Those movements were again contrary to Eisenhower's directive to concentrate 1AD but consistent with Eisenhower's waffling about the use of American units.

Ward, CG, 1AD, proposed recapturing one of the key Eastern Dorsal passes with a strong attack on Maknassy, nearly 100 miles south of the Ousseltia fight and

50 miles due east of Gafsa on the road and rail line to Sfax. Fredendall liked Ward's proposal, which would put American troops in striking distance of Rommel's line of retreat up the Tunisian coast. He directed the Maknassy assault to begin on January 30. To carry it out, Ward improvised a Combat Command C, under control of a headquarters consisting chiefly of the staff of the 6th Armored Infantry Regiment under Colonel Stack.

Before Maknassy, however, Fredendall wanted first to raid Station de Sened, a railroad water stop midway between Gafsa and Maknassy. Ward was apprehensive, predicting that the proposed raid would "give our hand away" and alert the Germans to American designs on Maknassy. "Fredendall dismissed the objection with an impatient wave..."[15] Welvert, CG, Constantine Division, also expressed his misgivings, but Fredendall insisted that 1AD first attack Station de Sened. He ordered Combat Command C (CCC) to carry out his desired hit-and-run incursion.

At 4:00a.m. on January 24, a raiding force of 2,000 American troops departed Gafsa in trucks for the trip to Station de Sened, about 28 miles eastward. Shortly before noon, U.S. artillery fire opened on the crossroads. In just over three hours from the opening artillery concentration to the last shot, the Americans overwhelmed their objective and CCC reorganized for the return march. By 6:00p.m., it was back in bivouac near Gafsa. The only American casualties were two men wounded, and one tank damaged by a mine and another by gunfire. CCC captured 96 enemy prisoners.[16] But the American cat was out of the bag and the Axis was alerted to II Corps's intentions.

"For the American troops, it had been principally a morale-building exercise. They were better prepared for the next operation." The official historian's observation is far too kind to Fredendall. Rick Atkinson's assessment of the skirmish seems on the mark: the actual psychological and military skills impact on the troops involved is unclear at best. Fredendall gracelessly trumpeted his small tactical success to his superiors. But for the Germans, the raid on Station de Sened signified sinister American intentions in the Gafsa sector. Generals Ward and Welvert had been correct. The Axis generals recalculated the likely timing of the expected Allied thrust against their supply line which they had long feared. Kesselring and his subordinates moved to accelerate their spoiling attack to counter that threat and to expand the Axis bridgehead in Tunisia.[17] Fredendall had pulled the tiger's tail and the beast would soon maul II Corps.

After the Station de Sened raid, it was left to Fredendall to decide whether to pursue the planned attack on Maknassy and the pass just east of it or to strengthen the Allied hold on Faïd Pass, as Generals Giraud and Juin fervently urged. Either operation would face the threat of an enemy offensive toward Gafsa and Tébessa. Fredendall reasoned that seizing Maknassy now would protect Faïd Pass and inflict direct damage on the enemy.[18] From his underground fortress, he ordered the attack on Maknassy to proceed on February 1. Two forces were directed against the objective in simultaneous assaults. Colonel Stack's Combat Command C was to advance on January 30 from Gafsa eastward along the northern side of the screening hills to enter the coastal plain via Maïzila pass and move to Maknassy. At the same time, another temporary armored force cobbled together for the mission and designated Combat Command D, under Colonel Robert V. Maraist, 1AD's artillery chief and now the CCD commander, was to march from the Bou Chebka area through Fériana, Gafsa and Station de Sened, then eastward along the route of the railroad to Maknassy. 1st Armored Division had placed a reserve of sorts near Sbeïtla.[19]

Maknassy is in the southeastern corner of central Tunisia on the lower eastern plain where the Eastern Dorsal bends to the southwest toward Gafsa. A narrow-gauge railroad and highway enter the Maknassy plain at the southwestern corner through an opening at Station de Sened and continue east through a defile between low hills. Entry from the north is by the Maïzila pass, between Djebel Maïzila (522m) and Djebel Gouleb (736m), through which runs a road from Sidi Bou Zid.

Von Arnim, commanding Fifth Panzer Army, had noted the skirmish at Sened, and had promptly reinforced both Maknassy and Station de Sened. But Faïd Pass, 30 miles north of Maknassy, and the only gap in the Eastern Dorsal still in Allied hands, worried him more. Faïd Pass was a defile between razorback ridges. Occupied by more than 1,000 tough French troops from Welvert's Constantine Division, under command of Brigadier General Jacques Schwartz, Faïd was considered by French strategists to be vital in controlling central Tunisia. Von Arnim called it "my nightmare." Five hundred yards deep and half a mile wide, the pass led to the broad, flat coastal plain to the east and the broad, arid Tunisian plateau to the west. Von Arnim decided to eliminate the Faïd threat before the Allies made their position there too strong to reduce.[20]

CHAPTER 13

The Enemy Attacks to Seize Faïd Pass

Fifth Panzer Army launched its offensive at Faïd Pass on January 30, 1943, one day before the II Corps's attack on Maknassy. The Axis charge was spearheaded by the now refreshed and rearmed 21st Panzer Division, supported by elements of Imperiali's Italian 50th Special Brigade and other Italian army troops. The Axis object was to gain control of the pass, to install security detachments on the chain of mountains from north of Faïd Pass to Sened village, and to reconnoiter halfway to Sbeïtla. Upon completion of its mission, the main body was to withdraw after leaving strong security detachments at key points in the Eastern Dorsal. Italian troops would hold the area of Station de Sened, blocking the narrow plain there and maintaining liaison with 131st (Centauro) Armored Division east of Gafsa, at a pass between Sened village and Sakket.[1]

Faïd Pass was a broad but shallow opening, between the sharp ridges of Djebel Sidi Khalif (705m) on the north and Djebel Bou Dzer (473m) on the south, through which ran the main hard paved highway from Sfax to Sbeïtla, and beyond. There were two lesser gaps in the Eastern Dorsal, which were crossed by rough dirt roads or trails, one about six miles north of Faïd Pass, near Sidi Khalif, and the other just south of Djebel Bou Dzer at Aïn Rebaou.

An attacking force passing through the Faïd defile in a westerly direction from the coastal plain would approach Faïd village one mile to the southwest of the western opening of the pass. The village was a small collection of block-shaped, white masonry houses. The road forked at the village, with the main road leading seven miles straight across the level plain to Poste de Lessouda and the secondary road running west-southwest for eight miles to Sidi Bou Zid. Just to the north of Poste de Lessouda was the isolated hill mass of Djebel Lessouda (644m), a striking, steep-sided hill with excellent views of the wide stretches of plain which encircled it. About ten miles to the southwest were a series of similar hills of which Djebel Ksaïra (560m), near Aïn Rebaou pass, and Djebel Garet Hadid[i] (620m), west of

---

i   Modern Jabal Qarat al Hadid, Tunisia.

Djebel Ksaïra, were prominent. Sidi Bou Zid was about five miles south of Djebel Lessouda and four miles north-northwest of Djebel Garet Hadid. The village's bright stuccoed buildings were surrounded by cultivated fields and orchards in geometric patterns. Elsewhere were large irregular fields of cactus and thin grass.[2]

The 21st Panzer Division was commanded by Colonel Hans Georg Hildebrandt. It organized for the onslaught in two powerful groups, *Kampfgruppe Pfeiffer* and *Kampfgruppe Grün*. *Kampfgruppe Pfeiffer* was further subdivided into northern, central, and southern task forces. 21st Panzer Division attacked at 4:30a.m. on January 30. Hildebrandt's forces executed a brilliant set of complex and synchronized approach maneuvers, taking advantage of the open spaces. The small northern task force, the 2nd Tunis Battalion, reinforced by Italian elements, moved to protect the north flank and to hold Sidi Khalif pass. The center group, employing the 3rd Battalion, 104th Panzer Grenadier Regiment (reinforced), led by Major Georg Pfeiffer, attacked Faïd Pass from the east. One company of infantry from the 2nd Tunis Battalion climbed Hill 644 at the southern end of Djebel Sidi Khalif and struck the defenders of Faïd Pass from the northern flank at the same time Pfeiffer's assault began from the east. The southern task force, 1st Battalion, 104th Panzer Grenadier Regiment (reinforced) stormed ahead to seize and block Aïn Rebaou pass and to protect the southern flank against the French on Djebel Ksaïra. To the south, nearer Maknassy, *Kampfgruppe Grün* (1st Battalion, 5th Panzer Regiment, reinforced) made a longer encircling march through Maïzila pass to hit the French garrison at Faïd village from the rear and then to join in capturing the pass. *Kampfgruppe Grün* was screened by the 580th Reconnaissance Battalion which moved to a supporting position west of Djebel Boudinar (716m). The reconnaissance unit then scouted west as far as Bir el Hafey. A division reserve was held near the Sfax-Faïd road.[3]

"Rippling fire from thirty panzers drove the French back yard by yard, and body by body, until by late afternoon the valiant defenders [in the pass] were surrounded."[4] The northern and southern task forces of *Kampfgruppe Pfeiffer* attained their objectives on schedule, but the center task force and *Kampfgruppe Grün* were held up for five hours by unyielding French resistance. *Kampfgruppe Grün* drove off an American armored force that approached from the northwest, after which the *panzers* continued toward the western opening of the pass to envelop the defenders still there. The Germans finally forced the brave French defending Faïd village and the western end of the pass to withdraw to Sidi Bou Zid, but it took another 90 minutes of fighting for the Nazis to secure the village. By mid-afternoon, 21st Panzer Division had seized both ends of the pass, the surrounding minor passes of Sidi Khalif and Aïn Rebaou, and Faïd village. Well placed French mines had disabled four *panzers*. *Kampfgruppe Grün* contacted a company of the *2nd Tunis Battalion* and sealed off the pass on the west. Grün postponed the advance at nightfall.

The French colonial troops inside the pass stood strong. Major Pfeiffer's center task force was twice thwarted at the eastern end of the pass; in darkness it advanced only 200 yards into the opening before the French stopped them again. The French kept the area illuminated by parachute flares, forestalling night movement by Axis troops up the slopes to positions from which to make a renewed attack in the morning. During the night of January 30, the French defenders were surrounded but staunchly kept the Germans from seizing the pass.[5]

The French commanders begged Fredendall on January 30 for a counterattack at Faïd Pass. "Fredendall was reluctant to abandon his planned drive on Maknassy, which was scheduled to begin in a few hours with another 2,000-man raiding party. French pleas and a vague directive from Anderson to 'restore' the situation at Faïd, forced his hand... Fredendall... ordered a mincing sequence of half-measures destined to make a bad predicament truly dire..."[6] Major General Ward was in Gafsa supervising CCC's preparations for the attack against Maknassy. His tanks could have made a difference at Faïd, but Fredendall ignored him. Five hours after the 21st Panzer Division attacked, Fredendall bypassed 1st Armored Division headquarters and communicated directly with Combat Command A (CCA) headquarters, both of which were in Sbeïtla. He ordered CCA to counterattack in order to allow the French to reestablish their defense of the pass. But Fredendall imposed two limitations: CCA was to compromise neither the defense of Sbeïtla, nor the ability to reinforce the Fondouk and Pichon Passes. "CCA, whose previous mission was simply to reinforce the [Fondouk and Pichon] passes ... received a commander's intent from two levels up with three competing end states."[7] There was no supporting intelligence with Fredendall's orders, because Fredendall, in his bunker at Speedy Valley, had virtually no contact with the isolated French forces at Faïd. He also did not task 1AD or other II Corps assets to conduct reconnaissance east of Sbeïtla prior to CCA's advance. Fredendall, therefore, had no idea that he had committed only a fraction of CCA to a counterattack against the bulk of the 21st Panzer Division. These CCA elements were somehow to execute their mission without any additional fire or aviation support from corps or division. They would also be 78 miles away from the closest supporting unit. Despite the obvious situational uncertainty and danger, II Corps did not give CCA sufficient resources. Fredendall set up CCA to fail.[8]

At about 10:00a.m. Brigadier General McQuillin directed a reconnaissance company to reconnoiter the Djebel Lessouda–Faïd area. A short time later he sent a group consisting of a company of perhaps 17 tanks, a company of armored infantry of about 193 plus vehicle drivers, and an artillery battery with four guns southward to Sidi Bou Zid along a secondary route via Bir el Hafey. The reconnaissance company reported at about 2:00p.m. that the enemy had secured the sector from Rebaou pass to Faïd village with infantry and tanks. Axis aircraft interdicted and delayed American reinforcements moving in daylight. Despite urgent and repeated requests from the French, the American reinforcements failed to travel the 30 miles in time to prevent the loss of Faïd village or the encirclement of Faïd Pass and Allied air action was simply too weak to stop the enemy.

At 2:30p.m., McQuillin decided to postpone his counterattack until early on January 31 and to move into attack position under cover of darkness. Dividing his command, he ordered a northern group to assemble in the vicinity of Poste de Lessouda, and a southern group in the Sidi Bou Zid area. About 3:30a.m., January 31, McQuillin, accompanied by Truscott, then assigned to AFHQ Advance Command Post, issued orders from Poste de Lessouda for a 7:00a.m. onslaught. One part of his force under Lieutenant Colonel William B. Kern was to strike through Rebaou Pass from Sidi Bou Zid to get east of the enemy at Faïd Pass, and the other under Colonel Stark was to advance against the Faïd area from Djebel Lessouda.[9]

But McQuillin's decision to delay overnight settled the contest. The enemy was able to secure the defense of Faïd before dawn came on January 31. The official history says in understatement: "American efforts to relieve the French in Faïd pass on January 31 were not successful." The enemy had dug in, establishing a gun line of concealed anti-tank cannons, machine guns, and mortars. The Germans had emplaced artillery at a convenient distance further back to cover the approaches and had put *panzers* in defiladed positions.[10]

> After thirteen hours of planning, BG McQuillin issued his plan of attack at 0330 on January 31. Task Force (TF) Stark, the main effort, would occupy an assembly area just south of Djebel Lessouda and conduct a frontal attack to seize Faid Pass. On its right flank, TF Kern would occupy an assembly area in [the] vicinity of Sidi bou Zid, penetrate the Ain Rebaou Pass, and envelop the Axis positions from the south. The attack would begin at 0700. This left his subordinate formations three and a half hours to plan. There were no written orders or rehearsals. Major General Ward, sidelined from this action by MG Fredendall, was physically present for, but did not contribute to the orders brief.[11]

The American assault on Faïd by elements of 26IR, 1ID and of CCA, 1AD, consisting in the north of a dozen M4 Sherman tanks and a battalion of infantrymen following Highway 13 toward the pass, began as ordered at 7:00a.m. on Sunday, January 31.[12] It was met with a coordinated and powerful combined arms defense. Axis aerial, artillery, anti-tank, tank, and infantry fires induced panic, confusion, fear, and indecision in the CCA troops as the Americans marched straight into the German artillery trap. The American infantry pushed into the lower foothills north of Faïd Pass and were promptly hit by a thick curtain of bullets and shrapnel. The 1st Battalion of the 26th Infantry Regiment, after scaling two ridges north of the pass, was pinned down for the rest of the day by an impenetrable wall of Axis fire from the third crest. The Germans had hidden towed 88mm dual-purpose guns as anti-tank weapons above the western approach to Faïd Pass. "[American troops] knew that the greatest single weapon of the war, the atomic bomb excepted, was the German 88mm flat-trajectory gun, which brought down thousands of bombers and tens of thousands of soldiers. The Allies had nothing as good, despite one of them designating itself the world's greatest industrial power."[13] It was not until late in the war that the U.S. Army fielded the 90mm gun M3 in towed dual-purpose and tank main gun variants; its high-velocity armor piercing rounds could defeat the *PanzerKampfWagen* VI, the famous Tiger I.

The M4 medium tanks of Company H, 3rd Battalion, 1st Armored Regiment, CCA, were lured within range of those well-sited and concealed weapons, which opened fire from three sides. Within ten minutes, nine American tanks were ablaze and there were more than 100 American casualties. The surviving American tankers and infantrymen would angrily blame one another for the losses and for the complete failure to achieve tank-infantry cooperation.[14]

The supporting U.S. artillery was shelled by long-range counterbattery fire and was relentlessly attacked by German dive bombers. Advancing eastward out of Sidi Bou Zid further south, a battalion from CCA's 6th Armored Infantry tramped across irrigated vegetable fields, but its approach was delayed and then broken off under Stuka attacks, machine guns and heavy *panzer* fire.[15] By 2:00p.m. on January 31, the enemy had succeeded in holding Faïd Pass. The only decisions McQuillin made that day were to withdraw, reorganize, and plan for a second frontal attack the following afternoon, Monday, February 1 at 1:00p.m.

CCA's February 1 attack met a similar fate. Two infantry battalions assaulted the ridgeline three miles south of the pass. German gunners "held their fire until we were practically at the foot of the objective," an officer wrote. "The men got a terrific raking over by the enemy as they fell back." Fifteen *panzers* drove out from Faïd Pass and shot up the infantry from their left flank until driven away by M4 tanks of 3rd Battalion, 1st Armored Regiment, 1AD. Four American self-propelled 75mm guns, augmented by the tanks and tank destroyers, pursued the *panzers* until they reached the cover of German anti-tank guns. The disorganized U.S. infantry was able to withdraw with the armor support. But the tanks and self-propelled guns were then subjected to severe shelling from the hidden enemy guns and fell back under the galling fire.[16]

The Americans had failed the French again. The American attack had not relieved the French in Faïd Pass or prevented the enemy from bringing up reinforcements.[17] Faïd Pass was gone, and with it the Eastern Dorsal. The Germans were now firmly established on the Eastern Dorsal from Djebel Sidi Khalif to Maïzila pass where they had gained a foothold south and west of that gap.[18]

> On February 2nd, CCA shifted to an area defense just east of Sidi bou Zid and Djebel Ksaïra, a hill five kilometers to the southwest of Aïn Rebaou Pass. In its first major action, CCA lost 210 men. The French Constantine Division suffered 900 casualties. While the Allies lost men, equipment, and mutual trust, the Axis gained two key passes and the initiative in central Tunisia.[19]

At 9:30a.m. on February 1, General Giraud ordered Lieutenant General Welvert to make a vehement protest to Fredendall regarding the dilatory American movements and the impotence of U.S. air and artillery.[20] By February 1, however, the French in the pass could not be relieved nor the pass recaptured with the resources available.

Nevertheless, under orders from the underground leaders of II Corps, American troops continued useless efforts to drive the enemy from the Eastern Dorsal. This irresponsible disregard for human life and failure of leadership on the part of the senior commanders, who lacked any first-hand knowledge of the battle situation, was not attributable to Fredendall alone. Deficiencies of command, judgment, and intelligence corrupted the entire chain of command right up to Eisenhower. The Allies had spread too thin along too great a line with U.S. forces dispersed in small combat groups which would have to be committed piecemeal to meet any enemy attack.[21] This grave situation begs the question now why AFHQ did not direct the abandonment of the weakly held Allied positions and make a general withdrawal to the Western Dorsal before the enemy forced them to do so. If in fact no immediately mounted effort could have achieved success, it would have been wiser, as Rick Atkinson observes, to fall back to defensible positions in the Western Dorsal, there to receive and defeat the anticipated counterattack, and to resupply from available and enormous stores, assemble fresh troops and new equipment, and mount an overwhelming attack to crush an increasingly disadvantaged foe.[22]

CHAPTER 14

Failure at Maknassy

Although the enemy's capture of Faïd threatened the entire Allied position in Tunisia, Fredendall's attention had remained fixed on Maknassy in the south. He believed he had to make a solely tactical decision: whether he should send Colonel Stack's force, Combat Command C, to join the counterattack at Faïd or to use it instead for the attack on Maknassy. Giraud and Welvert recommended that the force be brought south of Djebel Ksaïra to the Aïn Rebaou area by a route enabling it to strike the enemy from the rear. For once, Fredendall concurred, and at 1:00p.m., January 30, II Corps ordered Stack directly by telephone (again not through 1AD command channels) to start northeastward from Gafsa toward the area of Sidi Bou Zid with the mission of striking "in flank the force of enemy tanks and infantry thrusting at SIDI BOU ZID from the east, and also to strike any force moving from MAKNASSY toward SIDI BOU ZID."[1] During the night of January 30–31, Stack was out of direct contact with McQuillin and CCA at Faïd; he and CCC spent that night in bivouac about 30 miles southwest of Sidi Bou Zid.[2]

Then Fredendall reversed himself. Just as CCC was nearing the Faïd battle area on January 31, Stack received radioed orders from II Corps at 4:00p.m. to "turn south and join in coordinated effort with Maraist on Maknassy." During that fateful night (January 31 – February 1) when CCC could have been of help at Faïd and was only a few miles northeast of Maïzila pass, Stack was still unable to communicate with CCA. Following his latest instructions, he blocked the northern mouth of Maïzila pass and prepared for a morning attack, leaving the fight at Faïd Pass to Combat Command A and General Schwartz's exhausted troops.[3]

Instead of concentrating 1st Armored Division's two available combat commands as Eisenhower "desired," Fredendall had further divided his armored forces. He had directed the new Combat Command D under Colonel Maraist to seize Maknassy.[4] His orders sending CCC south were based on an uninformed assumption about what was happening at Faïd and Aïn Rebaou. He and the II Corps staff, safely ensconced in their heated tunnels in Speedy Valley, believed that CCA troops were advancing north along the eastern side of Djebel Bou Dzer when in fact they had been trapped and brutally ambushed. The opportunity for McQuillin's CCA and Stack's CCC to cooperate late on January 31 had been declined in favor of combining Stack's attack on Maknassy with that by Maraist's CCD. In the opinion of the official historian, it still would have been feasible during the night of January 31 – February 1 to postpone the Maknassy operation and to recall Combat Command C to the Faïd area.[5]

General Welvert had remained convinced of the advantages of reinforcing the Allied troops at Faïd. He sought out Stack that night and urged him to raise the question again with Major General Ward, commanding 1st Armored Division. Stack contacted Ward, who might justifiably have concluded that he had been effectively removed from direct command of his own units by II Corps and Fredendall, who had repeatedly bypassed him. But Ward was a good soldier. He confirmed his superior's orders for Stack to join with Maraist and CCD in an attack toward Maknassy, while McQuillin and the French units under Schwartz made one last attempt to recover Faïd Pass from its Axis occupants.[6]

McQuillin acknowledged candidly and with distress late on February 1 that CCA had failed to accomplish its mission. His right wing had been thwarted and the infantry on the left had been driven back "in disorder" from a point close to the enemy's positions by the concealed *panzers* which had poured enfilade fire on the GIs attacking toward Faïd Pass.

On February 2, II Corps ordered CCA to pass to the defensive. The message was sent in this instance from II Corps to Major General Ward. It read: "Mission: Contain enemy at Faid and Fondouk. Active defense. Patrolling, Active use of arty fire. Insure no exit by enemy. Notify McQuillin at once." CCA organized positions on Djebel Ksaïra and set up a line east of Sidi Bou Zid. The enemy had already moved onto other high ground east of Djebel Ksaïra and directly south of Rebaou pass, onto the heights north of that pass, and along the western slopes of Djebel Sidi Khalif. Enemy observation posts had excellent vantage points from which to observe all approaches to the Faïd area from the west. The Axis troops watched every American movement and took due note of the placement of troops and machines and the timing of unit routines. The *panzers* withdrew into the passes, remaining a hidden menace. The enemy emplaced artillery as heavy as 210mm howitzers to interdict Allied movement toward Axis infantry positions and to outrange American and French guns in counterbattery fire. The Italians remained in Faïd village while the Allies occupied Sidi Bou Zid.[7]

The course of Maraist's assault on Station de Sened, of McQuillin's battle at Faïd Pass, and of the enemy attack northeast of Rebaa Oulad Yahia still posed a tactical problem for Fredendall and II Corps staff. As if they were in a classroom analyzing and assessing variants of textbook scenarios, they worried about how best to employ Combat Command C. Considering the directives from AFHQ and First Army, II Corps definitely should have ordered CCC into a defensive posture as corps reserve.

However, as CCC opened its attack on Maïzila pass on February 1, under II Corps's orders, it ran into the enemy reinforcements that Arnim had deployed during the night. Enemy infantry and armored cars, supported by artillery, counterattacked at 7:30a.m. CCC drove off the enemy, but new orders from General Ward at 1st Armored Division postponed the commitment of CCC inside the pass until that afternoon. At 2:00p.m., orders ending the delay and indecision came through to Colonel Stack: "Secure Maïzila Pass, including both exits, Reconnoiter to south with view to attack on Maknassy."

The afternoon assault opened with a 20-minute artillery preparation followed at 5:10p.m. with an advance by the tanks and two companies of infantry on foot. Half-tracks carried other infantry to objectives already in American hands to organize those places quickly for defense. Soft ground and anti-tank fire delayed the American advance, but the GIs gained the southwestern side of the pass and part of the northeastern side before darkness forced them to suspend fighting. CCC suffered three killed, 20 wounded, and 43 missing, but Stack insisted that CCC could reach and take Maknassy the next day. He was planning his morning strike when II Corps abruptly recalled CCC from the Maïzila pass during the night of February 1–2 and sent it north to Hadjeb el Aïoun as part of a general shift to a defensive posture to counter a suspected enemy threat against that sector of the Allied line.[8]

Fredendall now issued a flurry of confused and confusing orders and countermands directly to units of 1AD, yet again bypassing the division's ostensible commanding officer, Major General Ward. He did not, however, issue any orders for reconnaissance of the ground or of the Axis forces to the east. "That left Maknassy to CCD, *now reinforced with the first units in Tunisia from the 34th Infantry Division and specifically the Iowa boys of the 168th Infantry Regiment...*"[9] The destinies of the troops of the 34th Infantry Division and of the 1st Armored Division were to be intertwined from here on in many future operations.

Maraist's attack plan was straightforward: artillery, tanks, and infantry would again storm Station de Sened in a manner similar to the January 24 raid, and then press on 20 miles to Maknassy.[10] Screened by elements of the 81st Reconnaissance Battalion, CCD marched on Station de Sened from Gafsa early on January 31. "Infantrymen from the 1st Battalion of the 168th [Infantry Regiment] packed into open trucks late Sunday morning, January 31, for the trip from Gafsa to Sened Station. Having just arrived from Algeria, many still carried their bulky barracks bags. An engineer officer detected 'a sort of Sunday School picnic atmosphere in the morning as we started out.'"[11] The reconnaissance force worked its way around Station de Sened to occupy high ground east of it. The infantry moved in trucks cross country on a wide front toward a point about ten miles west of the objective. There the troops were to dismount to make the approach on foot, attacking from the south with two companies abreast and a third echeloned to the right rear. The tanks were to approach parallel to the road to bypass the objective on the north and then strike in an enveloping maneuver from the east. The artillery supported the attack from positions northwest of the village.

The American attack was to have started late in the day. The tanks and artillery were in position at 1:45p.m., but the 1st Battalion of the 168th Infantry was not. The green troops of 168RCT were for the first time making a cross-country movement in the face of violent Axis opposition. They were caught completely off guard. The "Sunday school picnic" truck convoy carrying 1/168's deficiently trained and inexperienced soldiers was slow, kept driving past the assigned detrucking point and was insufficiently dispersed. Eight enemy Stuka dive bombers attacked it at 1:30p.m., emerging from sunward, one trailing another with sirens shrieking, as their bombs impacted among loaded trucks bunched bumper to bumper. The sirens and the bomb blasts induced the same kind of terror in the Americans as they had in the French in the spring of 1940.[12] "All down the road men were lying, some terribly hurt, some dead, some shocked beyond control," one witness wrote.[13] Fifty soldiers had been killed or wounded, the worst toll from a Stuka attack in the entire Tunisian campaign. Another officer wrote:

> It was the most terrible thing I had ever seen, not the bodies and parts of bodies near smoking vehicles, some sitting, some scattered, some blue from powder burns—it was the expressions on the faces of those [who] wandered listlessly around the wreckage, not knowing where to go or what to do, saying, "This can't happen to us."[14]

Sergeants shouted, driving the troops back into the remaining trucks. Twenty-four enemy planes returned at 4:56p.m. including Messerschmitt Bf109s firing 20mm cannons. They inflicted yet more casualties and sowed greater panic among the survivors. Badly frightened men scattered and ran into the desert. "Maimed and twisted bodies, some of them still burning, made the men overcautious," wrote First Lieutenant Lauren E. McBride.[15] Again, the men were loaded on their trucks, only to flee in blind terror with each rumor of approaching aircraft. Finally, the battalion abandoned the trucks. The soldiers staggered toward Station de Sened in two parallel columns 500 yards on both sides of Highway 14. Arriving at dusk in an olive grove three miles from the village, too late to attack at 5:00p.m. as planned, the devastated battalion bivouacked for the night.[16]

Three different colonels had come and gone as commanding officers of the 168th Infantry Regiment during the last six months of 1942, and a fourth took command in January 1943. He was Thomas D. Drake, an experienced, steady soldier who had enlisted at age 16, was a much-decorated veteran of World War I, and had returned to the Army as an officer after college.[17] Drake was not present or in command when 1/168 had been caught in the open and its men slaughtered. He had spent the past two days on the road finding and visiting the scattered elements of the regiment and being briefed by the entire Allied chain of command. At 6:30p.m. on January 29, Drake, after his tour of inspection, received a telephone message to report to

AFHQ. There he was instructed to travel by road to Constantine and to report to Lieutenant General Anderson, commanding First Army. When Drake asked about his 3rd Battalion, and his Service and Headquarters Companies, he was informed that First Army continued to retain the 3rd Battalion as security troops. He called the chief of staff of First Army, Major General Colin V. O. McNabb, in Constantine, who granted Drake permission to bring the other two companies with him. After an all-night journey, Drake arrived at First Army at 4:30a.m. He instructed his executive officer to bivouac the troops. He waited there until 9:30p.m. when the British staff returned from dinner. Anderson instructed Drake to proceed to the command post of U.S. II Corps east of Tébessa and report to Fredendall for detailed orders. Drake understood that the mission of 168RCT would be to attack and secure some high ground overlooking the coastal plains of Tunisia.[18]

Drake arrived at Speedy Valley about 3:30p.m. on January 31, where he met Fredendall. That evening, as his 1st Battalion hid in the Sened Station olive groves trying to recover from the day's horror, Drake stood with Fredendall in the II Corps tunnels, before a map of southern Tunisia. Fredendall told Drake that the 168th Infantry Regiment was already forward and that 1/168 had been "badly used" in the abortive assault on Station de Sened when they were strafed and bombed by German aircraft. Fredendall drew Drake's attention to the high ground east of Gafsa that rose above the coastal plain over which Rommel must move northward to join Fifth Panzer Army. Emphasizing to Drake that his regiment was needed badly at the front, Fredendall ordered Drake to support the attack to the east by Colonel Maraist's CCD. "You will attack tomorrow morning and seize" the ridges east of Maknassy.[19] With what seems today bizarre irony, Fredendall directed Drake to execute the attack under orders from Major General Ward, commanding officer of the 1st Armored Division. When Drake protested that he did not have the Antitank Company or the 3rd Battalion, Fredendall directed his II Corps staff to call First Army with instructions to release 168RCT's 3rd Battalion, Antitank Company, Engineer Company and Collecting Company to join the main body of the regiment.[20]

Drake then drove to Gafsa, arriving at about 12:30a.m. on February 1 at the rear echelon command post of the 1st Armored Division. The duty officer reported to Drake that the 1st Battalion, 168th Infantry Regiment was at the front under Maraist, commanding CCD, that 2/168 was up the road forward waiting for darkness to board trucks to move to the assembly area for the next day's attack, and that the 175th Field Artillery Battalion was also on the move. The duty officer informed Drake that Major General Ward wanted to see him at the front as soon as possible and inquired if Drake would assume responsibility for the troop movements. With the wisdom of a seasoned officer, Drake emphatically declined, as 1AD had made the arrangements and should carry on.[21]

Drake next visited the bivouac of the 175th Field Artillery Battalion, commanded by Lieutenant Colonel Kelly, and the camp of the 2nd Battalion, commanded by

Lieutenant Colonel Baer. He found that the units had full loads of ammunition. He informed both unit commanders that the regiment would attack in the morning under orders yet to be issued by Ward at 1AD. Drake took care to look into 1AD's arrangements for the convoy that was to take 2nd Battalion and the 175th FA Battalion to the assigned assembly area in the dark. He learned from a military policeman at the crossroads that a certain Captain Frederick K. Hughes of 1AD was there as a guide. Drake sought out Hughes, who confirmed that he had been sent to meet the artillery and infantry and to conduct them to their assembly area. Drake questioned Hughes about the arrangements, but Hughes brusquely assured Drake that he knew exactly where to place the troops and that they would be where Colonel Drake wanted them in the morning. Hughes said he would report the arrival of the column at the assembly area to CCD headquarters.[22] With a final word of caution from the experienced Drake to Hughes to be careful not to overrun the front line in the dark, Drake drove on to Ward's command post about 20 miles southeast of Gafsa on the road to Sened Station.

Drake arrived at Ward's command post (CP) about 2:30a.m. Ward mordantly told Drake that Colonel Maraist had "everything left in the division" under his command, as Ward's entire division, Combat Commands A, B and C, were away on other tasks under Fredendall's direction, and that he had nothing left but his staff to command. Ward briefed Drake about the previous day's attack and the 1st Battalion's losses and informed him that in the renewed assault Drake would command all the remaining infantry.

Drake took his leave, and drove the several miles to Maraist's command post, arriving at about 4:30a.m. The CCD command post staff reported that the convoy carrying the infantry and artillery units of the 168RCT had passed the command post while Drake had been with Ward and should already be closing into the bivouac areas. Lieutenant Colonel John Petty, commanding 1/168, came to the CP; he reported to Drake that while his troops had been seriously shot up the survivors would be ready to fight that day. As Maraist was not expected until 5:30a.m., the conscientious Drake drove to the supposed bivouac of the 2nd Battalion. He planned to reinforce 1st Battalion's morning attack with the 2nd Battalion.[23]

The 175th Field Artillery Battalion and the 2nd Battalion, 168th Infantry made the road march during the night with their guide, Captain Hughes, who proved to be as incompetent as he was disrespectful. Hughes had led the battalion convoy past a Military Police checkpoint at speed. Except for the small group of elements of 168IR with Drake, and a portion of the 2nd Battalion's support troops, the soldiers of 2/168 and 175FA were driven past the American lines directly into the enemy's positions. When Drake later arrived at the assigned bivouac, he could not find his troops. Where 800 men should have been at the staging area north of the road, the desert was bare except for a few tanks and half-tracks. Military Policemen on Highway 14 reported that 80 trucks, including the 2nd Battalion's field kitchen, had run through roadside checkpoints and into the no-man's land outside Station de Sened. An MP told Drake that the long column of trucks had passed him headed for the enemy lines between 3:00 and 3:30a.m. He had not stopped them, he explained, because he had no orders to do so.

Drake, already disturbed by the arrogantly casual and careless leadership style of the Allied chain of command, and the lack of military diligence and initiative in the lower ranks, feared the worst, which was quickly confirmed. Parachute flares and violent firing of all calibers suddenly erupted from the east within the German lines. Lieutenant Colonel Petty summoned the men he had assigned to the outpost and came back with two frightened privates. Those men admitted that they had manned the most advanced outpost. They claimed that they had halted the column but that the officer leading it had said he knew what he was doing.[24] A subsequent investigation proved that the feckless Captain Hughes had indeed led his charges past the American picket line and into the enemy's position.

The 2nd Battalion was pinned down less than a mile from Station de Sened and remained there under fire for the next ten hours. Terrified soldiers of 2/168 jumped from their truck beds and scraped shallow foxholes with helmets and hands. A barrage of enemy mortars and machine guns raked the convoy, destroying 17 vehicles. "They were," an officer in another unit later noted, "in a very bad spot."[25] In the morning, most of the 2nd Battalion was either captured or immobilized by enemy fire and quite unable to participate in any attack. A few chastened soldiers managed to find their way back to the American lines before noon.[26]

Enemy strength and dispositions at Station de Sened were quite different from what had existed when the Americans had first raided the place. Combat Command D had expected to find about 250 men with eight machine guns, four 47mm anti-tank guns, and two 75mm field guns emplaced behind minefields west of the village. A few armored cars had also been observed there, but the main enemy force was presumed to be east of Maknassy. Contrary to that uninformed presumption, Arnim had concluded that Sened was still threatened and had sent strong reinforcements from Gabès. The village was now very well defended.[27]

Colonel Maraist appeared in the early morning on February 1 to issue the orders for the attack. The infantry under Drake was to attack supported by tanks and artillery, with the objective to retake Sened. No artillery preparation was to be made. The tanks would advance on the left of the infantry, not as part of a coordinated combined arms assault. The attack was to begin at 7:30a.m., but no sooner had Maraist spoken than German dive bombers, which Drake estimated at 50 in number, attacked the assembly areas, littering the desert with burning tanks and half-tracks. After the air raid, Drake emphatically told Maraist that an attack at 7:30a.m. was not possible as he had not even seen all his troops nor made a ground reconnaissance of the objective or its approaches. The earliest the regiment could attack, Drake insisted, was 9:30a.m.; Maraist agreed with Drake's assessment and postponed the attack.[28]

The second fight at Station de Sened turned into a daylong pitched battle. At 9:30a.m., Drake rallied the 1st Battalion from their protective olive grove. By noon, the troops remained more than a mile from the village, harassed by Stukas and swarms of bullets that prompted one man to ask if anyone else could hear "all those bees buzzing?" Men lay on their backs kicking at jammed rifle bolts with their boots. "We learned in battle that sand and oil don't mix," a lieutenant recalled. The brave Lieutenant Colonel John Petty was firing from his knees when enemy bullets struck him in the abdomen; he died 12 days later. Petty's executive bled so much from a head wound that his submachine gun clogged with blood. An enemy shell blew through the battalion intelligence officer, First Lieutenant Woodrow N. Nance. "He was torn almost in two in the middle." Drake later wrote: "Men were dying everywhere. The sand was kicked up in clouds and the air was filled with whining bullets."[29]

The American attack advanced but only slowly against enemy fire, finally penetrating the village in the later afternoon. At mid-afternoon, as Maraist directed CCD's artillery and tank fire on the village, Drake ordered a flanking attack on the right by the 1st Battalion's Company B, commanded by Captain Bird. Three rifle platoons fixed bayonets, fanned out in a skirmish line, and charged toward the village, passing charred corpses laying across the turrets of three smoldering American tanks. Station de Sened fell at 4:00p.m. under the weight of 1st Battalion's assault, but a swift enemy counterattack retook the town long enough to capture the 2nd Battalion surgeon and 15 medics who had rushed in prematurely to treat the wounded. In a final burst of close quarter fighting with grenades and bayonets, the village fell to the Americans for good at 5:30p.m. The booty included 52 Axis prisoners. Most of the enemy troops skillfully withdrew toward Maknassy.[30] 2/168 was reorganized because Lieutenant Colonel Baer, the former commander of the 2nd Battalion, had been lightly wounded in his hand, but was psychologically disabled by the day's action. Baer was replaced by his executive officer, Major Moore. CCD and 168IR established perimeter defenses, held Station de Sened during the night and prepared to continue the advance the next morning, to the east.[31] Meanwhile, of course, Fifth Panzer Army had assembled greater forces, also to the east.

Fredendall urged Maraist to move east more quickly: "It is of vital necessity for you to get forward and place the infantry on its objective four (4) miles east of Sened Station." Fredendall again made his exhortation directly to Maraist at CCD, not through Ward at 1AD headquarters, and absent any first-hand knowledge of the ground or of enemy dispositions "four miles east of Sened Station." "Too much time has been wasted already," continued Fredendall. "*I shall expect you to be on the objective not later than 1000 hours, 2 February.* Use your tanks and shove. From 1800 hours, this date, (1 February) General Ray E. Porter, USA,[i] will be in

---

i   Brigadier General Ray E. Porter was at that time assigned to II Corps's advanced command post.

command of your operation until completion of your mission, after which you will revert to Corps control in the Gafsa area."[32]

That same night, Major General Ward, unaware of II Corps's most recent orders to CCD because Fredendall and II Corps staff had not bothered to inform 1AD's headquarters, sent his own orders to Maraist. The two battalions of the 168th Infantry and the 175th Field Artillery Battalion were to revert to General Porter's command after CCD had gained the position east of Station de Sened. CCD was then to move to the Gafsa area to enter corps reserve, and the 81st Reconnaissance Battalion would shift to Sbeïtla, where the 1AD headquarters would open at 2:00p.m., February 2. Ward lastly directed Maraist to secure a position favorable to defense "three to four miles east of Sened Station." After the position had been organized by the two battalions of the 168th Infantry Regiment, Maraist was to remain there in a supporting posture until instructed by Porter.[33]

The orders issued by Fredendall and Ward were confusing enough by themselves. Worse, both sets of orders contradicted a directive made by Eisenhower that same morning. Eisenhower, in a meeting with Generals Anderson and Truscott at Télergma airfield, had ordered that the central front was to be securely held by employing the 1st Armored Division as a concentrated force, even if that involved pulling back the line from the Eastern Dorsal, evacuating Gafsa, and forfeiting the use of Thélepte airfield. "If Maknassy is not taken by tonight, the whole division should be withdrawn into a central position and kept concentrated," Eisenhower had insisted.[34] Both Fredendall and Ward appear to have been unaware of Eisenhower's order. GIs on the firing line deserved to be excused for wondering with dismay if their commanders, up to and including Eisenhower, knew what they were doing or ever coordinated their planning and direction.

At 2:00a.m. on Tuesday, February 2, Colonel Maraist issued his orders for the continued attack to the east to begin at 5:00a.m. The objective was to seize the high ground overlooking the plains extending toward Sfax. The armor would precede the 168RCT's infantry. Maraist would personally direct the attached Cannon Company of the 39th Infantry Regiment. Colonel Drake ordered the 168th Infantry Regiment to advance in column of battalions, 1/168 in the front, with 2/168 to follow at 1,000 yards. The 175th Field Artillery Battalion was to displace and re-emplace by bounds and provide fire support on call. 168RCT's Cannon Company (75mm guns mounted on half-tracks) was to follow on the right flank of the 1st Battalion. Drake was forward with the 1/168, while the regimental command post followed the 1st Battalion. The renewed advance began promptly at 5:00a.m. on February 2, and within a few minutes German aircraft appeared and began bombing and strafing. This time, however, the enemy planes were themselves attacked by fast and heavily armed U.S. Army Air Corps P38 "Lightning" fighters, which quickly drove the Germans away.[35]

The drive toward Maknassy proceeded rapidly against light artillery and machine-gun fire until about 9:30a.m. when progress was abruptly ended by a dive-bombing attack on the tanks. Under enemy long-range artillery fire, the now steadier infantry kept advancing and by about 12:00 noon seized the objective, the high ridges six miles east of Sened. CCD's tanks quickly concentrated to meet a counterattack, the 168th Infantry Regiment dug in on the heights, the 81st Reconnaissance Battalion took up positions protecting the north and south flanks, and the 701st Tank Destroyer Battalion's reconnaissance elements pushed five miles farther east. 1/168 occupied the center of the objective; 2/168 was placed on the left rear. 175th Field Artillery Battalion was in the center rear to cover the entire front and both flanks. The 39th Infantry's Cannon Company was placed behind the easternmost ridge to protect the front and left flank against an enemy armored attack, and engineers arrived to plant mines to close the valley on the left. An enemy column of trucks and some tanks was bottled up by U.S. artillery and mines in a defile on the right flank, but without sufficient American troops to attack and destroy it, the enemy column and several enemy air raids continued to menace the American force.[36]

What the official Army history calls a German counterattack came at about 4:00p.m. A dive-bombing attack by 24 Stukas from the west and rear surprised and again demoralized the infantry. When a group of 16 *panzers* approached on the left flank, an officer of the 2nd Battalion, 168IR ran in panic through the lines. "There has been a breakthrough!" he bellowed. "Save yourselves! Save yourselves!" Panic infected some troops who left their positions and started running west. Caught up in the fear, others jammed the road west with vehicles. Hundreds rose from their trenches and foxholes and ran toward the rear or threw themselves into the fleeing vehicles.[37] Drake reported that the men "were wild-eyed as they roared along at full speed. The column was made up of half-ton weapon carriers, jeeps, half-tracks, tanks—anything that would roll."[38] An artillery battalion commander later recalled, "A sort of hysteria took hold of everyone. The [enemy] tanks were knocked out, but the hysteria continued." A combat engineer added, "All of the infantry soldiers I could see anywhere around were hightailing it to the rear." The engineers also fled. Desperate officers worked frantically to stop the rout and turn the soldiers around; they organized a straggler line from north to south across Highway 14 at Sened Station to snare those running away. There the hysterical horde was finally turned by officers and soldiers as unyielding as those hard-handed Union Army cavalry patrols who had curtly demanded of stray soldiers, "Show blood!"[ii] Sergeant James McGuiness of Company F, 2/168, wrote to his parents:

> Some of the fellows have run off and leave us fighting and don't think for one minute that I haven't had the urge to get up and leave. A fellow isn't yellow, but those shells bursting above and around you day in and day out is really tough.[39]

---

ii   Catton, Bruce. *A Stillness at Appomattox*. New York: Doubleday, 1953, 82.

The wise Drake did not believe there ever had been a serious counterattack. He had gone forward to investigate movement to the east when he became aware of what he called "some desultory firing" around 5:00p.m. He then observed his men's panicked flight. Drake wrote later that only part of one battalion (2/168) and some rear units had been affected. His investigation found that 1AD's screen tanks had been withdrawn without notice to his infantry, causing a platoon of *panzers* to move forward to investigate, advancing into the 168RCT's position. At first the GIs, with no great exposure to armored fighting vehicles, had mistaken them for friendly tanks until the *panzers* opened fire at close range. That attack triggered the frayed nerves of the GIs and led those in the immediate vicinity to believe that the *panzers* were among them in numbers. Quick action by Drake and other officers averted general panic without any loss to the position.[40] Five *panzers* had managed to reach the main position of 168IR, but they were driven off an hour later by American tanks and tank destroyers. By 7:00p.m., the American hold on the ridges east of Sened was generally restored and held throughout the night.[41]

CCD's advance toward Maknassy began once more at daylight on February 3 with tanks, tank destroyers, and assault guns out in front of the infantry line to repel any Axis counterattack. Several tank destroyers from the reconnaissance unit of the 701st Tank Destroyer Battalion moved cautiously to within six miles of Maknassy by noon. American artillery fired on enemy detachments that came within range, and in a rare second appearance of Allied air power, 15 American B-25 medium bombers bombed enemy tanks near Maknassy at about 3:30p.m.

But in accordance with orders, that was as far as CCD was to advance. The enemy had lost seven light tanks, two French 75mm guns, two 88mm dual-purpose guns, considerable transportation equipment, a small quantity of ammunition that was destroyed or captured, and about 160 troops taken prisoner. The Americans lost four light tanks, nine half-tracks, one self-propelled 105mm howitzer, one 75mm pack howitzer, two self-propelled and one towed 37mm guns, as well as lesser weapons and transport vehicles. American casualties were 51 killed, 164 wounded, and a troubling 116 missing.[42] The American attack was over. By dawn on February 4, pursuant to II Corps's orders, CCD had pulled back to Gafsa, abandoning Station de Sened for the second time in ten days. The offensive had failed to seize Maknassy, failed to relieve enemy pressure on Faïd Pass, and failed to help McQuillin's CCA. A 1st Armored Division account concluded that "no decisive objective was gained."[43]

CCD and the attached battalions of 168IR had had an appalling first battle experience against *Kampfgruppe Strempel*, a hastily organized collection of enemy reconnaissance units reinforced with artillery and a few tanks and with close air support. The American attack on Maïzila pass and Fredendall's foolish raid on Station de Sened a week earlier had disclosed Allied intentions and timing and had convinced Fifth Panzer Army of an imminent Allied threat to the 21st Panzer Division's operations in the Faïd pass area. Colonel Hildebrandt, commanding the 21st Panzer Division, organized a provisional headquarters under his chief of staff, Lieutenant Colonel Strempel, and ordered Strempel to defend the sector from Djebel Matleg (477m) to Djebel Bou Hedma (790m) at the boundary with the Italian 131st "Centauro" Armored Division. *Kampfgruppe Strempel* controlled four German battalions reinforced by some Italian troops and by artillery and flak: the 334th Reconnaissance Battalion, 29th Africa Battalion, 580th Reconnaissance Battalion, and miscellaneous units of the Italian 50th Special Brigade. The 190th Panzer Battalion, which since its murderous encounter with Lieutenant Colonel Waters's 1/1AR at Chouïgui Pass had become known as the "fire brigade" of the Tunisian bridgehead, was held in tactical reserve in the Meheri Zebbeus area.[44]

> [D]uring these four days [January 30 – February 2, 1943], three constants [of First Army's and II Corps's] actions were the micromanagement, dispersal, and unsynchronized employment of 1st AD forces. When the fighting subsided, MG Ward still did not control any forces outside of his Division Reserve. First Army held CCB in reserve at Maktar. II Corps held CCD in reserve at Bou Chebka, CCC in 1st AD—in name, but not in practice—reserve at Hadjeb el Aioun, and CCA in an area defense of Sidi bou Zid. The division was spread out over a 150 by 125 kilometer area. Two of its combat commands were reeling from unsuccessful, independent attacks against superior forces. Its other two had been kept out of the fight by higher headquarters' indecision. Given the demonstrated Axis threat along both XIX and II Corps's extended and weakly held fronts, there was a clear doctrinal need to adopt a mobile defense and form a decisive counterattack force. It was also clear that a concentrated 1st AD should be this force. GEN Eisenhower knew this, and insisted on it with LTG Anderson. He and his subordinate commanders would have a short respite from Axis attacks to implement this guidance.[45]

In 1945, Colonel Drake recalled that 168RCT spent Wednesday and Thursday, February 3 and 4, digging into its positions on the ridge and making artillery and mortar range charts, punctuated by frequent enemy air raids. Shortly after daylight, an errant engineer half-track blundered into a dump of fused mines, detonating the mines and certainly attracting the attention of the enemy perched on the hills to the east. The Antitank Company arrived at 9:30a.m. on February 3 after a long road march and was placed in a defensive position. Thursday, February 4 was quiet except for more air attacks. Fighting by other units was in progress near Maknassy where Combat Command A was struggling to reach Maknassy from the north. The soldiers of 168RCT observed the enemy in their front refueling vehicles about eight miles to the east. At about 3:15p.m. a flight of bombers dropped ordnance in the rear area of the 168RCT's position. Happily, little damage was done.

At 5:00p.m. on February 4, Brigadier General Ray Porter sent orders to 168IR to withdraw that night under cover of darkness and to assemble near Gafsa by daylight on February 5. Drake assembled his officers at 6:00p.m. and gave painstaking orders for the withdrawal. The engineers were to prepare all installations and equipment, including railroad engines and a roundhouse, for demolition; they were then to mine Highway 14 behind the rear guard. Rear and support units and the artillery were to march away at 8:00p.m., with the special units, the Headquarters Company, and

2nd Battalion behind the artillery. 1st Battalion was next in line, followed in turn by a company of tanks. The executive officer commanded the withdrawing column, which was to clear the western ridgeline by 10:00p.m. Colonel Drake remained with the rearguard screen, consisting of Company B of 1/168 reinforced by the heavy machine guns (water cooled .30 caliber M1917) of the heavy weapons platoons of Companies B and D. The engineers carried out the demolitions at midnight, set the mines, and quickly rejoined the screen. By daylight, the last elements of 168RCT had assembled near Gafsa.[46]

II Corps Goes on the Defensive

The enemy's attacks southwest of Pont-du-Fahs, in the Ousseltia valley, and at Faïd Pass drew Allied forces into dispersed holding positions which extended perilously far out from the Western Dorsal. II Corps now halted its operations to seize Maknassy, and at noon, February 3, Headquarters, 1st Armored Division (Major General Ward) issued new orders based upon the loss of Faïd Pass. The poorly armed French forces in the Fondouk el Aouareb-Pichon area were now vulnerable to an attack similar to the horrific action at Faïd.[47] 1AD's new mission was to contain the enemy from Fondouk el Aouareb gap to Maïzila pass, a distance exceeding 50 miles. It was to reinforce the French troops quickly wherever needed, to engage in active reconnaissance and patrols, to use artillery freely, and to employ mobile striking forces in swift counterattacks against any enemy outpouring from the eastern mountain chain.[48]

Operations thus far had cost II Corps a total of 699 casualties: 50 killed, 487 wounded, 152 missing, and 10 captured. The soldiers of II Corps had also lost of much of their innocent verve as well as their confidence in themselves and their leaders. 1AD remained dispersed. Combat Command B, still withdrawn by Anderson from both II Corps and General Ward's control, was at Maktar in First Army reserve.[49] Combat Command C was only nominally under 1AD's control because of Fredendall's continued malpractice of issuing orders directly to subordinate units and ignoring intermediate headquarters. His most recent orders had directed CCC to cover the 20-mile zone from north of Djebel Trozza to a ridge southeast of Hadjeb el Aïoun, while Combat Command A covered the rest of the chain of mountains as far as Djebel Meloussi, west of Maïzila pass.

First Army directed II Corps to recall Combat Command D from the operation toward Maknassy to enter II Corps Reserve at Bou Chebka in place of the detached Combat Command B. The 81st Reconnaissance Battalion (less Company B) was placed in 1st Armored Division Reserve at Sbeïtla. The 168th Infantry Regiment (1st and 2nd Battalions) passed to direct II Corps control and was ordered to move from Gafsa to Sbeïtla and then to Sidi Bou Zid. The 3rd Battalion, 168th Infantry, went into II Corps Reserve at Fériana. To enhance the mobility of U.S. forces across the rear of the northern sector, Company B, 16th Armored Engineer Battalion, and engineers from the U.S. 34th Infantry Division were tasked to build a hard surfaced road from Hadjeb el Aïoun to El Ala.[50] That road-building project was soon to pay great dividends by accelerating Allied movements behind their extended line.

On Saturday, February 6, 1943, 168th Infantry Regiment, less 3rd Battalion, passed Sbeïtla and bivouacked in the open desert. Relying on dispersal for protection against air attacks, the regiment dug in both its men and vehicles. At 3:00p.m. the II Corps chief of staff appeared with detailed orders for the 1st Battalion to move to Sidi Bou Zid at dark to relieve a French battalion. Colonel Drake protested II Corps's prescription of the means to carry out the mission, and the order was changed to read "send a battalion." Drake again requested the release of the 175th Field Artillery Battalion to his control, but II Corps instead provided the 17th Field Artillery Battalion (155mm guns), retaining 175FA Battalion at Gafsa. On Sunday, February 7, 168RCT received new orders attaching the regiment once again to 1st Armored Division, with directions for Drake to report to Major General Ward.

Ward commanded 168RCT to move to Sidi Bou Zid during the night of February 7–8 and there to report to Brigadier General McQuillin, commander of CCA. Ward directed that the 3rd Battalion, 168RCT was to rejoin the regiment, but that the 1st Battalion of the 168RCT was to move back to Fériana that night to be placed in II Corps reserve. Command and control of 17th Field Artillery Battalion was also to pass to McQuillin. Drake issued the necessary orders for the movements, then drove to Sidi Bou Zid to report directly to McQuillin. McQuillin told Drake to complete the movement of the regiment that night and to relieve the 26th Infantry Regiment (detached from 1st Infantry Division) the next day. Despite intermittent enemy long-range artillery fire, the 168RCT (2nd and 3rd Battalions) and the 17th Field Artillery Battalion marched to Sidi Bou Zid and moved into assembly areas without incident.[51]

Early in the morning of February 8, 1943, Drake accompanied McQuillin on a reconnaissance of the ground east of Sidi Bou Zid. McQuillin selected the positions for the units of the 168th Infantry Regiment to occupy, then he and Drake returned to the command post of the 26th Infantry Regiment at 10:00a.m. 168RCT carried out the relief in daylight because II Corps had directed that 26IR was to enter II Corps reserve by 5:00p.m. The two infantry regiments made use of folds in the ground and of available vegetation to screen their movements and by 7:00p.m. 168IR had replaced 26IR in the line. For the next five days, February 9 through 13, 168RCT consolidated and improved its positions, putting up wire entanglements, laying mines, shifting troops, and emplacing weapons.[52]

Anderson and Fredendall intended to hold as much of the forward areas as possible while the Allies prepared for offensive action in March. Eisenhower's concurrence in holding positions so far out on the plain was another military mistake that Eisenhower should have corrected. The senior Allied commanders wrongly presumed that the enemy would remain quiescent behind the Eastern Dorsal. They reasoned that when an opportunity arose to strike at the Axis line of communications on the coastal plain arose, the Allied forces could somehow assemble on the plain west of the Eastern Dorsal, in which all the gaps were now held by the enemy and from which the enemy could observe all movement to the west, and then miraculously bash through the defile that offered the best hope of success. The gorges in enemy hands, however, were two-way portals behind which the enemy could assemble its own mobile forces. "[I]t was hardly to be expected that the enemy would quietly permit strong forces to be organized for the purpose of piercing the barrier and wreaking havoc in the rear of Field Marshal Rommel's army."[53]

The loss of Faïd Pass and enemy control of all the Eastern Dorsal passes rendered the Allies dangerously vulnerable to destructive Axis attacks by mobile armored formations emerging out of the Eastern Dorsal gaps. The retention of the areas east of the Western Dorsal was hazardous at best. Anderson, Fredendall, and their chiefs of staff, by the evening of February 5, had reached decisions on the dispositions of their forces that events would once again show to be tactically unsound.[54] Eisenhower, Anderson and Fredendall kept underestimating the enemy. German aggressiveness and the tools to exercise it existed in plenty in Tunisia in mid-February 1943.

PART III

"CITIZENS OF DEATH'S GREY LAND": THE KASSERINE BATTLES

CHAPTER 15

The Axis Strikes at II Corps

Allied Dispositions

AFHQ and its subordinate commands expected another enemy attack in central Tunisia; again the only question was *where*. There were indications from some sources that an attack might be made toward Pichon, either by way of the Fondouk el Aouareb Gap or by one of the routes north of it.[i] Other signs seemed to point to enemy attacks along more than one axis. The withdrawal of 10th Panzer Division from positions along the northern front into a mobile reserve farther south was a fact that should have caused alarm among the Allies. While the enemy was planning and preparing its onslaught, British First Army was reorganizing its V Corps front. First Army returned scattered small units to their parent organizations and took steps to establish a substantial First Army reserve. The arrival of the British 46th Division in the forward area, and the introduction into the French sector of elements of the U.S. 1st and 34th Infantry Divisions, made it possible in Anderson's mind to withdraw the British 6th Armoured Division from the Bou Arada valley into First Army reserve.[i]

Units of the 34th Infantry Division not already at the front had been moving from Algeria toward and into Tunisia for some days. On February 2, 1943, the 135th Regimental Combat Team, with the 109th Quartermaster Battalion attached, rolled east out of Algeria toward Tunisia. 135RCT set up bivouac at night on the outskirts of Sidi-bel-Abbes, headquarters of the French Foreign Legion. On February 3, the regiment was in a bivouac area outside Orleansville. The following day, Colonel Parkin and Lieutenant Colonel Carley L. Marshall were relieved of assignment to the regiment, and Colonel Robert W. Ward was assigned and assumed command of 135IR. The bivouac that day was near L'Arba. Marshall was assigned as commander, 1st Battalion, 133rd Infantry Regiment.

The threat of Axis air raids now precluded movement in daylight. Under cover of darkness, bivouacs were established in succession near Bi-bou-Arrerdij, Guelma, and Le Kef as the regiment continued into central Tunisia. 135RCT moved again during the night of February 8–9 to an area ten miles east of Maktar, Tunisia. Initially attached to

---

i   Modern Haffuz, Tunisia.

the 1st Infantry Division, 135RCT and 133RCT were ordered to relieve elements of the French Army XIX Corps in the Pichon area. Upon relieving them, the regiment was to defend its sector to prevent any enemy advance in a westerly direction.[2]

Lieutenant General Anderson thought that the forward areas could be held during the reorganization by a smaller concentration of infantry. He directed that each likely route of approach by enemy armor be heavily mined, that the minefields be covered by infantry and artillery, that a mobile reserve be kept in each sector, and that observation be continuous, supplemented at night by energetic and vigilant patrolling. Once established, the First Army reserve would make it possible to counter an Axis thrust without improvising troop formations for each defensive operation. When the 133rd and 135th Regimental Combat Teams completed their long wintry journey by truck from the Oran area to Tunisia during the second week of February, they relieved French units from the Algiers Division. Colonel Ward's 135th Infantry Regiment had barely completed that process near Pichon before the enemy began its assault. The 133rd Infantry Regiment, commanded by Colonel Ray C. Fountain, was farther west and moved to the vicinity of Hadjeb el Aïoun. The 34th Infantry Division, under Major General Ryder, reassumed division command and control of both 133RCT and 135RCT just as the enemy's attack started.[3]

The complex operations to relieve the French troops were carried out on successive nights. The 1st Battalion, 135RCT relieved the 3rd Battalion of the *1st Régiment Tirailleurs Algérien* (Regiment of Algerian Tirailleurs (RTA or Sharpshooters)) and the 3rd Battalion, 9th RTA, on February 10–11. 3rd Battalion, 135RCT relieved the 1st Battalion of the 1st RTA on February 11–12, and the 2nd Battalion, 135IR relieved the 1st and 2nd Battalions, 9th RTA, on February 12–13. The 125th Field Artillery Battalion relieved two batteries of French artillery on February 13–14. All remaining French artillery and anti-tank protection and the British Royal Artillery Anti-Aircraft and Anti-Tank units remained in the area. When the last of the designated French units had been relieved, the 135th Infantry Regiment assumed responsibility for the sector.

The left flank of the 135th Infantry Regiment was protected by French irregulars, the dreaded Moroccan Goumier[ii] mountain fighters in their striped djebalas and sandals carrying fearsome curved knives, and by elements of the U.S. 1st Infantry Division. 135RCT's right flank, however, was exposed to attack from the Fondouk Gap and Djebel Aïn al Rhorab, both of which were now in enemy hands. As of 12:00 midnight, February 14, with the enemy's attack imminent, the 135th Infantry Regiment also reverted to the control of the 34th Infantry Division under Major General Ryder.[4] As the enemy launched its offensive against II Corps, 135IR suffered its first casualties in the Pichon sector. Private First Class John J. Dresser, Company B, 1/135, was wounded while on patrol on February 14. On February 15, a five-man patrol from Company B failed to return. Early that evening during

---

ii   The Goumiers were indigenous Moroccan soldiers who served in four groups of about 12,000 men each attached to the French Army of Africa under French officers.

an air attack, Captain Charles A. Fanning and Second Lieutenant Charles B. Keys, both of Company C, 1/135, were wounded, and Private First Class Erwin L. Nichols, Company C, and Technician Fifth Grade Herbert K. Schneider, Band, were killed by bomb fragments.[5]

Axis Attack

On Sunday, February 14, 1943, Axis forces launched a powerful armored and motorized infantry attack with the objective of annihilating the Allies on the Eastern Dorsal range and expanding the Axis bridgehead around Tunis. Over the next two weeks German armor and infantry would seriously damage 1st Armored Division (under nominal command of Major General Ward but in fact still directed by Fredendall) and would push the U.S. and French forces 50 to 85 miles westward to the Western Dorsal. Rommel fervently desired to oust the Allies from Tunisia altogether by continuing the attack against the Americans through the Western Dorsal at Kasserine Pass toward Tébessa.[6] The Axis assault commenced two weeks of almost continuous maneuvering and fighting from Faïd Pass in the east to Djebel el Harma and the Bou Chebka pass in the west, and Thala and Sbiba in the north. Remembered by Americans as the battles of Kasserine Pass, the Axis offensive was not a complete surprise, but the Allied plans and force allocations to meet it were once again tactically incompetent and too weak. Rick Atkinson harshly critiqued the Allied dispositions.

> The folly of the Allied battle plan was clear: after losing Faïd Pass in late January, the Americans should have either recaptured the Eastern Dorsal—at whatever cost—or retired to defensible terrain on the Grand Dorsal. Instead they had dispersed across a vulnerable open plain where the enemy could defeat them in detail.[7]

The tactical failures would be compounded by the technological mismatch between the American armor and the superior German *panzers*.

The Enemy's Intentions

The enemy had been studying how to achieve the destruction of the Americans and drive the Allies out of Tunisia ever since Rommel in November 1942 had first pointed out the advantages of combining his retreating force with Fifth Panzer Army, already in Tunisia, to gain the margin of superiority over the Allies for a drive into Algeria.[8] As Rommel's German-Italian Panzer Army completed its prolonged withdrawal into southern Tunisia, the Axis bridgehead numbers would swell to 190,000 combat soldiers and over 300 tanks, a temporary but substantial advantage of 14 Axis divisions to nine for the Allies. Rommel's German units as they moved into Tunisia were at far less than half strength, with barely 30,000 combat soldiers, but those formations were still formidable.

Rommel and Arnim knew the Axis grasp on Tunisia was tenuous. Their strategic assessment was simple: the high command must either provide enough supplies to the two African armies or abandon Tunisia. "We cannot afford a second Stalingrad,"[iii] Arnim told Rommel. "Right now the Italian fleet could transport us back."[9] The German-Italian Panzer Army had been partly resupplied and some of its losses in men and equipment replaced, but the volume of logistical support to Tunisia had not reached a level which could support either a lengthy offensive or a prolonged defense. On February 4, Rommel sent yet another memorandum to *Comando Supremo*, proposing to leave part of his army at the Mareth Position and use its mobile units to strike Gafsa from the southeast while mobile elements of Arnim's command hit simultaneously from the northeast.[10]

The situation, Rommel contended, was temporarily propitious. The longer the attack was postponed, the greater the likelihood that the British Eighth Army would hamper its full execution and that American forces would become too strong to defeat. On the other hand, should no such attack be attempted, the Allies would be far more likely to succeed in pinning down Arnim's Fifth Panzer Army while striking the German-Italian Panzer Army from both the front and the rear. If the Axis troops in Tunisia were to avoid a diet like the grimly restricted rations in Stalingrad, the bridgehead would have to be widened beyond the current 50-mile coastal strip and supply lines would have to be reopened. Soon Rommel and Arnim would have to defend a 400-mile front against an enemy steadily growing in power, with new tanks in large numbers, more artillery tubes including heavy howitzers, new, more effective anti-tank weapons, and exponentially increasing airpower. In the past month, the Anglo-Americans had flown more than 11,000 air sorties over Tunisia, a foreshadowing of total Allied domination of the air. Allied ground strength would increase quickly from nine divisions to 20.[11]

Rommel, like the Allies, was convinced that the greatest potential threat to the Axis bridgehead in Tunisia was an American lunge from Gafsa toward Gabès to sever the two Axis armies. If the Germans were to survive in Tunisia, they must "break up the American assembly area in southwest Tunisia." The slow pace of Montgomery's pursuit would allow Rommel's troops at least a fortnight to wreak havoc in Tunisia while a rear guard held Eighth Army at Mareth, the old French fortified line near the Libyan border. After crushing the Americans, the German-Italian Panzer Army could swing back south to deal with the British Eighth Army.

Kesselring agreed and the attack plan quickly coalesced. Arnim's Fifth Panzer Army would strike first in Operation *Frühlingswind*—Spring Breeze—a thrust by

---

iii   In the Battle of Stalingrad (August 23, 1942 – February 2, 1943), Germany and its satellites fought the Soviet Union for control of the city of Stalingrad (now Volgograd) in Southern Russia. At the end of the battle, the Red Army launched a gigantic offensive that surrounded and destroyed or captured the entire German 6th Army.

two *panzer* divisions through Faïd Pass on the Americans positioned near Sidi Bou Zid. Spearheaded by more than 200 Mark III and Mark IV tanks, plus a dozen Tigers [*PzkpfW. Mk. VI*], *Frühlingswind* was intended to "weaken the American by destroying some of his elements and thereby confuse and delay his advance." Rommel's German-Italian Panzer Army, including the German Africa Corps (*Deutsche Afrika Korps* or *DAK*), would then strike further south through Gafsa in Operation *Morgenluft*, Morning Air. When reinforced by armored units of 5th Panzer Army, Rommel—who lusted after the vast Allied fuel and supply dumps at Tébessa—would have 160 tanks. "We are going all out for the total destruction of the Americans," Kesselring declared.[12]

The conditions for success, as Rommel saw the situation, were a swift and surprising attack within the next few days; a concentrated assault by superior Axis forces; and a unified command disregarding the boundary between the two Axis Army zones. But a unified command was not a feature of the Axis forces in North Africa. The German high command had decided to establish a unified command only when the presence of two Axis armies in Tunisia made it necessary, and Hitler was not yet ready to implement that plan. Thus, Rommel's prospective offensive was to lack unity of command and control until the Kasserine battles were effectively concluded.

Axis strategy required the extension westward of the bridgehead near Tunis so that it included at least the Djebel Abiod–Medjez el Bab road. The plans for the attacks on Sidi Bou Zid and Gafsa were therefore essentially defensive in concept. If a chance for offensive exploitation by the Axis forces were to arise, the divided Axis command would be handicapped in quickly making decisions to determine objectives to be attacked and the forces to be used. As Eisenhower had already discovered, because the Axis ground forces were coordinated rather than commanded, speedy adjustments across commands to take advantage of opportunities were not likely be made.[13]

Von Arnim had his own plans for the employment of both 10th Panzer Division and 21st Panzer Division. His Fifth Panzer Army also included the Italian 131st "Centauro" Armored Division. Until February 12, Fifth Panzer Army's southern boundary extended to the 34th parallel. German-Italian Panzer Army's area of responsibility was extended on that day northward to include Gafsa, Sened, and Sfax, covering an area that was critical to its security but which it could not defend effectively against strong simultaneous attacks there and at the Mareth position. Von Arnim's objective was to push back that part of the Allied forward line which ran between Pichon and Maknassy, using all his mobile troops not inextricably engaged elsewhere.[14] Rommel in the meantime had devised his own plans for the "Gafsa operation" that required the employment of units controlled by 5th Panzer Army.

Comando Supremo then ordered an attack against the Gafsa area, primarily to destroy Allied forces, and only secondarily to gain territory. In that proposed operation Rommel would command all armored and mobile elements of the two *panzer* armies not committed to operations on other fronts. The 10th Panzer and 21st Panzer Divisions from the northern army and the 15th Panzer Division from the southern force would be supported by the Luftwaffe's *Fliegerkorps Tunis*.[15]

Kesselring, Rommel, and Arnim met on February 9 to discuss in person *Comando Supremo's* orders. They analyzed reconnaissance reports indicating that American units were leaving Gafsa for more northerly stations, and the two army commanders revised their plans. The attack would now consist of an initial operation against Sidi Bou Zid by Fifth Panzer Army, using 10th Panzer and 21st Panzer Divisions, and a later joint attack under Rommel's command against Gafsa by a *Kampfgruppe* taken from the *Deutsche Afrika Korps* and supported by elements of the 21st Panzer Division. *Comando Supremo* revised its directive and Kesselring approved the plans to execute it.[16]

The armored strength of the Axis forces for the attack at Sidi Bou Zid exceeded 200 Mark III and Mark IV *panzers* plus about 12 Mark VI Tigers. The 10th Panzer Division had 110 tanks in four battalions; 21st Panzer Division, 91 tanks in three battalions; and *Division Superga* had an attached German company with several Tigers. By delaying the attack on Gafsa until the elements of the 21st Panzer Division could also take part, a force of some 160 tanks might be deployed there. The armored units to be drawn from southern Tunisia included 53 German and 17 Italian tanks.[17]

The Axis forces were matched by the U.S. 1st Armored Division, which had 202 medium and 92 light tanks in operation, and lighter armored vehicles and artillery that considerably outnumbered those of the attacking force.[18] The American division, if concentrated, could be a formidable opponent in the expected battle. Although some of the new M4 tanks were available in battalion strength, the American medium tanks were still mostly M3 'Grants,' with lighter armor and a main gun of shorter range and lower muzzle velocity than their German antagonists. 1st Armored Division would have to outnumber its opponents to survive, let alone win.[19]

The allocation of Axis mobile forces between the two successive operations was discussed for about a week. Rommel, notwithstanding Axis intelligence reports, argued vehemently that the Allies would make a strong fight at Gafsa. He obtained an assurance that a large part of the 21st Panzer Division and others of Arnim's mobile armored units would be available to him.

The German strike at the southern flank of the British First Army in February therefore began as two separate but related, and only loosely coordinated, operations under different commands. The first was the effort by Arnim to complete his hold on the Eastern Dorsal from Faïd north to Pichon, and to push the Allies well to the west. The second was Rommel's spoiling attack to disperse and destroy the American II Corps in the general vicinity of Gafsa. If the first were successfully completed, the second could begin. Von Arnim planned, after relinquishing the 21st Panzer Division to Rommel, to bring as much as possible of his 10th Panzer

Division northward along the western edge of the Eastern Dorsal to gain full possession of the gaps at Fondouk el Aouareb and Pichon, and drive in the Allied flank north of Pichon. At that time, the German commanders understood that after the operations at Sidi Bou Zid and Gafsa, Fifth Panzer Army was only to engage in reconnaissance toward Sbeïtla and Rommel's force was only to probe toward Fériana.[20]

II Corps Dispositions

At 6:30a.m., Valentine's Day, 1943, 1st Armored Division's CCA, under the command of Brigadier General McQuillin, with the infantry of the 2nd and 3rd Battalions, 168th Infantry Regiment attached, was waiting, if not as ready as it might have been, for the enemy column which came through Faïd Pass. Following II Corps's orders on February 11, the "Lessouda Force" of infantry, tanks, artillery, and tank destroyers, was dug in on and around Djebel Lessouda, north of Sidi Bou Zid. It was commanded by Lieutenant Colonel Waters, now executive officer of the 1st Armored Regiment. Waters had 900 troops for the defense of Djebel Lessouda, including a company of 15 tanks and a four-gun artillery battery. The infantry force comprised the survivors of the shaken 2nd Battalion, 168th Regimental Combat Team under their new commanding officer, Major Moore. 2nd Battalion's Company E and two platoons of Company H were detailed to provide security for CCA's self-propelled artillery. Waters controlled Company G (15 tanks) and Reconnaissance Company, 1st Armored Regiment, Battery B, 91st Field Artillery Battalion (four guns), and one platoon of Company A, 701st Tank Destroyer Battalion (four GMC M3s, half-tracks mounted with 75mm guns).[21]

McQuillin, commanding Combat Command A, had instructed his engineers to lay barbed wire and mines across the entire CCA front, roughly 40 miles. "Hell," observed one bewildered young lieutenant, "there isn't that much barbed wire in all of North Africa."[22] The tanks, tank destroyers, and artillery occupied varying positions on the flat during the day and retired after dark to laagers within the defensive area until just before daylight. The Americans' daily activities, of course, continued to be observed and documented from Axis positions to the east.

On February 12, Moore's infantrymen of the 2nd Battalion, 168th Infantry Regiment fashioned fighting positions in crevices and behind piles of shale along the steep slope fronting the Lessouda position. Moore considered Fredendall's battle plan "excellent to defend against a flood," but not effective for stopping Wehrmacht tanks. Since he had commanded the battalion for barely a week, he kept his assessment to himself. 2nd Battalion's Company E had been detached by McQuillin and placed in positions on the desert floor as a forward picket line, an obsolete artifact of the Civil War that left the infantrymen dangerously exposed in a war of mobile armored fighting vehicles. "Each day the brass shoved [Company E] farther east until it now spanned a five-mile front in the shadow of Faïd Pass, more than an entire battalion should have covered."[23]

Ten miles southeast of Djebel Lessouda and east of Sidi Bou Zid, 2/168's sister unit—the 3rd Battalion of the 168th Infantry Regiment—dug in on Djebel Ksaïra (560m). The GIs entrenched as best they could in the stony soil. Bent like a horseshoe, with the open end facing north toward Highway 14 and Faïd Pass, Ksaïra was shelled daily by enemy howitzers, punctually at 8:00a.m., 1:00p.m., and 6:00p.m. Colonel Drake, CO of 168RCT, had nearly 1,700 troops on Ksaïra, including the band and some soldiers without rifles. The last hot food was served on February 10 and then the men were restricted to cold rations and a single canteen of water per day.

Drake ordered that any soldier leaving the line under fire was to be "killed at once." There was to be no mercy for the enemy, either. "Teach all personnel to hate the Germans and to kill them at every opportunity," he declared to his unit leaders. "I will notify you when I want prisoners taken." The engineers laid mines along the base of Ksaïra. Artillerymen near Lessouda registered[iv] their guns on known features around Faïd. As ordered by Fredendall, but against Drake's better instincts, the Americans sent out nightly reconnaissance patrols that ventured into the Eastern Dorsal, poking at the pass and smaller defiles in the ridgeline. Some patrols got into firefights; some did not return at all. Out on the edge of the American line, in front of Company E [2/168], a single strand of barbed wire was hung with rock-filled cans.[24] How rattling pebbles were to be heard over wind and tank motors is baffling.

McQuillin unreasonably expected the Lessouda Force and 3/168 on Ksaïra to block an Axis attack until a counterattack could be mounted by CCA's mobile armored reserve. Even with the few artillery pieces they had, the infantry placed on the two hills lacked the anti-armor punch to delay a strong combined arms assault for long. CCA's mobile force had about 40 tanks of 3rd Battalion, 1st Armored Regiment, under Lieutenant Colonel Louis V. Hightower, stationed closer to Sidi Bou Zid than the Lessouda Force and 3/168. An artillery observation post on Djebel Lessouda opened communications with the command posts of both Lessouda Force and CCA in Sidi Bou Zid, and a similar arrangement was established by 3/168 on Ksaïra. The 91st Field Artillery Battalion (less Battery B which was with Waters at Lessouda) and 2nd Battalion, 17th Field Artillery Regiment (155mm guns), were placed astride the Sidi Bou Zid–Aïn Rebaou road at the base of Djebel Ksaïra, where they were protected from air attack

---

iv   The procedure of adjusting the fire of guns onto their targets by observation, and recording (hence "registering") the final data of elevation and deflection needed to hit particular targets.

A regiment of the 34th Infantry Division on the Camp Claiborne, Louisiana parade ground, *circa* 1941. Note the soup bowl steel helmets. (U.S. Army photo)

Two 34ID riflemen in a training camp. (Minnesota Military Museum, U.S. Army photo)

34th Infantry Division troops debark on the Belfast docks, January 26, 1942. (U.S. Army photo)

LTG H. E. Franklyn, commander of British troops in Northern Ireland (L) conferring with MG Russell P. Hartle, commander of U.S. Army Northern Ireland Force. (U.S. Army WW2 Signal Corps photograph collection)

34ID troops on meal break in Ireland. (U.S. Army photo)

34ID troops practicing with a 37mm AT gun in Ireland. (U.S. Army photo)

LTC William Darby, Commander, 1st Ranger Infantry Battalion, and former member of the 34th Infantry Division. He often used a motorcycle as a mode of transportation in North Africa. (U.S. Army WW2 Signal Corps Photograph Collection)

MG Charles Wolcott Ryder. (January 16, 1892– August 17, 1960) CG, 34th Infantry Division in the Mediterranean Theater of Operations, and CG, IX Corps in the Pacific Theater of Operations. (U.S. War Department, 1945)

British Army commandos and 34ID Ranger volunteers in Northern Ireland. (U.S. Army photo)

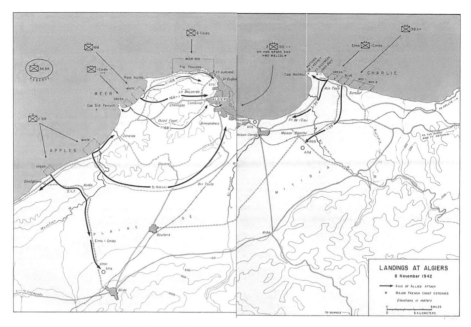

Landings at Algiers. (NWAf, Map 3, pp. 232–233)

The vicinity of the city of Algiers and the western landing beaches, showing Beer White, where 168IR should have landed, and Apples White, 17 miles to the west, where most of the regiment came ashore. (Prepared by the author using Google Earth Pro)

The vicinity of the city of Algiers and the eastern landing beaches, where 39IR, under Ryder's command, hit the beaches. (Prepared by the author using Google Earth Pro)

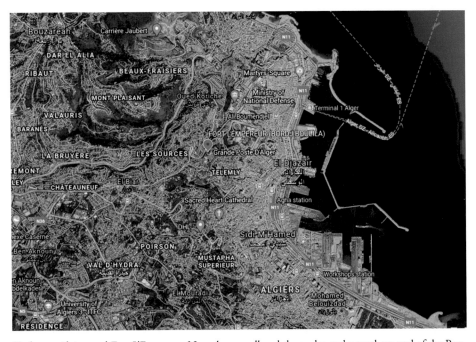

Harbor at Algiers and Fort L'Empereur. Note the seawall and the moles at the southern end of the Port, where Terminal Force landed and made their stand. (Prepared by the author using Google Earth Pro)

Near Algiers, on November 8, 1942, troops of 39RCT hit the beaches near Surcouf behind a large American flag (left), hoping the French Army would not fire on them. (U.S. Army. National Archives and Records Administration, Franklin D. Roosevelt Library, National Archives Identifier: 195301)

Members of the 168th Infantry Regiment prepare a machine-gun position at a U.S. airfield in Algeria soon after landing on November 8, 1942. (U.S. Army. National Archives and Records Administration)

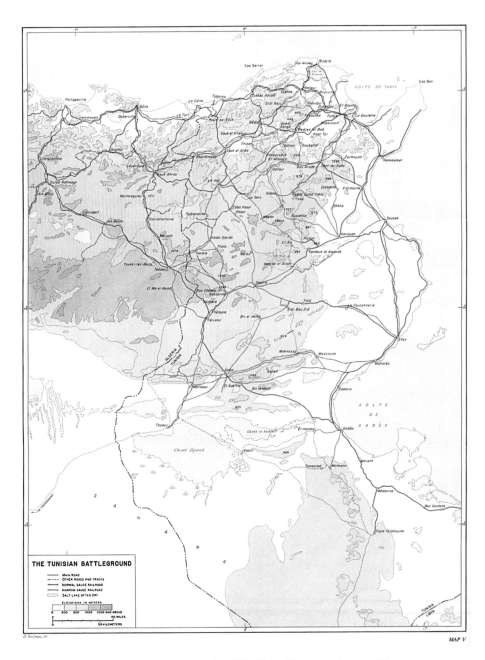

The Tunisian battleground. (NWAf, Map V, map pocket, p. 754)

MG (later LTG) Lloyd Ralston Fredendall, CG, II Corps, Tunisia. (Wikimedia Commons; Ben Weiner. Creative Commons Attribution-Share Alike 4.0)

MG Orlando Ward, Commanding General, 1st Armored Division. (U.S. Department of the Army)

Crew of M-3 Tank #309503, 1st Armored Division, at Souk el Arba, Tunisia, November 23, 1942. (Cooper, U.S. Army Signal Corps (NA-COO-42-211))

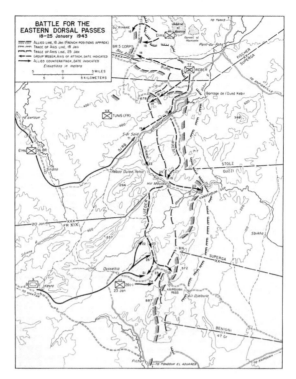

Overview of terrain and opposing forces as they began the battles for the Eastern Dorsal Passes (NWAf, Map 8, p. 375)

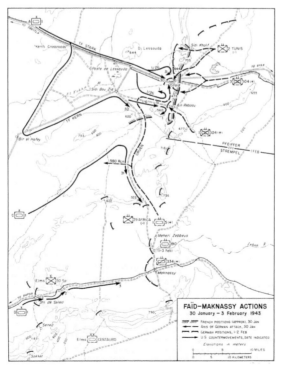

Faïd-Maknassy actions, January 30–February 3, 1943, depicting four days of fighting and frustration for the Allies. (NWAf, Map 9, p.389)

Field Marshal Rommel (left), with General Fritz Bayerlein, confers with Field Marshal Kesselring (right) in North Africa, *circa* late January–early February 1943. (Bundesarchiv, Bild 146-1989-089-00/ CC-BY-SA 3.0)

M4 of Alger's 2nd Bn, 1AR, destroyed at Oued Rouana February 15, 1943. The tank suffered a catastrophic internal ammunition explosion that blew the turret off and collapsed the floor, killing the entire crew. (U.S. Army photo)

M4s of F Company, 2nd Bn, 1AR, destroyed at Oued Rouana while attempting to rescue troops of 168IR at Garet Hadid. The tank in the foreground was hit by a 75mm round. The tank in the background was hit by a 50mm round. None of the deployed 48 tanks returned. (U.S. Army photo)

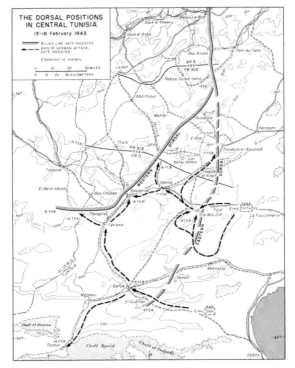

Overview of positions of Allied and Axis forces, and Axis attacks after the fall of Faid Pass. The American forces were too few and too dispersed to defend their extended line. February 13–18, 1943. (NWAf, Map 10, p. 404)

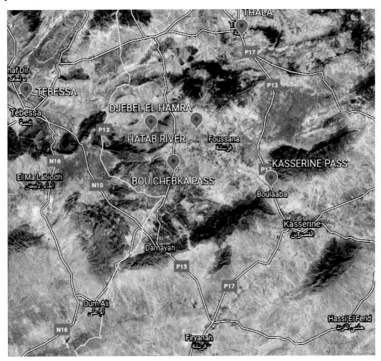

Central Tunisian Battlefield from Tèbessa, Algeria to Kasserine, Tunisia, depicting the relation of Kasserine Pass to Thala, Dj. el Hamra and Bou Chebka, where the Allies stopped the Germans. (Prepared by the author using Google Earth Pro)

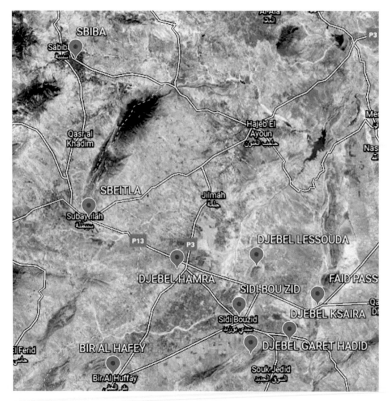

Central Tunisian Battlefield from Sbiba to Faid Pass, showing the scenes of the German victories at Sidi Bou Zid and Sbeitla. 34ID repulsed 21st Pz. Div. at Sbiba (top left). (Prepared by the author using Google Earth Pro)

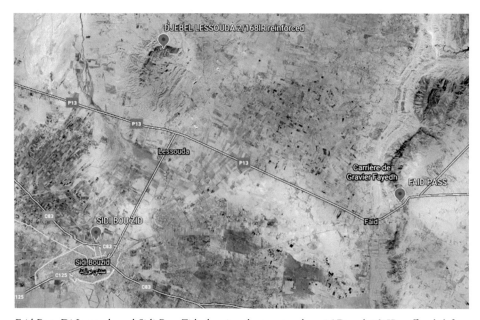

Faid Pass, Dj Lessouda and Sidi Bou Zid, showing the terrain where 1AD and 168IR suffered defeat. 2/168 was on Dj Lessouda (top center). (Prepared by the author using Google Earth Pro)

M3 Grant medium tank of 1st Armored Division advancing to support American forces during the battle at Kasserine Pass, Tunisia, 1943. (U.S. Army Signal Corps WW2 photograph collection)

U.S. 37mm AT gun emplaced near Kasserine Pass. (U.S. Army Signal Corps)

New River, North Carolina testing of the Bantam jeep, 1941. "Cute as Bambi" (as Fussell wrote), the 37mm gun proved woefully inadequate in combat. (U.S. Army Signal Corps. Date 1941, Library of Congress, Prints and Photographs Division, digital ID fsa.8e012)

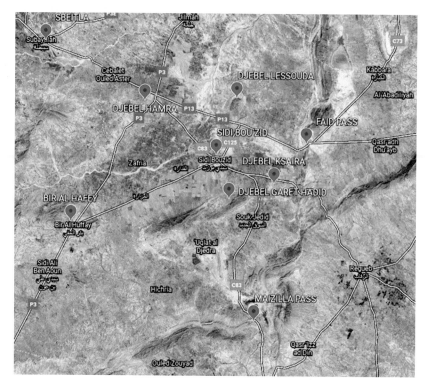

The Sidi Bou Zid battlefield, where the Axis had an unexpectedly easy and overwhelming victory. (Prepared by the author using Google Earth Pro)

The terrain southeast of Sidi Bou Zid, showing Dj Ksaira and Dj Garet Hadid where Drake's troops made their brave but losing stand. (Prepared by the author using Google Earth Pro)

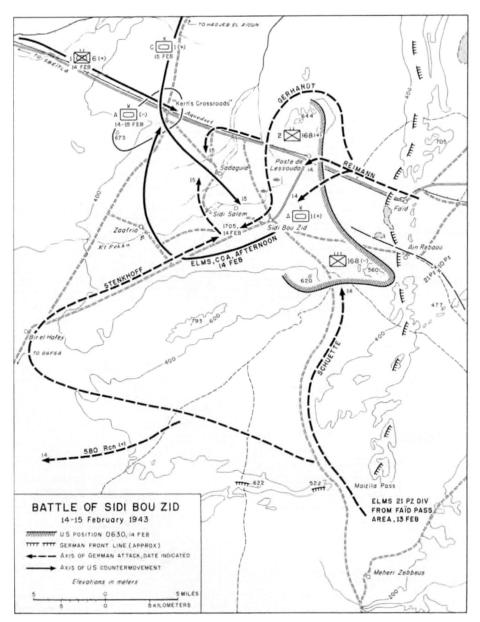

BATTLE OF SIDI BOU ZID
14-15 February 1943

- U.S. POSITION 0630, 14 FEB
- GERMAN FRONT LINE (APPROX.)
- AXIS OF GERMAN ATTACK, DATE INDICATED
- AXIS OF U.S. COUNTERMOVEMENT

Elevations in meters

5 MILES

5 KILOMETERS

Battle of Sidi Bou Zid, February 14–15, 1943. 2/168 was on Hill 644 (Dj Lessouda), north of Sidi Bou Zid, and 3/168 was further south on Dj Ksaira, Hill 420 and Dj Garet Hadid, Hill 560. Note the movements of counterattacking American armored units and of the German *panzer* units that destroyed them (upper left) on the second day. (NWAf, Map 11, p. 408)

LTG Patton (left) confers with General Eisenhower at the beginning of the II Corps offensive in Tunisia, 1943. Note Eisenhower's standard issue canvas puttees, later replaced by improved combat boots. Patton is wearing his riding boots. (U.S. Department of the Army)

From left to right, Brigadier General Theodore Roosevelt Jr., deputy commander 1ID, Major General Terry de la Mesa Allen, CG, 1ID, and Lieutenant General George Patton, CG, U.S. II Corps observe the successful American action against 10th Pz. Div. at el Guettar, March 1943. (U.S. Army; National Archives and Records Administration)

by elements of the 443rd Coast Artillery (AA [Anti-aircraft]) Battalion (SP [self-propelled]).[v]

Soldiers of 3/168, from an observation post on Djebel Ksaïra, saw enemy activity in their front throughout the day on Saturday, February 13. Hostile vehicles in the distance were moving south to the observers' right, on a road east of Djebel Kretchem toward Meheri Zebbeus. The scale of the traffic indicated a large force in motion toward Maknassy. Later that evening, even the roaring northwest wind could not drown out the noise of tank motors and treads to the east. An attack was clearly imminent. Drake ordered the regiment's heavy trucks to move back to Sbeïtla after dark, sent a quartering party to Sbeïtla that afternoon to prepare to receive the vehicles, ordered breakfast to be served at 4:00a.m., and ordered the regiment to "stand to" in the manner of World War I trenches at 5:00a.m. All units were alerted, and the supply vehicles retired to Sbeïtla. At 9:30p.m. on February 13, Lieutenant Colonel Waters conferred at Combat Command A's command post in Sidi Bou Zid with Brigadier General McQuillin and Colonel Peter C. Hains, III, commanding officer of the 1st Armored Regiment. Waters then returned to Djebel Lessouda to await the enemy.[25] At 11:30p.m. Drake was summoned from Ksaïra to McQuillin's CCA command post in the village of Sidi Bou Zid. There, on the eve of a perilous battle that required his attention, he met Eisenhower, who presented Drake a Silver Star for the action at Station de Sened. All night, listening posts on Djebel Ksaïra reported the noise of large tank formations in the regiment's front to the east.[26]

Axis Forces Concentrate into Armored Battle Groups

Fifth Panzer Army's attack against Sidi Bou Zid (Operation *Frühlingswind*) was commanded personally by Arnim's chief of staff, General Heinz Ziegler. General Ziegler's plan required careful timing of the approach march of each battle group to its assault position. His objective was to outflank, surround and annihilate Combat Command A of the 1st Armored Division and to destroy the attached infantry battalions. The 10th Panzer Division (now commanded by von Broich) had moved by night marches from its position near Kairouan, assembled east of Faïd Pass, and now advanced through the pass before daybreak on February 14, to attack along the Faïd–Sbeïtla road.[27] The non-motorized units of the 21st Panzer Division (Hildebrandt), which had been stationed near Faïd since January 31, were assigned to the second phase of the attack against Sidi Bou Zid; meanwhile the 21st Panzer Division's mobile elements had passed along the eastern side of the mountain chain to Maïzila pass, about 20 miles farther south, where they would turn to approach Sidi Bou Zid from the south and southwest.[28]

---

v   M3 half-tracks armed with dual or quad .50 calibre machine-gun mounts.

10th Panzer Division organized three assault groups for its attack on Djebel Lessouda and Sidi Bou Zid: *Kampfgruppen Gerhardt* and *Reimann,* and a reserve force, *Kampfgruppe Lang. Kampfgruppe Gerhardt* began the operation by advancing west through Faïd Pass, then swinging to the northwest around Djebel Lessouda (Hill 644) to neutralize its defenders and to bar intervention from the direction of Sbeïtla or Hadjeb el Aïoun. This force was built around the 7th Panzer Regiment (less a battalion) and a battalion of the 69th Panzer Grenadier Regiment. *Kampfgruppe Reimann* moved along the highway from Faïd to Sbeïtla toward the southeastern corner of Djebel Lessouda, and then turned southwesterly to strike at Sidi Bou Zid. *Kampfgruppe Reimann* included the 86th Panzer Grenadier Regiment (less a battalion), a company[29] of 14 heavy *PzKpfW VI* Tiger Is and a platoon of towed 88mm dual-purpose guns, as well as supporting infantry, engineers, and artillery. The reserve, *Kampfgruppe Lang,* consisted of the 10th Motorcycle Battalion reinforced by armored engineers, an anti-tank gun platoon and two towed 88mm dual-purpose gun detachments. Most of the artillery of both the 10th and 21st Panzer Divisions was positioned in the hills east of Faïd to support the German infantry attack.[30]

21st Panzer Division also organized itself into battle groups, each having a battalion of *panzers,* supported by armored infantry mounted on armored personnel carriers, organic artillery, and anti-aircraft guns. *Kampfgruppe Schuette* comprised Headquarters, 104th Panzer Grenadier Regiment and Headquarters, 5th Panzer Regiment. *Kampfgruppe Schuette* was first to open the Maïzila pass for the main body of the division, and then would turn north to attack Sidi Bou Zid, driving the Americans back to the village and containing them there. Meanwhile, *Kampfgruppe Stenkhoff,* reinforced by a second battalion of tanks, and screened on its southern flank by the 580th Reconnaissance Battalion (reinforced), would make a wide flanking maneuver west to Bir el Hafey, about 25 miles across country from Maïzila Pass. From Bir el Hafey, *Kampfgruppe Stenkhoff* was to swing back to the northeast and bear down on Sidi Bou Zid from the southwest. That movement would enable *Kampfgruppe Stenkhoff* to join forces with units of the 10th Panzer Division, *Kampfgruppe Schuette,* and the nonmobile elements located at Aïn Rebaou pass. Together those units were to surround the American forces in and around Sidi Bou Zid and destroy them piecemeal. Another force was to remove any irksome Americans who might be on Djebel Garet Hadid (620m) and put an end to its usefulness as an observation post.[31]

The Axis operation against Gafsa (Operation *Morgenluft*) was planned and conducted by the *Deutsche Afrika Korps.* A composite German-Italian force in division strength consisting of infantry and armored units supported by artillery, anti-aircraft weapons, and other detachments, *Kampfgruppe DAK* was commanded by Colonel Kurt Freiherr von Liebenstein, formerly commanding officer of the 164th Light Africa Division.[32] *Kampfgruppe DAK* was first to join mobile Italian units near El Guettar and then move against Gafsa from the southeast. Other mobile elements were to be drawn from the 21st Panzer Division in the area of Sidi Bou Zid to reinforce the *DAK* for its drive on Gafsa. The objective was the Gafsa basin, but Rommel constantly had in mind the possibility to exploit as far as those tempting Allied supply depots at Tébessa.[33]

CHAPTER 16

Combat Command A and the 168th Infantry Regiment at Sidi Bou Zid

More than 100 10th Panzer Division tanks had moved south toward Faïd Pass undetected by Allied air reconnaissance. American scouts had reported that a small gorge below Faïd Pass was "impassable for armored vehicles"; they had not discovered the enemy engineers re-grading the trail.[i] Lieutenant Colonel Waters in his rocky den on Djebel Lessouda had sent a patrol with a radio to Faïd Pass, but the scouts stopped three miles short of the Eastern Dorsal range. "I didn't go out to check them," Waters later admitted. "My error." The patrols soon heard a faint rumble from the direction of the pass, the sound of massed tanks. The noise was reported and noted; some CCA supply vehicles were sent to the supposed safety of the not-too-distant rear.[1]

Elements of the 86th Panzer Grenadier Regiment and the 7th Panzer Regiment emerged from Faïd Pass about 6:30a.m. on February 14. That morning the plain west of Faïd was covered in mist and fog. As the Germans turned northwestward to go around the north side of Djebel Lessouda they encountered and attacked, as they had planned and expected based on earlier observations, some of the patrolling tanks of Company G, 1st Armored Regiment, under command of Major Norman Parsons. Early in the action Major Parsons' tank was knocked out, and all radio communications with Waters at Lessouda were lost. The early morning haze obscured the tank fight from the view of the infantry on Djebel Lessouda.[2] Now the American field commanders on and near Djebel Lessouda were deaf, mute, and blind, so they did not request a prepared artillery barrage on Faïd Pass.[3]

The tanks of 10th Panzer Division drove from the Eastern Dorsal onto the plain. Having watched the Americans' routine each day for a week, the Germans knew exactly where to find them. One astonished sergeant likened the noise to "half of the Krupp Iron Works moving out of the German Ruhr Valley." The enemy proceeded to use on a smaller scale the sweeping envelopment tactics already familiar to the

---

i   The Americans learned this lesson the hard way and would benefit from it. The Germans made the same mistake in the Alban Hills of central Italy where in June, 1944 U.S. Army engineers graded a mountain goat track into a road for tanks that would lead to Rome.

world from the early annihilating battles in the Soviet Union during the summer of 1941.[4] Three miles east of Djebel Lessouda, the attackers divided. A group of 80 tanks and half-tracks of *Kampfgruppe Gerhardt* steered north and then west to encircle Djebel Lessouda, isolating some CCA tanks and the infantry troops of 2/168 under Lieutenant Colonel Waters. The other two 10th Panzer battle groups turned south towards Sidi Bou Zid. Enemy scouts seized four ambulances, each jammed with wounded GIs; most of the medical detachment of the 168th Infantry and the collecting company of the 109th Medical Battalion were captured with the loss of 100 men, including ten physicians.[5]

CCA headquarters was in Sidi Bou Zid with a company of tanks from Lieutenant Colonel Hightower's 3rd Battalion, 1st Armored Regiment. The Headquarters Company of 168RCT was in the regimental command post in an olive grove about mile and a half farther east from the village. Colonel Drake and the 3rd Battalion of 168RCT were on and around Djebel Ksaïra about four and one-half miles east of the 168RCT command post. CCA's artillery, including the 155mm howitzers of 17FA Battalion, was out on the plain between the 168RCT command post and Djebel Ksaïra.[6]

CCA headquarters quickly became aware that a tank battle was in progress west of the Faïd Pass, but its immediate significance and the enemy's strength were uncertain. "To clear up the situation," CCA ordered Colonel Hains, commanding 1AR, to deploy Company H, 2nd Battalion, and Company I, 3rd Battalion, 1st Armored Regiment (M3 'Grants') and most of Company A, 701st Tank Destroyer Battalion (GMC M3s, 75mm guns on half-track chassis) by road from Sidi Bou Zid to Poste de Lessouda. As those units started forward, they were bombed by the first of several Axis air strikes in the area that day. Then observers on Djebel Lessouda warned the armored force that about 20 *PzKpfW IV*s were at Poste de Lessouda, in addition to the enemy fighting Parsons' Company G, 2/1AR, near the pass. The American armored force under Colonel Hightower came within sight and range of the enemy a few minutes later and was fired upon by towed 88mm dual-purpose guns and by a platoon[7] of Mark VI Tiger tanks, also mounting 88mm guns. Hightower's tanks were completely outranged, and their return fire was ineffective either to drive off or to destroy the German tanks and guns. The Americans on the firing line realized with horror the strength and firepower superiority of the Axis forces attacking Sidi Bou Zid. Their higher headquarters, however, were still in doubt about the relative proportions of the U.S. and German forces engaged.[8]

Two groups of German tanks and infantry closed on Djebel Lessouda from the north and east. Colonel Drake, watching through his field glasses from Djebel Ksaïra, counted 83 enemy tanks in front of Lessouda. There were flashes of gun fire as the two German groups shot directly into the Americans on Lessouda. The enemy fire destroyed all the U.S. tanks and several self-propelled guns attached to Lieutenant Colonel Waters' command. Company E of the 2nd Battalion, 168th Infantry Regiment, in foxholes on the desert floor in front of Lessouda, was immediately overrun. Drake later wrote that the "men from that company said that… enemy tanks would put a track in the fox hole, turn around on them and crush the soldier into the ground."[9]

When the first wave of 80 German tanks and half-tracks had looped north around Djebel Lessouda at dawn, the bad visibility and uncertainty about the identity of the approaching vehicles initially persuaded Major Moore to have his 900 infantrymen hold their fire. Colonel Hains radioed Waters from Sidi Bou Zid. "There must be something going on," Hains said in understatement. "There is an awful lot of firing out there in front of you now." Better visibility and dire reports from the routed forces to the east soon clarified the American predicament. By 8:30a.m., German tank commanders stood on their tank turrets out of rifle range, scanning Lessouda with field glasses. The *panzers* then systematically raked every visible target on the hill with main gun fire. An enemy column led by motorcycle troops pressed up the lower eastern slopes through a narrow *wadi*.[ii] At a range of 300 yards, Moore gave the command for 2/168 to fire. A deluge of massed rifle, BAR (Browning Automatic Rifle) and light machine-gun fire poured down on the enemy from the rocks. The Germans fell back, leaving their dead and wounded. Two Wehrmacht officers and six enlisted men were taken prisoner. At noon, the enemy assaulted again, this time attacking up the southern face where Waters' command half-track was hidden in a gulch. Grenadiers in *feldgrau* battle dress darted through the olive trees and tuft grass below. Unable to reach Moore by radio to warn him of the threat from the south, Waters sent his driver up the hill to find him. A few minutes later the soldier stumbled back, bleeding from a hole through his chest inflicted by one of 2/168's own riflemen. Waters wrapped him in a bedroll with two shots of morphine and stayed with him until he died. Moore was now marooned with his infantry on the upper slope. About 4:00p.m. Waters was discovered and captured by German troops, placed in a motorcycle sidecar, and driven through Faïd Pass to eventual incarceration in a Bavarian prison camp.[10]

By 9:00a.m., the enemy's strength on the western side of Djebel Lessouda was already 39 Mark IV *panzers* and four of the new Mark VI Tigers, accompanied by mobile infantry in armored carriers. This force moved gradually southward toward the road from Faïd to Sbeïtla, firing continuously on the slopes of Djebel Lessouda as it passed. Hightower, warned of the approach of this second force which might cut him off, redirected Company H, 3rd Battalion, 1st Armored Regiment, to slow the enemy's advance by fire and maneuver. Lieutenant Colonel Charles P. Summerall, Jr.'s 91st Field Artillery Battalion, less Battery B, which had been in the path of the first attack and was now about to be caught again, from the rear, also opposed the northern prong of the enemy attack by fire. Hightower started the fight with

---

ii   In Arabic, "*wadi*" generally means a gully, arroyo or shallow valley created by stream erosion but that is usually dry except when it has rained, common in desert areas of North Africa and Western Asia.

47 tanks. Although greatly outranged and outnumbered, his crews fought bravely against the more effective German tanks. By mid-afternoon, all but seven of his tanks had been destroyed. During the battle, some American artillerymen panicked and abandoned their guns and posts. German tanks surrounding Ksaïra thrust forward toward Sidi Bou Zid and captured a reconnaissance company, rendering the 1st Armored Division's Reconnaissance Battalion impotent to rescue Drake's men on Djebel Ksaïra or to counterattack. The surviving American reconnaissance units withdrew and ran for Sbeïtla.[11] American armor losses were heavy, and, in the last hour of the morning, the unequal contest ended when Hightower withdrew southwestward. Of 52 CCA M4 medium tanks in action near Sidi Bou Zid, only six would survive the day.[12]

Axis dive bombers and fighter-bombers bombed and strafed the Americans between 10:00 and 11:00a.m. in support of enemy ground attacks on Sidi Bou Zid from Faïd village and Aïn Rebaou Pass. The ground assaults pinned down General McQuillin's forces and permitted the German armored pincers to close in on Sidi Bou Zid from the northwest and southwest. CCA now recognized that the enemy's drive was too powerful for the defenders, but McQuillin held in place under Ward's orders as the situation deteriorated. McQuillin ordered the 2nd Battalion, 17th Field Artillery, to move from its exposed positions east of Sidi Bou Zid to an area southwest of the village, but as it moved back by batteries, enemy dive bombers like vultures repeatedly struck and destroyed it.[13]

Zeigler's charge from Faïd Pass was now strengthened by the 21st Panzer Division's debouchement from Maïzilla Pass 20 miles south. During the late afternoon of February 13, the mobile main elements of 21st Panzer Division had moved southward to Maïzila Pass. Those were the vehicles the American observers on Ksaïra had seen. After darkness on February 13, 21st Panzer Division started through the pass. The first elements of *Kampfgruppe Schuette* followed by the 5th Panzer Regiment marched over a path through a minefield and emerged from Maïzila Pass shortly after 6:00a.m. on February 14. At 9:40a.m., Company C, 81st Reconnaissance Battalion, reported to 1st Armored Division that 20 unidentified vehicles were moving away from Maïzila Pass, ten going west and ten turning north toward Sidi Bou Zid.[14] The enemy was moving to positions to take CCA and the 168IR in a double envelopment. At 1:45p.m., half a dozen Tigers attached to 10th Panzer Division passed through Sidi Bou Zid's northern outskirts. At 5:05p.m., tanks from the 21st Panzer Division in the south and those from 10th Panzer Division in the north met two miles east of Sidi Bou Zid on Highway 125. The violent encirclement of the Americans on the hills east of Sidi Bou Zid took less than 12 hours.[15]

On Djebel Ksaïra the battle went badly from the first for Drake and his men. While the battle of Djebel Lessouda was developing, observers on Ksaïra spotted a large group of vehicles, including *panzers*, coming toward Sidi Bou Zid from the southeast. Then it was reported that CCA's artillery and the guns of 17th FA

Battalion near Djebel Lessouda were withdrawing to the rear. Drake later wrote that the withdrawal of the artillery precipitated what he characterized as "a rout in some cases." He called McQuillin at 8:00a.m. on a field phone to report the situation and the panic of some of the troops. McQuillin said to Drake: "You are on the spot. Take command and stop it." Drake inquired: "You mean for me to take command of all troops in the area?" McQuillin replied: "Yes."[16] It was already too late. The imminent arrival of the 21st Panzer Division from the south precluded any chance for Drake to "stop it."

Martin Blumenson, one of the U.S. Army's official historians of World War II and a famous chronicler of the war in North Africa, wrote of Drake in the ensuing stand of the 168IR at Ksaïra and Garet Hadid that, "It takes one hell of a soldier to look good in defeat." Drake and the more than a thousand men under his command were about to fight a good fight, a "supreme moment, a moment of agony, but a moment above all of glory" for Drake and his regiment.[17]

Drake knew now that his regiment's position on Djebel Ksaïra was untenable. Enemy tanks near Sidi Bou Zid appeared to be deliberately moving over slit trenches to crush the remaining defenders. The soldiers of several American units around Djebel Ksaïra attempted to leave for the rear but their officers cudgeled them back into the line.[18] About half an hour after his first conversation with McQuillin, while Drake was watching the battles to the north at Lessouda and to the west at Sidi Bou Zid, Lieutenant Colonel Gerald Line, executive officer of 168RCT, came to Drake and said: "General McQuillin is on the telephone and said he is pulling out and you are to stay here." Drake understood that 168RCT had been tasked to hold its positions to the last man. He went to the phone to speak personally to McQuillin, but the phone line was dead. Signalmen under First Lieutenant Edgar P. Moschel reported that the telephone at the far end of the line was simply gone. The CCA command post had temporarily moved seven miles west, then joined the absconders heading toward Sbeïtla.[19]

At about noon, an outpost reported the enemy column approaching from the south to attack Djebel Ksaïra. Drake knew that enemy tanks already had passed north of Djebel Lessouda and moved west to cut the road junction seven miles west of Lessouda, blocking any attempt to exit Sidi Bou Zid to the west. Morale among the defenders on Djebel Ksaïra plummeted. Some officers pleaded with Drake to withdraw as CCA had done, but Drake was a tough old professional soldier. He decided to attack, rather than to withdraw, by taking higher ground across the highway west of Ksaïra. With nearly a thousand troops already dug in on Djebel Ksaïra, Drake saw advantage in moving about half of his men, then waiting in *wadis* on the base of Ksaïra, onto Djebel Garet Hadid, a higher ridge four miles west of Ksaïra.[20] The enemy was approaching the position of 2/168 from both north and south. Drake ordered the soldiers of the regimental band, under Second Lieutenant Seymour R. Bolten, to lead the advance as scouts along the road to Garet Hadid.

Drake and his men on the hill had not been wholly abandoned by other Americans near Ksaïra. Captain William R. A. Kleysteuber, commander of Company A, 16th Engineer Battalion, 1st Armored Division, reported to Drake with orders from McQuillin to render any assistance possible. Company E, 2/168, commanded by Captain Donald L. Wilkinson, had been relieved of providing security to CCA's artillery, and the survivors now returned to Drake's command. Drake ordered both those units, and Headquarters Company, 168RCT, under Captain Bernard U. Bolton, with several hundred men picked up from other units, to follow the band members, advance to Garet Hadid, and there to secure and fortify the place.[21]

On the way to Garet Hadid, Drake, personally leading the provisional force, discovered an orphaned platoon of M3 light tanks; the lieutenant in command announced that he had orders to withdraw. Drake told the lieutenant firmly that he, Drake, was now in command of all troops in the vicinity, and that the tank platoon was now subordinate to him. He instructed the lieutenant to have his tanks join the advance to Garet Hadid. On arriving at Garet Hadid, the first platoon, Company C, 109th Engineers, under First Lieutenant Royal I. Lee, mined the road leading northeast past the hill; Company A, 16th Engineers laid another minefield at the southeastern end. Meanwhile, the remnants of Company A, 81st Reconnaissance Battalion, Captain Otto C. Amerell commanding, joined the force on Garet Hadid, along with the Cannon Company of the 39th Infantry Regiment, Captain "Buck" Waters commanding, and seven 37mm towed anti-tank guns that the engineers of Company A, 16th Engineer Battalion had brought with them. Drake's adjutant, Major Merle A. Meacham, had made a head count and reported that about 950 men were now present on Garet Hadid, of whom about 300, men from artillery, armor, and service and support units, were not armed. Drake found that he had ten officers from his regimental headquarters, three officers and 11 men of the medical detachment, a single officer and 53 men of the attached platoon of engineers, 39 members of the regimental band, seven officers and 201 men of Company E, 2/168, an officer and 40 machine gunners and mortarmen of Company H, 2/168, and four officers and 89 men of the attached Cannon Company of the 39th Infantry. Additionally, he had about 150 engineers who were laying a minefield across the road coming from the Maïzila Pass, along with 40 survivors of the 1st Armored Division's reconnaissance battalion. Some of the unarmed men scrounged firearms and ammunition from damaged vehicles and dead or wounded soldiers, but many remained without personal weapons. The riflemen, tankers, artillerymen, musicians, cooks, bandsmen, and clerks took positions on the barren rock.[22]

The road from Maïzila pass to Sidi Bou Zid, Highway 83, ran between Djebel Ksaïra on the east, where most of 3/168 was dug in, and Djebel Garet Hadid on the west where Drake and his mixed force of about 950 men were now positioned. Drake's soldiers had completed the occupation of Garet Hadid and had just deployed for the defense when an advance element of *Kampfgruppe Schuette* came within gun range. There was a small exchange of fire, then the enemy deployed and began a siege of the hill from all sides.²³ The main body of *Kampfgruppe Schuette* soon arrived and joined in the siege by late afternoon.²⁴ Meanwhile, *Kampfgruppe Stenkhoff*, the main force of the 21st Panzer Division, pushed west from Maïzila pass along the northern edge of Djebel Meloussi (Hill 622), screened to the west and south by the enemy's 580th Reconnaissance Battalion. Except for muddy *wadis* and rough dips in the plain or mechanical failures, there was no interruption or American opposition to Stenkhoff's advance. *Kampfgruppe Stenkhoff* reached Bir el Hafey on the Gafsa–Sidi Bou Zid highway about noon, assembled, and at 1:45p.m. marched in force northeastward along the highway toward Sidi Bou Zid, some 18 miles distant.²⁵

Ward's headquarters near Sbeïtla received frantic messages from the units engaged with the enemy and was making regular battle reports to II Corps headquarters near Tébessa. The successive appearances of the enemy's armored groups left CCA and 1AD in doubt about the total numbers and unit identifications of the Axis forces. 1AD reported CCA's loss of artillery and identified Mark VI Tigers among the enemy tanks. Ward requested more artillery. In response, II Corps ordered a mere battery of the 68th Armored Field Artillery Battalion and two platoons of Company A, 805th Tank Destroyer Battalion, to move from Fériana to Sbeïtla.²⁶ At Speedy Valley, the fog of war was thickened by wishful thinking.

Eisenhower and Truscott had returned to Speedy Valley from Sidi Bou Zid at dawn on Sunday morning. After resting for two hours in a sleeping bag spread across a cot, Eisenhower conferred with Truscott, Fredendall and Anderson. Information was sketchy and imprecise, they admitted, but the enemy attack appeared to be a local affair. "There was no reason to think that McQuillin would not be able to hold on his own," Truscott later wrote. But Anderson now wanted to evacuate Gafsa in the far south as a precaution, retracting the Allied right flank to the more defensible Grand (Western) Dorsal. Eisenhower agreed.²⁷

The arrival of the 21st Panzer Division closed the trap on the GIs of 3/168 holding Djebel Ksaïra and Drake's mixed force occupying Djebel Garet Hadid. After *Kampfgruppe Stenkhoff* had marched cross-country to the west to the Gafsa–Sidi Bou Zid road, it had turned up the highway to hit Sidi Bou Zid from the southwest as planned. *Kampfgruppe Schuette* had turned to its right after clearing Maïzila Pass and had driven straight north along Highway 83, into the gap between Djebel Garet Hadid and Djebel Ksaïra. The Americans engaged the Germans in the flats between the hill masses all afternoon and into the evening. American troops on the two hills threw enough firepower at the attackers to slow down *Kampfgruppe Schuette*'s advance six miles from Sidi Bou Zid, but enemy gunners answered with artillery, mortars, and direct *panzer* fire, and they kept coming. "It seems like everything the enemy uses is designed to harass a man," one American private concluded.²⁸

At 2:00p.m. Drake was able to reach McQuillin by radio. He asked for permission to pull his men off Djebel Ksaïra and Garet Hadid. In textbook bureaucratic fashion, Brigadier General McQuillin passed the request to Major General Ward, who relayed it to Lieutenant General Fredendall, who was 100 miles away from the battlefield, where the fighting appeared on maps and papers less dangerous than reality warranted. After eight minutes, McQuillin was told: "Too early to give Drake permission to withdraw." McQuillin radioed the message to Garet Hadid: "Continue to hold your position." Drake recognized that he had considerable strength on Hadid and Ksaïra. He thought he might be able to hold out but not without help. His force would need supplies, especially water and ammunition, and an Allied counterattack by strong forces capable of driving off the enemy either to hold the ground or even to evacuate. He wrote a hasty note on British-issue toilet tissue to Ward at 1AD headquarters.

> Enemy surrounds 2d Battalion located on Mt. Lessouda since 0730 this morning. Forty tanks known to be around them.... All artillery pulled out at 1300, still trying to locate them. McQuillin's headquarters pulled out at 1100 to southwest, did not notify except by message. Talked to McQuillan [sic] by radio and he said help had been requested. Germans have absolute superiority, ground and air. Have stopped retreating tank destroyer unit and am attempting to hold my command post position. Unless help from air and armor comes, immediately, Infantry will lose immeasurably.[29]

Drake gave the message to a brave young lieutenant named Marvin E. Williams and told him to take it to 1AD's headquarters. Williams, "feeling like an Indian scout carrying a message from Custer," slipped off the hill and careened cross country in a jeep to Sbeïtla. Just before nightfall, he delivered Drake's message.[30]

Ward's grasp of the fighting around Sidi Bou Zid was blurred by distance, delays, incomplete reports, his superior's opinions, and the inevitable chaos of battle. He just did not realize how grave the situation actually was.[31] About mid-day, however, 1AD received reports from CCA that Hightower's 3rd Battalion, 1st Armored Regiment had lost about half its tanks. The German formation south of Sidi Bou Zid was characterized as very substantial. Ward, who had disdainfully described the dispositions east of Sidi Bou Zid to Eisenhower only the night before, and who had heard Robinett's fervent criticism of the dangerous placement of the American infantry, now perceived the crisis with growing alarm. Not only had Djebel Lessouda been surrounded, but Colonel Drake's troops were besieged on Djebel Ksaïra and Djebel Garet Hadid. All elements of CCA in and around Sidi Bou Zid were being driven out and would have to move without delay to avoid being caught and flayed on both flanks. The armored units could not assist the infantry on the hills. Ward authorized Combat Command A to pull out, and by 2:05p.m., CCA's command post was already seven miles southwest of Sidi Bou Zid. Hightower's surviving tanks staunchly covered the withdrawal, fighting off *Kampfgruppe Stenkhoff* on the southwestern flank. 1AD nonetheless ordered 168th Infantry Regiment and the other troops with Drake to remain on the hills until it could be relieved by a counterattack the next morning. The infantry could not have withdrawn in daylight in any event. The surrounded GIs would have been quickly overwhelmed.[32]

At dusk, the survivors of CCA, without the trapped 168th Infantry Regiment battalions and the other troops Drake had herded into his command, began arriving at a rally point near Djebel Hamra (673m), where they reorganized to defend Sbeïtla.[33] Some troops had fought bravely and well. Many unnerved, stunned, and bone-tired soldiers were not fighting at all. The gallantry of Hightower's 3rd Battalion, which made the fighting retreat through Sidi Bou Zid at the cost of losing most of its tanks and their crews, coupled with the obstinate defense by 2nd Battalion, 168th Infantry Regiment at Djebel Ksaïra and Garet Hadid, had allowed hundreds of McQuillin's CCA GIs to escape. Several thousand others were trapped, captured or dead. Of the five battalions initially controlled by CCA, two were surrounded and three were on the way to destruction. Nine German battalions had smashed into the Americans. Although those nine barely added up to a full-strength standard *panzer* division, among them were two of the Wehrmacht's most renowned formations filled with tough and experienced fighters: the 10th Panzer Division, spearhead of General Heinz Guderian's breakthrough at Sedan in May 1940, and the 21st Panzer Division, perhaps the most experienced desert fighters on Earth. Meanwhile the second phase of the Axis offensive, *Morgenluft*—Rommel's attack in the south toward Gafsa—had yet to begin.[34]

By 3:30p.m., General Ziegler considered that his initial mission had been achieved. He ordered the 10th Panzer Division to reconnoiter aggressively to Hadjeb el Aïoun, 25 miles north of Sidi Bou Zid. He directed the 21st Panzer Division to assemble for a rapid move against Gafsa, probably starting at noon next day. But he also ordered both divisions to use some of their nonmobile units to finish off the fragmented but stubborn American units around Sidi Bou Zid. The tenacious defense of Djebel Lessouda, Djebel Ksaïra, and Djebel Garet Hadid by the soldiers of 168IR and the other men with them was more than irritating. The American infantry seriously hindered the execution on schedule of Operation *Frühlingswind*. Now the enemy was compelled to lay siege to the hills to destroy the doughty American garrisons, losing even more precious time. Still, the reality was that the 2nd and 3rd Battalions of 168RCT were surrounded, could not be reinforced, and were unable to move. The possibility of an American counterattack, however, deterred Ziegler from immediately moving his forces further west.[35]

Like the French, the American units in the Sidi Bou Zid sector were not equipped with weapons suited to a successful counterattack on a fearsome enemy who employed late-model medium and heavy tanks with high-velocity guns and armor-piercing munitions, 88mm dual-purpose guns, and other modern arms. While the Americans were better equipped than the French in their armament, especially artillery, artillery fire control, and mechanized mobility, that firepower and mobility were denied them around Sidi Bou Zid by the enemy's proximity and superior firepower. That situation could be corrected only by bringing sufficient additional firepower to the battlefield to drive away the enemy.

To make the next day's counterattack and to attempt to rescue the men on Djebel Lessouda, Djebel Ksaïra, and Djebel Garet Hadid, Ward deployed from Hadjeb el Aïoun what remained of Stack's Combat Command C. He also persuaded Fredendall to obtain the transfer of control by First Army to 1AD of CCB's 2nd Battalion, 1st Armored Regiment, led by Lieutenant Colonel James D. Alger. First Army agreed and the arrangements were completed in the afternoon of February 14. Alger's battalion took to the road that afternoon using the new 22-mile route between El Ala and Hadjeb el Aïoun which had been constructed recently by American engineers, including troops from 34ID.[36]

Soon after 5:00p.m. *Kampfgruppe Stenkhoff* contacted elements of the 10th Panzer Division west of Sidi Bou Zid, completing the envelopment. By nightfall, the village was firmly held by the Germans. Those Americans who could escape had withdrawn toward Sbeïtla. The others were isolated, trapped on Djebel Lessouda, Djebel Ksaïra, and Djebel Garet Hadid. Abandoned, burning, or broken-down vehicles were scattered across the desert west of Sidi Bou Zid. Combat Command A's known losses were severe: six killed, 22 wounded, 134 missing, 44 tanks, all but two tank destroyers, nine 105mm guns of the 91st Armored Field Artillery Battalion, and all the 155mm guns of the 2nd Battalion, 17th Field Artillery Regiment.[37]

Shock and disbelief permeated the American command hierarchy.

> A battlefield bromide cautions: "Never believe a straggler and rarely believe a casualty." Both breeds had begun trickling into 1st Armored Division headquarters, and their collective tale of prodigious German strength fell on deaf ears. Colonel Louis Hightower, CO, 3rd Bn., 1st AR, 1AD, whose Sherman tank "Texas," after killing four panzers, had been shot from under him that day along with most of the rest of his battalion in a gallant but futile fight, arrived at Ward's headquarters in a Sbeïtla cactus patch on Sunday night. He was, a witness reported, "badly used up and declared that his battalion had been wiped out." Hightower confirmed that Tigers were involved in the attack along with scores of other panzers. Messages from Djebel Lessouda and Djebel Ksaïra provided detailed if fragmentary intelligence about enemy tanks, guns and troop concentrations.[38]

The enemy had rapidly consolidated its striking power and its forces on the battlefield were much stronger than the American hierarchy had yet envisaged. Every level of American command lacked an accurate knowledge and appreciation of the size and firepower of the attacking formations. Consequently, 1st Armored Division had requested, and II Corps had sent, what would yet again prove to be inadequate reinforcements. General Welvert saw the situation much more clearly. When II Corps demonstrated its leisurely pace of decision making, the irrepressible Welvert tried to expedite leadership action on February 14 through French channels at Anderson's First Army headquarters. He vehemently requested chief of staff, French XIX Corps to have First Army send all of Combat Command B to Sbeïtla at once. First Army flatly dismissed him, refusing to release CCB from Maktar for commitment near Sbeïtla based on the situation as then understood by the British.

Incompetent and inexperienced senior leadership, communications failures, inadequate armaments, bad intelligence estimates, and the confusion of the real-time battle situation slowed the Allied decision cycle. No unit of the 10th Panzer Division had yet been identified in the Sidi Bou Zid attack, in large part because so few American soldiers at Sidi Bou Zid were any longer physically or mentally able to make accurate reports. The total number of tanks, thought to be from 90 to 130, might be the 21st Panzer Division and the separate 190th Panzer Battalion only, without any from the 10th Panzer Division. If that calculation were correct, First Army reasoned, the 10th Panzer Division was still opposite the French XIX Corps preparing for an attack there, and Combat Command B would be needed. British and American generals did not even conjecture that the Germans, accepting the risk to achieve the goal of forcing a general Allied retreat out of Tunisia, had rapidly moved and concentrated all their available forces into powerful mobile armored fists quite capable of overwhelming the Allied formations at the spearpoint.[39]

Eisenhower left II Corps headquarters late in the morning of February 14, after his nap and meeting. With Truscott and others, he drove to AFHQ in Constantine, sight-seeing at the ruins of the Emperor Trajan's second century city at Timgad en route. He and his senior officers did not then believe that the attack at Sidi Bou Zid was the enemy's spearpoint. He had agreed to hold Allied strength in central Tunisia and to evacuate Gafsa rather than withdraw to more defensible positions in the Western Dorsal. But dire reports of the battles continued to arrive at AFHQ's advance command post and AFHQ at last concluded from the enemy's evident strength that the Allies could not successfully defend Gafsa. The evacuation of Gafsa was accomplished during the night of February 14–15 in a dusty cloud of confusion, shouted orders, and desperately excited activity. The troops at Gafsa pulled back to Fériana.[40]

II Corps pulled in its southwestern flank from Gafsa and moved reinforcements from north of Sbeïtla. First Army shifted the northern boundary of II Corps's operational zone. After midnight, February 14–15, Thala (north of Kasserine), Sbiba (north of Sbeïtla), and Fondouk el Aouareb gap were assigned to the sector of the French Lieutenant General Koeltz's XIX Corps.[41] All scheduled reliefs of French units were suspended. The 133rd Regimental Combat Team, 34ID, moved to cover the gap between Djebel Trozza (997m) and Djebel el Abe'id (697m), south of El Ala. The road leading into Sbiba from the east was blocked with a French force, the 1st Battalion, 1st Algerian Infantry, and with artillery, tanks, and anti-tank guns. East of Kasserine village, the 19th Combat Engineer Battalion (Colonel Anderson T. W. Moore) began to arrive during the night of February 14–15 to organize a hasty defense line, a task for which they were entirely untrained and singularly unsuited. Despite the reports of disaster from the field, a peculiar form of group-think amounting to collective denial set in throughout the Allied high command, which no eyewitness statement could dispel.[42] Shortly after 8:00p.m. Anderson sent and late on February 14 Fredendall received the following instructions, already made inapposite by the success of the German attack.

> As regards action in the Sidi bou Zid area, concentrate tomorrow on clearing up situation there and destroying enemy. Thereafter collect strong mobile force in Sbeïtla area ready for action in any direction… Army Commander deeply regrets losses suffered by CCA, but he congratulates them on their fine fight, is confident they will decisively defeat the enemy tomorrow, and is sure the enemy must have suffered losses at least as heavy as their own… Press on with defenses as ordered… 7 February.[43]

"This hallucination whisked through Speedy Valley without challenge and on to Ward."[44] Ward and his operations officer, Lieutenant Colonel Hamilton Howze, dutifully issued orders for a counterattack the next day with a force weaker than that which had already been destroyed or driven from the battlefield. Ward ordered Lieutenant Colonel Alger's 2nd Battalion, 1st Armored Regiment to lead the counterattack. 2/1AR was equipped with new early model M4 Shermans but had absolutely no combat experience. "Ward, ostensible commander of the 1st Armored Division, told his diary: 'Alger was more or less on his own.'" Brigadier General Robinett, CO, CCB, from which Alger's battalion had been detached, reported that Alger "saluted and smiled as he passed."[45]

The decision to counterattack with Combat Command C, reinforced by Alger's 2nd Battalion, had been made before II Corps had received First Army's wildly unrealistic order. Fredendall, from his myopic seat in Speedy Valley, also ordered Ward to see to the relief and withdrawal of the isolated infantry troops during the morning of February 15, while the counterattack was being launched.

> Desire you carry out plan to withdraw 168th Infantry from positions on Djebel Lessouda and Djebel Ksaïra. Details of withdrawal left to your judgment but should be designed for maximum security of infantry withdrawing.

That both Anderson and Fredendall believed that the forces assembled for the counterattack could defeat the enemy and rescue the trapped infantry reflected the appalling ignorance of the higher commands of what had really happened on February 14. Their failure to assess properly the intelligence and situation reports from the field was exacerbated by the fragmented and confused command and control arrangements at Sidi Bou Zid and to the west.[46]

Ward and Howze wrote the mission of Stack's reinforced CCC in straightforward U.S. Army doctrinal terms.

MISSION TO COMBAT COMMAND C
This force will move south, and by fire and maneuver destroy the enemy armored forces which have threatened our hold on the Sbeïtla area. It will so conduct its maneuver as to aid in the withdrawal of our forces in the vicinity of Dj Ksaïra, eventually withdrawing to the area north of Dj Hamra for further action.

The American planning and execution of the counterattack at Sidi Bou Zid was too slow, too late, and by any military measure assigned forces too weak for the task. There had been a short window of opportunity to strike the Germans while they were recovering from their offensive to entrap and destroy the U.S. forces around Sidi Bou Zid, but the Americans lost that opportunity because the German operational tempo was so much faster than the Americans' ability to make and execute decisions. Welvert was aware of this failing and had desperately tried to persuade First Army to urge Fredendall to take faster and more powerful action, but without success.[47]

CCC's orders were prepared by 1st Armored Division headquarters with the aid only of small-scale maps of the anticipated battle area. Ward's staff had drawn the 2nd Battalion's march route with blue pencil and a straight edge on a 1-to-100,000 scale sheet on which each mile of desert terrain was represented by less than an inch of paper. Two officers from the Reconnaissance Company, 1st Armored Regiment, and Colonel Hains, CO of 1AR, all of whom had been in the preceding day's battle, tried to provide some supplementary real-life information. Stack understood the enemy's strength to consist of 40 tanks north of Sidi Bou Zid and 15 to 20 tanks south of it, belonging to as yet unknown enemy units.

As planned, CCC, reinforced by Alger's 2nd Tank Battalion after its arrival from Maktar, marched south from Hadjeb el Aïoun early on February 15 by road to an assembly area northeast of Djebel Hamra. Stack intended somehow to push a column through or beyond Sidi Bou Zid, with the object of screening the withdrawal of the 2nd Battalion, 168th Infantry Regiment and other troops, under Lieutenant Colonel John H. van Vliet, Jr., on Djebel Ksaïra and Colonel Drake on Djebel Garet Hadid. The troops of the 3rd Battalion, 168th Infantry Regiment on Djebel Lessouda under Major Moore were substantially closer to Sbeïtla (about 22.5 air miles) than those on Djebel Ksaïra (about 31.2 air miles) and would be evacuated in a later operation.[48] Ward's and Stack's plans, so blithely developed, never came to fruition.

Just before the counterattack began, CCC comprised a mix of units, most of which were well under full strength: the 3rd Battalion of the 6th Armored Infantry Regiment; Alger's inexperienced but complete 2nd Battalion, 1st Armored Regiment; Company G, 13th Armored Regiment; the 701st Tank Destroyer Battalion (less Companies A and C); the 68th Field Artillery Battalion (less Battery A); the 1st Platoon, Company D, 16th Armored Engineer Battalion; the 1st Platoon, 443rd Coast Artillery (Antiaircraft) Battalion (Self Propelled); a detachment of Company B, 2nd Battalion, 13th Armored Regiment; and Company A, 47th Armored Medical Battalion. This motley and undersized force was expected to mount the counterattack and to destroy the enemy at Sidi Bou Zid.[49]

CCC's lead elements reached the assembly area by 9:45a.m. on Monday, February 15. Unlike the day before, "[t]he day was dry and sunny… Sidi Bou Zid [was] thirteen miles distant. Beyond the town… Djebel Ksaïra sat on the horizon. Djebel Lessouda loomed to the left… A landscape that from a distance seemed flat as a billiard table was in fact corrugated with subtle folds and dips…"[50] Just before 1:00p.m., Alger's 2nd Battalion appeared on a camel track from the north. The column wheeled and headed southeast for Sidi Bou Zid at eight miles per hour. Alger had been told to push beyond Lessouda and Ksaïra "and then hold until friendly infantry could withdraw" from the hills where they were trapped. No ground reconnaissance had been conducted by Stack's own troops. Allied intelligence estimated enemy strength at 60 tanks at most, which was less than half their actual number.[51] The Americans went charging forward without adequate reconnaissance to attack and somehow overpower an experienced and wily foe perhaps four times their strength, an enemy that made excellent use of every fold and depression in the ground to conceal the positions and number of their forces.

The enemy observed the approaching column on the ground and from the air. Enemy planes strafed CCC near the end of its march and it was not reorganized until just after noon, when it began the attack. From Stack's command post on Djebel Hamra, the battlefield stretched out below with unimpeded view for miles through the clear dry air of a sunny afternoon. Even through field glasses, Sidi Bou Zid, about 13 miles distant, was only a tiny spot of dark-hued evergreens and white houses behind which rose the hazy slopes of Djebel Ksaïra where 3/168 was trapped. To the left in the distance was Djebel Lessouda where 2/168 was beleaguered. The road from Sbeïtla ran straight toward Lessouda, where Major Moore radioed reports of what could be seen from the heights. On the right, the road from Bir el Hafey slanted northeastward to Sidi Bou Zid, and roughly parallel with it lay the long ridge of Djebel el Kebar (793m). The sun-heated desert air wavered and shimmered, blurring the view of the Allied spectators on Djebel Hamra. The dips and folds of the plain were gradual, but several steep-sided deeper *wadis* crossed it roughly from north to south. The monotonous brownish-gray landscape was marked at various points by patches of darker cactus, by the geometric shapes of cultivated fields and orchards, and by clusters of low, block-shaped white buildings. At 12:40p.m. the American formation started over this expanse until from the perspective of American observers its vehicles were reduced by distance to pinpoints and obscured by clouds of dust.[52]

Going into their first battle, 2nd Battalion's tanks, 42 M4 Shermans with short-barreled 75mm guns in turrets, were up front. They started slowly southeastward in a column of companies, led by Company D, followed by Company F, the assault guns, and finally Company E. Tank destroyers were grouped on each wing. The artillery and then the infantry in half-tracks followed. At 1:40p.m. a formation of 10 to 12 enemy fighters and nine enemy bombers swept over the column, strafing and bombing it not far from Djebel Hamra. They caused little damage to personnel or equipment but deranged Alger's formation, making it perfectly clear that German commanders knew of and were ready for the counterattack. At 2:45p.m. Ward heard CCC report: "Tanks now approaching Sidi Bou Zid. Enemy's lack of reaction suspicious... enemy force must be small or sucking us in." Howze also sent a radio message alerting Drake and the men on Garet Hadid and Djebel Ksaïra to the planned evacuation: "Keep your eyes peeled and be ready to jump on the bandwagon."[53]

Radio reports from Djebel Lessouda and Djebel Ksaïra to CCC through 1AD's command post described German movements and the large but dispersed Nazi forces. Both Moore and Drake urged Stack to press the attack aggressively while he retained that apparent advantage.[54]

> [W]e found the commanding colonel [Stack], standing beside a radio half-track. We stood close enough to the radio to hear the voice of the battalion commander [Alger], who was leading the tank attack. At the same time we watched the fantastic surge of caterpillar metal move forward amidst its own dust... Far across the desert, in front of us, lay the town of Sidi bou Zid. Through the glasses we see it only as a green oasis whose green trees stood out against the bare brown of the desert. On beyond were high hills, where some of our troops were still trapped after the... attack of the day before.[55]

Alger's tanks were able to cross the series of *wadis* in the path of the counterattack only at a few points. Toward these crossings his tank companies converged temporarily before again spreading out in attack formation. The tanks, with one exception, crossed the first *wadi* successfully and resumed the advance toward the second. As they arrived at the one good crossing point there, the enemy fired on the now concentrated tanks with air bursts and then with anti-tank artillery fire. On the northern flank, an enemy battery of four 88mm and two 47mm anti-tank guns had been waiting quietly in concealment. Fortunately, those guns were observed and overrun by the leading platoon of Company D, 1st Battalion, 1st Armored Regiment before the enemy weapons were able to fire on the Americans.[56] At 4:30p.m., the Germans dive-bombed the armored infantry just as it passed through the American artillery positions, presenting a conveniently concentrated target.[57]

While CCC and the 2nd Battalion were delayed by enemy air attacks, the Germans organized to repulse the counterattack. Three companies of *Kampfgruppe Stenkhoff* maneuvered to strike the American south flank while elements of *Kampfgruppe Gerhardt*, from a position northwest of Sidi Salem, moved to envelop CCC from the north. Three heavy and two light anti-tank batteries withheld their fire to conceal their positions until the 2nd Battalion's tanks were near their objective, then began firing steadily when the U.S. tanks were all in range. Meanwhile, enemy Stukas diverted the attention of the Americans from a slow shift by elements of the 5th Panzer Regiment aimed at turning the southern flank.[58] Muzzle flashes appeared near the town; 20 seconds later, enemy artillery air bursts again exploded over the American artillery batteries, spreading burning shrapnel. Alger reported enemy tanks approaching on his left and, ten minutes later, coming from his right. CCC had driven straight into the Nazi trap.

Ernest "Ernie" Taylor Pyle (August 3, 1900–April 18, 1945) was a Pulitzer Prize-winning American journalist and war correspondent best known for his stories about ordinary American soldiers during World War II. After winning acclaim for his columns depicting the London Blitz and the coming of war to America, by August 1942 Ernie was back in England writing about American soldiers' lives and their relations with the British. He petitioned for a draft deferment to remain a war correspondent. He accompanied American and British soldiers in the invasion of North Africa in November 1942 and remained until the end of the Tunisian campaign. He wrote insightful, compassionate columns about military policemen, quartermasters, and airmen, but he had the most sympathy for the plight of the infantryman, particularly the infantrymen of the 34th Infantry Division. Ernie's column was a resounding success. Increasingly dismayed with the horror of battle and the deaths of soldiers he held in friendship, he nonetheless was to be found at the front, close to the fighting. He would fall to a Japanese sniper's bullet on Ie Jima during the Battle of Okinawa. On February 15, 1943, Pyle was in the literal thick of the ill-fated American counterattack to rescue his 34ID buddies.

> Both sides had crossed and recrossed these [Arab] farms in the past 24 hours. The fields were riddled by deep ruts and by wide spooky tracks of the almost mythical Mark VI tanks… Evidence of the previous day's battle was still strewn across the desert. We passed charred half-tracks. We stopped to look into a burned out tank, named *Temes*, from which a Lieut. Col. friend of [Ernie Pyle] and his crew had demolished four German tanks before being put out of commission themselves… We moved closer to the actual tank battle ahead, but never went right into it—for in a jeep that would have been a fantastic form of suicide. We stopped, I should judge, about a mile behind the foremost [American] tanks… Later we learned that… German tanks had maneuvered in behind us, and were shooting up our half-tracks and jeeps. But… we didn't know this at the time… Then we could see the dust kick up a couple of hundred yards away. The shells hit the ground and ricocheted like armor-piercing shells, which do not explode but skip along the ground until they finally lose momentum or hit something.[59]

"Brown geysers of earth and smoke began to spout," wrote Pyle, who with his Army officer driver had driven up with the attacking column. Pyle's fellow correspondent A. D. Divine was observing the attack from Djebel Hamra west of Sidi Bou Zid in the company of Major General McQuillin, CO, CCA, Stack, CO, CCC, Hains, CO, 1st Armored Regiment, Alger's superior, and Lieutenant Colonel Hightower, commander of the now destroyed 3rd Battalion, 1st Armored Regiment. Divine, standing close to McQuillin, reported that "within a matter of minutes the golden dust that trailed 2nd Battalion's tanks like banners had turned black… We saw the counterattack falter and break and shatter."[60]

The air burst shells were fired by German artillery concealed on the shoulders of Djebel el Kebar and other vantage points to the southeast. Flying shards of hot metal forced the tank crews to close their hatches and to continue moving with restricted vision. The tanks arriving at the third *wadi* came under much heavier fire, especially on the southern flank. Company D on the north was able to get tanks into the village of Sidi Salem, where they blasted the buildings and a motor pool to the east and stopped an enemy tank force trying to slip by the village's northern edge. But when Company D emerged northeast of the village, heavy long-range fire from the north forced the tanks back to cover. In defilade, Company F moved toward the area south of Sidi Bou Zid along a route to which Alger had directed them.[61]

Company E, in the meantime, came forward and pressed toward Sidi Salem when, at about 4:30p.m., it encountered the spearhead of the enemy armored force striking from the northern flank. Company F at about the same time engaged *panzers* making a similar thrust from the south. On both flanks, the enemy sent additional enveloping forces. The German southern pincer escaped detection until it had reached a threatening position, but it was driven off by Battery C, 68th Armored Artillery Battalion. The threat of encirclement remained high, and the American forces now began to withdraw from the trap as quickly as they could. Observers on Djebel Lessouda reported a slowly advancing column of *panzers* including some Mark VI Tigers, heading toward the deep northern flank. CCC committed its reserve company of medium tanks (Company G, 13th Armored Regiment, equipped with M3 Grant medium tanks) to intercept that northern pincer. Company G took a course too far to the northwest and entirely missed the enemy, who turned southward into the battle area, avoiding both the reserve tanks and long-range fire from the 91st Armored Field Artillery Battalion near Djebel Hamra.[62] The ensuing massacre of the American tanks occurred mostly in an onion field 1,000 yards square near a *wadi* two miles west of Sidi Bou Zid called Oued Rouana. Main gun tracer shells filled the air and ricocheted over the plowed fields, many of them striking armor plate with morbidly brilliant scintillations. By 4:30p.m. American tanks were burning from Company D in the north, Company E in the center, and Company F in the south.

At 4:50p.m., Stack radioed Alger from the command post on Djebel Hamra. He asked Alger to report his situation and to state what he needed. "Still pretty busy," Alger answered laconically. "Situation in hand. No answer to second question. Further details later." Then his radio went silent. Alger's tank, while heading back toward Sidi Salem to rejoin Company D, was disabled; an enemy round struck the gun barrel and jammed the turret, then four more rounds sliced through the engine and the turret, killing the radio operator. Leaping from the hatch, Alger and two other soldiers ran north. They were soon captured by the enemy and Alger later joined Waters in a German prisoner-of-war camp. His detailed report was delayed until 1945, when he was released and wrote an account of the fighting based on the recollections which he and his fellow POWs from the battalion had shared during their imprisonment.[63]

At 4:45p.m., Stack had reported to Ward that it was doubtful that CCC would reach Djebel Ksaïra before sundown.[64] Even that cautious statement proved to be overly optimistic. Stack had ordered his infantry battalion to hold in place rather than risk encirclement.[65] But an hour later the armored infantry was forced to move back to escape that very envelopment. The tank battalion, whose losses were already severe, started back through a gauntlet of enemy anti-tank fire. A few dismounted crews also escaped.[66] A reserve platoon of four M4s assembled below Djebel Hamra to cover the retreat of the other 52 Shermans. But as the battalion war diary recorded, "None returned."[67]

After dark, the 68th Armored Field Artillery Battalion (less Battery A), marched from the battlefield where it had been briefly cut off at dusk. The enemy now held the field, illuminated by burning American tanks and half-tracks. The Germans salvaged their own equipment and recovered or demolished vehicles left behind by the Americans. Another American tank battalion had been destroyed in battle with heavy losses. Two months later, more than 40 rusting U.S. tanks and other vehicles were found when Allied troops again advanced over that ground.[68] The American estimate of the damage inflicted by CCC upon the enemy was 13 Mark IV tanks, five 88mm and ten other artillery pieces damaged or destroyed, and upwards of 50 men killed. The few survivors of the 2nd Battalion, 1st Armored Regiment, reported on February 16 that, in addition to the catastrophic loss of tanks, guns and other vehicles, 15 officers, including Alger, and 298 enlisted men were missing in action and one officer was wounded and was evacuated.

The Germans claimed to have salvaged all of their damaged *panzers*. The enemy listed as American matériel captured or destroyed: 39 tanks, 17 armored personnel carriers, four anti-tank guns, three self-propelled guns, eight machine guns, one 105mm howitzer, and about 100 vehicles.[69] By morning on February 16, CCA would estimate casualties from the past two days at 1,600 men. Nearly 100 tanks had been lost, along with 57 half-tracks and 29 artillery pieces. "Also lost, after such obviously inept generalship, was whatever confidence the ranks still held for the high command."[70]

The senior American commanders still did not grasp that they had lost another tank battalion. "We might have walloped them, or they might have walloped us," Ward reported to II Corps just before midnight on February 15. In fact, the Germans were surprised by the weakness of the counterattack and were on alert for a second assault. But the enemy already knew from captured orders and signal intercepts exactly which U.S. units had been engaged, what forces remained to oppose them, and what the Americans intended to do. 1st Armored Division and other II Corps units maintained a line near the road junction east of Sbeïtla and reorganized for defense.[71]

CHAPTER 17

The Destruction of Two Battalions of the 168th Infantry

On February 15, Anderson realized that his plan to hold the forward positions, with which Eisenhower had agreed, had been a mistake. The Axis attack from Faïd and Maïzilla had exposed First Army's southern flank, and the whole Allied force was in danger of being outflanked and cut off from the south. It was now impossible to concentrate an armored formation to counter the threat. The Allies had lost too many tanks too quickly. "I feel therefore," he wrote to Eisenhower, "that it is wise to consider in good time whether we should not voluntarily withdraw to the main ridge of the Grande Dorsal from Djebel Bargou southwards, linking up with Kef el Ahmar and down to the Sbeïtla area." He told Eisenhower that a retreat with the surviving forces intact was preferable to a costly effort to hold the Pichon area and the Eastern Dorsal. "I think it is essential that we hold the Grande [Western] Dorsal itself, and I am prepared to fight all out to insure this." He warned that even holding the Grande Dorsal might not be possible if the Allies first lost heavily while being driven out of their easterly positions. As before, Eisenhower concurred.[1]

First Army issued a warning to II Corps at 5:00p.m., February 15, that withdrawal had been decided and that First Army would direct the methods for protecting the retreat and for establishing a new, more defensible line. In the meantime, Anderson directed II Corps to extricate the infantry of the 168th Infantry Regiment from the hills near Sidi Bou Zid, and then to withdraw to positions from which to defend Sbeïtla, Kasserine, and Fériana. Anderson also ordered II Corps to maintain a mobile reserve capable of operating to the northeast, east, south, and southwest. First Army expected II Corps to be prepared to engage the enemy should Axis forces move west or southwest from the Fondouk el Aouareb-Pichon gap, or northward toward Hadjeb el Aïoun from the Faïd area. Anderson's understanding of the forces available to II Corps bordered on fiction. In fact, II Corps no longer had enough armored forces under its control to effectively execute any of those missions.[2]

Orderly retreat in the presence of the enemy is one of the most complex and difficult of military operations. But a successful withdrawal to more defensible positions supported by shorter supply lines may require the enemy to exert a much greater effort and to expend disproportionately greater resources to gain any further military advantage. British Eighth Army's advance against the Mareth Position was imminent. The Germans would have to win the battle in Central Tunisia quickly. To fight through the Western Dorsal against Allied reserves in positions favorable for defense could be made costly to the Axis. The large reinforcements streaming from the west might render it impossible. The Allied decision to fall back to the Western Dorsal required abandoning the forward base at Sbeïtla and the air base at Thélepte. The defenses of the passes in the Western Dorsal had to be hastily improvised. Defensible points to the north, including Thala and Sbiba, and to the west, at Djebel el Hamra and Bou Chebka pass, had to be reinforced strongly to contain and then halt the Axis thrust. The troops only recently brought eastward, including the elements of the 34th Infantry Division near Pichon, would have to move back to defend the critical points. While the Allies correctly estimated the Axis supply situation to be bad, the Allied commanders could not be certain that the momentum of the Axis offensive would not solve the enemy's supply problem by capturing the enormous dumps of Allied fuel and supplies at Tébessa, precisely as Rommel desired.[3]

The Allied withdrawal was of no help whatsoever to the soldiers of the 168th Infantry Regiment beleaguered on the hills east of Sidi Bou Zid. The destruction of Alger's 2nd Battalion had happened in the sight of Moore and his trapped infantrymen of the 2nd Battalion, 168IR on Djebel Lessouda. Although the enemy kept the Lessouda position under a strait siege, Moore now received orders to get out of the trap somehow. Ward, unaware that Waters had been captured, sent orders addressed to Waters to get his force back during the night.[4] At dusk on Monday evening, February 15, a lone U.S. P40 fighter flew over Lessouda and dropped a U.S. mail sack tied to a small parachute. Inside, Moore found the message from Ward: "You are to withdraw to road[i] west of Blid Chegas where guides will meet you. Bring everything you can. Ward." Suspecting a typically devious Nazi trick, Moore radioed McQuillin's command post for confirmation, asking for the division commander's nickname. 1AD's reply was "Message okay. Pinky."[5]

During the night of February 15–16, the 2nd Battalion, 168IR attempted to escape the encirclement. At 10:30p.m. on Monday, Moore gathered his men on Lessouda's southwestern slope. Hundreds of tired, thirsty, and scared GIs despondently listened to his instructions. Heavy weapons were to be spiked and abandoned. They would march in the dark in two columns, 30 yards apart, parallel to and a mile north of Highway 13. The rendezvous point was nine miles west, near the cross-roads below Djebel Hamra on the road to Sbeïtla. Wounded men were to be carried on litters. If a German prisoner uttered a sound, he was to be bayoneted at once. Moore then led

---

i   Modern Highway P3 at the base of Djebel Hamra.

his surviving soldiers through the enemy's outpost line in utter silence. They walked, stooped over, beneath a rising full moon, in two lines led by Company F, which Moore had commanded in Iowa in what must have seemed to him to have been a long-ago fantasy. At the base of the hill, they passed an 88mm gun, "so close that we could have easily reached out and touched it," one officer later reported. Half an hour later, Moore heard voices to his left. He veered from the column toward a line of trees, where a man called to him *auf Deutsch*. Moore circled back to the column. "He didn't speak our language," he whispered to a young captain. The voice called once more, and then machine-gun fire ripped across the desert. "Scatter!" Moore yelled. "Run like hell." The men did so. As some fell to the machine-gun fire, Moore ordered the others to drop and crawl. Artillery from the western edge of Lessouda slammed, followed by the reports of German mortars. The battalion chaplain, First Lieutenant Eugene L. Daniel, Jr., told the litter bearers and medics to flee while he remained with the wounded to await capture.[6] In the end, the courageous sacrifices of men like Daniel and many thousands of other American and Allied soldiers would carry the Allies to victory over the Nazi Reich a little over two years later.[ii]

At about 5:00a.m. on Tuesday, February 16, Moore and a small group of soldiers from Company F reached the crossroads near Djebel Hamra where Ward had posted sentries. Haggard and thirsty, they found there some three dozen others from Company F. Soon, part of Company H joined them with a dozen German prisoners in tow, followed by Company G. By sunrise, Moore counted 231 troops. Others arrived throughout the day in Sbeïtla, where the quartermaster passed out blankets and overcoats. After another head count, Moore reported that out of the 904 men he had commanded two days before, 432 remained.[7] Three officers and 58 men had been taken as prisoners immediately after their flight was discovered and more were captured later.[8] Some of the missing were dead.

Truscott described in his memoirs his telephone conversations with Fredendall on the morning after the defeat of the American counterattack.

General Fredendall telephoned me at 0800, February 16th, to say:

"The picture this morning does not look too good. The counterattack force—Colonel Stack with two battalions of infantry, some artillery and a battalion of medium tanks under Colonel Alger—got into the fight at Sidi bou Zid just before dark. Then their radio went out and there was no news until they phoned at three A.M. and recommended that the railhead be moved back from Sbeitla. Information is confused but G-3 has them on the phone now getting the latest information. I will have a full report and will call you back in a few minutes. It does not look good. The worst will be the loss of two battalions of tanks."

A little later, General Fredendall telephoned me again:

"At dark last night, Alger's tank battalion and its supporting artillery were hit in the flank. They ran into two battalions of German tanks in concealed positions. Stack had infantry and

---

ii   Daniel continued his pastoral work in German POW camps until his release at the end of the war. He wrote and published a memoir entitled *In the Presence of Mine Enemies: An American Chaplain in World War II German Prison Camps*. 1985, ISBN 9780961750107.

artillery on Djebel Hamra behind them, but he could not continue the attack without support. There has been no contact with Alger's battalion since dark last night, and we fear that it is lost. There is a possibility that it has gone on to join Drake's battalion on Djebel Ksaira, but I doubt it… The first day's losses will include sixty-two officers and 1536 enlisted men, about half killed or missing."

In reply to my question, General Fredendall informed me that General Anderson had finally released Combat Command B and that Robinett had joined Ward at Sbeitla. He had told Ward to get his division straightened out and to hold defensively east of Sbeitla. The infantry battalion on Djebel Lessouda had started to fight its way out during the counterattack, but there was no further word from it. This was the bitter picture, at 1000 hours the morning of February 16th, which I had to convey to General Eisenhower. More than one hundred American tanks destroyed in two days, along with two battalions of artillery overrun, and two battalions of infantry lost, and no one knew how much more!

General Eisenhower decided that his best contribution would be to return at once to AFHQ and put impetus behind the measures to make good our losses…[9]

The men of 3/168 and other troops with Drake and van Vliet were in even worse trouble than their fellows of 2/168 had been. On February 15, the Germans violently pressed their attack on Djebel Garet Hadid. Around 7:30a.m., they began to put pressure on both hills with artillery shelling and an infantry assault. About 200 Germans penetrated the positions on Garet Hadid held by the engineers, who expelled them with hand grenades. The 30-some members of the regimental band, who usually doubled as litter bearers, "made beautiful music on rifles accompanied by machine guns." Three times the *panzergrenadiers* penetrated as far as Drake's command post. Enemy snipers were at work and the GIs were constantly hunting them. Because of the rough ground and the artillery pieces available to them, the besieged were able at first to hold enemy tanks at bay. But as the day went on, *panzer* guns and artillery fire steadily picked off the American guns. As the enemy pushed in from the right flank, a counterattack by two platoons pushed the Germans back.

The "rear" on Garet Hadid was controlled by a tall, inverted cone of rock. Drake had been able to spare only a section of six men to garrison that rock formation. The enemy scaled the side of the rock, killed three men, and drove off the others, who immediately reported to Drake. Drake then ordered Second Lieutenant Bolton with six men of the Regimental Band to retake the cone position. The counterattack succeeded and temporarily prevented the enemy from breaking into the American ranks.[10]

The situation for the defenders on Garet Hadid had become desperate by late on February 15. The soldiers had not had water or food since the evening of February 13, casualties were heavy, and no medical assistance other than first aid was available for the wounded. Van Vliet's command on Ksaïra was similarly beset. By sunset on February 15, an estimated 300 *panzergrenadiers* backed by *panzers* had infiltrated the lower slopes of Ksaïra. 3rd Battalion kept them at bay with heavy doses of mortar fire, then American counterattacks temporarily repulsed the enemy with showers of hand grenades. But minutes later the Germans were again racing up the *wadis*. Enemy machine gunners and snipers fired at any movement. The men of the 168th Infantry and their fellow soldiers were no longer confused about where or whom to shoot. There were many individual acts of extraordinary courage arising out of hatred for their tormentors, bitterness about the situation, and lust for revenge. The regimental band's bass drummer was slain carrying ammunition to the perimeter; a clarinetist was killed while avenging him.[11]

The enemy resumed its ground assaults at 7:00a.m. on February 16, and by noon all the defenders' artillery on Garet Hadid had been destroyed by direct fire. Casualties continued to mount. The rear and right flanks were driven in. The troops stranded in two groups on Djebel Ksaïra and Djebel Garet Hadid continued to be subjected to scourging machine-gun and mortar fire until they had been squeezed into ever-shrinking perimeters on the crests of the hills. By any path that would avoid the enemy formations between them and sanctuary, the 1,900 men of 3/168 were at least twice as far from Djebel Hamra as the troops of 2/168 at Lessouda. They also were hungry and thirsty and low on ammunition. Drake had contacted CCA by radio, using a code pre-arranged with the 1st Armored Division's communications officer, but his radio would function only in daytime when the sun warmed its rundown battery. His repeated requests for supplies of water, food and ammunition were not acknowledged. No supplies arrived. Some men were so overcome with fright and anxiety that they abandoned their fighting positions on various pretexts. Drake had to instruct the regimental bandleader to form firing squads to keep the lines intact. The men were marginally safer within the perimeter than running down the slope into ground infested with the enemy.[12]

German intelligence mistakenly believed that only one company occupied each hill. In fact, despite their losses, the entire American force still equaled roughly two battalions. German attempts to maneuver the defenders out of their positions grew increasingly bold. The enemy attacked the remaining positions of 3/168 on Djebel Ksaïra early in the afternoon of February 16. The 3rd Battalion was able to withstand the attack initially, but by 2:00p.m. the left flank on Djebel Ksaïra collapsed, and it became clear that 3/168 could not hold for another day.[13]

At 2:30p.m., McQuillin sent an unencoded radio message to Drake that 1st Armored Division could do nothing to rescue the troops marooned on Djebel Ksaïra and Djebel Garet Hadid. The decision to stay or withdraw was left to Drake, but CCA's message made it clear that the troops beleaguered on the hills could expect no relief. "Fight your way out. Time and place yours. Air cover will be provided. Instructions will be dropped by plane this afternoon." The message contradicted Drake's previous orders from McQuillin to hold the position to the last man, and Drake was exasperated and confused. He did not disclose the content of the message to the troops, but instead radioed a coded message to van Vliet, the 3rd Battalion commander on Ksaïra: "How long would it take to cut your way out and join me at Garet Hadid? Be prepared for prompt move but make no change in disposition until you receive direct order from me." Van Vliet replied promptly: "Will not attempt until after dark on order. There are eight 88s between you and me." As if on cue and to preclude any escape plan, the enemy had pulled artillery onto the ground between the two hills, "unlimbered his guns, and shelled our men at will," a lieutenant recalled. "We had no artillery to reply to him and he was out of range of our smaller weapons."[14]

At 3:00p.m. Drake received another message from CCA. "Look for dropped message at 1700 hours." Drake assumed that 3/168 and the other troops under his command would be ordered to leave their positions, and he directed his GIs on Garet Hadid to prepare for withdrawal that night. He selected a route westward along the foot of Djebel Garet Hadid, then southwest following the foothills, and further northwest across the desert toward a feature he referred to as El Hamir (Djebel Hamra). At about 5:43p.m. three U.S. fighter planes flew over and dropped a parachute sack containing two typed sheets that landed on Ksaïra rather than Garet Hadid. Van Vliet spent more than an hour decoding the lengthy message and then encoding an abridged version for radio transmission to Drake. The gist of the message was as Drake had expected. The troops on Djebel Ksaïra and Djebel Garet Hadid were ordered to withdraw during the night of February 16–17 and to make their way to Sbeïtla. "Drake was to take his troops off the hills and try to get them to safety. That was all. Not even a definite location for meeting friendly forces. In what would be his last message, Drake acknowledged the permission finally granted. He showed no bitterness, only unbroken spirit. 'Besieged,' he radioed, 'good strength, good morale.'"[15]

Drake called his unit commanders together at 6:30p.m. and gave his instructions. The withdrawal would start at 11:00p.m. with all units on Garet Hadid leaving their positions simultaneously. The route of march, a modified version of his original plan, was to be around the northeastern nose of Garet Hadid, back along the foothills to the southwest for about five miles, then northwest for another five miles to a small hill in the desert. There the troops would stop and take cover, to rest during the day for the final breakout—five miles farther to Djebel Hamra and the crossroads—to be made on the following night. The men were to leave their helmets and wear overseas caps, which resembled those of the German *Afrika Korps*. They were to carry out all the light machine guns and the 60mm mortars; they were to destroy all the equipment they could not take, but without lighting fires; motor vehicle parts were to be buried, radios were to be smashed. One medic was to remain with the wounded at the aid station on each hill.[16]

Drake next sent a coded message to van Vliet on Djebel Ksaïra directing the main body of 3/168 to withdraw that night. The soldiers on both hills destroyed their weapons and gear except what they could carry. Working as quietly as possible so as not to alert the enemy, they rendered weapons and equipment unserviceable. They slashed tires with bayonets and battered equipment with hammers. A sergeant walked through the motor pool, firing .45 caliber pistol bullets into every engine block. Engine and radio parts were removed and smashed or buried, and machine-gun bolts were hidden. Men too gravely wounded to walk—60 on Ksaïra alone—had to be left behind, draped with canvas, and accompanied by a single medic at the aid station on each hill, in the optimistic and honorable expectation that they would be captured and properly cared for by the Germans.[17]

The withdrawal commenced at 10:00p.m., when Drake sent out the code phrase to decamp—"Bust the balloon" and the main body of 3/168 on Ksaïra crept westward in column before the men on Garet Hadid, to allow van Vliet's troops to close up with Drake's column.[18] A German patrol in a captured American half-track challenged the rear of the column of troops from Ksaïra. The vehicle was promptly incinerated with rifle grenades and its occupants shot, but for one man who escaped. Fortunately, the incident did not alert the Germans.[19] The withdrawal continued. The troops on Garet Hadid left next, leaving rearguard outposts in position.[20] Hundreds of soldiers crept down the rocky slopes beneath a full moon behind wind-driven clouds. Almost at once Drake discovered he was leading his men through a German tank park and bivouac area. A *panzer* came toward him, and the commander shouted in German. When Drake ignored him, the tanker hesitated, then turned aside and rumbled away. The men worked their way out across plowed fields onto the plain, moving toward Djebel Hamra in the darkness. With one delay and another, the last troops did not leave Ksaïra until nearly midnight.[21] The straight distance by air from the Garet Hadid position to a point just south of Djebel Hamra is at least 15 miles, but Drake's men could not proceed in a straight line on the ground. They marched all night, with only one rest break. Drake had realized at once that his troops could not reach Sbeïtla before dawn; he had made their goal El Hamri (Djebel Hamra), the only high ground between Sbeïtla and Garet Hadid. He fervently hoped that they would find U.S. Army units still there. He would later learn that the 6th Armored Infantry Regiment had been withdrawn from Djebel Hamra during the evening of February 16, just hours before Drake's command left Djebel Garet Hadid.[22]

"We marched all that night across the sand, in gulleys or dry washes, wherever we could find a path other than being silhouetted on a skyline," wrote one soldier. "Whenever the moon would come out, or a real or imagined sound was heard, we would halt and crouch down." Hungry and in pain from thirst and wounds, GIs soon tossed away the machine guns and mortar tubes, then ammunition, blankets and even rifles. Columns disintegrated into noisy bands of disorganized stragglers. The men scurried through the scorched battlefields south and west of Sidi Bou Zid where Hightower and Alger had fought, now strewn with the corpses of their fellow soldiers and burned-out tanks.[23]

The basic battlefield survival lessons of concealment and silent march had been thoroughly learned, but to no avail. "Dawn caught them all in the open, scattered across five miles of desert west of Sidi bou Zid. Their objective, Djebel Hamra, loomed on the horizon, shrouded in mist."[24] The column was about five miles from Djebel Hamra when Drake ordered his officers to adopt a proper approach formation, dividing the troops into two files about 50 yards apart, and continuing the march.[25] As the columns of escaping soldiers attempted to cross a road leading toward Djebel Hamra, German trucks carrying *panzergrenadiers* came up on the left flank. The enemy motorized troops gave chase, circling out of range like Genghis Khan's horse archers. The enemy vehicles then halted about 1,000 yards away and German soldiers emerged from beneath the canvas awnings. "Those," a lieutenant informed Colonel van Vliet, "are not our vehicles." The *panzergrenadiers* took firing positions. Three Allied planes came into sight; one pilot fired into the line of German trucks, then all three aircraft flew away. So much for the air cover that had been promised. The Germans then opened fire with machine guns, rifles, and mortars; the Americans scattered. There was little cover in the large open fields of the Sbeïtla plain, and control and discipline began to disintegrate.[26]

Retaining control over several hundred men, Drake formed a perimeter, with himself in the center directing a desultory firing against the Germans, who soon brought up several *panzers*, all of them appearing to Drake as "huge monsters, with a yellow tiger painted on their sides." Drake rallied the 400 men still within earshot, deploying them and ordering them to open fire with every available weapon, knowing that only about half the men were still armed. He asked for volunteers, one officer and GIs, to take position on a hillock in their rear where the German infantry was trying to encircle them and there to fight a delaying action. First Lieutenant William Rogers, 91st Armored Artillery, volunteered to lead a group of 12 men. The squad "gained the desired ground, a little knoll in the desert," Drake reported, "and there they were able to hold the enemy off for about an hour." Flanked and overrun by *panzergrenadiers,* the valiant Rogers and his heroic band of fighters were all killed after buying that precious hour for their fellow soldiers.[27]

At 10:00a.m., Drake ordered First Lieutenant William W. Luttrell to assume command of another squad. "He took one look at me and screamed, 'Lieutenant, take those men and charge!'" Luttrell later recounted. Luttrell formed a hasty skirmish line of frightened and exhausted riflemen. "Move out," he barked, then led the men into the fight, where they were soon cut to ribbons. "They just went down in front of me—some slow and some quick, some forward and some backward." Luttrell survived to be taken prisoner.

The "monster" *panzers* bearing the emblem of a yellow tiger opened fire on the Americans. The *panzergrenadiers* set up machine-gun positions and lay down fire as they surrounded the American positions. The hopeless battle lasted about three and a half hours; American fire steadily decreased as GIs fell or ran out of ammunition. The enemy lashed the fugitives with machine guns, broke the Americans into small groups with *panzers* and armored cars, drove the survivors into cactus patches, and captured all but a few. A German armored scout car approached bearing a white flag but followed immediately by *panzers*. Those GIs who did not surrender at once were killed. Drake defied a demand to surrender from one *panzer* commander, but he was stopped by a German major who spoke good English and politely invited Drake to enter the major's car. Drake complied and was taken to the headquarters of a German general he believed was named Schmidt.[iii] The German officer saluted Drake and said, "I want to compliment your command for the splendid fight they put up. It was a hopeless thing from the start, but they fought like real soldiers." "I saw that it was hopeless and put my white handkerchief on a stick and waved. That was that," van Vliet later reported. The debacle was complete. Of van Vliet's men from Djebel Ksaïra, some 800 were captured, along with another 600 from Garet Hadid including Colonel Drake.[28]

A burial detail of captured GIs was forced to collect and dump the American dead in a mass grave. They then joined the column of prisoners shuffling east. A few hundred GIs of 3/168 and other units eluded capture and reached Allied lines, many having survived a week or more on stolen eggs and fried cactus leaves. Drake's second in command, Lieutenant Colonel Gerald C. Line, made his way into the American lines, the only officer to escape. The two infantry battalions of the 168th Infantry Regiment and parts of their supporting units had been obliterated. "It is pardonable to be defeated," observed Luttrell, who would spend the rest of the war in a German prison camp, "but unpardonable to be surprised."[29] Nevertheless, as Martin Blumenson observed, "On the plain of Sbeitla, in the ashes of defeat, had been born a legend of a fighting man and a fighting regiment. It takes one hell of a soldier to make more than a thousand men look good in defeat."[30]

The experience of the captured Americans as prisoners of war was an unqualified misery. As soon as Drake was taken from the field, the captured U.S. medical personnel were marched away as prisoners and were not permitted to care for their injured comrades. Drake learned from reports of other soldiers that the American wounded were abandoned to be beaten and robbed by Arabs in the sight of German soldiers. The other prisoners were subjected to thoroughly invasive searches by German soldiers and junior officers, who took not only military papers and service items but valuables of every kind. The Americans were then lined up in a column of fours, officers at the head, and forcibly marched that night to Lessouda. They were held overnight at Lessouda without shelter, water, or food. At dawn on February 18, trucks arrived and transported the American POWs to Sfax. There the prisoners were held in a wire compound under guard towers with no sanitation facilities. They were given water and black bread. On February 19, the Americans were locked into livestock railcars and moved by rail; there were no toilets in the cars. They stopped in Sousse for latrine purposes. The train continued to Tunis, where some men were

---

iii   It is possible the officer was Schuette.

subjected to brutal interrogation. From Tunis, most of the men were flown to Capua, Italy, but others were taken to Capua by sea at risk of destruction by Allied air and naval attacks. After two weeks at Capua, the American POWs were transferred to prison camps in Germany and in Poland.[31]

CHAPTER 18

Sbeïtla

The Axis Attack Pauses

With Sidi Bou Zid and Gafsa in enemy hands, the Allies expected the Germans to exploit their successes and to do so quickly. The Axis forces were not, however, under a unified command structure and exploitation of the victory at Sidi Bou Zid was not at first coordinated or energetic. The Germans spent most of the day on February 16 fighting to clear the obdurate Americans from Djebel Ksaïra and Djebel Garet Hadid and attempting to learn Allied intentions. Von Arnim and Rommel bickered over what further actions to take and with what forces.[1] The Axis triumph at Sidi Bou Zid left them off balance. *Frühlingswind* had been a stunning success, and the Allied abandonment of Gafsa had made *Morgenluft*—Rommel's thrust in the south—superfluous. The Axis commanders now debated what they should do.

Atrocious Allied communications security helped the enemy to answer that question. Unencrypted radio transmissions told German eavesdroppers what the Allies intended. Following Anderson's order at 10:40a.m. on February 16 that II Corps was not to counterattack further, German commanders knew that American troops in II Corps would fight only a delaying action at Sbeïtla as part of a general retreat. Kesselring, then on a flying visit to Hitler's headquarters, ordered the strike on Sbeïtla to proceed. Von Arnim ordered his troops to Sbeïtla, the gateway to Kasserine Pass and the Grand or Western Dorsal.[2] Ziegler, shortly after midnight February 15–16, directed the 10th Panzer Division to reconnoiter toward Sbeïtla early in the morning and to storm the town during the day. At about the same time Ziegler conferred by telephone with Arnim, insisting that he would not be able to attack successfully toward Hadjeb el Aïoun in the general direction of the Fondouk el Aouareb Gap unless he could retain command over the 21st Panzer Division. Therefore, at 7:45a.m., February 16, Arnim informed *Kampfgruppe DAK* [Rommel] that he would not send the 21st Panzer Division to the Gafsa area now in Axis possession. Von Arnim then ordered Ziegler to strike against Sbeïtla on February 17 with a brief, powerful blow to destroy the Allied supply dumps, and then to turn north against Fondouk el Aouareb with the mission of destroying the Allied forces south of the gap. The main bodies of both divisions assembled near Sidi Bou Zid. The less mobile elements of the 10th Panzer and 21st Panzer Divisions were meanwhile still engaged in the final effort to eliminate the Americans on Djebels Lessouda, Garet Hadid, and Ksaïra.[3]

As the German forces moved to seize Fériana and Thélepte and to attack Sbeïtla on February 17, the possibility arose of a much deeper Axis penetration into the Allied southern flank than had been planned. Rommel still favored a thrust against Tébessa, perhaps advancing the entire Axis forward line to the west. He asked Arnim if the latter intended to exploit his successes in such a way. Arnim replied that he intended to use the 21st Panzer Division around Sbeïtla and the 10th Panzer Division, as originally planned, in the Fondouk-Pichon area. He would advance his main line of resistance only to the crests of the Eastern Dorsal in view of the state of his forces and supplies. Without command coordination from above, the two commanders made no preparations on February 18 to press beyond the Western Dorsal, but only reconnoitered from Sbeïtla and Thélepte. Rommel went so far as to order his only substantial reserves to start back to the Mareth Position, while Arnim committed the 10th Panzer Division with *Kampfgruppe Buhse* near Fondouk. Axis air reconnaissance west of Kasserine indicated that the Allies were not assembling for a strong counterattack.[4]

The Allied Line Swings Back

During the night of February 16–17, while U.S. 1st Armored Division fought around Sbeïtla and the unfortunates of 3/168 were trying to escape, Allied troop movements continued for the second night to swing the Tunisian front from the Eastern to the Western Dorsal. British armored forces moved southward to shield westward withdrawals by American and French units. Then the British forces also moved west and southwest to reinforce defensive zones along the new line. On February 15, the easterly bulge in the Allied front north of Sbeïtla–Sidi Bou Zid was flattened first at the south where it was largest. North of this point the bulge was pulled back to the Ousseltia valley, where French and American troops moved to defensible positions on the rocky heights bordering the valley on the west. The 34th Infantry Division assumed responsibility for the Pichon-Djebel Trozza (997m) section of the Allied front under Lieutenant General Koeltz. But 34ID was without its 168th Regimental Combat Team, the beat-up remnants of which were straggling back into American lines on the eastern front of the Western Dorsal, and also without its 2nd Battalion, 133rd Infantry Regiment, performing guard duty at AFHQ in Algiers.

When the withdrawal was ordered on February 16–17, 34ID moved to the Sbiba gap.[5] The 16th Regimental Combat Team of the U.S. 1st Infantry Division was withdrawn from the Ousseltia heights southwestward to the II Corps area between Tébessa and Fériana. Elements of the British 6th Armoured Division and 1st Guards

Brigade moved into Sbiba and Thala. The artillery of the U.S. 9th Infantry Division began a rapid road march over difficult terrain from beyond Oran to Thala. First Army had finally released Combat Command B, 1st Armored Division, to II Corps on February 15 for deployment in the defense at Sbeïtla. CCB reached Sbeïtla by two routes that night and passed to 1st Armored Division control. Late on February 16 CCB advanced into positions southeast of the village.[6]

Sbeïtla, site of an ancient Roman town, lay about one mile south of a tip of Djebel Mrhila (1,378m), a long and lofty ridge extending more than 18 miles north–northeastward. About five miles south of Sbeïtla was a lower chain of hills, with widely spaced crests, running roughly westward from Djebel Hamra (673m). To the northeast of those hills, Combat Command A maintained a thin outer screening line. As one approached from the east over the rising plain, Sbeïtla sat in a wide gap between the hills. To the west of the village another wide expanse of open plateau reached to the base of the Western Dorsal, from Kasserine north to Sbiba. Two streams, one the Sbeïtla river, the other a tributary from the southwest, converged some five miles east of the village and drained northeasterly, eventually joining the Zeroud river, which flowed through the Eastern Dorsal near Hadjeb el Aïoun. The Sbeïtla river ran in a deep-sunk channel along the northeastern side of the town. There were many olive groves and cultivated fields along the streams. A narrow-gauge railway that connected Sousse on the coast with the mining town of Metlaouï in the southwest ran through Sbeïtla to Kasserine and beyond. A railroad bridge and another bridge of three arches, formerly an aqueduct, crossed the Sbeïtla river about half a mile east of the village. For almost two miles east of the highway bridge, the road from Faïd ran through the olive groves. The Americans expected the Axis assault toward Sbeïtla and on to Kasserine to the west to come along that road, first to a bridge five miles east-southeast of Sbeïtla, and from there to fan out on either side of the road to search for vulnerabilities in the main American defense line nearer the village.[7]

At 1AD's command post, the smog of war persisted. Major General Ward was still for a time without enough accurate information about the situation near Sbeïtla to exercise effective command and control. Rarely leaving his command post, he could not form a coherent picture of the battlefield from the many alarming messages streaming into his headquarters from subordinate commands. Ward had initially remained strangely unperturbed despite reports that the Americans had lost two armored battalions, two infantry battalions, two artillery battalions, and several smaller units and that a powerful enemy striking force was coming his way. But the news that McQuillin and many CCA troops not already dead or captured had left the battlefield and were stampeding westward finally succeeded in shocking Ward out of his leadership stupor and his resentment at having been bypassed by Fredendall. Stack, the CCC commander, watched McQuillin and his battered troops roll past. "I told General Ward," Stack recounted, "that if he thought that CCA was his front line, he was mistaken." Ward angrily radioed McQuillin and found him "some miles in the rear," Stack added. "Ward ordered McQuillin to stop the retreat of CCA and return to his original position."[8]

II Corps ordered the 1st Armored Division to screen the Allied troop movements into the Sbiba sector by a delaying action at Sbeïtla, but Fredendall did not tell Ward that a withdrawal from Sbeïtla was under consideration until First Army directed II Corps to evacuate. The loss of Sbeïtla would immediately open the northward route to Sbiba. II Corps instructed Ward to use defensive tactics both to gain an indefinite amount of time and to preserve itself "as a fighting force." 1AD must not be pinned down nor enveloped and cut off.[9]

Ward's delaying action had to be conducted in an area where Djebel Mrhila on the north and the lower ridge on the south protected the flanks, but which had little depth. From Djebel Hamra westward for about eight miles there was little cover, and the ground offered no defensible positions. Still, Ward's state of mind improved as he and his entire division were reunited for the first time since Northern Ireland. He established his main line of resistance three miles east of Sbeïtla, at the edge of extensive olive groves, with CCB on the right holding the southern sector and the remnants of CCA on the left holding the northern sector. Highway 13, the Faïd–Sbeïtla road, was the boundary between them. On February 16 Ward attached CCC to CCA for McQuillin's use as a reserve west of the town. McQuillin's command now consisted of a great many pieces: his own CCA with 1st Armored Regiment (less 1st Battalion), 1st Battalion, 6th Armored Infantry, 3rd Battalion, 13th Armored Regiment, 701st Tank Destroyer Battalion (much reduced in strength), 91st Field Artillery Battalion, one battery, 68th Field Artillery Battalion, C Company, 16th Engineer Battalion, five guns of the 106th Coast Artillery, one battery, 213th Coast Artillery (90mm guns); and CCC consisting of 3rd Battalion, 6th Armored Infantry, 1st Battalion, 13th Armored Regiment, the other batteries of the 68th Field Artillery Battalion, the main body of the 16th Engineer Battalion, elements of the 701st Tank Destroyer Battalion, and one company, 805th Tank Destroyer Battalion. The main line of resistance was to be held until a time to be determined by II Corps order.[10]

Panzers of *Kampfgruppe Gerhardt* of the 10th Panzer Division advanced slowly over the plains southwest of Djebel Lessouda toward the forward defenses of Sbeïtla on February 16. In mid-afternoon, the Americans observed other enemy tanks farther southwest assembling for an attack. McQuillin and Hains reconnoitered and assigned positions to CCA's units. At 4:00p.m. CCA sent the 3rd Battalion, 13th Armored Regiment (less Company G) forward from its reserve position south of Sbeïtla to reinforce the screen and to prolong the defense until CCA could move into its newly assigned positions. Ward ordered the infantry and artillery units to withdraw to the new locations in the latter part of the afternoon, leaving as a covering force Colonel Hightower's company-strength provisional unit. Company G (Captain

Herman McWatters), 2nd Battalion, 13th Armored Regiment and elements of the 701st Tank Destroyer Battalion were placed on the southern flank.

The American defensive arrangements were not yet completed when the German spearhead crashed into the screen at around 5:00p.m. on February 16. Sharp fighting erupted in the late afternoon and continued after dark. The enemy's forward elements attempted to turn the northern flank of Company G about 5:00p.m., but reinforcements from 2/13AR led by Lieutenant Colonel Ben Crosby arrived in time to catch the Germans by surprise and quickly drive them back. Hightower's tanks successfully stopped yet another German column and then withdrew. Darkness was falling when the American troops saw a strong enemy armored force in three columns approaching along the axis of the Faïd–Sbeïtla road behind Company G, as that unit followed the remainder of the 3rd Battalion, 13th Armored Regiment, back into Sbeïtla. A rearguard action with sporadic firing ensued, while the bulk of CCA, after replenishing fuel and ammunition supplies from dumps in the olive grove about two miles east of Sbeïtla, moved into fallback defensive positions. The American tank destroyers, after being cut off on the south flank at Djebel Hamra, dispersed, ran pell mell from the Germans, and filtered back farther south during the night.

On the southwestern side of a wide, deep, straight-sided *wadi* about one mile east of Sbeïtla, the 213th Coast Artillery Battalion had emplaced its 90mm guns. The 68th Armored Field Artillery Battalion stood ready behind its 105mm howitzers under olive trees along the Faïd–Sbeïtla road. The 91st Field Artillery Battalion was to take adjacent positions when it arrived. The 3rd Battalion, 6th Armored Infantry, had orders to protect the artillery and to support CCA's armor, which was assigned to defensive positions at points along the line north of the Faïd road, astride the railroad, and in front of the artillery. 3/6AR was also ordered to be ready to counterattack.[11]

But the Germans already knew that the American force would not fight long to keep Sbeïtla. *Kampfgruppe Gerhardt* headed for the bridge on the Faïd–Sbeïtla road about five miles east-southeast of Sbeïtla. *Kampfgruppe Pfeiffer*, consisting of one tank battalion, one armored infantry battalion, two field batteries, and some anti-tank units of the 21st Panzer Division, was expected to pass through *Kampfgruppe Gerhardt* near the bridge and make the attack. The Germans intended to hasten the Allies' withdrawal from Sbeïtla by following closely on the heels of 2/13AR and of Company G. It was an overcast, frosty night under a pale moon gliding between patches of moving clouds. When Pfeiffer's point detachment came near enough to the American rear guard to see the dim outlines of its vehicles, the Germans opened fire. Scattered rounds carried into the olive groves beside the highway and hit near the CCA command post or fell among troops refueling vehicles or on supply dumps under the trees. Arnim's three armored columns continued the onslaught on Sbeïtla, pressing the fight in the dark until the early hours of February 17.[12]

The extreme stress of the unrelenting German attacks in the darkness unnerved some soldiers of the 1st Armored Division and the situation began to get out of hand. Around 8:30p.m. on February 16, as American engineers detonated explosives to wreck bridges, culverts, an aqueduct, and an ammunition dump, some American troops panicked and fled the battlefield. For most of the troops it was a first experience of a night attack. The Americans were exhausted by three days of defeat, intensified by a pervading sense of being let down by those in command who appeared to be 'playing it by ear.' The firing at the front and the roar of the engineers' demolitions combined in a hellish noise, and the explosions of the scattered enemy rounds were too close for comfort. Some soldiers took vehicles from the olive groves, where scattered enemy fire was falling, onto the road and started westward. Soon the road was a mass of bumper-to-bumper traffic streaming west out of Sbeïtla in the darkness, choking the roads and threatening to leave Sbeïtla undefended. But resolute troops of other elements of CCA stood fast, including the tankers of the 3rd Battalion, 13th Armored Regiment, and the provisional company, 1st Armored Regiment. The enemy, apparently unaware of the actual situation despite their accurate intelligence that the Americans would wage only a delaying fight, recognized that Sbeïtla was being evacuated but reported that the Allies were still resisting strongly rather than making a full withdrawal.[13]

By dawn on February 17 the Allied situation at Sbeïtla had at least been clarified if not improved.[14] Ward received first-hand oral reports at about midnight on February 16–17 and concluded correctly that CCA had lost substantial combat power and was under imminent attack by a large, armored force. At 1:00a.m. on Wednesday, February 17, he reported by telephone to Fredendall in Speedy Valley that the situation was extremely grave. The Germans were at the edge of Sbeïtla with about nine Mark VI and 80 Mark IV tanks. The enemy's spearhead had already pierced the outer line three miles to the east. CCA had buckled beyond repair. Ward did not know how long his division could stand and fight. Fredendall transmitted Ward's dire report to Brigadier McNabb at Advance Headquarters, First Army, to General Anderson, and to General Truscott at the Advance Headquarters, AFHQ in Constantine. Truscott wrote: "[Fredendall] considered situation extremely grave, and uncertain of ability to hold." Truscott had sent Colonel Don E. Carleton to Sbeïtla during the day, as Truscott's personal agent to observe and assess the situation. Carleton now made a confirmatory firsthand report to Truscott. Truscott concluded that 1st Armored Division would soon be overrun. Fredendall collapsed in a shameful panic. He ordered Speedy Valley evacuated and moved to a new corps headquarters in the primary school at Le Kouif, 17 miles northeast of Tébessa. The ridiculous and expensive tunnel project was abandoned forever.[15]

The news was bad enough, but in accord with the adage about not believing the wounded and stragglers, not entirely true. The German advance during the evening of February 16 was slowed and then stopped by the growing determination among many GIs not to be kicked around anymore. "Strong enemy resistance," 21st Panzer Division reported after several skirmishes. With only 65 operational *panzers*, Hildebrandt, with the concurrence of Arnim, decided to await daybreak before pressing his attack. Von Arnim, in accordance with his intentions expressed over the preceding days, diverted part of 10th Panzer Division for a thrust 25 miles northeast toward Pichon in an effort to cut off the Allied forces there.

At 1:30a.m., February 17, Anderson via McNabb authorized Fredendall to withdraw 1AD command from Sbeïtla. First Army also directed II Corps to withdraw from Fériana the force under Colonel Stark that had previously withdrawn from Gafsa. Stark's command comprised the 3rd Battalion, 26th Infantry, the 1st Ranger Battalion, the 175th Field Artillery Battalion, detached from 34ID, E & C Squadrons, British Derbyshire Yeomanry, French units of the Constantine Division, and, beginning February 8, the intact 1st Battalion, 168th Infantry, also detached from 34ID and held in Fériana after that date as II Corps reserve. But Anderson also instructed Fredendall to order Ward to hold until the evening of February 17 to allow the preparation of Allied fallback positions at Kasserine Pass in the west and at Sbiba in the north. Fredendall protested that by then the 1st Armored Division would be reduced to smoking scrap. Anderson agreed to give Fredendall more discretion. Fredendall instructed Ward to hold at all costs until hearing otherwise. CCB received a division order at about 3:00a.m., February 17, directing that Sbeïtla must be held at all costs until 11:00a.m. That order was superseded by another about an hour later which directed CCB to hold on a line south and east of the town until ordered to withdraw.[16]

The enemy did not storm Sbeïtla at dawn. Beginning at 7:15a.m., *Kampfgruppe Gerhardt* stayed in close contact, watching Allied truck convoys leave Sbeïtla, but did not advance, and the main body waited for additional units from Sidi Bou Zid. A full-scale assault was planned to begin at noon. Both sides kept up harassing artillery fire. The Germans made several probing attacks during the morning, only to encounter terrain on the northeastern approaches that was unsuitable for armored operations. Hildebrandt decided to launch his main effort with *Kampfgruppe Stenkhoff* of the 21st Panzer Division south of the Sbeïtla–Sidi Bou Zid road. He ordered Colonel Pfeiffer's infantry to attack at the same time directly from the east. At about noon, Axis infantry advanced down Highway 13 and the *panzers* attacked CCB on the American right.[17] The Americans, who had learned much from and about their enemy in the past two days, had used the morning lull to reposition their tanks and guns to take every available advantage of the corrugated terrain, and now made good use of every opportunity to hide, shoot and move.[18] Despite careful planning and a greater force, the initial German assault ran into carefully hidden anti-tank guns, artillery traps, and defiladed tanks, which waited patiently until the enemy was at point-blank range and then fired a volley that disabled five *panzers* and slowed the attack. But the depleted and outgunned Americans could not hold for much longer.[19]

II Corps now suffered more adverse consequences of its overextended and undermanned defense against the enemy's rapidly concentrated armored forces. The holding action at Sbeïtla, despite several satisfying instances of local tactical success, was a calamitous American defeat. At 2:30p.m., Ward authorized CCB to withdraw behind the other combat commands. For three hours 2nd Battalion, 13th Armored Regiment, under Major Henry E. Gardiner, fought a deft and gallant rearguard battle at a cost of nine obsolete M3 medium tanks, including the battalion commander's tank, "Henry II." Gardiner stayed on the battlefield with his men until all the survivors had withdrawn, then his own tank was hit. With his driver dead, himself wounded, and his tank in flames, Gardiner hid until sunset, then fled west.[i] [20]

The Americans had managed to stay in Sbeïtla most of the day but began to retreat in the late afternoon as ordered. They passed west of Kasserine by midnight to bivouacs between Kasserine Pass and Thala. By 5:00p.m. German and Italian troops edged into Sbeïtla and organized their defense without impeding the American withdrawal. The town was rubble, an empty, burning heap of demolished buildings and bridges and smashed water mains.[21]

First Army organized the defense of the Sbiba gap further north with Allied units which moved in on the night of February 16–17 and on the following night. Finally convinced that the attack from the Faïd Pass toward Sbeïtla was the enemy's spearpoint, Anderson ordered emergency daylight moves by the British 1st Guards Brigade (less one battalion), with the 18th Infantry Regiment, 1st Infantry Division, attached. Those units were further reinforced first by the 34th Infantry Division (five infantry battalions and supporting artillery battalions), which marched northwest from Pichon to Maktar, and then south to Sbiba, and then by the British 26th Armoured Brigade (less 16th/5th Lancers) under command of Brigadier Charles A. L. Dunphie. Somewhat later in the day, Major General Sir Charles F. Keightley's Headquarters, 6th Armoured Division, was transferred to French XIX Corps with the mission of defending Sbiba gap. The corps boundary was redefined to extend from a point four miles south of Sbiba to Hadjeb el Aïoun.[22]

At about 9:30a.m. on February 17, Brigadier McNabb, chief of staff at First Army, telephoned Truscott at the AFHQ Advanced CP to report that one brigade of the British 6th Armored Division with artillery and anti-tank guns had been ordered from the north to Thala, and that the 34th Infantry Division on the right of what had been the French sector was to hold the high ground east of Sbiba. At about 10:45a.m., Fredendall reported that Fériana and Thélepte had been evacuated and that other units were retreating through the Kasserine Pass. Fredendall told Truscott that Ward (1AD) was to start west at 11:00a.m. through the pass and take

---

i   For his courage and leadership at Sbeïtla, Gardiner was awarded the Distinguished Service Cross.

position south of Tébessa. McQuillin (CCA) was to move to Sbiba by nightfall. Then Fredendall added:

> We are going to have to write Drake and his battalion off. I am going to get a plane over him and tell him to give in. There is no out. He is completely surrounded. He had two days' ammunition and two days' rations. He had been out for twenty-four hours. There is no use prolonging the agony. We have got to write him off.

Truscott later wrote: "That was bitter news."[23]

Fredendall called Truscott again at about 1:30p.m. on February 17; Truscott, whose practice was to have a stenographer record his telephone conversations, recalled later what Fredendall reported.

> I am holding a lot of mountain passes against armor with three and one-half battalions of infantry. If they get together any place a couple of infantry battalions, they might smoke me out... I haven't got a damn bit of reserve. I need a combat team of infantry worse than hell. All I have got are three and one-half battalions of infantry. They are not enough. And we just got a little dope from First Army that indications are that the enemy is going to attack from Fériana with the objective of Tébessa.

Truscott "explained to General Fredendall that the artillery and cannon companies of the 9th Infantry Division were on their way, but that even they could not be expected for several days." He suggested that Fredendall call Anderson for infantry to meet the emergency.[24]

As night fell, a long column of Allied support units, followed by combat elements, motored west beyond Kasserine Pass.[25] The Allies were dejectedly learning, again, how to retreat. "But in the glooming a spark kindled among those who had stood fast and fought well at the end. Pride, vengeance, anger came... and a sense that enough was enough, that from this havoc a ruthless killing spirit would emerge. The war was coming inside them now."[26] Among those tramping through the passes of the Grand Dorsal was Ernie Pyle, who considered the retreat "damned humiliating" even as he wrote of the soldiers around him:

> Personally, I feel that some such setback as this—tragic though it is for many Americans, for whom it is now too late—is not entirely a bad thing for us. It is all right to have a good opinion of yourself, but we Americans are so smug with our cockiness. We somehow feel that just because we're Americans we can whip our weight in wildcats. And we have got into our heads that production alone will win the war...
>
> As for our soldiers themselves, you need feel no shame nor concern about their ability. I have seen them in battle and afterwards and there is nothing wrong with the common American soldier. His fighting spirit is good. His morale is okay. The deeper he gets into a fight, the more of a fighting man he becomes...[27]

Rick Atkinson wrote: "Pyle was telling his readers what they wanted to hear. Oddly enough, it was true."[28]

Fredendall, continuing his practice of personally directing the placement of subunits in tactical positions, ordered Colonel Anderson Moore, commanding a force consisting of the 19th Engineers and the 1st Battalion, 26th Infantry Regiment, detached from the 1st Infantry Division, then defending a line east of Kasserine village, to hold that line until 1st Armored Division had passed through, and then to organize Kasserine Pass for defense. During the night of February 17–18 this order was executed.[29] Colonel Moore's force, ill-disposed and without strong armor support, would bear the brunt of the initial German armored attack through Kasserine Pass.

CHAPTER 19

The Red Bull's Fight at Sbiba

The Enemy's Indecision

The first phase of the enemy's exploitation after the battles near Sidi Bou Zid ended when Gafsa, Sbeïtla, Fériana and the airfield at Thélepte were abandoned by the Americans. On February 17, the two main enemy forces, *DAK* at Fériana and 21st Panzer Division at Sbeïtla, had accomplished their separate missions. The 10th Panzer Division had contacted the Axis forces at Fondouk el Aouareb Gap and, in conformity with Arnim's orders, was on its way to an assembly area north of Kairouan to prepare for a renewed attack into First Army's flank. By February 18, Axis reconnaissance units were probing the gaps in the Western Dorsal from Sbiba to El Ma el Abiod. Enemy air reconnaissance discovered the Allied troop formations moving westward from the Kasserine Pass and Bou Chebka areas. It appeared to the Axis leaders that the Allies were concentrating their forces around Tébessa, and perhaps leaving only rear guards to defend the passes through the Grand Dorsal. The initiative was still with the Axis forces.[1]

Field Marshal Rommel strongly believed his forces could successfully pursue and destroy the retreating Allies. He now evinced what the official Army history characterizes as "an uprush of sanguine anticipations," contrary to the pessimism he had expressed on the previous evening (February 17) when he had averred that his own forces were not strong enough to undertake an attack against Tébessa and that such an operation would be feasible only if reinforced by the main body of Arnim's mobile forces and supported by a holding attack along the Fifth Panzer Army's northern and central sectors.[2]

Von Arnim had his marching orders, but Rommel's next move was less clear. Axis successes thus far had revived the opportunity to accomplish the ambitious operation that Rommel had earlier advocated as a reason for bringing the hard-hitting mobile units of his army swiftly back from Libya to Tunisia. But the enemy's momentum now waned for want of a unified command and a shared offensive vision. To the Allies' great good fortune, the Axis lost more than two days because the German generals were not able to decide how to take advantage of their unexpectedly rapid success. In a message to Kesselring and Italian *Comando Supremo* in Rome, Rommel requested that both the 10th and the 21st Panzer Divisions be placed under his command. At 2:20p.m. in the afternoon of Wednesday, February 18, after a flurry of messages and a telephone conversation in which Arnim expressed his unyielding opposition to Rommel's proposals, Rommel sent a message to *Comando Supremo* and to Kesselring, the German commander in chief, South.

> On the basis of the enemy situation as of today, I propose an immediate enveloping thrust from the southwest on Tébessa and the area to the north of it, provided Fifth Panzer Army's supply situation is adequate. This offensive must be executed with strong forces. I therefore request that 10th Panzer and 21st Panzer Divisions be assigned to me and move immediately to the assembly area Thélepte-Fériana.[3]

Von Arnim again disagreed, in a phone call to Rommel and in messages to Kesselring.

Allied intelligence detected part of this protracted debate, but the most important message, conveying Rommel's request for the two armored divisions, was not decrypted. Kesselring had just returned to the German offices in the Frascati district of Rome after a visit to Hitler at his headquarters in East Prussia. He was at first uncharacteristically indecisive, but quickly recovered his customary confidence, concluded that opportunity outweighed risk, and fully approved Rommel's proposal, giving it his full endorsement in a message to *Comando Supremo*. But in Kesselring's absence from Rome, an ambiguous order from *Comando Supremo* had been issued on February 16, directing exploitation of the successes gained at Sidi Bou Zid, but making Arnim instead of Rommel responsible for such operations. This was a departure from Kesselring's intent.[4] He radioed the two army commanders in Tunisia.

> I consider it essential to continue the attack toward Tébessa and northward by concentrating all available forces on the left [southern] wing and exploiting our recent successes with a blow that can still have vast consequences for the enemy. This is for your preliminary information. I shall speak in this sense to the Duce and [General] Ambrosio today.[5]

Early in the morning of February 19, Kesselring flew to Tunisia to confer with Arnim and to ensure the prompt execution of *Comando Supremo*'s directive. Kesselring wanted to guarantee that everything possible was done to make the Axis offensive succeed. He had reason to be apprehensive. *Comando Supremo*'s vague instructions had sown confusion and misunderstanding among the Axis commanders. Kesselring learned that Arnim had interpreted the directive to read that Group Rommel "was to break through [the Allied front] between Le Kef and Tébessa" and that Arnim expected Rommel to move on Tébessa with only the forces Rommel had in hand, meaning *Kampfgruppe DAK*. Von Arnim had prepared a counterproposal which he felt would bring decisive and speedy success, provided the required combat forces and supplies were made available. He wanted to strike the Allies with a concentric or enveloping attack toward Le Kef, and thence down the Medjerda river, with Béja as the objective. Kesselring was having none of this and unequivocally rejected Arnim's concept; he had intended a wide envelopment of the main Allied forces including both Tébessa and Le Kef as essential objectives. Not until later would Kesselring discover that *Comando Supremo*'s directive had failed to make his intention clear to Rommel.[6]

Comando Supremo gave its approval at 1:30a.m. on Friday morning, February 19. Rommel could have the two *panzer* divisions, but with a proviso. Rather than lunging as far west as Tébessa, Rommel was to aim due north of Kasserine, at Le Kef, where the roads were better, and he could cut off Anderson's First Army.[7] The directive stated that "a unique opportunity is now offered to force a decisive success in Tunisia." It directed Rommel to make a deep thrust toward the north to threaten the rear of British V Corps, if possible, to isolate and damage it, but in any event to force an Allied retreat from Tunisia. With all available mobile elements of his own German-Italian Panzer Army, as well as the 10th Panzer and 21st Panzer Divisions now assigned to him, Rommel was to attack toward Maktar-Tadjerouine with Le Kef[i] as his initial objective. He was to concentrate his forces along a line from Sbeïtla to Tébessa. Other forces would provide flank security along the line Tébessa-Tozeur. The directive from *Comando Supremo* greatly disappointed Rommel, who still wanted to charge on to Tébessa, and he reiterated his view to *Comando Supremo*.[8]

To the extent the orders prescribed an objective deep inside the Allies' rear in the north it was in accord with Rommel's intention to induce an Allied withdrawal into Algeria. Making Le Kef the objective of the mission, however, was contrary to Rommel's proposal to make a wide circling movement to the northwest through Tébessa. Rommel's interpretation of the *Comando Supremo* directive was that Tébessa was now to be only the western anchor of the drive in the direction of Le Kef instead of being the first objective of a wide enveloping sweep toward Bône. Rommel regarded the prescribed more easterly axis of the northern attack as shortsighted. The main Axis thrust would drive directly into the Allied reserves, assuring a much more difficult fight to achieve Rommel's goal of seizing, looting, and destroying the huge supply depot and command center at Tébessa in Algeria.[9] Rommel ranted at "an appalling and unbelievable piece of shortsightedness" by [his] superiors.[10]

Meanwhile, the Axis high command directed Arnim to prepare the rest of Fifth Panzer Army to launch a holding attack on a wide front between the coast and Pont-du Fahs. Fifth Panzer Army was to tie down and harass the Allies by frequent local attacks.[11]

Rommel worried about any further delay. He had interpreted *Comando Supremo*'s orders to make Le Kef, not Tébessa, the objective of his drive to the north. He calculated that most of his mobile forces would be required to reach Le Kef quickly. He commanded them to converge for an advance on a direct, northwesterly axis to

---

i   Le Kef lies about 78 miles northwest of Sbeïtla, north of Kasserine, and northeast of Tébessa. The
     line Maktar-Tadjerouine is well north and east of Tébessa.

Le Kef, either through Kasserine Pass or Sbiba, depending on which was determined to be less firmly held. Rommel ordered his commanders to begin the first phase of the renewed attack at first light on February 19. The 21st Panzer Division started at 8:00a.m. along the road from Sbeïtla to probe the Sbiba Gap. Ksour,[ii] 50 miles north on the road to Le Kef, was the objective. *Kampfgruppe DAK* was to strike into the Kasserine Pass to clear it in one swift push. Rommel directed the 10th Panzer Division to return immediately from the Pichon-Kairouan area to Sbeïtla, reserving its later commitment for decision until he could determine the relative progress at Sbiba Gap and at Kasserine Pass. Mobile elements of the *131st "Centauro" Armored Division* were called up from Gafsa and instructed to strike toward Tébessa from the southeast.[12]

Rommel meanwhile sent a message to *Comando Supremo* at last insisting that the overall command arrangements must be clarified. During the night of February 19–20, *Comando Supremo* issued its order for reorganization of command. Under the designation Group Rommel, the field marshal was to command the combined forces of the *First Italian Army* (General Messe), charged with the defense of the Mareth Position, and a force now designated *Angriffsgruppe Nord* [Northern Attack Group] including 10th Panzer Division, 21st Panzer Division, and *DAK*. Rommel personally would lead *Angriffsgruppe Nord* in the operation now underway. The change, long overdue, went into effect at 6:00a.m. on Friday, February 20.[13]

34th Infantry Division Moves to Sbiba

While the Axis commanders were arguing about their next moves, American, British, and French troops moved to positions in the new Allied line to defend locations where the enemy was likely to make thrusts. Now satisfied that the Axis attack in the south was the main enemy offensive, Anderson had taken steps early on February 17 to expedite the reinforcement of Sbiba by the British 1st Guards Brigade (less one battalion), with the 18th Infantry Regiment, 1ID, attached, greatly reinforced first by Ryder's 34th Infantry Division (less 168IR and 2nd Battalion, 133IR), and next by the British 26th Armoured Brigade (less 16th/5th Lancers) under command of Brigadier Dunphie. AFHQ and First Army also made changes in the chain of command, most of which were yet again unhelpful.

By the morning of February 19, when Group Rommel began to probe at Kasserine Pass and to move toward Sbiba, Allied troops had already assembled at both places. While the 21st Panzer Division was capturing Sbeïtla on February 17, *Kampfgruppe Gerhardt* of the 10th Panzer Division had marched toward Pichon in conformity with Arnim's plan for the sequel to Operation *Frühlingswind*. His intention had been

---

ii   Ksour is about halfway between Maktar and Tadjerouine on the Maktar–Tadjerouine line.

to have *Kampfgruppe Gerhardt* and *Kampfgruppe Buhse* attack from the east, seize Pichon, and cut off the Allied forces in the Eastern Dorsal. *Kampfgruppe Gerhardt*, approaching via Hadjeb el Aïoun, contacted *Kampfgruppe Buhse* at 4:00p.m. on February 17. But their advance was slowed down by mines, and except for a rear guard at Pichon the Allies, including elements of 34th Infantry Division, had extricated themselves from both positions well in advance of the enemy's attempt to cut them off. Von Arnim's estimate of Allied strength and intentions had been mistaken. The Axis drive to the north was a blow into thin air.[14]

Ryder summoned his regimental commanders to 34ID headquarters during the evening of February 16 and instructed them to prepare to withdraw from the Pichon sector beginning at 7:00p.m. on Tuesday, February 17. Nervous observers from 135th Regimental Combat Team reported several times on February 17 that there were enemy tanks nearby, but none appeared. At about 5:30p.m. the enemy launched a small probing strike by infantry supported by mortar and artillery fire. That attack was beaten off and the 133rd and 135th Infantry Regiments proceeded to pull out. To screen the withdrawal of 135RCT, Major Garnett E. Hall commanded a rear guard of three rifle platoons, one each from Companies B, G, and I, supported by their respective .30 calibre light machine gun and 60mm mortar sections. 1/135 withdrew into division reserve near Sbiba by way of Maktar. By 5:30a.m. on Thursday, February 18, 135RCT, less the 1st Battalion, was established at Er Rbeiba. At 6:00a.m. that day, 34ID ordered 135RCT to move immediately to the vicinity of Sbiba and take up defensive positions in a sector southeast of the town assigned to the division. Motor transport was not available. The 135th Infantry Regiment marched by foot some 30 miles. They reached the designated position southeast of Sbiba at about 11:00p.m. on February 18. That was a feat worthy of the toughest of the regiment's Civil War forebears.[15]

The Allies completed their withdrawal to the Western Dorsal during the night of February 17–18. At Sbiba, after 1st Armored Division's CCA had cleared the pass as it withdrew from Sbeïtla, British engineers closed the minefield. The Sbiba position, behind two belts of mines, was held at first by two units under command of Headquarters British 6th Armored Division: the British 1st Guards Brigade, and the 18th Infantry Regiment, detached from 1ID. To the left or east on a line southeast of Sbiba and east of the road from Kasserine, five battalions of the 34th Infantry Division, two from the 133rd Infantry Regiment (Colonel Fountain) and three from the 135th Infantry Regiment (Colonel Ward), as well as attached French troops, were moved into position. The 135th Infantry Regiment was in contact on its left with elements of the 1st U.S. Infantry Division farther north. On 135IR's right was the 133rd Infantry Regiment, and on the 133IR's right was the 18th Infantry Regiment. Late on February 18, reconnaissance elements of 21st Panzer Division began to probe the new Allied lines of defense south of Sbiba.[16]

Sbiba was in the zone of the French XIX Corps commanded by the Lieutenant General Koeltz. The British 6th Armoured Division, directly under First Army, opened its headquarters at Rohia, nine miles north of Sbiba, at 8:00p.m., February 18 to control the defense of Koeltz's southwestern sector. On the same night one component of that division, the Headquarters, 26th Armoured Brigade (Dunphie), shifted from Sbiba to Thala, with part of its subordinate units. The British 1st Guards Brigade, with the U.S. 18th Regimental Combat Team, and the battalions of the U.S. 34th Infantry Division coming into the line, remained to hold Sbiba. First Army now placed 18RCT under Ryder's command. 18RCT's three battalions took up positions south of Sbiba and just east of the Sbeïtla–Sbiba road. Before dawn on February 19 the 133rd and 135th Infantry Regiments of the 34th Infantry Division, supported by three artillery battalions, had extended the line along the ridge southeast of Sbiba. The infantry were backed up by the tanks of the 16th/5th Lancers and elements of the 72nd and 93rd British Antitank Regiments, Royal Artillery. The French Light Armored Brigade and a small unit, Detachment *Guinet*, maintained roadblocks between Sbiba and Rohia.

Meanwhile, at Thala, Dunphie's force assembled during the night of February 18–19. The Thala sector was crucial for opposing the enemy's main effort but Dunphie knew that his tanks were obsolete, and that he was out-gunned, and out-armored. He planned to provide reserves at either Sbiba or Kasserine Pass, or at any secondary pass which the enemy might attempt to envelop. At 6:00a.m., February 19, the units under Dunphie's command passed to the nominal control of U.S. II Corps.[17] The higher Allied commands, however, were again quite unable from their distant and limited perspectives to exercise full command and control over the coming battles at Thala, Sbiba and the Bahiret Foussana valley.

On February 19, Fredendall's II Corps was spread among three forces along the Western Dorsal with a fourth in a supporting position on the south flank and a fifth to be brought into position the following night. An ill-fated mixed force of badly equipped, disgruntled, and indifferently led engineers and infantry, with a few tanks and some artillery, was at Kasserine Pass. Northwest of Fériana, guarding the Dernaia position and the routes from Fériana to Tébessa through Bou Chebka, was a relatively large American and French force commanded by the battle-wise Welvert. It included the U.S. 1st Ranger Battalion (many members of which had been recruited from 34ID); the 1st Battalion, 168th Infantry Regiment, detached from 34ID and not involved in the debacle at Sidi Bou Zid; the U.S. 36th (155mm guns) and 175th (British 25-pounder QF howitzers) Field Artillery Battalions, the latter also detached from 34ID; Company D, 16th Armored Engineer Battalion; Company B, 19th Combat Engineers; Battery A, 213th Coast Artillery (Anti-Aircraft) Battalion; three battalions of French infantry and four batteries of French artillery. At the extreme southwestern flank, south of El Ma el Abiod, was 3rd Battalion, 26th

Regimental Combat Team (reinforced), detached from the 1st Infantry Division, and known as Bowen Force. It was backed by what remained of the battered CCA, 1st Armored Division.[18]

The Enemy Is Turned Back at Sbiba

During the Axis assault at Kasserine Pass and then after the enemy breakthrough there, three separate battles were fought in central Tunisia. These were Sbiba, Thala and the Bahiret Foussana valley. The latter involved two related actions, one at Djebel el Hamra on the far western edge of the valley and another at the Bou Chebka pass on the southwestern edge. For the Allies, the result of one of the three fights was poor, but the Germans did ultimately withdraw. The results of the other two actions were decidedly good. The engagements occurred from east to west in geographical space and in temporal sequence. First and of most importance to the history of the 34th Infantry Division was the defeat at Sbiba of the northern German thrust up Highway 71 by 21st Panzer Division.

As the armored fighting vehicles of the right wing of Rommel's double thrust against the Allied defenses advanced toward Le Kef on Friday morning, February 19, German intelligence incorrectly reported that the troops straddling the road at Sbiba, 25 miles above Sbeïtla, were French and British and not in great numbers. In fact, eight American infantry battalions drawn from the 34th Infantry and 1st Infantry Divisions, backed by American and British artillery, and with substantial British infantry and some armor close by, now held the terrain east of the road. The main body of 21st Panzer Division started north from Sbeïtla at 9:00a.m. on February 19 with its objective a road junction at Ksour. The head of the column arrived shortly before noon at the first narrow belt of Allied mines across the road about six miles southeast of Sbiba, where they were able to open a gap while covering the operation with artillery fire on the higher ground to the northwest. The Germans then came up against the second, better laid minefield, well within the range of British artillery. Enemy observers, assisted by Arabs, now saw the strength of the Allied positions held by a considerable number of infantry on the high ground on either side of the road, three to four miles farther north, supported by 20 Allied tanks and at least two battalions of artillery. Allied shells now fell on the oncoming Germans.

21st Panzer Division was preparing its assault on the Sbiba defenses when Rommel arrived at Hildebrandt's command post to urge an aggressive, concentrated attack for a breakthrough rather than the planned wide frontal attack. But Hildebrandt's attack on February 19 was stopped short before he was able to commit his infantry. While the enemy main column stopped, one armored battalion from 5th Panzer Regiment and some truck-borne infantry swept to the east out of range of the Allied artillery and then northward directly into ground held by the battalions of the

18th Infantry Regiment. A detachment of the British 16th/5th Lancers tried to move within range to deter the attack but lost four of its light tanks to the longer-range guns of the enemy's vehicles. The Germans brought up several batteries of light field howitzers, emplaced them, and began counterbattery and preparation fire on the Allied ridge positions while the infantry of 104th Panzer Grenadier Regiment prepared to attack.[19]

The American and British gunners at Sbiba now demonstrated a competence and confidence which would grow into a truly fearsome destructive force in the coming weeks and months. With the benefit of good observation positions, the 151st Field Artillery Battalion and the other Allied artillery units supporting the 34th Infantry Division and 1st Guards Brigade had plotted more than 100 fire concentrations on the approaches to Sbiba. The Germans quickly began bleeding *panzers*.[20] By mid-afternoon on February 19 a dozen *panzers* had been wrecked by artillery fire, and enemy corpses littered the ground. One GI likened the effect of 105mm shells on armor hulls to "taking shoe boxes and shoving them flat."[21] The remaining tanks were driven back. The enemy's infantry attack came to a complete standstill and the *panzers* retreated out of artillery range. The whole day's enemy offensive was ineffective and irresolute, owing in large part to the devastating volume and accuracy of Allied artillery.[22] British engineers went out after dark and demolished seven of the enemy's vehicles. Hildebrandt pulled his armored units behind a defensive line of infantry, sent the 580th Reconnaissance Battalion to the eastern flank, and covered the west flank by the 609th Flak Battalion. The Americans near Sbiba used the night to dig in their machine guns and mortars and to lay yet more mines and barbed wire in front of their line in expectation of another attack the next day.[23]

The Red Bull soldiers were right. *Panzers* and two Wehrmacht infantry battalions made a renewed assault on the American positions the next morning, February 20. The enemy attacked first in the area controlled by the 18th Infantry Regiment, but the assault quickly collapsed in a hail of Allied artillery fire. The enemy then tried to make a two-battalion infantry attack, with artillery support, on the American ridge positions to the east, while sending an armored force of 33 Mark III and six Mark IV *panzers* with a battery of field artillery, on another wide sweep around the eastern flank. The *panzers* were to take the Allied ridge positions from the rear, and then envelop Sbiba and cut the road north of it. The enemy operation was beset with difficulties. Fog and rain over the battle area and elsewhere in Tunisia deprived the 21st Panzer Division of preparatory Stuka attacks or promised fighter support. The Germans found that the terrain to be traversed to the east was extremely difficult, with deep *wadis* and extensive soft areas. The armored force's route of advance was quickly determined to be impassable. Allied artillery observers, however, could see quite well the ground over which the Germans tried to approach. The Allied gunners again adjusted pre-plotted artillery barrages with murderous accuracy on German troops, vehicles, and batteries.

The German infantry stubbornly continued to advance under the British and American shelling, and by noon they came within 600 yards of the positions on the ridge held by 133IR and 135IR. The Americans laid down heavy small-arms and mortar fire and the German infantry faltered and fell back. Four *panzers* did manage to penetrate the 34th Infantry Division's perimeter before they were knocked out by anti-tank weapons. The rest were driven back. Although enemy casualties were light, the *panzergrenadiers* could not gain any ground, and the armor again pulled back in the early afternoon. With Rommel's reluctant approval, 21st Panzer Division backed off and dug in below Sbiba.[24] Rommel ordered 21st Panzer Division's troops to organize an active defense from a base line running between Kef el Korath (1,100m) on the northwest and the apex of Djebel Mrhila (1,378m) on the southeast, more than five miles from Sbiba village, and to stand ready for an Allied counterattack. 21st Panzer Division had about 30 operational tanks, two battalions of armored infantry, six batteries of field artillery, and two companies of anti-aircraft artillery. The Allies before Sbiba were even then receiving powerful reinforcements. A provisional British tank unit equipped with 25 new Churchill tanks came to Sbiba from Le Kef during the night. Already concentrated there by Monday, February 22 were the eight American and three British infantry battalions, numerous field artillery battalions, and other units.[25]

The regimental history of the 135th Infantry describes a solid defensive fight at Sbiba. 2/135 was positioned on 34ID's center left with 133IR on its right flank. 3/135 was on the division's extreme left (northeasterly) flank with a platoon on Hill 476. 3/135 maintained a vigilant liaison with elements of 1ID on 34ID's left flank. 1/135 was held in division reserve. Around noon on Friday, February 19, enemy tanks from the direction of Sbeïtla attacked the British 1st Guards Brigade on 34ID's right flank, west of the road. Further armored attacks followed, supported by infantry, against 34ID's positions; they continued unabated for the ensuing two days. The brunt of the attacks was borne by the 133rd Regimental Combat Team holding the center of the 34ID sector. American and British medium and light artillery battered the enemy units even before they reached the main line of resistance. Germans who managed to infiltrate close to the 34ID infantry's positions were immediately killed or captured. The 34th Infantry Division at Sbiba sustained approximately 50 men killed, 200 wounded, and 250 missing in what was an important Allied victory.[26]

After the southern German charge broke through Kasserine Pass and advanced toward Thala, First Army ordered 34th Infantry Division to withdraw during the night of February 22–23 to the vicinity of Rohia. There the division assumed a defensive posture in new lines to oppose a possible enemy attack from the Thala sector in the south toward First Army's positions to the north. 34ID smoothly executed the movement amidst some grumbling by GIs who felt that they had the situation in hand at Sbiba. 135RCT built up a new defense line near Rohia with minefields and wire at all positions and mutually supporting and pre-sited firing positions covering all approaches. Where the soil permitted excavation, each soldier dug out a four-foot-deep foxhole. Ward, commanding 135RCT, ordered that the Rohia positions were to be held at all costs. Underscoring the grim change in the psychology of the American troops, all Arabs passing through the lines in either direction or who came under suspicion in the rear were shot. Other Arabs were only detained for a day.[27]

The enemy also noted the new determination of the Americans. The evening intelligence report from German-Italian Panzer Army to *OKH* at Rome on February 20, 1943, related that "the enemy opposed violent resistance to our attacks at Sbiba... At Sbiba, the enemy who received constant reinforcements especially in artillery, was able to put a stop to the attack of the 21st Pz. Div., from his improved, dominant positions; the division had gained little ground and was forced to pass to the defensive."[28]

CHAPTER 20

The Axis Breakthrough at Kasserine Pass

The Grand (or Western) Dorsal extended northeast to southwest for 200 miles. There were three passes through the range in the south, connecting Tunisia's interior plateau to the Algerian highlands. Kasserine Pass, 25 miles west of Sbeïtla, had for millennia provided a two-way door for invasion. The pass was at an elevation of some 2,000 feet, between crests which climbed about 2,000 feet higher still, so that winter clouds and mist limited visibility, as was the case on the morning of February 20, 1943. The meandering Hatab river bisected Kasserine Pass northwest to southeast. A steeply banked stream, the Hatab was in spate to its banks from the winter rains, impeding mobility between the northern and southern halves of the pass.

Kasserine's appearance and land would be familiar to anyone who has traveled in the American Southwest: a badland of eroded hills and canyons. In the throat of the pass the road forked. Highway 13, the left tine, continued winding westerly along the Hatab for another 30 miles to the Algerian border near Tébessa. From Djebel Zebbeus to Tébessa, the road extended west-northwest for some 15 miles to Djebel el Hamra[i] (1,112m) at the far northwestern edge of the Bahiret Foussana valley. That road skirted the northern edge of a rough area, almost one third of the valley, which tipped northward from the mountain mass west of Djebel Chambi toward the Hatab river. The Hatab terrain has been described as a "gigantic, crudely corrugated shed roof draining into a badly bent and twisted gutter." The right tine, designated Highway 17, skirted Djebel Semmama due north for 30 miles to the town of Thala and then another 40 to Le Kef.[1]

As the official history notes, Kasserine Pass was not impregnable, but it "offers such advantages to defense that a sufficient force could exact an exorbitant price from a foe determined to take it at all costs." Properly armed troops entrenched on the heights on either side, a basic requirement of any such defense, could dominate the triangular area of approach from the Kasserine side. That area provided no cover and any force attempting to take the heights could easily be seen. A force seeking to push into the gorge by moving along the valley floor would come under punishing

---

i   To be distinguished from Djebel Hamra west of Sidi Bou Zid.

enfilade fire from one side or the other, or both. The eastern opening was less than a mile wide and defenders could observe and fire on any attacking force. An attacker could be restricted by minefields to narrower approaches leading to killing zones covered by prearranged fires.[2]

II Corps had enough force to defend the Kasserine Pass, but that strength was not concentrated at the pass, and the units that were sent to Kasserine were not sufficient in numbers nor competently organized or commanded. Some units in or near the pass were simply not capable of executing a defense against a combined arms attack. The remnants of 1st Armored Division had been sent to the uplands south of Tébessa to protect the supply dumps; the rest of II Corps was concentrated in other danger spots.[3] The forward defense of Kasserine was therefore initially assigned to the hapless 19th Combat Engineer Regiment, 1,200 men unprepared and ill-suited for the part of combat soldiers. The regiment had not even completed rifle training before deployment overseas. Since arriving at the Tunisian front six weeks earlier, the engineers had been building roads. Late at night on Tuesday, February 17, these men formed a thin three-mile-wide skirmish line across the throat of the pass, where they sat for the next 36 hours, without doing much else except to lay a few mines. The engineers should have been ordered to dig in on the elevated shoulders of the pass, and to establish overlapping zones of fire for machine guns and pre-plotted fire concentrations for mortars. Their foxholes were inadequate, and they failed to set up barbed wire entanglements or to place enough mines to encumber the avenues of approach and drive the enemy into kill sacks.[4] Lack of trained leadership resulted in fatal errors in both positioning the troops and preparing defenses.

Even Fredendall, many miles away in the schoolhouse at El Kuif, recognized the vulnerability of Kasserine Pass and the precarious state of the 1,200 engineers. He ordered a battalion of the 26th Infantry Regiment from the scattered 1st Infantry Division to join them, along with a four-gun French battery and some tank destroyers. At 8:00p.m., February 18, Fredendall personally phoned Colonel Alexander Stark, commander of 1st Infantry Division's 26th Infantry Regiment and in a desperate tone said: "Alex, I want you to go to Kasserine right away and pull a Stonewall Jackson. Take over up there."

"You mean tonight, General?" asked Stark.

"Yes, immediately; stop in my CP on the way up," was the answer.

The first defensive organization in Kasserine Pass had been executed by Colonel Moore, who began with a small mine-laying group on February 16. Moore had then shifted all units under his command from the line east of Kasserine village into the pass during the night of February 17–18. When 1st Battalion, 26th Infantry Regiment arrived, Moore placed it astride the Thala road about two miles northwest of the fork in the pass, and his own unit on the southwestern side of the gap, from the Hatab river to Hill 812 (Djebel Zebbeus), on a line through Hill 712 and crossing the Tébessa road. Moore covered the road to Tébessa with about 200 engineers and infantrymen armed with small arms and automatic weapons and supported by two batteries of U.S. 105mm howitzers, a battery of French 75s, and a battalion of tank destroyers in the rear. The main line of resistance extended almost three miles. Moore held it with only about 2,000 badly positioned and inadequately armed men.[5]

It took Stark nearly 12 hours to travel over the rugged terrain from El Kuif to Kasserine. Before morning, he had assumed command of the provisional force from Moore, directly in the case of the infantry from his regiment along the Thala road, and indirectly through Moore of the reinforced 19th Combat Engineers on the other side of the gap. The German advance elements arrived at the same time as Stark. "A quick inspection of the misty pass revealed a predicament even Stonewall Jackson would have been hard put to salvage…" A single rifle platoon was positioned on the height of Djebel Semmama. All four infantry companies of the 1st Battalion, 26IR were in a line on the low ground on the left side of the pass. On the right side, one engineer platoon held Djebel Chambi, while three companies of engineers-turned-infantry held, if tenuously, the flats.[6]

The delay in the Axis attack on Kasserine Pass and the successful defense at Sbiba on February 19 and 20 had caused Rommel to reconsider his original plan to commit the 10th Panzer Division through Sbiba toward Ksour and Le Kef, while merely sealing Kasserine Pass behind a feint toward Tébessa. He had decided, consistently with his more ambitious plan to strike at Tébessa, that the prospects at Kasserine Pass were better.[7] He now ordered General von Broich's 10th Panzer Division to come back from the Pichon-Kairouan area, and to continue through Sbeïtla to Kasserine. There it was to pass through *Kampfgruppe DAK* in Kasserine Pass and to proceed northward toward Thala. *DAK*, after clearing the pass, would proceed northwestward to Djebel el Hamra, seize the passes there, and leave strong defensive elements facing west. Rommel's decision to employ the 10th Panzer Division in the western wing of his attack rather than closer to the 21st Panzer Division followed the directive from *Comando Supremo*, which specified that the greater weight should fall near Kasserine and the Thala axis. It also reflected the tactical situation as then known to Rommel, which promised quicker success at Kasserine Pass.

The friction of war, however, had affected the Germans as well as the Allies. The 10th Panzer Division was to have assembled at Kasserine village by daybreak on February 20; that did not happen. The division was at only half strength because other units including the heavy *panzer* battalion (with some Tigers), remained committed in Arnim's sector. Its available units were delayed by poor, soggy roads and the same harsh weather plaguing the Allies. As late as the night of February 19 its advance elements had arrived only at Sbeïtla.[8]

At dawn on February 19, *DAK* tried to seize Kasserine Pass in a sudden and violent rush. That attack was turned back by good shooting from the French battery of 75mm guns. By 10:00a.m., however, enemy artillery began falling around Stark's command tent three miles west of Kasserine and the Germans renewed their advance in force. Trucks brought up enemy infantry at 10:15a.m., moving toward the high ground on both the left and right of the pass. American reinforcements, including the regimental band, a tank platoon, and three companies from the 39th Infantry Regiment, 9th Infantry Division arrived during the fighting in the early afternoon. The tempo of enemy artillery increased after dark. The Germans deployed for the first time the *Nebelwerfer*,[ii] a six-barreled rocket mortar that "stonked"[iii] targets with a half-dozen 75-pound high-explosive rounds soon known to GIs as "screaming meemies."[iv] At 8:30p.m., enemy patrols overran the infantry battalion command post. German infiltrators cut off the solitary company on the slopes of Djebel Semmama, then seized Point 1191, the mountain's most important ridge. Many GIs who eluded capture were later robbed of their clothes and weapons by Arab brigands.[9]

Mist and fog had settled on the Kasserine Pass in the early morning of Saturday, February 20. Rommel was displeased both with the weather and with the slow progress of his troops, as he had been at Sbiba. General Karl Buelowius had ordered two grenadier battalions to resume their assault, but they advanced only haltingly. Rommel himself ordered three more mobile infantry battalions including motorcycle troops, to reinforce the attack—10th Panzer on the Axis right, *Deutsche Afrika Korps* on the left—for a six-battalion push supported by five artillery battalions. Despite the bad weather and roads, the Germans ferociously attacked the motley group of Americans defending Kasserine and then broke through against resolute but costly fighting by some American units. The power of the German attack disrupted communications between Allied units and between those units and their higher commands. By late morning, the Americans collapsed under German numbers and firepower. The units so precariously positioned on the isolated djebels were overrun or surrounded and destroyed or captured. Survivors jumped on any available vehicle and fled beyond the western outlet of the pass, chased to the Allied rear by the banshee screams of *Nebelwerfer* rounds.

Colonel Theodore J. Conway, sent forward by Truscott to assess Stark's plight, was astonished to see troops streaming past him west and north out of the pass. Conway promptly joined them, but Stark held until after 5:00p.m., when grenades began detonating near his command post in a gulch by the Hatab river. He hurried upriver with his staff before moving overland toward Thala. Casualties among infantrymen alone totaled nearly 500 dead, wounded, and missing. Italian tanks drove west five miles on Highway 13 toward Tébessa without seeing a trace of the Americans except for burning wreckage.

Fredendall, his chief of staff, Colonel John A. Dabney, and others reconnoitered toward the pass along the Kasserine–Thala road late in the morning, February 20,

---

ii   A deceptive euphemism meaning "smoke mortar."

iii   "Stonk" is verb derived from British artillery usage, meaning to strike a target with a concentrated artillery bombardment.

iv   Or as "moaning mimis."

while Robinett's command echelon, far ahead of Combat Command B's main column, moved south through Thala toward Kasserine Pass. When the two groups met south of Thala, Fredendall was returning, convinced that the enemy had broken through on the Kasserine–Tébessa road, and had overwhelmed and crushed the infantry and combat engineers there but not the artillery, tank destroyer, or tank units. It was no longer possible to implement his earlier plans for CCB.

> At corps and higher headquarters... the actual situation was not well understood... [T]he enemy's success of the previous night on the northeastern side of the pass... made it seem likely that he might first thrust toward Thala.[10]

At 3:35a.m. on February 21, a week after the Axis offensive had begun, Fredendall's headquarters warned:

> Enemy reliably reported in possession of heights on either side of Kasserine Pass... Attack also going toward Thala on a four-thousand-yard front and had advanced about two thousand yards beyond the pass.

For the moment, Kasserine Pass was lost, and the Germans pushed ahead west and north.[11]

CHAPTER 21

The Battles on the Roads to Thala and Tébessa

The successful defense at Sbiba Gap on February 19 and 20 allowed First Army to shift combat power westward on February 20 to meet the enemy's spearpoints. The Allied command and particularly Anderson at First Army, however, were still unclear about the situation at the front. The lack of clarity was not relieved by Fredendall's frantic efforts to establish areas of command responsibility or by conflicting directives from First Army. Anderson, at last convinced that the enemy's main effort was directed at Kasserine rather than Sbiba, inserted yet another link in the chain of command. First Army designated Brigadier Cameron Nicholson, second in command of the British 6th Armoured Division, to control, on behalf of II Corps, the operations of all the increasing number of units—British, American, and French—then assembling south of Thala. The new provisional organization was named "Nickforce."

At midnight on February 20–21, while Nicholson was making his way over mired roads from Rohia, Robinett, commander of CCB, and his operations officer, Lieutenant Colonel Edwin A. Russell, Jr., met in conference with Brigadiers McNabb and Dunphie, and others, at Thala. Those men agreed upon a sensible plan of battle: Dunphie would organize south of Thala; Robinett was to cover the routes to Tébessa and Haïdra; both forces were to await and receive the Germans, and both would counterattack, making their strongest efforts on the enemy's flanks once the enemy was committed. At 7:00p.m. on February 20, II Corps had 99 medium (still mostly M3 Grants), 47 light (M3 Stuarts) and 74 nonoperational tanks. Allied tanks were therefore to be conserved and the battle was to be fought mainly with other arms. The meeting was over before Brigadier Nicholson reached Thala at 3:15a.m. on the 21st. Being wise and a prudent leader with confidence in his subordinates, he confirmed the battle plan.[1]

Fredendall's new arrangement also prescribed two distinct defense forces. American troops were to cover Tébessa; British units were to defend Thala. II Corps directed Robinett to assume command of all the troops in the vaguely defined area south of the Hatab river and to defend the passes at Djebel el Hamra. Robinett was expected to stop the enemy's advance toward Tébessa, then drive them back into the Kasserine

Pass and restore the Allied positions there. Fredendall gave Dunphie a similar mission within the Thala sector. Dunphie was to take command of all troops remaining on the north side of the Hatab, including the survivors of Stark's group from Kasserine. He was to use Stark's communication lines to report to II Corps.[2] "For the coordination of this attack, Robinett comes under your command," Fredendall instructed Dunphie, who was now to be directly under U.S. II Corps. Direct communication between Robinett and Dunphie by liaison officer was arranged later in the day.[3] The official history's assessment of Fredendall's order to Dunphie is scathing.

> The II Corps had in effect passed to Dunphie a responsibility which he lacked the means to carry out, requiring him not only to command his own force in battle but also to co-ordinate these operations on one side of the broad [Bahiret Foussana] valley with Robinett's on the other, despite inadequate means of communication.[4]

Fredendall had evaded his responsibility as corps commander to control the battle in the II Corps sector, instead placing that responsibility on his field commanders. He remained without adequate personal knowledge of the ground, of the state of the available Allied forces, and of the enemy's force and dispositions, even after his own inexcusably belated personal reconnaissance of the area south of Thala.

A new chapter in the battles began on the night of February 20–21, after Rommel's *Angriffsgruppe Nord* had gained possession of the northwestern exits from the Kasserine Pass and begun to move west toward Tébessa and north toward Le Kef. Allied troop movements, the preparation of defensive positions on the previous day, and the reinforcements marching toward the battle area were about be tested by the Axis forces moving north and west of Kasserine. The enemy, while somewhat reduced in combat power, was still aggressively bellicose. The military task facing the Allies was to contain the German onrush after it was far enough along the diverging roads to be too widely separated for its units to provide mutual support.

Because Rommel did not have enough forces for strong attacks along both routes, the Axis problem was to decide which road to block and which to use to attack a major objective. The Germans took two days to clear Kasserine Pass, committing both *Kampfgruppe DAK* and 10th Panzer Division in the process. Rommel was again hesitant, once more evidencing an attitude of pessimism and depression which was most unusual for him. Nonetheless, on the night of February 20–21 he directed his troops to make ready for an Allied counterattack and to send out reconnaissance forces along each road.[5]

The finale of the Kasserine battles was now to be enacted, in two cotemporaneous actions. The Allies had established holding forces barring the road to the north below Thala, the main northwesterly route to Tébessa at Djebel el Hamra (1,112m), and the secondary routes southwest from the Bahiret Foussana valley through the Bou Chebka Pass onto the Bou Chebka plateau. Twenty miles west of Kasserine Pass and parallel to the Algerian border, the jagged escarpment known as Djebel el Hamra ran north to south, crossed by the packed-dirt roadbed of Highway 13 from Kasserine. The main body of Robinett's CCB marched over a muddy dirt road leading southward from Haïdra to the Djebel el Hamra area. Behind a light forward screen, CCB took up positions along the eastern face of the ridge and in the passes at its center and northern end. Many stragglers from Kasserine Pass and survivors from Djebel Lessouda had been assembled at the base of the ridge. They were given water, food, and ammunition and organized in provisional companies in a line along the eastern side of Djebel el Hamra to defend the passes. The enemy made its preparations around the edges of Bahiret Foussana valley all morning on February 21. Each opponent expected an imminent attack by the other.[6]

The Battles at Djebel el Hamra and Bou Chebka Pass

At 11:25a.m. February 21, 1943, 33rd Reconnaissance Battalion reported to Rommel that only small numbers of American forces had thus far appeared east of Djebel el Hamra. The German scouts, however, were in error. Djebel el Hamra and its lesser foothills were now occupied by American infantry and armored formations, on good ground and in strength, supported by powerful artillery. Present and dug in were the 16th Infantry Regiment, 1st Infantry Division, and Combat Command B, 1st Armored Division. The Americans had a combined eight infantry battalions and 11 artillery batteries with 44 105mm guns. Based on the bad intelligence, Rommel, without waiting for confirmation from air reconnaissance, opted to resume the offensive against the Allied forces south of Thala with the 7th Panzer Regiment of the 10th Panzer Division, which had been organizing within sight of American observers and was already under harassing U.S. artillery fire. But he also directed *Kampfgruppe DAK* under General Buelowius to seize the passes at Djebel el Hamra to secure the German western flank.

Northward from Kasserine, Nicholson, who had opened "Nickforce" headquarters at 6:00a.m., February 21 in Thala, sent more infantry to the defensive position established by Dunphie south of the village. Nicholson expected reinforcements to arrive at Thala during the next two or three days. The portentous question was whether Nickforce could hold out long enough for those reinforcements to reach Thala before the Germans smashed the defenders.

Robinett's repeated attempts to coordinate with Dunphie had been disrupted by the air bombing of the liaison officer's communications vehicle, and II Corps had only intermittent contact with both commands. The battles of February 21–22 along the two roads, therefore, were fought simultaneously but independently. Again, Headquarters, II Corps possessed inadequate information from the battlefields and was hampered by the confusion of responsibility and authority that Fredendall and Anderson had themselves created. The coordination of Allied forces was impaired by the defective communications and confused channels of command. Luckily, Allied forces along the western and southern edges of the Bahiret Foussana valley and at Thala had been timely reinforced on February 21. The battle was now in the hands of the American, French, and British soldiers and their individual field commanders on the ground facing the enemy.[7]

The main body of Robinett's reinforced CCB had entered the Bahiret Foussana valley during the morning of February 21. Although not completely deployed, CCB was well established by the time Buelowius's *Kampfgruppe DAK* approached. CCB opposed *DAK* with courageous determination, and in Rommel's opinion, "very skillfully."[8] *DAK's* main force left Kasserine Pass at 2:00p.m. on February 21 moving generally northwesterly. German tanks came at CCB's front as *DAK* surged forward along the Hatab's south bank with 40 *panzers* followed by infantry in trucks. They were hit almost at once by increasingly strong artillery fire from unseen American guns hidden on the German southern flank.

Within an hour the weight of massed American howitzers began to tell. Buelowius lacked enough guns for effective counter-battery fire. By 4:00p.m. the attackers had drawn within range of defiladed American tanks and plunging fire from anti-tank guns concealed in the rocks. Even for the *Afrika Korps* it was too much: at 6:00p.m. Buelowius broke off the attack, still four miles short of Djebel el Hamra. *Kampfgruppe DAK* had lost ten tanks, and CCB only one. Between *DAK* and its objective the ground was flat, a level plain without cover and under constant Allied observation from the scrub-covered hills on three sides. Frontal attack in daylight seemed out of the question and, even at night, would be met by Allied troops in strength and on terrain well suited to defense. In the face of the galling defenses, Rommel authorized a wide march to the south during the approaching night.[9]

Repulsed on the right at Sbiba, Rommel directed a now familiar sweeping attack to flank the Americans in the south (the Axis left) and roll them up from the rear. The enemy renewed the attack against CCB the next day, February 22, at the southwestern corner of the Bahiret Foussana valley against positions held by the 2nd Battalion, 16th Infantry Regiment, and 2nd Battalion, 6th Armored Infantry, supported by the 12 105mm guns of the 33rd Field Artillery Battalion. The enemy, in a column of infantry supported by artillery and tanks, was astonished and startled to find themselves hotly engaged at daylight not near Djebel el Hamra, but nearly seven miles to the southeast near the Bou Chebka Pass. A fierce fight erupted that initially went to the Germans. Two *panzergrenadier* battalions attacked at dawn just above Bou Chebka Pass, and by 8:00a.m., five American howitzers and three lesser guns had been captured, along with 30 vehicles. The American line buckled and fell back, leaving a feature known as Hill 812 held by the *panzergrenadiers*. *DAK* had by good luck struck the seam between CCB's zone and 1ID's sector.

It was here and now that the transformation phenomenon earlier described by Ernie Pyle matured into a full and concrete reality. American soldiers hardened and fought to kill. Despite the deafening noise and violent death around them, the men stood their ground. The American line stiffened. A German movement to assist Italian troops somewhat relieved the American pressure in the Italian sector, but immediately ran into U.S. anti-tank defenses and artillery fire of deadly effectiveness. *DAK* was 23 air miles from Tébessa; it would be allowed to come no closer. At 9:00a.m. the fog lifted, exposing the hundreds of Germans now isolated on Hill 812. Buelowius ordered 24 *panzers* and the infantry of the Italian 5th Bersaglieri to push northwest at Djebel el Hamra as a diversion to save his trapped infantrymen. That force came within two miles of the ridgeline before crumpling under ferocious American fire from three sides.[10]

The Americans had many guns but had at first lacked coordination and direction for their fire until "Mr. Chips" took them in hand. Brigadier General Clift Andrus, the 1st Infantry Division artillery commander, known to his gunners as "Mr. Chips," had been described by Major General Allen, CG, 1ID, as "the most skilled and practical artillery officer I know." Andrus now lived up to that well-deserved praise. In a demonstration of brave and inspired leadership, he personally rounded up batteries and gunners and put them into the line. When he told the GI gunners they were going to shoot in support of an American counterattack, "most of them started to cry" in sheer relief. Artillerymen felled pines on the djebel's front slopes to clear fields of fire. "An artilleryman's dream," Andrus reported. "The valley floor was covered with targets of every description, from tanks and eighty-eight batteries to infantry and trucks." A single battalion, the 27th Field Artillery, fired more than 2,000 rounds, and others were just as profligate, flagellating the enemy with nonstop clouds of shells. By 2:00p.m., the *Afrika Korps* was in retreat as terrorized Axis soldiers ran eastward. Enemy dead lay scattered across the Bahiret Foussana valley.

Without reliable communications, Allen had tried unsuccessfully that morning to mount a counterattack. He was at last able to contact Robinett through the command post of 2nd Battalion, 6th Armored Infantry. The commanders coordinated preparations and the Americans moved against their foe at 4:00p.m. The 3rd Battalion, 16th Infantry, advanced against Hill 812, supported by fire from the 2nd Battalion, 16th Infantry, on the right and from the 2nd Battalion, 6th Armored Infantry, on the left. Aided by a sortie of tanks from Company G, 13th Armored Regiment, the 16th Infantry Regiment drove the Nazi infantry from Hill 812, retrieving the eight American guns and 30 vehicles captured earlier that morning, all still in serviceable condition.[11]

The Germans suffered heavy casualties and withdrew in some disorder toward Kasserine Pass. Some Italian troops retreated but ran into the zone of other elements of the 13th Armored Regiment and were captured. Near Hill 732, in another action, the 5th Bersaglieri Battalion was overtaken at the end of the day by CCB's tanks, which forced the enemy to scatter in headlong retreat and captured many enemy vehicles and supplies intact.[12] It was now apparent to Buelowius that the effort to reach the passes of Djebel el Hamra could not succeed. The German attack toward Tébessa had failed.[13] The war diary of German-Italian Panzer Army described the outcome:

> The attempt made during the night by Kampfgruppe D.A.K. to seize the pass by a swift stroke fails. The Kampfgruppe reorganizes and at dawn advances again to the attack. As a consequence of the enemy's powerful artillery action and because of flanking fire on three sides coming from dominating positions in the hills, the attack meets with no success. The Kampfgruppe is forced to pass to the defensive toward noon and to meet several violent counterattacks executed by the enemy, some of them with tanks, until evening. In the course of this action our left flank is pressed back eastward; the fighting lasts until nightfall. In this counterattack the enemy has the advantage of possessing on the surrounding heights excellent observation posts dominating the entire battlefield.[14]

The Battles on the Road to Thala

As *Kampfgruppe DAK* prepared to pull back into Kasserine Pass after dark, Rommel's 10th Panzer Division was engaged in a series of intensely brutal contests. During the afternoon and evening of February 21, Dunphie's British light armor and infantry troops made a gallant stand against superior German armor and mobile infantry south of Thala. During the afternoon of February 20, Dunphie's 26th Armoured Brigade (less 16th/5th Lancers) had established a defensive line on the road from Kasserine to Thala about nine miles north of the pass. He placed the infantrymen of the 2nd Lothians on the east, the tanks of the 17th/21st Lancers on the west, and the infantry of the 10th Royal Buffs in the center with field artillery in support. Rommel's main attack toward Thala on the morning of February 21 destroyed the British rear guard by 9:30a.m. 10th Panzer Division continued its march north toward the British force of 50 tanks, mostly obsolete Valentines, and infantry, including the 2nd Battalion, 5th Leicestershire Regiment (Br. 46th Infantry Division). The Leicesters had arrived at Thala during the night of February 20–21 and had established a second line of defense on a ridge astride the road about four miles south of Thala. Except for five U.S. tank destroyers which joined the fight, a British officer reported that he had been unable to rally American stragglers passing by "at speed" with—as an American officer observed—"the usual story of being the only survivor." All day long, hundreds of fleeing Americans from Stark's shattered command sprinted through Thala yelling, "He's right behind us!" No one needed to ask who "he" was.[15]

In defense of Thala on February 21, the British 26th Armoured Brigade, part of Nickforce, was opposed by 30 *panzers*, 20 self-propelled guns, and 35 half-track personnel carriers of 10th Panzer Division. From the midnight conference with McNabb and Robinett at Thala, Dunphie understood his orders to be to defend Thala at all costs, gaining a day for the 2/5 Leicesters and others to prepare a main defensive position on the ridge just south of the village. He did not share Robinett's understanding that his tanks were to be conserved. The Valentines were so light and equipped with guns of such short range that they were at a severe disadvantage anyway against the improved German Mark IIIs and Mark IVs. Dunphie reasoned that as the British tanks were about to be replaced by American M4 Shermans, they could be expended and that to gain the necessary time against a formidable and determined foe without heavy losses was simply not reasonable.[16]

On a ridge about nine miles south of Thala, Dunphie had stopped and dug in. A mile away, the enemy assault line massed on another ridge. Rommel, having made his dispositions for the fight at Djebel el Hamra, had spent most of the early afternoon with von Broich's spearhead. Now he demonstrated his own ferocity and aggressiveness, for the last time in North Africa. Taking command of the situation himself at 3:00p.m., Rommel personally ordered the infantry to mount their trucks and half-tracks and follow just in rear of the *panzers* until they came up to the British line of defense. At Rommel's direct command, the panzers rumbled through the *panzergrenadiers* and the Germans advanced directly into the British line. A tank and infantry battle raged. The outgunned British Valentine tanks were blown apart. The British lost 15 tanks but engaged 10th Panzer Division until 4:00p.m. Dunphie then ordered his force to fall back, after an hour of exceptional courage, to the last ridge south of Thala where the 2/5 Leicesters were waiting on the final line of defense.[17]

The British fell back until they reached the ridge held by the Leicesters about four miles south of Thala. They made skillful use of smoke in a delaying action which permitted the survivors to slip through a gap in the defensive line in front of Thala just before 7:00p.m., when Dunphie's command vehicle followed his troops through. Rommel pressed the pursuit. In a ruse using a captured Valentine tank, *panzers* followed directly after Dunphie through the center of the British infantry positions guarding the ridge. The "Trojan Horse" trick worked and after the Germans had penetrated well within the defenders' lines, they opened a devastating fire on the British infantry.[18] The northern slope of the ridge erupted in a wild brawl lit by burning vehicles, flares, and pointblank fire from both German and British tanks amidst non-stop firing by British artillery. The German ruse resulted in the loss of the Leicesters' position and the capture of hundreds of British soldiers. The German gunners first found and knocked out the British signal vehicles, preventing reports and alarms to Thala. German infantry with machine guns following the *panzers* took positions along the heights and demolished the British trench lines. The British kept fighting with every man and weapon.

Two thousand yards north, Dunphie's remaining tanks had laagered in a grassy hollow just below the town when the German tanks rushed upon them, guns blazing. For three hours the British engaged in another chaotic and savage battle. "It was a tank fight in the dark at twenty yards' range and under," reported Dunphie. Dunphie was able to reach his superior Nicholson by radio to warn that the Leicesters had been overrun and that the tanks faced annihilation. But when he proposed pulling back to the edge of Thala, Nicholson refused: "Hold at all costs."

The British held, and the cost was gruesome. Dunphie's original 50 tanks were reduced to 21 when the last German vehicle fired a final burst at midnight and sullenly withdrew. The Germans took with them more than 500 British prisoners. The Leicesters now counted only 40 able-bodied men. The British had incurred 800 casualties, mostly captured but many dead. Dunphie ordered every cook, driver, and clerk in Thala into the firing line. Barely a mile away, Rommel was assembling his remaining force of 50 tanks, 2,500 infantrymen, and 30 guns. At that moment there simply were not enough Allied forces at Thala to thwart a renewed Axis attack at daylight on February 22.[19]

The British, however, were not done. Nicholson, to offset the loss of the ridge position in front of his artillery, sent some of his remaining tanks on an insanely brave counterattack just before dawn. The British lost at least five tanks, and the survivors brought back alarming but inaccurate reports of great enemy strength. Their cutthroat ferocity, however, had a monitory effect on the German commanders. Von Broich also had received erroneous intelligence that the Allies in Thala were preparing a substantial counterattack. He decided to postpone his renewed attack until the anticipated Allied attack had been repulsed. After personal reconnaissance, Rommel approved von Broich's delay but instructed his subordinate to continue the drive north through Thala immediately after stopping the counterattack.[20]

Meanwhile, Eisenhower was trying to get control of the battle, directing reinforcements to the most critical points, and preparing for an Allied counterattack. Fredendall had shifted the 1st Armored Division northeastward and placed its commander, Major General Ward, in charge of operations by all units, American, British, and French, west and northwest of Kasserine Pass. But he had also blamed Ward for the debacle and suggested to Eisenhower that Ward should be replaced. Eisenhower was initially prepared to approve Ward's relief by Major General Ernest N. Harmon, then commanding general, 2nd Armored Division, under Major General Patton in Morocco. While Harmon was flying east, Eisenhower was advised by calmer heads not to fire Ward. He listened and concluded that a change of command of 1AD was inexpedient. He instead sent Harmon to the front in the capacity of "a useful senior assistant" to Fredendall in the "unusual conditions of the present battle," for the corps commander to employ as he chose.[21]

With dramatic timing befitting an American western movie, powerful Allied reinforcements did arrive at Thala. During the afternoon and evening of February 21 the U.S. 9th Infantry Division's artillery had approached Thala from Tébessa. Eisenhower at AFHQ had ordered 9ID's artillery to move from a bivouac near Tlemcen in western Algeria when Sbeïtla was being evacuated. In a stunning example of the mobility of the entirely mechanized U.S. Army, the artillery train had made a motor march of over 700 miles, in a column more than ten miles long, across the icy, rutted Atlas mountains in only four days. The arrival of its firepower commanded by Brigadier General Stafford Leroy Irwin, another expert gunnery officer, "could not have been more opportune."[22] Irwin commanded 2,200 men and 48 medium (155mm) and light (105mm and 75mm) guns. The 12 155mm howitzers of the 34th Field Artillery Battalion were emplaced during the early hours of February 22 along a road running west from Thala, with the six 75mm howitzers of the 47th Infantry Regiment's Cannon Company protecting their westernmost flank. The 24 M2A1 105mm howitzers of the 60th and 84th Field Artillery Battalions went into position about 3,000 yards farther south, with six 75mm howitzers of the 60th Infantry Regiment's Cannon Company on their right. About 2,000 yards still farther south was the new main line of defense. Twelve hundred yards south of that, on the dominating ridge, formerly the Allied main defense line, were the Germans.[23]

During the night of February 21–22, Harmon arrived at Fredendall's new command post at Djebel Kouif. The situation was still not well known, and II Corps had not issued orders for an Allied counterattack. In his typical manner, Fredendall gave Harmon written orders placing him in direct command of the U.S. 1st Armored Division and such elements of the British 6th Armored Division as were within the II Corps area. Harmon had no staff, only the aide who had accompanied him from Morocco and an assistant operations officer (Lieutenant Colonel Barksdale Hamlett) from the II Corps Artillery Section. II Corps loaned Harmon a radio-equipped vehicle with driver and radio operator. He drove during the night to see Ward at Haïdra and Nicholson at Thala. Although Harmon did not officially relieve Ward of his command, he did assume Ward's mission and was given Ward's staff and command post. Harmon insisted that Hains' provisional unit of M4 medium tanks with diesel motors and British radios be sent to occupy a defensive position near Thala.[24]

Major General Harmon, after encouraging and instructing Ward, set out for Thala and his first "confrontation with the British." As he rode to Thala, he considered his situation. Eisenhower had handed him a no-win assignment. If he helped win the battle, he would get no credit. If the battle were lost, he stood to take blame. The Germans were shelling Thala when he arrived. Harmon dodged down streets and alleys hugging walls on the way to Nicholson's cellar. After identifying himself he asked Nicholson about the situation of the British forces. "Well," Nicholson said, "we gave them a bloody nose yesterday and we are damned ready to give them another one this morning!" Harmon admired the fighting talk. "I knew that [Nicholson] and I were going to get along together just fine." But Harmon did not really know just how bad the situation was. Most of Nickforce's infantry was gone. What tanks he retained from the eviscerated Lancers and Lothians were then engaged in combat. It was only thanks to his artillery that the line was holding at all. Harmon informed Nicholson that American armor was on the way and that if Nickforce could hold that day, Harmon was determined to counterattack.

As Harmon and Nicholson were speaking, a tall red-headed soldier came into the cellar. He was Brigadier General Irwin. He told Nicholson and Harmon that he had just received an astoundingly inexplicable order from Anderson to leave Thala and to move to Le Kef, 60 miles away. Nicholson was horrified. "You can't do that. If my men see your brigade pulling out it will be a terrible blow to their morale." Harmon agreed. With real leadership, he turned to Irwin, saying "Irwin, you stay right here," countermanding First Army's orders on his personal responsibility. Irwin smiled with relief. "That's just what I wanted to hear." Moments later Irwin left to continue directing the emplacement and fire of his guns.[25]

Other reinforcements were en route to the Thala area. Thirty-five M4 tanks and crews by rail and 17 more M4 tanks by sea and rail were sent from Morocco to Tébessa, while 25 British Churchill tanks were sent to Sbiba. Eight hundred replacement troops per day and the main body of the 9th Infantry Division were marching east in accordance with plans and schedules made before the German offensive, but now expedited by Eisenhower at AFHQ. Still other reinforcements were scraped together from combat units in the west and sent east to make good the earlier losses inflicted by the enemy. Before the Axis offensive was defeated, two tank destroyer battalions, one tank battalion (separate) with 56 more medium tanks, elements of the 17th Field Artillery Regiment and the entire 13th Field Artillery Brigade, and more anti-aircraft units were en route to Tunisia. The organizational and logistical planning and execution were conceived, directed, and inspired by Eisenhower, who now demonstrated his native leadership capacity and his skills in assembling and employing military power on a large scale.[26] II Corps ordered 1AD's CCB "to bring all possible forces to bear in order to assist" Nicholson's command, but Robinett was already moving units to support the Thala defenders.[27]

Dawn came on Monday, February 22; the expected Axis attack on Thala did not. Irwin nonetheless judged the predicament at Thala "extremely critical." By first light on February 22—despite wretched maps, squally weather, and British misapprehension over the enemy's whereabouts—Irwin had emplaced 9ID's guns, and every additional gun in the area that he could find, in a three-mile arc so that the first German shells of the morning were answered in kind. The forward lines were barely a thousand yards apart and each side could see the other's positions. Snipers effectively discouraged forward observation. The American gunners began firing hundreds of shells blindly toward the reverse slope of the ridge where the Germans were.[28]

The cataract of Allied shells of all calibers admonished the Germans to be cautious. At 7:00a.m. von Broich noted that the size of some of the explosions erupting on the reverse slope of the ridge indicated 155mm guns, from which he Inferred that an entire infantry division had arrived to defend Thala. He phoned Rommel, who had returned to Kasserine, saying that he had planned to attack, but now Allied shells were falling thickly and that in his opinion an even more serious counterattack could follow. Von Broich suggested that they should wait once again. Rommel agreed.

Generalfeldmarschall Rommel had shot his bolt, both militarily and personally. His army was low on ammunition, with but four days' rations left, and only enough fuel to travel less than 200 miles. Axis reconnaissance along the north Tunisian front on February 22 indicated that the advanced positions of British V Corps and French XIX Corps had not been seriously weakened or deprived of local reserves.[29] Air reconnaissance west of the Allied southern flank revealed that strong reinforcements were approaching Thala from Le Kef and moving from Tébessa toward the Bahiret Foussana plain. Rommel now understood that his offensive could not succeed. The mud and mountain terrain were ill-suited to armored action, rain and fog impeded air support, and the combat power of the Axis units was greatly diminished, while fresh troops and more equipment and supplies were streaming east into the Allied lines. The Axis plan to penetrate to Le Kef and beyond was impossible. Rommel's offensive to the northwest collapsed, but it had achieved the tactical objective of delaying for at least several weeks an Allied march to the sea near Sfax to break communications between the German armies.[30]

The Axis Withdraws; the Allies Are Dilatory

Field Marshal Kesselring visited Rommel's command post northwest of Kasserine on the afternoon of February 22. After his outburst of ferocious activity, Rommel was in a steadily declining emotional state. Kesselring landed at Kasserine in his little Storch airplane and motored to the command post in Rommel's staff car, where Rommel immediately disabused Kesselring of the notion that the Allies were defeated or even retreating. On the contrary, the Axis left flank was now exposed to powerful attacks from the west, where the American defense "had been very skillfully executed." The renewed attack on Thala, rescheduled for 1:00p.m., had been twice postponed. Kesselring's recollection in 1949 was that Rommel was inclined to exaggerate the threat posed by the British Eighth Army to the First Italian Army, whose rear guard was the veteran 15th Panzer Division, and that Rommel was unable to appreciate or exploit the advantages of the initiative which he still possessed. "Rommel was in a depressed mood," Kesselring observed. "I thought it best to raise his self-confidence by expressing my confidence in him." Despite his best efforts, Kesselring's encouragement failed to improve Rommel's mood. Both commanders agreed, however, that they should advise *Comando Supremo* to withdraw Axis forces from western Tunisia. They proposed to move quickly to the Mareth area and to hit British Eighth Army with a sudden attack before it could become a serious menace. Meanwhile, Rommel ordered his troops to begin the retirement into Kasserine Pass. General Ambrosio issued his order for retreat shortly before midnight.[31]

The morning of February 22 passed without an Allied counterattack. The Allies carried out air strikes, artillery exchanges, and what the enemy took to be small probing ground attacks along the front. The 9th Infantry Division's artillery sustained 45 casualties, fired 1,904 rounds on February 22 and the following day, and had only 15 minutes of 105mm ammunition left at the end of the battle.[32] The lines remained unchanged. Neither side was able to coordinate low-level air attacks with attempts to move on the ground. Axis aircraft opposed the arrival of Allied reinforcements at Thala by strikes on columns north and northwest of the village.[33] Rommel ordered von Broich to pass to the defensive, and with that order the enemy's last opportunity to penetrate the secondary mountain barrier beyond Kasserine Pass toward Le Kef was abandoned. By February 23 reinforcements arriving at Thala made the Allied position much stronger. The Germans tallied Allied losses at the end of the action at Thala as 571 prisoners, 38 tanks, 12 anti-tank guns, one anti-aircraft gun, 16 heavy mortars, three self-propelled guns, nine motor vehicles, and three aircraft.[34]

Thala was the high-water mark of the Axis campaign in northwest Africa. Upon arriving back in Rome, Kesselring formally authorized the withdrawal. On Monday night, February 22, Axis troops left their trenches and slipped back through Kasserine Pass. The 21st Panzer Division served as rear guard, but there was nothing to guard against. "The enemy follows only hesitantly," the German-Italian Panzer Army war diary noted on Tuesday, February 23.[35]

The Allies did not pursue closely the retreating and used-up Axis units. II Corps hesitated just when the enemy was most vulnerable. At Fredendall's headquarters, preparations had been made to withdraw the II Corps front into Algeria in case of an enemy breakthrough at Thala. The total evacuation of Tébessa had seemed a real possibility to Fredendall. For more than a day after the Axis decision to abandon the attack, Rommel's actual situation was neither recognized nor acted upon by First Army or by II Corps. First Army forces defending Sbiba, including the 34th Infantry Division, were moved further back to positions near Rohia during the night of February 22–23 to counter an enemy attack from Thala northeastward toward Rohia and then south toward Sbiba. The 21st Panzer Division might have entered Sbiba village unopposed, but instead they just watched, as ordered, until the Allies cautiously returned after an absence of about 24 hours. Aside from the delay in correctly understanding that the Axis forces had retreated, the U.S. Army's official history contends that the shuffling of the Allied command was the fundamental cause for the failure in direction of operations to strike the enemy as it pulled back.[36] That indeed may have been part of the problem, but the real culprit was the now chronic lack of leadership in the commanders of II Corps and First Army and, it must be said, of Allied Force. The senior responsible officers appeared to be concerned only to place more layers of responsibility between themselves and their soldiers. Their badly conceived command and control solutions and their bumbling confusion of orders and directives stood in striking contrast to the performance of fighting Allied officers on the ground like Harmon, Robinett, Andrus, Dunphie, Nicholson, Irwin, Ryder, Allen, and Welvert, who had and exercised in noble fashion the essential martial leadership skills.

Eisenhower desired II Corps to pursue the fleeing foe, but he had not yet acquired his command voice and did not give imperative orders for the pursuit. On the evening of February 22, he phoned Fredendall and tried to persuade his subordinate to lead. "The proper time" had come to counterattack and pursue. Intercepted German radio traffic "suggested a broad withdrawal." Fredendall would be "perfectly safe" in counterattacking immediately to catch Rommel in the open. Fredendall, unmanned and fearful after the recent violent battles, demurred. The enemy had "one more shot in his locker;" it would be wiser to spend another day on the defensive as a precaution. No one knew exactly where Rommel was. Both II Corps and First Army senior leadership were too paralyzed by anticipated misfortunes to pursue the vulnerable enemy. "Having been knocked about for more than a week, senior commanders wanted only to put some distance between themselves and their tormentors. Little effort was made to seize the initiative."[37][i] Rommel was gone but it took more than a day for Allied troops to cross the Western Dorsal eastward in strength. Even the usually pugnacious Harmon did not exhibit his customary aggressive leadership and follow-through that the situation required. "Our follow up was slow," Major General Harmon later conceded, "and we let them get away."[38] When the Allies did counterattack to retake Kasserine Pass on February 25, they:

> ... attacked against a phantom foe... [T]hey prepared with appropriate care. But the actual operation turned out to be an unopposed march, impeded only by road demolitions, mines, and booby traps... The pass was free of the enemy, and once the mine fields could be cleared, the Allies would be free to guard it against attack from the east and to prepare for the time when they would regain the initiative in central Tunisia.[39]

---

i   Here Atkinson gives ironic play to the subtitle of George Howe's volume of the Army official history: "Seizing the Initiative in the West."

"Each with his feuds, and jealousies, and sorrows": Balance Sheet of the February Battles

American casualties in the Kasserine battles exceeded 6,000 of the 30,000 GIs engaged in the battle. Of those, half were missing, mostly prisoners of the Axis, including many of the men of the 2nd and 3rd Battalions of the 168th Infantry Regiment. II Corps lost 183 tanks and most of their crews, 104 half-tracks including many of the obsolete tank destroyers, more than 200 guns, and 500 jeeps and trucks. Some American units were mauled beyond repair. "The proud and cocky Americans today stand humiliated by one of the greatest defeats in our history," Lieutenant Commander Harry Butcher, Eisenhower's naval aide, wrote in his diary.[i] "There is definite hangheadedness." From Faïd Pass to Thala, the Americans had been driven back 85 miles in a week, farther than they would be two years later in the Battle of the Bulge.[1]

The news from Tunisia reached the hometowns of the men of Iowa's 168th Infantry Regiment through newspaper articles describing the escape of the survivors. The *Red Oak Express* ran a front-page story by the Associated Press on February 26, 1943, beneath the headline "Moore Leads Escape from Nazi Lines." Datelined "on the Tunisian Front," the article recounted how Robert Moore had led many in his battalion to safety from a hill surrounded by German soldiers. But few other details emerged over the next two weeks other than sketchy dispatches about a fight in a remote place called Kasserine. The dreaded War Department telegrams began arriving on the evening of March 6, 1943; by midnight there were more than two dozen in Red Oak alone, nearly identical: "The Secretary of War desires me to express his regret that your son has been missing in action in North Africa since February 17."

Southwestern Iowa's losses at Kasserine were grim. Clarinda had lost 41, Atlantic 46, Glenwood 39, Council Bluffs 36, Shenandoah 23, Villisca nine. Red Oak's toll reached 45, nearly a third of Company M, which altogether lost 153 men. Total losses for the 168th Infantry Regiment included 109 officers and 1,797 enlisted

---

i   Butcher came from a career in broadcasting, which he continued after the war. His diary, authorized by Eisenhower, became the basis of Butcher's gossipy book published in 1946 under the title *My Three Years with Eisenhower*.

men. When letters began arriving through the International Committee of the Red Cross from German prison camps, there was some consolation and hope in the fact that most of the missing had been taken prisoner. Many ended up in *Stalag* III-B, while officers typically went to an *Oflag* in Polish Silesia.[2]

The Axis had pursued two objectives in the offensive against Sidi Bou Zid, Gafsa, Sbeïtla, Fériana, and through the Western Dorsal at Kasserine. The enemy had wanted both to decisively reduce Allied offensive combat power by the destruction of men and matériel, and to compel British First Army to withdraw westward in the north by a deep penetration of First Army's southern flank, expanding the area of the Axis bridgehead in Tunisia and facilitating its defense. The Axis offensive failed to achieve either objective, despite its short-term tactical success. "In short, the Axis had achieved a tactical success rather than a major victory influencing the strategy of the campaign."[3] As gruesomely painful as the two weeks of the Kasserine battles had been, the Allies had suffered a tactical, temporary setback rather than a strategic defeat. Rommel had failed to reach the Allied supply depots. Von Arnim had failed to force British First Army to withdraw from Northern Tunisia. Both failed to reduce the offensive capacity of Allied forces. The Allies had already made good their losses and they were vastly accelerating the growth of their air and ground combat power. The only enemy achievement was to force the Allies to delay their planned attack to cut the link between Fifth Panzer Army and German-Italian Panzer Army.

The consequences to Allied soldiers and units had been nonetheless devastating. The enemy had inflicted substantial losses in men and matériel on the British, Americans, and French. Two battalions of the 168th Infantry Regiment of the 34th Infantry Division were destroyed and had to be reconstituted with fresh troops. The 2nd and 3rd Battalions of 1st Armored Division's 1st Armored Regiment had been massacred at Sidi Bou Zid. The survivors were temporarily combined as an understrength 23rd Battalion. The American troops overrun at Kasserine and the British defenders of Thala had also suffered disproportionate losses compared to the enemy.[4]

Severe Allied deficiencies in battle technique and equipment were now obvious. Portions of five American divisions had fought around Kasserine, but almost never as intact, integrated combat organizations. Eisenhower, Anderson and Fredendall had lost sight of the cardinal principles of concentration of forces and mutual support. Unit cohesion had disintegrated as leaders came and leaders went, and smaller units were separated from their parent commands. The overarching problem, however, was one of competent command in combat.

> [Fredendall]… like several of his subordinate commanders [e.g., McQuillin]… was overmatched, unable to make the leap from First World War's static operations to modern mobile warfare… Robinett made a fair point after the war: that it was "dead wrong" to blame Fredendall exclusively… Possibly one would have to search all history to find a more jumbled command structure than that of the Allies in this operation."[5]

Others made a strong argument that the blame for the February 14–15 disasters rested squarely on Fredendall. He was in charge of combat operations. Anderson and McQuillin were also accountable to a lesser extent.

> Faulty interpretation of intelligence—radio interception—led officers at AFHQ and British First Army Headquarters at Constantine to believe that the main German attack was to strike further north than it did… That interpretation caused General Anderson to hold Robinett's Combat Command B at Maktar until Rommel had overrun McQuillin's Combat Command A… While Anderson's decision set the stage for the attack… at Sidi bou Zid, it was not responsible for the disaster… The responsibility for the debacle can be fairly laid upon the Corps Commander, General Fredendall, and upon Combat Command A itself. General Fredendall had prescribed detailed dispositions for McQuillin's command which were not in accord with what the conditions and the terrain demanded, although he had never been within many miles of the area in question…. General Anderson… was not responsible for the counterattack force blundering into an ambush in which an entire tank battalion was destroyed. This must be charged to lack of reconnaissance, poor security, and inadequate combat leadership.[6]

But the real fault was Eisenhower's, and he knew it. Fredendall might have been in charge, but Eisenhower was commander in chief. This was war where people died, not one of his duplicate bridge games with inanimate cards and iterative opportunities to do better. He later honorably acknowledged his fatal errors. He had confounded the Allied command structure. He had badly underestimated the vulnerability of the French, exposing them to be slaughtered without effective Allied support. He had acquiesced in dispositions that stretched the Allied line until it broke, and too many soldiers died. He wrote candidly after the war, "had I been willing at the end of November to admit temporary failure and pass to the defensive, no attack against us could have achieved even temporary success."[7]

Before the Kasserine battles, Eisenhower, in his role as the military leader of a fractious coalition, had striven for consensus and compromise within the highest ranks of the Allies, rather than asserting his own authority as supreme commander from the very start. He had lacked the ruthless self-confidence and forcefulness crucial for proficiency and success in combat command at his level. He had suggested but not commanded the concentration of the 1st Armored Division in mid-February. He had recommended but not demanded that Fredendall counterattack vigorously on February 22.

There were other shortcomings. He and many others in the American army had failed to grasp the tactical significance of the technological disparity between already obsolete American weapons and the superior machines and guns deployed by the Axis. Although the deficiencies had been known for months, he claimed surprise in late February that the 37mm "squirrel rifle," both as towed AT gun and as main armament on the M3 light tank, and the half-track tank destroyer M3 mounting a 75mm gun, had been wholly ineffective against the German *panzers* and anti-tank weapons. The rapid development of battle tank technology on the Eastern Front in 1940–2 was not a secret to the Allies. Yet the German deployment of the new upgrade of the *PzKmpfW* IV with a high velocity 75mm gun and the all new *PzKmpfW* VI (Tiger) mounting an 88mm gun, built to counter the new Soviet T34 medium and KV and IS-1 heavy tanks, was a surprise to American combat leaders like Waters. Both of these new German fighting vehicles were deployed with terrible effect in North Africa, albeit, fortunately for the Allies, in limited numbers.[8]

Eisenhower and his subordinates should not have been surprised and blindsided by the war making prowess of the enemy. But their wonderment was of a piece with the naiveté and self-delusion of most Americans early in World War II. The combat veteran Paul Fussell saw the cultural and psychological problem clearly.

> Watching a newsreel or flipping through an illustrated magazine at the beginning of the American war, you were likely to encounter a memorable image: the newly invented jeep, an elegant, slim-barrelled 37-mm gun in tow, leaping over a hillock. Going very fast and looking as cute as Bambi, it flies into the air, and behind, the little gun bounces high off the ground on its springy tires. This graceful duo conveyed the firm impression of purposeful, resourceful intelligence going somewhere significant, and going there with speed, agility, and delicacy—almost wit.
>
> The image suggests the general Allied understanding of the war at the outset. Perhaps ("with God's help") quickness, dexterity, and style, a certain skill in feinting and dodging, would suffice to defeat pure force. Perhaps civilized restraint and New World decency could overcome brutality and evil…
>
> At first everyone hoped, and many believed, that the war would be fast-moving, mechanized, remote-controlled, and perhaps even rather easy… [B]y 1940 the Great War had receded into soft focus, and no one wanted to face the terrible fact that military successes are achieved only at the cost of insensate violence and fear and agony, with no bargains allowed. Even the official history of the U.S. Army's Quartermaster Corps admits how innocently far off the mark were early estimates of the numbers of graves registration units ultimately needed. It would take a skilled pessimist and satirist like Evelyn Waugh to estimate more properly what the war would mean. He notes in his diary in October 1939: "They are saying, 'The generals learned their lesson in the last war. There are going to be no wholesale slaughters.' I ask, how is victory possible except by wholesale slaughters?"[9]

The Allies had been overextended along the line between the Western and Eastern Dorsals in south central Tunisia. This was in small part a consequence of Eisenhower's failed gamble to get to Tunis before winter set in, but the major cause was the failure of II Corps and First Army to heed Eisenhower's repeated instruction to establish and maintain a concentrated armored reserve, a *masse de manoeuvre*. The American armored forces in the south were dispersed in small combat groups that could not mutually support one another and were in consequence in mortal danger when they encountered a sudden powerful concentration of the enemy's large mobile units. The same was true of American infantry units. The rout at Sidi Bou Zid was a distressing example of the consequences of overextension of forces.

No amount of personal bravery or steadfastness would have prevented the American defeat at Sidi Bou Zid. The Germans had assembled their striking forces skillfully and quickly and brought large and powerful formations to bear on the hapless defenders of Sidi Bou Zid on February 14 and on the ill-fated counterattack by Combat Command C, 1st Armored Division the next day. The enemy's local preponderance of force and superior weapons were exponentially magnified by the dispersed dispositions of American infantry on the hills near Sidi Bou Zid. Fredendall had placed the American units where they could not be mutually supported. The Germans isolated the battalions of the 168th Infantry Regiment on the hills, employing overwhelming firepower to prevent maneuver or movement, and sealing them out of the tank battle on the plain. The enemy then proceeded to destroy or capture the separated American units in detail. On February 14–15 the enemy was not only better equipped and more numerous but also more savagely cunning and skillful than the American adversaries. As the Axis offensive thrust through Sbeïtla and then Kasserine, battle-hardened German soldiers had proved themselves wily and ruthless.[10]

Axis troops forced the breakthrough at Kasserine Pass against a haphazard, ineffective defense. The organization of the pass for defense was late in coming and badly undermanned. After Kasserine Pass fell, however, German attacks were adroitly parried and obstinately fought by American soldiers, who were then much better led and artfully arrayed in advantageous positions, and accordingly grew in confidence, determination, and battle skill. Rommel later wrote that he considered the defense after the breakthrough stubborn and the performance of the U.S. troops superior.[11] Rommel and his colleagues failed to exploit fully the potential of the breakthrough because the defenses west and north of Kasserine pass were quickly reinforced and became formidable. Most happily for the Allies, the Axis high command, despite the training and battle experience of its forces, was much more greatly hindered by its internal rivalries and inefficiencies than its Allied counterpart. The Axis commanders' two-day delay in deciding what to do after Sidi Bou Zid allowed the Allies to retreat and prepare strong defenses.

> Allied resistance cannot be given all the credit for stopping the Axis advance. To a large extent Rommel's failure may be attributed to an aggregate of Axis mistakes. The most consequential was the lack of unity of command and the indecision demonstrated after the successes gained in the battles near Sidi Bou Zid.[12]

The battles during the week of February 14 through 21 leading to the American routs at Sidi Bou Zid, Sbeïtla, and Kasserine Pass were the low point of U.S. Army combat performance in North Africa. "A great sorting out was underway: the competent from the incompetent, the courageous from the fearful, the lucky from the unlucky. It would happen faster in the American Army than it had in the British."[13] Eisenhower evaluated his own performance honestly, even if he did not always publicly acknowledge his failings. He had not been professionally interested in, and in consequence had not exercised sufficient diligence about, the tactical disposition of Allied forces, despite the alarms sounded by commanders in the field. He had failed to issue, and was reluctant to compel compliance with, direct commands when both were required. It is worth remembering that he was at the same time expected to counsel and negotiate with the most important personages on the planet at the highest strategic level.

Eisenhower had done some things quite well. He had transferred troops and equipment from the U.S. 2nd Armored and 3rd Infantry Divisions to serve as reinforcements and replacements for the units in combat. Some of the troops from 3ID were sent to bolster 34ID, including fully trained junior officers, non-commissioned officers, and riflemen. He had expedited the 9th Division artillery's march to success at Thala. He purged and reorganized his intelligence operations, accelerated the rearmament and retraining of the French, redesigned American training methods, and brought in the British General Alexander to exercise overall operational command in Tunisia and to restore order to the chain of command. Meanwhile, Eisenhower patiently parried the intrusive meddling of Churchill.

> [Eisenhower] studied his mistakes—this practice was always one of Eisenhower's virtues—and absorbed the lessons for future battles in Italy and western Europe... [He] could take heart that for the first time—... in the successful defense of Djebel el Hamra—American commanders had demonstrated some capacity for combined arms combat, the vital integration of armor, infantry, and artillery and other combat arms. That art, like fighting on the defensive... had been given short shrift in stateside training; soldiers were forced to learn where lessons always cost most, and are often given only once, on the battlefield.[14]

American troops had learned in the most brutal manner possible their enemy's methods and the requirements for survival and effective fighting on a porous battlefield. German tank attacks were made at dusk as well as at dawn and were pressed even in complete darkness with star shells and flares until American tank forces were scattered or destroyed. The enemy understood American divisional and regimental deployment practices; they expected two thirds of a force in the assault and one third in support, and routinely opposed an attack by a double envelopment counterattack to defeat all three. Germans lured brave but unwary Americans into encircling traps of hidden tanks and into ambuscades of anti-tank guns. German high-velocity anti-tank ammunition generated white-hot metallic spall when it penetrated the less well armored American tanks, igniting the fuel and ammunition in a catastrophic explosion; later versions of the medium tank M4 would put the ammunition under the floor. American solid shot armor-piercing shells, if they pierced the armor at all, immobilized Nazi tanks but did not destroy them, allowing the enemy to salvage and repair equipment from the battlefield. German tanks advanced at a slow pace, reducing dust clouds and noises which would attract attention and allowing enemy gunners to acquire targets more easily and accurately. In battle, a *panzer* might halt and feign being damaged when fired upon, and when its adversary turned to a different opponent, the German would resume rapid and accurate fire.[15]

Other even worse fights and more failures lay ahead, but the survivors had begun to learn the lessons of war. The Americans were forced to recognize the many deficiencies in their weapons and tactics. The M3 light tanks were useful only for reconnaissance, not for tank-on-tank combat. The 75mm half-track gun motor carriage M3 with which almost all tank destroyer units were then equipped was extremely fragile and obsolete. A soldier, when asked if enemy aircraft bullets went through the half-track's half-inch armor replied, "No sir, they only come through the wall and then they rattle around." In GI jargon, the half-tracks were sadly known as "Purple Heart boxes." The M3 medium tank was obsolete, with inadequate armor and an outmatched main gun. The M4 medium tank was mechanically reliable and fast, but the early versions, designed for infantry support, were under-armored with a low velocity main gun that could not penetrate the frontal armor of the enemy's newer medium and heavy tanks even at point blank range. The 37mm towed anti-tank gun with standard ammunition was effective only against scout cars and light vehicles, except at suicidally close ranges and only against the older, less thickly armored *panzers*. The soldiers of 34th Infantry Division's anti-tank units would use their 37mm guns as flat trajectory weapons against entrenched enemy infantry.

The U.S. Army needed longer-range, higher-velocity guns with better telescopic sights on tanks and for anti-tank roles. Basic infantry tasks, especially the practical hands-on familiarization of all front-line fighters with the basic infantry weapons, had to be better taught and continually practiced. Training and equipment for the avoidance, detection, and removal of mines, and for the use of mines against the enemy, had to be greatly improved and extended to all troops.

Allied air-ground coordination was practically non-existent. The Axis dominance in its air-to-ground support role had been so great that Allied training in enemy aircraft identification was a waste of time. After the Kasserine battles, Allied troops knew never to fire at any airplane, for fear of drawing attack, unless that airplane fired first. Air reconnaissance, with careful interpretation, was of some value to higher headquarters but of little use to tactical units which needed it in real time. Air bombing missions by medium bombers had been executed too slowly to influence most battles in real time and tactical air support by fighter-bombers had been available only rarely.[16] Eisenhower and his battle commanders had much work to do to retrain and re-equip the Army and expand its air arm if it were ever to have the capacity to meet Axis forces on even terms.

As March came, the opposing lines took roughly the same shape they had held before the Valentine's Day offensive had pushed the Americans nearly into Algeria. The final campaign in Africa would be fought on a shrinking battlefield: the eastern third of Tunisia. In a rough rectangle 50 miles wide and 300 miles long, three Allied armies would confront two Axis armies in a climactic struggle for control of the continent and of the Mediterranean basin. In the center of the Allied line, where II Corps remained under Anderson's tactical command, the Americans buried their dead, turned their backs to Kasserine Pass, and waited to see who would lead them forward.[17]

PART IV

"SOME FLAMING, FATAL CLIMAX": THE FINAL BATTLES IN TUNISIA

CHAPTER 23

The Allies Prepare to Destroy the Axis Armies in Tunisia

Both the Allied and Axis coalitions reorganized after the February battles with new army group commands in Tunisia. General Sir Harold R. L. G. Alexander took command of the new 18 Army Group late on February 19. Field Marshal Rommel was designated commander of Army Group Africa on February 23, though this proved to be temporary and brief. Each commander had immediately to deal with the demoralizing aftermath of the recent battles and the prospect of future offensive operations under his control.[1]

Alexander assumed command of the Allied forces with an unfortunately deprecative, even denigrative attitude toward the wrong people. He condemned the American soldier and American field officers, instead of their senior commanders. The combat behavior of American troops, in Alexander's view, demonstrated inferior fighting ability. He was completely unaware and unappreciative of the sense of gritty resolve that had grown in the American soldier. He intended in future operations to depend more heavily upon British units. Alexander's bias was to have consequences for 34th Infantry Division until General Bradley became II Corps deputy commander and demanded that the division be given a chance to prove itself in battle.

Upon assuming command, Alexander's leadership behavior and management style were exemplars of all that had been lacking in the senior Allied commanders. Despite his biases, he issued clear, direct orders reflecting careful thought, organizational capability, and a firm resolution to win the war. He directed that the Americans should first receive battlefield experience in limited roles assuring small successes that would restore morale. This was in accord with Eisenhower's thinking. But Alexander also planned not to commit the Americans to the larger undertakings until late in the campaign, if at all. His was initially inclined to improve American battle leadership by the relief and replacement of existing American field commanders by new ones and the swift production of more competent American field grade and junior officers by special training under British tutelage. Alexander was constrained, however, both by Eisenhower at AFHQ and by the growing relative predominance of the American forces. To avoid damaging Allied unity of effort, he could not risk offending American national sensitivities.[2]

The Allied objectives now were to drive all the Axis forces in Tunisia within a wall of guns and tanks in the narrow northeastern corner of Tunisia, to complete their isolation from Europe by air and sea interdiction, and then to split them into segments for piecemeal annihilation. Operations to constrict the enemy within its bridgehead were to consist of two major phases. First, the British Eighth Army (General Sir Bernard Law Montgomery, commanding) would push northward along the coast through the Gabès narrows and central Tunisia beyond Sousse. Second, Allied engineers would construct new airfields and reconstruct captured enemy airfields close to the new front so that rapidly increasing Allied air power could be used with full effect against the enemy, and most importantly against the enemy's air and sea supply lines, in the final stage of the campaign.[3]

Alexander planned for the British Eighth Army's drive northward to be the Allies' primary operation in the first phase of a spring campaign. He initially expected the British First Army to engage only in small holding attacks along the northern front and, of course, to hold the approaches to Tunis and Bizerte. U.S. II Corps in central Tunisia would also play only a small auxiliary role. While the Eighth Army attacked the Mareth and Chott Positions near Gabès, the II Corps would threaten the enemy's line of communications through well timed, well prepared, and carefully controlled attacks. II Corps was to be restricted to operations designed only to attract and divert enemy reserves from opposing the British Eighth Army. The limited missions, Alexander believed, would also serve to advance the training of II Corps, increase its self-confidence, and improve its morale. He had no intention of employing II Corps to thrust beyond the Eastern Dorsal onto the coastal plain. There was to be no revival of Operation *Satin*. The Eighth Army's attack on the Mareth Position would begin in the middle of March, and the auxiliary operations in central Tunisia were adjusted to that schedule.[4] Alexander's operational approach and judgment of American fighting ability, however, were offensive to the American commanders.

Alexander had arrived in Algiers on February 15 to confer with Eisenhower at AFHQ. AFHQ completed the arrangements for Alexander's new headquarters at Constantine and prescribed 18 Army Group's responsibilities. For this purpose, Eisenhower prepared a directive to instruct Alexander, with specific provisions to make clear the roles and responsibilities of AFHQ and of 18 Army Group.[5] Headquarters, 18 Army Group was to assume command and control of all Allied combat operations in North Africa. British troop training was to be under Alexander's control but that of American troops was reserved for G-3, AFHQ. Logistical support, including transportation, remained outside the army group's province; 18 Army Group exercised control only over level of supply and assignment of priorities in delivery. Although it was an Allied headquarters with some American officers, 18 Army Group would be staffed predominantly by British personnel. Alexander's chief of staff was Major General Sir Richard L. McCreery. Brigadier L. C. Holmes oversaw operations, and an American, Brigadier General William C. Crane, was his deputy.[6]

The three headquarters directly subordinate to 18 Army Group were British First Army, U.S. II Corps, and British Eighth Army. The French XIX Corps remained under First Army's command while its front was narrowed, and most French troops were rearmed with modern weapons and re-trained.[7]

Alexander commenced his command by surveying the Tunisian front and the performance to date of his principal subordinates. Eisenhower had empowered Alexander to decide who to retain and who to dismiss. Alexander regarded Anderson as a sound soldier with leadership potential. But his assessment of the performance by the U.S. II Corps commander, Fredendall, during the recent battle was vehemently and correctly unfavorable. Alexander demanded that II Corps be led by someone in whom he had confidence and who, in turn, could command the confidence and respect of the American division commanders.

Neither Major General Ryder, commanding 34ID, whose 168th Infantry Regiment had been so severely battered as a direct result of Fredendall's orders for the dispositions at Sidi Bou Zid, nor Major General Ward, commanding 1AD, whose relief Fredendall had demanded during the Kasserine battles, had any faith or trust in Fredendall. Both held Fredendall accountable for assigning missions and then prescribing both insufficient and ineffective means and methods to accomplish them. Those charges carried great weight when both men expressed their views to Eisenhower's trusted observers. Fredendall had told Eisenhower to make the choice between himself and Ward if either were to be retained. Alexander concluded on March 3 that, contrary to Fredendall's evaluation, Ward, and his subordinates, with the notable exception of McQuillin, had provided sound leadership to the 1st Armored Division, which retained substantial combat power. In light of Alexander's sharply critical assessment of Fredendall, Eisenhower determined to bring in a new corps commander. His conclusion was validated by the information and observations provided by his chief of staff, Major General Walter Bedell Smith, his trusted special representative, Major General Omar Bradley, his former deputy chief of staff at the Advance Command Post, AFHQ, the competent Major General Truscott, and his G-3, Brigadier General Lowell W. Rooks. Eisenhower, as Atkinson observes, had not yet learned to move quickly to remove subordinates who could not meet the demands of their positions. He did not need a committee to tell him that Fredendall had failed as a combat commander and had to be relieved.[8] And yet at that moment he hesitated. In time Eisenhower would develop the capacity to fire incompetent people promptly, without remorse, hesitation or second guessing. He would learn, and teach others, that in military command at the higher levels, the mission trumps the person.

Atkinson concludes that the ultimate responsibility for the Allied command and control failures was at the top: with the Supreme Allied Commander. Mistakes had been made and soldiers had died because of his mistakes. After Kasserine Pass was retaken, Eisenhower immediately replaced those whose battle performance had been unhelpful at best and catastrophic at worst. The axe fell on both field commanders and AFHQ staff. Eisenhower fired his G-2 [intelligence] chief, British Brigadier Eric E. Mockler-Ferryman, for relying over much on one type of intelligence, ULTRA intercepts and decryptions, discounting real-time and first-hand information from front-line units, and failing to detect the imminent German offensive. Those errors, especially at First Army, had led to the fatal misinterpretation of the enemy's objectives and the debacle at Sidi Bou Zid. The AFHQ intelligence position was held by a British officer in view of the extensive use of British sources of information in the Mediterranean. Brigadier Kenneth D. W. Strong, a former British military attaché in Berlin, was sent from the United Kingdom by General Sir Alan Brooke, chief of the Imperial General Staff, to become the new G-2 at Algiers.[9] Other heads soon rolled too, including that of Colonel Alexander Stark, who had been unable to hold the line at Kasserine Pass. He was sent home on March 2 but would later serve with distinction in the Pacific. McQuillin's relief came soon after. Tunisia, as Robinett observed, became "a professional graveyard, particularly for those in the upper middle part of the chain of command."[10]

In the case of Fredendall, however, Eisenhower still wavered. While telling others in private that he should have assigned Patton to II Corps instead, Eisenhower had given Fredendall greater deference and authority than was appropriate. The commander in chief was now in an embarrassing situation of his own making. He had recently and most inconveniently written notes lauding Fredendall for his leadership during the Algiers operations and had praised him to Marshall as a "stouthearted" leader worthy of a third star.[11] Now, in the harsh light of Fredendall's personal collapse and his total abandonment of command and control of II Corps in battle, Eisenhower's praise was farcically unmerited and reflected badly on his own judgment. Firsthand reports from the front could not be ignored. Harmon was scathing. "He's no damn good," he told Eisenhower on February 28, on his way back to Morocco. "You ought to get rid of him." From their first meeting on February 22, Harmon had disliked Fredendall, who had appeared to Harmon to be drunk and panicked. With evident haste and relief, Fredendall had appointed Harmon deputy corps commander with tactical control of II Corps, effectively abandoning his command and his oath as an officer. Fredendall was a "common, low, son-of-a-bitch," Harmon added, "a physical and moral coward." Truscott opined that II Corps was unlikely to "ever fight well under his command." Alexander was unequivocal. "I'm sure," he told Eisenhower, "you must have a better man than that." Eisenhower solicited the opinions of other subordinates rather than do the difficult but necessary thing. "What do you think of the command here?" Eisenhower asked Major General Bradley. "It's pretty bad," Bradley replied. "I've talked to all the division commanders. To a man they've lost confidence in Fredendall as the corps commander."

Fredendall was quietly relieved of command of II Corps on March 6, 1943. He was not deprived of rank or otherwise disciplined. Eisenhower explained to

Harmon that this was done to avoid shaking public confidence and trust in the high command, including himself. Fredendall received his third star, command of a training army in Tennessee, and a hero's welcome home.

Eisenhower rationalized to Marshall that Fredendall "has difficulty in picking good men" and "has shown a peculiar apathy in preparing for a big push." This was at best solicitous of Marshall's feelings, at worst disingenuous, reflecting Eisenhower's only nascent mettle as a leader. Major General Smith, Eisenhower's highly competent chief of staff, gave a pithy and damning final assessment of Fredendall: "He… was a good colonel before the war."[12]

Major General George S. Patton came to Tunisia from I Armored Corps in Morocco "to participate in operations for which he had been thirsting."[13] He took command of II Corps on March 7, bringing with him a new chief of staff, Brigadier General Hugh J. Gaffey, and other staff officers. His command of II Corps was a temporary interruption in the planning and preparation for him to command the new American Seventh Army in the invasion of Sicily. Major General Bradley was designated deputy corps commander; he was to succeed Patton in command of II Corps as soon as operations in the southern Tunisian sector were completed and Patton was transferred from II Corps to Seventh Army.[14]

When Patton arrived at the Maison Blanche airfield outside Algiers, he and Eisenhower had a brief conference over the hood of Eisenhower's car. Eisenhower expected Patton to command II Corps for only three weeks or so before resuming his preparations for the invasion of Sicily. He instructed Patton to rehabilitate II Corps with all possible speed to get the troops ready for the offensive operations which 18 Army Group was planning. He told Patton to give priority to intensive combat training, re-equipping, reorganization, and the practical application of the battle lessons thus far learned. Patton was also to undertake careful planning of the logistics of II Corps for the prospective offensive, not one of Patton's personal strong points but a task of which II Corps staff was more than capable. Finally, the supreme commander urged Patton to demonstrate and instill in the American forces a spirit of genuine partnership with the British forces, a task not at all to Patton's generally Anglophobic taste.[15] Eisenhower added:

> You must not retain for one instant any man in a responsible position where you have become doubtful of his ability to do the job… This matter frequently calls for more courage than any other thing you will have to do, but I expect you to be perfectly cold-blooded about it… I will give you the best available replacement or stand by any arrangement you want to make.

Patton arrived with sirens shrieking at the schoolhouse headquarters of II Corps at Djebel Kouif on the late morning of March 7.[16] "[H]e wasted no time leaving his boot-prints on II Corps. One definition of military morale is a will to fight that is stronger than the will to live…"[17] Patton saw that the Americans plainly needed inspired leadership to embolden them for the coming battles. "Determined and energetic, Patton could also be boorish and abusive, incapable of distinguishing between the demands of a disciplinarian and the caprices of a bully."[18]

Morale improved, but whether Patton actually contributed to the fighting spirit of II Corps remains unclear. Hot showers, new and clean clothes, socks and boots, hot food and timely mail did wonders for body and mind. Beginning on March 8, II Corps was no longer part of Anderson's First Army but directly under Alexander and his 18 Army Group as the result of Alexander's reorganization of Allied forces. The American divisions—the 1st Armored and 1st, 9th and 34th Infantry—were each at last united. Their regiments and battalions were welded into coherent combat units in a way that had been impossible during the first four months of the campaign when command and control had been in a continuous state of flux. The U.S. divisions regrouped and trained intently as entire, integrated units for several weeks, while preventing further Axis attacks by installing thick, deep minefields. There was no escaping, however, the soldier's irremediable long-term fate. Major General Theodore Roosevelt's letters to his wife Eleanor captured the mood of many men who now understood that they were in a fight to the death for the duration of the war.

> I guess nations going to war must go through a stumbling period before they purge the incompetents... I think this is a five-year war. It won't be over until another winter has passed, until we are firmly on the Continent, and until Germany is faced with still another winter... Now we know too much. Now we know that the world we knew is a long time dead. We know there'll be troubles of every sort.[19]

General Roosevelt's sentiments about a long war were not shared by the rank and file. The commanders would have to tell the soldiers explicitly that the only way home lay through the rubble of a conquered Germany. Most did not want to hear it.

CHAPTER 24

II Corps and 34ID Prepare to Attack

When the February battles ended, and the Allies slowly felt their way eastward as the Axis units withdrew, the Allied main battle line extended from Cap Serrat to El Ma el Abiod, running east of Sidi Nsir, Medjez el Bab, Bou Arada, Djebel Bargou (1,266m), Djebel Serdj (1,357m), Kesra, the Sbiba Gap, Djebel Semmama (1,356m), and Djebel Chambi (1,544m). It covered the lateral road from Djebel Abiod to Bèja, which was a logistical advantage to British V Corps. Importantly, the Allies held the approaches to the plain of Tunis along either side of the Medjerda river. The front protected the main gaps in the Western Dorsal from Maktar to Sbiba, and from there to the southwestern extremity of the mountain chain. The main landing fields in the Medjerda valley, the air landing grounds between Le Kef and Thala, and the airfields near Tébessa were protected and operational. The Thélepte airfields, abandoned during the recent enemy offensive, were to be recaptured as a preliminary step in the Allied spring offensive.[1]

U.S. II Corps held the southern part of the Allied front. The 34th Infantry Division under direct command of II Corps held the northeast part of the corps sector around Sbiba, about 25 miles west of the positions it had held in January. The 1st Infantry Division held the southwest sector until February 27, when the 9th Infantry Division relieved 1ID and assumed control of the position on 34ID's right flank. The 1st Armored Division, in bivouacs between Tébessa and El Ma el Abiod, and the 1st Infantry Division, assembled near Morsatt, were refitted and made ready for the upcoming offensive. Headquarters, II Corps, stayed at Djebel Kouif.[2]

The American divisions in II Corps required new equipment, rest and rehabilitation for the survivors, reorganization and reconstitution of battered units, replacements for casualties, and intense practical combat training. The remnants of 168RCT rejoined 34th Infantry Division, which was then, except for 2/133, fully consolidated for combat operations for the first time in the war. 34ID reconstituted and reorganized the 168th Infantry Regiment, which had lost its valiant commanding officer (Colonel Drake) and much of its strength near Sidi Bou Zid. Colonel Frederic B. Butler, from G-3, II Corps became the new commander of

168IR. Major General Ryder requested the return to the 133rd Infantry Regiment of its 2nd Battalion, which was still assigned as the AFHQ security detachment at Algiers, but AFHQ declined for that time. In fact, the battalion would not rejoin 34ID until almost a year later, in March 1944, in Italy. Ryder also requisitioned 36 new M2A1 105mm howitzers to replace the well-worn British 25-pounder guns used by the division's artillery battalions since their arrival in Ulster.[3] The new guns did not arrive until May 3, 1943, when the division was already in the closing days of the Tunisian Campaign.[4]

Patton worked relentlessly to instill in II Corps soldiers an aggressive and martial spirit. He vigorously carried out the preparations for the battle he so desired. He single-mindedly drove his principal subordinates and moved with restless energy throughout the II Corps area. His regime substituted strict military protocol for unsoldierly casualness. He required attention to detail, even of dress, to establish in every soldier a high level of practiced care and competence. Some of Patton's methods seemed trivial "chickenshit" to those on whom they were imposed.[5] The observable improvements which some might attribute to Patton's methods were perhaps also traceable to the lessons learned by troops in combat. The GIs had matured as soldiers, working at their jobs, looking ahead more than they looked back, and needing more than anything else successes in battle to boost their morale.[6] The GIs of the Red Bull Division would still have to gain experience in the attack and endure rough treatment by an entrenched enemy before they would qualify as combat veterans, but they were no longer the grinning "Sunday school picnic" crowd that had come out of the Midwest.

The process of replacing lost soldiers did not work well. Problems with replacements sent to fill casualty-depleted ranks had been evident even before Kasserine. Now, as thousands more replacement troops moved into Tunisia, it was clear that the War Department's personnel system was not meeting the needs of the Army's combat units. Soldiers were viewed by the military bureaucracy in the continental United States as fungible, like equipment parts. As troops were killed, wounded, transferred, or rotated, new troops were deployed to keep units at close to full strength as possible, at least on paper. This assembly-line model had invidious flaws. When troops were transferred from units in the rear to units at the front as reinforcements, many were capable. But most combat commanders could not resist the chance to dump their troublemakers and incompetents as well. Worse yet, the War Department had assumed entirely without evidence that airpower would play a greater role in destroying enemy ground forces and that infantry losses therefore would be less than they had been in World War I. Worst of all, the War Department bureaucracy, including Marshall and the Army Ground Forces commander, Lieutenant General Lesley McNair, had not foreseen what should have been obvious: riflemen and other front fighters would be wounded, killed, or become physically and mentally disabled much faster than cooks or clerks.

Combat wears down line-fighting units and wears out the soldiers in them. The combat generals came to realize that fighting divisions and regiments should not be left in the line longer than 30 to 40 days, at most, without rest. It also became clear that merely filling the ranks with inexperienced and often poorly trained replacement soldiers, who lacked both basic combat skills and emotional ties to their new comrades, did nothing to improve unit cohesion or combat efficiency. These defects, and more, had appeared in Tunisia. The losses among riflemen were real and the need for trained combat soldier replacements was urgent.

The most valuable military occupational specialties (MOS) to the leaders of infantry units were naturally those which involved the use and control of infantry weapons, most of all the rifleman, the trigger puller, the increasingly precious and rare MOS 745.[7] Many of the men sent forward in response to combat unit requisitions for replacements, however, had not even finished basic combat training, and many were physical or disciplinary misfits. One study estimated that 80 percent of the infantry replacements had not qualified in their basic weapons. Of 2,400 men sent to the 34th Infantry Division, a startling proportion was overage and in poor physical shape. One batch of 250 men included 119—almost 50 percent—who were 39 or older. Combat unit commanders began sending their agents to replacement depots to choose new soldiers, "somewhat as one would buy a horse."[8]

"Paralyze a man with memories"

A large rise in the number of mental breakdowns also began to threaten the combat capacity of the United States Army. Any man exposed to extended combat became "a bit windy of shellfire" in a British reporter's phrase. Beginning in late 1942 and continuing through mid-1943, the number of American soldiers who could not continue fighting because they were suffering from neuropsychiatric syndromes increased dramatically. In the course of fierce and prolonged combat, many soldiers broke down and suffered from debilitating anxiety attacks, repetitive nightmares, tremors, stuttering, mutism, and amnesia. During the 1943 Tunisian campaign, after the violent engagements with Axis forces, 20 to 34 percent of all casualties were neuropsychiatric in nature. To U.S. Army physicians of that time, these patients were baffling because their symptoms changed rapidly, no physiological cause could be found, and none of the available treatments proved effective. War neuroses successfully mimicked the symptoms of organic disease, confusing and frustrating physicians. Military officials realized that the policy of evacuating every man with a neuropsychiatric diagnosis could not be maintained because more men were leaving the North African Theater of Operations than were entering it.[9] Eisenhower worried in a memo to Patton that "an increasing number of these cases are now being reported." First known as "shell shock" because of a World War I era misunderstanding that neuropsychiatric disorders derived mainly from brain damage caused by concussions suffered in artillery barrages, the syndrome in Tunisia was renamed "combat exhaustion," a term borrowed from the British. The Army's chief psychiatrist described a typical patient: "He appeared as a dejected, dirty, weary man. His facial expression was one of depression, sometimes of tearfulness. Frequently his hands were trembling or jerky."[10]

Ernie Pyle had tried to convey to his uncomprehending audience something of the indelible trauma inflicted by war.

> The scream of an approaching shell is an appalling thing. We could hear them coming—(You sort of duck inside yourself, without actually ducking at all.)… War has its own peculiar sounds. They are not really very much different from sounds in the world of peace. But they clothe themselves in an unforgettable fierceness… because born in danger and death… The clank of a starting tank, the scream of a shell through the air, the ever-rising whine of fiendishness as a bomber dives—these sounds have their counterparts in normal life, and you would be hard put to distinguish them in a blind-fold test. But, once heard in war, *they remain with you forever…* These nervous memories come back to you in a thousand ways—in the grind of a truck stating in low gear, in high wind around the caves, in somebody merely whistling a tune. Even the sound of a shoe, dropped to the floor in a hotel room above you, becomes indistinguishable from the sound of a big gun far away. A mere rustling curtain *can paralyze a man with memories.*[11]

By the end of the war more than 500,000 men from the Army ground forces alone would be discharged for psychiatric reasons. That number did not include the approximately 1.8 million men, out of 15 million draftees examined, who were immediately rejected as mentally or psychologically unfit after their induction physicals. Today these symptoms are known as Post-Traumatic Stress Disorder and are recognized as a predictable type of brain injury caused by exposure to violence, including the extreme violence of combat. The traumatic stress of the constant and immitigable prospect of maiming or death in battle could unseat even the healthiest of minds. For every six men wounded, another became a neuropsychiatric casualty. Men by the hundreds, then by the thousands, had tremors or paralysis in their limbs, dysfunctional bowels, vacant stares. An Army study concluded that commanders fostered "an attitude closely akin to the old Puritan approach to the venereal problem—the ostrich attitude, the 'we don't discuss it' idea, or 'it just isn't so.' Unfortunately, it is very much so… The front-line soldier wears out in combat."[12]

Physicians soon learned to treat soldiers as far forward in the combat zone as possible. The three common treatments in North Africa included electroshock, an accepted practice at the time but now regarded as ineffective and unethical except under carefully controlled conditions; large doses of barbiturates, to induce sleep for two to seven days; and sodium pentothal, intended to bring supposed demons to the surface. None of these produced consistently satisfactory outcomes. Nearly three-quarters of treated soldiers resumed military duties in some form, but less than two percent returned to combat. Tunisia made it clear to Army psychiatrists that "the average soldier reached his peak effectiveness in the first ninety days of combat and was so worn out after 180 days that he was rendered useless and unable to return to military service." Another study noted that "no man is removed from combat duty until he [has] become worthless. The infantryman considers this a bitter injustice... He can look forward only to death, mutilation, or psychiatric breakdown." After months of fearful stress and mental trauma, of close calls, of witnessing violent death and horrible wounds, even the bravest men wondered, as one fighter squadron commander did, "Am I becoming uncourageous?"[13]

Modern combat could break any soldier. But the notion that the experience of combat might mentally destroy a human being was not acceptable to the U.S. Army hierarchy. The very idea was anathema to Patton, who had little tolerance for human limits. In his personal and inflexible world, combat exhaustion was an illegitimate diagnosis for cowards to hide behind.[14]

Another general affective reaction resulted from combat with the Axis. After the Kasserine battles, a murderous hatred for the enemy arose in the American soldier. These former civilians evolved into killer riflemen, who practiced their art with growing skill and savagery. Ernie Pyle, writing of men in the 34th Infantry Division, now definitely sensed a vivid change in the Red Bull troops.

> The... change is the casual and workshop manner in which they now talk about killing. They have made the psychological transition from their normal belief that taking human life is sinful, over to a new professional outlook where killing was a craft. To them there is nothing morally wrong about killing. In fact it is an admirable thing...
>
> [The GI's] blood is up. He is fighting for his life, and killing now for him is as much a profession as writing is for me... He wants to kill individually or in vast numbers. He wants to see the Germans overrun, mangled, butchered in the Tunisian trap...
>
> The front-line soldier wants [the war] to be got over by the physical process of his destroying enough Germans to end it. He was truly at war. The rest of us, no matter how hard we worked, were not.[15]

The trauma of 6,000 casualties in three weeks—including 845 dead—did what no exhortations by the commanders or training exercise could do. "They lost too many friends," Pyle observed with his characteristic direct simplicity. Visiting combat pilots flying P40 "Warhawks" but surely having in mind his friends in the infantry, Pyle wrote:

> Now it is killing that animates them... They were all so young, so genuine, so enthusiastic. And they were so casual about everything—not casual in a hard, knowing way, but they talked about their [fights] and killing and being killed exactly as they would discuss girls or their school lessons.
>
> Maybe they won't talk at all when they finally get home. If they don't it will be because they know this is a world apart and nobody else would ever understand.[16]

CHAPTER 25

The Battle of Supply: The Buildup for the Allied Offensive

Admiral Ernest J. King, chief of Naval Operations during World War II, is credited with saying: "I don't know what the hell this 'logistics' is that Marshall is always talking about, but I want some of it."[1] Marshall and Eisenhower both understood how critical to victory it was to supply the front-line units in Tunisia with their enormous requirements for food, water, clothing, shoes, ammunition, vehicles and fuel and to build up reserves and forward supply dumps for the anticipated offensive. United States Army doctrine required the chiefs to get the supplies to the troops.

> Supply is a command responsibility. A commander may charge certain members of his staff and other administrative personnel with certain supply functions, but they act only in the name of and for the commander. The responsibility for insuring the proper supply of the unit is that of the commander alone. He is also responsible for the supply of attached elements...
>
> An inseparable alliance exists between tactics and supply. The supply plan must support the tactical plan. The most brilliantly conceived and executed tactical plan will fail unless supported by a sound supply plan.[2]

Perhaps Eisenhower's chief contribution to the 1943 spring campaign was ensuring that the matériel needed to finish the job was available at the front on time and in quantities large enough to make difference. For the Allies, at last, there would be no shortage of transport or supplies with which to crush the Axis bridgehead. Rick Atkinson sagely observes that modern industrialized war is a clash of systems: political, economic, and military. The Allies proved to be much better than the Axis powers at effectively integrating and efficiently managing the three pillars of national power: industrial capacity, national character, and an educational system that produced people able to organize global war. "The battle," Rommel famously observed, "is fought and decided by the quartermasters before the shooting begins." In early spring 1943 the quartermasters truly came into their own and the advantage in industrial production and organization lay with the Americans, despite the deficiencies in some weapons systems.[3]

The Allied rear, or "Zone of Communications," from Casablanca across the rim of Africa through Oran and Algiers to Tébessa in eastern Algeria, and on to Tunisia, was reorganized and massively augmented for the resumption of the Allied offensive in March. The "North African Theater of Operations, U.S. Army" (NATOUSA), was activated at Algiers on February 4, 1943, to direct and manage the logistical and personnel needs of the growing United States Army forces in the area. By April, AFHQ alone exceeded 2,000 officers and enlisted men tasked to administer the supplies and personnel of NATOUSA.[4] Reviled by some front-line troops in vulgar terms, the rear echelon supply organization was vital to the very survival of those troops.

The supply organization in the North African communications zone was also created in February to meet the requirements of the March offensive. Brigadier General Everett S. Hughes, who had been engaged in ETOUSA on the logistical problems connected with Operation *Torch*, arrived on February 12 in Algiers to be deputy theater commander and commanding general of the communications zone. An Eastern Base Section at Constantine, constituted on February 13 under command of Colonel (later Brigadier General) Arthur W. Pence,[i] opened on February 27 to supply the requirements of U.S. II Corps. With the Atlantic Base Section at Casablanca and the Mediterranean Base Section at Oran, the Eastern Base Section came under the direct control of Brigadier General Thomas B. Larkin as commanding general, Services of Supply, NATOUSA. The flow of matériel to II Corps occurred within the broader pattern of the Allied buildups for the operations in Tunisia, the campaign being planned for Sicily, and other as yet unspecified Mediterranean operations. In addition to storage, inventory control, requisition fulfillment, packing, loading and shipping, logistics personnel had to ensure that supplies for II Corps were dispatched with minimal interference with the British line of communication to First Army.[5]

Allied plans for logistical support were sketched on February 27 at AFHQ in a conference over which Major General Humfrey Gale (British), the chief administrative officer, AFHQ, presided, and at which Major General C. H. Miller (British) of 18 Army Group briefed the plan. First Army's supply base would be at Bône, while II Corps would draw on the new Eastern Base Section at Constantine, Algeria.[6] Each army respectively was responsible for deliveries to the battle areas forward of the advanced bases. The principal maintenance center for tanks (US M3 and M4 mediums and M3 light) was at Le Kroub near Constantine, with facilities at Bône for servicing British Churchill tanks.[7]

The US Army's Eastern Base Section at Constantine was assigned use of the port of Philippeville. That port was dredged to a depth of 22 feet, which permitted four partially loaded Liberty ships and two coasters to discharge cargo simultaneously. It was equipped with cranes, hoists, and other cargo-handling machinery to expedite

---

i   Brigadier General Pence would later be commanding general, Peninsular Base Section (Italy), NATOUSA 1943–4.

the unloading process.[8] During March, 1943 the 91,000 tons of supplies and equipment which passed through Philippeville in addition to the tonnages carried by rail and road from the west not only supplied the requirements of the U.S. II Corps and the XII Air Support Command, but allowed the accumulation of reserves on which the British Eighth Army would be able to draw when it moved into the Tunisian battle area.[9]

Prodigies of American industrial production and logistical organization provided in superabundance everything that would be needed to defeat the Axis in North Africa. Railroad and highway infrastructure across French North Africa was greatly improved and expanded during March through the work of combat engineers and the Transportation Corps, U.S. Army. An exceptionally large requisition for railway rolling stock from production in the continental United States had been made when the Allied drive on Tunis failed in December 1942. That equipment began to arrive in March 1943; the management and operational personnel were already in North Africa to receive it and put it in service. Before the end of April, as II Corps was fighting its way through the northern hills toward Mateur and Bizerte, 43 trains averaging over 10,700 tons daily were passing through Constantine toward the combat zone.[10]

Additional road and rail transport was essential for the rapid accumulation of matériel for the Allied campaign of spring 1943.[11] In Oran, engineers built an assembly plant near the port and taught local workers to assemble a jeep from a box of parts in nine minutes. That plant turned out more than 20,000 vehicles. Another new factory nearby assembled 1,200 railcars, which were among 4,500 cars and 250 locomotives ultimately added to North African rolling stock. In aggregate, the upgraded roads, trucks, railroads, and railcars solved the long-distance heavy hauling problems that had bedeviled the Allies since the *Torch* landings.

In late January 1943, Eisenhower had made a special request to the War Department for more trucks. At a meeting on January 25, 1943, at the Hotel St. George in Algiers with General Marshall, Admiral King and Major General (later Lieutenant General) Brehon B. Somervell, chief of the Army Services of Supply (SOS, later renamed Army Service Forces[12]), and British staff officers, Eisenhower told Marshall and Somervell that the need for wheeled vehicles in North Africa was desperate. He told Somervell that the greatest single supply obstacle in the forthcoming Tunisian campaign was the absence of adequate transportation in North Africa. There was an urgent need for both truck and rail equipment. The deficit had in part arisen from AFHQ's decision in November 1942 to prioritize troops over vehicles because of the shortage of shipping for the Operation *Torch* landings. Eisenhower's forces had not yet received all the trucks left behind. In addition, the Algerian railways were in a poor state of repair and were inefficiently operated. Although knowledge of this situation had been conveyed to them in general terms, few in the War Department had realized how serious the transportation problem really was and how it hindered combat operations. Eisenhower recommended that fast freighters filled with trucks be substituted for troop transports in the next convoy.[13]

By this time, in actuality, vehicles were already arriving in considerable numbers. More than 4,500 had come in a convoy at the end of December, and 5,300 were on the way in a convoy then at sea. In that convoy also were the expert technicians and equipment for assembling crated vehicles, capable of putting on the road 3,000 trucks per month. Somervell, however, viewed Eisenhower's request and AFHQ's situation as a challenge to his Services of Supply organization. Eisenhower needed trucks, on wheels, in a hurry. SOS had an opportunity to prove its ability to deliver in an emergency. Somervell turned to Marshall and King and said that if the Navy could find escorts, he would have a special convoy ready to sail in three weeks. King promised to produce the escorts, and Somervell immediately cabled instructions to his own chief of staff in Washington: 5,000 2½-ton trucks (1,500 on wheels), 400 1½-ton trucks (200 on wheels), 72 large tank transporters, 2,000 trailers for the trucks, and some rolling stock, all to be loaded and ready by February 15, along with certain service units. Nothing must be allowed to stand in the way.[14]

Two days after Somervell's message arrived, Major General Wilhelm D. Styer, chief of staff of SOS, cabled back that the job could be done. "We will not let you down. However, if you want the Pentagon Building shipped, we would like to allow more time." Ships were lined up, to sail from New York, Baltimore, and Hampton Roads, designated UGS-5 1/2.[15] There were additions to Somervell's original order. The Army Air Forces requested 80 P-38 fighters, some special vehicles and ammunition; the Navy added a tankerload of diesel fuel. Twenty thousand tons of Lend-Lease filler cargo were also added, and at the last minute passage was arranged for three small V-mail detachments. The V-Mail operation was emotionally as critical to GI wellbeing as the new equipment.

SOS carried off the operation with admirable skill and speed. Procedural bottlenecks were bypassed altogether to facilitate the urgent mission. Depots shipped to the ports without clearance, and cargo was loaded as it arrived without priorities, any residue being held for a later convoy. By February 9, it was clear that all ships would be fully loaded. By the 11th, all cargo was in port at Hampton Roads and Baltimore, and practically all at New York. When convoy UGS-5 1/2 sailed, as scheduled, on February 15, it carried, in 22 ships, 200,000 tons of matériel including: 5,000 2½-ton trucks, 2,000 cargo trailers, and 400 dump trucks, plus the 80 fighter planes, and, for ballast, 12,000 tons of high-grade coal for locomotives and other uses, 16,000 tons of flour, 9,000 tons of sugar, 1,000 tons of soap, and 4,000 submachine guns, all of which arrived in Casablanca and Oran on March 6–7. "It was," the official Army account of its global logistical operations noted with justifiable pride, "a brilliant performance."[16]

Large assembly plants, quickly built, processed the twin-unit-packed crates of trucks. Companies and battalions of truck drivers to operate them were combed out of other units.[17] One battalion which was formed in the Casablanca area had its trucks loaded with high-priority cargo, and, within a week of arrival, started in convoy to Ouled Rahmoun about 1,000 miles away. Road maintenance, traffic control posts and stations, and good organization stepped up highway traffic. By late March, the average number of eastward bound vehicles reaching Orleansville was 600 per day. In the Eastern Base Section's area, some 1,500 trucks and 4,500 troops were supplementing the railroad. From Ouled Rahmoun and Bône to Tébessa, the daily transportation was 500 tons or more.[18] Including local hauling, the Eastern Base Section recorded movement in April of a total of 51,541 truckloads amounting to almost 84,000 tons.[19]

During World War II almost all supplies for American forces were shipped directly from the continental United States, in addition to the immense tonnages sent to the Russians, British, French, and other allies. The demands of modern combat were unprecedented. Although a World War II U.S. Army infantry division was about half the size of its World War I predecessor, it typically used more than twice as much ammunition—111 tons on an average fighting day. In Africa, total supply requirements, including ammunition, amounted to 13 tons per soldier per month. Five hundred miles of extra communications cable was shipped from Algiers to the front a day after it was requested. When Patton demanded new shoes for the entire II Corps, 80,000 pairs arrived within days. From late February to late March 1943, 130 ships sailed from the United States for North Africa with 84,000 soldiers, 24,000 vehicles, and a million tons of cargo. Although U.S. II Corps lost more armor at Kasserine than the Germans had massed at the beginning of the battle, the American losses were replaced almost immediately. So much ammunition arrived in Tunisia that it was stacked in pyramids and thatched with branches to simulate an Arab village.[20] The Axis armies in Tunisia would be starved of food, ammunition, and fuel for lack of air and sea communications with Europe, while the Allied armies would continuously receive a flood tide of supplies and equipment of all kinds.[21]

Not all was efficiency and order in such large and urgent operations. Transport holds contained far too many crates of Coca-Cola. Sixteen boxcars manifested to contain field rations were filled with peanut butter. Truck chassis and truck cabs were loaded on different ships and sent to different ports, hampering assembly operations. The same happened to artillery projectiles and bags of propellant, radios and radio batteries, and many other components that only operated together. Shipping manifests and inventories were confused, often beyond reconciliation. Nonetheless, the colossal effort worked. In 72 hours, American engineers built five new airfields around Sbeïtla, all of which were quickly filled with Allied warplanes and base facilities to challenge the Axis for domination of the skies. In all, more than 100 airfields were built during the Tunisian campaign and filled with American and British bombers and fighters. Americans on the home front did everything they could so that the enemy would not be merely defeated in Tunisia. It would be overwhelmed.[22]

The German military had pioneered modern military logistics, but as the war entered its 43rd month, Wehrmacht logisticians simply could not keep pace with the Allies and the Soviet Union on all fronts simultaneously. Axis supply lines to North Africa ran from Italy on and over the Mediterranean Sea, depending heavily on the Italian fleet for protection which it could no longer provide. The Royal Navy and the Allied air forces relentlessly ravaged the Axis ships and barges. From the beginning of *Torch* to May 1943, the Italians lost 243 ships and boats on the Tunisian run, with another 242 damaged; most of the shipping losses were inflicted by Allied air forces. The Sicilian Channel became what a German officer described as a "roaring furnace." To Italian sailors it was "the death route." Ships still afloat were often immobilized in Italian ports for lack of fuel. Allied long-range bombers battered Italian naval yards so relentlessly that at any given moment two-thirds of all escort vessels were unfit for service. As spring advanced German supply officers calculated that they needed four times the available number of the heavily armed, shallow draft vessels known as Siebel ferries, but their requirements could not be met because of German steel shortages.

As Allied air strength grew, Italian ports and their docks and warehouses were ever more frequently and effectively bombed. The North African ports still held by the Axis were also increasingly damaged by air attack. The Axis was compelled to haul more and more supplies on a fleet of 200 Ju-52 transport planes, but each plane carried less than two tons and was highly vulnerable to the heavily armed long-range Allied fighters now appearing in the skies over the Mediterranean in growing numbers. Trains carrying Axis matériel within Tunisia required coal imported from Europe; as supplies dwindled, crews turned to local lignite, which greatly reduced locomotive efficiency. Even as the Allies withdrew westward during the Kasserine battles, an inspection team from Berlin reported that if Axis ships kept sinking at the current rate none would remain afloat by early summer. Von Arnim warned *OKW* that "if no supplies reach us, all will be up in Tunisia by 1 July." The Axis bridgehead, he added, was becoming "a fortress without ammunition and rations." The Axis dictators made and repeated empty promises of support, but without stripping the other battlefronts or rebuilding the Italian Navy, little could be done. Even less was done. "Hitler wanted to be stronger than mere facts, to bend them to his will," Kesselring's chief of staff observed. "All attempts to make him see reason only sent him into a rage."[23]

CHAPTER 26

An Axis Spoiling Attack Fails

However difficult their supply problems, the Axis commanders on the ground in Tunisia were not biding their time until a renewed Allied offensive. At a conference in Rome on February 24 between Kesselring and Arnim, the principals agreed upon a plan to secure a better defensive line for the Axis bridgehead in Tunisia. Kesselring issued a direct order to Arnim: Fifth Panzer Army, despite the strikingly small size of the forces then available to it, was to launch an offensive along its entire front from the coast to the Bou Arada valley. The main effort was to be directed at Sidi Nsir with Béja as its objective. The attack was to be executed with the only armored force Arnim still had, reinforced to a total of 77 tanks by the temporary transfer of 15 Mark IV panzers from 21st Panzer Division.[1] Kesselring intended to gain an extension of the bridgehead westward to a new main line of resistance running from Djebel Abiod through Béja to Testour and El Aroussa. Rommel's reaction to the orders was again uncharacteristically hesitant, even pessimistic. He was stunned by this "completely unrealistic" idea by what he later called the "nincompoops at Comando Supremo." He seems to have had a better sense of the correlation of Axis and Allied forces than the avuncular Kesselring. Nonetheless, the Fifth Panzer Army's attack order was issued on February 25 and the attack began the next day.[2]

Kesselring and Arnim had erroneously assumed that Allied reserves had been withdrawn from the Fifth Panzer Army front because of Rommel's drive on Thala. To exploit that supposed advantage, Arnim planned a deep thrust toward Béja. He charged *Korps Gruppe Weber* with the main effort to Béja and a smaller force under General Manteuffel with a secondary attack nearer the coast. Simultaneously Weber was to capture Medjez el Bab in a double envelopment operation that would also destroy Allied forces at Bou Arada and gain the Siliana river between El Aroussa and Testour. Manteuffel was ordered to reduce the Allied positions at Djefna and to occupy the Ez Zouara river sector near Djebel Abiod. Von Arnim's plan was boldly ambitious. If any two adjacent attacks succeeded, the Allies would be forced to pull back their lines and yield to the Axis forces a substantial advantage of position. But the situation on the front of Fifth Panzer Army was not as Arnim imagined; in fact, it was decidedly unfavorable to an Axis attack.

The renewed fighting in the north foreshadowed actions by the 34th Infantry Division on that same ground in late April during the final battles of the Tunisia campaign. Von Arnim's main attack against the British 46th Division on February 26 came in the sector of the 128th Infantry Brigade (Brigadier M. A. James) along the road from Mateur to Béja through Sidi Nsir. Sidi Nsir was a small agricultural village nestled in the valley of the Bou Oissa river at the junction of a secondary road to Tunis and the railroad to Mateur. The railroad continued northeast along the gentler grades and twisting course of the Bou Oissa and the Djoumine rivers. The highway climbed almost due eastward over heights which separated Sidi Nsir from the broad Tine river valley. Among the many grass-green and gray limestone hills, Djebel Tahent (609m, later to become famous as Hill 609) was the most prominent. Over two miles northeast of Sidi Nsir, Djebel Tahent rose to a broad crest from which Mateur was visible, and from which troops could observe movement over a wide area in all directions. The Germans opened the attack with heavy mortar fire on Djebel Tahent, and enemy infantry took the hill about 10:00a.m., February 26.[3]

The British then fought a delaying battle near Sidi Nsir. Enemy infantry clambered along the hills on the northwest and southeast of Sidi Nsir until they enfiladed the British soldiers from both flanks. They then made a frontal assault with *panzers*, led by a single Mark VI Tiger. By 6:00p.m., the main British position had been overrun, and shortly afterward, the British abandoned Sidi Nsir. But the enemy's attack on Béja the next day failed, as British artillery and RAF bombers were ready in force and ravaged the *panzers*. On March 2, the enemy broke off action near Medjez el Bab. Two days later the Axis assumed a defensive posture between the Medjerda river and the Sidi Nsir sector and established its line of main resistance in the north on the high ground from Toukabeur to Ksar Mezouar, then north and northwest to Tamera.[4] Later, it would be the 34th Infantry Division's task to recapture Sidi Nsir, to retake Hill 609, and to break up the enemy's defensive line.

Weber's attack south of the Medjerda river was by any measure a costly fiasco. Executed with insufficient strength by inexperienced officers, it was repulsed with substantial casualties and the loss of irreplaceable matériel. The Axis main effort was suspended. Von Arnim withdrew a mountain regiment and shifted it to the sector northwest of Medjez el Bab as the action south of the Medjerda faded out and the front there was again stabilized along the original lines.[5]

Fifth Panzer Army claimed the capture of 2,500 Allied prisoners and the destruction or capture of 16 tanks, 20 guns, 17 anti-tank guns, seven planes, and other matériel. But Weber's forces had suffered over 1,000 casualties, the total loss of 22 irreplaceable *panzers*, and disabling damage to 49 *panzers*, leaving Weber with only six operational tanks on March 1. German armor losses were greater than those of the Allies.[6] Rommel scathingly criticized the tank losses, amounting to almost 90 percent of Weber's available armor, raging that the armor had been committed in violation of sound tactical principles.[7] Von Arnim had paid the price for a poorly timed and hastily prepared operation. He had sent his tanks into rugged mountainous terrain where they were unable to maneuver, became trapped and were knocked out. The bulk of his infantry had been wasted in the open country of the Bou Arada valley. There were lessons in this enemy failure of which the Allies, in the person of Major General Omar Bradley, took careful note and would apply in the coming weeks. Worse for the Axis, the attack had come too late. It might have succeeded had it been coordinated with Rommel's drive on Thala. Once more, the failure of the Axis to establish a unified command in North Africa had caused an Axis offensive to fall short of its objective.[8]

34ID Feints toward Pichon

American forces participated only briefly and on the outer fringe of the battle against the Axis offensive in the north. The 135th Infantry Regiment had drawn a short straw after the Kasserine battles and was sent to find the retreating enemy. A group designated Wulf Force, consisting of 2/135, supported by artillery and reconnaissance units, made a reconnaissance in force on February 25 to determine the enemy's presence east of the Western Dorsal. One group of Wulf Force, commanded by Lieutenant Colonel Clarence J. Lee and including Company E, 2/135, moved over the ground from Sbiba south down to Sbeïtla. Another group, led by Captain Frank A. McCulloch and including Company F and a platoon of the 34th Reconnaissance Troop, went east to Kef el Ahmar Pass. The northern group, including Company G, explored toward El Ala. Discovering that the enemy had departed, the 34th Infantry Division moved eastward from Rohia during the night of February 26–27 to reoccupy its former lines near Sbiba. A new defensive position was established with thick minefields and wire obstacles. The positions at Rohia were further strengthened and made ready as a fallback line if required.[9]

By March 4, 1943, Allied reconnaissance of the enemy's dispositions on the 34th Infantry Division's front indicated to 18 Army Group and II Corps that it was possible to resume aggressive action. In furtherance of Alexander's orders to develop the battle skills and confidence of the Americans in small engagements, the 34th Infantry Division was deployed to make a demonstration in force in the direction of Pichon-El Ala, where the division had first entered the line in Tunisia, about 25 miles east of the front it now held. The operation was intended as a feint in support of an attack in the south near Gafsa and El Guettar, directed by Patton and executed by 1st Armored Division and 1st Infantry Division. On Thursday, March 5, 34ID's "Ward Force," comprising the 3rd Battalion, 135th Infantry Regiment, augmented by its now returned soldiers who had served with the Commandos and by transfers from 3rd Infantry Division, with attached tanks, anti-aircraft artillery, field artillery, combat engineers and the Reconnaissance Troop, and commanded by Colonel Robert W. Ward, commanding officer, 135IR, executed the mission. Ward Force was to march in substantial strength to the east in the direction of Pichon and El Ala, to locate the enemy's positions and to divert reinforcements away from II Corps's attacks in the south.[10] Elements of the 133rd Infantry Regiment established blocking positions to the southeast, guarding the route of approach.

Starting from Sbiba and advancing via El Ala, Ward Force reached its objective phase line and engaged the enemy early in the afternoon of March 5 along the road leading from El Ala to Pichon and Fondouk el Aouareb in the area just north of Djebel Trozza (997m). The Americans quickly learned that the Germans were dug in along a well-prepared defense line, and Red Bull observation posts spotted a German force assembling for a counterattack to the battalion's left rear. At 5:00p.m. Ryder ordered Ward to withdraw. After its armored reconnaissance vehicles penetrated to the edge of Pichon and confirmed that the enemy occupied the place in strength, Ward Force withdrew. Hampered by rain and "ice-slick" muddy roads, Ward Force returned to its original position near Sbiba by a circuitous route that took elements of the command through the enemy's outpost line. Ward Force suffered only a few casualties.[11]

Following the diversionary action, which was quite well done, the main line of resistance of the 34th Infantry Division was moved six miles to the east where its units organized defensive positions and observation posts in a line running due north and south. The re-occupation of the Kasserine Pass by strong Allied formations removed any threat of enemy action from the south. By the middle of March, the 34th Infantry Division occupied a line on a range of hills some 30 miles west of the German positions. The no-man's-land between 34ID and the Axis forces was rocky and sandy, uninhabited except for small bands of Arabs and one or two families of European settlers who farmed some of the land near water holes. For the most part, the mountains were steep with vegetation only on their lower slopes; the summits were barren rock. Cross-country movement by armor would have been easy had it not been for the pestilential artillery fire accurately directed by both sides from good observation points. The only natural barriers were the *oueds* and *wadis* which crisscrossed the countryside but were not formidable tank barriers. Clumps of cactus or stunted olive trees were scattered over the ground and the deeper *oueds* and *wadis* provided the only concealment.[12]

Rommel, the "Desert Fox," left Tunisia on March 9, never to return. The Kasserine battles were the final victories of his military career. He was succeeded on that day as commander of Army Group Africa by Arnim, who in turn yielded command of Fifth Panzer Army to *General der Panzer Truppen* Gustav von Vaerst. Messe's command over First Italian Army remained only nominal with respect to its German elements, after General Fritz Bayerlein took up his duties as the German chief of staff with that army. The German 10th Panzer and 21st Panzer Divisions were now directly controlled by Arnim's headquarters as components of the Army Group Africa reserve, with only the 15th Panzer Division remaining for a time under Messe's command.

Rommel's departure from Tunisia was kept a deep secret. He stopped briefly in Rome, and paid his respects to the Führer at his advanced headquarters at Winniza in the Ukraine on March 10, then continued to Wiener-Neustadt, Austria on sick leave to cure a severe nasal infection. The Allies continued to believe that he was in Tunisia, and for weeks press reports nurtured the widely held belief that "Rommel's Africa Corps" was the only fighting force in Tunisia. In this respect, the Allied public was as badly informed as the Germans themselves, who had to wait for the Axis defeat in May to discover that the much-publicized German commander had not been leading Axis operations in Africa for the past two months.[13]

Meanwhile, during the night of March 9–10, 135RCT established strong combat outposts near Er Rbeiba.[i] Red Bull soldiers patrolled constantly to detect enemy movements from the east, and units frequently engaged German troops probing in the El Ala-Pichon area. At 11:50a.m. on Wednesday, March 10, patrols from 135IR had a fierce firefight with German troops west of El Ala. 3/135 advanced east of El Ala with the 34th Reconnaissance Troop. The Germans then made a now familiar enveloping counterattack. At 2:00p.m., the 125th Field Artillery Battalion came under direct fire from *panzers*, but direct fire returned by the artillery drove the enemy tanks away. 3/135 and 34th Reconnaissance Troop came under machine-gun and mortar fire at 3:30p.m. and at 4:00p.m. 135RCT troops observed enemy infantry dismounting from trucks in the left rear of 3/135. 34ID reported other *panzers* advancing north from Hadjeb el Aïoun in the right rear of 3/135.

3/135 and its supporting units were ordered to withdraw. The anti-tank towed gun and tank destroyer units were placed at the rear to counter the armor threat. 34th Reconnaissance and four platoons of 3/135 formed a covering force supported by Battery B, 125th FA Battalion. The cover force executed a withdrawal during the night but took a wrong turn and had to exfiltrate through enemy lines to reach the assembly area near Er Rbeiba. The next day, 3/135 with all its supporting units left Er Rbeiba before dawn and marched west to the 135RCT's original positions near Sbiba.

---

i   A mountain peak about 37 miles north of Sidi Bou Zid, about 18 miles east of Sbiba, and about 18 miles west of Pichon (modern Haffuz).

CHAPTER 27

The Crucible of Combat

By mid-March Eighth Army had at last pushed the Axis forces westward out of Libya and into Tunisia, where the enemy took up defensive positions in the old French fortifications known as the Mareth Line. About 25 miles long, it extended northeast from the vicinity of Cheguimu in the Matmata Hills toward the Wadi Zigzaou, and along the *wadi* to the Gulf of Gabès. Eighth Army defeated a German spoiling attack out of the Mareth Line with overwhelming artillery fire power, and Montgomery then sent a large flanking force west of the Mareth Line. The Eighth Army was to begin its attack against the Mareth Line during the night of March 16.

On Friday, March 12, 1943, while 34ID prepared for an attack toward Fondouk, Patton was promoted to lieutenant general.

II Corps, now under Patton's command, was to play a supporting role in Alexander's plan. The Americans were to capture and hold Gafsa, which would then serve as a logistical base for Eighth Army. After taking Gafsa, II Corps was to advance toward Maknassy to threaten Axis lines of communication and supply. The plan required the 9th and 34th Infantry Divisions to defend the approaches to Rohia, Sbeïtla, Kasserine, and Bou Chebka while the 1st Infantry Division took Gafsa. The 1st Armored Division was to attack toward Maknassy. During the night of March 16, Major General Terry Allen's 1ID made a 45-mile approach march in the rain, fiercely attacked and drove off the enemy, and seized Gafsa in the morning of March 17. 1ID then advanced another ten miles on the road toward Gabès and took El Guettar.[1]

After the II Corps' drive by 1ID and 1AD on Gafsa in the south was successfully completed, Patton directed 34ID to clear the plain between its line and the Germans' main line of defense in preparation for an operation to seize Kairouan. 34ID pushed a reconnaissance in force to Kef el Ahmar and Sbeïtla, where it encountered an enemy ready to fight. The regimental history of the 135IR recounts ruefully that "being inexperienced in warfare our troops were sometimes out-witted by the enemy, notably at Kef el Ahmar where… one of our rifle companies was ambushed by the Germans at heavy cost to ourselves." Even so, the Red Bull probing force turned northeastward at Sbeïtla and made continued progress along the road to Hadjeb el Aïoun. 34ID GIs frequently encountered typically malignant German minefields and the thorough demolition of every culvert and bridge. Aggressive screening operations by mobile German elements "made this phase of our activity very exciting." Other motorized elements of the 34th Infantry Division penetrated to El Ala and then turned south toward Djebel Trozza, reaching the highway near Hadjeb el Aïoun where the division's regiments linked up again. It was truly open warfare now; there was no flank, no front and practically no rear. 34ID GIs had to be prepared for the enemy to approach from every direction. The German air force was an ever-present threat and any considerable movement of troops had to be made under the cover of darkness with total black-out.[2]

On March 19, Patton returned to his headquarters in Fériana to find the British Major General Sir Richard L. McCreery, chief of staff, 18 Army Group, with new plans and orders for II Corps from General Alexander. II Corps was now to capture the high ground east of Maknassy and to send a light armored raiding party to the enemy's Mezzouna airfields and destroy them. No large forces, however, were to pass beyond a line extending from Gafsa through the Maknassy heights, Faïd, and Fondouk el Aouareb. Later, after the British Eighth Army had passed up the coast beyond Maknassy, II Corps was to be reduced by the transfer of the 9th Infantry Division to British V Corps to relieve the British 46th Division on the far northern flank, where that division would operate within British First Army. The 34th Infantry Division would at about the same time march north to attack Fondouk el Aouareb Gap along the axis Maktar-Pichon. II Corps was directed to move other units to Maknassy and toward a defile east of El Guettar, on the southern side of Djebel Orbata. The purpose of II Corps's actions in the south was primarily to draw off enemy troops which might otherwise strengthen the defense of the Mareth Position. Eighth Army's main attack at Mareth began on the night of March 20–21.

Alexander issued to Patton at noon, March 25 a revised directive for II Corps. Its base line was advanced from the Western Dorsal to extend between Gafsa and Sbeïtla. 18 Army Group released the 9th Infantry Division to II Corps to undertake offensive operations. 9ID, less the 60th Infantry Regiment, was to attack with the 1st Infantry Division southeast of El Guettar. Alone but under British operational control, the 34th Infantry Division (less the 133rd Infantry Regiment) was to attack the Axis-held gap through the Eastern Dorsal at Fondouk el Aouareb.[3]

In a series of battles in the vicinity of El Guettar between March 16 and April 1, the 1st Infantry Division repulsed 10th Panzer Division with a deadly artillery trap. The 1st and 9th Infantry Divisions then pursued the Axis forces toward Sfax, incurring heavy losses against ferocious German artillery and stubborn infantry. But the II Corps operations in the south had fulfilled the mission. They had diverted a *panzer* division that most certainly would have opposed the British Eighth Army's attack against the Mareth Line and the subsequent pursuit.

First Battle of Fondouk

The Allied high command had given 34th Infantry Division an important mission, despite its limited scope. 18 Army Group did not, however, commit sufficient force to achieve even Alexander's modest objective. The possibility remained of interfering effectively with the withdrawal of First Italian Army and *DAK* into the northeastern Tunisian bridgehead, and there joining Fifth Panzer Army, but the Allies would have to move quickly and in great strength. A combined arms force would first have to capture and drive through the Fondouk el Aouareb Gap and then a strong Allied armored force would have to debouch onto the coastal plain and attack the retreating enemy on its western flank while the Eighth Army pressed from the south.[4]

Pursuant to Alexander's directive of March 25, the 34th Infantry Division passed from II Corps control to the operational control of British IX Corps. The main force of II Corps, three divisions under Patton's command, was engaged in the battles for Gafsa, Maknassy, and El Guettar when the 34th Infantry Division made their first undermanned and irresolute attempt to capture the gap through the Eastern Dorsal near Fondouk el Okbi. If they could dislodge the Germans from the hills abutting the pass, the Allies would be able to threaten Kairouan and possibly cut off the enemy's forces in the southern portion of the Tunisian bridgehead. Alexander's plan of March 25 specified that the 34th Infantry Division should attack as early as possible on the axis Sbeïtla–Hadjeb el Aïoun–Fondouk el Aouareb, to seize the heights on the Eastern Dorsal south of the Fondouk Gap. "This ground will be firmly held," the directive stated, "to enable mobile forces to operate from there into the Kairouan plain." Lieutenant General Patton passed on these instructions to Major General Ryder in an evening conference at Fériana on March 25. His orders to Ryder were brief and clear. The 34th Infantry Division was to make what amounted to a large-scale demonstration; the capture of Kairouan was not 34ID's objective. The attack was, however, to capture Fondouk Pass and, after intermediate objectives had there been taken, to make a show of force in the direction of Kairouan to mislead the enemy about 18 Army Group's intentions. The means and method were left to Ryder's discretion.[5]

Ryder moved one regiment on the night of March 25–26, and a second on the following night from the area of Sbeïtla to the vicinity of Hadjeb el Aïoun. He left the 133rd Infantry (less the one battalion still on guard duty at AFHQ in Algiers) to defend Sbeïtla. Ryder prepared the 135th and the reconstituted 168th Infantry Regiments for an attack at daylight on Friday, March 27. The 175th Field Artillery Battalion was to support the 168th Infantry Regiment, and the 125th and 185th Field Artillery Battalions supported the 135th Infantry Regiment. II Corps made available battalions of the 178th (155mm howitzers) and 36th (155mm guns) Field Artillery Regiments, which were to remain in position near Sbeïtla, at the ready and on call by Ryder. The 813th Tank Destroyer Battalion and the 751st Tank Battalion assembled near Hadjeb el Aïoun and stood by in reserve on the right wing of the attack. Antiaircraft batteries of the 107th Coast Artillery were attached to the field artillery. The enemy's routes of approach for enveloping counterattacks through a secondary pass east of Hadjeb el Aïoun and by the western side of Djebel Trozza were covered by reconnaissance elements.[6]

Only a small amount of time remained to intercept Marshal Messe's Italo-German Army before it reached the relative safety of the enemy's defenses in northeastern Tunisia. Midway between El Guettar and Tunis, the Marguellil river threaded a narrow pass through the Eastern Dorsal where Fondouk Gap straddled Highway 3 as it ran toward Kairouan 20 miles to the northeast. Fondouk Pass, where First Army had mistakenly predicted the enemy would launch its February 14 attack instead of Faïd Pass, was about 16 miles northeast of Hadjeb el Aïoun. At that time, the shallow stream of the Marguellil river flowed from the northwest and in an elbow turn swung eastward at the pass through a wide, marshy valley. North of the opening was the Djebel ech Cherichera (462m) and its foothills. Immediately to the south, several precipitous knobs along parallel ridges of the Djebel Haouareb (306m) led to a higher hill mass. The Oued Zeroud wound around first southeasterly, then northeasterly, for 10 to 20 miles south of Fondouk, past the southern end of Djebel Haourareb. The gap itself narrowed at the village of Fondouk el Aouareb and the ground was almost flat both east and west of the gap. Less than 1,000 yards wide, the defile was bracketed on the north by a stony pinnacle named Djebel Aïn el Rhorab and on the south by the equally stony northern slopes of Djebel Haouareb.

The Djebel Aïn el Rhorab[i] (290m) rose just to the west of the pass, on the northern side of the stream, a steep-sided ridge above a large Arab village and spring. From Rhorab all the roads from the west and southwest that met in the pass en route to Fondouk el Aouareb could be well observed and brought under fire. Indeed, Djebel Aïn el Rhorab would prove to be a thorn in the side of 34ID in both of the division's fights to take the Fondouk Gap. The roads converging on the village from the west and southwest were dominated also by the massive Djebel Trozza, with a crest over 3,000 feet high. These roads ran over a bare, undulating plain cut by *wadis* but devoid of cover or screening vegetation except for widely scattered cactus patches and small olive groves.

Germans occupied the slopes and fissures of Djebel Aïn el Rhorab north of the gap and of Djebel Haouareb to the south, and the enemy had been busy there for weeks. In a scenario which would be repeated often in the future history of the 34th Infantry Division, the enemy had blasted gun positions from the rock and built bivouac dens within the cliffs, complete with heating stoves, beds, and rude kitchens. German gunners had registered their artillery on the open approaches from the west and calibrated their mortars on all the dead spaces below the ridges. Fields

---

i   Modern Jebel Ayn el Ghorab.

of fire were nearly perfect.[7] Major Roland Anderson, supply officer for the 135th Infantry Regiment, summed up the terrain: Fondouk was protected by "two spiny ridges which closed in on the village from the north, east and south. The Pass lay between the spiny ridges." Along the southern slope of the ridge was a wide *wadi* running from Pichon to Fondouk.[8]

The Axis defensive zone of which Fondouk Pass was a part was controlled by the Italian XXX Corps headquarters at Sousse (Lieutenant General Vittorio Sogno), through *Gruppe Fullriede* at Kairouan. The German soldiers defending the gap were not in great numbers and were not exceptionally well equipped. The Germans were rather thinly strung from outposts near Pichon southward to the Zeroud river. The hills northwest of Fondouk el Aouareb toward Pichon were held by two companies of the 1st Battalion, 961st Infantry Regiment, each with three rifle platoons with the usual squad machine guns, one platoon with two heavy machine guns and two mortars, and one anti-tank platoon with two guns. This unit of the 999th Africa Division consisted chiefly of court-martialed German soldiers to whom combat duty was "permitted" or rather offered in lieu of brutal imprisonment or execution. The defense of the Fondouk Gap was its first important battle.

Along Djebel ech Cherichera and northeast of that hill the ground was held by the 190th Reconnaissance Battalion, reinforced with some artillery. To the south, the 27th Africa Battalion was stationed along the crest of Djebel Haouareb, the objective of 34ID's planned attack, and the area from there to Djebel Hallouf (481m) was held by Headquarters, 961st Infantry Regiment (*Kampfgruppe Wall*). It consisted of the 1st Battalion (less some elements) and the 2nd Battalion, 961st Infantry Regiment, supported by artillery and anti-tank guns. As reinforcements for his sector, *Oberstleutnant*[ii] Fritz Fullriede could also draw on the 34th Africa Battalion, the 2nd Battalion, Italian 91st Infantry Regiment, and some native Arab units. Information gleaned on March 26 from German prisoners revealed that the enemy expected an attack.[9]

The first, unsuccessful effort to force Fondouk Pass was made in only loose coordination with the II Corps attacks at Maknassy by 1AD and at El Guettar by 1ID and 9ID. On March 25, Patton had ordered 34th Infantry Division to "go out in that area and make a lot of noise, but don't try to capture anything." The division's three infantry regiments—the 168th, 133rd (less 2/133), and 135th—had finally been reunited, but the two available battalions of 133IR remained in reserve at Sbeïtla. The reconstituted 168th Infantry Regiment was now under the command of Colonel Butler, a relentless, driving officer.[10] Despite casualties, reinforcements and replacements, the regiments of 34ID still had many of their original soldiers, men from Iowa and Minnesota. 168IR, in particular, was still an unnerved group. Defeat and heavy losses at Sidi Bou Zid had left deep and permanent wounds of

ii   Lieutenant colonel.

trauma and grief. Morale was poor and fighting spirit was worse. In a March 11 message to his officers, Ryder decried "this military creeping paralysis present in our division," and the want of "offensive spirit."[11] The first attempt to take Fondouk proved his point.[12]

By March 25, 1943, scouting operations had been completed and the 34th Infantry Division received the order for its first major attack as a unified division in the war.[13] The plan was to place two regiments abreast, with one battalion in reserve, covering a front of about five miles, to make a frontal assault on Djebel Haouareb with the objective of gaining the high ground on the south side of the Fondouk Gap and the valley of the Marguellil River. The boundary between the assault regiments was Route 3, the Hadjeb el Aïoun–Fondouk road.

Friday, March 26, 1943

The 34th Infantry Division made its approach march to the pass during the night of March 26–27. The 135th Regimental Combat Team moved through Kef el Ahmar Pass, where it had only weeks before suffered casualties in a German ambush. The battalions moved out from the river line about three miles northeast of Hadjeb el Aïoun advancing easterly along either side of Highway 3, on the axis Hadjeb el Aïoun-Fondouk El Okbi. Shortly after crossing the line of departure, the assault troops encountered an unmarked minefield which other Americans had laid during the mid-February fighting. The mines caused 18 casualties and demobilized eight or nine vehicles, with explosive light and noise that were undoubtedly seen and heard by German sentinels.[14] The distance from Hadjeb el Aïoun to the base of the primary objective at Djebel Haouareb was about 14.5 miles, and 135IR and 168IR quickly reached all intermediate ground objectives. There was no concealment on the ground except the undulations in the surface of the plain.[15] The assault regiments advanced astride the highway toward the long ridge of mountains which ran in a semi-circle southward and then westward from the pass.[16]

Saturday, March 27, 1943

The Germans had tactical advantages that not only compensated for their lack of numbers but also greatly multiplied their force. The enemy was in fortified positions on the hills north and south of the Fondouk Gap with excellent daylight observation to the north, west and south. The timing of the assault ensured that the GIs would be in the open when dawn came. The two assault regiments lined up abreast with the 168th Infantry Regiment (Colonel Butler) on the right closer to the enemy's principal hill positions and the 135th Infantry Regiment (Colonel Ward) on the left or north.[17] On the left side of the road, the 2nd and 3rd Battalions of 135IR assaulted, 3/135 on the right in contact with 168IR on its right. 2/135 was echeloned in depth to the left and rear. 1/135 was in division reserve assigned to protect the division's left flank, exposed to enfilade fire from Aïn el Rhorab. The regimental command post of 135IR was in a *wadi* about seven miles northeast of Hadjeb el Aïoun.[18]

The attack opened in the early morning with a four-battalion front. Each regiment echeloned its leading battalion and put a second battalion behind the outer company of the assault battalion. The GIs reached the first phase line four hours after marching from Hadjeb el Aïoun in good order and had not yet come under hostile fire. The steeply sloped hills of the Eastern Dorsal crossed their path of approach obliquely, with Hill 306 on Djebel Haouareb, the first objective, still several miles away. As the assault units advanced from the first phase line, the leading elements reached ground that sloped up to the foot of Djebel Haouareb and was within range of shelling from both the objective hills in front to the east, and on the northwest flank from Djebel Aïn el Rhorab. The enemy began shelling, and most of the fire fell at first on the 168th Infantry Regiment.[19] By 10:00a.m., the 135th Infantry Regiment on the north or left, the 168th Infantry Regiment on the south or right, and the 109th Engineer Battalion in a screening role further to the right, had managed to reach points about 1,000 yards from the base of the mountains.[20] 3/135 attacked to its front. 2/135 was echeloned to the left rear as flank protection. 1/135 remained in division reserve.[21]

168RCT's advance, clearly visible to the enemy, was opposed by heavy mortar and artillery fire which slowed it to a literal crawl. 2/135 also moved forward haltingly across the bare landscape under artillery fire. The assault advanced steadily but ever more slowly until about 11:00a.m., when the 168th Infantry Regiment reported that they were held up by heavy mortar and artillery fire. 3/135 paused its attack to allow 168RCT to come abreast. About ten minutes later 2/135 was attacked by a small, combined arms force from its left rear. A German reconnaissance group of scout cars and two light tanks had approached from the northwest and struck two squads of the 135th Intelligence and Reconnaissance Platoon at close range. Company F of 2/135 now engaged the enemy force by fire and called in artillery support that drove off the enemy.[22] The Red Bull soldiers were beginning to apply the lessons of combined arms operations on a porous battlefield where the combatants were mounted on fast motorized transports and fighting vehicles.[23]

But just after 11:45a.m., 3/135 also reported enfilading artillery fire from its left. Enemy artillery fire became general and intense; by noon it effectively halted all forward movement by 3rd Battalion.[24] By mid-afternoon, after struggling forward beneath the German guns, 34ID's assault stalled 500 yards short of its objective on Djebel Haouareb.[25] It would come no closer. As the volume of fire from atop and behind the hills intensified, the 135th Infantry Regiment, ahead and on the left, stopped a little before 2:00p.m., and the GIs sought cover from both the frontal and enfilading fire of enemy machine guns, artillery, and mortars, scrabbling in the hard soil to dig shallow trenches. The northern flank of 135IR was under constant enfilading fire by flat-trajectory weapons on Rhorab which swept the ground and made daylight movement impossible.

Several battalion officers, including Lieutenant Colonel Lee, commanding officer of 2nd Battalion, 135IR were wounded; leadership changes had to be made while the units were heavily engaged in battle. Lieutenant Colonel Albert A. Svoboda, regimental executive officer, was placed in command of 2/135, and the regimental S-1, Captain Ray Erickson, became Svoboda's operations officer. The executive officer of the 1st Battalion, Major Hall, was sent to replace Lieutenant Colonel Swenson in command of the 3rd Battalion. These reassignments of officers from headquarters further degraded the ability of the regimental staffs to exercise command and control.[26]

The 1st and 2nd Battalions, 168th Infantry Regiment, heading for somewhat separated objectives on their sector of the front, had not succeeded in reaching those objectives.[27] Colonel Ward issued night attack orders for 135IR. As nightfall drew near, the 2nd and 3rd Battalions, 135th Infantry Regiment attacked abreast in fading light, but both battalions drew murderous fire from all arms and took casualties. The attack reached the enemy's main line of resistance, but in the darkness the unit commanders lost control and the battalions could not hold their gains. During their respective fights, a gap developed between the 135th Infantry Regiment and the 168th Infantry Regiment on its right.[28] 135RCT became disordered with heavy casualties. Ward ordered his regiment to withdraw and reorganize.[29]

Sunday, March 28, 1943

During the night, 135RCT sorted itself out, collected its wounded and dead, and regained contact with 168RCT. The enemy kept up machine-gun fire over the field all night, illuminating the ground with green tracers.[30] The assault regiments renewed the attack to gain the high ground early in the morning of March 28, after another artillery preparation. At 7:00a.m. 2/135 struck but again encountered heavy flanking and frontal fire from artillery and mortars. The GIs were not able to return fire effectively or to hold their ground. They could not get past the base of Djebel Haouareb. Farther south, elements of the 168th Infantry gained some isolated crests, but further infiltration attempts were unsuccessful. Meanwhile, 1/135 while in division reserve patrolled toward Djebel Trozza, the high hill to the left rear of 135RTC. From there, enemy self-propelled guns (SPGs)[iii] shelled the 135th Infantry Regiment, inflicting yet more casualties. Every available bed, cot, and floor space at the 15th Evacuation Hospital in Sbeïtla was soon occupied by bleeding

---

iii   The regimental history of 134IR recalls that the shelling was from two "tanks."

soldiers from Fondouk. Nurses were forced to send late-arriving ambulances to other medical units.[31]

The official historian is pointedly critical in his judgment of the 34th Infantry Division's performance after reaching the base of the objective: "[N]either then nor later did assaulting forces risk enough troops to gain full possession of the exposed upper slopes. Infiltration tactics were unsuccessful."[32] There is merit to that criticism. Ryder had three battalions in reserve but did not commit any of them. Given its orders to capture the south side of Fondouk Pass, and the urgency of intercepting the retreating Italo-German Army, the division might have achieved its objective with more troops and the employment of all its artillery. But numbers were not the only problem. In their first attempt at Fondouk, the GIs of 34ID were still not quite yet the determined battlefield killers they would become.

March 29–31, April 1–2, 1943

Three days of small infantry skirmishes followed. On March 29, 168th Regimental Combat Team staged a diversionary strike following artillery preparation, and the 2nd Battalion, 135IR, again charged to its front without success. The attack crumpled. On the morning of March 31, a small American armored screening force challenged an enemy group lurking in the cactus and olive groves on the northwestern slopes of Djebel Touil (665m), about five miles south of the main battle area. The GIs drove them out despite strong fire from adjacent hills and an attack by Axis dive bombers. Two tanks were lost, but the skirmish forestalled an enemy strike at the 168th Infantry Regiment's southern flank.[33]

On the nights of March 31–April 1 and April 1–2, with the division's combat condition reported as only "fair," the infantry units fell back to defensive positions four miles to the west, to wait and rest. There they were well out of the range of the enemy's machine guns and artillery still holed up in their protected emplacements on Djebel Aïn el Rhorab, Djebel Haouareb, Djebel el Djeriri, and Djebel Hallouf. On April 1 the 34th Infantry Division was ordered to abandon its efforts toward Fondouk Pass and to withdraw to a temporary defensive line. Then on division orders 135IR retired two miles further westward to positions prepared by 1/135 for the assault battalions. 1/135 rejoined 135RCT from division reserve. All of the division's movements were completely exposed to enemy observation from the high ground to the east and north.

Although the 34th Infantry Division had not captured the Fondouk Gap, the Red Bull soldiers believed that they had forced the enemy to concentrate in the division's front. As Patton had requested, the division had made a lot of noise, but at a cost of 527 casualties. Almost 60 percent of the losses fell on the 168th Infantry Regiment, full of replacements after the Sidi Bou Zid debacle.[34] The regiment reported casualties: 17 killed, 108 wounded, and 178 missing.[35] Even after breaking contact with the enemy, the division was subjected to a week of harassing attacks by the German air force and artillery. The GIs could not reconnoiter the enemy's positions but the Germans could observe all American movement in daytime.[36]

The 34th Infantry Division's attack was stopped short of the Fondouk Gap on March 28 and 29 and never actually reached it. Ryder had acted in accord with Patton's oral instruction to make a noisy demonstration but not to run overly grave risks merely to gain ground. But Ryder and 34ID had failed to capture the high ground on the south side of the pass. Command and control of the attacking units were inadequate, and the performance of the American troops in the assault lacked a firm resolution to win, reflecting still-vivid memories of recent defeats. The German troops in consequence formed a derisively low, if arrogant and shortsighted, opinion of American soldiers. "The American gives up the fight as soon as he is attacked. Our men feel superior to the enemy in every respect."[37] Many British officers, no doubt encumbered by anti-American bias, also concluded that the soldiers of the 34th Infantry Division and their junior officers were not yet capable of successfully carrying out large-scale combat assignments.

The divisional history written by 34ID personnel takes a decidedly personal view of the first fight at Fondouk, from the perspective of the Red Bull soldiers who were exposed on the ground under fire. To the GIs, the mission was well-nigh impossible because the Germans held well-protected positions on the high ground, as earlier reconnaissance had revealed. The enemy had spent weeks preparing its positions in solid rock, many of them reinforced with railroad ties and steel girders. The approaches to the objective were bare and flat, completely devoid of cover. The objective was fortified by dense barbed wire entanglements and thick fields of anti-personnel mines on the lower slopes. These obstacles, as the enemy intended, slowed the infantry's movements, and greatly increased the effectiveness of defensive fire against the GIs. Maneuver went from difficult to impossible because the enemy could see everything on the flat land.

> [T]he operation was simply a head-on assault in the face of withering fire from an opponent having ample ammunition and virtual immunity from counter-fire. With great bravery [34th Infantry Division] troops attacked the enemy position again and again, each time being halted by a wall of fire before they could even carry the first ridge line. Casualties were heavy and grew… heavier. In their first large-scale action our troops were stunned to find themselves up against an almost impossible task." [38]

First Lieutenant (later Major) Arnold Brandt, commander of D Company, 1st Battalion, 135th Infantry Regiment, wrote an account after the war that addressed the real and persistent problems of insufficient training, lack of basic combat skills, and absence of combat experience. In his view, the assaulting regiments at Fondouk Pass suffered not only from adverse terrain, but also from errors in judgment and inexperience in the performance of basic military tasks. He acknowledged that the area was held in strength from positions prepared in solid rock and that the infantry battalions sallied repeatedly over bare, flat approaches through wire and mines, only to be thrown back. He summarized the battle as a series of head-on attacks over exposed terrain where the GIs could not see their tormentors, let alone hit the enemy with counterfire or normal infantry weapons. He concluded that the 34ID's soldiers had been forced to learn the hard way about aggressive assault under fire.[39]

The divisional history insists that "[i]t must not be thought, however, that nothing had been achieved by this gallantry." The men of the 34th Infantry Division evaluated their performance as satisfactory although not successful in the face of what they assessed as overwhelming enemy firepower from hidden and fortified positions. 18 Army Group had wanted German units to be diverted to the center of the line, that is, to the 34th Infantry Division sector. As the GIs of 34ID saw it, the German troops in the front of 34ID had been locked in place and so distracted by 34ID's attack that they were unable to influence the large-scale American attack in the south toward Maknassy. The assault on Fondouk, in their view, had thereby contributed to the mission to draw German strength away from British Eighth Army and gave the rest of II Corps an opportunity to interdict Panzer Army Africa's line of retreat. That assessment, however, did not consider either the relatively small numbers of Axis troops engaged at Fondouk or the fact that the Axis high command felt the situation was well in hand and did not commit reinforcements to meet the American threat. Patton had told Ryder not to take risks with his division but that did not excuse the hesitant, uncoordinated attacks. There was, nonetheless, a core of truth to the soldiers' insistence that they had been given an impossible task. They had suffered 527 casualties under ineffective battle leadership, in no small part because Alexander and First Army had not allocated enough forces to accomplish the objective of seizing control of the gap at Fondouk el Aouareb.[40]

CHAPTER 28

"Death Rides With Us"

Second Battle of Fondouk

Alexander, bloodily repulsed after testing the defenses at Fondouk el Aouareb with five battalions of the 34th Infantry Division, belatedly realized that he had committed too small a force. Nearly 90,000 Americans had indecisively poked at the Eastern Dorsal in several places, while First Army had been stationary for the past month. Captured Axis generals would later tell the Allies that the African campaign might have ended a month earlier if 18 Army Group had struck a harder blow at Fondouk. Alexander now directed his staff to plan a renewed attack to take the pass as part of a larger offensive on a front of 15 miles from Fondouk el Aouareb northeastward along the mountain chain to the northern extremity of Djebel Ousselat (887m). The 34th Infantry Division was to fight again at Fondouk, but this time under the command of British IX Corps with British and French troops participating, which more than tripled the attacking force. Infantrymen, both American and British, were to seize the sides of the Fondouk Gap along the Marguellil River, allowing the British 6th Armoured Division to sweep onto the coastal plain toward Kaiouran. Messe's Italo-German Army, fleeing Montgomery and Patton in the south, was to be intercepted and destroyed before it merged with Arnim's Fifth Panzer Army in the north.[1] For this offensive, Alexander decided to use Koeltz's French XIX Corps, operating under British First Army, and the British IX Corps, commanded by Lieutenant General Sir John Crocker. Crocker would come to be loathed by American soldiers of all ranks for his rigidity of thought, careless disregard for intelligence, flawed planning, and callous willingness to spend American lives. British combat units for the prospective operation would be in position by April 7. As the enemy forces marched north toward Tunis along the eastern coastline, little time remained to break through the Fondouk Gap if the enemy were to be destroyed on the coastal plain.[2] In the end, however, the renewed attack would be too late.

The Red Bull soldiers were distraught and weary during the week between the first attempt at Fondouk and the second. The survivors tried to rest and not to dwell on their wounds and lost comrades. Major Roland Anderson, regimental supply officer in the 135th Infantry Regiment, recalled that after the first attack on Fondouk:

> [P]atrols were the order of the day. At no time were the enemy front lines definitely established... [34ID] patrols and enemy patrols had frequent fire fights... [The] patrols brought information [about] the road net and... terrain features to the [division's] immediate front, which proved valuable in the [second] attack upon Fondouk... Approximately 150 personal [sic] replacements were received in the regiment... 2nd Battalion received this entire allotment because of the heavy casualties in the [first] battle [at Fondouk]... Enemy air was active and successful in knocking out several of [the regiment's] vehicles... Morale in all units of the Division was very low... [A] big build up was necessary prior to the second attack on Fondouk Gap. Hundreds of artillery pieces were massed, tanks assembled, and the Allied [air forces were] to give close support during this attack... Resupply and evacuation... were accomplished by one quarter ton vehicles [jeeps] and by carrying parties under cover of darkness... After darkness on the 7th of April the [135th] regiment moved to a new assembly area in the valley directly west of Fondouk Gap, approximately 1000 yards behind the line of departure... H-hour was to be at 0500 hours on 8 April 1943... [T]he Regiment would attack in column of Battalions, 3d Battalion in the lead, 2d Battalion following and 1st Battalion in reserve.[3]

On Saturday, April 4, the 34th Infantry Division received the orders that attached it to the British IX Corps for the second operation to seize Fondouk Gap.[4] The 34th Infantry Division, the British 6th Armoured Division,[5] the British 128th Infantry Brigade, and two squadrons of the 51st Royal Tank Regiment (temporarily released by British First Army) were now to be under Crocker's command.[6] The ultimate objective was defined as the interception and destruction of the retreating Axis forces.[7] French and other British units were to sweep the enemy from the hills north of Fondouk Pass, and 34ID was to win control of the southern hills.

The Germans, however, were adamantly determined not to be pushed off their ground until they were ready to go.

> Up to this time the troops of I Company [3rd Battalion, 133IR] had been given little opportunity to engage the enemy. Other units of the division had attacked Fondouk Gap the week before but were not successful... [T]he fighting spirit of the men of I Company to engage the enemy in an offensive operation was high... [T]he company was considered in the category "green troops" in comparison to the experience of the opposing forces.[8]

The fighting spirit of the men of I Company was likely bravado born of that amateurish greenness. Aside from brushing off the desultory enemy attacks at Sbiba while supported by large artillery concentrations and manning defensive positions at Sbeïtla, the men of Company I and the entire 133rd Infantry Regiment were unready for the shock and trauma of offensive combat. The second attack on Fondouk Gap would highlight the hard fact that the troops of 34ID had not been prepared for real fighting under defensive fire. Most of the men in the division had not had proper training in basic infantry tasks and tactics. There would be inadequate fire support from heavy weapons within the battalions both because of a lack of fire direction and control, and because of a complete failure to plan and organize the placement and protection of positions for the heavy weapons. Junior and field grade officers without experience were expected to solve tactical problems under fire. They generally lacked aggressive leadership and initiative, in large part because they did not see those virtues practiced by their superiors. A repeated example from the attacks at Fondouk was platoon leaders allowing the men to dig foxholes rather than encouraging them to go forward under fire using their weapons on the enemy. As Company I's executive officer, 1st Lieutenant Virgil Craven, later observed: "[B]ecause the company received... an initial setback... [this] need not... cause loss of the initiative. If proper training is conducted under competent leadership this situation would not exist."[9] The outcome of the second attack at Fondouk was, once again, the consequence of a total absence of realistic, practical training in basic infantry tactics and movement and the use of infantry weapons in teams, including the basic personal weapon, the M1 rifle. First Lieutenant Craven explained:

> During the limited... training the troops of I Company [3/133] had never fired the weapons they were armed with as much as they should have because of the scarcity of ammunition. All training prior to [Second Fondouk] consisted of road marches and defensive positions [as at Sbiba]. If an attack is going to be successfully carried out, then rehearsals with ball ammunition must be held in a realistic manner. The success of nearly every operation is the result of effective fire and movement.[10]

Similarly deficient, of course, was advanced training in combined arms combat, the intricate coordination of infantry, armor, and artillery. First Lieutenant Craven wrote after the war that the GIs just did not know how to follow an artillery barrage onto the objective.

> [T]he capabilities of artillery were overestimated... [I]t was considered very dangerous for friendly troops to be within several hundred yards of exploding artillery. It is imperative that infantry, regardless of possible casualties, follow close upon the shadow of an artillery barrage. Had this procedure been followed by our infantry at Fondouk Gap it is certain the pass would have been taken without delay and... unnecessary... casualties would have been avoided.[11]

And although tanks, both American and British, were employed at Fondouk, there was no synchronization or cohesion between armor and infantry.

> It has been said that... "ignorance is no excuse" for the failure to perform a job satisfactorily... [But] the men of I Company had never been taught the value of tank-infantry coordination. Even though the infantry failed to assist the tanks in [the second] attack [at Fondouk]... the employment of tanks [at Fondouk] can be criticized. Given the value of the vast amount of fire power, shock action and mutual support available [in an armor-infantry attack], it must also be... recognized by commanders that armor is vulnerable and cannot take an objective until the infantry has broken the initial crust of the enemy position. If armor is to be used it must [not be] frittered away.[12]

From April 1 to 5, the 133rd Infantry Regiment, less the orphaned 2nd Battalion, was in a defensive position at Sbeïtla, 30 miles from the main body of the 34th Infantry

Division.[i] On April 5, the regiment was released from its mission of protecting Sbeïtla and ordered to rejoin the division in a defensive position in the vicinity of Hadjeb el Aïoun and Djebel Trozza. That evening, trucks arrived and moved the regiment. The regiment's leaders understood that it was to make an attack with both available battalions, to seize Djebel el Haourareb as the first objective, and to continue the attack across to a feature behind Haourareb called "Hill A," which was less than 500 yards distant from the crest of Haouareb.[13]

Tuesday, April 6, 1943

On April 6, Lieutenant General Crocker held a command conference at Ryder's command post in an orchard near the village of Djebel Trozza, nine miles northwest of Fondouk. Crocker, accompanied by his principal subordinates and by Lieutenant General Koeltz, presented the British IX Corps plan and the orders for each of the participating major units. The design for the second attack against Fondouk was entirely Crocker's and he fumbled it badly. He had established the northern boundary of the 34th Infantry Division's zone along the southern edge of the Marguellil river, thus splitting the Fondouk Gap itself, as well as the approach from the west, into American and British areas of attack. This might have made for impressive classroom drawings, but it did not account for the enemy's carefully conceived, mutually supporting defenses or for the crucial need for the Allies to coordinate their actions seamlessly. Crocker's plan put Djebel Aïn el Rhorab, from which the entrenched enemy could pour enfilade fire across the river directly upon the American left flank, into the British sector. A British force on the 34ID's northern or left flank was tasked to take Pichon, and only when it had completed that task was it to turn south to reduce the enemy on Rhorab. 34ID was again to take the high ground south of the Fondouk Gap on its own, without coordinated support or reinforcement. Crocker's design did not provide any coordination between the British attack from Pichon and the 34ID attack toward the southern hills of the gap.[14] Moreover, Crocker was wrong about the enemy's strength and dispositions at Djebel Aïn el Rhorab. All evidence to the contrary notwithstanding, he was convinced that Rhorab was either unoccupied or that the enemy had few troops and weapons on the hill.

Major General Ryder very much disliked the IX Corps' plan for 34th Infantry Division's role in the second battle for Fondouk. He immediately recognized Crocker's plan as deeply flawed. At the April 6 conference, Ryder learned for the first time that the British 128th Infantry Brigade would attack initially the heights east of Pichon, and only later move southward toward Djebel Aïn el Rhorab. He argued that even under the best circumstances the 128th Brigade could attack Rhorab only after several hours of daylight had already passed on April 8. The 34th Infantry Division

---

i   The 133rd Infantry operated throughout the Tunisian Campaign without the 2nd Battalion.

would have already assaulted Djebel Haouareb and would have been fully engaged for hours before the British arrived at Rhorab. Djebel Aïn el Rhorab was only about 500 yards (less than 0.3 mile) north of where 34th Infantry Division's left flank assault troops would advance, well within the effective range of Axis machine guns, mortars, and light artillery on Rhorab.

Relying on earlier understandings, Ryder's own plan had prescribed the employment of all three of his regiments (including the two available battalions of the 133rd Infantry Regiment) and more armor and artillery than in the first attack, after first marching northward from their current positions southwest of the gap.[15] Ryder wanted the assault to be made directly eastward toward the heights south of the Fondouk Gap. He argued that the left flank of his assaulting regiments should be protected by a simultaneous attack by the British 128th Brigade to prevent the enemy from using Djebel Aïn el Rhorab as a convenient platform for concealed artillery, mortars, and machine guns delivering enfilading fire to the west and south. He pointed out that the ground over which the 34th Infantry Division must attack was so open as to make the frontal assault on Djebel Haouareb's steep and craggy slopes a formidable task. But enfilading fire from the left from Djebel Aïn el Rhorab might destroy the exposed assault troops.[16]

Crocker asserted baldly that Rhorab was only weakly held, a view he stubbornly continued to maintain after the battle and after the war despite the conclusive evidence that Rhorab was occupied and even received reinforcements during the battle. The British infantrymen, Crocker claimed, would deny Rhorab to the enemy but not actually occupy it until the American attack on Djebel Haouareb was well under way. American artillery was to blanket Rhorab with smoke shells, but, contrarily, not with high explosives lest they hit arriving British troops.

Ryder spoke out to Crocker and the other generals present. He argued urgently against an attack subject to enfilading fire from Rhorab. He well knew from his division's recent experience in frontal assault on that same objective that fire from Rhorab could and would stop the operation. His soldiers would have to go to ground to avoid the enemy's unopposed fire. He vehemently objected to the planned attack in range of Rhorab without first interdicting the enfilading fire. Lieutenant General Crocker summarily dismissed Ryder and his objections, curtly stating that Djebel Aïn el Rhorab would be lightly held and should not be a concern to the 34th Infantry Division. He ordered his subordinate Ryder to carry out the defective plan.

> Later recollections of the discussion are somewhat conflicting, but General Ryder's misgivings concerning the exposed northern flank of his attack, however clearly, he may have expressed them, produced no change in the corps orders. General Crocker and his chief of staff, Brig. Gordon MacMillan, then believed, as they did after the operation, that Djebel Aïn el Rhorab was much less strongly held than the heights east of Pichon and was not a serious menace to Ryder's attack. General Ryder's division could not add the seizure of Djebel Aïn el Rhorab to

its other responsibilities or even gain permission to reply to fire received from it, except to cover it with smoke shells during the critical opening phase.[17]

Ryder was understandably distressed and did not back off from his objections. Less than a week earlier, his division had been savaged by fire from Rhorab. Surely the Germans had since strengthened that already formidable position. He earnestly pointed out the vulnerability of his troops, who would face galling fire from both north and east, much like Longstreet's situation on the third day at Gettysburg.[18] Crocker, as Lee had done to Longstreet, waved away what he considered to be irksome distractions. Speed and maneuver would overwhelm the enemy's thin defenses.

Lieutenant General Koeltz, commander of the French XIX Corps, spoke in French. He knew the terrain very well. His corps had been driven out of the Fondouk Gap in January after holding the pass since the first push toward Tunis in November 1942. He had planned several times to retake it and had analyzed the ground situation thoroughly. He pointed out that the approaches over which the Americans must march were "entirely flat and completely exposed except for a row of cacti." His own reconnaissance proved that a frontal attack would fail. Koeltz suggested, "We could take out Djebel Rhorab from the north, because in this region the infantry could be supported by tanks." The rolling terrain and dense olive groves there would offer the Allied attackers more cover than the naked ground approaching Djebel Haouareb. Koeltz agreed with Ryder's assessment that the 34th Infantry Division was being committed under a faulty plan which threatened to result in failure. Major General Harold R. Bull,[ii] on his arrival at General Ryder's command post during the afternoon before the attack, reached the same conclusion. Crocker listened politely, then reaffirmed his own plan,[19] obstinately maintaining that it was too late to amend the plan of attack.[20]

Ryder was a good tactician and a good soldier. Eisenhower's orders were clear: subordinates were to salute and carry on, disregarding nationality. He issued orders for the attack in accordance with Crocker's directive.[21]

Elements of British IX Corps began assembling within sight of enemy outposts on Djebel Trozza on April 5–6. The 133rd and the 135th Infantry Regiments would make a second assault against Fondouk on the south or right flank. The objective was to take Djebel el Haouareb, the northern side of which overlooked the Fondouk Gap from the south. The Americans had to get on the crest of the high ground east of Highway 3, over steep and rocky slopes studded with German machine guns and minefields. The northern boundary for the 34th Infantry Division would be the southern bank of the Marguellil. The heights at Djebel Aïn el Rhorab and on the north side of the pass remained in the British sector.[22] Crocker's illusions notwithstanding, Rhorab was occupied by heavily armed and determined Germans.

---

ii   Bull was head of the Replacement School Command, Army Ground Forces, sent to North Africa by Marshall as a special observer.

Ryder was in a delicate and difficult leadership position. Time was short but he continued to think his way through the problem and his options. He knew better than anyone else the strengths and the weaknesses of his GIs. Once they had been pinned down by heavy enemy fire it would be impossible to get the survivors in motion again. He did not want to expend his soldiers uselessly. As Ryder considered the matter, he conceived the idea that his infantry might, despite their inexperience in night attack, make an approach march to the hills under cover of darkness.[23] An attack in darkness might at least mitigate the danger of enfilade fire from Rhorab.[24]

Wednesday, April 7, 1943

The second Fondouk operation, as British IX Corps planned it, was to occur in three phases. First, the British 128th Infantry Brigade would seize crossings over the Marguellil river west of the village of Pichon early on the night of April 7–8, enabling engineers to construct bridging for tanks and other vehicles before daylight. At dawn, the brigade would continue to the east to the heights beyond Pichon, then turn southward toward Fondouk el Aouareb Gap to neutralize and occupy Djebel Aïn el Rhorab. The second phase would consist of parallel but not coordinated attacks by the 128th Infantry Brigade and the 34th Infantry Division on opposite sides of the river to drive the enemy from the heights. There was no requirement that the British troops attack Djebel Aïn el Rhorab before or simultaneously with 34ID's attack. In the third phase, the British 6th Armoured Division was to pass through the gap.[25] Crocker deferred his decision whether the tanks of the 26th Armoured Brigade would be sent through the pass first or be preceded by the British infantry of the 18th Guards Brigade. He would wait to see how the battle went and what it revealed about the strength of the defense. That contingency proves that Crocker himself entertained at least some doubts about the strength of the enemy on Rhorab. Even if Crocker had to use the 18th Guards Brigade to clear Djebel Aïn el Rhorab, he would in any event have had to use British armor at the head of the column forcing a way through the gap.[26]

General Ryder, measuring the time, distance and topography factors affecting 34ID's part of the attack, concluded that he should get his assault battalions on the objective in the early darkness on April 8. Perhaps, with luck, the division could pass undetected past Djebel Aïn el Rhorab before dawn.[27] He requested, and Crocker granted, permission to advance 34ID's attack time from 5:30a.m. to 3:00a.m. But IX Corps in the meantime determined that a planned preparatory air bombardment of Djebel Haouareb should be cancelled. IX Corps notified 34th Infantry Division just before midnight, April 7–8, that there would be no Allied air attack. By then, the leading infantry units were already marching in a northeasterly loop to the line of departure at a large *wadi* running generally north and south some 5,000 yards (about 2.8 miles) from the base of the objective hills. At 2:20a.m., a liaison officer left division headquarters with orders for the assault regiments to cross the line of departure at 3:00.[28] That was perhaps the last moment in which 34ID's commander and his staff had control of events.

Ryder's plan for the attack called for two regiments abreast, each in column of battalions, the 135th Infantry Regiment on the north (left) and the 133rd Infantry Regiment on the south (right). Each regiment put its 3rd Battalion ahead on a 1,500-yard front. The 1st and 3rd Battalions, 168th Infantry Regiment, were screening the tank and artillery assembly areas and sent patrols south toward Djebel Touil, five miles south of the objective. The 2nd Battalion, 168th Infantry, was initially placed near the division command post subject to division orders. One company of the 751st Tank Battalion assembled behind the south end of the line of departure for commitment with the assault infantry on division order. The remainder of the tanks, with the 813th Tank Destroyer Battalion (less one company), took up positions yet farther to the south for commitment on the right or elsewhere as required. To the south and rear of the line of departure, six battalions of artillery were emplaced for massed fires. Farther to the rear, the 155mm guns of the 36th Field Artillery Regiment (less 1st Battalion) were placed to provide yet greater firepower. The deep northern flank was protected by a company of the 813th Tank Destroyer Battalion. The 2nd Battalion, 168RCT was soon ordered to move to join the tank destroyers on the northern flank.[29] Ryder reserved discretion, however, to attach 2/168 to the 133rd Infantry Regiment on the right wing of the assault. The 135th Infantry Regiment was directed to smoke appropriate targets on its left flank by mortars.[30]

On April 7, 3rd Battalion, 133rd Infantry Regiment, was in a defensive position at the base of Djebel Trozza. The officers of I Company had heard discouraging reports from personnel who were with the units of the 34th Infantry Division at the first unsuccessful attack on Fondouk Gap. The terrain did not afford any cover or concealment in most of the sector. The side of the mountain objective was rocky. The enemy was on the forward slope of Djebel el Haouareb in well-fortified positions. Just behind Haouareb was Hill A which provided protection for the enemy artillery, mortars, and tanks on the reverse slope of Djebel Haouareb. The enemy had registered mortars and artillery on every conceivable inch of the flat terrain, while the German infantry was well protected by overhead covers of steel girders and concrete. The enemy was well disposed to resist a frontal assault toward Djebel Haouareb over the flat terrain to the west. Machine gun positions were carefully sited to permit the maximum amount of overlapping grazing fire.

The commander of 3/133 understood the problems. He also understood his orders and planned to attack his assigned sector with two companies abreast. The battalion would attack with I Company on the left, K Company on the right, and L Company in reserve. The heavy weapons of M company would be employed to support the attack by fire from a central position.[31]

34ID GIs by the thousands had bought U.S. government life insurance on the eve of the first attack at Fondouk, reflecting a widely felt despondency. The Red Bull soldiers were keenly aware that they had failed in their first unsupported attack against the very objective they were now again to assault virtually alone. With the second attempt imminent, Alexander blithely told Eisenhower that troops in the 34th Infantry Division "seem reasonably confident about tomorrow's operation, and do hope it will go well." Alexander was being disingenuous and patronizing; to General Sir Alan Brooke, chief of the Imperial General Staff, he said that the Americans were "soft, green and quite untrained... Is it surprising then that they lack the will to fight?" As the 135th Infantry Regiment's commander later conceded, no officer in the division favored the attack or believed it could be successful, "but no one was saying so to the others." British planning was derided as "brittle and axiomatic... inflexible." Ryder had been wary of the British since the invasion of Algiers and now he was convinced that they wanted to win the war at the cost of American lives and matériel. At Fondouk, that meant expending the 34th Infantry Division and the lives of his soldiers so the British 6th Armoured could push through to Kaiouran unscathed.[32]

During the morning of April 7, the officers of Company I, 3/133, conducted a shakedown inspection of personnel and equipment. All weapons were examined. The troops were also scrutinized to ensure that they did not carry any information that could possibly aid the enemy if they were captured. To conceal the concentration of the division, the soldiers of I Company were instructed to remain under cover in daylight; only platoon sergeants and messengers were allowed to move around the area. About 11:00a.m., 12 replacements arrived. First Lieutenant Virgil Craven, the company executive officer, questioned the new men and discovered they had been in the Army less than a month. None had any knowledge of infantry tactics. Ten of the new dozen did not know how to load or fire the M1 rifle. Craven took the 12 men down in a *wadi* and showed each of them how to load and fire their weapons. The arrival of the 12 replacements brought the company up to 162 officers and men, but numbers do not always mean strength.

At 3:00p.m. all company commanders in 3/133 were called to battalion headquarters where they were given verbal fragmentary orders for the assault to be made on Fondouk Gap the next morning, April 8. There could be no reconnaissance by the company commanders over the area to be attacked because it was some 26 road miles away and any movement forward during daylight might reveal Allied plans and intentions. From the line of departure to the objective, which was about 4,500 yards, a little over 2½ miles, there was little or no cover. The enemy was well entrenched and exceedingly difficult to locate, although they would be looking "down our throats." Division's reconnaissance patrols had no useful information, except to emphasize that the high ground was well fortified and occupied by determined troops.[33]

While the company commanders were receiving the battalion attack order that they all recognized as fatally flawed, the soldiers of I Company were allowed to sleep. They would be up all night preparing for the operation and moving to the assembly area. In April in central Tunisia, the afternoons were hot, but the desert nights were cold, and the GIs wore their standard issue woolen overcoats for comfort. Despite logistical progress, inter-Allied supply problems persisted. The hot meal that was served at 6:00p.m. had to be supplemented by the British ration of "hard tack" and "ox-tail soup" of the thousand bone variety.[34]

> Ryder's men laced toilet paper in their helmet nets so they might see one another in the dark, while rehearsing the challenge—"Grocery?"—and countersign—"Store." They picked at a final meal... then nibbled the single slice of white bread served each man for dessert. At eight p.m. on Wednesday night, April 7th, 1943, the regiments of 34ID packed into trucks that carried them to the assembly areas west of Fondouk. A half-ton truck for carrying out the dead trailed the convoy, bold white letters on its side that read: "The Stuka Valley Hearse—Death Rides With Us."[35]

As planned, the 133rd and 135th Regimental Combat Teams moved from concealed positions northwest of Fondouk to the assembly areas west of the gap. 135RCT lined up on the right, or north, and 133RCT on the left, each with its 3rd Battalion in front of a column of battalions, then moved under cover of darkness during the night of April 7–8, 1943, to their lines of departure in a shallow *wadi* below Djebel Haouareb. Upon arriving at a predesignated phase line[iii] about 1,500 yards (more than 0.8 miles) from the base of Djebel Haouareb, the two leading battalions on the assault line were to pause for reorganization while Major Garnett Hall, commanding officer, 3rd Battalion, 135th Infantry Regiment, fired a green and white star cluster flare as a signal for the beginning of the artillery preparation.[36]

Thursday, April 8, 1943

At 2:30a.m. on Thursday, April 8, in the *wadi*, 34th Infantry Division's GIs took off their overcoats and shed all unnecessary gear and baggage, retaining only what they needed for combat operations. Each man was issued two extra M1 ammunition bandoliers, each carrying six *en bloc* clips with eight rounds per clip, and each weighing 3½ pounds.

Soldiers had to carry all their basic and essential equipment with them at all times. Individual load-carrying equipment was designed to allow the soldier to carry a basic load of weapons, ammunition, food, water, and first-aid gear. By World War II, the load had grown to include equipment such as knives and bayonets, entrenching tools, gas masks, maps, compasses, and radios. American soldiers in World War II used several different versions of the basic load-bearing gear. In the early phase of

---

iii   The regimental history of the 135th Infantry Regiment refers to an "81st coordinating line."

the war, the War Department issued a web equipment carrying system based on World War I designs.[37]

Colonel Fountain, commanding the 133rd Infantry Regiment, informed his officers: "I have been told that there will be tremendous aerial bombing support which will flatten everything—something we haven't seen to date." There would be nothing new to see that day either. There would be no bombing. Communications between 34ID and IX Corps were poor and despite Ryder's consultation with Crocker, there was confusion over the new attack time. IX Corps had cancelled the air strike, but that information never reached the line units.[38]

The assault elements of 3/135, Companies K and L on the right and left respectively, moved under cover of darkness from defensive positions near Hills 342 and 329. The advance elements arrived at the assembly area at 1:50a.m. and contacted 133RCT on the right. The rest of the 3/135 reported to the assembly area at 3:10a.m. Colonel Ward ordered the 3/135 not to proceed until further orders.[39] 1/135 was regimental reserve and was to cover the hill mass at Rhorab with fire.

For I Company, 3/133, the line of departure was about 1,000 yards in front of 133IR's assembly area, a little further south or to the right of the 135RCT in the same dry *wadi*. The company moved by foot from the assembly area to the line of departure in a column of platoons, with 1st Platoon in the lead followed by 2nd Platoon, company headquarters and light machine-gun section, 3rd Platoon and the 60mm mortar section. Upon arrival at the line of departure all extra equipment was placed in a company pile. The battalion aid station was set up in the *wadi* at the line of departure.

After crossing the line of departure, the platoons were to shift into a spread diamond formation with the 1st Platoon on the right, 2nd Platoon on the left, company headquarters and the light machine-gun section in the center and to the rear about 50 yards, followed by the 3rd Platoon and then the 60mm mortar section. The route to the objective was on an azimuth reading of 100 degrees for nearly 5,000 yards (about 2.8 miles). K company was on I Company's right; elements of 135IR were on the company's left. The platoons were maneuvered by voice, hand signals and the unreliable Signal Corps Radio [SCR] 536 ("walkie-talkie") from the company commander's position in the center of the two assault platoons. The company was supported by the heavy machine guns, 81mm mortars, and 57mm anti-tank weapons of M company, as well as the supporting field artillery battalions.[40]

Company I advanced from the line of departure at 3:30a.m. and assumed the spread, or wide, diamond attack formation as planned. The two assault platoons occupied a frontage of about 250 yards each. The light machine-gun section moved with the company headquarters and under First Lieutenant Craven's command until the initial deployment of the weapons. The 3rd Platoon was instructed to maintain a dispersion of 10 yards between each man. First Lieutenant Wayne D. Frazier, the

Weapons Platoon leader, was with the 60mm mortar section, about 50 yards behind the 3rd platoon.[41]

Just after 5:00a.m., two hours after Ryder's designated start time, two battalions of the 135th Infantry Regiment, on the left or north, attacked with the two battalions of the 133rd Infantry Regiment, on the right or south, each moving toward the high ground in its respective front just south of Fondouk Gap. Communications difficulties, loss of direction on the approach march, and lack of coordination delayed the strike by 135IR. As the two assault regiments pressed forward from the line of departure on a two-mile front, Major Hall's battalion, 3/135, lost its way in the darkness, veering north into the river bottom, and creating a gap between it and the 3rd Battalion, 133rd Infantry Regiment. To close the gap, the 1st Battalion, 135th Infantry Regiment, led by Lieutenant Colonel Robert P. Miller, rushed across the flats toward the assault line as dawn came and hostile fire from the left and the front intensified. That derangement delayed the start of the attack until 5:30a.m., the original H-hour.[42] The Red Bull soldiers could not reach the objective before daylight.

Progress, such as it was, was minimal from the beginning. In the growing light, the troops of the assault battalions were quickly pinned down by machine-gun and mortar fire from enemy positions so well camouflaged and so perfectly sited that it was virtually impossible to neutralize them even with barrages of artillery fire. Forward artillery observers were forced to take cover and keep their heads down, which hampered efforts to locate the enemy's positions. At about 6:30a.m. the leading elements signaled they had reached the coordinating line about 1,500 yards west of the base of the objective. Dawn had broken by the time Hall fired the star shell to initiate the prepared artillery attack at about 6:35a.m. The American gunners saw the green and white signal and began intensively shelling the objective. After the bombardment lifted to the higher ground, 34ID's assault troops advanced until about 7:30a.m. The troops halted about 2,000 yards from the objective, following orders intended to protect the troops from the air bombing attack on the objective that the field commanders still expected.[43]

Major General Ryder then learned that the artillery had been signaled when the troops had not reached the coordinating phase line and were still west of the 2,000-yard bomb line. He directed at 7:45a.m. that the infantry be stopped, the artillery alerted to mark the target by smoke shells, and the air bombing mission reinstated for the half hour between 8:00 to 8:30a.m. At about 8:00a.m., as plunging fire from Rhorab on the left and Haouareb straight ahead lashed the field, Ryder's orders arrived to pull back to the 2,000-yard buffer line for the bombing raid. Some of the infantry were able to move back. 34ID Headquarters attempted to get a bombing mission on the objective at 9:00a.m., but because of IX Corps's earlier cancellation of the raid, it never happened. Probably because the infantry advance had stopped, enemy fire from Djebel Haouareb diminished somewhat in the center and on the right, but the enfilading fire from the north continued unabated. Another artillery barrage, starting as planned at 9:30a.m., again covered the hill with smoke and high explosive. At the same time the enemy fired on the attacking infantry with mortars and machine guns. Some 34ID artillery rounds fell short, causing several casualties in Company E, 2/135 and in Company K, 3/135. But the attack pressed on.[44]

Company I, and its sister companies in 133rd Infantry Regiment, suffered similar experiences. After advancing about 200 yards from the line of departure, a messenger from battalion headquarters reported to I Company's commander with orders for the company to pause the advance until the unit on the left, from 135IR, caught up. The signal for the company to halt in position was given. At 6:00a.m. the 3rd Battalion commander ordered both assault companies to continue. As the sun rose over Djebel el Haouareb, I Company could clearly see the terrain and the objective. The GIs could not see the enemy, but the enemy could clearly see them. The terrain below the base of the objective was flat; the only available cover and concealment in the area were beds of poppies and blades of grass some four inches high growing in the hard soil.[45]

When at 6:30a.m. the flare signal had been fired, the leading platoon of I Company was more than two miles from the objective. The company continued to move forward slowly but as yet had not been fired upon. At 7:45a.m., orders came over the SCR 536 [walkie-talkie] radio to halt, as Allied bombers were supposedly on the way to work over the enemy positions. The troops waited in position until 8:30a.m. The bombers never arrived, and the advance resumed. At 9:00a.m., I Company came under long-range mortar and artillery fire from the direction of the objective, Djebel Haouareb. By 10:00a.m. the enemy fire was falling in heavy concentrations. The two assault platoons were forced to take up a dispersed formation extending over 500 yards in width as they advanced by leaps and bounds until they were within 1,000 yards of the base of the mountain. The rest of the company followed until the enemy's fire became so intense that the entire company was pinned down on the flat open prairie some 700 yards from the objective.[46]

At this point the company commander ordered the light machine-gun sections to come forward to support the attack. The machine guns were placed between the two assault platoons and opened fire simultaneously. They swept the forward slopes of the mountain, firing into likely enemy positions. After firing for several minutes, however, the enemy identified the locations of the American machine guns. Enemy mortar and artillery fire began to hit around the machine-gun sections and the crews were forced to cease firing.

At 11:00a.m. the commander of I Company informed his battalion commander of the situation, giving the location of the forward platoon. The commander promised to request artillery support. While the company stood by, the enemy swept the field with fire from weapons of every kind and caliber. Even when artillery shells began falling again on the side of the mountain, I Company was still not able to advance. Soldiers in the two forward platoons used their entrenching tools, bayonets, and even the lids from their mess kits to scrape out shallow slit trenches for cover from the bullets and shrapnel.[47]

At 12:00 noon, I Company reported to the battalion commander by radio that it was impossible to proceed further without some kind of supporting fire or reinforcement. Thirty minutes later, the battalion commander informed I Company that friendly tanks were on the way and should arrive at 1:00p.m. At the appointed time ten tanks of the 751st Tank Battalion, then attached to 34ID, rolled up between I Company's position and that of 135IR on the left, drawing the enemy's hostile attention. But I Company now found itself on the receiving end of enemy fire from all weapons directed at the tanks. The executive officer counted some 30 rounds of enemy artillery that fell within a radius of 25 yards of his prone position, but fortunately for him only two exploded. The others were duds. In less than 15 minutes four Sherman tanks were in flames within about 200 yards from I Company's front. When the surviving tanks withdrew, I Company's troops were again caught in the midst of artillery and anti-tank fire chasing the tanks away.

At 2:00p.m., 3rd Battalion ordered I Company to make a renewed coordinated attack with the entire battalion, to begin in one hour, to move onto and seize Djebel Haouareb. At 3:00p.m., the 1st Platoon, commanded by Second Lieutenant "Paddy" Padfield, crawled forward in bounds, and had gained about 100 yards when Second Lieutenant Padfield was struck down and killed by enemy machine-gun fire.[48] But only the brave Padfield and his 1st Platoon had executed that attack order. The soldiers of 3rd Battalion did little more than peek out of their slit trenches like turtles, only to go back and dig deeper. When the 2nd Platoon of I Company was ordered to move up and join the survivors of 1st Platoon, a few heroic GIs crawled forward only to expose themselves immediately to vicious machine-pistol and machine-gun fire. Two courageous GIs were wounded while crawling forward. By this time positions had been dug for the machine-gun sections of the weapons platoon. I Company was able to direct fire on the side of the mountain again, but after only a few bursts from each gun, enemy artillery fire poured down in such concentrations that the company commander directed further firing to cease.[49]

The 3rd Battalion commander advised I Company by radio that a tank attack with supporting artillery was to be made at 5:00p.m. He ordered all officers to get up out of their foxholes and go forward with the tanks, leading their men in an assault on Haouareb. At 5:00p.m. as promised, 15 tanks of the 751st Tank Battalion arrived backed by an artillery barrage on the hill. Even with reinforcements, the men of I Company would not be moved to join the tanks in the assault. Without infantry support, the tanks again reached a line about 200 yards in front of I Company. By this time, the American artillery fire had lifted and was firing on the reverse slope of the mountain, allowing the enemy on the forward slopes to return to their gun positions. Six more tanks were soon burning.[50]

"We were like a pea on a plate"

The 34th Infantry Division's attack on Djebel Haouareb had started forward in spurts under increasing enemy fire which raised an opaque cloud of dust. Like the 133rd Infantry Regiment, the soldiers of 135th Infantry Regiment crawled forward without any coordinated artillery or armor support. They were in the beaten zone of the machine guns almost before they realized it. "A wave of flying dust and steel and lead was always before us," one soldier recalled. In the morning light, 6,000 American infantrymen could be seen crawling and stooping over ground that provided no cover. "We were like a pea on a plate," a sergeant reported. Every attempt to answer the enemy fire brought a quick counterpunch from well-registered enemy mortars and artillery. The men then reacted exactly as Ryder had anticipated they would. They dug shallow trenches, found dry *wadis* in which to take cover, or lay behind sand hummocks for shelter for any conceivable shelter from the flying metal. Troops of 135IR on the northern flank simply would not move forward into a deadly curtain of fire such as they had never previously encountered or trained for.[51]

The entrenched Germans had the Americans' range; artillery blasted the flats, machine-gun rounds zipped overhead, and anti-tank shells ricocheted off the rocky soil. "We continued to move forward toward the enemy, standing erect like the British regulars charging up Bunker Hill," a young officer wrote. Those who tried to remain upright were quickly dissuaded. By noon, all forward movement had stopped, 700 yards from Djebel Haouareb. Terrified soldiers scraped at the shallow dirt with bayonets and mess-kit lids, then lay motionless so as not to attract attention. "The mere raising of an eyebrow attracted enemy fire," one sergeant in the 135th Infantry Regiment reported.[52]

A renewed assault of the objective was ordered at 3:45p.m. while the artillery kept up a harassing fire of enemy positions. The assault again failed under artillery fire from Rhorab into the left rear of the 135th Infantry Regiment.[53] At 5:45p.m. more tanks from the 751st Tank Battalion were again committed to support yet another assault. Companies K and L, 3/135, led the assault with the tanks in front, but they could not hold their gains under the continuing enfilade fire from Rhorab, just as Ryder had foreseen.[54] Red Bull soldiers encountered such heavy automatic weapons, mortar and small-arms fire from well-concealed positions protected by wire and minefields that they were not able to make any further progress. Enemy observation and firepower made maneuver impossible, and the troops attempted in vain to dig in on the stony terrain.[55]

At 7:00p.m., the 2nd and 3rd Battalions of 135RCT were ordered to launch a night assault to take the objective and obtain positions from which to clear the reverse side the next day. The attack did not succeed, but during the night of April 8–9, 135RCT troops did manage to infiltrate the German lines on the northern part of Haouareb.[56]

While the Americans were suffering under the infernal fire from Rhorab and Haouareb, the British 128th Infantry Brigade, supported by Churchill tanks of the 51st Royal Tank Regiment, had attacked through Pichon to the heights east of the village but quickly fell behind Crocker's uncompromising schedule. Finally turning south at 3:00p.m., the brigade was brought to a halt by German fire about a mile and a half from Djebel Aïn el Rhorab. The enemy that Crocker had insisted were not present in strength on Rhorab buried the British under heavy mortar fire northeastward, all the while keeping up vicious fire into the American flank to the south. The 34th Infantry Division was not the only unit under IX Corps's command that could be charged with less than satisfactory combat outcomes.

About 4:00p.m., when 34ID's assault battalions, supported now by tanks, were attempting their second doomed assault toward Djebel Haouareb, the British 26th Armoured Brigade passed unannounced and unexpected through 34th Infantry Division's attack area, much to the Americans' surprise and confusion.[57] The 135th Infantry Regiment's soldiers, after withdrawal, were now interspersed among vehicles of the British armored force, which remained deployed in attack formation. Under enemy observation and subject to even more fire attracted by the British vehicles, 135RCT had to reorganize before it could resume the attack. At all points, the first day of 34ID's second attempt at Fondouk el Aouareb Gap had been unsuccessful. As the Americans were learning through this trial by fire, however, modern firepower causes a battle to unfold and progress with an unhurried, bone-grinding pace on both sides. Their enemy, fighting a determined delaying action, had also been hurt, requiring the commitment of scarce reserves. The enemy would not be able to recover its losses.[58]

The surviving Red Bull soldiers felt better than circumstances warranted about their performance on the first day of the second battle of Fondouk el Aouareb, probably and justifiably because they were to a man elated to be alive. They acknowledged that they had not taken the objective, but they believed as they had after the first attempt to take Fondouk. The determination and disposition of the enemy resistance had made their task well-nigh impossible. Tipping their collective hat to the British troops, the Americans had the erroneous impression that the British attack on the left toward Rhorab had gone better than their own fight in the southern hills. The actual British experience had been punishing and bloody. When Major General Keightley, commanding British 6th Armoured Division, returned to his command post about 6:30p.m. on April 8 from a reconnaissance toward the pass, he found more orders from Lieutenant General Crocker. His division was to discover or make a path through the enemy's minefield during the night, and push the 6AD tanks through early next morning, April 9. Keightley was to protect his own flank from enemy guns and mortars on Djebel Aïn el Rhorab by sending one battalion of infantry to occupy it before daylight.[59]

Crocker continued to believe in a chimera, again contending that Djebel Aïn el Rhorab was lightly held or possibly even abandoned and must not be "re-occupied." As the Americans knew quite well, Rhorab was robustly defended by a small force of two stout companies which were about to be reinforced. On April 8, the enemy was compelled to commit reserves to prevent the Allies from breaking through to the Kairouan plain. *Oberstleutnant* Fritz Fullriede, commanding the *Kampfgruppe* defending the gap, had been instructed to fight a delaying action with grim determination until nightfall on April 10. On April 9, he reinforced the two companies of the 27th Africa Battalion defending Djebel Aïn el Rhorab and the hills to its north by sending into the line the 26th Africa Battalion. As his situation further deteriorated, he committed one company of the 334th Reconnaissance Battalion to regain lost ground on Rhorab. An anti-tank company, armed with seven self-propelled anti-tank guns and a captured and converted American armored car, took up positions near the village of Fondouk el Aouareb to the south of the Marguellil river and Highway 3, the Kairouan road. To reinforce the anti-tank defenses of the pass north of the river, Fullriede borrowed six self-propelled 47mm anti-tank guns from the Italian 135th Armored Battalion and two 88mm dual-purpose Flak guns. In the thickly mined pass were at least 13 heavy anti-tank guns on the southern side of the river and two more on the north. That was the gauntlet that the British armor would have to run to get to the eastern end of the pass.[60]

Meanwhile, the enemy was taking advantage of the delay in taking the pass caused by Fullriede's obdurate defense. During the night of April 8–9, the Italian First Army's formations passed unmolested across the Kairouan plain. But the Axis needed yet more time. The German units under General Fritz Bayerlein were more slowly moving up the coast, east of Kairouan, under light pressure from the British Eighth Army.[61] The 34th Infantry Division was for the moment in the eye of the storm.

> The arrival of darkness was a blessing… [T]he troops [had] an opportunity to get out of the prone positions, where most of them had been, and get onto their feet without the fear of receiving enemy fire. All men of I Company now had been exposed to their initial fire… [T]here were some 8 to 10 known stretcher cases… [I]t had been impossible to render aid during the day because of the intensity of enemy machine gun fire. After the wounded had been located the question arose as to how and by whom the evacuation would be made. Finally a litter was brought from the battalion aid station and the support platoon evacuated the wounded.[62]

Battalion headquarters, 3/133, requested all companies to report on ammunition requirements and the status of personnel, and informed them that rations would arrive about 8:00p.m. Nothing was said about any further attacks or about night patrols to the objective. Without waiting for instructions, the company commander of I Company formed a five-man patrol from each of his platoons and ordered them to determine the enemy's dispositions and to search for ground that offered more protection. The first patrol, from the 2nd Platoon, started at 9:00p.m. and was followed by scouts from the 1st Platoon and the 3rd Platoon. These *ad hoc* patrols of tired, frightened men proved to be quite uninformative.[63]

At 8:00p.m. crates of the combat type "C" rations were brought forward by the kitchen personnel to Company I's position, but the mess sergeant in his haste to get the food to the men had not opened them. The noise of breaking the boxes attracted the attention of the enemy. Another ferocious barrage of artillery and mortar fire fell on Company I, turning a pleasant anticipation of a meal into shocking fear and pain. Before the vulnerable men could dive into their foxholes three had been wounded by flying shrapnel. The incident emphasized to First Lieutenant Craven another battle lesson that had not been taught. "[T]he troops lacked knowledge or training of the importance of quietness when in contact with the enemy." After the enemy artillery and mortar barrage had ceased, I Company's commander ordered all platoon leaders to reorganize their units. The noble Second Lieutenant Padfield had died during the day. The 1st Platoon survivors were badly shaken, and 1st Platoon was reassigned to support duties. The 3rd Platoon took up the assault position.

After taking roll, I Company's officers discovered that each platoon was missing ten or more men; more than 50 men were unaccounted for overall. The mess sergeant reported that several men were in the kitchen area some eight miles from the company's position. Craven was instructed to return to the kitchen area and return with the stragglers. He found five men at the kitchen area and while returning with them, he found 45 more men in the *wadi* that had been the line of departure. They had made their way off the battlefield, unnoticed by their platoon leaders. When questioned about their status, the answer was "we were lost and couldn't locate the front." Craven turned the 50 idlers over to the company commander about 11:30p.m.; after a tongue lashing, they were returned to their platoons. By this time, the first patrol had returned, but the patrol leader was unable to give any useful specifics about the enemy's location and disposition. But all the company officers knew with certainty that the enemy had sent patrols to within 100 yards of the company's position that very evening. Second Lieutenant Padfield had worn a treasured gold nugget ring that had been removed before his body was carried away at 11:00p.m.[64]

Friday, April 9, 1943

At 12:00 midnight on April 9, all the company commanders of 3rd Battalion, 133rd Infantry Regiment, were summoned to battalion headquarters in the rear to receive orders for the following day. When I Company's commander returned, he was forced to tell his subordinates that all leaders from General Ryder on down were thoroughly disappointed by the division's failure to take Haouareb. Orders for the next day included breakfast at 4:00a.m. and a coordinated attack after the artillery had again pummeled the enemy positions. As the troops came for their rations, they were informed of the mission. At 4:30a.m., Craven checked the two assault platoons and found all in readiness.[65]

The men of 34ID spent a hard, painful night, April 8–9, with little rest, followed by another excruciating day under murderous fire. During the night, the troops of I Company, 3/133 had prepared and emplaced all attached and supporting weapons in protected positions. The company officers of I Company expressed a belief that a new attack might be successful this time. "The sun rose over the formidable Haouareb this day the same as the day before. However, this time the hill looked bigger than ever and even more quiet and peaceful." There was of course no peace at hand. At 6:00a.m. the American artillery began to detonate across the forward slopes of Haouareb. This was the signal for all units to start moving forward. But "not a soul could be seen moving" although the enemy was not firing. Every single soldier remained in his foxhole.[66]

At 8:00a.m. orders came from the battalion commander at battalion headquarters, still in rear of the assault companies. Haouareb was to be taken without delay, the commanders of I Company and K Company were to coordinate the time of attack, and they were then to report by radio to the battalion headquarters. After conferring, the company commanders set the time for their assault at 9:00a.m. Just before 9:00a.m., enemy dive bombers bombed the area on the left and to the front of I Company's position. The bombing was a last straw for the company commanders. Amidst the smoking bomb craters and their bleeding soldiers, they postponed the attack. At 9:30a.m. the battalion commander again contacted his company commanders by the SCR 536 [walkie-talkie] radio and demanded a progress report. I Company's commander dissembled. He stated that his unit was going forward slowly but meeting stiff resistance, when in reality no soldier could be moved to look up from his foxhole.[67]

34ID was still not able to coordinate combined arms operations. At 9:00a.m., April 9, before Crocker's orders to the British armored units had been executed, 31 U.S. tanks from the 751st Tank Battalion, under Ryder's orders, advanced toward Djebel Haouareb. The tanks passed through the infantry positions to arrive at the base of the hill without benefit of either artillery preparation or coordination with the infantry. Even with the surprising appearance of the tanks on the slopes in their front, the infantry remained pinned down under now intensified ground fire and enemy dive-bombing. In the early morning of April 9, 1/135 had passed through the positions of 3/135 to an assembly area; at 10:15a.m., 1/135 made another assault on Djebel Haouareb with the tanks in nominal support. But the American tanks had outrun both the artillery cover and the infantry support. They reached the objective under heavy fire, but the infantry, under constant heavy fire of all arms, was unable and unwilling to risk advancing to take it. The armor was forced to withdraw after 15 minutes. Five tanks were lost without gain.[68]

Across the 34th Infantry Division's entire front, troops went to ground and simply would not move except to skulk rearward on various pretexts. "There was no cover or concealment," a company commander in the 135th Infantry Regiment reported. "Mortar and artillery fire were so heavy that the dust formed by the shell fragments looked like a smoke screen." There were, however, stirring acts of valor. Private Robert D. Booker, a machine gunner of the 133rd Infantry, was awarded posthumously the Congressional Medal of Honor for his self-sacrifice, fidelity to duty, and leadership on April 9, 1943. He was the first Red Bull recipient of the Medal of Honor, the only one in the North African campaign.[69]

"We are going to get on top of that mountain and brew tea on the backs of those dead Germans," shouted a private; his platoon leader replied, "Private, you are now a sergeant. Let's go!" They went but the battle was not over.[70] A second attempt by the GIs about 11:30a.m. on a narrower portion of the front reached the lower slopes of Hill 306 but was then smothered by fire, mainly from the pestiferous north flank, which persisted until mid-afternoon. At about 3:45p.m. hours the positions of 1/135 were dive-bombed, and the battalion suffered many casualties and another blow to morale.[71] The remaining U.S. tanks were then sent to the rear, out of range. The British 6th Armoured Division would have to bash through the gap on its own.[72]

Company I, 3/133, received a radio message that friendly tanks would arrive on its positions and directing that the troops were to move forward to assault the objective with the tanks. At 11:30a.m. the tanks arrived. As there had been scarce enemy fire during the morning, it was not difficult to get the platoons to move forward. American artillery pounded the forward slope of Haouareb with a barrage that appeared to cover every foot of the mountain. The GIs allowed themselves to believe that the artillery would have a devastating casualty effect upon the enemy. Perhaps even the few enemies who did not become casualties would be so stunned that they would mount only a feeble and half-hearted resistance.

It was not to be. Ryder's misgivings were realized. I Company was gaining ground when a hailstorm of artillery, mortar and anti-tank fire accompanied by wicked machine-gun fire fell from the left flank, the direction of the now reinforced Rhorab. I Company was again pinned to the open ground less than 800 yards from the base of the objective. Enemy anti-tank fire forced the U.S. tanks to withdraw into a row of cactus for concealment. From 2:00p.m. until 3:30p.m. it seemed to the GIs that the enemy was all around, pelting them with every mortar, artillery tube, and machine gun available. Casualties mounted with the passing of each minute. The 3rd Battalion's commander, who had yet to come forward from his command post to lead his troops in the battle, advised Colonel Fountain, commander of the 133rd Infantry Regiment, that it was impossible to advance against the murderous enemy machine-gun fire and asked that he be placed under arrest, rather than have his men under the enemy fire any longer. His request was granted.

3rd Battalion's acting commander, upon his assignment, ordered the company commanders to submit strength reports stating the actual number of men available for the next attack, scheduled for 5:00p.m. I Company reported a total effective strength of 80 men out of 162 who had gone into the fight. The acting battalion commander ordered the reserve company forward to make the attack in lieu of I Company, but a few minutes later, on the left flank in the direction of Rhorab, the GIs heard the noise of a terrific firefight erupting. "The British had caught up at last and only two days late," moving with what seemed to the GIs such lightning speed that the enemy's position on Rhorab crumbled.

The enemy in 133IR's front, however, was not done yet. A relief of Company I was attempted at 4:30p.m. but failed due the intensity of enemy fire from on and behind Haouareb. About 5:00p.m., American tanks again moved into I Company's position and went forward to the base of the hill, receiving only spasmodic machine-gun fire. But before the infantry could advance, I Company received orders to hold its position and prepare for a night attack.[73]

Major General Keightley had sent the 3rd Battalion, Welsh Guards to patrol as far as Djebel Aïn el Rhorab during the night (April 8–9) with orders to attack and clear Rhorab as early as possible in the morning of April 9. When Crocker learned that the British troops had not yet opened a path through the minefields, he ordered the 26th Armoured Brigade to advance into the pass, ordered the entire 1st Guards Brigade, if necessary, to occupy Djebel Aïn el Rhorab, and directed the 128th Infantry Brigade to assist them.[74] Crocker was still dementedly convinced that Djebel Rhorab had been neutralized or abandoned. It most certainly had not. By mid-afternoon, enemy skirmishers and mortars immobilized the British infantrymen more than a mile from the crest. Throughout the day on April 9 the 3rd Battalion, Welsh Guards fought a ferocious battle on the rocks of Rhorab. All the officers in two British companies were killed or wounded.[75]

Finally, at 3:30p.m., April 9, 34 hours after the Allied attack began, the valorous 3rd Battalion, Welsh Guards, supported by tanks of the 2nd Lothians, captured Djebel Aïn el Rhorab. "The Welsh Guards' losses alone totaled 114, a high price for a hill Crocker had considered inconsequential."[76] The remaining defenders of the hills north of the gap were mopped up with the help of the 3rd Battalion, Grenadier Guards. They took over 100 German prisoners from the 26th and 27th Africa Battalions, but at least that many escaped. The 135th Infantry Regiment was still receiving enemy fire from the left rear as late as 2:30p.m., to which they were ordered not to reply so as not to harm their British brothers in arms.[77] By the evening of April 9 the British had secured the northern opening of the gap. The Allies had the mouth of the pass but still had not yet broken through.

While the 3rd Battalion, Welsh Guards and the 34th Infantry Division were engaging the enemy on the hills north and south of the gap, the British 26th Armoured Brigade spent the morning and afternoon of April 9 attempting to get around or through a deep but irregular belt of mines across the pass.[78] Exasperated with the delay, Alexander himself ordered Crocker to open the valley and break through with a massed armored spearhead. IX Corps ordered the tankers to force the pass at once. "The gap must be forced… like a covey of partridges flying over the guns." Early in the evening the British 26th Armoured Brigade directed a company of tanks to move through the minefield. "Goodbye," one squadron commander told a comrade. "I shall never see you again. We shall all be killed." He died that day, just as he foresaw. The 17th/21st Lancers[iv] pressed forward a few hundred yards. Then the point tank radioed: "There's a hell of a minefield in front. It looks about three hundred yards deep. Shall I go on?" The reply came immediately: "Go on. Go on at all costs."[79]

> Mines ripped the front ranks and fifteen German antitank guns took most of the rest. Crews spilling from their flaming turrets were machine-gunned before they touched the ground… Two surviving British Shermans clattered to the rear with dazed Tommies clinging to the hulls…[80]

The audacious, some would say foolhardy, assault nevertheless achieved a breakthrough. The few surviving tanks of the 17th/21st Lancers with some Royal Engineers pushed through the minefield and made a path through the pass. Following behind the destroyed 17th/21st, the 16th/5th Lancers found a narrow, navigable route that curved into the Marguellil *wadi*. The British armor traversed the muddy river bottom to emerge on the far side of the minefield more than a mile beyond the village late on Friday afternoon. After the 16th/5th Lancers had cleared the pass, the main body of British armor quickly followed. Allied fire had put some enemy anti-tank guns out of action, but Axis mines and guns had destroyed 34 British tanks.[81] Red Bull soldiers coming up from behind looked on in amazement to see the surviving British soldiers making tea in the shelter of their tanks, with shrapnel glancing off the hulls. Now outflanked, the enemy survivors withdrew. Only the dead remained at their posts, surrounded by piles of spent brass. "Their faces were as smooth and white as marble statues," an American lieutenant recalled.[82]

The 2nd Battalion, Coldstream Guards, 1st Guards Brigade, 6th Armoured Division was ordered to clear the enemy from the heights nearest the gap in the U.S. 34th Infantry Division's zone, which was accordingly narrowed to transfer the north-facing slopes of Djebel Haouareb to the 6th Armoured Division. The Allies now threatened to encircle the Germans from the north and west. Seven Axis battalions had fought at Fondouk against 11 Allied infantry battalions backed by the artillery of two Allied divisions and four tank battalions. Fullriede, having accomplished his mission to delay the Allied advance through April 10, now ordered his *Kampfgruppe*

---

iv The same unit whose brave and obedient horse cavalry ancestors in 1854 made the infamously stupid and bloody charge at the Russian guns at Balaklava, in the name of fidelity to duty.

to withdraw to Kairouan. The enemy in the hills facing General Ryder's troops prepared to join the main northward retreat during the night.[83]

Dismayed by IX Corps's losses in both men and tanks and angered by the failure of the American infantry to secure the southern hills on his schedule, Crocker now lost his earlier aggressive attitude and took counsel of his fears. Intelligence indicated that the wounded but still formidable 10th and 21st Panzer Divisions were somewhere ahead. British IX Corps with 34th Infantry Division had taken the gap, but Crocker considered the Allies' losses, the approaching darkness, and the possibility of a counterattack in the morning by *Panzerarmee Afrika*. He decided not to push out onto the plain until the next morning, April 10. The armored elements already through Fondouk Gap were called back into the pass to laager for the night of April 9–10.[84] The opportunity to strike the retiring enemy columns on the coastal plain had passed. Crocker and his staff understood that the enemy had intended its savage delaying action to hold the area between the gap and Kairouan through April 10. "The disappointment and sense of frustration engendered by the delay were profound."[85]

At 7:00p.m., I Company, 3/133, received orders to cover the withdrawal of the 3rd Battalion back to the *wadi* from which the attack had begun. When full dark fell, the company commander left First Lieutenant Craven in charge. GIs were placed in groups of two or three and spread across the battalion's sector to prevent enemy patrols from infiltrating. A litter was brought from the aid station and with the assistance of service company personnel, I Company methodically evacuated its casualties. By midnight on April 10, the 80 survivors of I Company, ragged and exhausted from two days of intense enemy fire, were back in the dry *wadi* from which they had set out two days before, "clustered around in small groups in the *wadi* eating their cold 'C' ration of meat and beans but thankful that they were away from the fire of the enemy."[86]

Saturday, April 10, 1943

In the darkness of early April 10, after infiltrating assault troops onto the objective earlier in the night, "a great effort" was made by the rest of 133rd Infantry Regiment to finally take Hill 306, the highest point on Djebel Haouareb. The 1st Battalion, 133rd Infantry attacked to gain the summit of Hill 306 and adjacent ground. 1/133 reached the crest and drove off the last of the defenders. By 1:15a.m., 1/133 had captured the hill. 135RCT, with the 1st and 2nd Battalions leading, also launched a final attack over the northern part of Haouareb. 1/135 advanced down the reverse slope into Fondouk Gap while the 2nd Battalion advanced on three hills behind the mountain. Colonel Miller's troops then moved through the gap to its eastern mouth. The 34th Infantry Division completed the occupation of the former enemy positions south of the Fondouk Gap. By noon, April 10, elements of the 34th Infantry Division including the 168th Infantry, which had relieved the 133rd Infantry Regiment, held at last the heights on either side of the Marguellil river. The British armored units were by that time hunting the enemy on the road to Kairouan.[87] A motorized infantry force from 34ID had been prepared to occupy Kairouan, but that mission was assigned to British troops.[88]

The Allied breakthrough had come too late at too great a cost. *Kampfgruppe Fullriede's* delaying action at the Fondouk Gap was a German military success. Fullriede's instructions had been to hold at the Fondouk Gap until April 10 to permit the passage to the north of the main body of *Deutsche Afrika Korps* (*DAK*), and then to withdraw. The retreating Italians in Messe's army had marched past Kairouan on the night of April 8–9.[89] Without interference from Montgomery or Crocker, the remnants of the 10th and 21st Panzer Divisions, of *Kampfgruppe Lang*, of 131st "Centauro" Armored Division, and the other units under the command of *Deutsche Afrika Korps* were on the line Faïd-Sfax during the night of April 8–9 and passed through Kairouan on the night of April 9–10.[90]

By 10:00a.m. on April 10 the British 6th Armoured Division completed the transit of Fondouk el Aouareb Gap and started for Kairouan, 18 miles away. With 110 Sherman tanks, it moved on a broad front astride the Fondouk el Aouareb–Kairouan road. Before the British reached the plain west of Kairouan, they had to overcome anti-tank guns east of the Fondouk Gap. At the cost of four Shermans, the British 16th/5th Lancers chased away the covering force at those guns late in the day.[91] In several small, armored engagements during the day, 6AD netted about 650 prisoners, destroyed 14 enemy tanks, and captured 15 guns. But the bulk of the enemy escaped to the north, staying just beyond artillery range as they had planned to do. At 11:10a.m., April 10, 18 Army Group issued a new instruction to British IX Corps. After cleaning up the area near Kairouan, which IX Corps occupied during the evening of that day after the enemy had withdrawn,[92] it was to turn toward Sbikha to cut off enemy forces stranded in the northern portion of the Eastern Dorsal.[93] IX Corps executed those orders on April 11. Meanwhile on April 10, Combat Command A, U.S. 1st Armored Division, pushed through Aïn Rebaou pass south of Faïd under General Patton's personal supervision and moved along the eastern side of the mountain chain. By late evening, its 81st Reconnaissance Battalion had joined elements of the 168th Infantry Regiment east of Fondouk el Aouareb village.[94]

From April 8–10, in the Fondouk el Aouareb Gap, the British 6th Armoured Division had 67 casualties: 19 killed, 48 wounded. It lost 34 tanks. The 2nd Battalion, Welsh Guards suffered over 100 casualties at Djebel Aïn el Rhorab. American losses in those three days totaled 439, including more than 100 killed in action. In the 34th Infantry Division, the 135th Infantry reported 73 men killed and 184 wounded. The 3rd Battalion, 133rd Infantry suffered 82 men killed, wounded, and missing. The 1st Battalion, 133rd Infantry, reported 15 men had died and 82 were wounded. The 168th Infantry Regiment was committed late and had at least three casualties.[95]

Among the wounded was Major Moore, commander of 2/168, who had been blown out of his foxhole by a German bomb that had killed his radio operator. Temporarily blind and deaf, Moore was evacuated to the rear where a soldier who had known him in Villisca, Iowa described him a week later as "still very dazed and shaky... a sad and worried man." He spoke of his wife Dorothy and his daughter Nancy, wondering if he would see them again. The dead Red Bull soldiers were wrapped in white mattress covers and their bodies placed in trucks to be interred in another new cemetery. "It is only by the grace of God that I am here to write this today," a soldier in the 135th Infantry told his parents in Minnesota.[96]

The mission to intercept and destroy part of the Axis forces in Africa had failed. Messe's troops closed on the Tunis bridgehead at Enfidaville, 40 miles south of Tunis, and took their places in the most formidable position occupied by the Axis since the loss of El Alamein five months earlier. The Tunisian campaign became a siege with the Axis holding in an iron grip the high and fortified ground. Alexander's strategy had been uninformed, shortsighted, clouded by bias, and slow. Crocker's tactics had been a complete disaster. The battleworthiness of the 34th Infantry Division was now even more suspect. Crocker's flawed plan resulted in a flawed execution by the green American soldiers, thrown without preparation into a veritable Hell on Earth. Although the Allies had captured 6,000 Germans and 22,000 Italians in a month, Eighth Army had moved too slowly.[97]

CHAPTER 29

34ID and the Aftermath of Second Fondouk

"Whale tracks at the bottom of the sea"

British appraisals of the 34th Infantry Division's performance in the second attack at Fondouk el Aouareb Gap were cast in uniformly pejorative language. The Americans retaliated with their own recriminations. The result was inter-Allied animosity and desperately strained relations between the Allied commanders and among the soldiers of the Allied nations. Crocker held the Americans responsible for the failure of his precious brainchild. He blamed the failure of the operation on the inability of the British armor to get through the pass expeditiously, and that failure, in turn, entirely upon the inability of the 34th Infantry Division to carry out its mission to occupy the southern hill mass. He recommended to Alexander that the 34th Infantry Division be withdrawn from the line for retraining by British officers, particularly of the American junior officers.[1]

In an unwise and bitter tirade to a group of officers visiting from Algiers on Sunday morning, April 11, General Crocker declared that "all commanders from Major General Ryder downwards in the 34th Division were too far in the rear of the troops they commanded" and that leadership "by junior officers was very weak indeed." Crocker publicly accused the 34th Infantry Division of being alone responsible for the outcome at Fondouk. Crocker or someone close to him fed his denigrating remarks to war correspondents, and unflattering stories soon appeared in newspapers across in the United States. The German retreat was described as though "Rommel" had again succeeded in outwitting the bumbling Americans. *Time* magazine reported in its April 19, 1943, issue that the second fight at Fondouk was "downright embarrassing for the American troops. All day the British worked their way efficiently along the ridges; all day the U.S. troops tentatively approached but never stormed the first of their heights." Ryder gallantly declined to rise to the bait, saying only, "The British were damn good." But disagreeable emotions flashed through the Allied ranks like wildfire. Eisenhower, depressed and angry, took the criticism personally. The undeniable defects in American combat skills, while hardly as irredeemable as the British suggested, left him feeling as low as "whale tracks at the bottom of the sea," Patton reported.[2]

Some American officers who were personally aware of the issues involved at Fondouk later made their opinions known. They condemned Crocker's plan of attack as being unnecessarily and carelessly profligate with American troops and matériel. Other American officers, some of whom were or became committed and open Anglophobes, sought to absolve the 34th Infantry Division from responsibility by emphasizing that the IX Corps plan had required Ryder to attack from the start with an exposed flank, to which he had objected and tried to avoid. There was merit in these defenses, but the fact remained that the Allies needed one another to win the war.

Eisenhower and Alexander intervened quickly and forcefully to suppress the mounting tide of accusations and to repair the fraying Allied bonds. Eisenhower made it clear to Alexander that American forces were to have a significant role in the closing fight in Tunisia. He cabled to Alexander: "I desire that you make a real effort to use the II U.S. Corps right up to the bitter end of the campaign, even if maintenance reasons compel it to be stripped down eventually to a total of two divisions and supporting Corps troops..."[3] He directed 18 Army Group to give II Corps a mission which would keep it committed aggressively. If any Allied sector were to be narrowed or pinched out by the northward progress of Eighth Army and the eastward drive by First Army, that sector was not to be that of the U.S. II Corps.

Eisenhower now became the leader he truly was. He made it clear that his orders served the best interests of a unified Allied military effort required to prevail over a terrible enemy. His commands were not to be gainsaid. The Americans in North Africa were to be fully employed in combat until the enemy capitulated. The American divisions being organized and trained in the United States represented the only great body of Allied reserves, and the best American officers and men from North Africa would be sent to the United States to train them. Confidence breeds confidence, and the resulting combat readiness and success in battle would improve American battle performance and morale.[4]

At the small unit level, it was of no benefit to the soldiers of the 34th Infantry Division to excuse or minimize the faulty aspects of the division's operations thus far. General Ryder knew this. Ryder and his staff acted energetically to improve the fighting skills of his Red Bull soldiers as well as the operations of the division and regimental staffs. The division moved to a training area near Maktar on April 15 and began at once a program of intensive training in all kinds of attacks: on open plains, by night, with tanks, in mountainous terrain, and behind a rolling artillery barrage. Ryder personally led the way right behind the exploding shells. After what was for too many of the troops their first training in true-to-life combat scenarios complete with the shocking noise of screaming men, roaring machines, and explosions, every participant was familiar if not expert with all infantry weapons and basic tactics.

Ryder asserted himself as commander and with some changes in command, the 34th Infantry Division was made battle ready.[5] The division's history recalls: "Without exaggeration it may be said that the [34th] Division was transformed during the next few days. After [its] grueling... and discouraging introduction to heavy combat all units passed through a most rigorous week of training with special emphasis on night attacks and... cooperation between infantry and artillery in the assault behind a rolling barrage."[6]

First Lieutenant Brandt, CO, D Company, 1/135, wrote after the war that his battalion had taken a beating at Fondouk Pass. He described the grueling ten-day training program at Maktar, conveying the combat-like urgency, maddening noise, continuous demands on wit and stamina. The training program emphasized familiarization with all weapons, coordination of units, night and day attacks, cooperation with supporting weapons including artillery and tanks, and the movement of assault troops closely behind the initial artillery fires on the attack. All the troops were taught how to fire their weapons under combat conditions. "All realized their mistakes and measures were taken to prevent... repetition... During this time the Division was [transformed] into a fighting machine."[7]

The officers and men of the 34th Infantry Division were in fact as hard on themselves as their British critics were. The 135RCT's history records that Major Garnet Hall, commanding officer of 3/135, which had been on the extreme left in the second attack on Fondouk el Aouareb, held the opinion that the battalion could have achieved its objective had the left flank not been open. Nonetheless, Hall related deficiencies in the Americans' battle performance from which lessons had to be learned.

> Most of the infantry attacks were not coordinated. Most attacks were too individual with little or no contact with units on the flanks. The tank attacks were not followed by the infantry; in many instances the infantry did not know which tanks to follow nor which way they would come, whether from rear or either flank. The artillery was not used to its fullest extent, communication was defective from forward observation to the batteries. Many times the artillery barrage would come down on our own troops, injuring many of them and took a lot of aggressive spirit from the men. Communications at best were poor, too many units on a wire, 536 radios [walkie-talkies] were not dependable, messengers were too slow and uncertain. O.P.s [observation posts] in this sector were very poor, the nature of the terrain being such that at their best the O.Ps had very little and limited view, as a result hardly any information was received from them. Supply of food and water was fair; not enough [ammunition] was expended to test that phase of supply. Morale at the beginning of the attack was very high, but due to misinformation, changes in plans, receiving fire from our own artillery and the nature of ground over which we operated, the men lost heart and confidence. The Medical Detachment, in [Hall's] estimation, was the only department worthy of any commendation. They did... exceptional... work under the worst conditions. Their personnel should be an inspiration and example to the rest of us.[8]

The intrepid First Lieutenant Craven, executive officer of I Company, 3/133, may not have been privy to the tactical debates of the general officers, but he grasped perfectly the implications and consequences of 34ID's performance at Fondouk.

Even though I Company failed to capture Fondouk Gap, along with all the other units [of 34ID], they did succeed in finding out some of their shortcoming[s] which were to be corrected in later training. Even if viewed from the Corps level this operation was not successful in [that] the enemy delayed the allied forces... long enough to allow the main forces of Rommel's Afrika Korps to complete their withdrawal to the north. There is no doubt as to the importance placed upon Fondouk Gap by the enemy since his positions were constructed out of solid rock and reinforced with steel girders and concrete... The attack at Fondouk Gap may be classified as [a] plan poorly executed.[9]

Influenced by Crocker, Alexander had indeed considered removing the 34th Infantry Division from the line for extensive retraining. Crocker's assignment of blame for the slow attack at Fondouk el Aouareb by the 34th Infantry Division only inflamed and deepened Alexander's existing bias against both the U.S. 34th Infantry Division and 1st Armored Division. He was reluctant to commit the U.S. 1st Armored Division, "owing to its present low state of morale and training." He wanted 1st Infantry Division withdrawn to prepare for Operation *Husky*, the invasion of Sicily. He did not want the Allied line of supply in the north burdened by the requirements of a four-division American corps. He insisted on a reduced role for the Americans in the final battles in North Africa.[10]

The Americans were having none of it. Lieutenant General Patton made known his comprehensive objections to 18 Army Group's intentions for his II Corps units. On April 12, discussing with Alexander the role of II Corps, Patton argued that II Corps, which had operated since March 8 directly under 18 Army Group, must not be subordinated once more to British First Army. The Americans had 467,000 troops in northwest Africa, more than 60 per cent of the Anglo-American army. Most of the Americans were earmarked for the invasion of Sicily or were part of the titanic American logistical operations. What Alexander had in mind for II Corps amounted to achieving victory in Tunisia without those almost half-million troops, with an almost entirely British force.

Later that day Patton documented his position. He wrote to Alexander that the 34th Infantry Division must be kept with II Corps to "restore its soul." He warned that because it was a National Guard unit "its activities assume local interest of great political significance" in their home states, implying that congressmen from Iowa and Minnesota would react very poorly to any humiliation of their thousands of military constituents by British officers. At Patton's direction, Bradley hand carried the letter to Alexander's headquarters in Haïdra. "Give me the [34th] division," Bradley told the field marshal, "and I'll promise you they'll take and hold their very first objective." Intrigued, Alexander, perhaps impressed with Bradley's passion, brushed off his staff's objections and told Bradley, "Take them, they're yours."[11]

On April 14, Lieutenant General Eisenhower flew to Haïdra to confer with Generals Alexander, Anderson, Patton, and Bradley on the plans for Sicily and for the final Tunisian offensive, and most especially the arrangements for II Corps' role in that offensive. In the interests of Allied comity, Alexander had been compelled to reconsider the subject of fully using American troops under American command in the end game of the Tunisian campaign. At the insistence of the Americans, he yielded to Eisenhower and Patton. On April 16, 18 Army Group issued the final plan.[12] All four American divisions in II Corps were to be included in the attack. American logisticians had demonstrated that they could supply U.S. troops without disrupting the British supply lines provisioning First Army. Patton repeated his objection to again subsuming II Corps into Anderson's command after it had been reporting directly to Alexander. Alexander acquiesced, authorizing Patton as the II Corps' commander to appeal any disagreeable order from Anderson directly to Alexander.[13]

"There was only tomorrow"

Colonel Ward, commander of 135RCT, issued on April 13, 1943, orders for renewed training entitled Training Program No. 1, opening with a note of grim ferocity that Patton at his most fervent had not exceeded.

> The Boche rat in the closing trap will now be more vicious than ever. The longer he holds Tunisia the longer he delays an invasion of the continent and thereby accomplishes his mission. You have seen and felt him use every means from booby trapped bodies to cannon-carrying airplanes to kill you. Your only chance is not to avoid him, but to close with him, and personally kill him first. Battles are won by closing with the enemy and killing him. The quicker you can reach his position the better your chance of not suffering heavy casualties.[14]

Rick Atkinson frames the Allied situation in a broader perspective.

> There was irony in all this carping, albeit visible only from the high ground of history. On average nearly a thousand Axis prisoners were tramping into Anglo-American cages every day. The Allies were inflicting crippling casualties on the already understrength Axis combat units. Allied forces were about to secure their fifth great battlefield conquest in a year, with a triumph that would join Midway, El Alamein, Guadalcanal, and Stalingrad as a milepost on the road to victory. More than 200,000 Axis troops were now penned like sheep in a Tunisian fold measuring roughly fifty by eighty miles, just large enough to bury two enemy armies. An entire continent would soon be reclaimed, and an entire sea, the Mediterranean, converted into an Anglo-American lake. If American troops still seemed callow at times, one need only consider how far they had come since the bumblings of TORCH and imagine how far they would go once the greatest industrial power on earth had fully flung itself into total war.[15]

The official history concludes that "the Americans in Tunisia and elsewhere would have been gratified if the II Corps had broken through the eastern mountain chain to deliver disastrous blows on the main body of the enemy. It was hard for them to accept the view that the II Corps was not yet equal to such a mission against the more experienced foe." [16] The Red Bull survivors of Fondouk cast sidelong looks at the rows of dead and forced themselves to move on.

Yesterday had never happened. There was only tomorrow, and the killing required tomorrow to reach the next day. Sergeant Samuel Allen, Jr., a former college student who had led his own swing band in peacetime, tried to explain in a letter home the hard nihilism that made young men at war seem so old when they contemplated the dead. "We have found that it is best to forget about those friends, not to talk about them," he wrote. "They don't even exist."[17]

CHAPTER 30

II Corps and 34ID Move to the North

On April 13, 1943, the middle period of the Allied campaign in Tunisia ended. During the second week of April, the Axis forces were corralled in northeastern Tunisia behind an arc extending from a point on the north coast east of Cap Serrat to Enfidaville and the Gulf of Hammamet on the southeast.[1] The Axis retreat had constricted the enemy, had exacerbated already dire supply problems, had eliminated any freedom of maneuver, and had cost important airfields. Alexander, at Eisenhower's insistence and despite the strong disapproval of other British officers and the recommendations of his own staff, assigned II Corps a critically important role in the final phase of the campaign. II Corps was to break the enemy's defensive line in the north and capture the port city of Bizerte. The Americans were to move north *en masse* to position themselves for their new zone of attack as part of a general Allied realignment in preparation for the annihilation of the remaining Axis forces.[2]

The front now defended by the trapped Axis forces extended over mountains and valleys, plains, and marshlands, 30 or more miles from the ports of Bizerte and Tunis. Five major regions comprised the enemy's bridgehead. The Allies made joint plans and conducted operations to destroy the Axis armies in each region: (1) that north of the Medjerda river; (2) that between the Medjerda and the Miliane river with its tributary, the Kebir river; (3) that from the Miliane and Kebir rivers to the foothills on the western edge of the coastal plain; (4) the coastal plain and the flats at the base of the Cap Bon peninsula; and (5) the Cap Bon peninsula.

The northernmost region, the area of II Corps's operations, was an almost rectangular area trending northeast-southwest, with Bizerte in the northeastern corner and Medjez el Bab at the southwest. Its western half was covered by hills and low, unforested mountains except close to the coast between Cap Serrat on the west and Bizerte on the east. The hills lacked any geologic pattern. They consisted of a series of widely varying complexes in which a higher crest and neighboring hills formed interlocking groups, favorable to defense. Foremost among these complexes was the one including Djebel Tahent (Hill 609) near Sidi Nsir, from whose summit it was possible to see Mateur. Fingers of high ground projected from the mountain area northeastward across the coastal plain, enclosing a section adjacent to Bizerte and separating it from a second, narrow area north of the Medjerda between Tebourba and the ocean. Two great shallow lakes, the Garaet Ichkeul and the Lac de Bizerte, southwest and south of Bizerte, restricted all overland approach to Bizerte to narrow belts between the shores and the hills. The Tine river ran northeast and north from sources south of Hill 609 to the plain near Mateur.[3]

On the northern flank, the U.S. II Corps was to advance eastward from Béja to Chouïgui, and at the same time, nearer the northern coast, to expel the enemy from Bald and Green Hills, known as the Djefna position. The Americans were to gain control of high ground dominating a road junction northwest of Garaet Ichkeul.[4]

The Allies maintained constant pressure on the enemy's forward line as they prepared their main offensive.[5] At the northern end, the British 46th Division forced *Division von Manteuffel* to give ground so that when the U.S. 9th Infantry Division took over the British positions at 6:00p.m., April 14, most of the area gained by Axis attacks since February 26 had already been recovered by the British. Just before the Allied attacks began on April 19, the northern portion of the Axis front ran from a cape on the coast north of Djebel Dardyss (294m) through the Djefna position to the vicinity of Sidi Nsir. The 334th Division (*Korpsgruppe Weber*) withstood the attacks of the British 4th Division toward Sidi Nsir and the hills south of it, but despite a tough defense northwest and north of Medjez el Bab, the British shoved the enemy from the crest of Djebel Bech Chekaoui (667m) and the neighboring heights. From these high ridges Allied observers could keep "Longstop Hill" (290m) under surveillance and see over it to the Medjerda river plain beyond.[6]

For Alexander's endgame, the Allies' realignment of their forces exploited their advantage in mechanized transportation. Despite the challenges of distance and terrain, the United States Army brought mobility to an unprecedented level of military effectiveness in the closing weeks of the Tunisian campaign. Eisenhower saw to it that his field units had an abundance of motorized transport and the fuel to operate it. The Allied regrouping along the new line in Tunisia involved the transfer of armored units from the British Eighth Army on the coastal plain near Kairouan to the zone of British IX Corps east of Le Kef, and also the movement of the entire II Corps and all its equipment and supporting units from central Tunisia to the new zone northeast of Béja.[7]

The Americans made their mechanized anabasis in trucks and jeeps on four trunk roads beginning Sunday, April 11. They motored north for 150 miles riding 30,000 vehicles. They left the desert and moved into the northern hills closer to the sea where some had fought in November and December. Every GI now studied the militarized topography with the expertise of a surgeon considering the anatomy of a patient. A streambed was not a streambed but defilade, pastures and wheat fields were exposed fields of fire. Laurel thickets, olive groves and cactus patches became ambush sites, and every grove of cork or olive trees, haystack or outbuilding might hide a German 88 or a machine-gun nest. A ford over a *wadi* was an artillery trap. The faces of ridges and all approaches to hills were killing zones sown with anti-personnel mines backed up by pre-sited mortars and artillery. Folds in the land could hide massed troops and tanks. No soldier could look at the terrain without feeling that it had become sinister and deeply personal.[8] The survivors of the 34th Infantry Division could now be called veterans, manifesting what Abraham Lincoln called "the tired spot" that nothing could touch or remedy.[9] Ernie Pyle, who was with the Red Bull soldiers again, wrote: "They were dead weary, as a person could tell even when looking at them from behind. Every little line and sag of their bodies spoke of their inhuman exhaustion. They were young men, but the grime and whiskers and exhaustion made them look middle-aged."[10]

The Allied plan was straightforward and brutal. More than 300,000 Allied troops in some 20 divisions, with 1,400 tanks and as many artillery tubes, would attack in three main groups along the 140-mile arc from Enfidaville south of Tunis to the Mediterranean coast west of Bizerte. On the far-left flank of the Allied line, the Americans would drive on Bizerte from the west with four U.S. divisions and three French battalions known collectively as the Corps Franc d'Afrique.[11] They were to break the Axis line of resistance, fragment and immobilize the enemy armies, and then kill or capture the broken foe.

The movement by U.S. 9th ("Old Reliables") Infantry Division (Major General Manton Eddy, commanding) to the northern end of the line had been scheduled for nearly a month. 9ID moved north as soon as the fighting near El Guettar had ceased. They marched through eastern Algeria along the main road between Tébessa and Souk Ahras, and then northeastward through the cork forest near Tabarka and the village of Djebel Abiod to the hills near Sedjenane. The 47th Infantry Regiment began relieving elements of the British 46th Division on the night of April 12–13.

The decision that the entire U.S. II Corps would attack in a simultaneous strike from the northern part of the Allied front was reached later. The planning and preparations to move the rest of II Corps had to be implemented more hurriedly. To regulate the movement of II Corps across the continually active east-west supply routes of British First Army, and to shift British armored troops from the east coast through the II Corps area to that of British IX Corps, required careful coordination and timely communication between the staffs of II Corps and of First Army. Most of the mileage covered by II Corps units lay within British First Army's existing zone of communications. A new II Corps bivouac and supply area was not established until after the bulk of the American troops had arrived in the north and all troop movements during the transfers of Allied forces were made under First Army's control. The actual arrangements were preceded by a road reconnaissance in which representatives of the G-3, provost marshal, and Engineer sections of II Corps worked collegially with officers of the Movement Controls Branch, British First Army. Together, they selected routes along which control points could be set up and agreed on a plan to control the traffic to that would ensure an average rate of 100 vehicles per hour northbound.[12]

The II Corps traffic crossed the two major west-east highway and railroad routes and made use of ten miles of one of these roads to reach the road junction at Le Kef.[13] Columns of II Corps vehicles assembled near the route's southern terminus in numbers calculated to completely fill each allotted time slot. II Corps had to transfer not only the 1st Infantry, 1st Armored, and 34th Infantry Divisions, but also its own headquarters and approximately 40 Ordnance, Armor, Artillery, Medical, Quartermaster, Engineer, Chemical Warfare Service, and Signal units of varying size. II Corps divisions were subdivided into combat teams, which along with the corps troops, were prioritized to allow for 2,400 vehicles per day. Between April 14 and 18, II Corps assembled its units in the Tébessa area at those periods which best suited the total volume of Allied transportation flowing within First Army's area. They were then moved from the assembly points to the southern terminus of the main route.[14]

To avoid clashing with the British 6th Armoured Division in the joint use of the road net between Pichon and Maktar, the 34th Infantry Division was brought northward in two large groups. They proceeded via Le Sers and east of Le Kef to Souk el Arba and the cork forest, the first group on the night of April 21–22 and the second during the night of April 23–24.[15] On April 23, 135RCT left its training area near Maktar and moved by truck. On the 24th, at 7:00a.m., it arrived at the new II Corps assembly area about nine miles northeast of Béja.[16] II Corps moved rapidly in great secrecy across the Allied lines of communication from southern Tunisia to the north where it became the extreme left flank of the Allied front. Initially, the 34th Infantry Division was placed in II Corps reserve.[17]

The II Corps Battle Plan

On April 15, 1943, command of II Corps passed quietly from Patton to his deputy commander of the past six weeks, Major General Omar Bradley. Bradley's active participation in the planning and operations of II Corps greatly facilitated and eased his assumption of command. On April 16, his headquarters moved from Gafsa to a site two miles northwest of Béja, where Bradley's staff had organized the II Corps command post on April 15 in tents on a farm belonging to the mayor of Béja, M. Jean Hugon. British V Corps retained control over all road movements and the relief of British units by the Americans until 6:00p.m., April 19, when Headquarters, II Corps, officially assumed command of its new sector under Bradley. Its forward line ran from the ocean east of Cap Serrat to Hill 667, five miles west of Heïdous.[18] On April 18, the corps commanders of First Army briefed their respective plans at a conference at Thibar. Bradley went over the plans in detail with his staff and division commanders the next day.[19]

On the morning of April 22, Bradley arrived by jeep on the crest of a hill outside Béja to address an audience of field officers and the press. Bradley was six feet tall, with a high forehead and thin hair that had been graying since his West Point days. He was 50. He wore a well-used olive drab field jacket and canvas leggings and carried his favorite Springfield Model 1903 .30 caliber bolt-action rifle. He was a descendant of Missouri farmers and one schoolteacher, his father. He had an infantryman's ingrained feel for terrain, with a detailed mental picture of every significant feature of the ground from Béja to Bizerte.

With a map pinned on an easel and a pointer in hand, Bradley elucidated the impending campaign to the assembled group of officers and civilians. "He laid down his schedule with no more panache than a teacher outlining the curriculum for the new semester," recalled the journalist A. J. Liebling. Mateur was the key to Bizerte, Bradley explained. The 9th Division would take the far-left flank along the sea—skirting Green and Bald Hills, where the British had found so much trouble. The other two U.S. infantry divisions—the 1st and 34th—would attack further south, through Sidi Nsir and the hill country below it. The 1st Armored Division would exploit any breakthrough on the coastal plain leading to Bizerte.[20]

Bradley did not tell his audience or even his division commanders that his first act as corps commander had been to disregard instructions from Eisenhower. The commander in chief had written that "the southern portion of your sector appears to be reasonably suited for tank employment and it is in that area that you will be expected to make your main effort." Bradley, however, had a better sense than either Eisenhower or Alexander of the ground beneath and in front of him and a better idea for winning control of that ground. AFHQ's proposed route, through the narrow Tine river valley, seemed such an obvious German ambush site that II Corps staff dubbed it "The Mousetrap." Bradley was a canny tactician, and he was certain that an attack on the exposed valley floor invited disaster. He turned a deaf ear to Eisenhower and ordered his commanders to avoid the low ground.

He called the coming fights in the hills "hunting wild goats." By attacking into the high ground—"djebel hopping"— American troops could avoid the vulnerable bottlenecks that had cost so many lives in the past five months. II Corps would take the battle directly to the enemy defenders on the rugged hills where they were entrenched. The hunt for those goats would take time, patience, and ingenuity. Axis engineers had spent months fortifying the enemy's hill complexes. In the II Corps sector, the enemy now mustered an estimated 12,000 infantry troops, and that number would more than triple in the next two weeks.[21]

Bradley's plan of attack "conformed only generally" to the directives of AFHQ and 18 Army Group. 18 Army Group gave II Corps the mission to secure the northern or right flank of British V Corps while V Corps made the principal Allied attack along the Medjerda river. Bradley, however, decided II Corps should fight with all its resources to gain control of the high ground between the Sidi Nsir–Mateur road and the Tine river valley, and of the hills rising on the southern side of that valley as far as the watershed between it and the Medjerda. He saw clearly that success in the hill country would break the Axis defensive front in northern Tunisia and would open the way to Mateur and the fragmentation of the Axis forces. The southwestern approaches to Mateur and the hills adjacent to Chouïgui pass (from the Tine valley to the coastal plain near Tebourba) were Bradley's ultimate objectives in the southern part of the II Corps zone. He chose the 1st Infantry Division and the 34th Infantry Division as his instruments to break the enemy in its hill forts above the Tine valley. The 9th Infantry Division would simultaneously threaten Mateur from the west, close the roads west of the Garaet Ichkeul, and then take Bizerte.[22]

Bradley's plan for II Corps's assaults toward Mateur and Chouïgui drew upon the lessons so painfully learned during recent weeks in central Tunisia. The upper Tine river valley favored by AFHQ and 18 Army Group was indeed a tempting route. The ground near the riverbanks, despite the lack of good roads, allowed easier transit for vehicles than the hillsides. The valley floor consisted of several broad alluvial plains connected by narrowing gaps between closely adjacent hills. The natural defensive advantages of the topography, however, allowed the enemy to contest the valley route from numerous mutually supporting hill forts, turning the flats into shooting galleries. The Germans during recent months had prepared minefields, machine-gun bunkers, anti-tank and artillery positions, and observation posts to direct the fire of those guns, all designed to drive an attacking force in the valleys into killing zones and there subject it to ruinous losses. With pneumatic drills and dynamite the enemy had excavated superbly situated defensive positions, and built dugouts and bunkers reinforced with concrete. They had placed countless mines and had emplaced six artillery battalions. Defiles between hills and approaches from the valley up the slopes and in the draws were targets for prepared artillery and mortar concentrations and were covered with antipersonnel mines. Routes likely to be used by American patrols, and good points of observation which the enemy would have to abandon upon withdrawal, were also heavily mined.[23]

Bradley wisely ruled out a doctrinal fight with the enemy on terrain where the Germans would have the advantages of observation and the ability to employ all arms. He planned an infantry battle, supported by every artillery piece he could muster and, when the opportunity arose, by tanks in close support. The precipitous terrain made the use of armor difficult and was a serious obstacle to rapid movement by other arms, but the battle in the hills would be on more even terms. II Corps would first occupy the hills west of the Tine river's headwaters. Then the Americans would hop from djebel to djebel on either side of the valley. They would avoid the Mousetrap until II Corps had won control of high ground from which the valley of the Tine could be dominated, and the myriad of malignant mines had been cleared from routes along the riverbank. Bradley kept 1st Armored Division concentrated for a later thrust out of the Mousetrap and into the more open countryside near

Mateur. Unlike Crocker, Bradley was not about to squander his precious mobile strength trying to bash a path through the enemy's anti-tank defenses. The 9th Infantry Division (reinforced) was also to be sent over the northern hills closer to the coast rather than along the lower ground in its zone. 9ID was first to flank and cut off the Djefna position, and then march on, its ultimate objective Bizerte.[24]

Bradley wanted the U.S. Army's superior artillery to be used on the enemy with maximum lethal effect. II Corps, including the weapons of the infantry regiments' cannon companies, had 24 heavy (M1 8-inch guns and M1 240mm howitzers), 72 medium (M1 155mm), and 228 light (M2 105mm and M1 75mm) artillery pieces. Huge supplies of artillery ammunition were now on hand. The 9th Infantry Division had four battalions of 105mm howitzers (of which one was armored), two battalions of 155mm howitzers, and one battery of 155mm guns. Bradley reinforced the Tine valley sector with II Corps's artillery of six battalions of 105mm (of which five were armored self-propelled guns), three battalions of 155mm howitzers, and two battalions of 155mm field guns (less one battery). 1ID had its normal complement of three battalions of 105mm howitzers and one battalion of 155mm guns.[25] The 34th Infantry Division was similarly equipped, including four battalions of British 25-pounder quick-firing howitzers and a battalion of 155mm guns. The hill fortresses hiding the enemy "goats" would be pounded by a hail of exploding American shells.

An Axis spoiling attack in the sector of Goubellat began in the British First Army's zone while the IX Corps and V Corps were organizing for their April 22 attacks. The Axis strike itself disturbed Alexander less than Montgomery's complete cessation of pressure against the Axis forces in the southeast, a development that the US Army official history characterizes as "a serious departure from the army group's general plan."[26] The relatively fresh Hermann Göring Division, less some elements, struck shortly before midnight on the night of April 20–21 against the heights southeast and south of Medjez el Bab, with the southernmost flank along the edge of the Goubellat plain. Its mission was to lighten Allied pressure on adjacent sectors and disrupt Allied offensive preparations.[27] The assault, favored by surprise, caused some shock and disorientation among British troops, as enemy troops penetrated the Allied lines along a 12-mile sector to a depth of about five miles. But at daybreak, as the enemy ran up against the main British position, the drive stalled. First Army's tanks and artillery moved in with a vengeance, forcing the attackers back to their original lines after nightfall. The enemy claimed to have taken over 300 prisoners and to have destroyed five batteries of artillery, about 80 trucks and motor vehicles, and seven tanks. But the Germans themselves paid a price of over 300 casualties, and the attack did not delay the Allied offensive.[28]

British First Army had a tough time making progress in its own attack. British IX Corps began its planned assault on April 22 when Crocker sent the 46th Division (Major General Harold A. Freeman-Attwood) to gain possession of the high ground west of the Sebkret el Kourzia marshes after an extraordinarily heavy artillery preparation. The Germans were ready and offered determined resistance, managing to hold its ground south of the marshy Sebkret el Kourzia. But north of the marsh, the British broke the enemy defense line. Crocker deployed his 6th Armoured Division (Major General Keightley) late on April 23 to exploit toward the Pont du Fahs–Tunis road. The armor rolled into the opening and broke through, forcing the remaining elements of the Grenadier Regiment back onto the hills to the east. The 6th Armoured Division rounded the northern edge of the salt lake and one element drove ahead toward Pont du Fahs.

Von Arnim ordered the *Deutsche Afrika Korps* to extend its front to cover the crumbling south wing of the Hermann Göring Division. He sent Fifth Panzer Army's last remaining mobile reserve, the 10th Panzer Division, also much reduced in strength, into the breach, initiating a prolonged seesaw battle with Keightley's tanks. During the following days, the armored clash was fought to a standstill in the area east and northeast of the Sebkret el Kourzia in the vicinity of a dominating hill known to the Germans as "Kamelberg" (Camelback Mountain).[29]

The British First Army's attacks were generally unsuccessful, despite the unshakeable intrepidity of the British soldiers and the dire logistical straits of their Axis opponents. On Friday, April 30, Anderson told Eisenhower that First Army in the past week had suffered 3,500 casualties, including about 900 killed. For the period from April 20–26 Army Group Africa claimed to have destroyed 162 British tanks, 24 guns, 67 motor vehicles, and 23 planes. But German and Italian losses were also severe. Von Arnim now had 69 operational tanks in all of Africa. German reserves consisted of a single depleted *panzer* battalion.[30] After two days of battle, the 10th Panzer Division was reduced to 25 functioning *panzers*. Reinforcements drawn from the First Italian Army and 15th Panzer Division increased its strength by April 26 to 55 German and 10 Italian tanks. At the same time Fifth Panzer Army held another armored force of about 14 *panzers* in support of the 334th Infantry Division, nearer the Medjerda river.[31] Alexander was irritated and disappointed by Montgomery's suspension of Eighth Army's attack against the Enfidaville position because the Axis was able to replace some of its heavy losses on the western front by withdrawing troops and tanks from the east.[32]

CHAPTER 31

"In the great hour of destiny they stand"

The Battle of Hill 609

The attacks of the British First and Eighth Armies had been halted. The concluding offensive of the Tunisian campaign was now to begin with the American II Corps's attack to break and derange the enemy defense east of Sidi Nsir. The attacks in the north by 9th Infantry Division (Eddy), and in the south by 1st Infantry Division (Allen), 34th Infantry Division (Ryder), and 1st Armored Division (Harmon), were as valorous, difficult, and frustrating as those of the British. Retrained, reequipped, and with casualties largely replaced, the 34th Infantry Division's soldiers would now fight relentlessly to destroy the German "goats" in their fortifications. Progress would be measured by hills taken, casualties suffered, ammunition expended, enemy dead, and enemy prisoners captured. One regiment of 34ID was in the fight from the start; the rest of the Division went into the attack two days later. The valor and stamina of the Red Bull GIs earned for the 34th Infantry Division "battle honors fairly won."[1]

The 168th Infantry Regiment reinforced 1ID's position on the northwestern flank and by April 23 had occupied and held Hills 344 and 533, northwest of Kef el Goraa (Hill 575).[2]

> The 168th Infantry, 34th Division was in a forward position extending across [what was to become] the 34th Division front. The remaining elements of the [34th] division were partly in the [divisional] assembly areas northeast of Béja and the rear elements were closing in from... the vicinity of Maktar... Many replacements had been received with the majority coming from the 3rd Infantry Division. In the group were well trained lieutenants and NCOs who readily filled the key positions of the smaller units. The general overall feeling of the command was relatively good because they were under an American Corps commander who was well known for his superior generalship in the field, and also the majority of the command could see the beginning of the end and wanted to end it as soon as possible...
> [O]n 22 April 1943 the 168th Infantry closed into the area in the vicinity of Béja... [I]t was necessary to move the [regiment] immediately into position... to accomplish [the] mission of protecting the left flank of the 1st Division... With the enemy's right flank anchored on Hills 407-473-375 the regiment ordered the 1st and 3rd Battalions to move to the vicinity of Djebel Grembil (Hill 489) and defend the left sector (northwest portion) of the [1ID] division area and be prepared to assume the offensive. The 2nd Battalion was ordered to move into the

high ground in the vicinity of Hill 344 and defend the right sector (southeast portion) of [what would be] the [34th] division area, establish contact with the 1st Division and be prepared to assume the offensive... [3]

Good Friday, April 23, 1943: "Hunting wild goats"

U.S. II Corps opened its attack during the early hours of April 23 with a tremendous artillery preparation in support of the 1st and 9th Infantry Divisions. The southern portion of the II Corps front was initially held by the 1st Infantry Division, greatly reinforced by the 168th Infantry Regiment and the 6th Armored Infantry Regiment. 1ID's sector extended southeasterly about 14 miles from the vicinity of Djebel Grembil (499m), west of Sidi Nsir, to that of Djebel Bech Chekaoui (667m), five miles west of Heïdous. The northern limit of this zone of attack stretched to the northeast along the heights between the Malah and Djoumine rivers, while the southern edge extended toward Tebourba and Djedeida, along the crest of Djebel Lanserine (569m). Like the 9th Infantry Division zone farther north, 1st Infantry Division's sector embraced two river valleys which trended generally northeastward and three belts of ridges and hills on either side of the two valleys. The center section was so rugged and so strongly defended that the full strength of the reinforced 1st Infantry Division was required from the beginning of the attack. The northern flank along the Djoumine river was protected by Company B, 81st Reconnaissance Battalion, which was in contact with the 91st Armored Reconnaissance Squadron on the southern flank of the 9th Infantry Division. The 168th Infantry Regiment was temporarily attached to the 1st Infantry Division and assigned to hold its left. [4]

The American infantry moved forward in Friday's first light, "a long, slow line of dark-helmeted forms silhouetted in the [artillery] flash," Ernie Pyle wrote. [5] As the 9th Division swept across a broad, 28-mile front on the left flank, Bradley threw the weight of his punch against the right with first the 1st Infantry Division and, two days later, the 34th Infantry Division, forming a 13-mile crescent on a northeasterly vector. [6] The 1st Infantry Division jumped off on a six-mile front, extending from the hills just south of Sidi Nsir to the Tine valley. The direction of the attack led into a belt of hills seven miles deep from Kef el Goraa (Hill 575) to the eastern end of Djebel Sidi Meftah, a long ridge north of the Tine river with heights known as Hill 347 and Hill 281. Three strongpoints, Hills 575, 400, and 407, formed the German outer defense line. For the next several days 1ID, reinforced by 168IR, struggled to capture them. Those heights fell in the zones of attack of the 26th, 16th, and 18th Regimental Combat Teams. [7]

"A belt of rugged hills"

The terrain over which the 1st Infantry Division attacked was covered with less dense underbrush than that to the north. The valleys held cultivated fields of short, maturing wheat and numerous olive groves extending up the lower slopes. The hills were rocky, covered at best with thin grass, but the contours were generally more rounded than those in the south. In this northern sector, however, most of the hills were in groups so close together that the enemy could easily deliver supporting fire from hill to hill. Unimpeded observation from higher hills allowed the Germans to direct accurately mortars and artillery batteries emplaced well to the Axis rear, some out of range of American artillery. Daylight operations by American troops were in full view of the enemy. The Americans adapted their tactics to compensate for the enemy's topographic advantages; they attacked several hills simultaneously and moved mostly under cover of darkness.

Of the higher hills, Djebel Tahent (Hill 609), three miles east of Sidi Nsir, was a menacing example of the tactical problem posed by a dominating height surrounded by lesser hills in an interlocking system of defense, requiring protracted and costly exertions by an attacking force to gain the ground.[8] But as Bradley had perceived, if II Corps, meaning the 34th Infantry Division, could capture and destroy the hill fort complex around 609, the enemy's defensive line before Mateur and Bizerte would be splintered and the entire Axis front in Tunisia would be ruined.

The reinforced 1st Infantry Division's operations on April 23 revealed the strength of the outer German defenses across 1ID's front. The 26th Infantry Regiment at Hill 575 (Kef el Goraa), the 18th Infantry Regiment at Hill 407, and the 6th Armored Infantry Regiment, detached from 1st Armored Division, at Hill 420, ran into violent resistance from well-shielded enemy positions on the main objectives and deadly mutually supporting fire of all weapons from adjacent heights. 1ID also encountered the enemy's murderous placement of minefields. The GIs learned to anticipate the enemy's disconcertingly rapid counterattacks to regain their lost ridges. As quickly as drawing a pistol, enemy counterattacks could catch and kill an American unit while it was still regrouping from an assault. The solution was for the Americans to attack closely behind their artillery fire, and then in an adrenaline-driven frenzy immediately prepare to receive the enemy by using available cover or erecting shelter, and rapidly emplacing heavy weapons. The first day's attack identified which hills in the 1ID sector were the key crests in the interlocking hill groups that II Corps must seize.[9] Bradley and Allen realized that the natural advantages for defense in the extraordinarily rough terrain required a considerably stronger effort if the infantry were to succeed in pushing ahead.[10]

Major Ross Frasher, in April 1943 an infantry company commander in 2nd Battalion, 168th Infantry Regiment, described in his post-war Infantry School thesis how II Corps maneuvered to gain positions from which it would later invest and capture the several hill forts in the complex.

> A belt of rugged hills that was 15 to 20 miles in depth lay between the II Corps and Mateur, the enemy's chief center of communications and the key to Bizerte. The hills in this area formed a jumbled maze providing no broad corridors for advance. The Tine River seemed to offer the

only likely approach for armor, but before this could be used the high ground on both sides had to be taken. The 1st Division with 6th Armored Infantry and 1st Armored Division [were] to attack the enemy in these hills. The flank north and south of the Beja–Mateur road was covered by the 168th RCT with the remaining units of the 1st Armored and 34th Division in reserve. The 168th Infantry was in a forward position extending across [what was to be the] 34th Division front. The remaining elements of the [34th] Division were in the rear assembly area northeast of Béja or closing in from Maktar.[11]

By April 23, 1943, 2/168 had occupied a defensive position along the forward or eastern ridge of Hill 344, south of the Béja–Nsir–Mateur road, southwest of Djebel Tahent (Hill 609). The battalion coordinated with the movements of 1ID.[12]

Saturday, April 24, 1943

Bradley recognized after the first day of fighting that he had to deploy additional combat power to break the enemy's hold on its hill fort complexes. During the night of April 25–26, Bradley directed the main body of the 34th Infantry Division to move into the line between the 9th Infantry Division on 34ID's left (northern) flank and the 1st Infantry Division on 34ID's right (southern) flank. The 168th Infantry was returned to 34ID control, and soon after the remainder of the division would join the fight on the 1st Infantry Division's left. The front assigned to 1st Infantry Division was shortened, allowing 1ID to concentrate its force.

The sector assigned to the 34th Infantry Division followed the railroad from Béja to Mateur along the Tine river valley through some of which ran a narrow serpentine road.[13] The Red Bull soldiers had to acclimate to the terrain of northern Tunisia, which was much different from that further south. This part of Tunisia was extensively cultivated, with orchards and fields. The hills, while just as steep, had considerably more vegetation and the lower slopes were cultivated. But the higher peaks, to the dismay of the GIs, were as bare and rocky as those further south, and often so steep that to climb them, even without weapons or enemy opposition, required great exertion and care.[14]

The German *Division von Manteuffel* held not only the enemy line in front of the 9th Infantry Division but also that part of the line in the southern portion of the II Corps zone of advance. Of immediate concern to the 34th Infantry Division was the area nearest Sidi Nsir and the sector extending northeast about ten miles which included Hill 609. That sector was defended by two battalions of Luftwaffe *Regiment Barenthin* and by the northern wing of the 334th Infantry Division, with a third *Barenthin* battalion held in reserve. Southward from this area, across the Tine river valley to the heights of Djebel Lanserine, was the main body of the 334th Infantry Division. The eight Nazi infantry battalions holding the front were organized in three regiments. North of the Medjerda river were the 755th Infantry, a provisional headquarters, and the 756th Mountain Regiment. Two more battalions and elements of the 504th Heavy Panzer Battalion were in tactical reserve. The 334th Division sector to the south, across the Medjerda river to the Medjez el Bab-Tunis highway (inclusive), was held by the 754th Infantry Regiment.[15]

On April 24, II Corps's artillery intermittently shelled enemy positions on Hill 575 (Kef el Goraa). The 3rd Battalion of the 26th Infantry Regiment was relieved from a position on the left of the 1ID sector by 168IR. 3/26 then moved up to support a renewed attack planned for April 25. Meanwhile, the 16th Infantry Regiment managed to outflank the enemy on Hill 575 by capturing three important hills to the southeast. According to a prisoner-of-war report, the enemy had pulled out of Hill 575 at 2:00a.m. on April 25, just as 1ID's attack began, leaving only a rear guard. 2/16 occupied the hill at 3:50a.m., and a few hours later 1/16 took possession of Hill 533 to the north. 3/16 advanced northeast of Hill 575 and continued along the ridge toward Djebel Touta (Hill 444), which they occupied by the afternoon. As the 1st Infantry Division pushed forward, the 2nd Battalion of the 168th Infantry Regiment moved southeast from Hill 344 and took over Hills 533 and 575. 2/168 first moved two companies (F and G) east to Hill 533 on April 24. Then 168IR, with Company C of the 701st Tank Destroyer Battalion attached, relieved the rest of the 26th Infantry Regiment, 1ID, on the night of April 24–25. G Company then moved to Hill 575 in the 1ID zone. The battalion established outposts and sent out patrols to find and contact the 16th Infantry Regiment, 1ID.[16]

After the second day's operations, Bradley and II Corps modified the plan of attack between Sidi Nsir and the Tine valley based on four considerations: the enemy's firm grip on the hills near Sidi Nsir, the advances made as 1st Infantry Division had fought its way into the hills, the resulting exposure of 1ID's left (north) flank, and the imminent arrival of the entire 34th Infantry Division.[17]

Easter Sunday, April 25, 1943

When 1st Infantry Division renewed its attack early on April 25, the enemy on 1ID's center had quietly pulled back four or five miles to a previously prepared main line of resistance. Only security detachments, booby traps, and minefields remained to cover the enemy's withdrawal, and German artillery had plotted numerous concentrations to strike the hills as the Americans occupied them. The enemy fire was so intense that at 4:00a.m. it drove 1ID's troops off Hills 469 and 394. The Germans remained in strength on Hill 473 (Djebel el Hara), a mile and a half west of Sidi Nsir. The 168th Infantry Regiment, attached to 1ID, was tasked to cover that threat to 1ID's left flank. 1ID advanced during the day on April 25 and occupied Hills 575 (Kef el Goraa), 407, and 420 as the enemy pulled back about four miles to the northeast, to a group of hills located at a point where the Tine valley pivots to the north.[18] By 8:00p.m. the 1st Infantry Division had occupied the western end of Djebel Sidi Meftah (Hill 281), and the hills leading to it from the southwest, Djebel Touta (Hill 444), close to the Sidi Nsir–Chouïgui road, and the hills directly west of Djebel Touta. In the Tine valley, 1ID was at a line which stretched southeastward to a point about a mile and a half north of Djebel el Ang (668m). Major General Allen intended to continue on April 26 toward intermediate objectives under II Corps' current plan of attack, but the 1st Infantry Division now held a salient that projected past adjacent enemy-held territory with a northern or left flank extending for 10,000 yards (over 5.5 miles) along the road to Chouïgui.

> The 1st Division [on April 23–25] moved forward approximately 5 miles leaving a dangerous open flank on their left. The II Corps decided it was time to commit the 34th Division in a coordinated attack with the 1st Division. On 25 April 1943 the 1st and 3rd Battalions of the 168th with the support of a heavy artillery barrage, launched their attack from Hill 489 upon the enemy-held hills [407 and 473]. The attack was pinned down and stopped by heavy MG fire and mortars. The 2nd Battalion moved approximately one mile east to more effectively protect the 1st Division flank.[19]

The 175th Field Artillery Battalion, detached from 34ID, and several battalions of Corps Artillery carried out the fire mission in support of the assault by 1/168 and 3/168 on Hill 473 (Djebel el Hara). Despite the cover of the barrage, enemy machine-gun and mortar fire halted the advance from Hill 489 north toward Hills 407 and 473 after only slight progress.

Monday, April 26, 1943

In three days of tough fighting the Americans had forced their enemy to shorten its line. The enemy, however, only moved back to yet more solidly built positions. On April 26 Axis resistance stiffened and the progress of II Corps's attack slowed. Bradley and his division commanders realized that the desperate Nazi troops intended to fight to the last bullet before a breach could be blasted open either by 9th Infantry Division at the north through the envelopment of the Djefna position, or by 1st Infantry Division at the south by driving the enemy from the hills on either side of the Tine river valley. The cornered enemy was not fighting a holding action now; they were fighting for survival, and they were fighting savagely. In the enemy's center, 1ID had pushed northeastward along the Sidi Nsir–Chouïgui road far enough to prevent its use by the enemy. The enemy had fought hard in a losing battle to defend Hill 575 (Kef el Goraa) and was fiercely holding on to Djebel Grembil (499m) and Djebel el Hara (473m) near Sidi Nsir on 1ID's left flank. The Germans had defended those hills west of Hill 609 successfully for the previous two days against the 1st and 3rd Battalions of the 168th Infantry Regiment.

For operations on April 26, the fourth day of the offensive, the 1st Infantry Division was deprived of the support of the 1st Battalion, 13th Armored Regiment, which returned to Major General Harmon's 1st Armored Division during the night of April 25.[20] To increase II Corps's combat power, the main body of the 34th Infantry

Division moved into the line. Early on April 26, Ryder's 34th Infantry Division assumed responsibility for the zone between the 9th Infantry Division on the left of 34ID and 1st Infantry Division on the right flank, from Djebel Grembil (Hill 499) and Djebel el Hara (Hill 473) on the northwest to Hill 575 on the southeast. The 168th Regimental Combat Team and 701st Tank Destroyer Battalion returned to 34ID control.[21]

> [On] 26 April 1943, heavy artillery fire was again placed on [Hills 407 and 473] to soften them up... [Headquarters, 168th] Regiment decided that a flanking move was necessary to take and reduce the right flank of the enemy. The 2nd Battalion located in the extreme right sector of the [34th] Division [area] was in the zone... that... [34th] Division decided was to be the area of the 135th Infantry. The [34th] division the same day committed the 135th Infantry into the zone... occupied by the 2nd Battalion, 168th infantry. The [168th] regiment coordinated with the 135th Infantry on the relief of the 2nd Battalion, 168th Infantry, then ordered the 2nd Battalion to prepare for a night attack on the strongly defended Hill 473 to be launched on the night of 26–27 April... The 1st and 2nd Battalions were to continue the attack on the morning of 27 April 1943.[22]

The reader will gain from a study of the maps of the terrain and of the unit movements in the 34th Infantry Division's sector a better understanding of the constantly changing positions of the infantry battalions in what Major Frasher called the "belt of rugged hills" during the ensuing six days of incessant combat to take Hill 609 and the surrounding hill forts. By April 26, 1st Infantry Division was already heavily engaged in attempts to take and hold Hill 529 south of Hill 609 and to advance east to Hill 455, through which ran the new inter-divisional boundary with 34ID. The sector assigned to the 34th Infantry Division was aligned in a northeasterly direction pointed directly at Mateur. Initially, as the 34ID's main body was still moving forward from its assembly area at Maktar, the 168th Infantry Regiment had held by itself what became the 34th Infantry Division's sector, on the 1st Infantry Division's left or northerly flank.

Through a heavy fog in the early hours of April 26, 1st Infantry Division troops fought and scrambled along the ridges of Djebel Sidi Meftah (Hill 281) and Djebel Touta (Hill 444), not quite reaching the eastern ends. Patrols crossed to the area north of the Sidi Nsir–Chouïgui road, southeast of Hill 609. As 34ID moved in on 1ID's left flank, Major General Allen and his staff modified the 1st Infantry Division's objectives. 1ID's front was narrowed from some ten miles to less than five miles, to be held by one battalion each from the 26th and 18th Infantry Regiments. The line ran eastward from the precipitous and strongly defended Hill 531 (about 1,000 yards south of Hill 609) over the western end of Djebel el Anz and then southeastward via the eastern slopes of Djebel Sidi Meftah (Hill 281) to the Tine river valley. American observers on recently captured hilltops spotted enemy troop movements and eagerly directed artillery fire on many targets, including the top of Hill 609. 1ID units carried out reconnaissance in preparation for the resumption of the division's advance. The 16th Infantry Regiment was alerted to move on the left of the 26th Infantry Regiment along the northern edge or left of the 1ID divisional zone, synchronizing its actions with the 34th Infantry Division's operations to reduce the Hill 609 hill fort complex.[23]

The terrain to the east in the 34th Infantry Division's zone was dominated by rocky hill masses. None was taller than Djebel Tahent. Von Arnim's troops had retreated across the II Corps's front to even more strongly fortified positions on and around it. From the 1st Division's sector, GIs could look down the road that ran diagonally from the rail station at Sidi Nsir across the "Mousetrap" valley toward Chouïgui. On the north side of the road, on the northern rim of the Tine valley, the tall white faces of Djebel Tahent rose into the North African sky.[24]

By April 26 Bradley recognized that until Hill 609 was taken, 1st Infantry Division could not progress further down the southern rim of the Tine valley. Hill 609 was the bulwark of the Axis bridgehead's defenses and conquering it was crucial to II Corps's mission to occupy Mateur.[25] But Hill 609 could be captured and held only by simultaneously driving the enemy from the adjacent hills which controlled the approaches and protected the inner keep. Three miles northeast of Sidi Nsir, 609 towered above all nearby features by virtue of its height and location. Almost 2,000 feet above sea level, it dominated all direct approaches from Béja to Mateur. The mountain was an enormous mass of rock, its lower slopes covered with vegetation and olive groves below almost vertical rock walls twisting along the southwestern and southeastern slopes. The top of Hill 609 was a barren mesa 800 yards long and 500 yards wide. From the top, GI observers with telescopes would later pick out individual house windows in Mateur 12 miles away and a blur on the horizon that was Bizerte another 20 miles beyond. The southwest and southeast sides were faced with 50-foot limestone cliffs. The direct approaches to Hill 609 from the west and from the south were almost impossible because the faces of the mountain rose nearly sheer. Except for small olive groves scattered around the southwestern slope, the terrain of the approaches from the west and southwest offered almost no cover to assault teams, while the limestone palisades provided many rocky nooks to hide defenders. Fissures in the rock formed natural chambers up the cliff walls; German machine guns were hidden in holes at the base. Neighboring heights—Hills 461, 490, 531, 455—provided overlapping fields of fire for more machine guns and mortars. On the northeastern face, however, a somewhat easier approach was possible.[26]

Hill 609 and its satellite hill forts were manned mostly by the *Regiment Barenthin*, soldiers drawn from the Luftwaffe's parachute and glider schools, who, in Alexander's assessment, were "perhaps the best German troops in Africa." The GIs of the 34th Infantry Division appraised their foe on a par with the best German paratroops. This enemy was boldly and determinedly led. Right at the top of Hill 609 enemy engineers had constructed a citadel blasted out of the rock, which was in range of supporting artillery, mortar, and machine-gun fire from the similarly fortified adjacent hills. Hill 609 was not only a defensive post; the Germans used Djebel Tahent as an artillery observation post. Considering the topography and the dispositions of the enemy defenders in the hill forts, and with faith in the innate toughness and hard-won battle wisdom of his troops, Major General Ryder made a brilliant tactical decision. 34ID would demolish the outer hill forts, surround Hill 609 and the lesser hills with maneuver battalions, assault simultaneously Hill 609 and the adjacent hill forts, and then force a way into the citadel from the German side by a relatively easier approach, ascending a goat trail which led up from the mountain's northeast corner.[27]

The 34th Infantry Division's history summarizes the situation.

> After stubborn fighting during which our troops showed that they had learned well how to follow an artillery barrage, the attack swung eastward into the hills which lay in the path of our advance to Hill 609. To further the Corps plan of seizing the important communication center of Mateur, to the northeast of our sector, it was first necessary to secure the dominating terrain—Hill 609…
>
> The 168th Infantry protected the left flank of the Division by seizing three high peaks on successive days while the 135th Infantry on the right proceeded to make progress at the rate of one hill a day, using the cover of night to deploy for its attack.[28]

The 34th Division's objective was to take the entire hill fort complex, attacking on a southwest to northeast axis against the westward bulge in the enemy's line on the hills north of the Sidi Nsir–Chouïgui road to bring Hill 609 under American control.[29]

> Hill 609's upper contours [rising] from a much larger, less steeply slanting base, when seen from above, resemble a crude Indian arrowhead pointing toward the east. From tip to base, this arrowhead extends for more than 800 yards, while the distance from the northern to the southern barb approximates 500 yards. Deep notches, bounded by precipitous slopes, pierce the northern and southern sides. Its top is divided into two major areas, a fairly level table rising gradually from west to east in the triangular section between tip and barbs, and an irregular amphitheater falling off to the west, with a narrow level shelf above the white southwestern escarpment. That cliff because of its great height masks from the adjacent ground to the south and southwest the existence of the higher slopes on the western portion of the crest and gives the appearance of a substantial mesa resting on a massive ridge. Low vegetation, mostly bunch grass, growing among rocky outcrops over much of Hill 609, offered little concealment, while the rocky ground made digging in with infantry tools out of the question.
>
> The triangular eastern section juts up from its base, while the western end rises gradually on the northwest and most steeply of the entire mass on the southwest. There a great palisade, looming brightly in the April sun high above the surrounding ground, was visible to the attacking forces for many miles. An unimproved road crosses the western part of the arrowhead to an Arab village which nestles at the base of the southern notch. Another track skirts the crest at the east, giving access to scattered olive orchards on the lower slopes. Hill 609 is no monadnock but its summit projects at least 200 feet above the crests of any neighboring hills, and it furnished excellent observation over much of the II Corps zone of attack.[30]

"By now, the 34th Division had moved into the II Corps sector after its unhappy experience at Fondouk. Remembering the promise [he] had made to Alexander,

[Bradley] picked the 34th to go after 609."[31] Bradley took a real risk in promising Alexander that the Red Bull soldiers would take their next objective. He chose men who had suffered from bad training and worse leadership, men who had never dreamed they would have to kill or be killed, men who had been criticized, denounced, and censured on both sides of the Atlantic for their battle performance, men whose souls and hearts and been broken. But Bradley trusted Ryder and had looked deep into the eyes of the Red Bull soldiers. He saw that they could and would follow Ryder and rise not only to the greatest challenge of their lives, but to the very acme of Hill 609. The 34th Infantry Division had spent every day since Fondouk in remedial combat training, learning, relearning, and practicing the craft of war.[32] Bradley told Ryder: "Get me that hill and you'll break up the enemy's defenses clear across our front. Take it, and no one will ever again doubt the toughness of your division."[33]

The mountainous mass directly west of Hill 609 had two great shoulders, Hill 490 and Hill 435 (northwest of Hill 490). A second massif northwest of Hill 609, divided by a narrow defile from Hill 490, was known as Hill 461. Opposite the southeastern quarter of Hill 609 and northwest of the Sidi Nsir–Chouïgui road was a wide hilly zone with two rows of crests or ridges. Soldiers on Hill 609 looking from south to east saw the crests designated on the map as Hills 529, 531, 455, 523, 545, and then 558. Almost parallel to these hills and between them and the Sidi Nsir–Chouïgui road was a lower series of heights rising from a second ridge, of which the most prominent hills were 428 and 476. The contours of these hills were rounded except at the northwest, where they were more sharply eroded, so that from Hill 609 this area appeared as a broad, rolling plateau extending back from a steep edge. From the southwest, even from observation points on the shoulders of hills within the American lines, the GIs could see the upper slopes only on some of these hills, *leaving important details of the terrain near their bases to be discovered by reconnaissance patrols.*[34]

The boundary between the 34th Infantry Division and the 1st Infantry Division sectors cut across the hills from the southwest to the northeast, requiring mutual support and coordination of fires between the units on either flank. The boundary ran over the southeastern slopes of the Hill 531 fortress, with the shorter southern part of that precipitous mile-long ridge inside 1ID's area, and the rest reaching its highest point at 531 meters in 34ID's sector. As the battle developed, both Ryder and Allen came to realize that Hill 531 was the real key to the German defense and that if their troops could capture it, the battle would be won.

The 16th Infantry Regiment of 1ID could best approach the southeastern portion of Hill 531 by passing through the saddle between Kef el Guebli and Hill 529, but It could not move to take other objectives to the east and northeast without being subjected to flanking fire from Hill 531. The 1st Battalion, 135th Infantry, could attack Hill 531 only over ground already occupied by elements of 16IR. Necessarily, battalion commanders of the 135th Infantry Regiment on occasion directed artillery fire on enemy targets in 16IR's area. Lieutenant Colonel Miller, commander of the 1st Battalion, 135IR was ruefully mindful of the disastrous consequences which a failure of coordination could cause because of his own recent experience on the left flank at Fondouk el Aouareb near Djebel Aïn el Rhorab. He arranged a field telephone connection with the command post of the adjacent battalion of the 16IR, and a regimental liaison was established. The difficulties of coordinated operations in the rugged hills severely strained the American units' efforts to stay in contact by any means.[35] But although it drained manpower and matériel, constant communication between front-line units was vital to the GIs' ultimate success.

One should hold in mind the relative sizes and dispositions of the defending and attacking forces. The Hill 609 complex in the 34ID sector was held by two battle-hardened battalions of *Regiment Barenthin*. Somewhat reduced by battle losses, they were protected in positions some of which had been blasted and drilled in solid rock and reinforced with concrete, rail ties and earth. They were well equipped with machine guns, mortars, and light artillery with adequate ammunition. A third battalion of *Regiment Barenthin* provided a limited source of reinforcements. The attacking Americans included two entire regiments and part of a third from the 34th Infantry Division. Two regiments from the 1st Infantry Division attacked the heights southeast of the Hill 609 complex, manned by Wehrmacht troops of the 334th Division. The numbers, mobility, firepower, and determination of the GIs defied the advantage that the terrain conferred on the defenders. It is probable that the attackers outnumbered the defenders by about two to one. In the fighting that was to decide the fate of Hill 609, the GIs were armed with the M1 Garand and a continually refreshed supply of ammunition clips, hand grenades, machine-gun belts, and mortar bombs, thanks to the energy and improvisation of supporting troops and their own ingenuity. They were backed by tanks and the artillery of two divisions and of an Army Corps. The Americans had the firepower advantage.

During the night and early morning of April 25–26, both II Corps and the 34th Infantry Division artillery fired a great many concentrations on Hills 407 and 473 to soften up the enemy positions. On the morning of April 26, the 135th Infantry Regiment was ordered to move about four miles northeast of the regimental assembly area to Hill 575 (Kef el Goraa) and to relieve the 168th Infantry Regiment from its positions west of Hill 609. 135RCT prepared to launch what its commanders understood were to be local diversionary strikes to support the main attack of the 34th Infantry Division, to be made by the 168th Infantry Regiment on the division's left or northern flank. That understanding was quickly corrected. 3/135 was ordered to complete the relief in time to allow both battalions to prepare for offensive operations on the morning of April 27. The relief started at 1:00p.m. and was completed seven hours later. The commander of 3/135, accompanied by the battalion S-3 and the company commanders, moved to the command post of

2/168 for a reconnaissance. 3/135 relieved 2/168 from outpost positions west and southwest of Hill 609, and then moved to the vicinity of Hill 334. 1st Battalion marched to the vicinity of Hill 533, and the 2nd Battalion went into regimental reserve on Hill 575.[36]

The enemy had demonstrated during the first days of II Corps's operations the primitive ferocity with which they would defend their possession of the inner hill fort complex. The 34th Infantry Division's operations staff, fully aware of the nature of the interlocking defenses of 609's satellite hills, had not at first appreciated that the relatively small enemy forces on the hills, distributed to unleash torrents of interlacing defensive fire, could drive off any direct attack on Hill 609. Ryder's initial plan of attack had assigned the seizure of Djebel Tahent to the 135th Infantry (Colonel Ward). During the day on April 26, 135IR had overcome light resistance on the heights west and southwest of Hill 609 but had discovered immediately that a direct approach to Hill 609 would be strongly resisted from Hill 490 (to the northwest), from Hill 531 (to the south), and from Hill 609 itself. Ward then presented and Ryder approved a plan to send one battalion against Hill 490 and a second battalion to occupy the part of Hill 529 in the 34ID zone and then to attack Hill 531.[37] The infantry battalions of the 34th Infantry Division would use simultaneous attacks, coordinated fire and maneuver, supported by artillery, heavy mortars, and both heavy and light machine guns to shatter the defenses and open a path into the Hill 609 citadel.

Bradley, however, was worried by Ryder's plan. To take Hill 609, 34ID had first to take both Djebel el Hara (Hill 473) and Hill 490, which covered the approaches from the west. Ryder proposed to take both hills in a single attack. Bradley felt that "Ryder proposed to take a bigger bite than I could guarantee on a starting attack."[38]

The commander of 1/135, Lieutenant Colonel Miller, with his staff and the company commanders, arrived near Hill 575 on 34ID's right (southeastern) flank a little after noon on April 26 for a reconnaissance before the march to the assembly area. As the officers discussed a plan of attack, a German prisoner captured by 168IR troops was brought in. The prisoner claimed to be a deserter. The German said Hill 609 was only lightly held by disloyal troops, that the main force had withdrawn, and that it would be easy for the Americans to capture the place if they attacked immediately. He claimed that 50 men could do the job. The prisoner was a liar. The American officers saw through his treachery, completed their reconnaissance, and made the final attack plans. "There was excitement in the air and the tone was for an immediate attack." 1/135's troops assembled behind Hill 575 by 6:00p.m. Ammunition and rations were issued. Miller planned to attack that night under cover of darkness to seize both Hill 490 and Hill 531 preliminary to seizing Hill 609. 135IR's plan placed the 1st Battalion on the right (south) to assault the enemy positions on Hills 529 and Hill 531 and the 3rd Battalion on the left to take Hill 490. The battalions were to move over Hills 374 and 484, the intervening heights on the route to their respective objectives. 2/135 was designated regimental reserve. 1/135's Company A had little more than 60 per cent of its authorized strength and Company B had about 65 per cent of its strength before they attacked Hill 531.[39]

Lieutenant Colonel Miller ordered Company A, 1/135 to secure Hill 484 and then move on toward the base of Hill 531, laying engineer tape to guide the rest of the battalion. Company B would follow, then shift to the left of Company A. The 1st Battalion moved out at 7:00p.m. in single file. The GIs had learned it was better to have fewer guns but an abundance of ammunition, so the weapons platoons of each company took only two machine guns each; all other personnel carried extra ammunition chests. The battalion command group followed Company A. The 81mm mortar crews came next, leading Company B. Company C brought up the rear with the men of one entire rifle platoon transformed into ammunition-carrying oxen for the heavy weapons company. It was impossible for the anti-tank platoon to drag the 37mm AT guns over the terrain they had to traverse, so those soldiers were also dragooned as ammunition carriers. The movement through the dark was slow. At times men had to be bodily lifted over rocks and their equipment or ammunition loads were returned to them when they reached the other side.[40]

Captain Donald Landon, commanding Company A, reached Hill 501 at about 10:00p.m., contacted elements of Company B on its left, and continued its march to Hill 484. The terrain was punishing, and the enemy threw occasional artillery rounds in the dark. There were casualties in Company A from the missiles and from falls from precipices. Company A arrived at Hill 484 at about 5:00a.m. on April 27; the rest of 1st Battalion stayed on Hill 501 as planned.[41]

Tuesday, April 27, 1943

Nine battalions from the 34th Infantry Division, supported by continuous artillery fire, attacked the hill fort positions around Hill 609 along a 6,000-yard front on April 27. Ryder, a capable infantry tactician, had recognized what he called the "checkerboard of interlocking defenses," which required his men to annihilate the enemy on the adjacent hills while at the same time attacking Hill 609 itself.[42] Only simultaneous suppressive fire on all the hills would allow the soldiers to get close enough to destroy the enemy on each hill. He made certain that all his battalion and company commanders well understood that to reach and destroy the enemy citadel on Hill 609, the surrounding key points had to be attacked and eliminated at the same time.

On 34ID's right, the hilly mass composed of Hills 531 and 529 rose out of the southern base of Hill 609. Hill 529 and Kef el Guebli were actually one hill, rising more than 300 feet above the Sidi Nsir–Chouïgui road which lay directly to the south. Hill 529 was separated from Hill 531 by a draw that provided an approach to the Hill 531 fortress. Hill 531 itself was a steep rock formation with jagged cliffs and crevices. It constituted a large natural bulwark blocking the approaches to Hill 609 from the west and south. On the west, facing Hill 529, Hill 531 was precipitous except for a more gradual slope in the center. Hill 531 was in turn covered from the northeast by two slightly lower but equally rugged features, one known as the Roman Ruins and the other as Hill 455, both rising from the base of Djebel Tahent.[43]

On 34ID's left, northwest of Hill 575 and west of the Bou Oissa river, Hills 473 (Djebel el Hara) and 375 lay in a northeasterly line. Those hills were the objectives of the 168th Infantry Regiment. All the objective hills were hard rock, impossible to dig in; some GIs blasted out foxholes in the stony northern Tunisian hills with "bee-hive" explosive charges.[44]

Red Bull soldiers ate "C" rations, filled their canteens, and smoked cigarettes in the twilight. As they had done before, each soldier tied a white cloth to the back of his helmet so the man behind him could follow him in the dark. Engineers marked paths through enemy minefields, with white tape or rocks wrapped in toilet paper. Every few minutes, platoon leaders huddled under their blankets with flashlights to check their compasses. "For the love of heaven and hell," a company commander's voice called in the darkness, "get going." As the GIs scrambled their way into the killing zones, the chainsaw noise of a German machine gun split the night, joined by a second and a third. "Our men crouched in gray shapes, running, falling flat, firing, running again," one witness reported. Enemy mortar rounds burst in prearranged concentrations on the saddles between the hills. The light of flares blossomed overhead. The men fell flat and froze silently in place. Machine guns killed or wounded some men; mines and booby traps took other GIs, exploding with sharp pops. "We lay there awaiting dawn, listening to the cries of a wounded man about a hundred yards down the side slope," a soldier later recalled. "He weakened and finally became silent."[45]

CHAPTER 32

Reducing the Outworks

135RCT's Attacks on Hill 490 and Hill 531

One company from each of 1/135 and 3/135 had moved forward after dark on April 26 to secure the line Sidi Nsir railroad station–Hill 374–Hill 484. From there, 1/135 was to attack, with its objective Hill 529, and simultaneously 3/135 was to attack objective Hill 490. Company I, 3/135 proceeded over the extremely rugged terrain from Hill 533 to Hill 374, reaching Hill 374 only at 2:30a.m. on April 27. Company A, 1/135 did not reach Hill 484 until 3:00a.m. Shortly thereafter, the forward companies were established as planned on the line Sidi Nsir–Hill 374 (Company I, 3/135)–Hill 484 (Company A, 1/135).

The other companies of both battalions had to cross the same unforgiving ground in a dense fog and did not reach the line of departure until 5:30a.m., so the attack had to be delayed until 6:00a.m. Now in daylight, the attack of 1/135 toward Hill 529 proceeded very slowly. By 8:35a.m., leading elements of Company A had reached Hill 501 and were pushing patrols toward Hill 529. At 10:50a.m. the advance units of the 1st Battalion had reached the reverse slope of its objective, Hill 529. They met extraordinarily strong resistance and were heavily engaged all day on the reverse slope of Hill 529, making no further progress on April 27. The 133rd Infantry Regiment supported the 135th Infantry Regiment during the attack to permit the periodic relief of the assaulting companies, physically and mentally exhausted by both the maneuvering and fighting.[1]

To the north, 3/135 left its assembly area at 5:30p.m. on April 26 and dismounted from their trucks on the south slope of Hill 575. From there, the battalion command group moved to a depression on the west slope of Hill 575 to establish the battalion's command post. 3/135 was to assault the enemy-occupied Hills 435 and 490 at 4:30a.m. on April 27. The battalion commander directed Companies I and L to lead the assault, with Company L on the left and Company I on the right. Company K was placed in battalion reserve and moved to Hill 374 at 5:00a.m. to assume Company I's previous positions, as planned. Two platoons from Company M (the weapons company of 3/135) were attached in support of Companies I and

L, respectively. The mortar platoon of Company M took up positions on the south slope of Hill 374 to support the assault.

The attack began at 8:50a.m. The 3rd Battalion command group moved from the command post to a vantage point on the north slope of Hill 575, while the approach march was made over open, rolling terrain toward Hills 435 and 490, with the main effort directed against Hill 490. The 3rd Battalion fought its way across the road by 10:05a.m. and the battalion's forward elements reached the southern slope of Hill 490, where the GIs were slowed up by wire entanglements in a zone under constant machine-gun and artillery fire from Hill 490 and from Hill 609. The enemy then poured in heavy automatic fire and artillery air bursts, supplemented by the booby traps and anti-personnel mines which were scattered everywhere.[2] At 11:15a.m., the 2nd Battalion was ordered to move by means of trails and *wadis* to the vicinity of Hill 484 in readiness for an enemy counterattack from Hills 490, 609, and 529.

Any attack by 1/135 on Hill 531 was impossible in daylight, but preparations moved ahead. Company A sent patrols to probe to the front and flanks and contacted 3/135 on Hill 374. 1st Battalion's heavy mortars assisted 3rd Battalion by firing on enemy automatic weapons in front of Hill 374. Before noon on April 27, Lieutenant Colonel Miller ordered Captain Landon to move Company A to Kef el Guebli, adjacent to Hill 529. The 81mm mortar battery remained on Hill 484 to stop any counterattacks and to engage the enemy on Hill 609 that was firing on Company A. As Company A marched in single file directly east over the southern slope of Hill 530, they were subjected to indirect machine-gun and artillery fires. As the lead platoon reached the road between Hill 529 and Hill 530 it turned south in error, but Captain Landon came forward and reoriented his platoon leader to move north.[3]

In the afternoon, the attacking companies of 3/135 maintained continual contact on their respective flanks. The 3rd Battalion commander ordered Companies I and L to hold their ground and to be prepared to resume the attack after dark. 3/135 made no further progress that day.[4]

Neither battalion of 135IR was able to achieve the entire seizure of its objective, but the GIs had nonetheless fought with grit, severely damaging the enemy forces opposing them, and then held the ground they had taken. The 1st Battalion, 135th Infantry Regiment discovered firsthand at Hills 529 and 531 what the 16IR already knew. American units could send patrols or small attacking forces without being resisted, but any substantial movement was likely to be observed from the heights and to be scourged with prepared mortar and artillery fire.[5]

3/135's commander planned for a renewed attack during the night of April 27–28 to complete the capture of Hill 490. The bases of Hill 490 and Hill 461 were to be the line of departure for an attack by 2/135 eastward to seize Hill 461 and then to reach the northwestern foot of Hill 609. At 4:00p.m. on April 27, Company L, 3/135 made a reconnaissance in force up the forward slope of Hill 435 preparatory to its renewed night attack. Once 3/135 had secured Hill 490 entirely, 2/135 could pass through the 3rd Battalion's positions to approach Hill 609 from the northwest. Company L was again to assault and take Hill 435, while Company K, 3/135, moving forward from Hill 374, was to attack Hill 490 with support from Company I, now the battalion reserve. The 3rd Battalion moved its command post forward to the foot of Hill 490.[6]

Attack by 168RCT on Hill 473 (Djebel el Hara) and Hill 375

By April 26, the 168th Infantry Regiment had occupied Hill 575 (Kef el Goraa) and Hills 344 and 533, northwest of Hill 575.[7] 168IR ordered its 2nd Battalion to move northerly to an assembly area and on the night of April 26–27 to assault the flank of the enemy on Hill 473 (Djebel el Hara) north of the Béja–Mateur road, on the northeast side of the Bou Oissa river. The battalion, and the rest of 168IR, had earlier been attached to 1ID on the extreme left flank of 1ID's sector. Now situated at the extreme right of 34ID's sector, 2/168 had practically no real-time information about the enemy positions or the terrain on the new objective, "and less knowledge of the obstacles and terrain between its position and the general objective."[8]

On April 26, as the main body of 34th Infantry Division moved into the sector on 1ID's left flank, elements of the 135IR had moved into the former 2/168 sector near Hill 575 and relieved 2/168. Company G, the designated assault company, was taken off the line first to give the GIs as much time as possible to prepare for the assault on Djebel el Hara. The officers and men of 2/168 now put into practice the lessons they had learned in the Tunisian campaign thus far. The battalion commander and the S-3 made a personal, eyes-on-objective reconnaissance from positions on Hill 533 with maps and field glasses directed at Hill 473 over three miles away. The command selected an assembly area, designated the Béja–Mateur road as the line of departure, and dispatched a patrol to reconnoiter the route from Hill 575 to the line of departure. The relief of 168RCT by 135th Infantry Regiment was completed by 8:00p.m. The men of 2/168 were in for a hard, rushed march over harsh territory. The distance to be covered and the nature of the terrain made time a crucial factor.[9]

The distance from the assembly area to the 168RCT's line of departure was 2,600 yards (about 1.5 miles) which the battalion had to reach on foot over rocky terrain, descending a steep slope to the valley 600 feet below. The railroad line lay 200 yards southeast of the line of departure. The distance from the line of departure to Hill 473 was about 2,800 yards (roughly 1.6 miles). Two hundred yards past the line of departure lay the Oued Bou Oissa. The battalion command group did not know whether it was fordable but because of the recent lack of rainfall they did not expect it to be deep. The ground from the line of departure to the base of the objective was rolling and covered with vegetation that appeared to be small grain.

There seemed to be a steep slope approximately 300 feet high from the rocky base of Hill 473 northeasterly to the summit of Hill 375. From their bitter experiences with enemy defenses and methods the battalion's leaders were now able to estimate the likely strength of the Axis opposition and the general location of its weapons. Hill 473's forward slope was the probable location of the resistance, and the foot of the hill probably would be heavily reinforced with machine guns well dug in. The enemy would have registered mortar concentrations from hidden batteries on all the approaches to the base of the objective. From the geographic arrangement of Hills 307, 473, and 375 in a northeasterly line and their relative sizes, the battalion officers deduced that the opposition would be a battalion of infantry reinforced with heavy weapons. Two days of dense clusters of high-explosive shells on the objective encouraged the battalion commanders to believe that "it was reasonable to assume that the enemy had softened up a bit and had prepared supplemental positions."[10]

While the information obtained from reconnaissance and the estimates of enemy plans and weapons were better than in earlier battles, the actual leadership during the fight would have to come from junior and field grade officers. The commander of 2/168 received his orders and conferred with his company commanders at the rear of Hill 533. H Hour was set at 2:00a.m., April 27 for 2/168's advance from the line of departure on the Béja-Mateur road. The order of march was Companies G, F, H, HQ, and E. Company G was to guide the battalion to the objective, using a compass, then assault the center of the objective and organize against a counterattack. Company F was to secure the ground on the right of Hill 473's base. Company E was to support Company G and to secure the left flank, opposing by fire the enemy on Hill 407. H Company (heavy weapons) was to move its machine guns onto the objective as soon as the assault troops had seized it and from there to resist any counterattack. II Corps and 34ID had arranged for artillery bombardment on Hills 307 and 473 from 4:10 to 11:30p.m. on April 26. Then the artillery would taper off and cease by 1:30a.m. Communication from battalion to division was to be by wire laid from the battalion command post as it moved forward to the base of Hill 473. But for communication from the companies to battalion, the notoriously unreliable SCR 536 walkie-talkies had to be used. The battalion commander accompanied Company G, the assault force. Silence was to be maintained until contact with the enemy; individual soldiers placed the now-familiar small white rags on the backs of their helmets. Each GI carried extra ammunition and two-thirds of a "C" ration. 168RCT assembled in the rear of Hill 533, where a hot meal was served to the troops.[11]

Guides from the reconnaissance patrol led 2/168 to the line of departure. The GIs moved out at about 11:00p.m., arriving at 1:30a.m. on April 27, just as the last explosions from the planned American artillery barrages erupted on Hill 473. The troops advanced in total darkness from the Béja–Mateur road over extremely hazardous steep slopes covered with loose rocks. The column had become extended, trailing far back into the darkness toward what was now the rear. The battalion commander held the head of the column at the road until the rear had closed in, especially the heavy weapons and ammunition carried by hand by the men of H Company. The commander of 168th Infantry Regiment and the battalion commander inspected Company G and briefed the leaders. By 2:30a.m. the column had closed up at the line of departure, and the battalion now crossed the road and moved toward Hill 473. Company G moved in two parallel columns. Two platoons of riflemen and a machine-gun squad were in the right column, and one platoon of infantry, a machine-gun squad, the 60mm mortar squads and the company headquarters group in the left. The company commander led the right column. A platoon leader led the left column, depending on the right column for direction in the near-total darkness and for maintaining the interval between the columns and between the files in his column.[12]

The advance to the edge of Oued Bou Oissa, some 300 yards over a flat cultivated field, was made without too much difficulty. Upon reaching the river, the two columns found it to be shallow and they crossed over. The ground on the far side of the river toward Hill 473 was rolling and climbing, with numerous eroded ditches running parallel to the direction of the advance. The ditches made control of the line of the attack difficult, and the company commander stopped the right column and directed the left column to move to its right and to join the base column in rear. The march was resumed in a single company column.

Upon learning the reason for the delay and reorganization into a single column, the battalion commander ordered the following companies to adopt a single column formation to avoid getting lost. By 3:30a.m., guided only by repeated compass checks, the assault column halted to allow the rear elements to catch up. The leaders estimated that Company G had advanced about 1,500 yards (about 0.9 mile) from the line of departure. The terrain was now steeper, with treacherously tangled undergrowth. It slowed the stealthy advance, and further drained the stamina of men who had had little or no rest in three days. The diligent battalion commander corrected the column's bearing when it had veered too far to the right (southeast).

At approximately 4:00a.m. the assault troops detected the enemy. They heard the banging of metal and the sound of voices from the left rear and right front of the column just as the first glimmer of dawn shone in the northeast. The dim outlines of German soldiers could be seen about 100 yards to the right front.[13]

The commander of Company G now released his rifle platoons for the attack. He directed the lieutenant leading 1st Platoon to deploy along a draw that extended to the right on a line at an angle to the direction of the company's assault and then to strike. A machine-gun squad followed directly in the rear of 1st Platoon. The sergeant leading 2nd Platoon was directed to deploy to the left along that same draw and to move in the direction of the objective, now outlined by the gray sky to the rear of the hill. But the third platoon was not yet at the release point; the lieutenant commanding 3rd Platoon had not maintained contact with the platoon ahead of his. The 2nd Battalion's commander directed Company G to proceed with only the two assault platoons.[14]

Just as the battalion commander turned to rejoin the rear elements, and as if upon a signal, enemy machine guns to the right front and left rear began firing. The German machine-gun pit on the right was the objective of the 1st Platoon. That gun was firing down a gully on a predetermined protective line which ran parallel to the battalion march route. 1st Platoon made short work of that machine gun. They were about 25 yards from the enemy position, maintaining silence and running very quickly. The GIs heard shouting from the machine-gun pit and almost immediately the sound of the weapon changed. The Red Bull assault had been discovered and the enemy was shifting the machine gun. But it was too late. The GIs had hand grenades for just this occasion and used them copiously. The enemy emplacement rocked from the explosions and the first machine gun was silenced. Meanwhile 2nd Platoon had deployed and was moving to the area from which voices had been heard. When the enemy in 1st Platoon's front began shouting and firing, the enemy facing 2nd Platoon was alerted and fired a second machine gun down another gully, again parallel to the battalion column's path. Two rifle squads and part of a third rifle squad of 2nd Platoon moved far enough to get inside the protective fire from the second enemy machine gun, about 50 yards from the gun pit. But some soldiers of the third squad were caught in the beaten zone and were hit. Some 2nd Platoon soldiers mistook their own grenade explosions for enemy mortar rounds and hit the ground. But others made use of more hand grenades, and after multiple explosions the second machine gun was silenced. Enemy machine guns further to the left of Company G were still firing, but only in occasional bursts, and soon they also ceased firing.[15]

Enemy mortar rounds began falling in the draw to the left. The commander of Company G moved to the left to reorganize 2nd Platoon. He located a few key men and ordered them to gather as many soldiers as they could, and to protect the ridge they now held from attack from the left or front. He then moved to the right and found that 1st Platoon's platoon leader and platoon sergeant were dead, several men were missing, and the survivors were already preparing to defend the ground they had taken. By then a Red Bull machine-gun squad had taken over the enemy emplacement. The company commander directed a squad leader to lead 1st Platoon and to deploy most of his men on the left front of the area to oppose any counterattack. He then returned to 2nd Platoon's position on the left, where the platoon sergeant had assembled a few men and ordered them to dig in. Company G's commander attempted to communicate with his battalion, but the SCR 536 radio was damaged beyond repair. He had to act on his own initiative and so he did, showing exemplary leadership under fire. In the growing light, he could see enough to locate his position. Company G's two platoons were about 400 yards from the crest of Hill 473 and inside the enemy defensive line. The company was taking rifle and machine-gun fire from the higher ground 300 yards to its left front. He stayed with his troops and sent a message to battalion by courier: "Held up. Machine gun fire 400 yards from objective."[16]

The other companies had halted when the assault company engaged the enemy. The battalion commander now determined that a wide flanking move was needed to overcome the resistance. He directed F Company to move to the right of G Company, in the direction from which the enemy fire originated. With no report from G Company, he judged by the noise level of the mortar and rifle fire that it was in trouble. As F Company scrambled to the right over the sharp rocks, the leading men tripped a hidden illumination flare. F Company's column was discovered just as the company commander directed his platoons to deploy and charge toward of the enemy. The Germans lay down rifle fire, and the GIs replied with their own heavy rifle and BAR fire. F Company's commander reported to battalion that his company was "advancing by fire." They kept moving and had reached a point near Sidi Nsir by about 8:45a.m., when an increasing volume of fire from the area of the railroad station slowed their advance to a standstill.[17]

As day broke on April 27, H Company, 2/168, the battalion heavy weapons company, was behind a ridge line near the 2/168's Battalion Command Post when it was ordered to move into action in support of F and G Companies. H Company's heavy machine guns were positioned on ridges in the rear of G Company and aimed at the heights to the left and above G Company's positions. H Company's heavy mortars were emplaced near the Oued Bou Oissa in the rear of F Company's elements fighting near Sidi Nsir. Throughout the day the mortars bombarded Hills 473 and 375, and the area around the railroad station. At 9:30a.m., when the battalion commander determined that Company F was making little progress and that Company G, on the battalion left, was pinned down, he ordered E Company to maneuver around the left onto Hill 375.

2/168's commander coordinated with the regimental command, never losing focus on his orders that the ultimate regimental objective was Hill 375. 1st Battalion's role was to attack Hill 407 and then continue the attack northeasterly against Hill 473. 2/168's commander directed the commander of E Company to lead his company up a draw to the rear of the line now held by the battalion and to occupy the top of Hill 473. It was slow going up the extremely steep draw toward the crest under occasional enemy rifle and machine-gun fire. But by 2:45p.m. the leading platoon of E Company had succeeded in taking the top of Hill 473 and was resolutely moving down the reverse slope toward the enemy positions on Hill 375. After advancing about 300 yards, however, the enemy halted Company E with heavy machine-gun fire from Hill 375 and artillery fire from beyond Hill 342. Nonetheless, E Company's threat to Hill 375 had relieved some of the pressure from G Company, at the base of Hill 473. Enemy fire from Hill 473 ceased, but G Company was still pinned down by fire from the slopes of Hill 375.[18]

With heavy shelling by the artillery, 168IR had attacked from the southeast and obtained a foothold on the southern slopes of Djebel el Hara.[19] It held the southeasterly half of Djebel el Hara but was stopped by continued enemy suppressive fire from Hill 375. The situation on 34th Infantry Division's left remained unchanged until the coming of darkness on April 27 allowed for movement. Then the 2nd Battalion performed a well-choreographed movement in the dark, rivalling a master chess game. The commander of 2nd Battalion, 168IR directed the front-line companies, F and G, to reorganize and to hold in place until that night when those units would move up a draw in the battalion rear and onto the northern side of Hill 473. Company G reformed and consolidated its positions in the area, evacuated its casualties, collected the dead, and prepared to move to Hill 473. Company F also reorganized and prepared to move to Hill 473. During the late afternoon, 1/168 crossed Hill 473 and went into a position from which to attack the regimental objective, Hill 375. 3/168 also moved forward along the reverse side of Hill 473 and prepared for its role in the assault on Hill 375. When 2/168's sister battalions were in position, the commander of 2/168 ordered Companies F and G to join E Company on Hill 473. With guides leading them, the commanders of F and G Companies arrived at the battalion forward command post at daybreak, April 28.[i] The 2nd Battalion was designated the regimental reserve, assigned to hold Hill 473 and to guard the approach to the hill from the north which was now the open left flank of the regiment and of 34ID. E Company occupied the nose of Hill 473 to enable it to place fire on Hill 375 in support of 3/168. G Company moved to the left (north) of Hill 473 to protect the open flank. F Company moved into the draw and sent out patrols around Hill 369.[20]

On the 34th Infantry Division's right flank, meanwhile, 135RCT was now ordered to support the 1st Infantry Division by attacking Hill 609 from the direction of Kef el Guebli and Hill 529.[21] Company A, 1/135 had reached its objective on Kef el Guebli but was immediately taken under heavy fire from enemy mortars, artillery, and machine guns. The GIs were wounded and killed by shrapnel and small-arms fire and by the concussive effect of exploding shells. Captain Landon told Lieutenant Colonel Miller by phone that the shock waves of enemy shells were amplified between the hill sides and that one of his men had "gone crazy." During the afternoon and evening of April 27 Companies B and C, 1/135, moved from Hill 501 to Hill

---

i   After the war, Bradley wrote that on the evening of April 27, an unspecified battalion of 34ID made a night attack on Djebel el Hara (Hill 473). According to the general's recollection, the battalion had "attempted an enveloping movement in the dark over a route that could not be reconnoitered by daylight." When morning came on April 28, Bradley claims, the battalion was so badly disoriented that it "found itself storming the hill from which it had moved out the night before." Bradley's account is not supported by the official Army history or the recollections of officers on the ground. See Bradley, Soldier's Story, 85.

529. Some 81mm mortars and heavy machine guns were positioned on Hill 530 southwest of the road. The GIs emplaced another set of machine guns on Hill 529.[22]

During the day on Tuesday, April 27, Lieutenant General Anderson, commanding British First Army, proposed that Bradley simply ignore Hill 609. Bradley was appalled by the suggestion and privately concluded that Anderson was "in over his head as an army commander." In a hastily arranged meeting that afternoon at Major General Allen's 1ID command post, Bradley, as was his way, clipped his map to another easel and explained the real-time battle situation as he saw it. 1.) The 1st Infantry Division had made enough progress to have exposed its left flank just a couple of miles southwest of Hill 609. 2.) German gunners on Hill 609 and other hill forts were placing accurate enfilading fire on 1ID troops. 3.) The 1st Infantry Division was more than 2,000 men understrength, including a shortfall of 60 officers. 4.) 1ID lacked the combat power to push against five enemy battalions on its front without risking a catastrophic counterattack from Hill 609 that would roll up its left flank. 5.) Finally, to ignore Hill 609 would mean returning to the vulnerable valleys, where, as Atkinson expresses it, the GIs would again draw fire from every *Gefreiter* with a mortar tube. "All this depends on our taking Hill 609," Bradley concluded.[23] By "all this" Bradley meant not only the present efforts of II Corps to take 609 but also the outcome of the Tunisian campaign and quite likely of the war.

> If Anderson meant what he said, he was ordering us to call off our attacks down the spine of the hills and crawl instead through the valleys where the enemy had zeroed in every plausible route of approach. Unless the enemy was already withdrawing from our II Corps front, we could not ignore those positions in the hills without running pell mell into the mouths of his guns.[24]

Two days of attacks by two battalions of the 135RCT with artillery support had failed as yet to take Hill 490 on the north and Hill 531 on the south. Both assaults on the night of April 26–27 and through April 27 were unsuccessful. The assault battalions gained footholds but failed to take their objectives.[25] The attacks by 168RCT to take Djebel el Hara and Hill 375 also fell short, despite artillery support and unwavering fighting by the Americans. But the GIs of 34ID never stopped fighting. They held the ground they could, retired out of the enemy's fire when necessary, evacuated their wounded, collected their dead, and prepared again to renew their multipronged attacks. The Red Bull soldiers did what they had to do.

Wednesday, April 28, 1943

The night attack by 2/168 had failed to capture all of Hill 375, but the assault companies had penetrated the enemy's main line of resistance and disrupted the defense of the hill. A fresh attack early on April 28 by 1/168 and 3/168 drove the enemy from Hill 375, the anchor of the German right flank in the Hill 609 complex.

By about 6:00a.m. on April 28, 168RCT at last occupied and secured Hill 375. In the afternoon of April 28, 2/168's brief respite as regimental reserve on Hill 473 ended abruptly when its commander received orders attaching 2/168 to the 133rd Infantry Regiment as reinforcement for an assault on the formidable Hill 609 itself.[26]

Meanwhile, 2/135's renewed attack on Hill 490 was slowed by the terrain and darkness until early in the morning of April 28. The push began at 4:15a.m. but immediately ran into trouble. Approaching its line of departure at 5:00a.m., 2/135 encountered murderous machine-gun and artillery fire. There was a fierce rifle firefight, with heavy casualties on both sides. The enemy launched a strong counterattack at 9:50a.m., but this time the GIs were supported by machine guns and mortars and prevailed. During the attack on Hill 490 Captain Vincent F. Goodsell of Company G, 2/135, saw German infantry with machine guns moving into a position from which 3rd Battalion would be enfiladed. He personally led three of his men forward to intercept and destroy the enemy. The Germans spotted Goodsell's group and fired machine guns at the GIs, but Goodsell drove home his attack. He and his men killed or captured the entire enemy group and took their three machine guns.[ii][27]

It took the rest of the day for the 2nd Battalion, 135RCT to knock out enemy machine-gun nests and eliminate the remaining enemy in its sector on Hill 490. The consequence was that 2/135 was not able to execute the planned attack toward Hill 609 on that day. Company L, 3/135 advanced and set up defensive positions atop Hill 435, drawing only spasmodic rifle fire. But Company I and the supporting Company K encountered more wire obstacles and booby traps below the crest of Hill 490. Engineers were sent forward to clear a path with bangalore torpedoes and dynamite. The assault troops fixed bayonets as Companies K and I then proceeded to the top of the hill. But the enemy there was also withdrawing. As the assault platoons moved up the paths, the GIs observed enemy outpost troops in the open. The Germans turned and ran when the assault elements reached a point about 75 yards from Hill 490's crest.[28]

3/135 at once consolidated its new location and prepared for counterattacks, which duly followed. As Companies I and K reorganized themselves for defense on Hill 490, the Germans attempted the expected counterattack on the 3rd Battalion's front at 10:50a.m. Companies I and K repulsed the enemy by massed rifle and BAR fire and clouds of hand grenades. Later in the morning a second enemy counterattack was similarly repulsed. By 3:00p.m. 135RCT had complete control of both Hills 435 and 490.[29] But the GIs on Hill 490 retained their hastily dug positions under continuing enemy mortar and artillery fire. The Germans attempted weak counterstrikes against Hill 490 at 4:00p.m. and 7:00p.m. which the GIs promptly squelched as well.[30] By mid-afternoon on April 28 Hills 435 and 490 belonged to

---

ii   Goodsell later was awarded the Distinguished Service Cross.

the Americans and 135RCT controlled the ground between Sidi Nsir and Hill 609 and an approach to the citadel.[31]

An additional battalion had been required, two attacks had failed with heavy casualties, and four German counterattacks had to be quelled, but by mid-day on that Wednesday, April 28, Hills 435 and 490 were in American hands. Now the 34th Infantry Division held ground over which it prepared to strike directly the exposed northwestern corner of Hill 609. "All day the valley rumbled with artillery fire; the crack of shells splitting rock carried from the hilltops. Hundreds of men fell sick in apparent reaction to Atabrine, a synthetic antimalaria drug. Weak and nauseated, they vomited down the front of their uniforms and fouled their trousers with uncontrollable diarrhea before rising on command in Thursday's wee hours to stumble forward again."[32] The Red Bull soldiers extended their control over the upper slopes of the large hill mass west of Hill 609 northwestward onto the Hill 435 shoulder.[33]

"Unshirted Hell"

In modern war, characterized by almost constant action in an environment of flying hot metal and other deadly dangers, there are few if any chances to celebrate victories or to appreciate progress made until after all the fighting is over. Such was the case with the developing battle in the hill fort complex and the deliberate pace of 34th Infantry Division's progress. Major General Allen, CG, 1ID, beloved by his own troops, complained bitterly that his 16th Infantry Regiment was catching "unshirted hell" in artillery and mortar salvos fired and directed from Hill 609. At 2:00p.m. on April 28, Allen ordered all three 1st Infantry Division regiments to halt and shelter in place until the 34th Infantry Division could better protect his left flank by capturing Hill 609.[34] In a phone call to Ryder, Allen asked how much longer the 34th Infantry Division needed to capture Hill "606." "Don't you mean Hill 609?" Ryder replied. "No, I mean Hill 606. My division artillery has put enough fire on that hill to knock it down three meters."[35]

Ryder then ordered 1/135 to demonstrate toward Hill 609 by movement and fire in support of an attack by 1ID elements to the northeast from Hill 529. The 1st Battalion was then to push over Hill 529 and attack Hill 531. North of Hill 609, 3/135 was fighting to capture Hill 461. At dusk, the 3rd Battalion of the 133rd Infantry Regiment was attached to 135IR and took over the defense of Hills 435 and 490.

The 1st Battalion, 135th Infantry Regiment at Hills 529 and 531 had a hard fight. Every American movement was immediately observed from one of the heights in enemy possession and deluged with prepared artillery fires. A striking force might crawl its way up a slope and reach the summit, only to be pinned down by heavy machine-gun fire from adjacent hills and pounded by enemy artillery air bursts. The enemy used a reverse slope defense, firing automatic weapons in quick bursts, then moving to cover, and dropping mortar and howitzer fire into draws and gulches through which attacking troops had to move. The routes of approach were always thickly mined. After gaining a summit, Red Bull soldiers who survived the prepared enemy fire from hidden weapons expected ferocious counterattacks. The GIs now knew the resilient Germans were exceptionally good at counterattacks and that the Americans had to be extraordinarily quick about preparing defensive positions to repel them.

At Hill 529, the 1st Battalion, 135th Infantry Regiment had temporarily driven the enemy off the top before noon, April 27, but Hill 531 remained out of reach on April 28 because of the damage the Nazis could still inflict from adjacent positions and from indirect enemy fire guided from their front-row seats on the higher hills.[36] The enemy troops still on Hill 531 delivered flanking fire both to the east on the 16th Infantry Regiment as it attacked toward Hill 523 and northwestward over the open area between Hill 490 and Hill 609 over which 3/135 had to advance. While Hill 531 appeared on a map much like any other Tunisian djebel, the development of the battle clearly reinforced Ryder's assessment that Hill 531was the key to the 1st Infantry Division's seizure of Hills 523 and 545, northeast of it, and to the success of the 34th Infantry Division's assaults on Hill 609 from the south and west.[37] The Red Bull soldiers simply had to take Hill 531. That task fell to the 1st Battalion, 135th Infantry Regiment.

As 1/135 advanced toward Hill 531 by fire, Companies A and C made several unsuccessful attempts to seize it. The 1st Battalion's 81mm mortars and machine guns operated in battery, providing flexible concentrations of fires on both Hill 531 and Hill 609. The American fire reached the reverse slopes of Hill 531 and a rocky knob just south of Hill 609's base, inflicting casualties and successfully disrupting the enemy's suppressive fires and counterattacks. First Lieutenant Brandt recalled later that "the mortars had a field day." 1st Battalion's mortar fire destroyed several observation posts on Hill 609 as well as several machine guns and artillery tubes. Mortar ammunition was supplied by jeep over a trail south and east of Hill 530. As Bradley had predicted, the battle took time and patience, but the GIs were making progress, and by nightfall on April 28, 1/135 controlled all of Hill 529 and Kef el Guebli, and had Hill 531 under constant fire.[38]

The inability of the 34th Infantry Division to occupy the stony Hill 609 citadel on April 28 frustrated once more the 1st Infantry Division, which on April 28 made costly attacks toward Hills 523 and 545. Those heights masked the enemy's line of supply and principal route of reinforcement. But Major General Ryder and his Red Bull soldiers persevered early on April 29 with his plan to take Hill 609 by envelopment of the mountain and its supporting forts from the north, west, and south. He ordered three coordinated attacks to be made by the three battalions of the 135th Infantry Regiment. The reinforced 3rd Battalion, 135IR had already captured

Hill 490 and the hill was secured by 3/133. 3/135 was to reorganize and replenish its ammunition on Hill 490, then advance southeasterly to clear the enemy from Hills 367 and 434, and then assault behind a rolling barrage on to the southwest slopes of Hill 609. The 2nd Battalion was to complete its mission of the previous day to capture Hill 461 north of Hill 609, then attack south toward Hill 609's northern slopes. The 1st Battalion was at last to eliminate the enemy from the Hill 531 fortress and then move east across the southern slopes of Hill 609 to capture Hill 455. All operations were to begin at 2:00a.m., April 29. Ryder directed all three battalions in the assault to strike simultaneously, believing that the defenders would be confounded by at least one of them.[39]

Thursday, April 29, 1943: "The Angry Chatter of a Machine Gun"

During the night of April 28–29, 1/135 attempted the seizure of Hill 531 against terrific opposition from the objective and from Hills 609 and 455. The soldiers made practically no progress and by morning on April 29, they were exhausted, beaten, and short of rations and ammunition. Most of the battalion's remaining manpower was needed just to resupply ammunition.[40]

The bone-tired 34ID GIs were not able fully to execute Ryder's plan on April 29. 2/135 and 3/135 on 1st Battalion's left had captured Hills 435 and 490 on April 28, so the enemy could no longer use those heights to place enfilade fire on Hill 531 and adjacent hills. But on the northern flank, 2nd Battalion, 135th Infantry Regiment ran into lethal resistance from Hill 461, while receiving enfilading fire from positions on Hill 537 and from the draw between Hill 435 and Hill 461 where enemy troops had infiltrated during the night of April 28–29. The enfilading fire struck the western flank of 2/135, already eroded by the bitter fighting of the previous day. 2/135 was pinned down short of Hill 461, unable to reach its objective, halting the planned northern envelopment before it really got started.

At 5:00a.m. on Thursday, April 29, Major Hall's 3rd Battalion, 135th Infantry Regiment, attacked from the base of Hill 490 toward the southwestern quarter of Hill 609 and advanced to the base across the intervening ground behind a rolling barrage as planned. Company K was in reserve in a gully extending southwesterly from Hill 609 along the base of Hill 490. Companies I and K moved forward. Company L was on the left moving almost easterly from Hill 490 toward the base of Hill 609.[41]

> Fog muffled every footstep as the 3/135 advanced 2,000 yards from Hill 490 to El Kadra, an Arab hamlet beneath the south wall of 609. Watching at first light, [the American journalist] Drew Middleton reported that he could trace "the path of these soldiers through the wheat just as you could follow the path of Pickett's charge through the summer wheat at Gettysburg."[42]

The infantrymen pushed ahead about 400 yards until the assault was stopped by the enemy's small-arms and machine-gun fire. Applying the division's recent training in coordinated artillery support, Hall called for another rolling artillery barrage to cover his troops. He ordered Companies I and K to attack at 10:30a.m. behind the barrage. Communication was by runners, like those from the Western Front of World War I, so the advance of the companies was not well coordinated. Company L received the order, but Company I did not receive it until 11:30a.m., and the assault companies lost contact with each other. Company L, with only 36 riflemen, less than a single platoon, attacked by itself at 10:30a.m. behind the rolling barrage. They gained about 300 additional yards into the enemy's positions against machine-gun fire. Meanwhile, 2/135's problems at Hill 461 made 3/135's flank vulnerable. When the American barrage stopped, the enemy fired into that vulnerability with small arms, machine guns, and mortar fire. "Muzzle flashes erupted across the face of 609 like 'tiny sparks, and the wind brought us the angry chatter of a machine gun,' Middleton noted. In disarray, the [3rd] battalion retreated 400 yards from the village to shelter in the olives."[43] Company L, which suffered another 11 casualties and was low on ammunition, withdrew with the battalion to reorganize.[44]

> Fleas from village huts so tormented some men that they stripped to their shoes, helmet, and ammunition belts, then dunked their infested uniforms in gasoline. Hundreds of shells crashed across the crest of Hill 609—"it resembles an erupting volcano," one soldier said—but the Germans held fast and the American momentum ebbed.[45]

3/135 immediately reorganized amid rocky outcrops along a low rise and started a second attack with fresh artillery support. That assault pushed part way up the slope of Hill 609 to the shelf at the base of the cliff, where the GIs could take cover from enemy riflemen and machine gunners firing from the buildings of the Arab village west of Hill 609. The indomitable few of Company L, 3/135, with only 25 effectives, engaged in close-quarters and hand-to-hand combat, using grenades, bayonets, and fists. By 4:00p.m. the fleabitten, dehydrated heroes of Company L retook the ground from which they had been driven and were again in occupation of the foot of Hill 609's southwestern escarpment.[46] But as night fell, Major Hall did not yet have full control of all his units.

On 34ID's southern (right) flank, the 1st Battalion, 135th Infantry Regiment continued its battle during the day on April 29 but could not get a firm hold at any point on Hill 531. An attack on the right was thrown back when the Nazi defenders dropped bundles of stick grenades on the GIs scaling the cliffs. The battalion's 81mm mortars were displaced to Hill 529, south of Kef el Guebli, from which they destroyed two enemy artillery positions on Hill 531 straightaway. The heavy weapons company also moved its machine guns to Hill 529 to provide suppressive fire. The shift of the heavy weapons was timely; within hours after the GIs and their weapons had moved, the enemy fired heavy concentrations of artillery at their former location. During the afternoon fighting, soldiers of Company A, 1/135, observed enemy movement in a cactus patch between Hills 531 and 609 but enemy fire prevented them from getting in positions from which to attack the enemy with small arms. The liaison corporal from Company D suggested using mortars to blast the assembling enemy, and then personally reported the tactical situation to the mortar platoon on Hill 529. The mortar battery bombarded the area, flushing the enemy into the open where American machine guns and riflemen picked them off one by one.[47] But then darkness fell, and the 1st Battalion withdrew toward Hill 529, leaving the enemy still in full possession of Hills 531 and 609.[48]

"Man cannot tell but Allah knows how much the other side was hurt!"

From Bradley's perspective at II Corps the attacks against the hill fort complex of the Tine river valley reached a critical point on April 29. Casualty numbers in the 34th and 1st Infantry Divisions were appalling: 183 were dead, 1,594 were wounded, and 676 were captured or missing in action.[49] 1st Infantry Division's battered units were still flagellated by fire from their left flanks as well as their fronts. The 16th Infantry Regiment, 1ID had incurred heavy casualties trying to reach Hill 523. The 26th Infantry Regiment, 1ID, fighting to occupy Djebel el Anz (289m), drew flanking fire from Hills 523 and 545 northwest of it. An American attack to seize Hills 523 and 545 before destroying the enemy on Hill 609 would be much too costly, if not wholly infeasible. Those hills, although farther from Hill 609, were as exposed to enemy fire from the citadel as Hill 531 was.

On the other hand, the Germans also had been badly hurt. The enemy had lost 408 prisoners and numerous dead and wounded. The *Barenthins* were weakening under the incessant pressure of greater American forces. German reinforcements and supplies were now under American observation and interdicting fire. The enemy's rations and ammunition were running critically low, and its troops were under severe strain, resorting to battlefield improvisations just to stay in the fight. Considering operations from Hill 609 to the Tine river valley as a whole, Bradley decided to keep pushing everywhere rather than to concentrate on some key objective as a method of winning the battle.[50]

> Seldom has an enemy contested a position more bitterly than did the German high on Hill 609. For he knew that once the rampart fell, he had no choice but to withdraw to the east and thus open a path to Mateur on the flank of his Tunis line.[51]

Battle attrition was working to the Americans' advantage. Bradley calculated that if the enemy failed to hold the Hill 609 complex, their enormous expenditure of men and supplies there and the tactical disadvantages that must result from abandoning the hill forts would render the Germans unable to hold the areas farther to the northeast. The Herculean American fight to remove a difficult obstacle to the U.S. offensive was also an opportunity to achieve the primary military objective of completely destroying the enemy's combat power.[52] Bradley's attitude about the inevitable and terrible American losses was coolly professional. Combat soldiers "were nothing more than tools to be used in the accomplishment of the mission," he wrote in his memoir. To many, Bradley's thinking is callous, even contemptible. He was driven perhaps by his own experiences of heartbreak. The way to survive the contemplation of so many deaths at his orders was to maintain a cold professional distance from the troops he sent into battle and to focus on saving as many lives as he could by ending the war as soon as humanly possible. "War has neither the time or heart to concern itself with the individual and the dignity of man."[53] Bradley told Ernie Pyle how he was able to make those bloody life-and-death decisions. "I have spent thirty years preparing a frame of mind for accepting such a thing."[54]

Despite skepticism from his armored commanders—"No one in his right mind would consider putting tanks in mountains," one colonel warned—Bradley decided now was the time for a combined arms attack with tanks. He ordered Ryder to use a company of tanks in support of his infantry in an attack along the western slope of Hill 609 at dawn on April 30.[55]

> When Ryder spoke to me of the possibility of flanking [Hill 609] from the rear, I offered him a company of tanks for mobile artillery support. He looked at me with mild surprise but readily accepted the help. The terrain certainly was not adapted to tanks, and no tactician would have recommended storming a cliff with Shermans. Yet their 75s were just what Ryder needed to blast the enemy out of those strong points.[56]

Ryder took the afternoon of April 29 to plan the attack with tank reinforcements to be carried out that night and early the next day. A company of medium tanks drawn from 1st Armored Division and a fresh infantry battalion, the 1st Battalion, 133rd Infantry, was attached to 135IR, Colonel Ward commanding. The tanks and infantry would make a combined arms attack advancing from a point 800 yards southwest of Hill 490 in the predawn hours of April 30. They were to assault in a northerly direction, crushing remaining resistance at the base of Hill 609, with the objective of gaining a foothold on the northwestern slopes of Hill 609 for later infantry exploitation. Captain Robert D. Gwin, commanding Company I, 1st Armored Regiment, 1AD, made his own reconnaissance before darkness and devised a detailed tactical plan. He coordinated with the infantry and artillery and received Major General Ryder's approval at the daily divisional command conference within sight of the area to be attacked.[57]

While 1/135 was still fighting without success to clear the northwesterly part of Hill 531, elements of 1ID were attempting to seize the southern part of the hill, also without success. Major General Allen, commanding 1ID, ordered an attack during the night of April 29–30 by the 16th Infantry Regiment with the objective of finally clearing and holding Hill 523. Colonel George A. Taylor, commanding 16IR, knew that Hill 545, the next crest directly east of 523, also had to be taken to prevent the enemy from using his troops on 523 for target practice. He devised a plan for the 1st Battalion, 16IR, Lieutenant Colonel Charles J. Denholm, commanding, to cross the open area south of Hill 523 in darkness and seize its crest before daylight, while the 3rd Battalion would clear the southern sector of Hill 531 by pushing north toward the reverse slope where the enemy was entrenched. The 2nd Battalion, 16th Infantry Regiment, was to assault and capture Hill 545 at the earliest opportunity.[58] Taylor's orders were executed on April 29–30 while the 1st Battalion, 135th Infantry Regiment, fought for its third straight day of combat to clear the northwestern slopes of Hill 531.

The 1st Battalion, 16th Infantry Regiment, bypassed Hill 531 early on the evening of April 29, moving south of it, and skirting Hill 455 to make a night attack on Hill 523. But the attack on Hill 523 by 1/16 ended in disaster. The 1st Battalion was able to reach and capture Hill 523 by 4:45a.m. on April 30, but as dawn broke, the enemy mounted a strong counterattack, enveloping the hill from the north and south. German reinforcements surrounded the hill and ferociously attacked at close range. The fight was hand to hand with knives and grenades, resulting in heavy American casualties, the capture of many men including Lieutenant Colonel Denholm, and the loss of the ground. In the next 24 hours, Hill 523 would change hands three more times.[59]

CHAPTER 33

Breaching the Citadel

Friday, April 30, 1943: "We Must Succeed or Die Trying"

Major Hall and his 3rd Battalion, 135th Infantry Regiment, moved during the night of April 29–30 to a position directly southwest of Hill 609. Company M moved to the left of Company L. 1st Battalion, 133rd Infantry Regiment, Lieutenant Colonel Marshall now commanding, was attached to 135RCT. At 5:00p.m. Ward ordered 3/133 to move to an assembly area on the southeastern slope of Hill 490 late in the evening of April 29, and to prepare for the attack with armor support from Company I, 3/1AR, 1AD, under Captain Gwin, also attached to 135RCT. The objective of the armor-infantry attack was to take and hold the northwesterly slopes of Hill 609. 1/133 assembled and began its approach movement at 9:30p.m. on April 29. The battalion moved under cover of darkness, troops on foot and weapons on motor transport.[1]

Ward did not rely on telephone or radio for his final attack orders; he had written orders delivered to Lieutenant Colonel Marshall personally. Ward directed 1/133, with the support of and in close cooperation with Gwin's tank company, to attack first in a northeasterly direction, destroying all enemy forces in the path of the advance, and then to pivot to the southeast to capture and hold the northwest slopes of Hill 609, advancing from the line of departure at 5:00a.m. on April 30. 1/133 and Company I, 3/1AR stood ready in their assembly area at 4:00a.m. on April 30. But many of the officers and men of 1/133 were ill, in part from physical exhaustion but like many others in 34ID chiefly from the anti-malarial drug Atabrine. The GIs were allowed to sleep while the infantry and armor officers made further local reconnaissance and coordinated their plans.[2]

On Friday, April 30, Ryder's 34th Infantry Division's battalions moved in concert to carry out Ryder's plan to completely encircle Hill 609 and to destroy the enemy around its base. 1st Battalion, 133rd Infantry Regiment attacked to the northeast and the southeast toward the northern side of Hill 609 supported by Gwin's tanks while 1/135 cleared Hill 531. Red Bull infantrymen would reach the summits of Hills 609 and 531, while Allen's tenacious 1ID troops would retake, lose, and then recapture and finally hold Hill 523 against determined enemy resistance and counterattacks. The danger was great, and some of those hills proved costlier than others.[3]

"God bless you all"

The 34th Infantry Division placed four battalions in a circle around the Hill 609 and, supported by Gwin's Company I, 1AR and by the heaviest artillery fire the division could muster, the final assaults began. "The bravery and discipline shown at Fondouk were now reinforced by the wisdom taught during the training period at Maktar and the infantry made encouraging progress."[4] The recent applied study and practical training in armor-infantry coordination paid dividends.

> … 17 tanks with Ryder's infantry on their tails moved up to Hill 609 from the flank and rear. They rumbled through machine gun and mortar fire until they sighted the enemy strong points, and soon the hill echoed with their guns as they slammed shell after shell into the enemy's positions.[5]

The early morning attack to reach the northwestern slopes of Hill 609 by Lieutenant Colonel Marshall's 1st Battalion, 133rd Infantry Regiment, and Captain Gwin's Company I, 1st Armored Regiment, succeeded admirably. The combined arms force jumped off at 5:15a.m. and progressed rapidly. Gwin's Shermans rolled northeasterly along the northwest slope of Hill 609 at dawn. Infantrymen of 1/133 trailed behind, some grabbing the skirt of a tank with one hand while firing their rifles with the other. "God bless all of you," a company commander of the 1/133 told his men. "We must succeed or die trying." Within two hours, the tanks and the infantry had covered almost a mile, machine guns rattling and main guns roaring. The dusty air reeked of gun propellant and the cacophony of combat, throbbing with gunfire, savage yells, and heart-rending cries for help.[6]

Bradley had been right. This was exactly the infantry support mission for which the early model M4 Shermans had been designed. In the terrain between the hills, the infantry identified the targets and the tanks effectively destroyed them with main guns and machine guns. The troops of 1/133 cooperated constantly with the tanks, directing tank fire against the enemy positions. Company A on the right and Company B on the left led the assault, with Company C following in reserve, and Company D [weapons] supporting. 1/133 troops and Company I's tanks advanced roughly northeast about 600 yards and then, as ordered, turned to the southeast toward the battalion's objective on the northwest slope of Hill 609. 1/133 cleaned out enemy gun positions on the intervening ground with tank-gun fire and a series of vicious rifle and grenade fights. The German defenders knocked out four of the tanks (two of which were recoverable) but the surviving tanks kept coming, rolling over the saddle between Hill 490 and Hill 609 to annihilate the remaining enemy.[7]

There was no hesitation on the part of the Red Bull soldiers now. The Americans fought with every ounce of strength, courage, and determination they had. By 6:45a.m., 1st Battalion, 133rd Infantry Regiment had completed the seizure of its first objective. Company A, 1/133, advanced against the foothills below Hill 609 to hunt the enemy there, cleaning out German positions at the base of the rocky precipice. It then pivoted to secure the northwest slope. The right flank assault platoon struck directly over the foothills, taking the Germans there by surprise from the flank and preventing enfilade fire from positions on the reverse slopes.[8] They took 21 German prisoners. Company B on the left had further to go but advanced rapidly to its objective and dug in.

Throughout the assault, the mortar platoon of Company D, 1/133 vigorously employed its weapons to protect and support the assault troops. After the objective had been taken, the mortar platoon skillfully displaced and reemplaced on the northwest slopes of Hill 609, moving to locations from which it was able to deliver high-trajectory fire to the top of Hill 609, smashing the enemy's citadel. Two heavy weapons platoons deployed machine guns on the right flank of 1/133 and provided powerful suppressing fire. At 9:00a.m. 1/133 and Company I, 1AR had reached their main objective.

2nd Battalion, 135th Infantry Regiment, pushed forward on the left at the same time and took possession of both Hill 389 and the tactically important Hill 461 north of Hill 609. From Hill 461 2/135 fanned out to the south and by 11:00a.m. had reached and connected with Marshall's battalion and Gwin's tanks, on 1/133's left on the northwestern slopes of Hill 609. With the 2/135 on Hill 461, and 1/133 on the north and northwest slopes of Hill 609, the two battalions communicated and coordinated the defense of Hill 461 to repel any enemy counterattack.[9]

At 6:00a.m., Hall's reinforced 3/135, simultaneously with 1/133's attack with tank support, surged forward, hunting German machine-gun emplacements and killing enemy snipers throughout the day as they bashed toward the southwestern side of Hill 609.

As the coordinated attacks to the north developed, Lieutenant Colonel Miller's 1st Battalion, 135th Infantry Regiment was heavily engaged in the final attack on Hill 531. By the morning of April 30, the locations of units of 1/135 had not changed appreciably. Company A still held its positions on Kef el Guebli with a heavy machine-gun platoon. Company B was on the reverse slopes of Hill 529. Company C was precariously perched on Hill 529 and a piece of Hill 531. The 81mm mortar platoon and a heavy machine-gun section were on Hill 529. Another heavy machine-gun section was emplaced on Kef el Guebli. Miller now ordered the 37mm AT gun platoon to place its weapons on the Sidi Nsir–Chouïgui road south of Hill 529 to protect 1st Battalion's right flank with flat-trajectory fire. Enemy machine-gun fire still swept the tops of the hills, and enemy mortars and artillery covered avenues of approach and interdicted the slopes held by the battalion.[10]

1st Battalion, 135IR attacked at 2:30a.m., April 30, to clear the enemy from Hill 531. The Germans fought desperately to maintain control of the southern approaches to Hill 609. 1/135's initial attack failed under torrential fire from Hills 455 and 523, but with incredible fortitude the soldiers of the battalion then repulsed repeated enemy counterattacks, making first-rate use of well-directed artillery fires. At 11:45a.m. Lieutenant Colonel Miller received orders for his battalion to make a renewed attack at 12:30p.m., this time synchronized with renewed assaults across the entire II Corps front. 1/135 was to seize Hill 531. Once on the primary objective the battalion was to outpost the ground and defend Hill 531, then push out combat patrols against the Roman Ruins and Hill 455 south of Hill 609. The attack was to be preceded by a ten-minute artillery and smoke concentration on Hill 531. Meanwhile, 1/133 was continuing its attack, supported by tanks, against the northwestern slopes of Hill 609. 1ID was also to make a combined arms attack in its sector.[11]

Miller realized he needed additional time to coordinate with his company commanders and to arrange for continuous communications and supply during the fight. He requested and received permission to delay 1st Battalion's attack for half an hour until 1:00p.m. In that brief interval, he directed each company to lay wire from their existing lines, which were already tied into the battalion CP and back to the rear. The network consisted of many sound-powered field telephones, connected to switchboards at command posts in what amounted to an overloaded party line. Company commanders and the battalion commander could all hear one another, monitor progress, and give orders, direct fires, or fulfill a request for resupply. Miller's plan for 1/135 was to have Company A move up the trail between Hill 529 and the adjacent Kef el Guebli, pass in front of Kef el Guebli under cover of smoke and capture the northeast part of Hill 531. Company C would move up the low ground in the center and up the side of Hill 531 to take the southeast part of the hill. Once the GIs had possession of Hill 531, both companies were to push out patrols to the Roman Ruins near the southern foot of Hill 609 and to Hill 455. Company B moved to the positions vacated by Company A to support the assaulting companies by suppressive fire and to repulse any counterattack. Company D [weapons company] continued to provide fire support for the assault from its emplacements. The 81mm mortars would supplement the artillery and smoke and continue to provide fire support when the artillery stopped.[12] 1st Battalion was now ready to take Hill 531.

Just as the assault was to begin, the enemy tried to preempt it with a strong counterattack by a large force. Lieutenant Colonel Miller observed the enemy assembling and took control. He ordered 1st Battalion to advance and keep fighting. He called in fire support from both 34ID and 1ID, as well as the 135RCT's regimental cannon company and the battalion's 81mm mortars. 1/135 had five 81mm mortars; three carried out the fire plan for the battalion's attack while two fired on the enemy concentration. The artillery was remarkably effective, the German counterattack collapsed, and the GIs saw the few remaining enemy soldiers running away.[13]

Covered by the artillery preparation and chemical smoke, and by mortar and overhead machine-gun fire from Hill 529, Company A, 1/135, worked up the northwestern bulge of Hill 531 while Company C, 1/135, fought their way up the southern slopes. The flank attacks were necessary because the hill rose in steep, tiered cliffs and escarpments at its ends, presenting a natural topographic barrier between the American companies.[14] The area between Hill 529 and Hill 531, including the cart track between the hills, was covered by enemy machine-gun fire. As the attack moved out, some short artillery rounds exploded in Company C's area and the troops went to ground. Lieutenant Colonel Miller rushed forward and urged Company C onward.

After moving a short distance Company C was again pinned to the ground by machine-gun and sniper fire, but Company C's weapons platoon and the heavy machine guns from Company D immediately engaged the targets. Observers on Hill 529 could see the enemy on a narrow shelf, but mortar fire could not reach them because of the shape of the hill. The commander of Company D, listening on the phone net, realized the tactical problem and ordered his 37mm AT guns to move to positions on Hill 529 from which to engage the enemy with direct, flat-trajectory fire. With the enhanced firepower, Company C managed to move slowly through hellish fire to the top of the southern half of 531, but the company found it impossible to continue into the depression in the center of the hill mass. As they crept up to the crest, they were hit by fire from the direction of the Roman Ruins and by small counterattacks by the Germans still on Hill 531, supported by enemy fire from the reverse (eastern) slope of the hill. The GIs stood their ground and beat off the counterattacks before carefully advancing.[15]

Meanwhile, Company A, 1/135 had moved quickly through the draw between Hill 529 and Kef el Guebli under cover of smoke, artillery, mortar, and heavy machine-gun fire. As planned, Company A's weapons platoon delivered supporting fire from Kef el Guebli. The battalion's 81mm battery kept up fire on Hill 531 after the artillery ceased firing. The heavy machine guns on Hill 529 provided close overhead suppressive fire on the objective as Company A moved to the assault. When the terrain masked the advancing GIs, the American machine guns elevated their fire just above the heads of the enemy, enabling Company A to move in for the kill. The hypersonic crack of bullets had the desired effect of confusing and disconcerting the enemy. Company A's 1st Platoon with a 60mm mortar continued toward the rocky knob south of Hill 609. 3rd Platoon, Company A valiantly stormed Hill 531, with every man firing as they followed the supporting fires. The mighty assault achieved the crest when it was stopped cold by a storm of stick grenades and by artillery and machine-gun fire still coming from the Roman Ruins.[16]

Company A's hand-grenade supply was exhausted. Apart from a few non-commissioned officers, the entire 2nd Platoon was in the rear carrying ammunition for the 4th [heavy weapons] Platoon. Captain Landon, CO, Company A, ordered five NCOs and some of the ammunition bearers into the fight with a fresh supply of ammunition and directed his weapons platoon to bring their light machine guns to the ground won on Hill 531. He also requested mortar fire on a field piece and a machine-gun emplacement on the Roman Ruins, from which the enemy was firing on the north slope of Hill 531. Company D [heavy weapons] did not have direct observation of the targets. Landon had to describe the target locations from visual observation and then Company D's commander located the enemy positions on a map. The initial round fell only 150 feet over and Landon adjusted the fires by radio relay. The next rounds were accurate and devastating. The targets were destroyed with less than 15 rounds.[17]

Company A, 1/135 then continued its assault into the enemy position on Hill 531. In close and violent fighting Company A at last took the northeast part of Hill 531. The remaining enemy troops retreated hurriedly down the eastern side and over the flat ground toward the Roman Ruins. 1st Platoon, Company A was only about 200 yards short of the objective. Company A alerted their counterparts of 3/135, on the left flank, who spotted and fired on the running enemy with rifles, BARs, and a section of heavy machine guns. None of the fleeing enemy reached the Roman Ruins.[18]

After the enemy artillery and machine-gun emplacements on the Roman Ruins had been destroyed, Company C, 1/135 under Captain Fanning moved further up the southern side of Hill 531. There was still a robust little pocket of enemy resistance about 35 yards wide between Company C and Company A. The terrain at the top of Hill 531 was scored with deep crevices and huge boulders that made it necessary for the GIs to clear every shadowy space. American observers on Hill 529 could see some enemy still on Hill 531 between the assault companies, but the GIs on Hill 531 were too close to the enemy to use mortars. Even rifle grenades might cause friendly casualties and it was not possible to move a 37mm gun into position on Hill 529.[19]

Then American observers spotted yet another large group of Germans approaching Hill 455 from the area north of Hill 523. They appeared to be an estimated battalion in strength, armed and carrying ammunition, and were moving in several columns toward Hill 523. The observers called in massed artillery from both 34ID and 1ID, boxing in and pounding the enemy troops from their rear and flanks. 1/135's mortar battery sealed the open end of the killing zone. The fire plan was to fire as one body on signal, with half of the weapons targeting the edges of the enemy formation and the other half moving fire in a scissors pattern inward and outward over the target area. Several rounds of mortar fire were directed between the enemy columns and Hill 523 as well to discourage the Germans from taking cover behind the hill. As the enemy swung toward Hill 523 and attempted to place mortars and other weapons, the signal to fire was given. The noise was deafening, and the air filled with black dust. When the air cleared, very few active enemy soldiers were to be seen. The German counterattack had been stopped.[20]

1st Battalion, 135th Infantry Regiment advanced slowly and steadily, but the assault companies suffered more casualties. Two platoons of Company A managed to get to the northwest tip of Hill 531.[21] The 3rd Battalion, 135th Infantry Regiment, near the Arab village, assisted the 1st Battalion at Hill 531 by firing on the enemy's reverse slope positions and interdicting repeated enemy attempts to reinforce and resupply Hill 531. The Germans again supplemented other weapons by dropping bundles of stick grenades on the attacking troops from higher crags. Company C, 1/135 was stopped just short of the top of Hill 531 by German rifle and machine-gun fire, but the enemy had exposed their positions. C Company's heavy weapons platoon returned the favor, hitting the enemy weapons pits with 60mm mortar bombs. The enemy fire ceased, and the Americans began the final assault, which now entirely consumed them. Their effort was the key to the battle and the campaign, and exemplified devotion to duty and sacrifice, reflecting great honor on themselves and their division.[22]

Company A's weapons platoon was in position on Kef el Guebli; most of another platoon was working as ammunition carriers. Late in the day, the light machine-gun squad and a detail heavily loaded with hand grenades crossed from Hill 529 to Hill 531 and climbed to the crest, where the attack was renewed. German machine-pistol fire hit Company C's position while machine-gun fire struck Company A. Company C returned fire into the pocket and prepared to assault, but the company commanders recognized that they were both receiving small-arms fire from the same area. Working together on the party line network, the commanders of Company C and Company A conferred. They determined that Company A was closer to the enemy's position and had employed several captured enemy weapons. To verify their respective locations and to avoid friendly fire casualties, each Company fired a signal flare. They were able to proceed cautiously and in constant radio contact into what had been the enemy's defended pocket, where they found that the enemy's survivors had run away. 1/135 had reached its objective on Hill 531 against fierce resistance. But the 1st Battalion was now in only intermittent contact with the 3rd Battalion on its left. German artillery, mortar, and machine-gun fire deluged Hill 531, disrupting phone wires and preventing movement. The enemy firing did not stop until, with the benefit of good observation from the newly captured heights, American artillery and mortar counterbattery fire destroyed the enemy weapons.[23]

By nightfall, April 30, 1st Battalion, 135th Infantry Regiment, controlled Hill 531. But Hill 455 still seemed out of reach. A gap remained between 1/135 and its left neighbor, the 3rd Battalion, 135th Infantry Regiment and the enemy continued to fire from the Roman Ruins. But the simultaneous assaults against Hill 609 had prevented the enemy from subjecting the top of Hill 531 to the usual intense and immobilizing enfilade fire.[24] 34th Infantry Division's capture of the crest of Hill 531 had at last secured the high ground. Now the Americans had the advantages of good observation and overlapping fields of fire over the terrain to the north, toward the southern base of Hill 609, and east toward other hill forts. The GIs had deprived the enemy of the key to its hill fort complex and the Germans could no longer pour fire from Hill 531 in support of the *Barenthins* on Hill 609 or against the troops of Allen's 1st Infantry Division to the south.

During the afternoon of April 30, Major General Ryder attached the 2nd Battalion, 168th Infantry Regiment, Lieutenant Colonel Bird commanding, to 135RCT for the closing operations against Hill 609. Colonel Ward now had five infantry battalions, three of which were depleted and tired, and a company of tanks under his control to close out the battle for Hill 609. At 2:30p.m. Lieutenant Colonel Bird contacted Colonel Ward for orders, then moved his troops to an assembly area north of the Sidi Nsir–Chouïgui road about 2,000 yards south of Hill 609. Ward directed 2/168 to move forward over the ridge between Hill 609 and Hill 531, destroying any enemy they found. The battalion was then to sweep counterclockwise around Hill 609, clearing the southeastern and northeastern slopes of machine guns and snipers. Finally, 2/168 was to assume a defensive position on the northeast side of Hill 609 and to coordinate with the 1st Battalion of the 133rd Infantry Regiment on their right (north) and the 1st Battalion of the 135th Infantry Regiment on their left (south).

2/168's assault began at 11:00p.m. in darkness.[25] As 2/168 moved toward the base of Hill 609, Company F surprised a platoon of enemy infantry trying to infiltrate up the western slopes of Hill 609 behind the 1st Battalion, 133IR. The GIs poured fire into the enemy formation and inflicted severe casualties. Lieutenant Colonel Bird then directed the battalion's advance over the ground in the saddle between Hill 531 and Hill 609, hunting and killing "wild goats" as Bradley had directed.

Continuing the attack around the southeastern and eastern base of Hill 609, 2/168 closed the Red Bull's ring around Hill 609 by joining the 1st Battalion, 133IR on its right, and tied in with the 1st Battalion, 135IR on its left at Hill 531.[26] At this point all the mutually supporting enemy positions had been eliminated except the citadel at the very top of Djebel Tahent. Although the Germans there were trapped, they could still direct artillery fire on the Americans from their excellent observation posts.

The Germans had underestimated the stamina and will to fight of the Red Bull soldiers. With Hill 609 surrounded, the GIs found and began to move up a goat track on the northeastern corner of the mountain. The enemy had uncharacteristically discounted the track as a feasible path of approach to the citadel. By mid-afternoon Friday, April 30, soldiers of 2/135 had fought their way up the sharply precipitous path and gained the summit. Riflemen of the 2nd Battalion, 135th Infantry Regiment, took the stubborn fighters of *Regiment Barenthin* by surprise from the rear. Following a screen of artillery shells, Red Bull infantrymen closed with the enemy. They blasted, shot, and stabbed the defenders from their breastworks. As darkness fell, a roaring frenzy of fighting and killing erupted on the mesa, with rifles, grenades, and bayonets. Only close control and diligent leadership in battle prevented friend from killing friend. The once-mighty *Barenthins* were overwhelmed and defeated. Some of *Regiment Barenthin* escaped, but many were slain, and even more were taken prisoner. Although the fighting on the mesa was not finished, the Hill 609 citadel was now the 34th Infantry Division's real estate, dearly bought at a dreadful cost. The Americans had driven the enemy from Hill 609, but their ability to hold it would be challenged by German counterattacks and attempts to infiltrate during the following night and on May 1. The other Red Bull battalions enveloped the hill.

By late on April 30, 34ID's 2nd Battalion, 168th Infantry Regiment, 1st Battalion, 133rd Infantry Regiment and the 2nd Battalion, 135th Infantry Regiment were working together to destroy the remaining enemy on the southeast and northeast slopes and the mesa of Hill 609. In the sector held by 1/135 on Hill 531, several local counterattacks over the northeast slopes were repulsed early in the evening. Lieutenant Colonel Miller ordered Company B, commanded by 1st Lieutenant Kimble Midkiff, to move to reinforce Company C, which was securing the north half of Hill 531, and to patrol toward Hill 455 and the Roman Ruins. During the night of April 30–May 1, 1/135 continued to take enemy sniper fire and harassing artillery rounds.[27] The bitter struggle of 16IR, 1ID, to maintain its hold on Hill 523 left the right flank of 1/135 dangerously exposed.[28] Fortunately for the Americans, and the Allied Force as a whole, the enemy, as Bradley had foreseen, was no longer in a condition to exploit the vulnerability.

It had been four days of continuous, grueling, and unspeakably horrible fighting. By late on April 30 the fall of the enemy's hill fort complex around Hill 609 was imminent. The troops of the 1st Battalion, 133rd Infantry Regiment, who had attacked with Gwin's tanks, had built up a coordinated defense of the northwestern sector below Hill 609 with elements of the 2nd Battalion, 135th Infantry Regiment on Hill 461. After spending the night in isolation in the area of the Arab village, troops from 3/135 patrolled around the western slopes of Hill 609, attained the summit at last, and set up an observation post at about 3:40p.m.[29] Now the military advantages were reversed. The Americans could see what they needed to see. Toward morning on May 1, 3/135 contributed supporting fire against an enemy counterattack against Hill 531.[30]

Saturday, May 1, 1943

During the night of April 30–May 1, 2/168 advanced around Hill 609 scouring the remaining foes, on its way to relieve 2/135 on the mesa. In the dark and fog of the early morning of May 1, Company E, 2/168 was making steady progress, stumbling through thick shrubbery and over rocks, into an olive orchard on the southeast slopes of Hill 609. When they thought they had reached the area where other 2nd Battalion soldiers were supposed to be, they stopped and listened, again exhibiting their new proficiency on the battlefield. As there seemed at first to be no one there, they moved on a little farther. Gradually, they became aware that they were not alone on the hillside, and they stopped again to listen. Close at hand, they heard a man stub his toe and swear softly *auf Deutsch*. The GIs realized that the enemy was near in the darkness, silently withdrew a short distance, and disposed themselves for fighting. After a time, First Lieutenant Marvin A. Good, a former shoe salesman from Shenandoah, Iowa, took a sergeant with him and stealthily returned to the position where they had first heard the enemy. The Germans were gone.

First Lieutenant Good brought his men forward and ordered them take positions in the olive orchard. The GIs again waited. As the first gray light exposed the forbidding cliffs of Hill 609 to their right, the Americans saw Germans coming at them and at once opened fire with M1 rifles and BARs. The firefight had lasted about half an hour when Nature entered the battle. A thick fog suddenly engulfed the scene, so obscuring that no one could see his own rifle in front of him. The fighting stopped. During the dark respite, Second Lieutenant Frank Cockett, formerly a tax clerk from Wailuku, Maui, Hawaii, helped his men to find better protected positions from which to fight. Some placed themselves at the bases of trees; others chose a pile or low wall of rocks to crouch behind.

The Germans also sought cover in the darkness, some behind a low rock wall. Then a gust of wind blew the fog away and the light came back. The Americans looked out from behind their rocks and saw the Germans only 15 yards away. The wall the Germans had chosen was just the other side of a goat track from the American position. The point-blank gunfight resumed in fury. The Germans had insufficient cover and bolt-action rifles, while the Red Bull soldiers now had better cover and M1 Garand semi-automatic rifles. When three Germans tried to flank the Americans, Cockett instantly shot them dead. A Stuka strafed the ground around the cliffs of Hill 609 but the GIs lifted machine-gun barrels and fired a barrage at it until the plane began to smoke and left. The enemy knew they were finished, but they were determined to take as many Americans with them as they could before they were killed. Two enemy soldiers stood up with their hands raised. When a GI rose to take them prisoner, the Germans murdered him. Two of his buddies at once shot and killed both the Germans. A sergeant stuck his head up to find more Germans and was shot between the eyes. The GIs kept firing with all weapons. The Germans had lost about 40 men when the survivors hurriedly withdrew.[i]

F Company, 2/168, had meanwhile ambushed and destroyed yet another enemy formation. Before dawn, the Germans had sent a company over Hill 455 in a futile attempt to reinforce their isolated troops. From their positions closest to the mountain, the veteran Red Bull soldiers observed and intercepted the enemy, waiting until their targets were within 100 yards, then pouring rifle, BAR, and machine-gun fire on them, inflicting heavy losses. F Company reported 35 German dead in its front.

As the battalion completed its mission around the base of the mountain, 2/168 took positions on the northeast slopes of Hill 609 adjacent to the positions of 3/135. Among the first reinforcements to reach the top early on Saturday, May 1 were Iowans from 2/168, including Company F of Villisca and Company E of Shenandoah,[31] who captured intact a German observation post with telephones. As the day brightened, 34ID artillery forward observers accompanying 2/168 to the summit almost giddily directed II Corps's fire upon the escaping enemy, causing great havoc.[32]

During the day on May 1, 1/135's combat operations to secure the hold on Hill 531, the Roman Ruins and Hill 455 continued. Early on Saturday morning, a rifle platoon, and the weapons platoon of Company B, 1/135 occupied the Roman Ruins after brushing off light resistance by badly battered enemy survivors. By mid-afternoon, the dead-tired GIs of 1/135 had succeeded. They had secured the long-contested stronghold of Hill 531 and finally closed the gap between it and Hill 609 by occupying the Hill 455 area. By 3:00p.m. on May 1, 1/135 had rooted out and destroyed the remaining resistance and were in complete control of their sector. A path was then cleared through a minefield between Hill 531 and Hill 609 to resupply the battalion, and that evening all the battalion's mortars and their ammunition were brought forward by trucks.[33]

The 34th Infantry Division's operations late on April 30 and during the day on May 1 closed the ring around and completed the occupation of Hill 609. The seizure and successful defense of Hills 531 and 455 placed Hill 609 and all the surrounding strong points firmly in the hands of 34ID. German countermeasures on May 1 were ineffective and un-coordinated. All enemy activity was now subject to American observation from the very same high ground which had served the enemy so well. Feeble German infantry counterattacks were smashed with heavy bombardments from the combined artillery of the 34th and 1st Infantry Divisions and by automatic-weapons fire from every American battalion.[34]

---

i   After the fight for Hill 609 was over, Second Lieutenant Lloyd Hardy, from Dayton, Oregon, and First Lieutenant Eldon Wilson, of Alva, Oklahoma, took the *Life* magazine artist Martin Fletcher over the scene of the firefight in the olive groves.

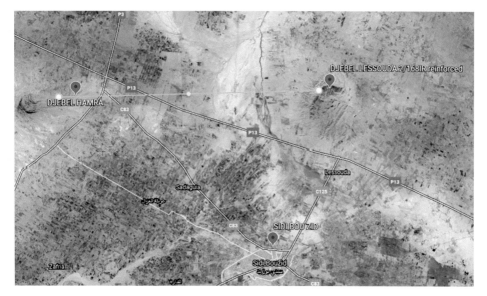

The successful moonlit escape of 2/168 from Dj Lessouda. (Prepared by the author using Google Earth Pro)

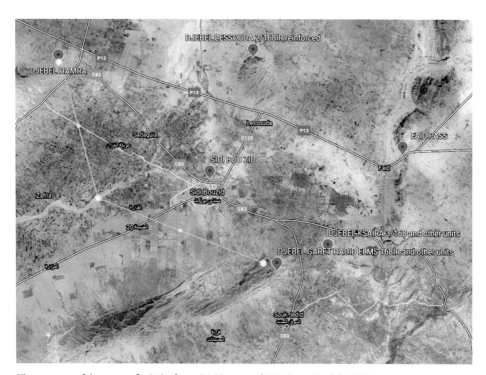

The unsuccessful escape of 3/168 from Dj Ksaira and Dj Garet Hadid. While most survived, most were captured as they attempted to walk to safety. (Prepared by the author using Google Earth Pro)

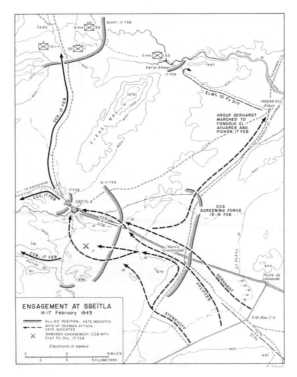

Engagement at Sbeïtla, February 16–17, 1943: Note position of 133rd Infantry Regiment at Kef el Ahmar (top center). The delaying action worked and although the Americans retreated, the GIs demonstrated a change in mindset that would end in victory in North Africa. (NWAf, map 12, p. 429)

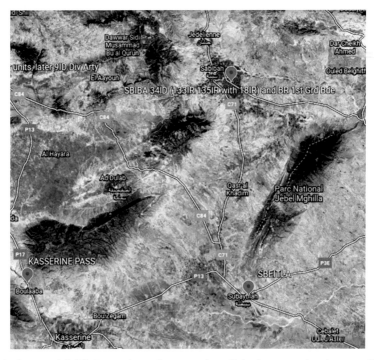

After Sbeitla (lower right) fell, Rommel sent forces north to Sbiba (top center) and west to Kasserine (bottom left). He found Sbiba, defended by 34ID, too tough and decided to press on through Kasserine Pass. (Prepared by the author using Google Earth Pro)

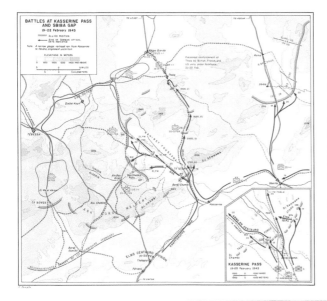

Battles of Kasserine Pass, Sbiba Gap and Thala, February 19–22, 1943. Note the positions of 133IR and 135IR of 34ID southeast of Sbiba (upper right), with Br. 1st Guards Brigade and US 18IR to the south and other elements of 1ID to the north, successfully blocking 21st Pz. Div.'s path to Ksour. (NWAf, p. 757)

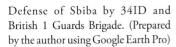

Defense of Sbiba by 34ID and British 1 Guards Brigade. (Prepared by the author using Google Earth Pro)

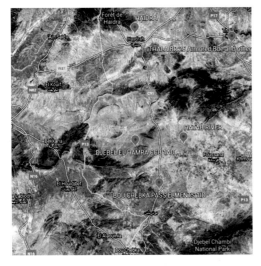

The terrain of the Allied victories at Djebel el Hamra (center) and Bou Chebka Pass (lower center), and at Thala (upper right). (Prepared by the author using Google Earth Pro)

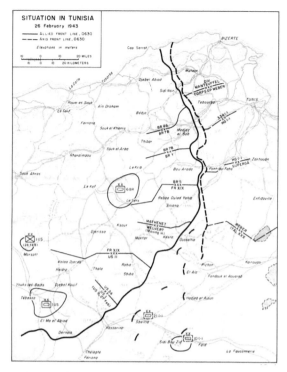

The new Allied line in Tunisia, February 26, 1943. 34ID occupied the area between Thala and Sbiba (lower left center). (NWAf, Map 13, p.491)

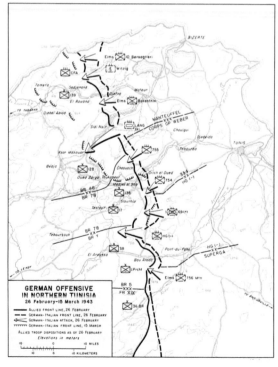

Fighting in northern Tunisia, February 26–March 15, 1943. The abortive German attack presaged 34ID's battle to take the hill fort complex east of Sidi Nsir (upper center) in late April. (NWAf, Map 14, p. 503)

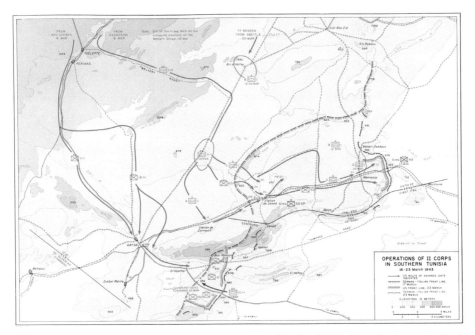

Operations of U.S. II Corps in Southern Tunisia while 34ID fought the bitter battles at Fondouk, March 16–23, 1943. (NWAf, Map X, map pocket, p. 759)

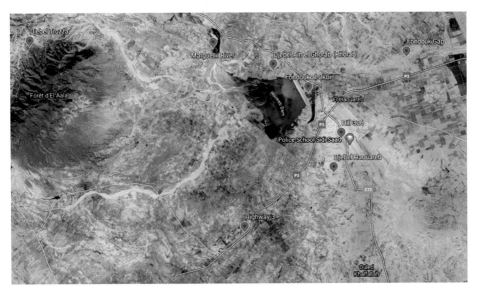

The Fondouk Gap battlefield today. After the war, the Marguellil River was dammed at Funduq al ʿUqbi. The land over which the enemy threw enfilade fire from Rhorab (upper center) against 34ID's left flank during its March and April attacks is now under water. (Prepared by the author using Google Earth Pro)

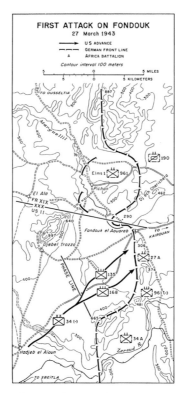

First Attack on Fondouk Gap, March 27, 1943. Note the movements of 135IR and 168IR toward Dj Haouareb (lower center). (NWAf, Map 17, p. 579)

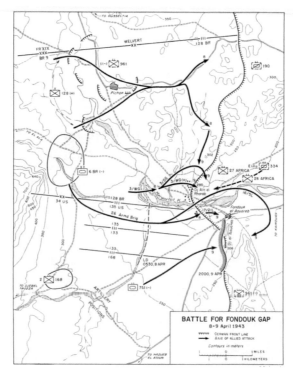

Second Battle for Fondouk Gap, April 8–9, 1943, based on a flawed British plan of attack to which Ryder objected but carried out like the good soldier he was. (NWAf, Map 18, p. 584)

A modern contour view of 34ID's approach to Dj Haouareb and the Fondouk Gap. In the spring of 1943, the only water was in the muddy bed of the Marguellil. (Prepared by the author using Google Earth Pro)

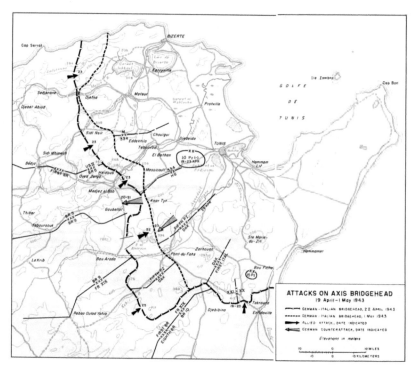

Final and victorious Allied attacks on Axis Bridgehead, April 19–May 1, 1943. (NWAf, Map No. 19, pp. 596–597)

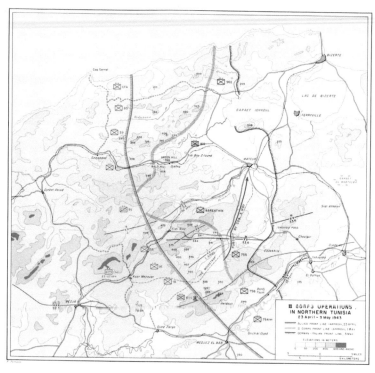

II Corps Operations in Northern Tunisia starting April 23. 168IR was attached to 1ID at the outset and rejoined the main body of 34ID for the assault on Hill 609 (lower center). (NWAf, Map XI, map pocket, p. 760)

British 1st Army commander Lieutenant General Anderson and U.S. Major General Bradley confer during the final Allied offensive against the Axis bridgehead in Tunisia. (U.S. DoD files)

Official portrait of General Omar N. Bradley, a Major General at the time of the Battle of Hill 609. (U.S. Army)

Mortar crews displacing to new positions near Hill 609, April 28, 1943. (U.S. Army Signal Corps)

Modern view of Hill 609 Battlefield and Hill Fort Complex from Hill 473 (Dj el Hara) and Hill 575 (Kef el Goraa) to Hills 490, 461 and 435. Hill 609 is out of the frame to the right. See next map. (Prepared by the author using Google Earth Pro)

Modern view of Hill 609 Battlefield and Hill Fort Complex, showing Hills 490, 461, 609 (upper center), 530, 531 (center), and 455. (Prepared by the author using Google Earth Pro)

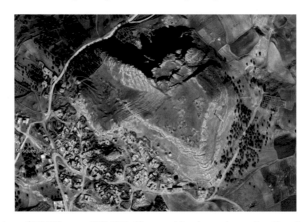

Modern view of Dj Tahent—Hill 609. (Prepared by the author using Google Earth Pro)

Another view of Hill 609 showing the olive groves on the slopes below the southeast palisade. (U.S. Army Signal Corps)

Skirmish of the Stone Walls by Fletcher Martin. GIs of 168IR are depicted on the right, Germans on the left. The firefight occurred in the final hours of the battle for Hill 609. (World War II Army Art Print Set 1, The Early Years. U.S. Army CMH Pub 70-46)

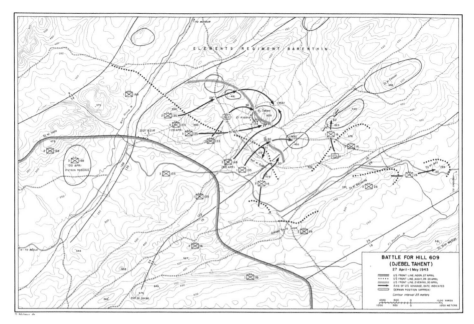

The Battle for Hill 609, April 27–May 1, 1943. The solid blue lines represent the movements of 34ID battalions. Red circles denote German pockets. (NWAf, Map XII, map pocket, p. 761)

Modern view of the Hill 609 battlefield in the final phase. Note the proximity of Hills 531, 455 and 609, which formed a triangle of mutually supporting fire. (Prepared by the author using Google Earth Pro)

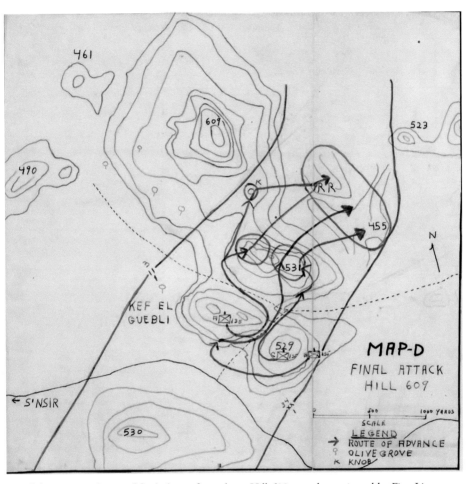

Hand-drawn tactical map of final phase of assault on Hill 609 complex, prepared by First Lieutenant Arnold Brandt, CO, D Company, 1/135. (See: Brandt, Arnold N. "The Operations of the 1st Battalion, 135th Infantry Regiment at Hills 609 and 531," Ft. Benning, Georgia, Infantry School, 1948, pp. 20–26)

General Hans Jürgen von Arnim, in Allied custody. (U.S. Army Signal Corps)

Axis prisoners by the tens of thousands were assembled in cages near Mateur, Tunisia, May 1943. (U.S. Army Signal Corps)

"The Herrenvolk like chickens in a yard." Thousands more Axis prisoners in the Allied cages at Gromalia, Tunisia awaited transport to England and the United States. (British Army Lieutenant Whicker, No 2 Army Film & Photographic Unit. Photograph NA 2866, Imperial War Museum (collection no. 4700-39))

Troops of the 135th Infantry Regiment, 34th Infantry Division, march in glory past the reviewing stand on Avenue Gambetta, Tunis, on May 20, 1943. (U.S. Army photo)

Soldiers of the 135th Infantry Regiment, 34th Infantry Division march through Tunis amidst a joyous reception in the victory parade of May 20, 1943. (U.S. Army)

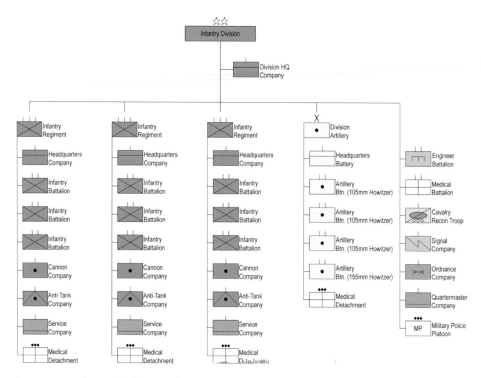

Organization of a standard U.S. Infantry Division, 1942. 34ID's three infantry regiments were the 133rd, the 135th, and the 168th. Its four artillery battalions were the 125th, the 151st, the 175th, and the 185th (the latter equipped with heavier 155mm guns). (Noclador, Wikimedia Creative Commons. Creative Commons Attribution-Share Alike 3.0 Unported license)

All along the line reconnaissance patrols reported the enemy forces to be retreating or surrendering.[35] The enemy responded to its defeat by pounding its former hill forts with artillery fire, using both ground and air bursts. The majority of 1/133's casualties occurred after Hill 609 was taken, in large part due to the unabated enemy artillery fire. 1/135's heavy machine-gun platoon moved from Hill 531 just in time to miss an enemy concentration there. 34ID units speedily dug in and prepared defensive positions against further counterattacks, but the surviving Germans were at last retreating.[36] A final German effort at dusk ended in failure. By the end of May 1, the enemy had failed to force the Americans from their positions.[37] The night of May 1–2 was relatively quiet.

The rocky tabletop of Hill 609 was burned and blasted. Corpses were strewn about. The dead Germans in their rock redoubts reminded one GI of Civil War photographs showing the dead along the rail fences at Antietam. The mesa "was literally covered with bodies," another wrote. "The stench was terrible." The hill was "pitted with shell craters, thick as currants in cake." Few holes were deeper than six inches: solid rock underlay the thin soil. After attempting in vain to bury the German dead in the shallow craters, GIs had to throw them into fissures where a bulldozer plowed them under. "Those who went through it," wrote Ernie Pyle, "would seriously doubt that war could be any worse than those two weeks of mountain fighting."[38]

The men of the 34th Infantry Division had proved themselves as worthy combat infantrymen with their victory at Hill 609, but there was a butcher's bill to pay. Ryder put his losses at 324 killed in action. The Red Bull soldiers collected their dead and their remains were removed from the hill in trucks. "All you could see," an artilleryman later remembered, "was their shoes hanging off the tail gate." American soldiers in II Corps were now fully in the grip of a merciless passion to kill their enemy. Across the Tine valley south of Hill 609, a staff officer in the 16th Infantry Regiment summoned a lieutenant preparing to lead a patrol back up Hill 523, which had changed hands four times in hand-to-hand fighting over the past 36 hours. "I don't believe I would take any prisoners on 523." "No," the lieutenant agreed, "no prisoners will be taken."[39] "Jerries approach our troops, some run, some fall on their faces, most of them weary, haggard, wild-eyed, terrified men who swing arms above their heads," the 16th Infantry Regiment reported. "A panorama of defeat, as vehicles, mules and men walk toward the [GIs] with white flags fluttering." The Red Bull soldiers were now aware that some enemy faked surrender to lure unwary GIs into the open. Staff Sergeant Clarence T. Storm of Villisca had been treacherously slain by such villainy; there were others. The GIs' loathing for the enemy became homicidal. All doubts were resolved by pulling triggers. "For twenty-four hours," Bradley noted, "few prisoners came from the 34th Division's front."[40]

The 34th Infantry Division's history claimed the laurels of victory in unpolished, ingenuous language that conveys both soldierly pride and a sense of affront and sorrow.

During this action the 34th Division found itself. After knowing the bewilderment, shock, and panic of battle, the bitterness of real war, the 34th ID now had an achievement of significance to the Tunisian campaign to its collective credit, in no small part due to the tactical skill of General Ryder and to the growing battle sense of the GIs. In his official report to the War Department, General Omar Bradley, commanding II Corps, stated regarding the fighting at Hill 609, "A strong enemy was repulsed. Fighting all day was intense and bloody. The enemy was engaged with bayonet and grenade, and there were many cases of outstanding bravery."[41]

The battle of Hill 609 was a combined arms victory. The infantry had been transformed by training and competent leadership into a formidable fighting force. The armor company detached from 1st Armored Division and assigned to support 34ID infantry battalions in close cooperation, and the reinforcement of the 135th Infantry Regiment by two fresh infantry battalions, had reinvigorated 34ID and provided unstoppable combat power, tipping the scales in the battle for Hill 609.[42]

Except for dead men and Lieutenant Colonel Denholm's map,[ii] the 16th Infantry Regiment found Hill 523 empty. The enemy was gone. As Bradley had foreseen, the capture of Hill 609 unhinged enemy defenses across the entire front, from the Mediterranean to the Tine river "Mousetrap." U.S. troops shouted, tanks clanked and clattered, and every gun in II Corps boomed as the final pursuit commenced. A reporter viewing the scene from atop Hill 609 wrote, "At our feet every road was thronged with [U.S.] troops, guns and supplies, pouring northward… Outside Béja, Bradley sat on a metal stool in his tent, reading dispatches. He studied the map on the easel, now crisscrossed with blue and red crayon marks showing an enemy in full retreat and pursuers close behind. He was in good humor…" He received a stream of ebullient reports from the 9th Infantry Division in the north, the 34th and 1st Infantry Divisions in the south, and the 1st Armored Division, advancing boldly through the Mousetrap and down the Tine valley on two mine-cleared routes the GIs had named Broadway and Riley Street. The enemy fell back as much as 15 miles to the far side of Mateur. When another dispatch noted signs of a possible counterattack, Bradley nodded grimly. "Let 'em come," he said. "We want to kill Germans…" Mateur fell on May 3. A dozen roads and rail lines converged at Mateur; its capture rendered impossible all enemy attempts to maneuver to concentrate against the British.[43]

The capture of the Hill 609 complex by the 34th Infantry Division and the unwavering attacks by 1st Infantry Division further south forced Arnim to choose between fighting with increasing disadvantage in the last narrow segment of hills or pulling back to a shorter line closer to Bizerte and the hills east of the Tine. 9th Infantry Division's successful attack in the northern part of the II Corps zone gave impetus to Arnim's decision.[44] By late on May 1 the Americans were positioned to cut the enemy off from both Bizerte and Mateur, and the Germans quickly

---

ii *See* p. 353, supra. Denholm and other prisoners would be released when the Axis forces in Tunisia surrendered on May 13.

abandoned the Djefna position facing the 9th Infantry Division. The Axis retreat behind Mateur along the Sedjenane road also forced them to withdraw from the hills adjacent to the Sidi Nsir road, in the area northeast of Hill 609. Axis units were now under Allied observation and open both to accurate artillery fire and to attack from the flank and rear. Von Arnim knew now that none of the Axis positions west and southwest of Mateur could be held against the power of the victorious II Corps. The Axis troops on II Corps' front fell back efficiently and quietly on the nights of May 1–2 and 2–3. Aggressive reconnaissance gave II Corps a real-time assessment of the retreat on May 2 and reconfirmed the enemy's general withdrawal from the II Corps front the next day. From Hill 609, a large fire was visible in Mateur. Elsewhere, explosions and fires indicated the Germans were demolishing bridges and destroying equipment.[45] II Corps now changed its dispositions, 1st Infantry Division crossing over to the left in II Corps's center. The 34th Infantry Division became II Corps's right flank division, aligned athwart the axis Sidi Nsir-Chouïgui, due east of Hill 609.[46]

CHAPTER 34

Victory in Tunisia

On May 2, 1943, 1st Battalion, 133rd Infantry Regiment, extended its lines in the morning and occupied the entire north slope of Hill 609. The 168th Infantry Regiment relieved the proud but suffering 135th Infantry Regiment which went into division reserve. 135RCT moved to positions on Hill 375 and Djebel el Hara. 2/135 relieved 3/133 in defense of Hills 342, 461, 435 and 490. 3/135 relieved a battalion of 168RCT. Night reconnaissance patrols reported many German corpses. In the morning of May 2, several weak counterattacks in the 1/135's sector were slapped away by U.S. artillery and 81mm mortar fire. When the enemy attempted to emplace three field guns, U.S. 81mm mortars, firing at a range of 3,900 yards by using extra increments of charge to propel the bombs, destroyed them. By the early afternoon, all enemy activity ceased.

Hill 531 and the vicinity were littered with dead Germans and destroyed weapons and equipment. The GIs collected maps and samples of equipment for Intelligence to analyze. Roughly 50 enemy corpses were found in the low area behind the knob south of Hill 609; those dead exemplified the terrible outcome of an infantry unit caught in the open by mortar fire. 1/135's 81mm mortars had fired over 6,000 rounds over four days. Its heavy machine guns had expended between 20 and 25 chests of ammunition each. The rifle companies had fired almost double the ammunition they had fired in any previous week of fighting. On inspection the GIs discovered that Hill 531 had emplacements for 70 machine guns, indicating that it had been defended by an entire *Barenthin* battalion. German prisoners now claimed that the southeast part of Hill 531 alone had been manned by 75 men, 50 of whom had been armed with machine guns or machine pistols. Hill 455 and the Roman Ruins also had many secreted positions for field guns and machine guns with fields of fire covering Hill 531. The chastened Nazi prisoners complained that the Americans never seemed to sleep but attacked all the time. During the night of May 2, 168IR completed its relief of 135IR on the southwest part of Hill 609 and Hill 531.[1]

On May 3, 3/135 was placed directly under II Corps command and sent to Djebel Lanserine where it took up defensive positions to protect II Corps's right flank. At

6:00p.m., 1/133 reverted to control of 133RCT and moved to an assembly area south of Hill 609. Under cover of darkness on the night of May 3, 1/135 relieved another battalion of 168RCT.[2]

Bradley recalled that "a prisoner from the Barenthin Regiment… protested our use of tanks in this attack. 'We could have held out against your infantry for another week,' he boasted, 'but we didn't expect to see tanks. As a matter of fact, you had no right to use them. We had been told that was not tank country and as a result we had few defenses.'"[3]

Eddekhila and Chouïgui

When the enemy did not counterattack after Mateur fell to the 1st Armored Division, II Corps completed its regrouping and reconnaissance preparatory to renewing its own attack. General Bradley moved his command post from the vicinity of Béja forward to Sidi Nsir. Eastern Base Section took over some of II Corps's supply points in the Djebel Abiod and Béja areas and established new dumps along the two major roads leading toward Mateur and Chouïgui Pass, while U.S. engineers bridged the streams near Mateur at several points. Meanwhile, northeast of Mateur, a reconnaissance in force by Combat Command B on May 5 skillfully drew enough anti-tank and artillery fire to locate the enemy's defensive positions.[4]

Bradley planned to resume II Corps's general attack on May 6. The 9th Infantry Division was to drive against the hills north of Garaet Ichkeul and eventually to overcome the fortified positions which the enemy had occupied in anticipation of an American attack on Bizerte. At the same time, the 1st Infantry Division on the north and the 34th Infantry Division on the south were to attack the enemy in the hills east of the Tine river. 34ID's target was the heights abutting Chouïgui pass, where the enemy was still present in force. The 1st Infantry Division continued its movement on an axis generally northeastward from Hill 609 while the 34th Infantry Division side-slipped southward from the vicinity of Hill 609 and then drove eastward along the Sidi Nsir–Chouïgui road. Both divisions crossed the route of advance of the 1st Armored Division but the main body of 1AD had already reached the vicinity of Mateur by May 5. Before daylight on May 6, from north of the Garaet Ichkeul to Pont-du-Fahs, the Americans and their allies were once more on the offensive.[5]

On May 4, the 135th Infantry Regiment minus the 3rd Battalion moved to assemble about ten miles east of Sidi Masour. The next day it again moved east to an assembly area in the vicinity of Hill 202. 3/135 reverted to control of 135RCT on Wednesday, May 6. The next day, May 7, 1/135 was on the right flank of 168RCT. There were more GI casualties from enemy artillery and mortar fire.

On May 6–7, II Corps persevered against an enemy that exhibited no diminishment of its will to fight. Following oral orders from Ryder to his commanders on

May 4, the 34th Infantry Division marched in power eastward to find and destroy any remaining enemy on the II Corps's right or southern flank. 34ID's mission was to take the Chouïgui Pass, the high ground north and south of it, and Chouïgui village, now held by the 1ID's former opponents, the German 334th Infantry Division. Before the general attack of the corps began on May 6, the 34th Infantry Division moved to occupy the village of Eddekhila in the southeastern corner of the Tine valley. Red Bull patrols on the afternoon of May 4 made no contact with the enemy in Eddekhila and the adjacent hills.[6] By now the experienced Americans had learned well the German practice of concealing their presence and strength until the main body of an attacking force came to the field. Accordingly, 34ID organized a reconnaissance in force for the next morning.

The ground commanders again chose a route along the rugged foothills at the southern edge of the valley rather than on the more exposed, but smoother, terrain near the river. The 168th Infantry Regiment, supported by the 175th Field Artillery Battalion, led the advance on May 5 in a column of battalions, with a reconnaissance platoon and the Antitank Company protecting the left flank. West of Eddekhila the head of this column met such strong resistance that its advance stopped. Artillery fire from the left and front, mortar and long-range machine-gun fire from the right and right rear, and unfavorable rising ground ahead without cover argued against a frontal attack. The Germans in 168IR's front would not be defeated in daylight without disproportionate losses. 168RTC planned a powerful night assault with two battalions abreast, each advancing on a 1,000-yard front behind a rolling barrage fired by four battalions of light (105mm) and two battalions of medium (155mm) artillery. A third battalion pushed over the hills to the south, protecting that flank and staying in contact with the British forces on 34ID's right flank. The attack that began on May 6 was to be the 34th Infantry Division's last operation of consequence in the general offensive by II Corps.[7]

168RCT fought its way beyond Eddekhila and into the heights east of it on May 6, but when the supporting artillery barrage was lifted, the Germans returned to their machine-gun and mortar positions and hurt both assault battalions while they reorganized for a second advance. Throughout the day, the three battalions of the 168th Infantry Regiment and the 1st and 3rd Battalions, 133rd Infantry Regiment, thrust into the hills south and east of Eddekhila toward the same area where the Germans had repulsed the first Allied attempt to reach Tunis in November 1942, almost seven months earlier. Progress was slow, and the 34ID GIs gained no high ground on May 6. On May 7, the 34th Infantry Division resumed its attack at 5:00a.m. The Red Bull assault battalions pushed northeastward over several crests. They were stopped just short of the Chouïgui Pass, but sustained pressure on the enemy until, just before dawn the next day, May 8, the Germans retreated in haste.[8] The Axis forces were quickly coming to the end of their ability to continue what had become for them a hopeless fight. Allied victory in Tunisia was near.

The 1st Armored Division raced east on the late afternoon of May 6 as the final II Corps offensive commenced. By the next morning, the Nazis had been violently disordered, leaving behind incinerated vehicles and more charred German corpses. 1AD tanks had effectively cut the Axis bridgehead in half. The 9th Infantry Division marched over the coastal hills toward Bizerte. The 1st Infantry Division, under Major General Allen, planned an attack across the Tine early on May 6 to continue the momentum of the Allied offensive. 1ID's target was elements of *Regiment Barenthin* holding a feature known as Hill 232. The *Barenthins*, as 34ID knew very well, were determined to make a last fight. Allen ordered the 18th Infantry Regiment, after crossing on two newly prepared bridges, to attack eastward against a djebel about seven miles southwest of Mateur, with the 26th Infantry on its southern flank. Company H, 1st Armored Regiment, furnished support. The attack opened auspiciously at 3:00a.m., but soon ran into difficulties. The 3rd Battalion, 18th Infantry, on the left, diverged to the northeast from its planned route of approach, lost contact with the 1st Battalion, and was trapped on the plain at daylight near the base of an enemy-occupied hill where it was subjected to devastating crossfire from machine guns and to crippling mortar barrages. The 18th Infantry Regiment lost 282 men and retreated across the Tine. The *Barenthins* slipped away in the night.[9]

Advance elements of 9th Infantry Division reached Bizerte in the early hours of May 7.

> They entered a dead city. The ancient port... lay empty, gutted by more than two dozen 4,000-pound bombs and many tons of lesser explosives. "Bizerte was the most completely wrecked place I had ever seen," Ernie Pyle wrote... The town had been without running water for three months. Typhus was here and cholera threatened... Warehouses and shipyards lay in rubble... By dawn, the last of the Germans had died or fled... [1AD] Shermans rolled to the edge of the Gulf of Tunis, took aim at a few Germans trying to escape by barge or skiff, and blew them out of the water.[10]

The end of II Corps's participation in the last great Allied offensive in North Africa came with darkness on May 7. The 9th Infantry Division held Bizerte, now clear of the enemy. The 1st Armored Division had cut the road and railway connections between Bizerte and Tunis via Ferryville or Mateur at several places. The 34th Infantry Division was in position to control the Chouïgui Pass and the town beyond. II Corps had driven the enemy Germans out of their last prepared defense line and had pierced that line east of Mateur and Ferryville. II Corps's mobile forces now stabbed deeply to the coast at the eastern limit of the II Corps zone, breaking the enemy's formations into small, disorganized fragments. The fighting elements of General von Vaerst's Fifth Panzer Army facing II Corps were now broken up into three isolated groups in the hills around the Lac de Bizerte, east of the Tine river. The number of surrendering Germans and Italians rapidly rose. The Allied operations to cut off the air and sea resupply routes to the Axis units had been tremendously effective. Shortages of water, food, fuel and of all types of ammunition had rendered the enemy unable any longer to defend itself.[11]

The 34th Infantry Division had captured the heights on the southern side of Chouïgui Pass in the fighting on May 5 and 6. During the night of May 7–8, 34ID prepared to attack the hills on the northern side at daylight, but after the success of the Allied attacks on Tunis and Bizerte, and the Axis evacuation of Tebourba and Djedeida on May 7, an operation to seize the hills became unnecessary. Daylight on May 8 revealed that the pass was defended by only a few infantrymen, either stragglers or an expendable rear guard, who were promptly snuffed out. By 8:00a.m., May 8, 1943, Red Bull soldiers dominated the heights adjacent to the pass and patrolled in Chouïgui village, east of the pass. The few fighting elements of the German 334th Infantry Division still able to move attempted to reach a line beyond the Mateur–Djedeida road; the rest were immobilized and awaited capture by the Allies. In mid-morning, a British patrol from the Tebourba area drove into Chouïgui to meet the men of the Red Bull Division. The last important tasks in II Corps's sector were to corral the thousands upon thousands of the enemy who sought to surrender and to mop up the encircled areas.[12]

British First Army began its final attack on Tunis with an enormous artillery barrage from more than 400 tubes at 3:00a.m. on May 6, 1943. At 5:40a.m. Allied aircraft carried out a bombardment unprecedented on the continent, smashing the enemy from Medjez el Bab to Tunis. British infantry advanced on a 3,000-yard front. The combat power of two divisions and a Guards brigade transferred from Eighth Army made First Army's attack overwhelming. Within hours the British 4th Division and the 4th Indian Division had blasted a gap two miles wide through the enemy defenses. Four tank battalions blitzed through.[13]

British armor columns captured Tunis at 3:30p.m. on May 7. General Barré, the first French general to fire on the Germans in Tunisia in November 1943, was given the honor of marching into the capital at the head of his troops.[14]

Once Bizerte and Tunis fell, Axis fuel shortages and Allied speed fixed the enemy in place, unable to maneuver or communicate. By the afternoon of May 8, the Axis forces under Fifth Panzer Army had been isolated in two shrinking pockets, both in range of powerful arrays of Allied artillery. The northern group included Fifth Panzer Army headquarters and the remainders of *Division von Manteuffel* and 15th Panzer Division (with elements of the 10th Panzer Division). Under the personal command of General von Vaerst in the hills north of Garaet el Mabtouha and El Alia, they prepared to make a last stand in El Alia and the hills to the northeast.[15] The southern group lay 20 miles away to the southwest, over ground occupied by the Allies and impassable salt marshes, where broken remnants of the 334th Infantry Division and small groups of other units were encircled by the 34th Infantry Division and British units in the hills between Mateur and Tebourba. Any hope that the southern group might fight its way out to join the main group to the northeast was abandoned early on May 8 when II Corps' soldiers cut the last Bizerte–Tunis road at daylight on May 9, closing U.S. combat operations in Tunisia. Now the remaining Allied mission was to kill the dead-end resisters and escort prisoners to their cages. At 9:30a.m. on Sunday, May 9 General von Vaerst sent his last situation report to Arnim: "Our armor and artillery have been destroyed; without ammunition and fuel; we shall fight to the last."[16] But those were only words. Von Vaerst knew it was the end and he was ready to capitulate. There would be no last stand.

Von Vaerst had already sought out his U.S. opponent to initiate an armistice. At 10:00a.m. on May 9 von Vaerst's delegates arrived under a flag of truce at the headquarters of Major General Ernest Harmon, now commanding the 1st Armored Division. On behalf of von Vaerst, the German officers requested an armistice while the surrender of all troops north of Tunis was being arranged. Bradley's headquarters sent instructions in the formula decreed at Casablanca: "The terms of surrender are unconditional." Bradley also instructed Harmon "to make certain they don't destroy their weapons. They are to collect their guns in ordnance piles and drive their vehicles into pools. Tell them if we catch them trying to destroy their stuff the armistice is off. We'll shoot the hell out of them." Von Vaerst's representative, Major General Fritz Krause, formerly artillery commander of the *Deutsche Afrika Korps*, asked Harmon for terms. As instructed by Bradley, Harmon replied, quoting Ulysses S. Grant to Simon Buckner at Fort Donelson: "Unconditional surrender. We propose to move immediately upon your works." Harmon gruffly added, "We will kill all who try to get away." By 12:00 noon, the Nazis had accepted the United States terms.[17] "Winning in battle is a lot like winning at poker or catching lots of fish," Ernie Pyle wrote. "It's damned pleasant and it sets a man up."[18]

At 12:50p.m., General Harmon reported to II Corps the surrender of the 10th and 15th Panzer Divisions. Eventually, the number of enemy prisoners reached the surprising total of almost 40,000.[19] Many more Axis soldiers would follow, trudging into soon overcrowded stockades.

> By mid-afternoon on May 9 II Corps had moved its CP from Sidi Nsir to a farmyard on the worn road west of Mateur. North of the highway, where a sandy plain stretched toward Djebel Achkel, our engineers had strung a barbed wire cage for the Germans. On the south side of the road a smaller enclosure had been reserved for their Italian allies. We anticipated 12,000 or 14,000 P[O]Ws. By nightfall, however the Germans had overrun our cages. German engineers were conscripted under their own noncoms to expand the enclosure. We doubled and soon tripled that original compound.[20]

Generals Gustav von Vaerst, Fritz Krause, Karl Buelowius, and Willibald Borowietz of the Wehrmacht, and Generals Kurt Bassenge and Georg Neuffer of the Luftwaffe, spent May 9–10 in custody at Headquarters, II Corps, near Mateur, and were then transferred to Headquarters, British First Army. Also captured was Major Hans Baier, the redoubtable commander of the *Regiment Barenthin*.[21] The Allies captured alive more than a dozen Axis generals. The four from the Wehrmacht and two from the

Luftwaffe who had yielded to II Corps "were fed C rations and beans on May 10 before being ushered into Bradley's intelligence tent—known as the Playhouse—where the competent and inquisitive Colonel Benjamin A. 'Monk' Dickson plied them with whiskey and cigars during a long chat around a plywood map board."[22]

On May 8, the 135th Infantry Regiment was alerted to move northwest of Chouïgui to eliminate any remaining enemy resistance. Beginning at 8:00a.m. on May 9, the regiment, with the 2nd Battalion in the lead, moved by truck to hasty defensive positions on Hills 325 and 350 near Chouïgui, and dispatched combat patrols forward which discovered no enemy. At about 1:40p.m. the troops of the 135th Infantry Regiment were informed that the Germans had unconditionally surrendered all enemy troops north of the Medjerda river and south of Bizerte on May 9. Notwithstanding the surrender of Fifth Panzer Army, 135RCT was ordered to continue operations and to pick up any enemy in the vicinity.[23] By nightfall on May 9, enemy forces along the lower section of the Medjerda river beyond 34ID's zone had been destroyed or captured. Wholesale surrenders were making the process of mopping up more tedious than risky.[24]

Some in the 34th Infantry Division might have been tempted to exploit the enemy's situation by continuing across the coastal plain, perhaps to Tunis. Ryder's men had struggled through the hills since April 23rd. They could be excused for wanting to be in on the final kill. But the boundary between U.S. II Corps and British V Corps had been carefully defined, and the Americans were under strict orders to remain northwest of the Medjerda river. The 34th Infantry Division reassembled its battalions, sent patrols to Djedeida, outposted the hills near Eddekhila, eagerly sampled some of the local fresh food, and sent the last of the Axis soldiers to the prisoner-of-war cages.[25] On May 11 the 135th Infantry Regiment and its sister regiments moved into a division bivouac area five miles west of Chouïgui. The regimental history of 135RCT laconically reported that "The African campaign was concluded."[26]

CHAPTER 35

"Time's Tomorrows"

On May 12, the Trident conference between President Roosevelt, Prime Minister Churchill and their military advisors began. The meeting in Washington, D.C. lasted until May 25. Among the chief outcomes was a unified Allied strategy in Europe for the period after the imminent invasion of Sicily. To implement that strategy, the high command considered how best to utilize the now experienced U.S. divisions in North Africa. Except for individual soldiers chosen to return to the United States to augment the training of the many new U.S. Army divisions, the veteran U.S. divisions were assigned to fight the Germans on the continent of Europe.

The remaining Axis forces in Tunisia surrendered on May 13, 1943. The prisoners came by the hundreds, then the thousands, then the tens of thousands; eventually there were more than 200,000, waving white flags. "Germans were everywhere," Ernie Pyle reported. "It made me a little light-headed." The surviving enemy soldiers flooded and then overflowed the stockades—"the Herrenvolk like chickens in a yard," the British author and journalist A. D. Divine wrote. Only a week before the Trident talks began, Eisenhower had assured Marshall that the "Axis cannot have more than a total of 150,000 men in Tunisia." He was wrong by a wide margin; the Axis prisoners included multitudes of rear-echelon troops and Italian colonial officials. Within a week after the Axis surrender the prison camp population grew to 225,000 and beyond. They were stuffed into compounds built to hold 70,000. In the end, Axis prisoners of war in Tunisia were kept in line by 8,600 guards, equivalent to half a division.[1]

The British forced the surrenders of the highest-ranking Axis officers further south. At 11:15a.m. on May 12, Mussolini authorized the capitulation of the First Italian Army. Fatuous posturing by the Italian generals followed, with white-flag emissaries sent to bargain for better terms from the British, who stiffly offered a stark choice of unconditional surrender or sudden annihilation by more than 700 massed artillery pieces. Ten minutes before the British deadline, the newly promoted Field Marshal Giovanni Messe gave up.[2]

Von Arnim and his staff had retreated to remote St.-Marie-du-Zit, 20 miles north of Enfidaville, where they camped with General Hans Cramer and the remnants of the *Deutsche Afrika Korps*. Von Arnim too knew that the game was over. He dispatched a colonel to find the British headquarters, who soon returned with Lieutenant General Charles Allfrey and Major General Francis Tuker—commanding respectively the mighty British V Corps and the tough 4th Indian Division—in Arnim's staff car. Von Arnim told the Allied generals that he "could not alter Hitler's orders" by surrendering all remaining forces in North Africa. Allfrey brusquely assured Arnim that that he and his troops would be blown off the map. Allfrey ordered the German to surrender his personal weapons and to present himself immediately for transport to a prisoner-of-war cage. Von Arnim complied and was later flown to Algiers and imprisoned. When Arnim requested to meet Lieutenant General Eisenhower, he was ignored. The Allied Supreme Commander would not speak to any German general until the final surrender of the Wehrmacht and the Reich at Reims two years later.[3]

In the early afternoon of Thursday, May 13, Alexander cabled a dignified message to Churchill, who was then again meeting with Roosevelt in the White House: "Sir, it is my duty to report that the Tunisian campaign is over. All enemy resistance has ceased. We are masters of the North African shores."[4] The breathy American statements common early in the campaign now yielded to eloquent brevity; Bradley's two-word cable to Eisenhower on May 9 read simply: "Mission accomplished."[5]

II Corps's casualties in the two weeks before the capitulation of Fifth Panzer Army had exceeded 4,400, with almost half the U.S. casualties from the 34th Infantry Division. Allied casualties in *Torch* and the subsequent Tunisian campaign had exceeded 70,000 men. The toll included 38,000 British—two-thirds in First Army and one-third in Eighth Army—of whom more than 6,200 were killed in action and 10,600 were missing or captured. French casualties exceeded 19,400, half of whom were dead or missing. There were 19,221 total American casualties from mid-November 1942 to mid-May 1943. These included 2,715 men killed in action, nearly 9,000 men wounded, and more than 6,500 men missing in action, in addition to about 1,000 *Torch* casualties.

As always, infantrymen bore the brunt. Although infantry units were only 14 percent of the U.S. Army's overseas strength in World War II, infantrymen suffered 70 percent of all American casualties. The 34th Infantry Division alone sustained more than 4,000 dead, wounded, and missing in North Africa—one quarter of the division's total strength. The 1st Infantry Division suffered nearly as many. Some units such as the 168th Infantry Regiment were shattered and had to be completely reconstituted.[6]

Axis casualties remain uncertain to this day. Enemy dead in just the last two weeks of the campaign were estimated at 3,000 in the U.S. sector, with another 41,000 captured. The German dead in Tunisia have been estimated at more than 8,500 and the Italians at more than 3,700. Combat wounded are usually more numerous than those killed in action by a factor of three or four, so an additional 40,000 to 50,000 Axis wounded can be approximated from the imperfect records. There is also substantial doubt around the number of German and Italian prisoners of war. Allied records in late May 1943 listed 238,243 unwounded prisoners in custody, including nearly 102,000 Germans. Von Arnim estimated the total prisoner count closer to 300,000, while Colonel Siegfried Westphal, Rommel's former chief of staff, put the German prisoner-of-war count alone at roughly 166,000. Rick Atkinson suggests that 250,000 is a reasonable estimate of those captured.

The war criminal Goebbels privately called the fall of North Africa a "second Stalingrad," telling his diary, "Our losses there are enormous." Half as many German divisions were destroyed in North Africa as at Stalingrad, but Allied prison camps in Tunisia overflowed with Axis rear-echelon support troops who would no longer be supporting the dictators. For the Axis, the campaign had ended in unmitigated disaster. Two armies had been destroyed. There were no Axis soldiers still fighting in North Africa. For the Allies, the North African invasion and the Tunisian camp had been a truly desperate gamble with the highest stakes. The campaign had ended in absolute triumph that indeed augured well for the future of the Allied nations and for human decency.[7]

The 34th Infantry Division marched proudly in the Allied victory parade in Tunis on Thursday, May 20, 1943. Under the palms on the *Avenue Maréchal Gallieni*, the 135th Infantry Regiment participated *en masse* as the United States representatives for the valor of the regiment's soldiers at Hill 609. While perhaps not as sharply "spit and polish" in appearance as the French, British and Empire troops, the Americans were gratefully and enthusiastically received by the liberated French. By 11:00a.m., the temperature in the shade was 92 degrees—"too damned hot to cuss," one soldier wrote. But it did not matter. Crowds six deep lined *Avenue Gallieni* and the broad *Avenue Jules Ferry* to celebrate the victorious end of the North African campaign.

The parade began at noon, after a convoy of limousines and open sedans pulled up at the reviewing platform and Lieutenant General Eisenhower took his place in the front row next to General Giraud. After the French came the Americans, with a band playing "Stars and Stripes Forever." The Red Bull GIs marched in new, olive-drab wool blouses, buttoned at the collar with the sleeves rolled down despite the heat, and M1 steel helmets that half hid their faces. Major General Harmon thought the troops shuffled like "Arkansas backwoodsmen," and Patton complained that "our men do not put up a good show in reviews. I think that we still lack pride in being soldiers, and we must develop it." But the cheering Tunis crowd saw the Americans as the heroes they truly were. From the sidewalks and the balconies, the crowd cried out "*Vive l'Amérique!*" and mobbed into the streets to hug the GIs.[8]

General Bradley left for Algiers on May 13 with some of his staff to attend conferences on the invasion and conquest of Sicily, and then set up a new II Corps headquarters at Relizane in the Oran area. The Eastern Base Section, which had held temporary control of an area adjacent to Mateur and Bizerte, released that control to the British First Army. Soon, of the former units of U.S. II Corps, only the U.S. 34th Infantry Division remained, serving for a time as a garrison force in northeastern Tunisia.

In his memoirs, Bradley expressed a mixed judgment of Major General Ryder and of the 34th Infantry Division, in a manner consistent with Bradley's practiced psychological distance from his subordinates and from the troops.

> In the 34th Division Ryder had confirmed his reputation as that of a skilled tactician. Lacking the dash of Terry Allen, he subordinated himself to the division. His weakness, however, lay in the contentment with which he tolerated mediocrity in his command. For rather than relieve ineffective subordinate commanders, he overlooked their shortcomings and thus penalized the division as well as himself.[9]

But Bradley did not hide his pride in the performance and sacrifice of the 34th Infantry Division.

> With [the] successful attack against Hill 609 the 34th rid itself of the poor reputation with which it had emerged from Fondouk. The following September Ryder sailed with his division from Tunisia to Italy. In two terrible years of campaigning in the mountains there 34th Division put in a total of 605 days in the line. Altogether in World War II it suffered approximately 20,000 casualties—almost one and a half times its full strength.[10]

"A Terrible Beauty"

"[O]ne continent had been redeemed," wrote Churchill with majestic brevity.[11] But the consequences of the Allied conquest of North Africa were greater than the occupation of the land, however strategically situated. The objective correlation of forces and military power between the Allies and the Axis had been permanently altered in favor of the Allies. The immediate military consequences were greatest for the Americans. Four U.S. divisions now had combat experience. U.S. soldiers of all ranks had learned the crucial importance of constant, realistic training and practice of military tasks and the need for complete familiarity with the use and tactical application of all weapons. They understood and could teach others the methods of combined arms teams, of reconnaissance and aggressive patrolling, of supply and sustainment in combat, of maneuver and stealth, of massed armor, and, it goes almost without saying, massed, coordinated artillery fire. They knew what it was like and how it felt to be bombed, shelled, shot at, and machine-gunned. They had experienced near starvation, exhaustion, filth, and bitterness at their lot, and they had kept fighting. Most of them were confident that they could do it again. They now provided the U.S. Army with a blooded hundred thousand hard-handed soldiers, "high-grade stock from which we must breed with the utmost rapidity," as one general urged.[12]

The Allied conquest of the northern rim of Africa and of the Mediterranean Sea had permanently seized the military initiative in the West from Hitler. Even the optimist Kesselring recognized the insurmountable and still growing power of the Allied forces. "It was in Tunisia," he later observed, "that the superiority of your air force first became evident." A Swiss newspaper reported that in Berlin people were "walking around as though hit in the head." The defeat and enormous losses of dead and captured were a terrible blow in Italy, which lost its African colonies and whose people at last clearly recognized the fatuous delusions of the ruling elite. The Italian people were more than ready for the end of the Fascist era.

Strategically, the campaign had bought the dictators some time by keeping the Mediterranean closed an additional six months. *Torch* and the Tunisian battles had strained Allied shipping and constrained long-term strategic planning by pulling Allied troops and supplies into the Mediterranean and away from an expedition into France. Most ominously for the Red Bull soldiers, the delay had given Kesselring and German engineers months to fortify and reinforce the Third Reich's southern flank in Italy, to which 34ID would be deployed.[13] The Axis was far from finished.

The GIs in North Africa were still growing in their mastery of the art of war and there was much yet to learn. There was no shortage of courage or physical toughness in the individual men of the Red Bull division. But Bradley believed that the campaign had shown that U.S. soldiers were still hesitant to close with and destroy the enemy. "That was his greatest worry," reported Major General Lucian Truscott, who added, "Why not at least be honest with ourselves!" Truscott himself was justly disturbed by what he saw as "too much satisfaction with a mediocre performance," and a tendency by some commanders to gloss over deficiencies. Some combat techniques—such as the critical coordination between armor and infantry—faded as time passed and many new soldiers joined the ranks of the veteran divisions. The historian Eric Larrabee wrote that North Africa had provided "a place to be lousy in, somewhere for the gift for combat and command to be discovered."

But in Rick Atkinson's poignant phrase, a "terrible beauty" had been born in the Americans in Africa. Most Americans had arrived in North Africa bitterly resenting their lot as soldiers in a war they did not want; most were now fully committed to ending the war by the complete destruction of their hated enemy. Drew Middleton wrote that after Tunisia, "the war has become a grudge fight, a personal matter." "There are three things that make a man fight," Ryder observed. "One is pride in himself, another is pride in his organization, and the third is hate. The 34th has all of them."[14]

The men of the 34th Infantry Division were becoming the sharp edge of America's "terrible swift sword." No one would ever call them "Sunday school picnic" boys again. But to win the war it would be necessary to develop and deploy trained teams of soldiers of all branches, infantry, artillery, armor, and air, in units of all sizes from squads to divisions under consistently competent and aggressive combat leaders. Soldiers had to be trained in realistic conditions and to possess and use in combat the skills needed for the coordinated use of all their weapons and systems across the battlefield.[15] To produce an army with those qualities required both talented leadership at all levels and the time for training, practice, and drill, and then more drill and more practice.

The soldiers of the Red Bull Division now needed and sought rest and healing. While they could, they bathed, slept, wore clean clothes and new boots, griped about the chow even when it was served hot, read mail from home, wrote letters, fished with hand grenades in Lake Bizerte, and drank beer and other beverages, some home-brewed and illicit. Soon enough, training resumed, and yet more training followed. Irony, cynicism, and nihilism still infested the ranks. Ernie Pyle had already seen enough of war to ask: "When you figure how many boys are going to get killed, what's the use anyway?" However realistic they were about war, even the most hard-handed and hardheaded men had delusive ideas, including the heartfelt belief that they had done their bit and should be sent home. Veteran GIs had no illusions, except perhaps that one. "Dame Rumor with her thousand tongues is running wild through all the camps in Africa," one soldier warned. The arrival of large numbers of new units and replacement troops in North Africa encouraged the false narrative that veterans at least would get some home leave now. Ryder became so alarmed at his men's self-deceptions that he assembled all the division's officers and sergeants on a hill near Mateur in mid-May.

> There are many rumors out there that the 34th Division [troops have] fought their battles, done their time, and are going back to the States. But, gentlemen, I am here to tell you today that the 34th Division will not go back until the war is over... As this war goes on it will get progressively worse and there will be progressively harder objectives to take, and more casualties as the German lines tighten. We shall fight in Europe, and we shall find that in comparison, the Tunisian campaign was but a maneuver with live ammunition.

Ryder told the brutal truth, and it was hard to hear. A Red Bull soldier mocked, "Ol' General Ryder's so homely that probably his wife doesn't care whether he gets back or not."[16]

In North Africa, the Red Bull soldiers had learned the privations and loss of real war, the brutal trauma of battle, the comradeship of professional soldiers, and the meaning of duty to one's fellows and to the country, often articulated in the sarcastic, vulgar language of the GI. Many GIs had discovered their own personal reserves of resilience and could now think clearly about the war and their place in it. "There is nothing over here to fog your vision of right and wrong," a soldier from Iowa wrote his parents. Underneath the ceaseless griping, typical of all U.S. combat soldiers, Red Bull soldiers felt what every man was really fighting for. "We all feel we've got something to fight for and something to live for, and we go along every day with the hope and the prayer on our lips that we can soon be on our journey home." North Africa had been their first step on that long journey.[17]

The protracted campaign in Tunisia delayed Allied European operations, beginning with *Husky*, the invasion of Sicily. The high command adjusted the planning schedules and recalculated the allocations of shipping and combat units. "War is a burden to be carried on a steep and bloody road," Marshall observed, "and only strong nerves and determined spirits can endure to the end." *Torch* had been a great risk—"the purest gamble America and Britain undertook during the war," the official U.S. Army Air Forces history concluded.[18] The victors, including the Red Bull soldiers of the 34th Infantry Division, deservedly celebrated their victory. "For the Anglo-Americans," Churchill wrote Eisenhower, the triumph was "an augury full of hope for the future of the world. Long may they march together, striking down the tyrants and oppressors of mankind."[19]

The certainty of more combat and death nonetheless cast a long shadow. To the soldiers of the "Red Bull" 34th Infantry Division, looking out over the Mediterranean from Africa, many more days of brutal battle lay ahead in Italy. Tens upon tens of thousands of GIs who had not yet even seen war were to be thrust over the next two years into that protracted and always uphill struggle known to history as the Italian Campaign. Among those men, and many women, was Second Lieutenant Robert N. Stokes, from Indianapolis, Indiana, soon to be assigned as a platoon leader in Company C, 1st Battalion, 135th Infantry Regiment. Like his fellow Red Bull soldiers, Second Lieutenant Stokes had been an ordinary American, torn away from his life, friends, family, and job by the tidal forces of war and transformed into a soldier. And with his fellow Red Bull soldiers he would fight, suffer, and be forever changed by battle and war. That American soldier was my father.

Documents

Document 1: General Order No. 3, Headquarters Iowa National Guard, Adjutant General's Office, February 3, 1941

HEADQUARTERS IOWA NATIONAL GUARD
ADJUTANT GENERAL'S OFFICE
Des Moines, Iowa

February 6, 1941

ADVANCE COPY

GENERAL ORDERS

NUMBER 3.

INDUCTION OF THE 34TH DIVISION INTO THE ACTIVE
MILITARY SERVICE OF THE UNITED
STATES.

1. The following Executive Order, ordering the 34th Division into the active military service of the United States is quoted:

EXECUTIVE ORDER

By virtue of the authority conferred upon me by Public Resolution No. 96, 76th Congress, approved August 27, 1940, and the National Defense Act of June 3, 1916, as amended (39 Stat. 166), and as Commander-in-Chief of the Army and Navy of the United States, I hereby order into the active military service of the United States, effective on dates to be hereafter announced by the Secretary of War, the following units and members of the National Guard of the United States to serve in the active military service of the United States for a period of twelve consecutive months, unless sooner relieved:

UNITS
All Federally recognized elements of:

*   *   *   *   *   *

34TH DIVISION

*   *   *   *   *   *

MEMBERS

All members, both active and inactive, of the units listed above.

All persons so ordered into the active military service of the United States are, from the effective date for each unit as respectively announced in War Department orders, relieved from duty in the National Guard of their respective States so long as they shall remain in the active military service of the United States, and during such time shall be subject to such laws and regulations for the government of the Army of the United States as may be applicable to members of the Army whose permanent retention in the active military service is not contemplated by law.

Commissioned officers and warrant officers appointed in the National Guard of the United States and commissioned or holding warrants in the Army of the United States, and affected by this Order, are hereby ordered to active duty on the dates to be respectively prescribed in War Department orders under such appointments and commissions or warrants.

All officers and warrant officers of the National Guard, appointed in the National Guard, who shall have been Federally recognized or examined and found qualified for Federal recognition, and shall have been assigned to units ordered to active duty under this Order prior to the effective dates respectively to be indicated for such units in War Department orders, who do not hold appointments in the National Guard of the United States in the same grade and arm or service in which they respectively have been most recently Federally recognized or have been most recently examined and found qualified for Federal recognition, are hereby tendered appointments in the National Guard of the United States in the same grade and arm or service in which they shall have been most recently Federally recognized or examined and found qualified for Federal recognition.

Each warrant officer and enlisted man of the National Guard, assigned to a unit ordered to active duty under this Order, who shall have been examined and found qualified for appointment as an officer in the National Guard of the United States, under the provisions of Section III, National Defense Act, as amended, and who shall not have been appointed in the National Guard of the United States in the grade for which examined and found qualified prior to the effective date to be prescribed in War Department orders for the induction of his unit, is hereby tendered appointment in the National Guard of the United States and commission in the Army of the United States, in the same grade and arm or service for which he shall have been so examined and found qualified, effective on the date of induction of his unit.

Each warrant officer and enlisted man of the National Guard who holds appointment as an officer in the National Guard of the United States and a commission in the Army of the United States, or who is tendered such appointment and commission by the terms of this Order, and who is assigned to a unit ordered to active duty under this Order prior to the effective date to be prescribed in War Department orders for the induction of such unit, is hereby ordered to active military service as a commissioned officer of the Army of the United States under that appointment and commission, effective on the date of induction of his unit.

<table>
<tr><td></td><td>Franklin D. Roosevelt.</td></tr>
<tr><td>The White House
January 14, 1941.</td><td>No. 8633</td></tr>
</table>

2. The processes of induction will be governed by AR 130-10, dated March 27, 1940, "Induction into the Service of the United States."

3. The Executive Order above quoted states "on the dates to be hereafter announced by the Secretary of War." Radiogram from the Secretary of War, dated January 16, 1941, which was quoted in mimeograph letter from this office, dated January 18, 1941, announced February 10, 1941, as the effective date of order into the active military service of the United States.

4. Officers responsible for the disbursement of State funds, will pay all current obligations prior to departure from home stations. They will dispose and account for unexpended balances of State funds in accordance with Memorandum No. 19, Headquarters, Iowa National Guard, dated December 5, 1940.

5. Final Report of National Guard Duty performed (WDNGB Form 100) for the period February 1 to February 9, 1941, incl., 1941, will be prepared as of February 9, 1941, and distributed through normal channels. Final Armory Drill Payroll for the period December 1, 1940 to February 9, 1941, inclusive, will be prepared immediately upon induction, and forwarded through normal channels.

By order of THE GOVERNOR:

CHARLES H. GRAHL,
Brig Gen AGD.,
The Adjutant General.

OFFICIAL: *R. A. Lancaster*

R. A. LANCASTER,
Lt Col AGD.,
Asst. Adjutant General.

Document 2: WDAG Order Detaching Ryder and for Travel to 34ID

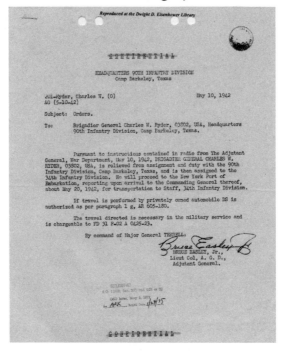

Document 3: V Corps Order Assigning Ryder as CG, 34ID

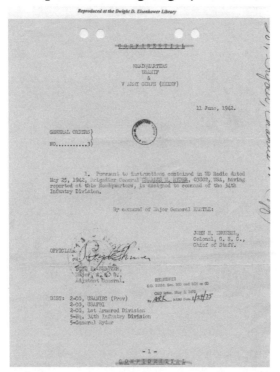

Document 4: MG Ryder's assumption of command of 34ID

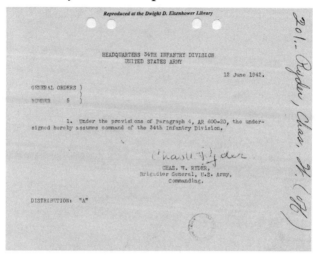

Document 5: Most Secret ULTRA Message from AFHQ to Ryder, November 6, 1942

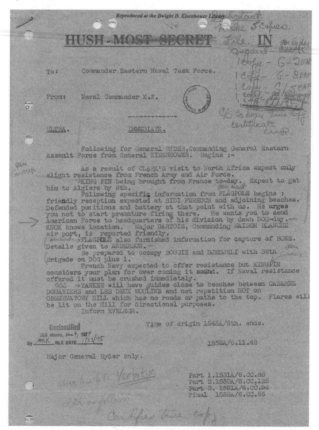

S. 1320b. **NAVAL MESSAGE.** Revised December, 1935.

S. 1320c. (For use with S. 1320b). **NAVAL MESSAGE.** (Revised October, 1935.)

S.1320c. (For use with S. 1320b). **NAVAL MESSAGE.** (Revised October, 1935.)

Write across	Number	Fire	Hq	AMP	23	55
	Out	42	-	Policy	Regarding	60
	Offensive	Action	-	and	strict	65
	compliance	therewith	.	I	rely	70
	on	all	to	carry	out	75
	the	spirit	of	these	instructions	80
			ENDS			85
						90
	Carbon copies to: Admiral Burrough					
	General Ryder					
	General Eveleigh					95
	G-2					
	G/1					100
						105
						110
						115
						120
						125
						130
						135
						140
						145
						150

S.1320. **NAVAL MESSAGE.** Revised December, 1935.

For use in Signal Department only				

Originators Instructions:
Indication of Priority,
Intercept Group, etc. URGENT

Codress Plaindress

No. of Groups:

TO: CC 57 160 - Eoran

FROM: Gen Ryder CG EAF

Write Across	Reliable	information	from	Allied	Headquarters	5
	shows	that	Gen	MAST	commanding	10
	French	Algiers	Division	with	headquarters	15
	at	HUEL	is	LA	DIVISION	20
	near	CATHEDRAL	and	PALAIS	D'HIVER	25
	(736 150)	is	favourable	to	us	30
	.	lend	a	force	of	35
	two	platoons	with	a	field	40
	officer	to	his	headquarters	by	45
	dawn	or	as	soon	as	50

System	P/L Code or Cypher	Time of Receipt	Time of Despatch	Operator	P.O.O.W.	Date
						135
						140
						145
						150

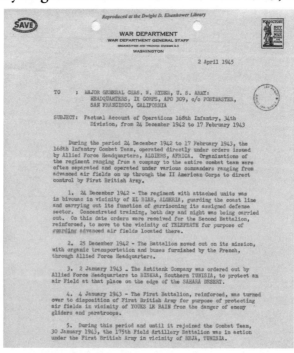

Reproduced at the Dwight D. Eisenhower Library

Document 6: Drake's Letter to Ryder: Factual Account of Operations 168th Infantry Regiment 24 Dec. 1942–17 Feb. 1943, April 2, 1945

6. Sometime during the first week in January 1943, Company C, 109th Medical Battalion and Company C, 109th Engineer Battalion, were both detached from the regiment and sent back to ORAN to rejoin the 34th Division, then arriving in AFRICA.

7. The Third Battalion, 168th Infantry, was held in Force Reserve in vicinity of ALGIERS by Allied Force Headquarters.

8. 15 January 1943 - The Regimental Commander, Colonel Thomas D. Drake, started on a visit of inspection of the widely spread regiment, covering 1500 miles during the next ten days and finding conditions far from satisfactory. The units placed out on guard had been given such varied duties and orders by persons unfamiliar with Infantry training and tactics that they were unable to carry on any proper training.

9. 29 January 1943 - At 1830 hours Colonel Drake received a telephone message to report to Allied Force Headquarters. Upon arriving there he was directed to leave for CONSTANTINE and there report to Lieutenant General Anderson, Commanding First British Army. Upon inquiry as to the disposition of the Third Battalion, Service Company and remainder of Headquarters Company he was informed that the Third Battalion would remain in place, but nothing was known about the other two organizations. Alerting the two companies the Colonel put in a telephone call for Brigadier McNabb, the Chief of Staff, First British Army and received his permission to bring the two companies along with him.

10. 30 January 1943 - At 0430 hours Saturday after a night spent in preparation and securing permission for the movement of the convoy along the over-crowded roads, the column passed the IP west of ALGIERS. Leaving the two companies under command of the Executive Officer for bivouacking, Colonel Drake proceeded on to British Army Headquarters at CONSTANTINE. All officers were out to dinner and he waited until 2130 hours at which time the staff returned. Orders were issued to him to proceed to the C.P. of the II American Corps located in a ravine just east of TEBESSA and there report to Major General L. R. Fredendall, U. S. Army, who would give him exact orders, but that in general his mission was to attack the Germans with the 168th Combat Team and secure some high ground overlooking the coastal plains of TUNISIA.

11. 31 January 1943 - Upon arriving at II Corps Headquarters about 1530 hours, Colonel Drake was greeted by General Fredendall who told

him he was needed badly at the front. General Fredendall showed him the situation map and indicated an area covering the high ground east of GAFSA and commanding the coastal plain over which Rommel's Army must move northward to effect union with the mass of German troops that had been pouring into Africa daily for the past two months. The order in substance was as follows: "You will attack tomorrow morning and seize this high ground (indicating). After taking up an all around defensive position you will conduct raids into Rommel's Lines of Communications, doing all the damage you can and prevent his uninterrupted movement north."

General Fredendall told Colonel Drake that his combat team was already up forward and for him to report to Major General Orlando Ward, First Armored Division for orders. Colonel Drake informed General Fredendall that neither the Anti-tank Company or the Third Battalion were with him. General Fredendall stated they were ordered to be present and that he had asked the First British Army for the entire Combat Team. General Fredendall then directed his Chief of Staff to get on the telephone and have the Third Battalion, Anti-tank Company, Engineer Company and Collecting Company released from their assignments and sent forward to join the Combat Team. General Fredendall then told Colonel Drake that one of his battalions (later found to be the First Battalion) had been pretty badly used that morning in an abortive assault upon the enemy positions when they were caught in their trucks by German dive bombers.

12. Going forward a few miles Colonel Drake reported in to the Rear Echelon C.P. of the First Armored Division. The officer (Lt Col) on duty said that the First Battalion, 168th Infantry, was at the front under the command of Colonel Maraist, Commanding Combat Command "D", and that General Ward who was up forward wanted to see Colonel Drake as soon as possible. He also stated that the Second Battalion, 168th Infantry, was down the road a couple of miles awaiting for darkness and the trucks that had been arranged to carry them forward; that the 175th Field Artillery Battalion was then moving in in that area. This officer then wanted to know if Colonel Drake would take charge and assume responsibility. Colonel Drake said, "No", most emphatically. He then explained that for him to take charge in the middle of their work would only tend to tie it up. That he, Colonel Drake, knew nothing about the arrangements that had been made, nor how many or where the trucks were to come from to haul the troops and nothing about road conditions or the enemy situation; that for the First Armored Division to carry-on until the troops were in their alloted assembly area was the only sensible thing to do.

13. Colonel Drake then visited both the 175th Field Artillery Battalion, commanded by Lt. Colonel Kelly, and the Second Battalion, 168th Infantry, commanded by Lt. Colonel Dewey H. Baer and assured himself that they had full loads of ammunition; told them that they would attack the next morning and that he would issue orders as soon as he found out the situation and received orders from the First Armored Division; further, that the First Armored Division would issue orders for their movement forward to an assembly area and upon reaching it, he wanted both of them to report to him at the advanced C.P. of the Combat Command. Shortly after midnight, about 0030 hours, the first of February, Colonel Drake reached GAFSA.

After identifying himself to the cross-roads military policeman, he learned what road led to General Ward's headquarters 20 miles southeast of GAFSA. Colonel Drake told the M.P. to watch for his column and the M.P. said a guide was right there to meet them. He then called Captain Frederick K. Hughes, 024471, First Armored Division, who came forward and told him that he had been sent there to meet the Infantry and Artillery to conduct them to their assembly area. When Colonel Drake questioned him Captain Hughes assured him he knew exactly where to place the troops and that they would be where Colonel Drake wanted them that morning. Also that the C.C. Headquarters had selected the places and as soon as they were in position he would report the fact to him at C. C. Headquarters. Colonel Drake told him he was going to stop and see General Ward first and then would go on to Colonel Maraist's C.P.

He appeared to know what he was talking about, so with a final word of caution to be careful about overrunning the Front Line, which Captain Hughes assured him couldn't happen, because he knew where to go and besides that the First Armored Division M.P.'s covered the road, Colonel Drake drove on.

Reaching General Ward's C.P. at 0230 hours, he explained the situation; said Colonel Maraist had everything left in the division under his command; that Maraist would be in command, but that Col Drake would command all of the Infantry; that his entire division, Combat Commands, A, B, and C were away on other Fronts and that he had nothing left but the General Staff to command. He explained that an attack had been started that day (Sunday); that the First Battalion, 168th Infantry, had been caught in trucks by Boche dive bombers and that they had suffered very heavily. He knew they were badly shaken, but hoped Colonel Drake would be able to pull them out of it.

After leaving him Colonel Drake drove on several miles and found Colonel Maraist's C.P. at about 0430 hours. The S-3 suggested he wait in their C.P. half-track until 0530 hours when Colonel Maraist would issue his battle orders. He further told Colonel Drake that all of his commanders had been, or would be, ordered to report at 0530 hours, so there wasn't anything he could do until then; that the units were closing in their bivouacs, having passed while he was with General Ward.

Lt. Colonel John Petty, Commander of First Battalion, came in shortly afterwards and explained to Colonel Drake that the First Battalion had been ordered sent forward in trucks to attack, along with tanks, and that they had been caught by dive bombers and badly shot up, but that they would be ready to fight again that day.

It still lacked some time before Colonel Maraist would appear to deliver his order of battle, so Colonel Drake started out to the bivouac of the Second Battalion. The sandy desert on the left of the trail where they should have been was completely barren except for a few tanks and half-tracks. As Colonel Drake's fears began to take more definite shape, violent firing of all calibers suddenly sounded from the east, well within the German lines. He knew the worst! In the darkness, the guide, Captain Hughes, had led this battalion well inside the enemy lines! The firing lasted about 30 minutes and then subsided. There seemed to be no alternative to their fate. The M.P. farthest to the front told Colonel Drake that about 0300 or 0330 hours, a long line of trucks carrying troops had passed him headed for the enemy lines. He was asked why he had not stopped them and he replied that he had had no orders to do so. Colonel Drake returned to the C.P. and inquired of Lt Colonel Petty how the truck column could have gotten through the front line and then sent him to get the outpost, which Petty said, he had placed on the road. Petty came back accompanied by two frightened privates who admitted to having been the farthest advanced road outpost. They both stated that they had halted the column, but that the officer leading it had gotten out of his machine and told them that he knew where he was going and that everything would be alright. (Nine months later I met Captain Hughes in a prison camp in Poland. He then stated to me that he had seen no such outpost and furthermore that he had never seen that terrain but one time and that during day light.) Colonel Drake's C.P. and Service Company had likewise failed to show up, but he was thankful for the appearance of Lt. Colonel Kelly, who assured him that the 175th Field Artillery would be right with him in everything he wanted.

Colonel Maraist now came to the group and issued in substance the following order: "The Infantry under Colonel Drake will attack, supported by tanks and artillery, and capture SENED. It will then push on and seize and fortify the high ground about eight kilometers east of SENED. No artillery preparation will be made. The tanks will advance on the left of the Infantry next to the mountain and will be available on call to Colonel Drake. Time of attack: 0730 hours". At this juncture about 50 German dive bombers suddenly appeared and started raining bombs down on the troops. No anti-aircraft artillery was available! Only the 30 and 50 caliber machine guns mounted on half-tracks and tanks, all of which went into action, as well as many of the rifles of the Infantry. The desert was soon littered with burning tanks and half-tracks. Several planes plummeted to earth in flames and many white parachutes dotted the sky as some were able to jump before going down. After dropping their bomb loads, the Germans withdrew.

The conference reassembled and Colonel Drake told Colonel Maraist that he couldn't possibly attack at 0730 hours as he had not had time to see the ground or his troops. He was asked what was the earliest time he could attack and he replied "0930 hours is the very earliest". Colonel Maraist then said, "Alright, time of attack 0930 hours".

14. At 0930 hours, Monday 1 February 1943, the attack started. As the Infantry moved forward it drew both enemy artillery and small arms fire. Lt. Colonel Kelly was forward with Colonel Drake at all times and was also in communication with the Armored Artillery. Prompt artillery fire was brought to bear on all targets located. Hard fighting resulted on the open plain. The tanks soon ran into emplaced 88's well dug-in in the cactus patches where they were completely concealed. Progress was very slow. About two kilometers advance had been made by 0120O hours with the town of SENED now in sight. To the north of the railroad, which ran east and west, were many blazing and smoking vehicles of the Second Battalion which were fired by the enemy. As the advance continued Colonel Drake saw what appeared to be hundreds of men break out of the cactus at the foot of the ridge on their left and start dashing toward them. It was the remainder of the Second Battalion. Colonel Drake arranged for a renewal of the attack with Combat Command D at 1430 hours. At the attack started out it was met by enemy fire of all descriptions, which soon stopped its advance and pinned it to the ground. Men were dying everywhere. The sand was being kicked up in the clouds and the air was filled with buzzing and whining

bullets. This appeared to be the end of the battle, because they had put everything into it time and again and still could not get forward. At this juncture Colonel Drake walked out in front of the First Battalion and started casually walking toward the enemy lines. At his urging they all got to their feet and charged forward. Enemy tanks were waiting in a row under the olive trees bringing direct fire upon them. They concentrated their small arms fire on these vehicles causing them to button up and continued their advance. Suddenly the enemy tanks, apparently not understanding this spectacle of riflemen attacking them, turned and streaked through the town. They had now gained the edge of the town when Colonel Drake sent Captain Bird, Commanding Company B, to envelope the town from the right. This he did and soon sent him a message that he had successfully reached the crossroad on the other side of the town. Colonel Drake went back to where he had last seen battalion headquarters and there found Lt. Colonel Petty had received a mortal wound through the stomach and that the battalion Executive Officer had been wounded. In addition to the capture of the town, including a railroad roundhouse and 12 engines, over 260 prisoners, about 100 Italians and a large amount of equipment, including new motorcycles in crates, were passed on to Combat Command D Headquarters. The Second Battalion was being reorganized under Major Moore, the Battalion Executive Officer, Lt. Colonel Baer having been wounded that day. The First Battalion now organized for all around defense, morale having been restored - everything looked better.

15. Tuesday, 2 February 1943, orders were issued at 0200 hours by Colonel Maraist for continuing of the attack at 0500 hours and to seize the high ground overlooking the open plains extending toward SFAX. The Tanks would precede Colonel Drake's Infantry; he would have the Cannon Company, 39th Infantry, attached to him for the battle. Colonel Drake issued orders for the attack in column of battalions; Second Battalion to follow First Battalion at 1000 yards; 175th Field Artillery displacing by bounds ready for instant support on call; Cannon Company follow right flank of First Battalion; Service Company remain where it was; O.P. follow First Battalion; Colonel Drake would be forward with the First Battalion. Promptly at 0500 hours the attack moved forwards. As Colonel Drake passed a large barn just before clearing the town, one of his inquisitive soldiers threw open the barn doors and about twenty Italians, who had huddled in there throughout the night, came pouring out with their hands raised over their heads. Within a few minutes the German Air Force appeared overhead and again they experienced the nerve racking scream of the dive bomber, accompanied by the heavy 'Crrunch'

of the exploding bomb. But this was going to be different - no more
than three of the Germans had gone into their dive when what appeared
to be black arrows came from over the range of hills to their left.
It was the first appearance of the American Air Force. These fast
'Lightnings' could fly rings around the Stukas and German planes soon
began falling everywhere.

Long range fire came against them, but nothing could stop the advance. Soon the first high ground was taken, then the next, and by
1400 hours the objective was reached.

Organization for defense was made while their tanks pushed on out
as a protecting screen on the open desert beyond and there gave battle
to German Panzers that were counter-attacking.

16. The First Battalion held the main part of the front; the
Second Battalion, the left rear, the 175th Field Artillery, a position
in center rear; the Armored Artillery, over which Colonel Drake had no
control, farther back and the Tanks toward the right rear flank, while
the remainder was used in front covering the organization of the ground.
The 39th Infantry Cannon Company was placed behind the first ridge in
the First Battalion sector where it could protect the front and left
against enemy armored attack. The Antitank Company had not arrived.
Engineers now came forward and were given the herculean task of plant-
ing mines to cover the valley to the left of the position.

Several dive bombing attacks and strafings, following the dropping
of their bombs, occurred throughout the day. During the days' attack
a long column of German trucks and tanks had been 'bottled up' in a
narrow rocky defile along the right flank by placing guns and mines at
both ends of it. The road being so narrow the enemy could not turn
their vehicles around, Colonel Drake asked for bombers to destroy them,
but headquarters sent word that they would be captured. This seriously
depleted his strength to maintain two fighting forces at the ends of the
pass. Neither could a sufficient force be detailed to fight and capture
them without deviating from the main mission. This enemy force was a
source of worry in that it might break out and over-run the rear area.

17. About 1700 hours Colonel Drake observed a movement near the
eastern exit of this pass which was about two miles away. Through his
field glasses he saw what appeared to be guns moving into position. At
first it was believed the enemy had debouched and were preparing to go
into action. The 175th Field Artillery was alerted and swung its guns
to cover this position while he went forward to find out who they were.

It was found that it was the Armored Artillery moving forward into
position.

Some desultory firing was going on at the front when from his
position Colonel Drake saw the road suddenly choke with fleeing
vehicles dashing madly to the rear. He started off cross-country
to intercept them, but several vehicles had already passed when he
reached the road. The men in the overcrowded vehicles were wild
eyed, as they roared along at full speed. The column was made up
of half-ton weapon carriers, jeeps, half-tracks and tanks - anything
that would roll. Colonel Drake stopped this rearward rush and placing a guard across the road, ordered all back to their position.
By personal direction and use of all available officers the troops
were returned to their former positions. Only part of one battalion,
plus some rear units had been effected. Investigations showed that
the screening tanks had been withdrawn without notification and that
a German patrol of one platoon of tanks investigating the withdrawal
had moved forward into the American position, being identified as
friendly tanks. Upon arriving there they opened sudden fire at point
blank range. This sudden development on the overwrought nerves of
troops led the men in the immediate vicinity to believe that the
German Panzers were among them in force. This near panic was averted
without any real loss to the defensive position.

18. 3 February 1945 - Wednesday - The day was passed in consolidating position, making range charts and of being dive-bombed by the
ever present enemy air at frequent intervals. A serious loss was sustained shortly before daylight when one of our half-tracks laden with
engineer personnel ran into a Dump of fuzed mines, setting off the
entire Dump. At 0930 hours the Antitank Company arrived, completing
their long journey from BISKRA and were placed in position. In the
late afternoon Brigadier General Ray Porter, who had been placed in
command of the entire sector, came forward and after inspection expressed his pleasure over the defensive set-up.

19. 4 February 1943 - Thursday - The entire day was quiet with
the exception of bombing attacks and continued strengthening of the
position. Heavy fighting was in progress north of them near MAKNASSAY,
where another combat command tried to break through to the south to
join forces. The enemy, however, was too strong for them, so there
they sat - two badly mauled battalions - 25 miles out in the heart of
the German Army. Considerable activity was observed out in front

where the enemy could be seen re-fueling tanks in a large olive
grove about eight miles forward. Air bombardment was called for
and was promised for 1400 hours, however, the attack did not
materialize. At 1515 hours a flight of fifteen flying fortresses,
accompanied by Spit Fires, came from the direction of the enemy
line, flying low over the American position and dropped their full
load of bombs on the rear area. Fortunately little damage was done.

20. At 1700 hours Colonel Drake received orders to withdraw
that night under cover of darkness and to secrete his command in the
vicinity of GAFSI by daylight. All roads would be at his disposal
from 2200 hours on and that he would destroy everything that might be
of use to the enemy. Hastily preparations were made and at 1800
hours all commanders were assembled and the order of march was given.
The order: "The Engineers to prepare all installations in SENED, including the roundhouse with the twelve locomotives they had captured
for demolition and to blow them at 2400 hours. They were then to
mine the road behind the Covering Shell which would pass at that hour.
The units in rear areas to march from their area at 2000 hours sharp;
Artillery the same. One Tank Company would follow the First Battalion
which would be in the rear of the Second Battalion, who in turn,
followed the artillery by fifteen minutes. Company B, Captain Bird
commanding, with two platoons of heavy platoons of heavy machine guns
from Company D to cover the front and withdrew on order. Trucks to
be spotted back of the first hill at 2200 hours. Special units with
the C.P., less the Commanding Officer, to follow artillery. Executive
Officer to command the column. Colonel Drake to remain with the shell".
Everything depended on timing and secrecy and the movement went like
clock work. All installations were destroyed immediately after the
troops moved out. At daylight the last of the Combat Team closed in
at its area in the vicinity of GAFSA.

21. 5 February 1943 - Friday - About 0800 hours Colonel Drake
went into GAFSA and talked with General Porter. There he received
orders to proceed to FERRIANA that night, leaving the 175th Field
Artillery behind. Some of the units of the Combat Team had been sent
on to FERRIANA during the withdrawal the previous night by orders of
higher headquarters. At 1500 hours a Colonel from Second American
Corps Headquarters came to Colonel Drake and issued orders for movement to continue on to SBEITLA that night. The movement started
promptly at 1900 hours with proper guides left along the road to
intercept and direct the troops.

22. 6 February 1943 - Saturday - After a hazardous all night
march the regiment, less one battalion, passed SBEITLA and bivouacked in the open desert, depending on dispersion for protection
from enemy bombers. Men and vehicles were dug-in. At 1500 hours
the Corps Chief of Staff, visited the command with orders for the
First Battalion to move to SIDI BOU ZID at dark to relieve a French
Battalion. Protest was made to a particular unit being designated,
whereupon the order was changed to 'send a battalion'. The First
Battalion had suffered very heavily in casualties during the battle
of SENED with approximately 20% casualties inflected on them.
Request was also made again at this time for the 175th Field Artillery Battalion, but instead orders were issued that the Seventeenth
Battalion of Corps, medium artillery would be sent forward to join
the regiment, because they had to have artillery at GAFSA and the
exchange would save moving the two units. However, promise was made
that the 175th Field Artillery would be sent forward within a few
days to rejoin its Combat Team.

23. 7 February 1943 - Sunday - Orders were received attaching
the Regiment to the First Armored Division and for Colonel Drake to
report to Major General Orlando Ward for orders. General Ward
issued orders for the command to move to SIDI BOU ZID that night and
there report to Brigadier General McQuillin, Combat Command A; that
the Third Battalion, 168th Infantry from ALGIERS would join the Regiment on the move forward and that upon reaching there the 17th Field
Artillery would revert to General McQuillin; that the First Battalion,
168th Infantry would move that night back to FERRIANA in Corp Reserve.
After issuing the necessary orders for the movement Colonel Drake went
forward to SIDI BOU ZID and reported to Brigadier General McQuillin.
General McQuillin ordered him to complete his movement that night and
to relieve Colonel Alexander N. Stark, commanding 26th Infantry, First
Infantry Division, the next day. That night the remainder of the
Combat Team, less the First Battalion, and with the Seventeenth Field
Corp Artillery moved forward and came under long range of enemy artill-
ery fire as they neared SIDI BOU ZID. However, the movement was completed into position without confusion.

24. 8 February 1943 - Monday - In early morning Colonel Drake
went on reconnaissance of position with General McQuillin, who selected
positions into which the units would move. Arriving back at the C.P.,
26th Infantry, at 1000 hours orders were issued for the relief of the
26th Infantry by Colonel Drake and movement into position for the other

units. Daylight relief was made necessary by orders that the 26th
Infantry must be relieved by 1700 hours, that day, as it was revert-
ing to the Corp Reserve. By dispersion and taking advantage of vegetation and folds in the ground, the movement forward was made and
the relief completed by 1900 hours.

25. For the next five days, the ninth to the thirteenth, inclusive, the time was spent in consolidating the positions, putting up
wire entanglements, laying the mines and shifting of units. On the
eleventh of February a typewritten order was received by General
McQuillin, signed by the Corp Commander, Major General Fredendall,
directing the exact location and disposition of each organization.
General Ward had written on the margin of this order in pencil,
"Show this to Drake." The order follows:

C
O   S E C R E T
  P
    Y   HEADQUARTERS II CORPS
                  APO #302

                                            11 February 1943

SUBJECT: Defense of FAID Position

TO   : Commanding General, 1st Armored Division.

1. You will take immediate steps to see that the following points
concerning defense of the FAID Position are put into effect:

    a. Scheme of Defense: DJ. KSAIRA on the South and DJ LESSOUDA
on the North are the key terrain features in the defense of FAID. These
two features must be strongly held, with a mobile reserve in the vicinity of SIDI BOU ZID which can rapidly launch a counter attack. Plans for
all possible uses of this reserve should be prepared ahead of time. A
battalion of infantry should be employed for the defense of DJ. KSAIRA,
and the bulk of a battalion of infantry together with a battery of artillery and company of tanks for the defense of DJ. LESSOUDA. Remainder of
artillery is at present satisfactorily located. It should, however,
furnish its own local protection, and be prepared to shift rapidly.

    b. Additional Reserves: The 1st Battalion, 6th Infantry, now
under your control, should immediately send a liaison officer to Hq. CC A.

Inasmuch as this Battalion will likely be employed by McQuillin should
an attack in the FAID area develop, the Battalion Commander in collab-
oration with McQuillin should prepare plans for the use of his Battalion. These plans should insure rapid movement and employment of this
Battalion once it has been ordered.

    c. Reconnaissance: It is extremely important that reconnai-
ssance and counter reconnaissance be conducted by you from HADJEB EL
AIOUN on the North to the pass between DJ. MAIZTLA AND DJ. GOULES on
the South. In this area strong listening posts should be established
24 hours a day from which raids, when appropriate, can be conducted.
It is essential that this reconnaissance and counter reconnaissance
link up with that now being conducted by the 1st British Derby Yeomanry.
The force now at McQuillin's disposal is not sufficient for the area
for which he is responsible. The bulk of your 81st Reconnaissance
Battalion should be used in the area HADJEB EL AIOUN - MAIZTLA - GOULES
PASS.

    d. Patrols: It is vital that strong infantry foot patrols be
sent forward at night from DJ LESSOUDA and DJ KSAIRA. These patrols
must be offensive. They must keep track of the enemy's strength and
organization. They should be especially watchful for any attempt of
the enemy to debauch from the passes at night. They must take prisoners.
It is also important that these patrols locate the presence of minefields,
if any, in areas like the gap between DJ REKHAIB and DJ BOU DZEL. The
latter would, of course, be of great importance in the event we decide
to capture FAID.

    e. Use of Wire, AT Mines, Trip Wire, etc.: I desire that you
make maximum use of all available means to strengthen the positions outlined above. The necessary material is available and should be used
immediately.

    f. Photography: I have instructed my G-2 to furnish you as
soon as possible a photographic strip covering the area: Pass at T8358 -
FAID PASS - REBOU - MATLEG PASS. I have asked that every effort be made
to secure good pictures of the Pass at T8358, FAID PASS, and MATLEG Pass.

2. I desire that a copy of this directive, together with your own
comments, be sent to McQuillin.

3. You will inform me when the instruction enumerated in this

directive have been complied with.

> L. R. FREDENDALL,
> Major General, U.S.A.,
> Commanding.

In other words I want a very strong active defense and not just a passive one. The enemy must be harrassed at every opportunity.

Reconnaissance must never be relaxed - especially at night. Positions indicated _must_ be wired and _mined_ now.

> L.R.F.

S E C R E T

The Second Battalion, less Company E, with two platoons of Company H attached, was placed at DJ. LESSOUDA, eight miles north of the city of SIDI BOU ZID and by General McQuillin's orders directly under the command of Lt. Colonel John K. Waters, First Armored Division; Company E, with two platoons of Company H, were placed with the Armored Artillery as local protection. He further directed that the Third Battalion would garrison DJ. KSAIRA and would be under the direct orders of General McQuillin; that Colonel Drake would command the Service Company and Headquarters Company; that the 17th Field Artillery would be attached to his Artillery and he would issue orders to it. Orders were also issued that the ground must be defended to the last man.

Each night patrols were made into the German lines on call from higher headquarters and prisoners captured and sent back. Some casualties were suffered during these patrols. On the twelfth General Ward sent forward instructions that Colonel Drake would command the Infantry. Upon delivering these orders to Colonel Drake, General McQuillin stated that the Second Battalion would remain under Lt. Colonel Waters at DJ. LESSOUDA and that any orders Colonel Drake saw fit to issue to the Third Battalion would be submitted to him for approval.

26. On Friday night the 12th of February replacements were received at the front. A total of 450 having been sent forward to the regiment, 250 of whom had been dropped off at the First Battalion in FERRIANA and the remainder coming on forward to SIDI BOU ZID. These replacements arrived, part of them without arms of any kind and all carrying two heavy barracks bags of clothing. The roster that accompanied them did not have all of their names on it, but id did contain names of men who were not present. Upon questioning these men it was found that a great many had never fired a rifle in their life. That none of them had entrenching tools, nor bayonets and some were without rifles. Many of them were medical corp men, artillery men, tank destroyer men and everything except infantrymen. These men were sent to the different companies throughout the day and had joined their companies for the attack which came Sunday morning.

That night six truck loads of "bazookas" and their accompanying ammunition was received. Distribution of these guns and rockets were made Saturday, but due to lack of them for instruction they were useless. Every effort had been made to get just one "bazooka" in the regiment for instructional purposes, but without success. They had been systematically forwarded to front line outfits where they were just as religiously thrown away.

27. 13 February 1943 - Saturday - During the afternoon an observer in the outpost on DJ. KSIARA spotted hostile vehicles moving south on the road east of DJ. KRETCHEM. The size of the movement indicated a large force in motion toward MACKNASSY. During the night listening posts on DJ. KSIARA reported noise of large tank formations in our front to the east.

Later that afternoon Colonel Drake issued orders to the Service Company that all heavy trucks of the 168th Infantry would be moved to SBEITLA at dark that night to go into bivouac there, and that a Quartering party would be sent out by infiltration that afternoon to prepare for their reception. Heavy enemy activities was observed in front of the position throughout the day and it appeared as though an attack was iminent. Orders were issued for breakfast at 0400 hours and to "Stand To" at 0500 hours the next morning. At 2350 hours a telephone call came through to the Regimental C.P. for Colonel Drake to report to the C.C.A.C.P. There he met General Eisenhower, the Allied Commander-In-Chief, who presented to him the Silver Star Medal for the action at SENED.

28. 14 February 1943 - Sunday - The enemy attacked at 0630 hours with two divisions of Panzers, the 10th and 21st. The German Group Commander of the Panzer Divisions was General Schmidt. The enemy first hit DJ. LESSOUDA with two battalions of tanks, one from the north and one from the east. The heavy north westerly wind had been blowing all night, during which the tanks moved up in the face of the wind without their noise being detected. Patrols had been ordered out every night by higher authority, in spite of the fact that there was but a restricted sector to patrol in the front. It was obvious to anyone that the enemy could locate the patrols and grab them at any time that they might wish to do so. One patrol stationed near FAID PASS on Saturday night was never heard of afterwards. Outside of one or two patrols to capture prisoners, it appeared that the patrols were unnecessary. Quite often most of them were killed, as the Germans would lie in wait for the patrols after the first couple of nights. Coming from the north and the east the two forces of German tanks closed on DJ. LESSOUDA. Through his field glasses Colonel Drake counted eighty-three German tanks in front of DJ. LESSOUDA. At daylight there were flashes of gun fire from the two German forces direct on the position. This almost instant action destroyed all seven of the American tanks with Lt. Colonel Waters. There were a few pieces of armored artillery which were knocked out at the same time. One company of infantry out on the desert dug-in in front of DJ. LESSOUDA was immediately overrun. What became of the infantry in those holes was never known, though two or three men from that company said that the men could be seen lying in the fox holes and the enemy tanks would put a track in the fox hole, turn around on them and crush the soldier into the ground. The remainder of the battalion was back in the hills just outside of DJ. LESSOUDA and later, under Major Moore, about half of them got through to the American lines.

29. Combat Command Headquarters was in SIDI BOU ZID, while the 168th Infantry CP was a mile and half farther east in a small olive grove. The Third Battalion of the 168th Infantry and the 17th Field Artillery were at DJ. KSAIRA, about four and one-half miles farther east. The remainder of the artillery of the armored command was out on the plains between the 168th Infantry CP and DJ. KSAIRA. One company of tanks under Lt. Colonel Hightower was in SIDI BOU ZID with the armored CP. While the battle of DJ. LESSOUDA was going on there was a large troop movement, including tanks, coming toward SIDI BOU ZID from the southeast. Air bombardment was called for, but did not

materialize. The armored artillery followed by the 17th Field Artillery, left their positions and withdrew to the rear. The withdrawal soon became a route in some cases. At this juncture Colonel Drake reported by telephone to General McQuillin that the troops appeared to be panicky. The general directed him, "You are on the spot, take command and stop it." Colonel Drake asked, "You mean for me to take command of all troops in the area?" General McQuillin's reply was "Yes." Steps were taken which effectively stopped the withdrawal. Troops infiltering to the rear were stopped and held in a state of readiness. About thirty minutes after this conversation the Executive Officer, 168th Infantry, Lt. Colonel Gerald Line came to where Colonel Drake was watching the battle of DJ. LESSOUDA through his field glasses and said, "General McQuillin is on the telephone and said he is pulling out and for you to stay here." Colonel Drake's instructions previously had been that he would hold his position to the last man. Colonel Drake went to the telephone but it was dead. The Communications Officer, First Lt. Edgar P. Moschel, 168th Infantry, reported that he had sent out two men to check the line. These men soon reported in and stated that they found that the telephone on the other end of the line was gone.

30. The outpost now reported an enemy column coming from the south. The enemy was flanking the position on three sides. Some of the enemy tanks had gone around DJ. LESSOUDA in a movement which cut a road junction seven miles west of DJ. LESSOUDA. All traffic leaving SIDI BOU ZID by road was now blocked. The morale of most of the men was low. Colonel Drake was repeatedly importuned if the troops should not pull out as the others had done. His reply was to the effect that he intended to attack; that it was his belief that an attack was his best defense, and that he was going to capture the high ground at GARET HADID, about a mile to the front. The enemy was coming up from both east and west and closing in. The Hdqrs, 168th Infantry, under Second Lt. Seymour R. Bolten, was immediately started forward as scouts along each side of the road leading toward GARET HADID. At this time Company A, 16th Engineers First Armored Division, reported to Colonel Drake. The Company Commander, Captain William R. A. Kleysteuber, 16th Engineers, said that he had been told by General McQuillin to report to Colonel Drake and there to render any assistance possible. Colonel Drake immediately sent forward this Engineer Company and Company E, of the 168th Infantry, Headquarters Company, less Dets. 168th Infantry, under Captain Bernard U. Bolten,

along with several hundred men that had been picked up from units outside the regiment, in an attack to seize GARET HADID. Company E, 168th Infantry, under Captain Donald L. Wilkinson had been on duty protecting the artillery and was now available to its regimental commander after the evacuation of the artillery. Outposts were left on the road to take care of anything that came through. On the way forward to GARET HADID Colonel Drake found a platoon of light tanks returning. The Lieutenant in command stated that he had been out as right flank outpost. He reported that the enemy was attacking in force with heavy tanks immediately behind him and that his instructions had been in such an event to withdraw. Colonel Drake explained to the Lieutenant that he was now in command of all troops in the area and that the tanks would now be under his, Colonel Drake's orders. The platoon of light tanks was immediately launched into the attack, and the improvised force, due to its speed of advance, was successful in reaching and seizing GARET HADID before the enemy could bring sufficient force to prevent them. The remnants of Company A, 81st Reconnaissance Battalion, under Captain Otto C. Amerell, were also placed in position, as they come back. The Cannon Company, 39th Infantry, Captain "Buck" Walters commanding, and the seven 37MM Towed guns that were with Company A, 16th Engineers. The First Platoon, Company C, 109th Engineers, under First Lt. Royal I. Lee, was given the task of mining the road leading northeast around GARET HADID, while Company A of the 16th Engineers, covered the mine field at the eastern end of it. All troops made hurried preparations for a last minute defense of GARET HADID. As the troops deployed for the defense of GARET HADID, the enemy came within gun range. There was a small exchange of fire whereupon the enemy deployed and then cautiously attacked. Had they gone on through the Americans would have been defeated. They did not attack in force at this time, but instead started a deliberate siege. The enemy besieged GARET HADID from all sides. By this time a check made by the Adjutant, Major Merle A. Meacham showed that about 950 men were employed in the defense of GARET HADID. About 300 of them were not armed, and these included men from tanks, reconnaissance units, tank destroyers and artillery units. Some of the men had procured side arms and guns that they had found in shot-up half-tracks. A hurried effort was made to secure arms from those found abandoned in an effort to arm everyone. This, of course, could not be done. The enemy made several attacks during the 14th, 15th and 16th of February.

31. On the 15th they began to drive in heavily and on three

different occasions penetrated as far as the CP. Several snipers worked throughout the position causing casualties and constant effort to wipe them out was exerted at all times. Due to the rough ground and the several pieces of artillery picked up in the move to GARET HADID, the enemy tanks could not get into the American forces to overrun them. All of the artillery was knocked out by the 16th of February by direct fire. Casualties were heavy and finally the enemy pushed in the right flank. A counter attack with two platoons was made and drove the enemy back to his original position. A tall inverted cone of rock controlled the whole rear position. Only six men could be spared to garrison this cone. The enemy succeeded in scaling the side and killed three of these men. The other three men came back and reported that they had been driven off. Colonel Drake sent one officer, Second Lt. Seymour R. Bolten, with six men of the Regimental Band to retake this position. They did retake it and their efforts saved the entire position from being penetrated. On the 15th the situation became very desperate as there had been no food nor water since supper on the 13th; casualties were heavy, no medical assistance other than first aid could be given to the wounded. The fighting did not let up day or night and finally on the 16th the enemy was able to get through. The entire rear and right flank were driven in. Losses began to mount. During this time Colonel Drake kept in contact with the armored forces to the rear by radio, using a code which had been arranged with the division Communications Officer before they went into action. The radio, however, would function only in the daytime. As soon as the sun went down the radio would fade out and there were no further communications with the outside world until the sun came up the next morning.

32. All guns of the 39th Cannon Company and all 37s were knocked out by noon 16th February. Reinforcements had been promised by the First Armored Division Headquarters, but each of the two attempts made were attacked in force by the enemy and failed to get through. Supplies were asked for by air. Ammunition was asked for but none came. Air bombardment on the numerous enemy artillery batteries in plain view was asked for but none materialized. On the 16th of February the enemy first attacked the Third Battalion, 168th Infantry, on DJ. KSAIRA. The Third Battalion was able to withstand the attack, although their position had become somewhat confused by the 17th Field Artillery which had moved back and forth and finally after leaving caused a collapse on their left. When the artillery moved out the Third Battalion was left in a scattered position. At 1400 hours on the

16th it became increasingly clear that the force could not hold out for more than one day longer.

33. At this hour the situation was thus: The rear of the position was driven in; the right flank was in process of being driven in; ammunition was running low; the center had been penetrated three times by tanks and the lack of water was becoming increasingly grave. The men having not eaten or had a drink of water for three days, along with the hot weather and nervous exertion, reduced many to a pitiful state.

At 1430 hours on the 16th of February 1943, Colonel Drake received a radio message from General Ward to this effect, "We can do no more for you. The decision is yours. I will try to have supplies dropped to you." The supplies were never dropped. This message which came in the clear was not understood because it presented problems which had not been in question! The orders were to hold this position. Was it intended that the decision was up to Colonel Drake, 'either to surrender, continue the defense or to withdraw'? No one was told of the contents of this message except the Communications Officer, Lt. Moschel, who received it, the radio operator, the Executive Officer, Lt. Colonel Line, the Chaplain, Stephen W. Kane, and the Commanding Officer, Colonel Drake. At 1500 hours on this date Colonel Drake received another message from General Ward, "Look for dropped message at 1700 hours." Colonel Drake assumed that they were going to order him to withdraw. He made all preparations for withdrawal that night and after a careful estimate of the situation, before which Chaplain Kane, standing in full view of enemy snipers with his hands raised in Benediction, asked the Blessing of God upon the decision, selected the route west along foot of GARET HADID, thence Southwest following the foothills until clear; thence Northwest across country to EL HAMIR. He sent a code message to Lt. Colonel John H. Van Vliet, Jr., of the Third Battalion to prepare to withdraw on order that night and then completed arrangements for the withdrawing of his own men from GARET HADID. He called a conference of his unit commanders for 1900 hours that night.

34. At about 1700 hours, three American fighter planes came over, flew directly over GARET HADID, and dropped a message on DJ. KSAIRA four and one-half miles to the north of his position, and at the point where the fighting was going on between the Third Battalion and the Germans. Fortunately the message dropped on the American Side. It

was about 2000 hours before Colonel Drake got the information it contained. It was not understood how the airplanes missed GARET HADID for this location was well known and identification panels were out. The message was long and the Commanding Officer of the Third Battalion had to decode and encode it. (See Incl. No. 1 for gist of the message contained in second paragraph.) It was then forwarded to Colonel Drake. Fortunately the message did not change any of the plans previously made. Colonel Drake was ordered to withdraw that night under cover of darkness. The route was left to his discretion. He was further ordered that all men would go to SBEITLA and that he was to be certain that each man understood that. The message added that an air umbrella would be provided and all support possible would be rendered for the withdrawal. These instructions were passed on to the unit commanders, the wounded were reassembled; the most seriously wounded were placed in ambulances and the rest of the wounded were covered with canvas in the area and left under suitable medical personnel with supplies. At 2200 hours the withdrawal started. First the troops from GARET HADID leaving outposts in position, followed by the Third Battalion in column. The tires of all vehicles were slashed, magnetos and radio parts buried, all machine gun bolts were hidden and everything done to make the abandoned equipment unserviceable without creating noise which would give the withdrawal away.

35. The Third Battalion started their march from their position thirty minutes before those from GARET HADID, so as to close the distance between the units. As the Third Battalion was attempting to cross the open desert between DJ. KSAIRA, a German scout car challenged them. One of our soldiers tossed a grenade into the scout car which set it on fire and burned it up. This did not excite the Germans as there was a great deal of confusion in the area, shooting, etc. The movement was not discovered. Colonel Drake lead the column through a German tank park and bivouac area without being apprehended. They marched all night covering between 22 and 26 miles with only one rest of a few minutes at midnight. Efforts had been made to get through by radio to General Ward to find out where the rendezvous point was located. It was perfectly obvious that he could not march to SBEITLA before dawn, so he set EL HAMIR, the only high ground between SBEITLA and his position, as the rendezvous point, and hoped that help would be there to meet him at that point. At dayling EL HAMIR could be seen in front of the column about a mile away. (Many months later it was learned that the 6th Armored Infantry Garrison had been withdrawn

from there the night before after the orders for the withdrawal
had been given).

36. The column had become somewhat disorganized in marching
and at this point proper approach formation was taken up. When
the returning men attempted to cross the road into the foot hills
of EL HAMRA a machine gun opened up on the right column from the
hills as a German motorized column came up the road. The enemy
stopped and started leaping from their trucks, while enemy tanks
immediately began encircling the American column. One U. S.
plane flew over at this point and opened fire on the column. Our
men, with surging morale, thought it was the promised air support,
but it apparently was a lone night fighter a little late getting
back from its mission. One German truck was hit and set on fire.
Colonel Drake immediately deployed his mixed command and opened fire
with the weapons that they had. By this time there were about 400
men in the command and not more than half of them were armed.
Colonel Drake asked for volunteers of an officer and men; the officer
to lead the group of men to a knoll in their rear as the German
Infantry was running to circle them. First Lieutenant William
Rogers, Artillery Liaison Officer of the 91st Armored Artillery,
volunteered to lead the twelve men and urged them to follow him.
They gained the desired ground, a little knoll in the desert, and
there they were able to hold the enemy off for about an hour. At
the termination of the hour Lt. Rogers and all of his men had been
killed.

The Germans brought up several tanks, all of them with yellow
tigers painted on their sides and opened fire. They also set up
machine-gun positions and supplemented that with rifle fire. While
they were doing this their infantry completely encircled the small
American force. After three and one-half hours of fighting the
American fire power diminished and then practically ceased as the
men were out of ammunition or had become casualties. Finally a
German armored car bearing a white flag came dashing into the American circle. Colonel Drake ordered his men to wave the car away.
When the car failed to respond he then ordered his men to fire upon
the German car. Some of the men began to fire, but others could
not as they had no ammunition and then they began surrendering in
small groups. German tanks came in following that vehicle without
any negotiations for surrender. The Germans had used the white flag
as subterfuge to come inside the circle of defense without drawing

fire. Their tanks closed in from all directions cutting Colonel
Drake's forces into small groups. The men who did not surrender
were killed by the Germans. One tank came toward Colonel Drake
and a German officer pointing a rifle at him called out, "Colonel,
you surrender." The Colonel replied, "You go to hell," and turned
his back. He then walked away and two German soldiers with rifles
followed him at a distance of about fifty yards. Colonel Drake
was then stopped by a German Major who spoke good English and was
asked to get in the German Major's car where he was taken to German
Divisional Headquarters. Colonel Drake was taken to General Schmidt,
Group Commander of the 10th and 21st Panzer Divisions at German
Divisional Headquarters where the German General immediately came
forward to see him, drew up at attention, saluted and said, "I want
to compliment your command for the splendid fight they put up. It
was a hopeless thing from the start, but they fought like real
soldiers." He also stated, "I called my regimental commander, who
held you at GARET HADID this morning, and asked him how the Americans
were". He replied that 'they were alright; that he hadn't heard a
sound from them', and I find you back here. I am glad to have you
for now I can go on to fight your comrades at SBEITLA." The German
Commander promised Colonel Drake that all the American wounded would
be cared for and that he could leave American medical personnel to
properly look after them, but immediately upon Colonel Drake leaving
the field, the American medical personnel was carried off as prisoners
and the American dead and wounded left to the ravages of the Arabs
who proceeded to immediately strip the dead and wounded and to beat
insensible those wounded who protested to the stripping of their
clothes. The American prisoners were assembled in a group and under
guard marched back that afternoon and night along the road to DJ.
LESSOUDA. Those Americans who were slightly wounded or who became
ill because of fatigue, lack of food and water and could not keep up
with the column were ruthlessly bayonetted or shot. Many were walking barefooted because the Arabs had taken their shoes from them
under the supervision of the German soldiers.

37. The statements of Lt. Colonel Van Vliet and First Lt. Moschel
are attached to this report as inclosures No. 1 and No. 2, respectively,
which cover the highlights of the report.

38. Prisoners-of-War

a. The men had been left to the systematic robbery of the

German soldiers, and some junior officers, for a period of about an half hour. During this time pockets and kits were thoroughly searched, often at the point of the rifle or the bayonet presented at the unprotected belly, while watches, rings, pocketbooks, pens and all valuables were ruthlessly seized. They were then formed in a column of fours, officers at the head, and started to the rear. Three German tanks brought up the rear of the column, which was flanked by armed guards, waiting to strike, bayonet or shoot, any who for any reason straggled.

b. All day they marched through desert sands with unrelieved thirst almost unbearable. Colonel Drake appealed to the German Commander in the name of common humanity to give the men a drink of water, but was met with the statement, "We only have enough for our troops." Near midnight they were finally halted for the remaining hours of darkness. The men were herded into a circle in the open desert and there practically froze in the piercing cold of the African night.

c. At dawn, 18 February 1943, trucks came, in which the men were packed, and thus transported to SFAX where THE FIRST FOOD WAS EATEN IN FIVE DAYS! Black sawdust bread was issued them along with water, as they were corralled into an open wired-in compound, roughly 100 yards square, and flanked by towers with machine guns in them. The men burrowed into the ground for warmth, scooping out the sand with their hands. No means whatsoever was provided for ordinary sanitation. Officers and men thrown in like pigs.

d. The next day trains were provided, 40 to 60 men in a live-stock car built for eight horses. The misery, squalor and suffering endured will remain fresh in their memories. Two days and one night were used to get to SOUSSE where the men were permitted to get out for latrine purposes. During all this time no provision had been made for men to answer the calls of nature as they were kept locked in the cars in darkness. One day in the yards at SOUSSE and then on to TUNIS under exactly the same conditions just described.

e. At TUNIS they were turned over to the inquisitors headed by a German called "Charley" who at the "School House" amused himself by stamping an iron shod heel onto a soldiers instep or twisting his fingers while backed up by loaded and bayonetted rifles, all in an effort to obtain military information. Another method was softly saying

a little trip out in the dark and the soldier's mother would never know what became of her darling boy. However, "Charley", although he had lived many years in America, was very gullible and was soon assiduously writing down fantastic stories that had no basis of fact.

f. From TUNIS the men were marched to the airport eight kilometers from the city and there most of them were transported by air in JU 52's to ITALY. Others went by water. All ended up at CAPUA, a collecting camp which stood out as a new low level. The men slept on the ground, which was dusty, and the nights were very chilly. No utensils were provided and the men procured rusty tin cans from a heap in the camp and with improvised spoons from boards which contributed proportinate dignity to the menu of cabbage water provided once daily. Two weeks of CAPUA and then they were ready to leave for the regular prison camps in Germany and Poland.

2 Incls:
1. Statement of Van Vleit
2. Statement of Moschel

THOMAS D. DRAKE, 015384
Colonel, G.S.C., WDGS
(Formerly Commanding 168th Inf)

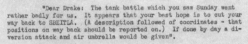

SUBJECT: Brief of Statement of Lt. Colonel John H. Van Vliet, Jr.
(To accompany Report on Operations of 168th Infantry
between 24 December 1942 and 17 February 1943)

1. Consolidated position of Third Battalion on DJ KSAIRA on
13 February 1943. Completed plans on 14th. Last ration for one
day arrived early morning hours 13th. Communication by telephone
lasted until 2020 hours, 16 February.

2. Dropped message by air at 1643 hours, 16 February - two
typewritten sheets. Gist of message:

"Dear Drake: The tank battle which you saw Sunday went
rather badly for us. It appears that your best hope is to cut your
way back to SBEITLA. (A description followed of coordinates - that
positions on way back should be reported on.) If done by day a diversion attack and air umbrella would be given".

The message was too long so it was condensed and encoded in
special regimental code and sent to Regimental CP at 1800 hours.

3. About 1430 hours, 16 February, received code from Colonel
Drake. "How long would it take you to cut your way out and join me
at GARET HADID? Be prepared for prompt move, but make no change in
disposition until you receive direct order from me." Reply sent
immediately, "Will not attempt until after dark on order. There are
eight 88's between you and me."

4. About 2025 hours received another code from Colonel Drake,
giving route to be taken on withdrawal to start at 2200 hours. "Withdraw to GARET HADID, proceed to west along there, thence S.W. following foothills until clear, thence N.W. to EL HAMRA." Left at 2310
hours (plans already having been made), one platoon (Lt Hatchett) left
engaged with enemy as covering force, to withdraw on three signal
flares, which were fired from flats near SIDI BOU ZID at about 0230
hours. Proceeded by route following in rear of Regimental Group. No
enemy encountered - tail of column had brush with a half-track (one
of ours manned by enemy). Rifle fire and grenades destroyed the half-
track, all killed in vehicle except one man who escaped. Near foot
of HADID mountain saw a shelter with light in it - heard voices - passed
within 75 yards, but not accosted. Passed through the enemy tank park

Inclosure No. 1   1

---

after turning northwest. During movement in dark over distance of
26 miles the battalion became divided into four groups besides the
platoon of Lt. Hatchett's which followed in rear.

5. About 0730 hours, Wednesday, 17 February, became engaged
with enemy. The sound of heavy firing came from ahead of us which
I though was the Regimental Group. Some small units of Second
Battalion had become mixed among my men. Organization was practically gone, due to lack of food, water and extreme fatigue. Ammunition was very scarce. Many M1 rifles were jammed and would not
function. After we had been exposed to their fire for some time I
saw it was hopeless and put my white handkerchief of a stick and
waved it - that was that!

6. The end of Lt. Colonel Van Vliet's statement to Colonel
Drake. Later he made the same statement to Colonel Drake in presence
of the Third Battalion's Executive Officer, Major Emanuel M.
Robertson.

I certify the above is a true statement made from the notes I
took down at the time it was made to me.

                                    Thomas D. Drake
                                    THOMAS D. DRAKE
                                    Colonel, G.S.C.

SUBJECT; Brief of Statement of First Lt. Edgar P. Moschel, Regimental Communications Officer, 168th Infantry. (To accompany Report on Operations of 168th Infantry between 24 December 1942 and 17 February 1943)

1. Sunday morning 14 February, 1943, maintained direct communication with Combat Command "A" until they were forced out of SIDI BOU ZID - radio contact, but no traffic. Call came from Combat Command "A" about 0630 hours to cut all lines to DJ. LESSOUDA road junction that enemy tanks were coming in their direction. Never heard from the two linemen afterwards.

2. About 0800 hours I heard Colonel Drake talking over the telephone to General McQuillin that Artillery was fleeing the battlefield in panic, and that he, Colonel Drake, was watching one battery at the time. Apparently there was some controversy as Colonel Drake said, "I know what I'm talking about. I know panic when I see it". I then heard Colonel Drake repeat after him that he was to take charge of the situation and the command of all troops in the area. Colonel Drake then sent word to Captain Wilkinson, Company E, to give artillery protection. The lines had been torn out by the fleeing artillery so two messengers were started out, but about five minutes later the line was repaired and the message cleared. The Third Battalion lines went out at the same time, but were soon repaired.

3. About 0830 hours Lt. Colonel Line, Executive Officer, 168th Infantry, received a call from General McQuillin that Combat Command "A" Headquarters was pulling out. He asked the General to talk to Colonel Drake who was forward observing the fighting at DJ. LESSOUDA and the action of the artillery. When Colonel Drake came to the telephone the line was dead and I heard Lt. Colonel Line repeat to Colonel Drake that Combat Command "A" Headquarters was pulling out and that Colonel Drake was to stay where he was. Efforts to contact Combat Command "A" Headquarters were fruitless, so I sent a lineman to Combat Command "A" CP, where he found a dead end. While he was there a staff officer of General McQuillin's came back to the scene and used the lineman's telephone to call Colonel Drake. Shortly after this the entire CP was alerted to move in either direction, to either go forward in attack or withdraw.

4. Some time before noon Colonel Drake sent an order to Captain

Wilkinson to move Company E to GARET HADID and shortly after this the CP was moved forward to GARET HADID. By this time German tanks were behind us and had occupied SIDI BOU ZID. All transportation around the CP, the Cannon Company, 39th Infantry, the AT Company and the Regimental Medical Section was moved forward to GARET HADID. After getting there, shortly before noon, I received a radio message from Headquarters First Armored Division that the SOI had been compromised and not to use it. During the afternoon numerous air targets were sent back, but none acted on. Late that evening during one of the attacks on us, three German tanks penetrated out CP position causing considerable damage, but they were forced back. A German Infantry attack was made on the left flank and every man, including messengers, was sent out to repulse it.

5. In the morning of 15 February a message was radioed by Colonel Drake to Armored Division Headquarters - "How are Moore and Waters?" The reply was, "Things look good for Moore and Waters", (referring to Lt. Colonel Waters, First Armored Division and Major Moore, Commanding Officer, Second Battalion, at DJ. LESSOUDA). (We later learned Waters had been knocked out and captured about 1500 hours the day before and Moore hadn't been heard from). Targets, gun positions, 88's, enemy troops and concentrations of vehicles sent by radio to First Armored Division Headquarters throughout the day. During late evening another tank attack made by Germans on our position, it too, repulsed though tanks again over ran our position as far as the CP. Before this a message was received, "Help on way - be prepared to climb on Band wagon and take a ride." About 1630 hours a heavy tank battle began just west of SIDI BOU ZID. As it became dark I could see 23 fires from burning tanks.

6. Tuesday, 16 February, 0830 hours inquiry from First Armored Division, "Have you seen anything of Stack or evidence of tank battle last night?" Evidence of tank battle was sent back with word that nothing had been heard from Stack. Usual air targets were reported throughout morning. By this time considerable numbers of German troops were between us and the Third Battalion. At 1400 hours radio message from First Armored Division to Colonel Drake. "Up to your decision. Air coverage and such counter action as possible will be given", signed Ward. Repeated calls were sent by Colonel Drake to General Ward asking for rendezvous. This was sent three or four times. Finally message came to be on lookout for plane to drop message. Panels were placed out for the planes. At 1430 hours a message from Colonel Drake to Lt. Colonel

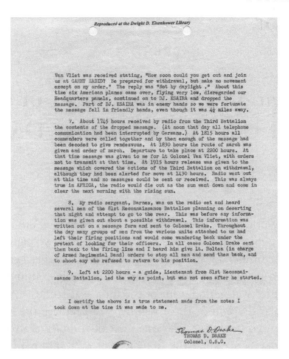

Van Vliet was received stating, "How soon could you get out and join us at GABET HADIDT Be prepared for withdrawal, but make no movement except on my order." The reply was "Not by daylight ." About this time six American planes came over, flying very low, disregarded our Headquarters panels, continued on to DJ. KSAIRA and dropped the message. Part of DJ. KSAIRA was in enemy hands so we were fortunate the message fell in friendly hands, even though it was 4½ miles away.

7. About 1745 hours received by radio from the Third Battalion the contents of the dropped message. (At noon that day all telephone communication had been interrupted by Germans.) At 1815 hours all commanders were called together and by then enough of the message had been decoded to give rendezvous. At 1830 hours the route of march was given and order of march. Departure to take place at 2200 hours. At that time message was given to me for Lt Colonel Van Vliet, with orders not to transmit at that time. At 1915 hours release was given to the message which covered the actions of the Third Battalion on withdrawal, although they had been alerted for move at 1430 hours. Radio went out at this time and no messages could be sent or received. This was always true in AFRICA, the radio would die out as the sun went down and come in clear the next morning with the rising sun.

8. My radio sergeant, Barnes, was on the radio set and heard several men of the 81st Reconnaissance Battalion planning on deserting that night and attempt to go to the rear. This was before any information was given out about a possible withdrawal. This information was written out on a message form and sent to Colonel Drake. Throughout the day many groups of men from the various units attached to us had left their firing positions and would come wandering back under the pretext of looking for their officers. In all cases Colonel Drake sent then back to the firing line and I heard him give Lt. Bolten (in charge of Armed Regimental Band) orders to stop all men and send them back, and to shoot any who refused to return to his position.

9. Left at 2200 hours - a guide, Lieutenant from 81st Reconnaissance Battalion, led the way as point, but was not seen after he started.

I certify the above is a true statement made from the notes I took down at the time it was made to me.

Thomas D. Drake
THOMAS D. DRAKE
Colonel, G.S.C.

Document 7: Ryder's Letter to Officers of 34th Infantry Division re Offensive Spirit, March 11, 1943

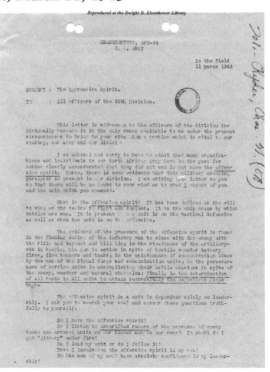

HEADQUARTERS, APO-34
U. S. ARMY

In the Field
11 March 1943

SUBJECT : The Aggressive Spirit.

TO : All officers of the 34th Division.

This letter is addressed to the officers of the division individually because it is the only means available to me under the present circumstances to bring to your attention a problem which is vital to our country, our army and our division.

I am ashamed and sorry to have to admit that many organizations and individuals in our North African Army have in the past few months clearly demonstrated that they did not and do not have the offensive spirit. Worse, there is some evidence that this military creeping paralysis is present in our division. I am writing this letter to you so that there will be no doubt in your mind as to what I expect of you and the unit which you command.

What is the offensive spirit? It has been defined as the will to win; as the desire to fight and conquer. It is the only means by which battles are won. It is as present when a unit is on the tactical defensive as well as when the unit is on the offensive.

The evidence of the presence of the offensive spirit is found in the flaming desire of the infantry man to close with the enemy with the rifle and bayonet and kill him; in the steadiness of the artillery-man in keeping his gun in action in spite of hostile counter battery fires; in the boldness and tanks; in the maintenance of communication lines by the men of the Signal Corps and communication units; in the perseverance of service units in accomplishing their battle missions in spite of the enemy, weather and natural obstacles; finally in the determination of all ranks in all units to attain successfully the objectives given them.

The offensive spirit in a unit is dependent solely on leadership. I ask you to search your soul and answer these questions truthfully to yourself;

Do I have the offensive spirit?
Do I listen to unverified rumors of the presence of enemy tanks and armored units on our flanks and in our rear? In short do I get "jittery" under fire?
Do I lead my unit or do I follow it?
Have I inculcated the offensive spirit in my men?
Do the men of my unit have absolute confidence in my leadership?

Organization and Equipment of a World War II U.S. Army Infantry Division[1]

The U.S. Army's World War I square divisions consisted of about 22,000 men each. Each division had two infantry brigades. Each brigade had two regiments. The square division possessed considerable hitting and staying power but lacked maneuverability and was difficult to supply. The War Department carefully examined the World War I division in the inter-war period. Out of the inter-war studies eventually came the plan for a triangular division of three regiments, to replace the square division of four regiments in two brigades.[2] The dilemma of military planners of the 1920s and 1930s was how to maintain the firepower of a 28,000-man infantry division while reducing it to 15,000 men. The Army's boards and branches considered the improvement of firepower with more or new weapons and the reorganization of the basic units within the division, especially the smaller units which bore the responsibility of physically closing with the enemy.

The new organization was accepted in principle in 1935. In January 1936, a special committee was appointed to conduct a study on the modernization of the Army. The committee's report proposing a triangular divisional organization was submitted six months later. The two brigade headquarters of the square division and one infantry regiment were eliminated. The combat power of the infantry division was placed in three infantry regiments of three rifle battalions each, with organic cannon and anti-tank companies. In 1939 the model of the new division was further developed through field tests. The 2nd Division was formed into a provisional unit to test the various proposals. For several months it tried out the suggested arrangements in the field. Test divisions were formed in accord with the various formations suggested; trial maneuvers on the ground were conducted under the direction of General Lesley J. McNair. McNair himself did the main work of transforming the new division from theory to actuality as chief of staff of the test division. His concepts of military formations for modern warfare were instrumental in shaping the World War II infantry division.

The result of two decades of Army experiments and studies was the "triangular" divisional organization. Out of the tests came a report recommending a triangular division of 10,275 men to replace the 22,000-man square division. McNair took it as a guiding principle that the combat units should be just that, equipped to fight offensively and unencumbered with merely defensive weapons or organic transportation not required for immediate needs. McNair held that larger formations, corps, and armies, should have responsibility for motor pools and specialist units.

The War Department, however, did not approve so drastic a reduction even though it approved the principal organizational patterns that emerged from the tests. It adopted a division of 14,981 men (later reduced to just over 14,000).[3]

The three-part infantry division consisted of the maneuver force of three infantry regiments, each supported by an artillery battalion and each with its organic mechanized transportation.[4] Notwithstanding McNair's objections, the new division was to have substantial organic support, including a motorized reconnaissance battalion (200 men), a signal company (197 men), an engineer battalion to include a traffic control detachment (500 men), and "service troops" (1,820 men). This last category would consist of a grouping, under a brigadier general, of the quartermaster, ordnance, medical, and all other divisional supply and maintenance units. The assignment of a brigadier to command service troops was as much a political sop as an organizational requirement. It was to provide a slot for brigadier generals dispossessed of their brigade commands. All technical signal communications, except within the artillery battalions, would be provided by the Signal Corps. The G-1 section was eliminated, its functions being transferred to the adjutant general's section. The plan provided for a specific support element for the division. For the first time supply and maintenance units were grouped within the division.[5]

The Table of Organization of the new triangular division was not approved until after the collapse of France in 1940. All Regular Army divisions were then reorganized in conformity with the new table. After Pearl Harbor, the National Guard divisions were required to conform. This situation was fraught with political repercussions because it eliminated grades and commands and over-age commanders were relieved.[6]

Within the National Guard, however, the square organization, somewhat modified, persisted even after many units had entered Federal service in 1940. The 34th Infantry Division remained a square division almost until the moment its units were ordered to Ireland in early 1942.

From 1937 to 1941 U.S. combat infantry organization and doctrine had undergone a real revolution. The infantry division's weapons were turned over completely, except for the .30-caliber water-cooled machine gun. A heavier mortar, the 81mm M1, was introduced, assigned to the heavy weapons companies of infantry battalions. The 60mm light mortar M2 replaced the old Stokes mortar and was assigned to the heavy weapons platoons of infantry companies. A light machine gun, the air-cooled Browning .30 caliber M1919, was adopted and provided to the company heavy weapons platoons. The Browning Automatic Rifle ("BAR") was so much improved as to be virtually made over. The BAR was assigned to a single specialized user in each squad of a rifle company. Finally, the Springfield 1903 bolt-action rifle was replaced by the revolutionary semi-automatic M1 Garand, except for sniper applications. The M1 rifle was issued to 11 of the 12 infantrymen in each infantry squad. New small arms including the M1/M2 carbines and the M1 (Thompson) and M2 submachine guns entered infantry armament, together with the larger machine gun, the .50-caliber M2.[7] The success of British and Russian anti-tank weapons proved that armor without infantry support was vulnerable. A splendid American anti-tank innovation, introduced to U.S. Army troops just before they boarded transports for the invasion of North Africa, was the famed "bazooka." The bazooka was a shoulder-launched rocket weapon with the great advantage of being recoilless. The rocket was fitted with a warhead utilizing hollow or shaped charge technology based on the "Munroe effect," resulting in a genuinely effective weapon against both armored fighting vehicles and fortifications.

The authorized strength of an American infantry division in 1944 illustrates the building-block character of military structure. The division totaled 14,253 officers and men:

Three rifle squads (each composed of nine riflemen and one BAR man, commanded by two non-commissioned officers, a sergeant and a corporal) made up a platoon, a unit of about 40 men commanded by a second lieutenant and a senior sergeant. The platoon leaders and senior non-commissioned officers were issued the .30 cal. carbine M1 and the .45 cal. pistol M1911A1. All infantrymen carried hand grenades on their battle harnesses.

Three rifle platoons with 143 M1 rifles, three Model 1903 sniper rifles, and nine (later 15) BARs, plus a weapons platoon (two Browning .30 cal. air-cooled machine guns M1919, one Browning .50 cal. heavy machine gun M2, three (later five) bazookas, and three 60mm light mortars M2) made up a company, a unit of about 193 men (6 commissioned officers and 187 enlisted men), commanded by a first lieutenant or a captain, an executive officer, and a senior sergeant. Officers, and senior non-commissioned officers, were issued 28 carbines and 10 M1911A1 pistols and, later, submachine guns.

Three rifle companies plus a weapons company (six 80mm heavy mortars M1, eight Browning .30 cal. water cooled machine guns M1917, one .50 cal. air cooled machine gun M2, and six bazookas), a headquarters company (three 37mm AT guns, later three 57 mm AT guns, two .50 cal. machine guns M2, four bazookas, 80 M1 rifles and 20 M1 carbines, and, later in the war, six .30 cal. machine guns and two submachine guns M2), made up a battalion, a unit of about 871 men and commanded by a major or lieutenant colonel, with an executive officer.

Three infantry battalions together with an artillery battalion (typically 12 105mm howitzers M1A2 in four batteries), a cannon company (initially six 75mm guns mounted on half-tracks, later six 105mm towed howitzers M3, four bazookas, and three .50 cal. machine guns M2), an anti-tank company (9 37mm towed AT guns, later 9 57mm towed AT guns, 19 bazookas, three .50 cal. machine guns M2, 72 M1 rifles, 48 M1 carbines, and 45 M1911A1 pistols), a service company (nine .50 cal. machine guns M2, 10 bazookas, 84 M1 rifles, 29 M1 carbines and one M1911A1 pistol), and a medical detachment, made up a regiment, a unit of about 3,100 men, commanded by a colonel, with an executive officer and a headquarters company.

Finally, three regiments plus an additional artillery battalion (12 155mm guns M1) and other supporting units (headquarters and headquarters company, engineer, signal, medical, transportation, maintenance, ordnance, collection, etc.) made up the division, a unit with a total complement of about 14,253, commanded by a major general, with an executive officer, an artillery chief, and a support services chief, all usually brigadier generals. For a graphic depiction of the organizational structure of a United States Army infantry division in World War II, see the final image in the second section of photographs.

Infantry Division Assault Doctrine

In all large ground combat formations, the final success of the attack depends upon the smallest units under the command of the lowest-ranking combat leaders. In World War II, the U.S. Army enlarged the infantry squad from eight men to 12. This was done despite evidence produced in the field tests that seven or eight men were all one corporal could hope to control in battle. The chief of infantry nevertheless strongly urged the increase. The span of control weakness of so large a squad was corrected late in 1940 when the leader was made a sergeant and his assistant a corporal. With two noncommissioned officers in charge, the infantry squad remained at 12 throughout World War II. Each 12-man squad had nine riflemen equipped with the M1 Garand rifle, one man operating the Browning Automatic Rifle as the squad automatic weapon, and was led by the corporal and the sergeant, who typically but not always also carried the M1 rifle. The platoon leaders, company commanders, and the senior non-commissioned officers might be armed with the .30 cal. carbine M1 and the .45 cal. pistol M1911/M1911A1, and later with the .45 cal. submachine gun M2. As the war progressed, experienced infantrymen armed themselves more or less as they pleased, sometimes with enemy weapons.

The Army's initial World War II infantry assault doctrine was based upon World War I experience. That doctrine was based upon the sound and traditional infantry doctrine of fire and movement, but it did not always work against determined and entrenched resistance. Each 12-man rifle squad was to have a two-man scout section, a four-man fire section and a five-man maneuver and assault section. The squad leader and the scout section would locate the enemy, and the leader would then call upon the second section's fire, which included the squad's Browning Automatic Rifle. Under that fire, the third section would advance. This method, however, directed only a fraction of the squad's firepower on the objective in the climactic advance, and the squad leader was frequently pinned down with the scout section. Extra power was needed; tanks attached to or supporting the infantry unit supplied that power. Tanks were regularly attached to all sizable infantry formations. A favored method of attack was a team of a tank platoon combined with an infantry company. Sometimes the tanks advanced first, sometimes they advanced with an infantry skirmish line, sometimes the infantry rode them or walked behind them. The tanks attacked centers of resistance, while the infantry eliminated anti-tank weapons and enemy infantry. This process was successfully used by the 34th Infantry Division during the battle of Hill 609 where an attached tank company supported infantry battalions.

Bibliography

Books

Ankrum, Homer. *Dogfaces Who Smiled Through Tears*. Lake Mills, IA: Graphic Publishing, 1987.

Atkinson, Rick. *An Army at Dawn*. New York: Henry Holt and Company, 2002.

Auphan, Paul and Jacques Mordal. *The French Navy in World War II*. Transl. A. C. J. Sabalot. Annapolis: United States Naval Institute, 1959.

Austin, A. B. *Birth of an Army*. London: Victor Gollancz, 1943.

Bailey, Leslie W. *Through Hell and High Water*. New York: Vantage, 1994.

Beck, Alfred M. *et al. The Corps of Engineers: The War Against Germany. US Army in World War II*. Washington, D.C.: U.S. Army Center for Military History, 1985.

Bennett, Ralph. *Ultra and Mediterranean Strategy*. New York: William Morrow, 1989.

Berens, Robert J. *Citizen Soldier*. Ames, Iowa: Sigler, 1995.

Binkley, John C. "A History of U.S Army Force Structuring," in *20th Century War: The American Experience Book of Readings*. Fort Leavenworth, Kansas: Command and General Staff College. 1996.

Blaxland, Gregory. *Alexander's Generals*. London: William Kimber, 1979.

Blumenson, Martin. *Kasserine Pass*. New York: Jove Books, 1983.

— *Patton: The Man Behind the Legend, 1885–1945*. New York: William Morrow and Company, Inc., 1985.

— "Kasserine Pass, 30 January–22 February 1943," in *America's First Battles, 1776–1965*. Charles E. Heller and William A. Stofft, eds. Lawrence, Kansas: University of Kansas Press, 1986.

Blumenson, Martin (ed.). *The Patton Papers, 1940–1945*. New York: Da Capo Press, 1996.

Bolstad, Owen C. *Dear Folks: A Dog-Faced Infantryman in World War II*. Self-published, 1993.

Bradley, Omar N. *A Soldier's Story*. New York: Henry Holt, 1951.

— and Clay Blair. *A General's Life*. New York: Simon & Schuster, 1983.

Brinkley, David. *Washington Goes to War*. New York: Ballantine, 1989.

Bryant, Arthur. *The Turn of the Tide*. London: Collins, 1957.

Burgett, Donald, *Seven Roads to Hell*. New York: Dell Publishing, 1999.

Burns, James MacGregor. *Roosevelt – The Soldier of Freedom*. New York: Harcourt Brace Jovanovich, Inc., 1970.

— *The American Experiment, Vol. III: The Crosswinds of Freedom*. New York: Alfred A. Knopf, 1989.

Butcher, Harry C. *My Three Years with Eisenhower*. New York: Simon & Schuster, 1946.

Bykofsky, Joseph and Harold Larson. *United States Army in World War II: The Technical Services. The Transportation Corps: Operation Overseas*. Washington, D.C.: Center for Military History, U.S. Army, 1990.

Camp, T. J., Brigadier General, USA. *Tankers in Tunisia*. 1943. Fort Knox, KY: Armored Replacement Training Center Republished: University Press of the Pacific, 2003.

Catton, Bruce. *A Stillness at Appomattox*. New York: Doubleday, 1953.

Chandler, Alfred, ed. *The Papers of Dwight David Eisenhower: The War Years.* Vols. 1, 2, 5. Baltimore: Johns Hopkins Press, 1970.

Churchill, Rt. Hon. Sir Winston S. *The Second World War,* Vol. III: *The Grand Alliance.* Boston: Houghton Mifflin, 1950.

— *The Second World War.* Vol. IV: *The Hinge of Fate.* Boston: Houghton Mifflin, 1950.

Clark, Mark W. *Calculated Risk.* New York: Harper & Brothers, 1950.

Clarke, Dudley. *The Eleventh at War.* London: Michael Joseph, 1952.

Clausewitz, Carl von. *On War,* edited and translated by Michael Howard and Peter Paret, Princeton University Press, 1984 [1976].

Collier, Richard. *The War in the Desert.* New York: Time-Life Books, 1977.

Cooper, Matthew. *The German Army 1939–1945.* Lanham, Maryland: Scarborough House, 1980.

Cowdrey, Albert E. *Fighting for Life: American Military Medicine in World War II.* New York: Free Press, 1994.

Craven, Wesley Frank and James Lea Cate, eds. *The Army Air Forces in World War II,* Vol. II: *Europe: Torch to Pointblank.* Chicago: University of Chicago Press, 1949.

Cray, Ed. *General of the Army: George C. Marshall, Soldier and Statesman.* New York and London: W. W. Norton Company, 1990.

van Creveld, Martin. *Supplying War.* Cambridge, UK: Cambridge University Press, 1977.

Curtis, Donald McB. *The Song of the Fighting First.* Self-published, 1988.

Curtiss, Mina, ed. *Letters Home.* Boston: Little, Brown, 1944.

Danchev, Alex and Daniel Todman, eds. *War Diaries 1939–1945, Field Marshal Lord Alanbrooke.* Berkeley and Los Angeles: University of California Press, 2001.

Davies, Kenneth Maitland. *To the Last Man.* St. Paul, Minn.: Ramsey County Historical Society, 1982.

Davis, Richard G. *Carl A. Spaatz and the Air War in Europe.* Washington, D.C.: Center for Air Force History, 1993.

D'Este, Carlo. *Bitter Victory: The Battle for Sicily, July–August 1943.* New York: Harper-Perennial, 1992.

— *Eisenhower: A Soldier's Life.* New York: Henry Holt & Co., LLC, 2002.

Doubler, Michael D. *Closing with the Enemy.* Lawrence, Kansas: University Press of Kansas, 1994.

Doyle, Hilary and Tom Jentz. *Panzerkampfwagen IV Ausf. G, H and J 1942–45.* Oxford, United Kingdom: Osprey, 2001.

Dunlap, Roy F. *Ordnance Went Up Front.* Plantersville, SC: Small-Arms Technical Publishing Co., 1948. Republished, Birmingham, Alabama: Palladium Press, 1998.

Eisenhower, David. *Eisenhower at War 1943–1945.* New York: Random House, 1986.

Eisenhower, Dwight David. *Crusade in Europe.* Baltimore: Johns Hopkins Press, 1948.

— *At Ease: Stories I Tell Friends.* New York: Doubleday, 1967.

Ellis, John. *Brute Force: Allied Strategy and Tactics in the Second World War.* New York: Viking, 1990.

— *On the Front Lines.* London: John Wiley, 1991.

Ellis, L. F. *Welsh Guards at War.* Aldershot, U.K.: Gale and Polden, 1946.

Engelmann, J. *Deutsche Schwere Feldhaubitzen 1934–1945* [German Heavy Field Artillery in World War II: 1934–1945]. Translated by Johnston, D. Atglen, PA: Schiffer Publishing, 1995.

ffrench Blake, R. L. V. *A History of the 17th/21st Lancers, 1922–1959.* London: Macmillan, 1962.

Foote, Shelby. *The Civil War: A Narrative: Fredericksburg to Meridian.* New York: Random House, 1963.

Forty, George. *United States Tanks of World War II in Action.* Poole, U.K.: Blandford, 1983.

Foss, Christopher. *Jane's Pocket Book of Towed Artillery.* New York: Collier, 1977.

Fraser, David. *Alanbrooke.* New York: Atheneum, 1982.

Funk, Arthur Layton. *The Politics of Torch.* Lawrence, Kan.: University Press of Kansas, 1974.

Fussell, Paul. *Wartime: Understanding and Behavior in the Second World War.* New York: Oxford University Press. 1989.

Gabel, Christopher R. *Seek, strike, and destroy: U.S. Army tank destroyer doctrine in World War II.* Fort Leavenworth, Kansas: Army Command and General Staff College, 1985.

Gander, Terry, and Peter Chamberlain. *Weapons of the Third Reich: An Encyclopedic Survey of All Small Arms, Artillery and Special Weapons of the German Land Forces 1939–1945.* New York: Doubleday, 1979.

Gelb, Norman. *Desperate Venture: The Story of Operation Torch, the Allied Invasion of North Africa.* New York: William Morrow and Company, Inc., 1992.

Green, Michael, and Gladys Green. *Weapons of Patton's Armies.* Osceola, Wisconsin: Zenith Imprint Press, 2000.

Green, Milo L., and Paul S. Gauthier, eds. *Brickbats from F Company.* Corning, Iowa: Gauthier Publishing, 1982.

Greenfield, Kent Roberts *et al. The United States Army in World War II: Organization of Ground Combat Troops.* Washington, D.C.: United States Army Center for Military History, 1987.

Grinker, Roy R. and John P. Siegel. *War Neuroses in North Africa.* U.S. Army, 1943, and see Roy R. Grinker and John P. Spiegel, *War Neuroses.* Philadelphia: 1945. This book was published as a confidential document in 1943 as Roy Grinker and John P. Spiegel, *War Neuroses in North Africa: The Tunisian Campaign.* New York: Josiah Macy, Jr. for Foundation for the Air Surgeon, Army Air Forces, 1943; see also: Grinker, Roy R., Lt. Col., M.C., USA and John P. Spiegel, Maj., M.C., USA. *War Neuroses.* Philadelphia: The Blakiston Company, Inc., 1982.

Harmon, Ernest, with Milton MacKaye and William Ross MacKaye. *Combat Commander: Autobiography of a Soldier.* Englewood Cliffs, N.J.: Prentice-Hall, 1970.

Heller, Charles E. and William A. Stofft, eds. *America's First Battles, 1776–1965.* Lawrence: University of Kansas Press, 1986.

Henry, Mark R. *The US Army in World War II (2): The Mediterranean,* Osprey Publishing, 2000.

Hill, Russell. *Desert Conquest.* New York: Knopf, 1943.

Hinsley, F. H. *British Intelligence in the Second World War,* vol. 2. New York: Cambridge University Press, 1981.

Hoffman, George F. and Donn A. Starry, eds. *Camp Colt to Desert Storm: The History of U.S. Armored Forces.* Lexington, KY: University Press of Kentucky, 1999.

Hogg, Ian V. and John Walter. *Pistols of the World (4 ed.).* David & Charles, 2004.

Hogg, Ian V. and John S. Weeks. *Military Small-Arms of the 20th Century.* London: Arms & Armour Press, 1977.

— *Military Small Arms of the 20th Century. 7th Edition.* Krause Publications. 2000.

Hougen, John H. *The Story of the Famous 34th Infantry Division.* Nashville: The Battery Press, 1979.

Howard, Michael. *Grand Strategy.* Vol. IV, August 1942–September 1943. London: Her Majesty's Stationery Office, 1972.

Howe, George F. *The Battle History of the 1st Armored Division.* Nashville: Battery Press, 1979.

—*The United States Army in World War Two. The Mediterranean Theater of Operations. Northwest Africa: Seizing the Initiative in the West.* Washington, D.C.: U.S. Army Center for Military History, 1993.

Hunnicutt, R. P. *Half-Track: A History of American Semi-Tracked Vehicles.* Navato, CA: Presidio Press, 2001.

Irving, David, *The Trail of the Fox.* New York: Thomas Congdon, 1977.

Jackson, W. G. F. *The Battle for North Africa.* New York: Mason/Charter, 1975.

Johnson, Franklyn A. *One More Hill.* New York: Funk & Wagnalls, 1949.

Jordan, Philip. *Jordan's Tunis Diary.* London: Collins, 1943.

Kammerer, Albert. *Du débarquement Africain au meurtre de Darlan.* Paris, France: Flammarion, 1949.

Keegan, John. *The Second World War.* New York: Penguin Books, 1989.

Kennedy, John. *The Business of War.* London: Hutchinson, 1957.

Kennett, Lee B. *G.I.: The American Soldier in World War II.* New York: Scribner's, 1987.

Kesselring, Albert. *The Memoirs of Field-Marshal Kesselring.* London: Greenhill, 1997, 2007.

Knickerbocker, H. R. *et al. Danger Forward: The Story of the First Division in World War II.* Atlanta, GA: Albert Love Enterprises, 1947.

Kreidberg, Marvin A., and Merton G. Henry. *History of Military Mobilization in the United States Army, 1775–1945.* Washington, D.C.: Department of the Army, 1955.

Kuhn, Volkmar. *German Paratroops in World War II.* Transl. H. A. and A. J. Barker. London: Ian Allan, 1978.

Larrabee, Eric. *Commander in Chief.* New York: Touchstone, 1987.

Lee, Ulysses. *The United States Army in World War II: Special Studies: The Employment of Negro Troops.* Washington, D.C.: Office of the Chief of Military History, United States Army, 1966.

Leighton, Richard M. and Robert W. Coakley. *The United States Army in World War II: Global Logistics and Strategy, 1940–1943.* Washington, D.C.: U.S. Army Center of Military History (1995).

Library of America. *Reporting World War II: Part One: American Journalism 1938–1944.* (Anthology). New York: Literary Classics of the United States, Inc. 1995.

Liddell Hart, B. H., ed. *The Rommel Papers.* Transl. Paul Findlay. New York: Collectors Reprints, 1995.

Lochner, Louis P. ed. and transl. *The Goebbels Diaries, 1942–1943.* New York: Doubleday (1948).

Lucas, James. *Panzer Army Africa.* San Rafael, Calif.: Presidio, 1977.

Macksey, Kenneth. *Crucible of Power: The Fight for Tunisia 1942–1943.* London: Hutchinson, 1969.

— *Tank versus Tank.* Topsfield, Mass.: Salem House, 1988.

MacVane, John. *Journey into War: War and Diplomacy in North Africa.* New York: Appleton-Century, 1943.

McKenney, Janice E. *The Organizational History of Field Artillery, 1775–2003.* Washington, D.C.: U.S. Army Center for Military History, Publ. No. CMH 60-16-1, 2007.

Mansoor, Peter R. *The GI Offensive in* Europe. Lawrence, Kansas: University Press of Kansas, 1999.

Marshall, Malcolm. *Proud Americans.* Self-published, 1994.

Martienssen, Anthony. *Hitler and His Admirals.* New York: E. P. Dutton, 1949.

Mauldin, Bill. *Up Front.* New York: Henry Holt and Company, Inc., 1945.

Meadows, Edward S. *U.S. Military Automatic Pistols: 1894–1920.* Richard Ellis Publications, 1993.

Messenger, Charles. *The Tunisian Campaign.* Shepperton, U.K.: Ian Allan, 1982.

Middleton, Drew. *Our Share of Night.* New York: Viking, 1946.

Miller, Clem. *Some Things You Never Forget.* Superior, Wisconsin: Savage Press, 1996.

Miller, Merle. *Ike the Soldier: As They Knew Him.* New York: G. P. Putnam's, 1987.

Millett, John D., Ph.D. *The United States Army in World War II: The Army Service Forces: The Organization and Role of the Army Service Forces.* Washington, D.C.: United States Army, Center for Military History, 1987 [1954].

Mollo, Andrew. *The Armed Forces of World War II.* New York: Crown, 1981.

Moorehead, Alan. *The End in Africa.* London: Hamish Hamilton, 1943.

Morison, Samuel E. *History of United States Naval Operations in World War II.* Vol. II, *Operations in North African Waters.* Boston: Little, Brown, 1950.

Murphy, Robert. *Diplomat Among Warriors.* New York: Doubleday, 1964.

Nicholson, Nigel. *Alex: The Life of Field Marshal Earl Alexander of Tunis.* New York: Atheneum, 1973.

Nicholson, Nigel and Patrick Forbes. *The Grenadier Guards in the War of 1939–1945*, two volumes. Aldershot, U.K.: Gale and Polden, 1949.

Palmer, Robert R. *et al. The United States Army in World War II: The Procurement and Training of Ground Combat Troops.* Washington, D.C.: Department of the Army, 1948, republished Washington, D.C.: U.S. Army Center for Military History, 1993.

Parkinson, Roger. *A Day's March Nearer Home.* New York: David McKay, 1974.

Parris, John A., Jr., and Ned Russell, with Leo Disher and Phil Ault. *Springboard to Berlin*. New York: Thomas Y. Crowell, 1943.

Pendar, Kenneth. *Adventure in Diplomacy*. New York: Dodd, Mead, 1945.

Persons, Benjamin S. *Relieved of Command*. Manhattan, Kan: Sunflower University Press, 1997.

Perrett, Bryan. *Panzerkampfwagen IV medium tank: 1936–1945*. Oxford, United Kingdom: Osprey,1999.

Playfair, I. S. O. and C. J. C. Molony. *The Mediterranean and the Middle East*, vol. IV, *The Destruction of the Axis Forces in Africa. History of the Second World War*. London: Her Majesty's Stationery Office, 1960,

Pyle, Ernie. *Here is Your War*. New York: Henry Holt, 1943.

— *Brave Men*. New York: Henry Holt, 1944.

Rame, David. *Road to Tunis*. New York: MacMillan, 1944.

Robinett, Paul McDonald. *Armor Command*. Washington, D.C.: McGregor & Werner, 1958.

Rolf, David. *The Bloody Road to Tunis*. London: Greenhill, 2001.

Rush, Robert S. *GI: The US Infantryman in World War II*. Oxford, UK: Osprey Publishing Ltd., 2003.

Ruth, Larry. *M1 Carbine: Design, Development & Production*. Highland Park, NJ: The Gun Room Press, 1979.

Sandburg, Carl. *Abraham Lincoln: The Prairie Years* and *The War Years*. One Volume Edition. New York: Harcourt, Brace & World, 1954.

Smith, Bradley. *The War's Long Shadow*. New York: Simon and Schuster, 1985.

Spielberger, Walter. *PanzerKampfWagen IV*. Berkshire, United Kingdom: Profile Publications Ltd. 1972.

Stewart, Richard W., ed. *et al. American Military History*, Vol. II: *The United States Army in a Global Era, 1917–2008*, 2nd ed. Washington, D.C.: U.S. Army Center for Military History, 2010 (Army historical series, CMH Pub. 30–220).

The Story of the 34th Infantry Division: Louisiana to Pisa. Compiled by members of 34th Infantry Division. Published by the Information and Education Section, MTOUSA, at Archetipografia di Milano, S: Milan, 1945.

Tapert, Annette, ed. *Lines of Battle*. New York: Times Books, 1987.

Thompson, Leroy. *Combat Handguns*. London: Greenhill, 2004.

— *The Colt 1911 Pistol*. Oxford, UK: Osprey Publishing, 2011.

— *The M1 Carbine*. Oxford, UK: Osprey Publishing, 2011.

Tobin, James. *Ernie Pyle's War*. Lawrence, Kansas: University Press of Kansas, 1997.

Tompkins, Peter. *The Murder of Admiral Darlan*. New York: Simon & Schuster, 1965.

Truscott, Lucian K. *Command Missions: A Personal Story*. New York: E. P. Dutton and Co., 1954; republished by Presidio Press, 1990.

Tuker, Francis. *Approach to Battle*. London: Cassell, 1963.

Tute, Warren. *The North African War*. New York: Two Continents, 1976.

20th Century War: The American Experience Book of Readings. Fort Leavenworth, Kansas: Command and General Staff College. 1996.

Vaughan, Hal. *FDR's 12 Apostles: The Spies Who Paved the Way for the Invasion of North Africa*. Lanham, Maryland: Rowman & Littlefield, 2006.

Vining, Donald, ed. *American Diaries of World War II*. New York: Pepys Press, 1982.

Vojta, Francis. *The Gopher Gunners of Minnesota: A History of Minnesota's 151st Field Artillery*. Self-published, 1995.

Warlimont, Walter. *Inside Hitler's Headquarters, 1939–1945*. Transl. R. H. Barry. Novato, Calif.: Presidio, 1964.

Weeks, John. *World War II Small Arms*. London: Orbis Publishing Ltd. and New York: Galahad Books, 1979.

Weigley, F. *History of the United States Army*, New York: The Macmillan Company, 1967.

Welles, Sumner. *The Time for Decision*. New York and London: Harper & Brothers, 1944.

Westphal, Siegfried. *The German Army in the West*. London: Cassell, 1951.

Whiting, Charles. *Disaster at Kasserine*. Secker & Warburg Ltd., 1984. Yorkshire, UK: Republished by Leo Cooper, an imprint of Pen & Sword Books, Ltd. Barnsley, S. 2003.

Williamson, Samuel Thurston. *These Are the Generals*. New York: Knopf, 1943.

Yeide, Harry. *The Tank Killers*. Havertown, Penn.: Casemate Publishers, 2004.

Zaloga, Steven J. *M3 Infantry Half-track 1940–1973*. Oxford: Osprey Publications, 1994.

— *US Field Artillery of World War II*. Oxford, UK: Osprey Publishing, 2007.

— *Armored Thunderbolt: The U.S. Army Sherman in World War Two*. Mechanicsburg, PA: Stackpole Books, 2008, Kindle ed.

Periodicals

Alexander, Field Marshal the Viscount Alexander of Tunis Harold R. L. G. "The African Campaign from El Alamein to Tunis, from 10th August 1942 to 13th May 1943." printed in Supplement, February 3, 1948, to *The London Gazette*, February 5, 1948. https://www.thegazette.co.uk/London/issue/38196/data.pdf.

Anderson, K. A. N. "Operations in North West Africa, 8 November 1942 to 13 May 1943." *London Gazette* (Supplement), Wednesday, November 6, 1946, https://www.thegazette.co.uk/London/issue/37779/supplement/5449.

Andrews, Peter. "A Place to be Lousy In." *American Heritage Magazine* (December 1991), Volume 42, Issue 8.

Betson, William R. "Sidi bou Zid—A Case History of Failure." *Armor*, Nov.-Dec. 1982.

Blumenson, Martin. "The Agony and the Glory." *Infantry Magazine*, Fort Benning Ga.: U.S. Army Infantry School, Vols 57–58, July–August 1967 ed., 48 *et seq*. Online at Google eBooks: https://books.google.com/books/download/Infantry.pdf?id=bLjAK1jMtFQC&hl=en&capid=AFL-RE72FsFZfD4fDj5qWT-yf7ejFYJsyiIwtAkdPNuEO7Y8gdb2paOybjw8ZDfP-imqfXoul90b-mhMlerertpWE4gKbtYd7irw&continue=https://books.google.com/books/download/Infantry.pdf%3Fid%3DbLjAK1jMtFQC%26output%3Dpdf%26hl%3Den.

Boyle, Harold V. Associated Press, account of "Texas," *Cavalry Journal*, March–April 1943.

Burba, Edwin H. "Battle of Sidi bou Zid." *Field Artillery Journal*, Sept. 1943.

Carvey, James B. "Faïd Pass." *Infantry Journal*, Sept. 1944.

Davis, Jr., Franklin M. "The Battle of Kasserine Pass." *American Legion*, Apr. 1965.

Dinning, Stephen, Letter, *Des Moines Register and Tribune*, March 21, 1943.

Fountain, Ray C. Letter, *Des Moines Tribune*, Aug. 5, 1943, Iowa GSMM.

Fussell, Paul. "The Real War 1939–1945." *The Atlantic*, August 1989.

Hoy, Charles J. "Reconnaissance Lessons from Tunisia." *Cavalry Journal*, Nov.–Dec. 1943.

— "The Last Days in Tunisia." *Cavalry Journal*, Jan.–Feb. 1944.

Irish, Kerry E. "Apt Pupil: Dwight Eisenhower and the 1930 Industrial Mobilization Plan." *The Journal of Military History*, Vol. 70, Number 1, January 2006.

Johnson, Jack K. "'Mr. National Guard': Ellard A. Walsh (1887–1975), Part 1." *Allies. Newsletter of the Military Historical Society of Minnesota*, Winter, 2012. Vol. XX, No. 1.

Middleton, Drew. "We'll Take 'Em Apart and Then Get Home." *New York Times Magazine*, July 1943.

McBride, Lauren E. "The Battle of Sened Station." *Infantry Journal*, Apr. 1945.

Murray, Brian J. "Facing the Fox." *America in World War II* (April 2006 issue), 28–35.

Nichols, Sheridan. "The United States Vice Consuls In North Africa, 1941 1942." *Proceedings of the Meeting of the French Colonial Historical Society* 4 (1979): 213–20. http://www.jstor.org/stable/45137349.

Norgaard, Norland. AP dispatch in *Red Oak Express*, Feb. 22, 1943, 1.

Smith, Col. Randy A. "The Technologically Hollow Force of the 21st Century." *Air Force Journal of Logistics*, Vol. 23, No. 2, Summer 1999.

Stewart, Richard W. "The 'Red Bull' Division: The Training and Initial Engagements of the 34th Infantry Division, 1941–43." *Army History*, Winter 1993. Department of the Army, Washington, D.C.: 1993.

"German Tanks Trapped" article in *The Times* (London), May 5, 1943.

Walker, David A. "OSS and Operation Torch." *Journal of Contemporary History* 22, no. 4 (1987). http://www.jstor.org/stable/260815.

Wanke, Paul. "American Military Psychiatry and Its Role Among Ground Forces in World War II." *Journal of Military History* 63, no. 1.

Wilson, Richard. "The Gallant Fight of the 34th Division." *Des Moines Register and Tribune,* 1943.

Manuscripts, Theses, Compilations

Altman, Robert F. "U.S. Army Interwar Planning: The Protective Mobilization Plan." Thesis, U.S. Army Command and General Staff College, Fort Leavenworth, Kansas, 2014.

Anderson, Major Roland. "Operations of 135th Infantry, 34th Division, in the vicinity of Fonduk (*sic*) el Okbi, North Africa, 26 March–11 April 1943 (Tunisian Campaign)," (MS., 1947). Donovan Research Library, U.S. Army Command and Staff College, Fort Leavenworth, Kansas.

Andrews, Major Samuel R., MN ANG. "Major General Charles Ryder: The Forging of a World War II Division Commander." Monograph, School of Advanced Military Studies, U.S. Army Command and General Staff College, Fort Leavenworth, Kansas, 2014.

Anonymous. Letter, Apr. 1943, *Minneapolis Tribune*, Mina Curtiss Collection, Yale University Library, Manuscripts and Archives.

Bailey, Major Leslie W. "The Operations of the 3d Battalion, 135th Infantry at Algiers, 7 November–10 November 1942." Manuscript, The Infantry School, Fort Benning, GA.

Berlin, Robert H. *U.S. Army World War II Corps Commanders*. Ft. Leavenworth, Kan.: Combat Studies Institute, 1989.

Brown, John S. "Winning Teams: Mobilization Related Correlates of Success in American World War Two Infantry Divisions." MMAS Thesis. U.S. Army Command and General Staff College, 1985.

Carr, Vincent M. "The Battle of Kasserine Pass: An Examination of Allied Operational Failings." Air Command and Staff College, Maxwell AFB, April 2003.

Craven, Virgil E. "The Operations of Company I, 133rd Infantry (34th Infantry Division) in the Attack of Fondouk Gap, North Africa, 8–9 April 1943 (Tunisia Campaign) (Personal Experience of a Company Executive Officer)." Typescript, Advanced Infantry Officers Course, 1949–50. U.S. Army Infantry School, Fort Benning, Georgia. Digital Collections, Donovan Research Library, Ft Benning, Ga. Online at https://mcoepublic.blob.core.usgovcloudapi.net/library/DonovanPapers/wwii/STUP2/A-F/CravenVirgil%20E.pdf.

Daubin, Freeland A., Jr. "The Battle of Happy Valley." Manuscript, 1948. Fort Knox, Ky. Armored School. U.S. Military History Institute.

Dennis, William G. "U.S. and German Field Artillery in World War II: A Comparison." Army Historical Foundation web article. URL: https://armyhistory.org/u-s-and-german-field-artillery-in-world-war-ii-a-comparison.

Dickson, Benjamin A. "G-2 Journal: Algiers to the Elbe." Unpublished memoir, n.d. U.S. Army Military History Institute (and in USMA Archives).

Fosdick, Roger Barry. "A Call to Arms: The American Enlisted Soldier in World War II." Ph.D. diss., 1985, Claremont Graduate School.

Gabel, Christopher R. "The U.S. Army GHQ Maneuvers of 1941." Ph.D. dissertation. Ohio State University. 1981.

Grinker, Roy R., Lieutenant Colonel, M. C., USA and John P. Spiegel, Major, M. C., USA. *War Neuroses*. Philadelphia: The Blakiston Company, Inc., 1982.

Hazen, David W. "Role of the Field Artillery in the Battle of Kasserine Pass," Master's thesis, U.S. Army Command and Staff College, 1973.

Heavey, Brigadier General William. F. "Down Ramp! The Story of the Army Amphibian Engineers." Infantry Journal Press, 1947.

Heymont, I. and E. W. McGregor. *Review and Analysis of Recent Mobilizations and Deployments of U.S. Army Reserve Components*. McLean, Va.: Research Analysis Corp., 1972.

Hudel, Major Helmut and Paul McD. Robinett. "The Tank Battle at Sidi bou Zid," in "Kasserine Pass Battles," n.d., vol. I, part 1, U.S. Army Center for Military History.

Johnson, Joanne E. "The Army Industrial College and Mobilization Planning Between the Wars." Washington, D.C.: The Industrial College of the Armed Forces, National Defense University, 1993.

Kesselring, Albert. "The War in the Mediterranean," part II, "The Fighting in Tunisia and Tripolitania." n.d. U.S. Army European Command. Foreign Military Studies, T-3.

— "Final Commentaries on the Campaign in North Africa, 1941–1943." 1949, U.S. Army European Command. Foreign Military Studies, C-075.

Kim, Don Y., Major, USA. "The United States 1st Armored Division and Mission Command at the Battle of Faid Pass." Monograph. School of Advanced Military Studies, United States Army Command and General Staff College, Fort Leavenworth, Kansas, 2017.

Larson, Ann, ed. "The History and Contribution to American Democracy of Volunteer 'Citizen Soldiers' of Southwest Iowa, 1930–1945." 1981, National Endowment of the Humanities.

Lavoie, Leon F., *et al.* "The First Armored Division at Faïd–Kasserine." 1949, Fort Knox, Ky., Armored School, U.S. Army Military History Institute.

Moore, Robert: "Induction of Company F," memo, Iowa GSMM; Villisca (Iowa) Review, Feb. 20, 1941.

Neal, Dennis F. "Dennis Frederick Neal, Soldier," typescript, n.d., Iowa GSMM.

Ney, Virgil. "Evolution of the U.S. Army Division: 1939–1968." Technical Operations, Inc., Combat Operations Research Group, under contract for U.S. Army Combat Developments Command, 1969.

— "Evolution of the U.S. Army Infantry Battalion: 1939–1968." Fort Belvoir, Va.: Technical Operations, Inc., Combat Operations Research Group, under contract for U.S. Army Combat Developments Command, 1968.

Von Arnim, Hans J. T., "Recollections of Tunisia." Transl. Janet E. Dewey, 1951. U.S. Army European Command. Foreign Military Studies, C-098.

Note on Foreign military studies

The US Army Foreign Military Studies (FMS), 1945–61 are a primary source for German military operations in World War II. They are the manuscripts of the US Army Historical Division's Foreign Military Studies program. These studies, written between 1945 and 1959 by former senior officers of the German Armed Forces, cover nearly every aspect of the German war effort. Many, but not all, manuscripts were translated into English. The Foreign Military Studies documents are found at the U.S. Army Military History Institute and in the National Archives and Records Administration, Archives II, College Park, Maryland.

Some 2,500 studies were produced and organized into nine series:

ETHINT-Series: a record of 80 interviews with high-ranking German officers conducted immediately after the war.

A-Series: transcribed oral interviews of selected German officers held as prisoners of war.

B-Series: narrative histories of units on the Western Front.
C-Series: 139 studies intended as source material for the history of the U.S. Army in World War II.
D-Series: studies of German operations in the Mediterranean Theater and Soviet Union, and several treatises on air and naval warfare, strategy, and tactics.
P-Series: a wide range of current and practical military topics of interest to the U.S. Army and other Federal agencies in the post-war period. Most concern operations on the Eastern Front.
T-Series: Comprehensive campaign-level topics written by committees of former German officers.
Air Force Studies: studies about the air war written for the U.S. Air Force by former Luftwaffe officers.
DA Pamphlet Historical Series: studies developed from the FMS manuscripts and then distributed as pamphlets within the U.S. military,

The FMS manuscripts vary in subject matter and quality. As with all historical documents, each study must be evaluated for accuracy and bias. The ETHINT and early A-, B-, and D-series manuscripts are the least factual because they were written from memory without access to official records. The C-Series are regarded as the most reliable. The academic consensus is that the German authors wrote a self-serving view of the war. However, many studies were valued enough by the US Army Center of Military History to be used in the official history of the United States Army in World War II and the Army Historical Series accounts of the War in the East. Reportedly, they were also used by German Armed Forces Military History Research Office (*Militärgeschichtliche Forschungsamt* or *MGFA*) as source material for its series on Germany and World War II (*Das Deutsche Reich und der Zweite Weltkrieg*).

Two guides were produced by the US Army Historical Division to catalog and index the studies:
• Guide to Foreign Military Studies 1945–54: Catalog and Index, published in 1954. It provides a summary of each manuscript and has a well-organized index.
• Supplement to Guide to Foreign Military Studies 1945–54, published in 1959. It lists and describes those C-, D-, and P-series studies produced after 1954.

34th Infantry Division Association website

http://www.34ida.org

135th Infantry Regiment

The Background of the 135th Infantry on deposit in the 34th Infantry Division Iowa Gold Star Museum. Camp Dodge, Iowa.

There are three collections of compiled records of the actions of the 135th Infantry Regiment on the 34th Infantry Division website. One such collection, largely prepared by Ray Rudolph, who was on the S-3 staff of the regiment, brought together the regimental monthly activity reports from Minneapolis (February 1941) to Monte Cassino (February 1944). His replacement continued the effort up to the breakthrough at the Gothic Line (September 1944) but was then captured by the Germans. Mr. Rudolph donated his personal copy of those papers to the 34th Infantry Division Association. The Ray Rudolph collection on the 34th Infantry Division Association website consists of the following listed documents:

Ray Rudolph

The Background of the 135th Infantry http://www.34ida.org/images/135inf/135inf_rr0000.txt.
Preparations for Combat, 1941 February http://www.34ida.org/images/135inf/135inf_rr4102.txt
- Induction into Federal Service.

- Camp Claiborne and Fort Dix.
- Northern Ireland and England.

Algerian Campaign—Landing At Algiers, 1942 October http://www.34ida.org/images/135inf/135inf_rr4210.txt.

Tunisian Campaign—Oran to Fondouk, 1942 November http://www.34ida.org/images/135inf/135inf_rr4211.txt.

- Landing at Oran.
- Pichon—First Action against the Germans.
- Defense of the Sbiba Valley.
- El Ala - Pichon Diversion.
- First Fondouk.
- Second Fondouk.

Tunisian Campaign—Hill 609, 1943 April http://www.34ida.org/images/135inf/135inf_rr4304.txt.

Italy and the Crossings of the Volturno, 1943 September http://www.34ida.org/images/135inf/135inf_rr4309.txt.

Montaquilla and Mount Pantano, 1943 November http://www.34ida.org/images/135inf/135inf_rr4311.txt.

Cassino, 1944 January. http://www.34ida.org/images/135inf/135inf_rr4401.txt.

Anzio and Rome Campaigns, 1944 March http://www.34ida.org/images/135inf/135inf_rr4403.txt.

- Anzio Beachhead.
- Rome.

Up the Coast to Leghorn, 1944 June http://www.34ida.org/images/135inf/135inf_rr4406.txt.

The Gothic Line, 1944 September http://www.34ida.org/images/135inf/135inf_rr4409.txt

Awards http://www.34ida.org/images/135inf/135inf_rr9999.txt.

Two of the three collections of compiled reports of the actions of the 135th Infantry Regiment list command and staff assignments to company level and identify casualties in detail. They are based in major part on the regiment's required monthly operational reports. The first of these collections, from the archives of the Gold Star Military Museum, Iowa National Guard, at Camp Dodge, Iowa, was scanned by the late Lieutenant Colonel (Ret.) Mike Musel. Further material, unique to this collection, includes unit strength and location reports, some communication logs, and many of the personnel citations and awards which tell the story of its soldiers—the hearts of the regiment—in detail. The Musel collection in the Iowa Gold Star Military Museum and on the 34th Infantry Division Association website consists of the following listed documents:

Iowa Gold Star Military Museum files

Camp Claiborne, Fort Dix, Northern Ireland, North Africa, 1941 February https://www.34ida.org/images/135inf/135inf_gs4102.pdf.

Salerno, Volturno, Cerasuola, 1942 May https://www.34ida.org/images/135inf/135inf_gs4309.pdf.

Cassino, Anzio, 1944 January https://www.34ida.org/images/135inf/135inf_gs4401.pdf.

Anzio, Lanuvio, Rome, Civitavecchia, 1944 April https://www.34ida.org/images/135inf/135inf_gs4404.pdf.

Cecina, Gothic Line, 1944 July https://www.34ida.org/images/135inf/135inf_gs4407.pdf.

Gothic Line, Winter Line, 1944 October https://www.34ida.org/images/135inf/135inf_gs4410.pdf.

Winter Line, 1945 January https://www.34ida.org/images/135inf/135inf_gs4501.pdf.

Po Valley, Combat Ends, Occupation, 1945 April https://www.34ida.org/images/135inf/135inf_gs4504.pdf.

French Border, Jugoslav Border, Going Home, 1945 July https://www.34ida.org/images/135inf/135inf_gs4507.pdf.

The third collection of compiled regimental reports of the 135th Infantry Regiment is from the personal papers of Colonel (Ret.) John Breit, who was commander of the 135th Infantry Regiment in the Po Valley Campaign and during the Italian occupation. Like the Musel collection, the Breit papers list command and staff assignments to company level and identify casualties in detail. They are based in major part on the regiment's required monthly operational reports. These papers were donated to the Gold Star Military Museum by William Breit, the colonel's son, and scanned by Pat Skelly. Extensive "Lessons Learned in Combat" and Awards and Citations reports are included at the end of this collection. The Breit papers collection at the Iowa Gold Star Military Museum and on the 34th Infantry Division Association website consists of the following listed documents:

Col. John Breit

Foreword http://www.34ida.org/images/135inf/135inf_jbforw.pdf.

Federal Service, Camp Claiborne, Pearl Harbor, 1941 February http://www.34ida.org/images/135inf/135inf_jb4102.pdf.

Northern Ireland, 1942 May http://www.34ida.org/images/135inf/135inf_jb4205.pdf.

Algiers, Tunisia, Kasserine, 1942 October http://www.34ida.org/images/135inf/135inf_jb4210.pdf.

1st Fondouk, 2nd Fondouk, Hill 609, 1943 March http://www.34ida.org/images/135inf/135inf_jb4303.pdf.

Waiting for Italy, 1943 May http://www.34ida.org/images/135inf/135inf_jb4305.pdf.

Salerno, 1943 September http://www.34ida.org/images/135inf/135inf_jb4309.pdf.

Volturno, Volturno, Volturno River, 1943 October http://www.34ida.org/images/135inf/135inf_jb4310.pdf.

Alife, Cassino, 1943 December http://www.34ida.org/images/135inf/135inf_jb4312.pdf.

Anzio, 1944 February http://www.34ida.org/images/135inf/135inf_jb4402.pdf.

Cisterna, Rome, 1944 May http://www.34ida.org/images/135inf/135inf_jb4405.pdf.

Tarquinia, Grosseta, Leghorn, Arno River, 1944 June http://www.34ida.org/images/135inf/135inf_jb4406.pdf.

Leghorn, Gothic Line, Winter, 1944 August http://www.34ida.org/images/135inf/135inf_jb4408.pdf.

Winter Line, Monte Belmonte, Highway 65, 1944 November http://www.34ida.org/images/135inf/135inf_jb4411.pdf.

Po Valley, Surrender of German 34th Div., 1945 April.

Lessons Learned in Combat http://www.34ida.org/images/135inf/135inf_jbless.pdf.

Appendix: Awards and Citations http://www.34ida.org/images/135inf/135inf_jbappx.pdf.

133rd Infantry Regiment

133RD INFANTRY REGIMENT • WWII NARRATIVE HISTORY

A detailed narrative history of the 133rd Infantry Regiment, 34th Infantry Division compiled by Mr. Pat Skelly from original reports found at NARA is online in a rough text form on the 34th Infantry Division Association website at http://www.34ida.org.

The history reports prior to September 23, 1943, when the regiment landed at Salerno, are quite different in form. The 2nd Battalion was attached to Allied Force Headquarters, first in England and then in North Africa, as security troops from September 17, 1942 until March 16, 1944. In their stead the 100th Infantry Battalion (Separate) served with the regiment from September 9, 1943, to May 23, 1944.

The early (Sep 1943–Aug 1944) and late (May 1945–Oct 1945) segments are all brief—1 to 6 pages in their original form. Those in between are much lengthier, typically 20 pages or more.

The 34th Infantry Division Association lists the following documents for the narrative history of the 133rd Infantry Regiment:

North Africa, 1st Battalion, Part One.

North Africa, 1st Battalion, Part Two.

North Africa, 3rd Battalion.

North Africa, Anti-Tank Company.

September–October 1943: http://www.34ida.org/images/133inf/4309.txt.

November 1943: http://www.34ida.org/images/133inf/4311.txt.

December 1943: http://www.34ida.org/images/133inf/4312.txt.

January 1944: http://www.34ida.org/images/133inf/4401.txt.

February 1944: http://www.34ida.org/images/133inf/4402.txt.

March 1944: http://www.34ida.org/images/133inf/4403.txt.

April 1944: http://www.34ida.org/images/133inf/4404.txt.

May 1944: http://www.34ida.org/images/133inf/4405.txt.

June 1944: http://www.34ida.org/images/133inf/4406.txt.

July 1944: http://www.34ida.org/images/133inf/4407.txt.

August 1944: http://www.34ida.org/images/133inf/4408.txt.

September 1944: http://www.34ida.org/images/133inf/4409.txt.

October 1944: http://www.34ida.org/images/133inf/4410.txt.

November 1944: http://www.34ida.org/images/133inf/4411.txt.

December 1944: http://www.34ida.org/images/133inf/4412.txt.

January 1945: http://www.34ida.org/images/133inf/4501.txt.

February 1945: http://www.34ida.org/images/133inf/4502.txt.

March 1945: http://www.34ida.org/images/133inf/4503.txt.

April 1945: http://www.34ida.org/images/133inf/4504.txt.

May 1945: http://www.34ida.org/images/133inf/4505.txt.

June 1945.pdf: http://www.34ida.org/images/133inf/4506.txt.

Mr. Skelly writes of these papers:

"The documents as presented here are—within the limits of my vision, alertness, and spell checker—a fair rendering of the original; but they are not a 'true copy'. Any annotations or significant corrections which I have made appear in 'square brackets.' There are clearly noticeable differences in style from segment to segment. These are due principally to the assignment of different clerks, historians, and adjutants to this task. I'm even now working toward providing some commonality of format without twisting the content. The original reports from which this collection has been made were obtained from the National Archives and Records Administration (NARA), College Park MD. A separate chronology for the Regiment covering the 1941–1945 period is available at: 133rd Infantry: http://www.34ida.org/history/133_narr_history.html."
- Patrick Skelly.

Government Publications

5 Fed. Reg. 3779–3791 (25 Sept. 1940).

6 Fed. Reg. 415 (16 Jan. 1941).

Comando Supremo: Italy at War, Library of Congress, Washington, D.C., 20540 USA http://www.comandosupremo.com/.

Center for Military History. *To Bizerte With II Corps: 23 April – 13 May 1943.* First printed by the Historical Division, War Department, for the American Forces in Action series, 1943, reprinted by the U.S. Army Center for Military History, CMH Publ. 100-6, 1989.

Dunham, H. H. *U.S. Army Transportation and the Conquest of North Africa. 1942–1943.* History Unit, Office of the Chief of Transportation, War Department, Jan 45.

Iowa National Guard, *General Orders No. 3:* Induction of the 34th Division into the active military service of the United States [Includes text of Executive Order No. 8633 and the instruction of the War Department], February 6, 1941: NARA, Dwight D. Eisenhower Presidential Library, Abilene, Kansas (hereinafter referred to as "DDE Presidential Library"): Collection: U.S. Army Unit Records, Box 1411.

Iowa National Guard. Biennial Report of the Adjutant General of the State of Iowa, 1940. NARA, DDE Presidential Library: Collection: U.S. Army Unit Records, Box 1411.

Biennial Report of the Adjutant General of the State of Iowa, Supplement to the 1941 Report, Archives and Records Department of Iowa, Camp Dodge, Johnston, Iowa. NARA, DDE Presidential Library: Collection: U.S. Army Unit Records, Box 1411.

Iowa National Guard. Biennial Report of the Adjutant General of the State of Iowa, 1942.

Industrial Mobilization Plan. War Department, Office of the Assistant Secretary of War, Washington, D.C. (1930).

U.S. Department of State. Publication 1983, *Peace and War: United States Foreign Policy, 1931–1941* (Washington, D.C.: U.S. Government Printing Office, 1943), 542–3. Online at http://www.ibiblio.org/pha/paw/ .

—*Department of State Bulletin,* Vol. II, Numbers 28–53, January 6 June 29, 1940 (Washington, D.C.: U.S. Government Printing Office, 1940, 529–36. Online at https://babel.hathitrust.org/cgi/pt?id=uiuo.ark:/13960/t0sr0fr17;view=1up;seq=7

— *Department of State Bulletin,* Vol. III, Numbers 54–79, July 6 December 28, 1940 Washington, D.C. Online at https://babel.hathitrust.org/cgi/pt?id=uiuo.ark:/13960/t7dr4f12b;view=1up;seq=7

—*Department of State Bulletin,* Vol. V: Numbers 106–31, July 5 December 27, 1941 Washington, D.C.: U.S. Government Printing Office, 1941.

Foreign Relations of the United States: The Conferences at Washington, 1941–1942 and Casablanca, 1943. Washington, D.C.: U.S. Government Printing Office, 1968.

Guide to Foreign Military Studies: Catalog and Index. Historical Division, Headquarters, United States Army Europe, 1954. https://www.ibiblio.org/hyperwar/Germany/FMS/index.html.

United States-British Staff Conversations report. Washington, D.C. March 27, 1941. www.ibiblio.org/pha/pha/pt_14/x15-049.html.

U.S. Army Ordnance Department (1917). *Description of the Automatic Pistol, Caliber .45, Model of 1911, with Rules for Management, Memoranda of Trajectory, and Description of Ammunition.* Washington: U.S. Government Printing Office (USGPO).

United States War Department. *German Infantry Weapons.* 25 May 1943. https://archive.org/details/GermanInfantryWeapons.

United States War Department. *German Military Abbreviations.* Special Series, No. 12, April 12, 1943. Prepared by U.S. Army Military Intelligence Service. [Declassified by authority of DOD Directive 5200.1R on May 23, 2003.]

United States War Department. FM 6-20 *Field Artillery Field Manual: Tactical Employment.* USGPO Washington, D.C. 1940, 1944.

—FM 6-75 *Field Artillery Field Manual: Service of the Piece 105mm Howitzer, M2, Truck-Drawn.* USGPO Washington, D.C. 1941.

—FM 7-10 *Infantry Field Manual: Rifle Company, Rifle Regiment.* USGPO Washington, D.C. 1942.

—FM 7-15 *Infantry Field Manual: Heavy Weapons Company, Rifle Regiment.* USGPO Washington, D.C. 1942.

—FM 7-20 *Infantry Field Manual: Rifle Battalion.* USGPO Washington, D.C. 1942.

—FM 7-24 *Field Manual: Communication in the Infantry Division.* USGPO Washington, D.C. 1944.

—FM 7-25 *Infantry Field Manual: Headquarters Company, Intelligence and Signal Communication, Rifle Regiment.* USGPO Washington, D.C. 1942.

—FM 7-30 *Infantry Field Manual: Supply and Evacuation: The Infantry Regiment; Service Company and Medical Detachment.* USGPO Washington, D.C. 1944.

—FM 7-35 *Infantry Field Manual: Antitank Company, Infantry Regiment and Antitank Platoon, Infantry Battalion.* USGPO Washington, D.C. 1944.

—FM 7-37 *Infantry Field Manual: Cannon Company, Infantry Regiment.* USGPO Washington, D.C. 1944.

—FM 7-40 *Infantry Field Manual: Rifle Regiment.* USGPO Washington, D.C. 1942.

—FM 8-35 *Medical Field Manual: Transportation of the Sick and Wounded.* USGPO Washington, D.C. 1941.

—FM 21-10 *Military Sanitation.* USGPO Washington, D.C. 1945.

—FM 23-5 *Basic Manual: U.S. Rifle, Caliber .30, M1.* USGPO Washington, D.C. 1943.

—FM 23-7 *Basic Manual: U.S. Carbine, Caliber .30, M1.* USGPO Washington, D.C. 1942.

—FM 30-40 *Recognition: Pictorial Manual on Armored Vehicles.* USGPO Washington, D.C. 1943.

—FM 25-7 *Field Manual: Pack Transportation.* USGPO Washington, D.C. 1944.

—FM 70-10 *Field Manual: Mountain Operations.* USGPO Washington, D.C. 1944.

—FM 70-15 *Basic Field Manual: Operations in Snow and Extreme Cold.* USGPO Washington, D.C. 1944.

—TM 9-710 *Basic Half-Track Vehicles (White, Autocar, and Diamond T).* Washington, D.C.: War Department, 1944.

—TM 9-1005-211-34 Technical Manual: *Pistol, Caliber .45, Automatic, M1911* 1964 edition. Pentagon Publishing, 1964.

—TM 9-1320 Technical Manual: *75mm howitzers and carriages.* USGPO Washington, D.C. 1944.

—TM 9-1326 Technical Manual: *105mm howitzer M3 and howitzer carriages M3 and M3A1.* USGPO, Washington, D.C. 1944.

—TM 12-427 Technical Manual: *Military Occupational Classification of Enlisted Personnel.* USGPO Washington, D.C. 1944.

—TM-E 30-451 Technical Manual: *Handbook on German Military Forces.* USGPO, Washington, D.C. 15 March 1945.

Glossary

The terms and abbreviations found here are used throughout the text and in the notes.

AA: Anti-aircraft.

AAA: Anti-aircraft artillery.

AAD: Atkinson, Rick. *An Army at Dawn*.

AAF: Army Air Forces.

ABC: American-British-Canadian Conversations.

AAR: After Action Report.

ACofS: Assistant Chief of Staff.

AD: Armored Division.

Admin: Administration.

Adv: Advance.

AF: Allied Force.

AFCP: Allied Force Command Post.

AFHQ: Allied Force Headquarters, led by the supreme Allied commander, General Eisenhower.

AFHQ micro: Allied Force Headquarters microfilm, NARA RG 351.

AGF: Army Ground Forces.

AGWAR: Adjutant general, War Department (Washington).

AIR: Armored infantry regiment, half-track mounted infantry integral to an armored division.

Amph: Amphibious, amphibian.

Angriffsgruppe Nord: German: Northern Attack Group.

Anlage: German: with reference to files of records, an appendix or annex.

Armd: Armored.

AR: Armored Regiment. A subordinate tank element of a U.S. armored division.

Army Group Africa: In February 1943, the Axis headquarters structure in North Africa was expanded and called Army Group Africa (*Heeresgruppe Afrika, Gruppo d'Armate Africa*) to manage the defense of Tunisia during the final stages of the North African Campaign. Army Group Africa included the German Fifth Panzer Army (*5. Panzerarmee*), and the Italian 1st Army. Command of the Army Group was turned over from Rommel to Hans-Jürgen von Arnim in March. He surrendered the Army Group on May 13, 1943, ending the Axis presence in Africa.

Arty: Artillery.

ASF: Army Service Forces, successor organization to the U.S. Army Services of Supply.

AT: Anti-tank.

Band: German, with reference to files of records, "volume."

BAR: Browning Automatic Rifle.

BG: Brigadier General (U.S. Army rank, O7), typically commanded artillery regiments or service and supply units, or was the executive officer or deputy commander of a division.

Bn: Battalion: (i)the highest-level subordinate element of an infantry regiment, with three rifle companies and a heavy weapons company, (ii) a subordinate element of an artillery regiment with 16 artillery pieces organized in four batteries; (iii) an independent unit of artillery or tanks attached to a division or a regiment. A U.S. Army infantry battalion typically had three rifle companies plus a weapons company (mortars and machine guns) and a headquarters company, a unit of about 871 soldiers commanded by a major or lieutenant colonel. In this book, battalions and their parent organizations may be denoted for brevity as, for example, "1/135," meaning the "1st Battalion of the 135th Infantry Regiment", or "1/1AR," meaning the "1st Battalion of the 1st Armored Regiment".

Br.: British.

Cannon company: In the U.S. Army, the cannon company was a novelty in 1942, recently added to the regimental table of organization. Under staff discussion for years, the cannon company of 1942 comprised 123 infantrymen manning six self-propelled 75mm howitzers, mounted on M3 half-tracks, and two self-propelled 105mm howitzers. Reports from the few companies in operation in North Africa were inconclusive. It was doubted at AGF headquarters that the cannon company was essential. The AGF tables of March 1943 abolished it, replacing it with three cannon platoons in the regimental headquarters company, equipped with six short-barreled, towed M3 105mm howitzers. Fifty-one men were saved in each regiment, or more than 150 in the division.[1]

Captain (CPT): U.S. Army commissioned officer rank, O4, typically a company commander.

CC: Combat Command, in U.S. armored divisions, the highest-level subordinate element of the armored division, organizationally analogous to a regiment in an infantry division. An armored division usually had four combat commands, each designated by a letter, e.g., CCA, CCB, CCC, and CCR (Combat Command Reserve). Each combat command was a combined arms force, with tank battalions, mechanized infantry, and artillery, with supporting units.

CCS: Combined Chiefs of Staff, the Anglo-American Allies' military high command, sometimes informally referred to as the "Charlie-Charlies."

CG: Commanding general.

CinC: Commander in chief.

Cmdre: Commodore

CMH: U.S. Army Center of Military History, Fort McNair, Washington, D.C.

Co: Company. In U.S. Army infantry branch usage in World War II, three rifle platoons plus a weapons platoon (machine guns and mortars) made up a company, a unit of about 193 men, commanded by a first lieutenant or a captain.

In the armor branch, as the war progressed, each tank company typically consisted of a Company HQ (two M4 75/76mm and one M4A3 105mm howitzer), a maintenance section, with one M3A2 half-track, two Jeeps, and one CCKW cargo truck, plus one M32 tank retrieval vehicle, and three tank platoons, each with five M4s with 75mm or 76mm guns.

CO: Commanding officer.

Colonel (Col): U.S. Army commissioned officer rank, O6, typically commanding a regiment.

Comando Supremo: Italian: During the Fascist regime in Italy, the head of state and commander in chief was nominally the reigning king. In fact, however, all power lay with Benito Mussolini as leader of the Fascists. With respect to military affairs, Mussolini exercised his authority through the Supreme Command (*Comando Supremo*). The Italian Supreme General Staff was reorganized in June 1941, and it became the most important organ of command. *Comando Supremo* functioned through its defense ministries and various high commands. The defense ministries included a Ministry of War, a Ministry of the Admiralty, and a Ministry of the Air. The high commands were based on geographic regions and included Army Group Libya. See Mollo, at 83.

Comdr: Commander.

Conf: Conference.

Conv: Conversation.

COS: Chiefs of Staff Committee (British).

CP: Command post.

CT: Combat team.

DA: Department of the Army.

Dept: Department.

D. D. Eisenhower or DDE: General Dwight David Eisenhower, supreme commander, Allied Force.

DDE Library: The Dwight D. Eisenhower Presidential Library, NARA, Abilene, Kansas.

Diss: Dissertation.

Div: Division. In U.S. Army infantry branch practice in World War II, three infantry regiments plus additional artillery and other supporting units (engineer, signal, medical, transportation, etc.) made up the infantry division, commanded by a major general. See the discussion in Appendix B: Organization and Equipment of a World War II U.S. Army Infantry Division. There were other kinds of divisions: armored, cavalry, motorized, airborne, mountain.

Djebel: Arabic: a hill or mountain. In modern times, Romanized as "jabal."

DMC: French: *Division de marche de Constantine* (Constantine Division).

Doc: Document.

EAF: Eastern Assault Force.

EBS: Eastern Base Section.

Engr: Engineer.

ETO: European Theater of Operations.

ETOUSA: European Theater of Operations, U.S. Army.

Exec: Executive.

FA: Field artillery; in U.S. usage, usually a battalion attached to a specific regiment or division, but also independent battalions or regiments attached to corps or army headquarters. Gun tube sizes ranged from 75mm to 240mm.

Flak: Flak is a contraction of German *Flugzeugabwehrkanone* (also referred to as *Fliegerabwehrkanone*) meaning "aircraft-defense cannon," the original purpose of the weapon. In English, "flak" became a generic term for ground anti-aircraft fire.

FM: Field manual, in U.S. War Department usage, *e.g.*, FM 7-10, Rifle Company, Rifle Regiment.

G-l: Personnel Officer of corps or higher staff. This function was performed by the Adjutant General's Office and by the adjutants general at army, corps, and division levels.

G-2: Intelligence officer of division or higher staff.

G-3: Plans and operations officer of division or higher staff.

G-4: Logistics and supply officer of division or higher staff.

GCM: General George Catlett Marshall, chief of staff, U.S. Army.

Gefechtsbericht: German: battle report.

Gefreiter: German military rank, equivalent to US Army private first class.

German Africa Corps ("*Deutsche Afrika Korps*" or "*DAK*"): The German expeditionary force in Africa during the North African Campaigns of World War II. Dispatched to shore up the Italian defense of their African colonies, the formation fought under various appellations, from March 1941 until its surrender in May 1943. The *Afrika Korps* was the major German component of *Panzerarmee Afrika*, which was later renamed the *Deutsche-Italienische Panzerarmee* and finally renamed *Heeresgruppe Afrika* (Army Group Africa). The unit's best-known commander was *General der Panzertruppen*, later Field Marshal, Erwin Rommel.

German-Italian Panzer Army: Panzer Army Africa was renamed German-Italian Panzer Army (*Deutsche-Italienische Panzerarmee, Armata Corazzata Italo-Tedesca*) in October 1942 during the long retreat after the defeat at the Second Battle of El Alamein during the Western Desert Campaign. Sometimes referred to as the Italo-German Army.

GenStdH: German: *Generalstab des Heeres* (General Staff of the Army).

GO: General order.

Gp: Group.

Heeresgruppe: German: Army group.

Hist: History or historical.

ID: Infantry Division. 34ID denotes the 34th Infantry Division.

Incl: Inclosure.

Inf: Infantry.

Info: Information.

Instruc: Instruction.

Intel: Intelligence.

Interv: Interview.

IGSMM: Iowa Gold Star Military Museum.

IR: Infantry Regiment. For example, 133IR denotes the 133rd Infantry Regiment.

JCS: U.S. Joint Chiefs of Staff.

Jnl: Journal.

Kampfgruppe: German: battle group, with a configuration determined by the assigned mission.

Kriegstagebuch or *KTB*: German: war journal or diary, a generally contemporaneous record of the plans, actions, and condition of a unit.

KwK: *KampfwagenKanone*: German: fighting vehicle cannon.

Lieutenant commander, U.S. Navy commissioned officer rank, O4.

Second Lieutenant (2LT): U.S. Army commissioned officer rank, O1, the most junior commissioned officer rank, typically a platoon leader.

First Lieutenant (1LT): U.S. Army commissioned officer rank, O2, typically a platoon leader, company executive officer, or company commander.

Lieutenant Colonel (LTC): U.S. Army commissioned officer rank, O5, typically a battalion commander or regimental executive officer.

Lieutenant General (LTG): U.S. Army commissioned officer rank, O9, typically a corps or army commander.

Maint: Maintenance.

Major (MAJ): U.S. Army commissioned officer rank, 04, typically a battalion executive officer or commander.

Major General (MG): U.S. Army commissioned officer rank, O8, typically a division or corps commander.

MHI: U.S. Army Military History Institute, Carlisle, Pa.

Micro: Microfilm.

Mil: Military.

Min: Minutes.

Misc: Miscellaneous.

MP: Military Police.

Msg: Message.

MSG: Master Sergeant, U.S. non-commissioned officer rank, E-8.

Mss: Manuscript.

MTOUSA: Mediterranean Theater of Operations, United States Army.

Mvmt: Movement.

NAf or N. Af.: North Africa.

NARA: National Archives and Records Administration.

NATOUSA: North African Theater of Operations, United States Army.

NCXF: Naval Commander Expeditionary Force.

n.d.: no date.

NWAf: George F. Howe, *The United States Army in World War II: Northwest Africa: Seizing the Initiative in the West.*

OCMH: Office of the Chief of Military History, U.S. Army.

OH: Oral history.

OB Süd: German: *Oberbefehlshaber Süd* (Headquarters, Commander in Chief South [southern Germany, North Africa, and several army groups on the Eastern Front]).

Oberkommando: German: Headquarters of an army or higher military organization.

Oberkommando des Heeres (OKH): German: High Command of the Army, which with *OKM* was subordinated to *OKW.*

Oberkommando der Kriegsmarine (OKM): German, High Command of the Navy.

Oberkommando der Wehrmacht (OKW): German: High Command of the Armed Forces, the staff mechanism through which Hitler as Führer exercised his control over the military establishment.

OCT: Office, chief of transportation.

OP: Observation Post.

Op Abt (H): German: *Operationen Abteilung (Heere)* (Operations Branch [Army]).

OPD: Operations and Plans Division, U.S. War Department. Omar Bradley called OPD the brain center of the U.S. Army in World War II.

Opn: Operation.

OSS: Office of Strategic Services.

Oued: Arabic: a stream or river, or its dry bed.

Panzer: The German word *panzer* derives through the French word pancier, "breastplate," from Latin *pantex,* "belly." *Panzer* refers to armored units or specifically to battle tanks and other armored fighting vehicles.

Panzer Army Africa: Panzer Group Africa was renamed Panzer Army Africa (*Panzerarmee Afrika, Armata Corazzata Africa*) on 30 January 1942. (A German *panzer* group was an army-level headquarters. As the war progressed all of the *panzer* groups were renamed Panzer Armies.)

Panzer Group Africa: When *Afrika Korps* was formed on 11 January 1941 it was subordinated to the Italian chain of command in Africa. In the middle of 1941 *Oberkommando der Wehrmacht* (*OKW*, Armed Forces High Command) created a new headquarters, Panzer Group Africa (*Panzergruppe Afrika, Gruppo Corazzato Africa*). On 15 August 1941, Panzer Group Africa was activated with *General der Panzertruppen* Erwin Rommel in command. The Panzer Group controlled the *Afrika Korps* and other units, notably the 90th Light Infantry Division), and the Italian X Corps and XX Corps.

Par: Paragraph.

Prep: Preparation.

Plat: Platoon: in U.S. Army infantry usage, in World War II, three squads (each composed of 10 riflemen and one BAR man, and commanded by a sergeant, assisted by a corporal) made up a platoon, a unit of about 40 men commanded by a second lieutenant, assisted by a senior non-commissioned officer.

PzKmpfW: *Panzerkampfwagen*: German: armored fighting vehicle.

QM: Quartermaster.

Rad (or Radio): Radiogram.

RAF: Royal Air Force.

Rcd: Record.

Rcn: Reconnaissance.

RCT: Regimental Combat Team. In a U.S. infantry division, an RCT included at least an infantry regiment and its attached artillery battalion, reconnaissance troop, and its supporting heavy weapons, anti-tank, supply, signals, engineer, medical and transportation units. Other configurations were determined by the mission.

Regt: Regiment. In U.S. Army usage, a major subordinate combat element of a division, consisting of three battalions, a headquarters company and supporting units, including reconnaissance, anti-tank, signal, medical, transport and quartermaster units. An infantry regiment had a cannon company equipped with M1 75mm pack howitzers or M3 105mm howitzers.

Rev: Revised.

RG: in NARA, a Record Group.

RN: Royal Navy.

Rpt: Report.

RTA: *Régiment Tirailleurs Algérien* (Regiment of Algerian Tirailleurs (Sharpshooters)), units of the French Army in North Africa with native Algerian soldiers and French officers.

S-1: Personnel section of a unit not having a general staff.

S-2: Military intelligence section of a unit not having a general staff.

S-3: Operations and training section of a unit not having a general staff.

SCR: Signal Corps radio set; each set was assigned a model number, such as SCR 536, the "walkie-talkie."

SD: SicherheitsDienste des Reichführers SS: German: The Nazi Party Security Service.

Sec: Section.

Secy: Secretary.

SGT: Sergeant, U.S. Army non-commissioned officer rank, E-5.

Sitrep: Situation report.

SOOHP: U.S. Army senior officer oral history program.

SOS: Services of Supply, the U.S. Army's procurement, logistics and supply organization.

SP: Self-propelled.

s.p.: self-published.

Spec: Special.

Sub: Subject.

Sum: Summary.

Tätigkeitsbericht: German: unit activity report.

TF: Task force.

TM: Technical Manual, in U.S. War Department usage, *e.g.*, TM 12-427. May also refer to a training manual prepared by Army units or commands.

Trans: Transportation.

Transl: Translation or Translator.

USFOR: U.S. Forces (London).

Wadi: Arabic: a dry gully or arroyo caused by stream erosion.

WD: U.S. War Department.

WDCSA: U.S. War Department, Office of the chief of staff of the U.S. Army.

WFSt: *Wehrmachtführungsstab*: German "Armed Forces Operations Staff".

Code Names

Anton: German occupation of southern France, which up to the time Operation *Torch* was executed had been unoccupied and under the administration of the French State with its capital in Vichy, France, November 10–11, 1942.

Arcadia: U.S.-British staff conference at Washington, December 1941 – January 1942.

Freedom: Signal code designation for Allied Force Headquarters, first on Gibraltar, later in Algiers.

Frühlingswind: German (Fifth Panzer Army) attack against Sidi Bou Zid, February 1943.

Gymnast: Plan of 1941 for invasion of French North Africa.

Husky: Allied invasion of Sicily in July 1943.

Morgenluft: German *(Deutsche Afrika Korps)* attack against Gafsa, after Operation *Frühlingswind,* February 1943.

Roundup: Various 1941–3 plans for a cross-Channel attack into France.

Satin: Proposed American II Corps attack toward Sfax, December 1942. Not executed.

Sturmflut: Operation by Rommel's *Angriffsgruppe Nord* against Kasserine Pass and Sbiba Gap, February 19–22, 1943.

Symbol: Casablanca Conference, January 14–23, 1943.

Terminal: Operation to seize the harbor of Algiers, November 8, 1942.

Torch: The Allied invasion operation in North Africa, November 8, 1942.

Trident: The Washington Conference of the Allied leaders in May 1943.

Endnotes

Introduction

1   Rick Atkinson. *An Army at Dawn*. New York: Henry Holt and Company, 2002, 53 (hereinafter cited as *AAD*) (emphasis supplied).
2   History of the 34th Infantry Division, Minnesota National Guard https://minnesotanationalguard. ng.mil/documents/2018/11/34th-infantry-division-history.pdf/ 4 of 7.

Chapter 1

1   United States-British Staff Conversations report Washington, D.C. March 27, 1941. www.ibiblio. org/pha/pha/pt_14/x15-049.html 1485-1550. HTML document created with GT HTML 6.0d 01/15/97 9:10 PM.
2   David Eisenhower. *Eisenhower at War 1943–1945*. New York: Random House, 1986, 72–4, citing Matloff and Snell, *Strategic Planning*, 29.
3   Bradley Smith. *The War's Long Shadow*. New York: Simon and Schuster, 1985, 103 (hereinafter cited as "Smith, *Long Shadow*").
4   Smith, *Long Shadow*, 103.
5   James MacGregor Burns. *Roosevelt – The Soldier of Freedom*. New York: Harcourt Brace Jovanovich, Inc. 1970, 41–3 (hereinafter cited as "Burns, *Roosevelt*").
6   Ibid.
7   Rt. Hon. Sir Winston S. Churchill. *The Second World War*, Vol. III: *The Grand Alliance*. Boston: Houghton Mifflin Company, 1950, 25 (hereinafter cited as WSC, vol III.).
8   Smith, *Long Shadow*, 104.
9   Burns, *Roosevelt*, 43–4.
10 Ibid., 45.
11 Ibid, 47–48
12 Ibid., 49.
13 WSC, Vol III, 427.
14 Ibid.
15 Ibid., 443–4.
16 Ibid., 444.
17 Ibid., 476.
18 Ibid., 477.
19 Ibid., 481.
20 Ibid., 482.
21 Ibid., 485. The then Shah abdicated in favor of his son and went into exile in South Africa.
22 Ibid., 490–1.

23   Ibid., 491.
24   Ibid., 493.
25   Ibid., 493.
26   Ibid., 540.
27   Churchill, instructions to General Sir Claude Auchinleck, commander in chief Middle East, 18 Oct. 1941, in WSC, Vol. III, 543. *See* Churchill Letter to Roosevelt, 20 Oct. 1941, 7, in WSC, Vol. III, 543–8.
28   WSC, Vol. III, 684–5 (emphasis supplied).
29   Ibid., 704–6.
30   *AAD*, 54.

Chapter 2

1   Ibid., 53.
2   Ibid.
3   The Army needed training in desert and armored warfare and in early 1942 directed Major General George S. Patton Jr., a Southern California native, to select a site and create what would become the Desert Training Center (DTC). Patton selected a 1,000-square-mile area in the Mojave desert across California and Arizona. Patton was called away from the DTC later in 1942 to lead the forces invading Morocco as part of *Torch*. None of the units that fought in North Africa had training at the DTC. The Army renamed the DTC the California-Arizona Maneuver Area (CAMA) in October 1943 to reflect its non-desert capacities. It served as a simulated "Theater of Operations" until spring 1944. The modern National Training Center is based at Fort Irwin, California in the same area.
4   Public Law (Pub. L.) 242, 41 Stat. 759, entitled "An Act to amend an Act entitled 'An Act for making further and more effectual provision for the national defense, and for other purposes,' approved June 3, 1916, and to establish military justice;" approved June 4, 1920. (Hereinafter cited as "NDA of 1920.")
5   Ibid., Chapter I, Section 1.
6   Ibid., Chapter I, Section 2 [Composition of the Regular Army].
7   Richard W. Stewart, ed. *et al.*, *American Military History*, Vol. II: *The United States Army in a Global Era, 1917–2008*, 2nd ed. Washington, D.C.: U.S. Army Center for Military History, 2010. Army historical series, CMH Pub. 30–220 (hereinafter cited as Stewart, *American Military History*), 59.
8   Stewart, *American Military History*, 69.
9   NDA of 1920, Chapter I, Section 5 [General Staff Corps].
10   Stewart, *American Military History*, 59–60.
11   NDA of 1920, Chapter I, Section 5.
12   Stewart, *American Military History*, 60.
13   Ibid.
14   NDA of 1920, Chapter I, Section 5.
15   Ibid.
16   Ibid.
17   NDA of 1920, Chapter I, Section 24a [Promotion List].
18   NDA of 1920, Chapter I, Section 2; Stewart, *American Military History*, 59.
19   Stewart, *American Military History*, 60; *see* NDA of 1920, Chapter I, Section 2.
20   Pub. Res. No. 59, 41 Stat. 1098, Ch. 40, approved February 7, 1921.

21 Pub. L. 27, 42 Stat. 68, Ch. 33, approved June 30, 1921.

22 Pub. L. 259, 42 Stat. 716, Ch. 253, Title I, approved June 30, 1922.

23 Stewart, *American Military History*, 60–1; Pub. Law No. 446, 44 Stat. 780, Ch. 721, entitled "An Act To provide more effectively for the national defense by increasing the efficiency of the Air Corps of the Army of the United States, and for other purposes." (Hereinafter cited as the "Air Corps Act of 1926.").

24 Stewart, *American Military History*, 64.

25 Air Corps Act of 1926, Section 2.

26 Stewart, *American Military History*, 61.

27 Report of the secretary of war to the president of the United States, 1933. Washington, D.C.: U.S. Government Printing Office 1933, Annual Report of the Chief of Staff, 48. (Hereinafter cited as "Chief of Staff Report 1933.")

28 Chief of Staff Report 1933, 20; Stewart, *American Military History*, 61.

29 Chief of Staff Report 1933, 20.

30 Stewart, *American Military History*, 61.

31 Ibid.

32 Ibid., 60.

33 Chief of Staff Report 1933, 21–5 [Effect of Reduced Appropriations on Training Efficiency and Personnel].

34 Ibid., 24.

35 Ibid., 24–5.

36 Stewart, *American Military History*, 66.

37 Ibid., 67.

38 Ibid., 66.

39 General Treaty for Renunciation of War as an Instrument of National History, June 1, 1933; online at https://www.loc.gov/law/help/us-treaties/bevans/m-ust000002-0732.pdf; Treaty for the Renunciation of War: Text of the Treaty, Notes Exchanged, Instruments of Ratification and of Adherence and Other Papers. The Department of State, Publ. No. 468. Washington, D.C.: United States Government Printing Office, 1933. Hathitrust Collection, online at https://babel.hathitrust.org/cgi/pt?id=uiug.30112021182107&view=1up&seq=1.

40 Stewart, *American Military History*, 67.

41 See WSC, vol III, 585.

42 Stewart, *American Military History*, 67.

43 Rogers Platt Churchill, *et al.*, eds. *Foreign Relations of the United States: Diplomatic Papers 1933–1939: The Soviet Union*. Washington, D.C.: US Department of State. Government Printing Office 1952; republished in electronic publication format by the Office of the Historian, Bureau of Public Affairs, U.S. Department of State, on May 26, 2018; Document 23: Letter, President Roosevelt to the Soviet Commissar for Foreign Affairs, M. Litvinov, dated November 16, 1933.

44 See Tydings–McDuffie Act, officially the Philippine Independence Act, Pub. L. 73–127, 48 Stat. 456, enacted March 24, 1934.

45 Franklin D. Roosevelt, First Inaugural Speech, 1933, online at https://catalog.archives.gov/id/197333 ("In the field of world policy I would dedicate this nation to the policy of the good neighbor—the neighbor who resolutely respects himself and, because he does so, respects the rights of others."), *see* Anti-War Treaty on Nonaggression and Conciliation, signed at Rio de Janeiro, October 10, 1933, text online at https://history.state.gov/historicaldocuments/frus1933v04/d141. Adhered to on behalf of the United States, subject to ratification, April 27, 1934; adherence advised by the Senate, subject to a reservation, June 15 (legislative day of June 6), 1934;

adherence ratified by the president, subject to the said reservation, June 27, 1934; instrument of adherence deposited with the government of Argentina, August 10, 1934; proclaimed by the president, March 11, 1936.; Stewart, *American Military History*, 65.

46　Report of the secretary of war to the president of the United States, 1934. Washington, D.C. U.S. Government Printing Office 1934, Annual Report of the Chief of Staff, 34 (hereinafter cited as "Chief of Staff Report, 1934"); *See*: Hearings before a Special Committee Investigating the National Defense Program, United States Senate, 77th Congress, First Session pursuant to S. Res. 71, 1941, USGPO. Washington, D.C. (Hereinafter cited as "Senate National Defense Hearings 1941.") Exhibit 36 [Reports on the state of the United States Army by Secretaries of War and Chiefs of Staff of the Army from 1926 to 1939], introduced at 304, appears at 364, cited material at 366.

47　Chief of Staff Report 1933, 29.

48　Ibid., 29–31.

49　Pub. L. 29, 49 Stat. 121, April 9, 1935; Title I, Finance Department, Pay and so forth of the Army, 49 Stat. 124; Pub. L. 598, 49 Stat. 1278, Ch. 404, May 15, 1936, see Title I, Finance Department, Pay of the Army, 49 Stat. 1282.

50　Stewart, *American Military History*, 66–7.

51　Senate National Defense Hearings 1941, Exhibit 36 [Reports on the state of the United States Army by Secretaries of War and Chiefs of Staff of the Army from 1926 to 1939], introduced at 304, appears at 364, cited material at 367.

52　James MacGregor Burns. *The American Experiment, Vol. III: The Crosswinds of Freedom*. New York: Alfred A. Knopf, 1989, 155.

53　Stewart, *American Military History*, 71.

54　Ibid., 69.

55　Ibid., 67.

56　Kerry E. Irish. "Apt Pupil: Dwight Eisenhower and the 1930 Industrial Mobilization Plan." *The Journal of Military History*, Vol. 70, Number 1, January 2006, 31–61; Joanne E. Johnson. "The Army Industrial College and Mobilization Planning Between the Wars." Washington, D.C.: The Industrial College of the Armed Forces, National Defense University, 1993; *Industrial Mobilization Plan*, War Department, Office of the Assistant Secretary of War, Washington, D.C. (1930).

57　Robert F. Altman. "U.S. Army Interwar Planning: The Protective Mobilization Plan." Thesis, U.S. Army Command and General Staff College, Fort Leavenworth, Kansas (2014)

58　Stewart, *American Military History*, 70.

59　Ibid., 68.

60　Ibid., 72.

61　Ibid., 70.

Chapter 3

1　Smith, *Long Shadow*, 103.

2　*Department of State Bulletin*, Vol. II, Numbers 28–53, January 6 – June 29, 1940 (Washington, D.C.: U.S., Government Printing Office, 1940, 529–36. Online at https://babel.hathitrust.org/cgi/pt?id=uiuo.ark:/13960/t0sr0fr17;view=1up;seq=7.

3　*Department of State Bulletin*, Vol. II, Numbers 28–53, January 6 – June 29, 1940 (Washington, D.C.: U.S., Government Printing Office, 1940, 531–2. Online at https://babel.hathitrust.org/cgi/pt?id=uiuo.ark:/13960/t0sr0fr17;view=1up;seq=7.

4   U.S. Department of State, Publication 1983, *Peace and War: United States Foreign Policy, 1931–1941* (Washington, D.C.: U.S., Government Printing Office, 1943), 542–3. Online at http://www. ibiblio.org/pha/paw/.

5   U.S. Department of State, *Department of State Bulletin*, Vol. II, Numbers 28–53, January 6 – June 29, 1940 Washington, D.C. [Addresses of President Roosevelt: Message to Congress re national defense, 529–36; National defense radio address], 591–6. Online at https://babel.hathitrust.org/ cgi/pt?id=uiuo.ark:/13960/t0sr0fr17;view=1up;seq=7 (emphasis supplied).

6   U.S. Department of State, *Department of State Bulletin*, Vol. III, Numbers 54–79, July 6 – December 28, 1940 Washington, D.C. [Meeting of the Ministers of Foreign Affairs of American Republics at Habana; Final Act of Habana, text; Act of Habana (Resolution XX of Final Act of Habana), text; 576; Addresses of Secretary Hull: Statements by Secretary Hull on danger to American republics; Alliance between Germany, Italy and Japan, 251; Danger to American republics from war in Europe; Foreign policy of U.S., text, highlights; Addresses of President Roosevelt Western Hemisphere, unity and defense], 291. Online at https://babel.hathitrust.org/cgi/pt?id=uiuo. ark:/13960/t7dr4f12b;view=1up;seq=7.

7   U.S. Department of State, *Department of State Bulletin*, Vol. III, Numbers 54–79, July 6 – December 28, 1940 Washington, D.C. [Meeting of the Ministers of Foreign Affairs of American Republics at Habana; Final Act of Habana, text; Act of Habana (Resolution XX of Final Act of Habana), text. Online at https://babel.hathitrust.org/cgi/pt?id=uiuo.ark:/13960/t7dr4f12b;view=1up;seq=7; U.S. Department of State. *Peace and War: United States Foreign Policy 1931–1941*. Washington, D.C. United States Government Printing Office, 1943, 82 and Documents 177 (Declaration of. Reciprocal Assistance and Cooperation for the Defense of the Nations of the Americas, Habana, July 30, 1940) at 562 and 178 (Statement by the Secretary of State, August 6, 1940), at 563. (Hereinafter cited as *PAW*.).

8   U.S. Department of State, *Department of State Bulletin*, Vol. III, Numbers 54–79, supra. See also "Final Act and Convention," Habana Meeting of the Ministers of Foreign Affairs. U.S. Department of State, *Department of State Bulletin*, Vol. III: No. 61. Publication 1498. August 24, 1940, 127–48. Online at https://babel.hathitrust.org/cgi/pt?id=uiuo.ark:/13960/t7dr4f12b;view=1up;seq=7.

9   U.S. Department of State, *Department of State Bulletin*, Vol. III, Numbers 54–79, July 6 – December 28, 1940 Washington, D.C. Addresses of Secretary Hull: Statements by Secretary Hull on danger to American republics, 42, 103, 176; Alliance between Germany, Italy and Japan, 251; Danger to American republics from war in Europe, 42, 103, 176; Foreign policy of U.S., text, 331, highlights, 337, text, 407; *PAW*, 82.

10 U.S. Department of State, *Department of State Bulletin*, Vol. III, Numbers 54–79, July 6 – December 28, 1940 Washington, D.C., at 199–207. Online at https://babel.hathitrust.org/cgi/pt?id=uiuo. ark:/13960/t7dr4f12b;view=1up;seq=7 ; *PAW*, 83–4, and Documents 179 (Message of President Roosevelt to the Congress, September 3, 1940) at 564, and 180 (Press Release Issued by the Department of State on September 7, 1940) at 568.

11 Pub. L. 783, 54 Stat. 582, Ch. 720, the Selective Training and Service Act, approved September 16, 1940.

12 5 Fed. Reg. 3779–91 (25 Sept. 1940).

13 *PAW*, 84 and Document 181 (Memorandum by the Secretary of State Regarding a Conversation with the French Ambassador (Henry-Haye), September 11, 1940) at 568.

14 *PAW*, 84 and Document 184 (Statement by the Secretary of State, September 27, 1940) at 573.

15 *PAW*, 85, and Document 185 (Memorandum by the Secretary of State Regarding a Conversation with the British Ambassador (Lothian), September 30, 1940) at 574.

16 *PAW*, 85–6, and Document 188 (Address Delivered by the Secretary of State at Washington, October 26, 1940) at 581.

17 Ibid.

18 *PAW*, 86–7, and Document 193 (Radio Address Delivered by President Roosevelt From Washington, December 29, 1940) at 599.
19 John Keegan. *The Second World War*. New York: Penguin Books, 1989, 574.
20 Stewart, *American Military History*, 70.
21 Ibid., 73.
22 Ibid., 71.
23 Ibid., 73.
24 Ibid., 73.
25 Message, Prime Minister Churchill to General Smuts, 9 Nov 41, WSC, Vol. III, 593–4.
26 Stewart, *American Military History*, 74–6.
27 Ibid., 74.

Chapter 4

1 6 Fed. Reg. 415 (16 Jan. 1941).
2 NARA, Dwight D. Eisenhower Presidential Library, Abilene, Kansas (hereinafter cited as "DDE Presidential Library"), Collection: U.S. Army Unit Records, Box 1411, HQ, Iowa National Guard, General Orders No. 3: Induction of the 34th Division into the active military service of the United States [Includes text of Executive Order No. 8633 and the instruction of the War Department], February 6, 1941. See Appendix A, Documents, Document 1.
3 *AAD*, 54; citing Francis Vojta. *The Gopher Gunners of Minnesota: A History of Minnesota's 151st Field Artillery*. Self-published, 1995, 124; David Brinkley. *Washington Goes to War*. New York: Ballantine 1989, 36; Homer Ankrum. *Dogfaces Who Smiled Through Tears*, Lake Mills, Ia.: Graphic Publishing, 1987, 32 ("World War II is a battle") (hereinafter cited as "Ankrum, *Dogfaces*").
4 The Institute of Heraldry, Office of the Administrative Assistant to the Secretary of the Army, says of the distinctive shoulder sleeve patch of the 34th Infantry Division that the patch shape simulates an *olla* (Mexican water flask) symbolizing the 34th Division's origin, formation and intensive training site at Camp Cody, New Mexico in October 1917. The bull skull also symbolizes the surrounding dry, desert-like area. Black denotes durability, firmness and stability and red is for courage and action. See https://tioh.army.mil/Catalog/Heraldry.aspx?HeraldryId=6467&-CategoryId=3653&grp=2&menu=Uniformed%20Services&ps=24&p=0. The Division's motto is "Attack, Attack, Attack." *The Army Almanac: A Book of Facts Concerning the Army of the United States*, U.S. Government Printing Office, 1950. See United States Army, Center for Military History, Combat Chronicles of U.S. Army Divisions in World War II https://history.army.mil/html/forcestruc/cbtchron/cc/034id.htm.
5 Richard W. Stewart, "The 'Red Bull' Division: The Training and Initial Engagements of the 34th Infantry Division, 1941–43." *Army History*, Winter 1993. Department of the Army, Washington, D.C., 1993, 1 (hereinafter cited as "Stewart, *Red Bull Division Training*"); John C. Binkley. "A History of U.S Army Force Structuring," in *20th Century War: The American Experience Book of Readings,* Fort Leavenworth, Kansas, Command and General Staff College. 1996, 139–55; see also John Ney. "Evolution of the U.S. Army Division: 1939–1968," Fort Belvoir, Va.: Combat Operations Research M-194, U.S. Army Combat Developments Command, 1969 (cited hereinafter as "Ney, *Evolution*"). [Dr. Richard W. Stewart was Command Historian, U.S. Army Special Operations Command, Fort Bragg, North Carolina.]
6 Martin Blumenson. "Kasserine Pass, 30 January–22 February 1943." In *America's First Battles, 1776–1965*. Charles E. Heller and William A. Stofft, eds. Lawrence, Kansas. University Press of Kansas, 1986. Chapter 8, 238–9.

7 Stewart, *Red Bull Division Training*, 1, and fn. 3: Biennial Report of the Adjutant General of the State of Iowa, 1942; and fn. 4: Martin Blumenson, "Kasserine Pass, 30 January–22 February 1943," in *America's First Battles, 1776–1965*. Charles E. Heller and William A. Stofft, eds. Lawrence: University of Kansas Press, 1986, 239; and fn. 5: Biennial Report of the Adjutant General of the State of Iowa, 1940, 5. Even field training at Camp Dodge in Iowa consisted of little more than range firing, marching, and small unit drill. There was no artillery range at Camp Dodge and little maneuver space. In addition, units had their training interrupted in earlier years by strikebreaking activity (*e.g.*, Maytag Washing Machine Plant Strike, July 1938) and other civil disturbance and emergency relief duties.

8 Stewart, *Red Bull Division Training*, 1 and fn. 6: John H. Hougen, *The Story of the Famous 34th Infantry Division* (Nashville: The Battery Press, 1949, 1979) (hereinafter cited as "Hougen") chapter VII; and fn. 7: Biennial Report of the Adjutant General of the State of Iowa, Supplement to the 1941 Report, Archives and Records Department of Iowa, Camp Dodge, Johnston, Iowa.

9 *AAD*, 96; Leslie W. Bailey, *Through Hell and High Water* (New York: Vantage 1994), 52 (hereinafter cited as "Bailey, *Through Hell*"); Hougen, 14–16.

10 *Regimental History, 135th Infantry Regiment*, Musel Collection, Iowa Gold Star Military Museum (hereinafter cited as *Regimental History, 135IR (Musel)*), IGSMM PDF file gs_4102.pdf, 3 of 103.

11 Pub. L. 11, 55 Stat. 31, Ch. 11, approved March 11, 1941.

12 Stewart, *American Military History*, 74.

13 *A Partial History of the 135th Infantry Regiment, 34th Infantry Division*. Approved for Publication, Allied Force Headquarters, Information News and Censorship Section. 34th Infantry Division Association and the Iowa Gold Star Military Museum, 1 (hereinafter cited as *A Partial History of 135IR (Rudolf)*); *Regimental History, 135IR (Musel)*, IGSMM PDF file gs_4102, 7 of 103.

14 *135th Inf. Rgt. History (Breit Papers, Iowa Gold Star Military Museum)*, (hereinafter cited as *135IR History (Breit)*) Phase I, IGSMM PDF file 135inf_jb4102: Federal Service, Camp Claiborne, Pearl Harbor, 1941 February, 5–6; *Regimental History, 135IR (Musel)*, IGSMM PDF file 135inf_gs4102, Camp Claiborne, Fort Dix, N Ireland, N Africa, 7 of 103.

15 *135IR History (Breit)*) Phase I, IGSMM PDF file 135inf_jb4102 Federal Service, Camp Claiborne, Pearl Harbor, 1941 February. 6; *A Partial History of 135IR (Rudolf)*, 2–3.

16 *Regimental History, 135IR (Musel)*, IGSMM PDF file gs_4102.pdf, 3–4 of 103.

17 *AAD*, 55, citing [Robert] Bob Moore: "Induction of Company F," memo, IGSMM; *Villisca (Iowa) Review*, Feb. 20, 1941.

18 *AAD*, 55.

19 *135IR History (Breit)*) Phase I, IGSMM PDF file 135inf_jb4102 Federal Service, Camp Claiborne, Pearl Harbor, 1941 February, 6.

20 Stewart, *Red Bull Division Training*, 2.

21 Hougen, Ch. VII [Claiborne Days]; *135IR History (Breit)*) Phase I, IGSMM PDF file 135inf_jb4102 Federal Service, Camp Claiborne, Pearl Harbor, 1941 February, 7.

22 Stewart, *Red Bull Division Training*, 4, and fn. 22: Four other National Guard divisions mobilized later (the 28th, 43rd, 40th, and 33rd Divisions).

23 Stewart, *Red Bull Division Training*, 2; and fn. 9: Training Orders, 34th Division, located in the Combined Arms Research Library. Fort Leavenworth, Kans., folder N-I9734. This folder includes a copy of the division master training schedule, the plan for setting up the intelligence classes as part of the overall schedule of classes, and a map of the training areas and ranges at Camp Claiborne. Areas were still set aside for the 67th and 68th Brigade headquarters. The division did not convert to a triangular configuration until some of its units were on their way overseas; and fn. 10: *The Background of the 135th Infantry* on deposit in the Iowa Gold Star Military Museum, Camp Dodge, Iowa.

24 Robert R. Palmer, *et al. U.S. Army in World War II: The Procurement and Training of Ground Combat Troops.* Washington, D.C.: Department of the Army, 1948, 2–3. Republished by the U.S. Army Center for Military History, CMH Pub. 2–2, 1991.

25 *135IR History (Breit))* Phase I, IGSMM PDF file 135inf_jb4102 Federal Service, Camp Claiborne, Pearl Harbor, 1941 February, 8.

26 Hougen, Ch. VII [Claiborne Days], 24.

27 *135IR History (Breit))* Phase I, IGSMM PDF file 135inf_jb4102 Federal Service, Camp Claiborne, Pearl Harbor, 1941 February, 8

28 Stewart, *Red Bull Division Training*, 4, and fn. 20: Christopher R. Gabel. "The U.S. Army GHQ Maneuvers of 1941." Ph.D. dissertation. Ohio State University. 1981, 198 (hereinafter cited as "Gabel: GHQ Maneuvers").

29 Jack K. Johnson. " 'Mr. National Guard': Ellard A. Walsh (1887–1975), Part 1." *Allies. Newsletter of the Military Historical Society of Minnesota*, Winter, 2012. Vol. XX, No. 1, 3; Stewart, *Red Bull Division Training*, 4.

30 *135IR History (Breit))* Phase I, IGSMM PDF file 135inf_jb4102 Federal Service, Camp Claiborne, Pearl Harbor, 1941 February, 8.

31 Pub. L. 213, 55 Stat. 626, Ch. 362, the Service Extension Act, of 1941 approved August 18, 1941; Stewart, *American Military History*, 73.

32 James W. Symington (former member of Congress), Letter to the Editor, New York Times, Sept 1, 1991; online at https://www.nytimes.com/1991/09/01/opinion/l-the-vote-that-saved-the-army-in-the-days-after-pearl-harbor-028191.html.

33 *135IR History (Breit))* Phase I, IGSMM PDF file 135inf_jb4102 Federal Service, Camp Claiborne, Pearl Harbor, 1941 February, 10.

34 Ibid., 8–9.

35 Ibid., 9.

36 Stewart, *Red Bull Division Training*, 2–3, and fn. 11: Interview, [Stewart] with Dewey Wood, medic in 3rd Battalion, 168th Infantry, 34th Division. at Camp Dodge, 7 March 1990; interview [Stewart] with Edward Bird, in 1941 a second lieutenant and later captain, commander first of the anti-tank company, then an infantry company, 1st Battalion, 168th Infantry, 34th Division, at Camp Dodge, 8 March 1990; and fn. 12: Ankrum: *Dogfaces*, 47–8.

37 Stewart, *Red Bull Division Training*, 3, and fn. 15: Gabel: GHQ Maneuvers, 167–95.

38 Stewart, *Red Bull Division Training*, 3, and fn. 16: Stewart, interviews of Edward Bird and Dewey Wood, cited at Stewart, *Red Bull Division* Training, at fn. 11.

39 Stewart, *Red Bull Division Training*, 3, and fn. 17: Lt. Gen. L. J. McNair, 2nd Phase. GHQ-Directed Maneuvers. quoted in Gabel, *GHQ Maneuvers*, 197. Lt. Gen. McNair later became commander, Army Ground Forces, which grew out of the GHQ structure and which was activated on March 9, 1942 to oversee the creation and training of the Army's ground units; and fn. 18: I. Heymont and E. W. McGregor, "Review and Analysis of Recent Mobilizations and Deployments of U.S. Army Reserve Components," McLean, Va.: Research Analysis Corp., 1972), 2–8.

40 Stewart, *Red Bull Division Training*, 4, and fn. 19: Gabel: GHQ Maneuvers, 198–200; and fn. 20: Gabel: GHQ Maneuvers, 198; and fn. 21: John S. Brown, "Winning Teams: Mobilization Related Correlates of Success in American World War II Infantry Divisions." MMAS Thesis. U.S. Army Command and General Staff College, 1985, 40.

Chapter 5

1 Stewart, *American Military History*, 77.

2   *Department of State Bulletin*, Vol. V: Numbers 106–31, July 5 – December 27, 1941 Washington, DC: U.S. Government Printing Office, 1941, 482. The American declarations of war on Japan, Germany and Italy are also set out in that Bulletin at 475–6.

3   Stewart, *American Military History*, 96.

4   Ibid.

5   Stewart, *Red Bull Division Training*, 5.

6   *135IR History (Breit))* Phase I, IGSMM PDF file 135inf_jb4102 Federal Service, Camp Claiborne, Pearl Harbor, 1941 February, 11.

7   *135IR History (Breit))* Phase I, IGSMM PDF file 135inf_jb4102 Federal Service, Camp Claiborne, Pearl Harbor, 1941 February, 11; *Regimental History, 135IR (Musel)*, IGSMM PDF file gs_4102, 10–11 of 103.

8   Pub. L. 338, 55 Stat. 799, Ch. 571, approved Dec. 13, 1941.

9   Ankrum, *Dogfaces*, 61–2; Stewart, *Red Bull Division Training*, 5, fn. 28.

10 *135IR History (Breit))* Phase I, IGSMM PDF file 135inf_jb4102 Federal Service, Camp Claiborne, Pearl Harbor, 1941 February, 11.

11 Ibid.

12 Hougen, 25.

13 *AAD*, 54; Stewart, Red Bull Division Training, 5; *135IR History (Breit))* Phase I, IGSMM PDF file 135inf_jb4102 Federal Service, Camp Claiborne, Pearl Harbor, 1941 February, 12; *Regimental History, 135IR (Musel)*, IGSMM PDF file gs_4102, 11 of 103.

14 Stewart, *Red Bull Division Training*, 4.

15 *Regimental History, 135IR (Musel)*, IGSMM PDF file gs_4102, 11 of 103.

Chapter 6

1   Stewart, Red Bull Division Training, 4.

2   WSC, Vol. III, *The Grand Alliance*, 490–1.

3   *See* note 28, supra, and WSC, Vol. III, *The Grand Alliance*, 684.

4   *AAD*, 54, citing Benjamin F. Caffey, Jr., oral history, Feb. 1950, Sidney Matthews papers, MHI; and Ann Larson, ed., "The History and Contribution to American Democracy of Volunteer 'Citizen Soldiers' of Southwest Iowa, 1930–1945," 1981, National Endowment of the Humanities, 22 (hereinafter cited as "Larson: *Volunteers*"); Hougen, 31.

5   Hougen, Chapter VIII; Stewart, *Red Bull Division Training*, 5.

6   Hougen, Chapter VIII.

7   Stewart, *Red Bull Division Training*, 5.

8   *A Partial History of 135IR (Rudolf)*, 2–3; *Regimental History, 135IR (Musel)*, IGSMM PDF file gs_4102, 12 of 103.

9   *The Story of the 34th Infantry Division, Louisiana to Pisa*. Compiled by members of 34th Infantry Division. Published by the Information and Education Section, MTOUSA, at Archetipografia di Milano, S.A., Milan, 1945, 2 (hereinafter cited as *Story of the 34th Infantry Division, Louisiana to Pisa*).

10 Stewart, *Red Bull Division Training*, 5. The Norman *bocage* countryside was marked by intermingling patches of woodland and heath, small fields surrounded by tall, impenetrable hedgerows, and orchards, excellent for infantry defense.

11 Virgil E. Craven. "The Operations of Company I, 133rd Infantry (34th Infantry Division) in the Attack of Fondouk Gap, North Africa, 8–9 April, 1943 (Tunisia Campaign) (Personal Experience of a Company Executive Officer)." Typescript, Advanced Infantry Officers Course, 1949–50. U.S. Army Infantry School, Fort Benning, Georgia. Digital Collections, Donovan Research Library, Ft

Benning, Ga. Online at https://mcoepublic.blob.core.usgovcloudapi.net/library/DonovanPapers/wwii/STUP2/A-F/CravenVirgil%20E.pdf. (Hereinafter cited as "Craven, V.").

12   Lt. Gen. Lucian K. Truscott. *Command Missions: A Personal Story*. E. P. Dutton and Co. 1954; republished by Presidio Press, 1990 (hereinafter cited as "Truscott").

13   *See* Maj. Samuel R. Andrews, MN ANG. "Major General Charles Ryder: The Forging of a World War II Division Commander." Monograph, School of Advanced Military Studies, U.S. Army Command and General Staff College, Fort Leavenworth, Kansas, 2014. See also Appendix A, Documents, Documents 2 and 3.

14   DDE Presidential Library, Collection: Ryder, Charles W. Papers 1917–1950 (hereinafter cited as "Ryder Papers"), Box No. 2, File: Ryder Personal 201 File 1942–1944, General Order, HQ 34th Inf. Div., 12 June 1942. See also Appendix A, Documents, Documents 2 and 3.

15   Dwight David Eisenhower. *Crusade in Europe*, Baltimore: Johns Hopkins Press, 1997 (hereinafter cited as DDE), 83.

16   DDE, 53 (emphasis supplied).

17   *135th Inf. Rgt. History (Breit)*, IGSMM PDF file jb_4205.pdf, Phase II, North Ireland, 2.

18   *Regimental History, 135IR (Musel)*, IGSMM PDF file gs_4102.pdf, 13 of 103; *135IR History (Breit))*, IGSMM PDF file jb_4205.pdf, Phase II, North Ireland, 2–3.

19   *Fifth Army History. Part I: From Activation to the Fall of Naples*. Chapter II, Training of Fifth Army. United States Army. Headquarters, Fifth Army. Florence, Italy. 1945–1947, 5–11.

20   *Regimental History, 135IR (Musel)*, IGSMM PDF file gs_4102.pdf, 13 of 103; *135IR History (Breit))*, IGSMM PDF file jb_4205.pdf, Phase II, North Ireland, 2–3.

21   *Regimental History, 135IR (Musel)*, IGSMM PDF file gs_4102.pdf, 13 of 103; *135IR History (Breit))*, IGSMM PDF file jb_4205.pdf, Phase II, North Ireland, 3.

22   *Regimental History, 135IR (Musel)*, IGSMM PDF file gs_4102.pdf, 13 of 103; *135IR History (Breit))*, IGSMM PDF file jb_4205.pdf, Phase II, North Ireland, 3.

23   Ryder Papers, Box No. 3, File: HQ 34th Inf. Div. Training Operations July – August 1942: Hq 34ID, 34ID Divisional Training Center, Third Day Exercise, Division Battalion Training Area, 19 August 1942.

24   Ryder Papers, Box No. 4: 34th Inf. Div. Training Manual, 1942–1943. File: 34th Inf. Div. Training Manual 1942–1943; Envelope: 34th Infantry Division Training Manual (maintained by MG Charles W. Ryder) 1942–1943.

25   Ryder Papers, Box No. 3; File: HQ 34th Inf. Div. Training Operations July – August 1942: Hq 34ID, Training Memorandum No. 30, 16 July 1942.

26   See Ch. 4, n. 34, supra.

27   Stewart, *American Military History*, 103.

28   DDE, 71; n. 27: Memorandum by the CCS, subject: Operations in 1942/1943, July 24, 1942, (SGS AFHQ 337.211, AGO).

29   DDE, 71–2, and n. 28: General Eisenhower was officially informed on August 14. Annex I to the Minutes of the Chiefs of Staff Committee, War Cabinet, August 14, 1942, in History of AFHQ, Part I, 3.

30   DDE, 72.

31   Howe, George F. *The United States Army in World War Two. The Mediterranean Theater of Operations. Northwest Africa: Seizing the Initiative in the West*. Washington, D.C. U.S. Army Center for Military History 1993, 35, and fn. 9 (hereinafter cited as "*NWAf*").

32   *NWAf*, 35, and fn. 10, 11.

33   DDE, 83.

34   Ibid., 75.

35   *NWAf*, 35, and fn. 12.

36 Ibid., 36, and fn. 13: These paragraphs appeared unchanged in the actual directive sent to General Anderson, 23 October 1942. Identical paragraphs were contained in the COS directives to Lt. Gen. Mason MacFarlane (Br.) at Gibraltar and Lt. Gen. Frederick Morgan (Br.), commanding general, Northern Task Force. The relation of national to Allied commander was thus made more subordinate than in 1918 after an initial proposal that it remain the same.

37 Ibid., and fn. 15.

38 Ibid., 35–7, and fn. 16.

39 *135IR History (Breit)*, IGSMM PDF file jb_4205.pdf, Phase II, North Ireland, 3; *Regimental History, 135IR (Musel)*, IGSMM PDF file gs_4102.pdf, 13 of 103.

40 *135IR History (Breit)*, IGSMM PDF file jb_4205.pdf, Phase II, North Ireland, 4.

41 *Story of the 34th Infantry Division, Louisiana to Pisa*, 3.

42 *NWAf*, 62–3, and fn. 10: Memo, Brig Gen Daniel Noce for Clark, 26 Sep 42, sub: Observation at amphibious training centers in Scotland. AFHQ AG 350.07-15, Micro Job 24, Reel 79D: and fn. 11: (1) Ltr, Adm Mountbatten to Gen Clark, Gen Anderson, and Vice Adm Bertram H. Ramsay, 25 Aug 42. AFHQ Micro Job 24, Reel 1360. (2) Msg, Clark to Anderson, 22 Sep 42. AFHQ Micro Job 24, Reel 790; and fn. 12: Ltr, Col S. E. Biddle to Gen Clark, 23 Sep 42. AFHQ Micro Job 24, Reel 1360. This outlines Clark's itinerary for an inspection trip.

43 Ibid., 61.

44 Ibid., 63.

45 *135IR History (Breit)*, IGSMM PDF file jb_4205.pdf, Phase II, North Ireland, 4.

46 *NWAf*, 50–1.

47 Ryder Papers, Box No. 3, File: Records relating to Operation *Torch*, May–September 1942, "Provisional Directive to Commander, Eastern Assault Force."

48 DDE, 83.

49 Ibid.

50 *NWAf*, 62, and fn. 7 and 8. The unit of fire (U/F) was a standardized quantity of ammunition for each weapon in service, varying for each type of weapon and, during World War II, in each theater of operation.

51 Ibid., 50–1, and fn. 61, 62, 63.

52 Ian V. Hogg and John Weeks. *Military Small-Arms of the 20th century*. London: Arms & Armour Press, 1977, 183, "US Rifle, Caliber .30in ('Garand'), M1-M1E9, M1C, M1D, T26" (hereinafter cited as "Hogg and Weeks, *Military Small Arms 7th ed.*").

53 Ibid., 53.

54 Ryder Papers, Box No. 3, File: Records relating to Operation *Torch*, May–September 1942, "Outline Plan for Seizing and Occupying Algiers."

55 Ryder Papers, 1917–1950, Box 3, Envelope: General Ryder Orders, File: Operation *Torch* – Eastern Assault Force Sept. 15 – Oct. 20 1942, FO #1 and Annexes.

56 *135IR History (Breit)*, IGSMM PDF file jb_4205.pdf, Phase II, North Ireland, 5.

57 *NWAf*, p.241–3; *135IR History (Breit)*, IGSMM PDF file jb_4210.pdf, Phase III, Algeria, 1; *AAD*, 96; *see* Owen C. Bolstad. *Dear Folks: A Dog-Faced Infantryman in World War II*, Self-published, 1993, 31, 63 (hereinafter cited as "Bolstad: *Dear Folks*"); Leslie W. Bailey. "The Operations of the 3rd Battalion, 135th Infantry at Algiers," 1948, 11 (Bailey was a platoon leader in Company I, 135th Infantry). See also Leslie W. Bailey. *Through Hell and High Water*. New York: Vantage 1994 (hereinafter cited as "Bailey, *Through Hell*").

58 Hougen, 31.

59 *NWAf*, 70 and fn. 33.

60 *NWAf*, 71; Brig, Gen. William. F. Heavey. "Down Ramp! The Story of the Army Amphibian Engineers." Infantry Journal Press, 1947, 21, 30.

61 *NWAf*, 71; citing as principal sources for these approach voyages: Incl 1 (Rpt of The Naval Commander, Center Task Force) and Incl 2 (Rpt of The Naval Commander, Eastern Task Force), in NCXF, Report of Proceedings, Operation TORCH. AFHQ Micro Job 8, Reels 16A–17A.

62 Ibid., 71.

63 See Hal Vaughan. *FDR's 12 Apostles: The Spies Who Paved the Way for the Invasion of North Africa.* Lanham, Maryland: Rowman & Littlefield, 2006. David A. Walker. "OSS and Operation Torch." *Journal of Contemporary History* 22, no. 4 (1987). Accessed February 26, 2021. http://www. jstor.org/stable/260815; Sheridan Nichols. "The United States Vice Consuls in North Africa, 1941–1942." Proceedings of the Meeting of the French Colonial Historical Society 4 (1979): 213–20. http://www.jstor.org/stable/45137349.

64 *NWAf*, 71.

65 DDE, 81.

66 Ibid.

67 *NWAf*, 97. These ships were designed as shallow-draught oil tankers to operate in Lake Maracaibo in Venezuela. They were requisitioned by the Royal Navy in December 1940 for conversion to tank landing ships. The oil tanks were removed to form a tank deck, and two large hatches and two 50-ton derrick cranes fitted to lift vehicles from the tank deck to the upper deck. The bows were cut off square and a heavy steel door fitted. A hinged extension, together with the door, provided a 100-foot (30m) ramp to unload vehicles. HMS *Bachaquero* (F110) could carry 18 30-ton tanks, or 22 25-ton tanks, or 33 heavy trucks. See English Wikipedia article HMS *Misoa* (F117). https://en.wikipedia.org/wiki/HMS_Misoa_(F117). See Royal Navy photograph at https:// commons.wikimedia.org/wiki/File:The_Royal_Navy_during_the_Second_World_War_HMS_ Bachaquero_at_Bone_IWM_A_15709.jpg.

68 *NWAf*, 72.

69 Ibid.

70 Ibid., 63.

71 *Regimental History, 135IR (Musel)*, IGSMM PDF file gs_4102.pdf, 14–15 of 103; *135IR History (Breit))*, IGSMM PDF file jb_4205.pdf, Phase II, North Ireland, 5.

72 *Regimental History, 135IR (Musel)*, IGSMM PDF file gs_4102.pdf, 31 of 103.

73 ROSTER OF OFFICERS OF 3RD BATTALION, 135IR, WHO PARTICIPATED IN OPERATION TERMINAL

3rd Battalion

Commanding Officer	LTC Edwin T. Swenson 0237257
Executive Officer	CPT William F. Snellman 0229963
Surgeon	CPT Vilhelm M. Johnson 0419941
Communications Officer	1LT Emory J. Trawick 0452091

COMPANY I

Commanding Officer	CPT LeRoy E. Dahlin 0325971
2nd in command	1LT William L. Muir 0386785
Platoon Leader	1LT Charles L. Matthews 0347921
Platoon Leader	1LT Hill P. Cooper 0407297
Platoon Leader	1LT Kimble E. Midkiff, 0452696
Platoon Leader	2LT Arnold F. Bradshaw WIA

COMPANY K

Commanding Officer	CPT Paul H. Thaler 0371590
2nd in command	1LT Thomas E. Chegin 0402781
Platoon Leader	1LT Leo G. Voss 0451700
Platoon Leader	1LT Leslie W. Bailey 24045
Platoon Leader	2LT John P. Flynn 01292861

Platoon Leader	2LT Luther L. Doty 0292844

COMPANY L

Commanding Officer	CPT Frank A. McCulloch 0279008
2nd in command	1LT Louis M. Smith 0385222
Platoon Leader	1LT Frank F. Gable 0371938
Platoon Leader	1LT John L. Bridgeman 0405746
Platoon Leader	2LT Irwin F. Hall 01292334
Platoon Leader	2LT James Koulgsorge 01292904

DETACHMENT OF COMPANY M

Commanding Officer	1LT Robert O. Foster 0425830
2nd in command	2LT George George KIA

On November 8, 1942, 2LT George was killed in action and 2LT Bradshaw was wounded in action. Fourteen enlisted personnel were killed in action and 33 enlisted personnel were wounded in the course of Operation *Terminal*.

See Regimental History, 135IR (Musel), IGSMM PDF file gs_4102.pdf, 55, 59 of 103.

74 *NWAf*, 241; 135th Inf Hist, Sec. IV, 18 Oct 42 – 15 May 43, 1.

75 *135IR History (Breit)*, IGSMM PDF file jb_4210.pdf, Phase III, Algeria, 1–2; *Regimental History, 135IR (Musel)*, IGSMM PDF file gs_4102.pdf, 31 of 103.

76 *NWAf*, 51–2.

Chapter 7

1   DDE, 78.

2   *See* David A. Walker. "OSS and Operation Torch." *Journal of Contemporary History* 22, no. 4 (1987). http://www.jstor.org/stable/260815.

3   *NWAf*, 229.

4   *NWAf*, 229, 185 (emphasis supplied).

5   *AAD*, 56.

6   *NWAf*, 230, and fn. 2: (I) Dir to CG EAF, 10 Oct 42. AFHQ G-3, Ops E/300/1 Micro Job 10A, Reel 5C. (2) Br. First Army Opn Instr No.4, IS Oct 42. DRB AGO.

7   *NWAf*, 230.

8   Ibid.

9   *NWAf*, 230–1.

10 Ibid., 231.

11 Ibid.

12 Ibid., 231–4.

13 Ibid., 186.

14 Ibid., 186, and fn. 2 and 3.

15 Ibid., 187.

16 Ibid., 73

17 Ibid., 74.

18 Ibid.

19 *NWAf*, 186.

20 Ryder Papers 1917–1950; Box No. 2; File: CWR Personal 201 File 1942–1944: Hush—Most Secret ULTRA Naval Communication to Commander Eastern Task Force, copy to and only for CWR, 1538 6 November 1942, 1. (See Appendix A, Documents, Document 5.).

21 Ibid., 2–8. (See Appendix A, Documents, Document 5.).

22 *135IR History (Breit)*, IGSMM PDF file jb_4210.pdf, Phase III, Algeria, 2.

23 *NWAf*, 234–5.

24 Ibid., 235.

25 *Story of the 34th Infantry Division, Louisiana to Pisa*, 3–4.

26 *NWAf*, 236, and fn. 7.

27 Ibid., 236–7.

28 Ibid., 237.

29 Ibid.

30 Ibid.

31 Ibid., 238.

32 Ibid.

33 Ibid., 239.

34 Ibid., 238–9.

35 *AAD*, 117, citing: letter, John O'Daniel to Orlando Ward, Orlando Ward papers, Jan. 1951, NARA RG 319, Office of the Chief of Military History,) 225; the first American battalion commander to die was Lt. Colonel George F. Marshall (CO, 3rd Bn, 6th AIR), killed in the disastrous Operation *Reservist* in the harbor at Oran; Robert J. Berens. *Citizen Soldier*. Ames, Iowa: Sigler, 1995, 36–7 ("ignoring orders") (hereinafter cited as "Berens: *Citizen Soldier*").

36 *NWAf*, 239.

37 Ibid., 241.

38 See Ch. 6, Note 67, supra.

39 *NWAf*, 241, and fn. 5.

40 Ibid., 241–2.

41 *NWAf*, 241–2 and fn. 14, citing (1) Operation TERMINAL (Rpt of Capt Fancourt), 11 Nov 42, in App. V to Incl. 2 of NCXF, TORCH Despatch. (2) Morison, U.S. Naval Operations, II, 207–8. (3) Maj Leslie W. Bailey, The Operations of the 3rd Battalion, 135th Infantry at Algiers; and fn. 15, citing 135th Inf Hist, Sec. IV, 18 Oct 42 – 15 May 43, I. Captain Fancourt's report (see contents of n. 14 (1) above) describes the *Terminal* forces as 725 U.S. troops and 60 Royal Navy personnel, and fn. 16, citing Lt Col Ray C. Fountain, U.S. Prov Div G-2 Report, 20 Sep 42. AFHQ G-3 Opns 22 / 7, Micro Job 10A, Reel 5C.

42 *NWAf*, 242–3.

43 Ibid., 243; *AAD*, 96–7.

44 Ibid., 243, and fn. 18, citing Bailey, Opns of 3rd Bn 135th Inf, 11–12, and fn. 19, citing (1) Br. Battle Sum 38, Opn "Torch," 29, (2) 135th Inf Hist, Sec. IV, 18 Oct 42 – 15 May 43, 2, and fn. 20, citing H.M.S. *Malcolm* (Rpt of Comdr Russell) in App. V to Incl 2 of NCXF, TORCH Despatch.

45 *AAD*, 97, citing: After Action Report, A.B. Russell, RN, "Operation Terminal," Nov. 11, 1942, Sidney Matthews papers, MHI; Bailey, *Through Hell*, 52.

46 *NWAf*, 243.

47 Ibid., and fn. 21: 21 (1) Bailey, Opns of 3rd Bn 135th Inf, 17. (2) H.M.S. *Broke* (Rpt of Comdr Layard) 11 Nov 42, in App. V to Incl 2 of NCXF, TORCH Despatch.

48 *135IR History (Breit)*, IGSMM PDF file jb_4210.pdf, Phase III, Algeria, 11–12 (personal statement of LTC Edwin T. Swenson); *Regimental History, 135IR (Musel)*, IGSMM PDF file gs_4102.pdf, 31–4 of 103.

49 *AAD*, 97–8, citing: After Action Report, A. F. C. Layard, in Bolstad, *Dear Folks*, 225 (*Then, on his fourth try*); Collier, Richard, *The War in the Desert*. New York: Time-Life Books, 1977, 14 (*Badly shaken*; "*light out like stripey-assed baboons*").

50 *NWAf*, 243.

51 Ibid., 244, and fn. 23: (1) Bailey, Opns of 3rd Bn 135th Inf, lB. (2) Br. Battle Sum 3B, Operation "Torch," 30; *135IR History (Breit)*), IGSMM PDF file jb_4210.pdf, Phase III, Algeria, 4, 12–13 (personal statement of LTC Edwin T. Swenson); *Regimental History, 135IR (Musel)*, IGSMM PDF file gs_4102.pdf, 31–4 of 103.

52 *Regimental History, 135IR (Musel)*, IGSMM PDF file gs_4102.pdf, 31–4 of 103; *AAD*, 98, citing: Warren Tute, *The North African War*. New York: Two Continents, 1976, 177; Auphan, Paul and Jacques Mordal, *The French Navy in World War II*. Transl. A. C. J. Sabalot. Annapolis: United States Naval Institute, 1959, 222; Layard, in Bolstad: *Dear Folks*, 225; Bailey, *Through Hell*, 46.

53 *AAD*, 98, citing: John MacVane, *Journey into War: War and Diplomacy in North Africa*. New York: Appleton-Century, 1943, 59 (hereinafter cited as "MacVane"); H. L. St. J. Fancourt, "Report of Commanding Officer, Force TERMINAL," Nov. 11, 1942, Sidney Matthews, MHI.

54 *NWAf*, 244, and fn. 26; *135IR History (Breit)*), IGSMM PDF file jb_4210.pdf, Phase III, Algeria, 3–4; 7–13 (personal statement of LTC Edwin T. Swenson); *Regimental History, 135IR* (Musel), IGSMM PDF file gs_4102.pdf, 31–4 of 103; *AAD*, 98; MacVane, 59; H. L. St. J. Fancourt, "Report of Commanding Officer, Force TERMINAL," Nov. 11, 1942, Sidney Matthews, MHI.

55 *AAD*, 99; Bailey, *Through Hell*, 49; "A Partial History, 135th Infantry Regiment," NARA RG 407.

56 *NWAf*, 244, and fn. 27: 135th Inf Hist, Sec. IV, 18 Oct 42 – 15 May 43, 3.

57 *AAD*, 99; Hougen, 36, "Terminal Force"; Kenneth Maitland Davies. *To the Last Man*. St. Paul, Minn.; Ramsey County Historical Society, 1982, 97 (hereinafter cited as "Davies, *To the Last Man*"); *NWAf*, 244; Bolstad: *Dear Folks*, 31, 95; *135IR History (Breit)*), IGSMM PDF file jb_4210. pdf, Phase III, Algeria, 4–6, 13–14 (personal statement of LTC Edwin T. Swenson); *Regimental History, 135IR (Musel)*, IGSMM PDF file gs_4102.pdf, 31–4 of 103.

58 *Regimental History, 135IR (Musel)*, IGSMM PDF file gs_4102.pdf, 31–4, 55, 59 of 103.

59 See Ryder Papers, Box No. 2, File: CWR Personal 201 File 1942–1944; Headquarters Eastern Task Force, Commander Eastern Assault Force to Commander in Chief, Allied Forces, Subject: Brief Report of Operations of Eastern Assault Force, 19 November 1942, 2, ¶d [Terminal Force].

60 *NWAf*, 243–4, and fn. 21–8.

61 See *135IR History (Breit)*, Phase III, 7–15.

62 *AAD*, 101; Jack Marshall, "Tales of a Timid Commando," typescript, n.d., Army Service Experience Questionnaire, 34th ID, MHI; After Action Report, "Company B, 168th Inf," Nov. 1942, IGSMM; Ankrum, *Dogfaces*, 122; *NWAf*, 236; Robert R. Moore, After Action Report, "Record of Events from 14 Oct. 1942 to Armistice, Nov. 1942, IGSMM; "The Tunisian Campaign,' 34th Div., Dec. 13, 1943, NARA RG 407, E 427, 334-0.3 ("not prepared").

63 *135IR History (Breit)*), IGSMM PDF file jb_4210.pdf, Phase III, Algeria, 6–7.

64 *Story of the 34th Infantry Division, Louisiana to Pisa*, 4–5.

65 Alain Darlan, the admiral's son, came to the United States in 1943 for treatment, at the invitation of President Roosevelt. The president had hoped to entice the father to the Allied cause by an offer to aid the son, but the admiral was assassinated on December 24, 1942. See *Time* (magazine), Milestones, December 9, 1946.

66 *NWAf*, 250–1, and fn. 49: Msg, S. Pinkney Tuck to Secy of State Cordell Hull, 8 Nov 42. Copy in OPD Exec 5, Vol. VI.; fn 50: Phone conv, Tuck and Atherton State Dept, 11:30 P.M., 8 Nov 42. Copy in OPD Exec 5, Vol. VI.; fn 51: The texts of Darlan's message to Pétain, and of Pétain's reply, are given in Albert Kammerer. *Du débarquement Africain au meurtre de Darlan*. Paris, France: Flammarion, 1949, 262, 267.

67 *NWAf*, 251.

68 *AAD*, 118, citing After Action Report, Jan. 3, 1945, NARA RG 226, E 99, OSS, box 40; Kenneth Pendar. *Adventure in Diplomacy*. New York: Dodd, Mead, 1945, 112.

69 *NWAf,* 250–1, and fn. 49. Message, S. Pinkney Tuck to Secy of State Cordell, Hull, 8 Nov 42. Copy in OPD Exec 5, Vol. VI, and fn. 50, Phone conv, Tuck and Atherton State Dept, 11:30 P.M., 8 Nov 42. Copy in OPD Exec 5, Vol.VI, and fn. 51.

70 Ryder Papers, Box No. 2, File: CWR Personal 201 File 1942–1944; Headquarters Eastern Task Force, Commander Eastern Assault Force to Commander in Chief, Allied Forces, Subject: Brief Report of Operations of Eastern Assault Force, 19 November 1942, 3, ¶ f; *AAD,* 118, citing: Charles W. Ryder, oral history, March 1949, Sidney Matthews papers, MHI (*"I will go anywhere"*); Murphy, *Diplomat Among Warriors,* 132.

71 *NWAf,* 251–2; *AAD,* 118–19; After Action Report, July 17, 1945 and Jan. 3, 1945, NARA RG 226, E 99, OSS, box 40; Pendar, *Adventure in Diplomacy,* 114; Hougen, 38 (*cavernous hall*); C. W. Ryder, oral history, March 1949, Sidney Matthews papers, MHI; After Action Report, C. W. Ryder, Nov. 19, 1942, NARA RG 407, E 427, Adjutant General, box 244; Murphy, *Diplomat Among Warriors,* 133.

72 *NWAf,* 252.

73 *NWAf,* 252, and fn.51.

74 *AAD,* 122–3; Murphy, *Diplomat Among Warriors,* 135, 138 (Clark's tacit threat); Berens: *Citizen Soldier,* 38 (Clark found General Ryder; "shoot their butts off"); Mark W. Clark. *Calculated Risk,* New York: Harper & Brothers, 1950, 108–13; Tompkins, Peter, *The Murder of Admiral Darlan.* New York: Simon & Schuster, 1965, 123 (*"J'accepte"*); "Record of Events," Feb. 22, 1943, NARA RG 338, Fifth Army, box 1, 1–13.

75 *AAD,* 122: Alan Moorehead. *The End in Africa.* London: Hamish Hamilton, 1943, 61 (*Clark immediately; Giraud announced*) (hereinafter cited as "Moorehead, *The End in Africa*").

76 *AAD,* 122–3, citing: "Record of Events," Feb. 22, 1943, NARA RG 338, Fifth Army, box 1, 13; Samuel E. Morison. *History of United States Naval Operations in World War II.* Vol. II, *Operations in North African Waters.* Boston: Little, Brown, 1950, 217; Benjamin A. Dickson, "G-2 Journal: Algiers to the Elbe." Unpublished memoir, n.d. MHI (and in USMA Archives), 29 (*"Mon Admiral, by order"*).

77 *AAD,* 156–7, citing: "Record of Events," Feb. 22, 1943, NARA RG 338, Fifth Army, box 1, 25–8; Murphy, *Diplomat Among Warriors,* 142.

78 *AAD,* 157, citing: Harry C. Butcher. *My Three Years with Eisenhower.* New York: Simon & Schuster, 1946, 190 (hereinafter cited as "Butcher"); Alfred Chandler, ed., *The Papers of Dwight David Eisenhower: The War Years.* Vols. 1, 2, 5. Baltimore: Johns Hopkins Press, 1970, 689,692,693 (hereinafter cited as "Eisenhower Papers").

79 *AAD,* 158, citing: Arthur Layton Funk. *The Politics of Torch.* Lawrence, Kan.: University Press of Kansas, 1974, 248; Eisenhower Papers, 680, 692, 698, 699, 701; "Record of Events," Feb. 22, 1943, NARA RG 338, Fifth Army, box 1; letter, Noguès to G. F. Howe, Jan. 1950, NARA RG 319, Office of the Chief of Military History, 2–3.7 CC1, box 225; Clark, *Calculated Risk,* 123. For the text of the Allied-French accords, of which there does not appear to be an English language version extant, see Kammerer, Albert. *Du débarquement Africain au meurtre de Darlan,* Annex XXVII, *"Les accords concernant l'Afrique du Nord française,"* at 681–5.

80 Ryder Papers, Box No. 2, File: CWR Personal 201 File 1942–1944; Directive by Commander Eastern Task Force to MG C. W. Ryder, 11 Nov. 1942.

81 Ibid.; Headquarters Eastern Task Force, Commander Eastern Assault Force to Commander in Chief, Allied Forces, Subject: Brief Report of Operations of Eastern Assault Force, 19 November 1942.

82 In his report, Ryder erroneously referred to the troops landed at *Beer* beaches as "CT 39," instead of the 168th RCT. He seems not to have had at that time full reports from his subordinates about the failure of the procedures to guide the 168IR's landing boats to the beach.

83 Ryder Papers, Box No. 2, File: CWR Personal 201 File 1942–1944; Headquarters Eastern Task Force, Commander Eastern Assault Force to Commander in Chief, Allied Forces, Subject: Brief Report of Operations of Eastern Assault Force, 19 November 1942.

84 DDE Presidential Library, Box: World War II Participants and Contemporaries: Papers. Folder: Chief of Staff, D Day, TORCH, 8 Nov 1942 to 9 Dec 1942. File: Chief of Staff D-Day Torch November 8 – December 9, 1942 (6). Message, Eisenhower to Marshall, November 11, 1942.

Chapter 8

1 *NWAf*, 255–6; *AAD*, 163–4; Ralph Bennett, *Ultra and Mediterranean Strategy*. New York: William Morrow, 1989, 190 ("a panther's leap").

2 *AAD*, 163–4; *Kriegstagebuch, 90th Panzer Armee Korps*, Nov. 16–30, 1942, NARA RG 319, Office of the Chief of Military History, box 225; Kühn, *German Paratroopers in World War II*, 158–61.

3 *AAD*, 164, citing: Kühn, *German Paratroopers in World War II*, 158; Walter Warlimont, *Inside Hitler's Headquarters, 1939–45*. Transl. R. H. Barry. Novato, Calif.: Presidio, 1964, 271 (hereinafter cited as Warlimont, *Inside Hitler's Headquarters*"); Anthony Martienssen, *Hitler and His Admirals*. New York: E. P. Dutton, 1949, 147; message, Hitler to Mussolini, Nov. 20, 1942, NARA RG 319, Office of the Chief of Military History, 2–3.7, box 225; Horst Boog, *et al.*, *Germany and the Second World War*. Vol VI, *The Global War*. Transl. Ewald Osers *et al*. New York: Oxford University Press, 2001, 793–4 ("*cornerstone of our conduct of the war*").

4 *AAD*, 167.

5 *AAD*, 166–7, citing: Kesselring, Foreign Military Studies, T-3 P1, part II, 6; Albert Kesselring, *The Memoirs of Field Marshal Kesselring*. London: Greenhill, 1997, 8–9.

6 *AAD*, 185, citing: W.J. Jervois, *The History of the Northamptonshire Regiment: 1934–1948*. Aylesbury, U.K.: Regimental History Committee, 1953, 119; *NWAf*, 302.

7 *NWAf*, 299.

8 Ibid., 301.

9 *NWAf*, 300–1, fn. 2 (1) Sitrep, *Div. Broich* to *XC Corps*, 26 Nov 42, in *Div. Broich, KTB*, Nr. 1. 11.XI.–31.XII.42, 26 Nov 42, and *Anlagenheft* II, *Anlage* 8. (2) 1st Bn 1st Armd Regt AAR, 31 Dec 42. (3) CPT Freeland A. Daubin, Jr., The Battle of "Happy Valley," MS. The Armored School, Fort Knox, Ky., 1948. (4) 1st Armd Div Hist and Jnl, Vol. 1. (5) *XC Corps, KTB I, 16.-30.XI.42.* 26 Nov 42.; *AAD*, 203–4; R. L. V. ffrench Blake, *A History of the 17th/21st Lancers, 1922–1959*. London: Macmillan, 1962, 97 (hereinafter cited as "ffrench Blake, *17th/21st Lancers*"); Belton Y. Cooper. *Death Traps*. Novato, Calif.: Presidio, 1998, 25; minutes, "Meeting of the Subcommittee on Armored Vehicles of the National Research Council," June 1943, 9.

10 Paul Fussell. *Wartime: Understanding and Behavior in the Second World War*. New York: Oxford University Press. 1989, 4 (hereinafter cited as "Fussell, *Wartime*").

11 *NWAf*, 255–62; *AAD*, 163–7.

12 *NWAf*, 347.

13 Ibid., 286–7, and fn. 19.

14 Ibid., 309.

15 Ryder Papers, Box 3 (includes statements of Col. Thomas G. Drake, Lt. Col. John H. Van Vliet, and 1st Lt. Edgar Moschel), Drake, Col. Thomas D., *et al*, Factual Account of Operations of 168th Inf., 34th Inf. Div., from Dec. 24, 1942 to Feb. 17, 1943, dated 2 April 1945, at 2, ¶ 8. (hereinafter cited as "Drake, *Factual Account*"). (A complete copy of Drake, Factual Account of Operations 168IR Apr. 1945, reproduced at the DDE Presidential Library, is appended in Appendix A, Documents, Document 6.)

16 *A Partial History of 135IR (Rudolf)*, 6.
17 *NWAf*, 347 and Map V.
18 Ibid., 347–8.
19 Ibid.
20 Ibid., 348–9 and Map V.

Chapter 9

1 *NWAf.*, 349.
2 Ibid., 349–50.
3 *NWAf*, 349–50; *AAD*, 270–1, citing: "Memorandum of Conference at Advanced Allied Forces Headquarters," Jan. 21, 1943, NARA, AFHQ micro, R-187-D; Butcher, 236.
4 *NWAf*, 349–50, and fn. 1 (1) Cbl, CinC AF to CCS, 29 Dec 42, XAF 61. (2) Butcher, 228–31. and fn. 2. (1) Memo, Lt Col R. H. Barry for Brig C. S. Sugden, 22 Jan 43. AFHQ G-3 Ops 58/1.6, Micro Job 10C, Reel 188D. (2) Msg, FREEDOM to AGWAR, 29 Dec 42, CM.IN 12717, and fn. 3. Msg, FREEDOM to USFOR (Eisenhower to Ismay for Churchill), 1550, 28 Dec 42. ETOUSA Incoming Cables, Kansas City Rcds Ctr.
5 *NWAf*, 350–1.
6 *AAD*, 271–2, citing: "History of Allied Force Headquarters," 1945, MTOUSA Historical Section, NARA RG 407, E 427, 95ALI-01, boxes 142–3.
7 *AAD*, 272, citing: "Outline History of II Corps," n.d., NARA RG 407, E 427, box 3112; Robert H. Berlin, *U.S. Army World War II Corps Commanders*. Ft. Leavenworth, KS: Combat Studies Institute, 1989, 5; *These Are the Generals*. New York: Knopf, 1943, 227; Benjamin S. Persons, *Relieved of Command*. Manhattan, KS: Sunflower University Press, 1997, 27; "World War II Generals," War Department, 1945. USMA Library.
8 *NWAf*, 350–1, and fn 5, citing Memo by Gen Eisenhower for the record, 25 Feb 43, in CinC AF Diary, Bk. V, 265a–265e.
9 DDE, 125 (emphasis supplied); see II Corps – Report of Operations, Tunisia, January 1 – March 15, 1943, AGO 202.03, 1, 2.
10 Ibid.
11 Ibid.
12 *NWAf*, 351, and fn. 6, citing: (1) DDE, 125.(2) Dir, Fr Army Detachment to XIX Corps, CSTT, *et al.*, 14 Jan 43. Transl. in AFHQ G-3 Ops 37/4, Micro Job 10B, Reel 81F. (3) Msg, Juin to II Corps, 16 Jan 43. AFHQ CofS Cable Log, 150.
13 *AAD*, 274, citing: Merle Miller, *Ike the Soldier: As They Knew Him*. New York: G. P. Putnam's, 1987, 472; G-1 report, HQ II Corps, Feb 14, 1943, NARA RG 492, MTOUSA, box 263.
14 *AAD*, 274–5, citing: blueprint, 19th Engineer Report, NARA RG 407, E427, box 19248; "Historical Record of the 19th Engineer Regiment," Oct. 1942 – March 1943, NARA RG 407, box 19248; "II Corps Engineer Section Journal," Jan 21 – Mar 1943, NARA RG 407, E 427, box 3234; DDE Presidential Library, James R. Webb Collection: "Diary Covering the Activities of General Fredendall," Jan 25, 1943.
15 *AAD*, 275, citing: Truscott, 146; MacVane, 195; Waters, John Knight, SOOHP, MHI, 175–6, 202 (some questioned).
16 *NWAf*, 351.
17 *A Partial History of 135IR (Rudolf)*, 6.; *Story of the 34th Infantry Division, Louisiana to Pisa,* 6–7.
18 *NWAf*, 352 and fn. 7, citing II Corps AAR, 2 May 43; fn. 8, citing (l)Msg, Eisenhower to CCS, 12 Jan 43. (2) Info supplied by Cabinet Office, London; and fn. 9, citing (1) Rcd of mtg between Anderson, Juin, and Fredendall, at Hq First Army, 11 Jan 43. Information supplied by Cabinet

Office, London. (2) Msg 101, Adv CP AFHQ to AFHQ, signed Truscott, 15 Jan 43. AFHQ CofS Cable Log, 144.

19 *NWAf*, 352, and fn. 10, During a conference with MG Fredendall at Télegma, Algeria. Memo, Gen Lowell W. Rooks for Gen Truscott, 14 Jan 43. AFHQ G-3 Ops 58/1.6, Micro Job 10C, Reel 188D; and fn. 11, citing (1) Memos: Chief Admin Officer AFHQ for CofS AFHQ, 12 Jan 43; G-4 AFHQ for Chief Admin Officer AFHQ, 12 Jan 43; Gen Rooks for Gen Truscott, 14 Jan 43; Brig A. T. de Rhe Philipe (sic) for Chief Admin Officer AFHQ, 15 Jan 43; Telegram, CinC AF to First Army, 1547, 12 Jan 43. AFHQ G-3 Ops 58/1.6, Micro Job 10C, Reel 188D. (2) In March 1943 II Corps began supporting almost 90,000 men over the same line of communications.

20 *AAD*, 271, citing: memo, AFHQ G-4, Jan 15, 1943, NARA, AFHQ micro, R-188-D ("*logistically out of hand*"); "Record of Conference Held by C-in-C Allied Force," Jan 10, 1943, NARA, AFHQ micro, R-188-D ("*fatal to do nothing*")."

21 *NWAf*, 353, and fn. 12.: The first conference was the Arcadia Conference held at Washington soon after the Pearl Harbor attack; and fn. 13: (1) See Official Casablanca Conference Book. (2) Sherwood, *Roosevelt and Hopkins*, Ch. XXVII. See *AAD*, 265–70, 280–300.

22 *NWAf*, 353.

23 *AAD*, 280–1; A. B. Austin, *Birth of an Army*. London: Victor Gollancz, 1943, 73 (hereinafter cited as "Austin, *Birth of an Army*"); DDE, 133, 135; Eisenhower Papers, 906n; *Foreign Relations of the United States: The Conferences at Washington, 1941–1942 and Casablanca, 1943*. Washington, D.C.: U.S. Government Printing Office, 1968. Jan 15, 1943, 567, 569.

24 *AAD*, 281–2; David Fraser, *Alanbrooke*. New York: Atheneum, 1982, 92–3, 297 (hereinafter cited as "Fraser, *Alanbrooke*"); John Kennedy, *The Business of War*. London: Hutchinson, 1957, 291; Alex Danchev and Daniel Todman, eds., *War Diaries 1939–1945, Field Marshal Lord Alanbrooke*. Berkeley and Los Angeles: University of California Press, 2001, 351, 352 ("*ridiculous plan*"); message no. COS (W) 430, British chiefs of staff, Jan 5, 1943, Watson Notes, G. C. Marshall Library; *Foreign Relations of the United States: The Conferences at Washington, 1941–1942 and Casablanca, 1943*. Washington, D.C.: U.S. Government Printing Office, 1968. Jan 15, 1943, 567, 574, 577; Arthur Bryant, *The Turn of the Tide*. London: Collins, 1957, 548 (hereinafter cited as "Bryant, *Turn of the Tide*"); *NWAf*, 353; F. H. Hinsley, *British Intelligence in the Second World War*, vol. 2, New York: Cambridge University Press, 1981, 570 (*ULTRA decrypt today*) (hereinafter cited as "Hinsley, *British Intelligence*").

25 *NWAf*, 353.

26 Ibid., 353–4.

27 *AAD*, 282–3; *Foreign Relations of the United States: The Conferences at Washington, 1941–1942 and Casablanca, 1943*. Washington, D.C.: U.S. Government Printing Office, 1968. Jan 15, 1943, 567–9 ("*any necessary adjustments*"); Butcher, 236; "Minutes of Meeting," Combined Chiefs of Staff, Jan 15, 1943, NARA RG 218, Joint Chiefs of Staff records, box 195.

28 *NWAf*, 353–4 (emphasis supplied), and fn, 14, citing: (1) Combined Chiefs of Staff, 57th and 58th Mtgs, 15 and 16 Jan 43. (2) Anfa 1st Meeting, plenary session, 15 Jan 43, Official Casablanca Conference Book. (4) First Army Sitrep, 31 Jan 43; and fn. 15, citing: (1) CinC Allied Forces Diary, Bk. V, A-160 (18 Jan 43). (2) DDE, 140, cites this passage of diary. (3) Ltr, Eisenhower to Anderson, 26 Jan 43. AFHQ G-3 Ops 58/2.1, Micro Job 10C, Reel l88D; and fn. 16, citing: Msg, AF Command Post to CG II Corps 1200, 20 Jan 43, par. 3. AFHQ CofS Cable Log, 190.

29 *NWAf*, 374–6, and fn. 4. General Fredendall's staff was headed by the following: Chief of Staff, Col. John A. Dabney; G-1, Lt. Col. Lon H. Smith; G-2, Col. B. A. Dickson; G-3, Col. Robert A. Hewitt; and G-4, Col. Robert W. Wilson. Other staff officers of Center Task Force had been reassigned to AFHQ, First Army, or the War Department; and fn. 5. Msg, Eisenhower to CCS, 12 Jan 43.

30   *NWAf,* 376, and fn. 6. (1) II Corps AAR, 2 May 43; 1st Armored Div G-3 Rpt 22; 26th Inf
     AAR. (2) Ltr, LTC Wrenn L. Larson to Atkinson, 27 Mar 51, with incl, Hist Rpt of 443rd CA
     (AA) Bn (SP). (3) Info supplied by Cabinet Office, London.
31   *AAD,* 303–4; D. D. Eisenhower to GCM, Jan. 30, 1943, Eisenhower Papers, 932; D. D. Eisenhower
     to CCS, Feb 3, 1943, Eisenhower Papers, 934 ("offensively defensive"); Harry Butcher diary, Jan
     18, 1943, DDE Presidential Library, A-161 ("I don't want anything"). (emphasis supplied)

Chapter 10

1   *AAD,* 304; *NWAf,* 377.
2   *NWAf,* 376.
3   *AAD,* 304.
4   Ibid.
5   *NWAf,* 377, and fn. 9. (1) *Fifth Panzer Army, KTB III,* 13–21 Jan 43. (2) AAR, *Kampfgruppe
     Weber,* in *334th Inf Div, la, KTB Anlagen, File Eilbote I.* (3) MS T-3 (Nehring *et al.*), Pt 3a.
6   *NWAf,* 376–7; *AAD,* 304.
7   *NWAf,* 377–8, and fn.10. (1) *334th Inf Div., la, KTB Anlagen, File Eilbote I.* (2) AAR, *501st Heavy
     Panzer Bn,* in *Fifth Panzer Army, Anlagen zum KTB III A, 2.-3l.I.43*; and fn. 11. (1) Giraud Hq,
     Rapport des operations. 35–7. (2) Info supplied by Cabinet Office, London.
8   *AAD,* 304–5; "Report of Ousseltia Valley Campaign," 19–29 January 1943," CCB, 1st AD,
     Feb. 12, 1943, NARA RG 407, E 427, 601-CCB-0.3; George F. Howe, *The Battle History of the
     1st Armored Division.* Nashville: Battery Press, 1979, 111–13 (hereinafter cited as "Howe, *1st
     Armored*").
9   *NWAf,* 378, 382; *AAD,* 304–5.
10   Vincent M. Carr, *The Battle of Kasserine Pass: An Examination of Allied Operational Failings.* Air
     Command and Staff College, Maxwell AFB, April 2003, Air University Press, Maxwell AFB, AL
     36112-6615, 18–21; republished as ebook by Pickle Partners Publishing, Auckland, New Zealand
     2014.
11   *NWAf,* 378, and fn. 12. (1) CCB 1st Armd Div AAR, 19–29 Jan 43, 12 Feb 43; and fn. 13: (1)
     Dir, Truscott to Anderson, Juin, and Fredendall. 1200. 20 Jan 43. AFHQ G-3 Ops 22/2. Micro
     Job 10A, Reel 5C. (2) II Corps AAR, 2 May 43. (3) Msg 6436, Algiers to Atlantic Base Section
     (SAL), 1752, 20 Jan 43, AFHQ CofS Cable Log.
12   *NWAf,* 378–9, and fn. 14: CCB 1st Armored Div AAR, 19–29 Jan 43, 12 Feb 43.
13   Ibid., 379, and fn. 15: (1) *334th Inf Div,* Ia, *KTB Anlagen, File Eilbote I.* (2) XIX Corps Jnl,
     19–21 Jan 43.
14   Ibid., and fn. 17: 11 (1) DMA Jnl, 20–1, 21 Jan 43. (2) 601st TD Bn AAR, 28 Feb 43. (3)
     Msg 138, Adv CP to AFHQ, 21 Jan 43. AFHQ CofS Cable Log, 199. (4) XIX Corps Jnl, 21–2
     Jan 43.
15   See Von Clausewitz, Carl. *On War (Vom Krieg).* Edited and translated by Michael Howard and
     Peter Paret, Princeton: Princeton University Press, 1976 and 1984, *Book One. On the Nature of
     War. Chapter 7. Friction in War,* 119.
16   *NWAf,* 379–80, and fn. 18: (1) *334th Inf Div. 1a, KTB Anlagen, File Eilbole I.* (2) CCB 1st Armd
     Div AAR, 19–29 Jan 43, 12 Feb 43: Chronological Sequence of Events in the Ousseltia Valley
     Campaign, 10 Feb 43, in 1st Armored Div Hist Records, Vol II.
17   Ibid., 380.
18   Ibid.
19   Ibid., 380–1. (emphasis supplied)

20 *NWAf,* 380 and fn.: 19. (1) CCB, 1st Armored Div AAR, 19–29 Jan 43; *Chronological Sequence of Events in Ousseltia Valley Campaign,* 10 Feb 43, in 1st Armored Div, Hist Records, Vol. II. (2) XIX Corps, Jnl, 23–27 Jan 43. (3) Info supplied by Cabinet Office, London. (4) 601st TD Bn AAR, 28 Feb 43; 26th Inf AAR, 25–28 Jan 43, 23 Apr 43.

21 Ibid., 381.

22 Ibid., 382.

23 *NWAf,* 382–3, and fn. 20. (1) Msg N22/29, Adv CP AFHQ to AFHQ, 30 Jan 43, AFHQ CofS Cable Log, 272. (2) Ltr, Gen. Allen to CinC AF, 7 Feb 43, AFHQ G-3 Ops 22/2, Micro Job 10A, Reel 5C. (3) 3rd Bn 16th Inf Battle Rpt, 8 Mar 43; CCB 1st Armored Div AAR, 19–29 Jan 43, 12 Feb 43. (4) XIX Corps Jnl, 24 Jan 43; fn. 21. 334th Inf Div, *Ia, KTB Anlagen, File Eilbote I;* fn. 22. CCB 1st Armored Div Intel Rpt, 21–28 Jan 43.

Chapter 11

1 *NWAf,* 401, n. 1:(1) [Foreign Military Studies] MS # T-3 (Nehring *et al.*), Pt. 3a. (2) AFHQ Rpt, G-2 Estimate of Axis Offensive Capabilities After Panzer Armee Rommel (sic) Is in Occupation of the Mareth Line, 7 Feb 43. AFHQ Micro Job 26, Reel 72 Spec. Msg 1784, USFOR to FREEDOM, 1700, 17 Feb 43, sub: Axis forces in North Africa. Non-Current Permanent Rcd File, Misc Cbls-1942–43, AG 311.22. (4) II Corps G-2 Estimate 8, 7 Feb 43; II Corps Periodic Rpts 39, 13 Feb 43, and 40, 14 Feb 43; 1st Armored Div G-3 Periodic Rpts 16, 9 Feb 43, and 18, 11 Feb 43. (5) *DMC [Division de marche de Constantine* (Constantine Division)] Journal, 9 Feb 43. (6) Msg, XIX Corps to II Corps (G-3), 2100, 9 Feb 43, in II Corps G-3 Jnl, 0641, 10 Feb 43.

2 Ibid., 402, n. 2: (1) Ltr, Eisenhower to Fredendall, 4 Feb 43. OPD Exec 3, Item la. (2) Msg, Adv CP Allied ASC to CinC AF, 6 Feb 43. AFHQ CofS Cable Log, 46.

3 Ibid., 363, and fn. 1: Msg, *Fifth Panzer Army* to *OB SÜD,* 15 Dec 42 in *Fifth Panzer Army, KTB Anlagen, Geh. u. Geh. Kdo. Sachen Band I, 16.XI.42-12.I,43;* and fn. 2. See *NWAf,* 322–3.

4 Ibid., 363–4.

5 Ibid., 363–4, and fn. 3: Minutes of Conf between Rommel and Bastico, 31 Dec 42, 1215 hrs, at Misurata, in *Panzer Army Africa, KTB, Anlagenband 6, Anlage 713/2;* and fn. 4: Memo, Rommel, *Panzer Army Africa* (Nr. 324/43), 22 Jan 43, Report Rommel to Cavallero for the Duce, in *OKH/ GenStdH/Op Abt, File A I-Afrika Berichte, Band 3, J6.J.-JB.V.43;* and fn. 5: [Foreign Military Studies] MS # D-072, *Aus dem Arbeitsgebiet des Kommandanten des Rueckwaertigen Armeegebiets Nordafrika* [The Activities of the Commanders of Rear Army Areas in North Africa], Teil II (*Generalmajor* Ernst Schnarrberger). Based on personal diary.

6 Ibid., 365.

7 Ibid., 364–5, and fn. 6: *OKW/WFSt,* KTB, 19 Jan 43.

8 Ibid., 368, and fn. 11: (1) See Appendix B, *NWAf,* 682–683; (2) (Opns Rpt, *Fifth Panzer Army, 0 Qu, Taetigkeitsbericht* ("activity report"), Abt Qu 3-0Q Tunis, 15.XI.-31.XII.42. (3) Rpt, *Afrika Transporte,* Nr. 1701/43, 7 Feb 43, in *OKH /CenStdH/Op Abt* (11), Afrika-A II Kraefte, I.I2B.V.43. (4) [Foreign Military Studies] MS # D-093 (Seibt).

9 Ibid., 370, and fn. 20.: Rpts, 10 Dec 42, 1 Jan and 1 Feb 43, in *OKH/GenStdH/Op Abt* (II), A IV-*Afrika-Transporte Allgemein,* 10.XII.42-29.VII.43.

10 Ibid., 371, and fn. 22: *Fifth Panzer Army,* KTB, Bands 2, 4, 12 Jan 43.

11 Ibid.

12 Ibid., 370–1, and fn. 23: (1) Tabulations, 1 Feb 43, in *Panzer Army Africa, KTB, Anlagenband R, Anlage 1031/9.* (2) Giovanni Messe, *La 1a Armata Italiana in Tunisia, Ministero della Difesa, Stato Maggiore Escrcito-Ufficio Storico.* Rome, 1950, 27; and fn. 24: *Panzer Army Africa,* KTB,

Band 2, 20 Jan 43. The main body of *21st Pz. Div.* crossed the Tunisian border on January 20. The division left its tanks and most of its heavy weapons with Rommel.

13   Ibid., 371–2.

14   Ibid., 370 and fn. 17 (1) Directive, *OKW/WFStjOp* Nr. 66214, 28 Jan 43, in *Panzer Army Africa, KTB Anlagen, Anlage 945.* (2) "January 24, 1943. General Messe informs me of a conference he had yesterday with the Duce in the presence of Cavallero. He has been made commander of the Italian forces that are flowing into Tunisia. ... What surprised Messe was the language of Mussolini, who spoke of certain successes, offensive possibilities, African recoveries, et cetera, et cetera. All this is due to the fact that Cavallero pictures a situation which is far from the truth and is deliberately deceiving the Duce." Hugh Gibson, ed. *The Ciano Diaries, 1939–1943. The complete, unabridged diaries of Count Galeazzo Ciano, Italian minister for foreign affairs, 1936–1943.* New York: Doubleday & Company, Inc., 1945. Republished by Simon Publications, Safety Harbor, FL, 2001, 574. Online at https://ia600200.us.archive.org/35/items/ GibsonHughTheCianoDiaries19391943TheCompleteUnabridgedDiariesOfCountGaleazzoCian/ Gibson%2C%20Hugh%20-%20The%20Ciano%20Diaries%201939-1943%20The%20 Complete%2C%20Unabridged%20Diaries%20of%20Count%20Galeazzo%20Ciano%2C%20 Italian%20Minister%20of%20Foreign%20Affairs%2C%201936-1943.pdf (3) *Panzer Army Africa, KTB Anlagen, Anlage 943/3, 26 Jan 43.* (4) Radio, *OKW/WFSt (H)*, Nr. 66185, 25 Jan 43, in *OKH/GenStdH/Op Abt* "Tunis."

15   *NWAf*, 370, and fn 18: (1) MS # T-3 (Nehring *et al.*), Pt. 3. (2) German Air Hist Branch (Abt 8), "German Air Force Activities in the Mediterranean. Tactics and Lessons Learned, 1941–1943," 30 Oct 44.

Chapter 12

1   *NWAf*, 383, and fn. 24: (1) CinC AF Diary, 21 Jan 43. (3) Msg 6436, AFHQ to Atlantic Base Section (SAL), 1752, 20 Jan 43, AFHQ CofS Cable Log; DDE, 127.

2   *NWAf*, 380–4.

3   *NWAf*, 384, and fn. 26: (1) Despatch, Lt Gen K. A. N. Anderson, 8. (2) Memo, Deputy CofS AFHQ (Truscott), for CGs of First Army, II Corps, and 1st Inf Div, 24 Jan 43, sub: Attachment of American troops to Br. First Army. AFHQ Micro Job l0A, Reel 5C; *AAD*, 305; memo, D. D. Eisenhower, Jan 19, 1943, Eisenhower Papers, 909; K. A. N. Anderson, *Operations in North West Africa, 8 November 1942 to 13 May 1943.*" Despatch to the Secretary of War printed in the *London Gazette* (Supplement), Wednesday, November 6, 1946 https://www.thegazette.co.uk/ London/issue/37779/supplement/5449 (hereinafter cited as "Anderson, *Operations in Northwest Africa*"); G-1 report, HQ II Corps, Feb 14, 1943, NARA RG 492, MTOUSA, box 263, DDE, 489; D. D. Eisenhower to Anderson, Jan 26, 1943, Eisenhower Papers, 922.

4   Ibid., 384–5 and fn. 27: Letter, Eisenhower to Anderson, 26 Jan 43, AFHQ G-3 Ops 58/2.1, Micro Job 10C, Reel 188D. (emphasis supplied)

5   *AAD*, 305; memo, D. D. Eisenhower, Jan 19, 1943, Eisenhower Papers, 909; Anderson, *Operations in North West Africa;* G-1 report, HQ II Corps, Feb 14, 1943, NARA RG 492, MTOUSA, box 263, DDE, 489; D. D. Eisenhower to Anderson, Jan 26, 1943, Eisenhower Papers, 922.

6   *AAD*, 305–6; Anderson: *Operations in North West Africa;* G-1 report, HQ II Corps, Feb 14, 1943, NARA RG 492, MTOUSA, box 263, DDE, 489; D. D. Eisenhower to Anderson, Jan 26, 1943; Eisenhower Papers, 922.

7   *NWAf*, 385, and fn. 29: (1) First Army Opns Instruction 11, 26 Jan 43. DRB AGO. (2) Fredendall and Juin agreed that Fondouk al Aouareb should be within II Corps's area in a conference at Tébessa on January 27, 1943, reported via AFCP to AFHQ and First Army in Msg 94/27, 28

Jan 43. AFHQ CofS Cable Log, 257; and fn. 30 (1) Giraud Hq, *Rapport des operations*, 39. (2) First Army Opns Instruction 11, 26 Jan 43. DRB AGO.

8 Ibid., 385–6.

9 Ibid., 385–6, and fn. 31 (1) Letter, Eisenhower to Anderson, 2 Feb 43. AFHQ C-3 Ops 58/2.1, Micro Job 10C, Reel 188D. (2) In addition to the 18th Regimental Combat Team (strength approximately 4,500), First Army had under command 62,456 British officers and enlisted men on 27 January 1943. Q (Maint) Tab Rpt of Admin Sitrep 10, 1800, 27 Jan 43 AFHQ CofS Cable Log; and fn. 32. Memo, Brig J. F. M. Whiteley for Gen Rooks, 22 Jan 43; Memo, Rooks to Whiteley, 22 Jan 43; Ltr, CinC AF to CG First Army, 26 Jan 43; Mins of Conf, 1 Feb 43. AFHQ G-3 Ops 58/2.1, Micro Job 10C, Reel 188D.

10 Ibid., 402, n. 3: Dir, CinC AF to CG First Army, 11 Feb 43. AFHQ G-3 Opns 58/2.1, Micro Job 10C, Reel 188D.

11 Don Y. Kim, Major, USA. *The United States 1st Armored Division and Mission Command at the Battle of Faid Pass*. Fort Leavenworth, KS: School of Advanced Military Studies, United States Army Command and General Staff College, 2017, 33. (Hereinafter cited as "Kim, *Battle of Faïd Pass*.").

12 *NWAf*, 386, and fn. 33. Msg, Cavallero, *Comando Supremo* (Nr. 027/ OP/A) to *Fifth Panzer Army*, 1830, 28 Jan 43, in *Fifth Panzer Army, KTB, Anlagen, g. Kdos. (Chefsachen), 16.I.-26.II.43, Tunesien*.

13 Ibid., 386–7 (emphasis supplied).

14 Ibid., 387 and fn. 34. Bir Mrabott is about 20 miles southeast of Gafsa on the Gabès road; and fn. 35. [1] II Corps FO 1, 19 Jan 43. (2) II Corps AAR, 3 May 43.

15 *AAD*, 306–7; Russell A. Gugeler, typescript, Unpublished biography of Orlando Ward, n.d. Orlando Ward Papers, MHI, X-62; diary, Jan. 23, 28, 1943, Orlando Ward Papers, MHI.

16 Ibid., 307.

17 *NWAf.*, 377–88, and fn. 36. Combat Command C consisted of: the 6th Armored Infantry Regiment (less two tank battalions and a tank company, amounting in total to a reduced tank battalion); Company C (plus one platoon of Company D), 81st Reconnaissance Battalion; Company I, 13th Armored Regiment, bringing the available armor up to one full battalion; Battery B, 68th Field Artillery Battalion; the 3rd Platoon of Company D, 16th Engineer Battalion; the 2nd Platoon of Battery B, 443rd Coast Artillery (AA) Battalion (SP); and detachments of the 141st Signal Company and 47th Medical Battalion. See 1st Armored Div Opns Instruction 1, 23 Jan 43; and fn. 37: 6th Armored Inf AAR, 23 Jan – 26 Feb 4, 1943; *AAD*, 307.

18 *NWAf.*, 388, and fn. 38: Rpt of Conf, Fredendall and Juin, Tébessa, 27 Jan 43, AFHQ CofS Cable Log, 252.

19 Ibid., 388, and fn. 39: 1st Armored Div FO 3, 30 Jan 43.

20 *AAD*, 307–8; Paul Carell, *The Foxes of the Desert*, Transl. Mervyn Savill. New York: Bantam, 1972, 333 ("*my nightmare*"); James B. Carvey, "Faïd Pass," *Infantry Journal*, Sep 1944, 8.

Chapter 13

1 *NWAf*, 388–90, and Map 9 [Faïd-Maknassy Actions], and fn. 40: *21st Panzer Div, la, KTB-Anlagen, Nr. 9, l.I.-31.III.43, Afrika*, (hereinafter cited as *21st Panzer Div, KTB Anlagen, Band 9*).

2 Ibid

3 Ibid., 390—1, and fn. 41: *21st Panzer Div*, FO for the capture of the Faïd strongpoint, 26 Jan 43, *21st Panzer Div, KTB Anlagen, Band 9*; *AAD*, 308.

4 *AAD*, 308; Akers, oral history, July 27, 1949, Sidney Matthews papers, MHI; Truscott, 150; Martin Blumenson, "Kasserine Pass, 30 January – 22 February 1943," in Charles E. Heller and

William A. Stofft, eds., *America's First Battles, 1776–1965*. Lawrence, KS: University Press of Kansas, 1986, 245.

5   *NWAf*, 391, and fn. 42: *21st Panzer Div, KTB, 1.I.-31.III.43*, 30 Jan 43.

6   *AAD*, 308; "Narrative of Events from 23 January 1943 to 26 February," CCA, 1st AD, NARA RG 407, E. 427, 601-CCA-0.3, box 14767 (hereinafter cited as "CCA Narrative of Events box 14767)"; Martin Blumenson, "Kasserine Pass, 30 January – 22 February 1943," in *America's First Battles, 1776–1965*, 108; Martin Blumenson, *Kasserine Pass*. New York: Jove Books, 1983, 108 (hereinafter cited as "Blumenson, *Kasserine Pass*").

7   Kim, *Battle of Faïd Pass*, 35.

8   Ibid., 36.

9   *NWAf*, 391–2 and fn. 43: 1st Armored Div FO 4, 30 Jan 43. The units available to Combat Command A were: the 1st Armored Regiment (less the 1st and 2nd Battalions, effectively a single battalion of tanks); the 1st Battalion, 6th Armored Infantry; part of the 26th Infantry Regiment (less Company C and 2nd and 3rd Battalions, amounting in total to an under-strength battalion of infantry); the 1st Reconnaissance Troop; the 33rd Field Artillery Battalion: the 91st Field Artillery Battalion; Company A, 701st Tank Destroyer Battalion; Company C, 16th Armored Combat Engineers; and Battery D (less two platoons), 43rd Coast Artillery (AA) Battalion (SP). In sum, CCA lacked a substantial part of its combat power as it entered battle; and fn. 44: Information supplied by Gen McQuillin to George Howe, in the Office of the Chief of Military History. See CCA 1st Armored Div AAR, 2:1 Jan–26 Feb 43; 26th Inf AAR, 11 Nov 42, 14 Apr 43, 23 April 43.

10   Kim, *Battle of Faïd Pass*, 37.

11   Ibid.

12   *AAD*, 309–11; Truscott, 148; Blumenson, *Kasserine Pass*, 109; Raphael L. Uffner, *Recollections of World War II with the First Infantry Division*, typescript, n.d., Cantigny, IL: McCormick Research Center, First Division Museum, 245–50 (hereinafter cited as "Uffner, *Recollections*"); "History of the 26th Infantry in the Present Struggle," Cantigny, IL: McCormick Research Center, First Division Museum, , 7/1–2, 7/2–3 (hereinafter cited as "History of the 26th Infantry").

13   Paul Fussell, "The Real War 1939–1945." The Atlantic, August 1989; Fussell, *Wartime*, 267–8.

14   *AAD*, 309–11; CCA Narrative of Events box 14767 (*the failed counterattack*).

15   *NWAf*, 392.

16   *AAD*, 309–11.

17   Ibid.

18   *NWAf*, 392, 394 (*Faïd Pass was gone*); *AAD*, 309–11; Truscott, 148; Blumenson, *Kasserine Pass*, 109; Uffner, *Recollections*, 245–50; History of the 26th Infantry, 7/1–2, 7/2–3.

19   Kim, *Battle of Faïd Pass*, 37–8.

20   *NWAf*, 392, and fn. 45: Phone Msg, Gen, Giraud to Capt Ciarlet to be transmitted to Gen Fredendall *et al.*, 1 Feb 43, in DMC Jnl, 1 Feb 43.

21   Ibid., 478.

22   *AAD*, 343.

Chapter 14

1   *NWAf*, 393.

2   Ibid.

3   Ibid., 392–3, and fn. 47 and 48: 47. 6th Armored Inf, Report of Combat Operations in North Africa, Nov 42 – May 43, Pt. II, 9.

4   Ibid., 392–6; *AAD*, 312.

5   *NWAf,* 393.

6   *NWAf,* 393, and fn. 49. II Corps Sitrep, 1700, 31 Jan 43; and fn. 50: *DMC Jnl,* 31 Jan 43. The French corps journal entry contains a special note by General Welvert describing his efforts to coordinate American operation at Faïd.

7   Ibid., 393, and fn. 51: (1) CCA 1st Armored Div S2 Rpt, 1800–2300, 1 Feb 43. (2) 3rd Bn 1st Armored Regt AAR, 1 Jan – 21 Feb 43, 30 Jul 43, (3) 26th Inf AAR, 23 Apr 43, which reports casualties of ninety wounded and six or seven missing; and fn. 52: (1) 6th Armored Inf AAR, 23 Jan – 26 Feb 43, (2) Memo, CG CCA to CG 1st Armored Div, in 1st Armored Div Sitrep, 1–2 Feb 43, (3) 1st Armored Div FO 5, 1200, 3 Feb 43, (4) Losses reported by the 26th Infantry [1st ID] were 1 killed and 56 wounded and for 6th Armored Infantry 4 killed and 16 wounded. (5) French losses known on 2 February were 905 officers and men, killed or missing in action. *DMC Jnl,* 2 Feb 43, (6) The enemy reported capture of 1,047 prisoners of war (mostly French), 25 armored cars, 3 guns, 2 anti-aircraft guns, 15 anti-tank guns, 8 mortars, 57 machine guns, 10 trucks, and 5 aircraft either destroyed or damaged. Msg, *OKH/GenStdH/Op Abt,* Nr. 1563/43, to army groups, 4 Feb 43, in *OKH/GenStdH/Op Abt,* File *Abendorientierungen Afrika,* 11-/3, V.43. (7) Msg, CG II Corps to CG 1st Armored Div, 1030, 2 Feb 43, in II Corps G-3 Jnl.

8   Ibid., 395–6; and fn. 54: 6th Armored Inf AAR, 23 Jan – 26 Feb 43.

9   *AAD,* 312 (emphasis supplied).

10 *NWAf,* 392–6, *AAD,* 312.

11 *AAD,* 312–13.

12 *NWAf,* 396, and fn. 37: (1) Memo, H. P. Dittemore for CG 1st Armored Div, 11 Feb 43, sub: Investigation. Copy in possession of Brig Gen Hamilton H. Howze. (2) 175th FA Bn War Diary, 31 Jan – 2 Feb 43. (3) Memo, Gen Fredendall for CinC AF, 10 Mar 43, sub: Notes on recent opns on the Tunisian front, par. 8.

13 *AAD,* 312–13; Atkinson interview, Aurelio Barron, Oct 19, 1999 (*"all down the road"*).

14 Ibid.; Edwin L. Powell, Jr., oral history, 1982, Lynn L. Sims, U.S. Army Corps of Engineers, Office of History, 102–7; (*"Sunday School picnic"*); "History of the 168th Infantry," Jan 31, 1942, NARA RG 407, E 427, boxes 9575–7; David Rame, *Road to Tunis.* New York: MacMillan, 1944, 229 (hereinafter cited as "Rame, *Road to Tunis"*); David Rolf, *The Bloody Road to Tunis.* London: Greenhill, 2001, 79 (*"It was the most terrible thing"*).

15 Lauren E. McBride, "The Battle of Sened Station," *Infantry Journal,* Apr 1945 (hereinafter cited as "McBride, *Battle of Sened Station"*).

16 *AAD,* 313; Wesley Frank Craven and James Lea Cate, eds., *The Army Air Forces in World War II,* vol. II: *Europe: Torch to Pointblank.* Chicago: University of Chicago Press, 1949, 142 (hereinafter cited as "Craven, *Torch to Pointblank"*); McBride, *Battle of Sened Station,* 30 (*"Maimed and twisted"*).

17 *AAD,* 314.

18 Drake, *Factual Account,* 1–2.

19 Drake, *Factual Account,* 2–3; *AAD,* 314; Stewart, Red Bull Training); 1; Drake, *Factual Account,* 2–3.; Dennis B. Bray, "Regimental Commander of the 168th Infantry, Colonel Thomas Davidson Drake: Battle of Sened and Sidi bou Zid, Tunisia," typescript, Nov 1977, Iowa Military Academy, IGSMM; Ankrum, *Dogfaces,* 174; Curtiss, Mina, ed., *Letters Home.* Boston: Little, Brown, 1944, 276.

20 Drake, *Factual Account,* 2–3.

21 Ibid., 3.

22 Ibid., 4.

23 Drake, *Factual Account,* 3–4; *AAD,* 314; "History of the 168th Infantry," NARA RG 407, E 427.

24 Drake, *Factual Account,* 5.

25 Drake, *Factual Account*, 4–5; *AAD*, 314, "History of the 168th Infantry," NARA RG 407, E 427.

26 Drake, *Factual Account*, 5; *NWAf*, 396, and fn. 57: (1) Memo, H. P. Dittemore for CG 1st Armd Div, 11 Feb 43, sub: Investigation. Copy in possession of Brig Gen Hamilton H. Howze. (2) 175th FA Bn War Diary, 31 Jan – 2 Feb 43. (3) Memo, Gen Fredendall for CinC AF, 10 Mar 43, subject: Notes on recent operations on the Tunisian front, par. 8. Hughes was captured; Drake, captured two weeks later at Sidi bou Zid, would meet Hughes nine months later in an *Oflag* in Poland. Hughes denied that there had been an outpost but admitted that he had seen the terrain only once and in daylight.

27 *NWAf*, 396–7.

28 Drake, *Factual Account*, 6.

29 Drake, *Factual Account*, 6. ("*Men were dying everywhere*"): *AAD*, 314–15; Ankrum, *Dogfaces*, 174 ("*all those bees*"); Hougen, 50; McBride, *Battle of Sened Station*.

30 *AAD*, 315; Berens: *Citizen Soldier*, 5, 47; "168th African History," in "168th Infantry Publications," IGSMM; Rame, *Road to Tunis*, 235.

31 *NWAf*, 396–7, and fn. 58: (1) Memo by Arty and Rcn Survey Officer 1st Armd Div. Copy in Office of the Chief of Military History. (2) *21st Panzer Div, KTB, l.l.-3l.III.43*, 31 Jan and 1 Feb 43.

32 *NWAf*, 397 (emphasis supplied), and fn. 59: (I) 1st Armored Div Hist Records, Vol. II. (2) Memo by Artillery and Reconnaissance Survey Officer. Copy in Office of the Chief of Military History.

33 *NWAf*, 397, and fn. 60: Copies in 1st Armored Div Hist Records, Vol. II.

34 Ibid., and fn. 61: Minutes of Conf between Eisenhower and Anderson, Feb 43. AFHQ C-3 Ops 58/2.1, Micro Job 10C, Reel 188D.

35 Drake, *Factual Account*, 7–8.

36 Ibid.

37 *AAD*, 316.

38 Drake, *Factual Account*, 9.

39 *AAD*, 316; T. J. Camp, ed. *Tankers in Tunisia*, 1943. Fort Knox, KY, Armored Replacement Training Center, 55. Republished: University Press of the Pacific, 2003 ("*A sort of hysteria*"); Edwin L. Powell, Jr., oral history, U.S. Army Corps of Engineers, Office of History, Alexandria, Virginia, 110 ("*hightailing it*"); letter, James McGuinness to parents, May 23, 1943, Co. F., 168th Inf., World War II Letters, 1940–1946, Western Historical Manuscript Collection, Columbia, MO: University of Missouri ("*Some of the fellows*").

40 Drake, Factual Account, 9.

41 *NWAf*, 398, and fn. 62: (1) Memo, Col Thomas D. Drake for ACofS G-2, 14 May 45, sub: Account of 168th Inf opns 24 Dec 42 – 17 Feb 43. DRB AGO [Ryder's copy of the Drake memorandum is Drake, "Factual Account of Operations 168IR, Apr. 1945"; see Appendix A, Documents, Document 6. (2) 175th FA Bn War Diary, 31 Jan – 2 Feb 43; *AAD*, 316.

42 Ibid., fn. 63: (1) Casualty List (omitting 81st Reconnaissance Bn after 1 Feb), 5 Feb 43. Copy in 1st Armored Division Historical Records, Vol. II. *About half the casualties were in the 168th Infantry.* (2) Ironically, General von Arnim considered that when Maraist's attack was called off, the means available to the Axis of defending Maknassy were insufficient. Foreign Military Studies, Mss #C-098 (von Arnim).

43 *AAD*, 316; "History of the 168th Infantry," NARA RG 407, E 427; After Action Report, 1st Armored Division, 27 Jan – 3 Feb, 1943, "Kasserine Pass Battles," vol. I, part I, U.S. Army Center for Military History ("*no decisive objectives*"); Howe, *1st Armored Division*, 129; *NWAf*, 398; Ankrum, *Dogfaces*, 174.

44 *NWAf*, 398 and fn. 64: *21st Panzer Div, KTB*, 1–3 Feb 43.

45 Kim, *Battle of Faïd Pass*, 42.

46 Drake, *Factual Account*, 9–10.
47 *NWAf*, 398 and fn. 65: Field Order 5.
48 Ibid., 399–400.
49 Ibid., 399, and fn. 66: The British 6th Armoured Division was being rearmed with U.S. M4 'Sherman' tanks at this time and was not, therefore, used as First Army Reserve. Memo, Eisenhower for the record, 25 Feb 43, in CinC AF Diary, Bk. V, 256a–256e.
50 Ibid., 400, fn 69: Msg, 10 Feb 43, Entry 174, II Corps G-3 Jnl.
51 Drake, *Factual Account*, 11.
52 Ibid., 11–12.
53 *NWAf*, 399.
54 Ibid., and fn. 67: (1) Msg, Gen Kuter to CinC AF, 6 Feb 43. AFHQ CofS Cable Log 46. (2) A plan for a counterattack to regain Faïd Pass to be led by General Porter was abandoned on 5 February 1943. Porter was transferred to AFHQ advanced command post from II Corps.

Chapter 15

1 *NWAf*, 402.
2 *Regimental History, 135IR (Musel)*, IGSMM PDF file gs_4102, 37.
3 *NWAf*, 403, and fn. 5: 133rd Inf and 135th Inf Histories.
4 *A Partial History of 135IR (Rudolf)*, 6–7.
5 *Regimental History, 135IR (Musel)*, IGSMM PDF file gs_4102, 37.
6 *NWAf*, 410, and fn. 22: (1) Report, *German-Italian Panzer Army* to *Comando Supremo*, 16 Feb 43, in *Panzer Army Africa, KTB, Anlagenband 9, Anlage 1081 / 4*. (2) FO, *Panzer Army Africa*, Nr. 1, in *Panzer Army Africa, Anlagenband 8, Anlage 1028/ 1*.
7 *AAD*, 343.
8 *NWAf*, 405; *see NWAf*, 322–3.
9 *NWAf*, 370, 372; *AAD*, 319–21; Harold R. L. G. Alexander, Field Marshal the Viscount Alexander of Tunis. "The African Campaign from El Alamein to Tunis, from 10th August, 1942, to 13th May, 1943," despatch to the Secretary of War printed in Supplement, February 3, 1948, to *The London Gazette*, February 5, 1948. https://www.thegazette.co.uk/London/issue/38196/data.pdf, 868, (hereinafter cited as "Alexander: *The African Campaign*); Anderson: Operations in Northwest Africa; "Rommel to Tunisia," NARA RG 319, Office of the Chief of Military History, box 227; war diary, *Panzer Army Africa*, Feb 3–4 and Feb 10–17, 1943, in "Kasserine Pass Battles," vol. I, part 1, U.S. Army Center for Military History; Helmuth Greiner diary notes, Feb 16, 1943, and personnel report, *Panzer Army Africa*, Feb 1, 1943, NARA RG 319, Office of the Chief of Military History, box 225; Albert Kesselring, "Final Commentaries on the Campaign in North Africa, 1941–1943", 1949, Foreign Military Studies, C-075, 17; Hans J. T. von Arnim, "Recollections of Tunisia." Transl. Janet E. Dewey, 1951. U.S. Army European Command. Foreign Military Studies, C-098, 48–9.
10 *NWAf*, 405, n. 10: Memo, *German-Italian Panzer Army* to *Comando Supremo*, 4 Feb 43, in *Panzer Army Africa, KTB, Anlagenband 8, Anlage 995*. A blow through Gafsa and Sbeïtla on Tébessa was earlier described as an objective of second priority on January 19, 1943 in *OKW /WFSt, KTB*, 19 Jan 43.
11 Ibid., 370, 372; *AAD*, 321–2; Warlimont, *Inside Hitler's Headquarters*, 310, 284 ("*restricted rations*"); Alexander, *The African Campaign*; I. S. O. Playfair and C. J. C. Molony, *The Mediterranean and the Middle East*, vol. IV, *The Destruction of the Axis Forces in Africa. History of the Second World War*. London: Her Majesty's Stationery Office, 1960, 273, 283–4 (hereinafter cited as Playfair, *Destruction of the Axis Forces*).

12 *NWAf,* 405–10; *AAD,* 322; B. H. Liddell Hart, ed., *The Rommel Papers.* Transl. Paul Findlay. New York: Collectors Reprints, 1995, 397 (*"break up the American assembly area"*) (hereinafter cited as Liddell Hart, *The Rommel Papers*); David Irving, *The Trail of the Fox.* New York: Thomas Congdon, 1977, 266–7 (*"Kesselring agreed"*, *"We are going all out"*) (hereinafter cited as Irving, *Trail of the Fox*); war diary (*Kriegstagebuch*), *Fifth Panzer Army,* Feb 8, 1943, in "Kasserine Pass Battles," vol. I, part 1, U.S. Army Center for Military History (*"weaken the American"*); war report, *Panzer Army Africa,* Jan 16 to Feb 12, 1943, in "Kasserine Pass Battles," vol. I, part 1, U.S. Army Center for Military History.

13 *NWAf,* 405.

14 Ibid., 406, fn. 11: *Panzer Army Africa, KTB, Band 2,* 3–13 Feb 43.

15 Ibid., fn. 12: Radio, *Comando Supremo* to *German-Italian* and *Fifth Panzer Armies,* 8 Feb 43, in *Panzer Army Africa, KTB, Anlagenband 8, Anlage 1016.*

16 Ibid., fn. 13: (1) *Panzer Army Africa, KTB. Band 2* ,9 Feb 43. (2) MS #T-3-P2 (Kesselring), Pt. 2. (3) MS #C-075 (Kesselring), comments on MS #T-3 (Nehring *et al.*), Pt, 3a.

17 Ibid., n. 14: Memo, *Kraeftegegenueberstellung* (Estimate of opposing forces), 19 Feb 43, in *OKH/ GenStdH/Op Abt,* File Tunis, 10.XI.42–2.V.43.

18 Ibid., n. 15: (1) 1st Armored Div Tank Status Rpt, 12 Feb 43, Entry 210, in II Corps G-3 Jnl. (2) Ltr, Eisenhower to Marshall, 21 Feb 43. Copy in CinC AF Diary, Bk. V, A-240-2.

19 Ibid., 407.

20 Ibid., 407, n. 16: (1) Radio, *Comando Supremo* to *Fifth Panzer Army* and *Panzer Army Africa,* 11 Feb 43, in *Panzer Army Africa, KTB, Anlagenband 8, Anlage 1038.* (2) *Panzer Army Africa, KTB, Band 2,* 11–13 Feb 43.

21 *NWAf,* 410–11; *AAD,* 326; Howe, *1st Armored,* 141.

22 *AAD,* 326; Ankrum, *Dogfaces,* 182 (*"isn't that much barbed wire"*).

23 *AAD,* 326; After Action Report, 2nd Bn, 168th Inf Regt, Feb 3–16, 1942, IGSMM.

24 *AAD,* 327; After Action Report, 168th Inf Regt, Feb. 27, 1943, IGSMM; After Action Report, 3rd Bn, 168th Inf Regt, n.d., IGSMM; After Action Report, 2nd Bn, 168th Inf Regt, Feb. 3–16, 1943, IGSMM (*"killed at once"* and *"when I want prisoners taken"*); Laurence P. Robertson, typescript, Army Service Experience Questionnaire, 1AR, 1AD, MHI.

25 *NWAf,* 411, n. 25: (1) Report by Col Hains, 12 Mar 43, in 1st Armored Div Hist Records; 1st Armd Regt AAR, 10 Jul 43; CCA 1st Armored Div AAR, 23 Jan – 26 Feb 43.

26 Drake, *Factual Account,* 15.

27 *NWAf,* 407, fn. 17: Von Broich took command when General Fischer was killed on 1 February by an Italian mine. *Fifth Panzer Army, KTB IV,* 1 Feb 43.

28 Ibid., and fn. 18: FO, *Fifth Panzer Army,* Nr. 260/43,8 Feb 43, in *21st Panzer Div, Ia, KTB-Anlagen, Nr. 9, I.I.-31.III.43, Afrika* (hereinafter cited as *21st Panzer Div., KTB Anlagen, Band 9*).

29 *PanzerKampfWagen* Mk VI Tigers were allocated to an independent *Schwere Panzer Abteilung* (heavy tank battalion) which was usually assigned to a corps or army headquarters. The battalion had a headquarters company with two Mk VI tanks, and three tank companies, each with a company headquarters with two Mk VI tanks and 3 tank platoons, each with 4 Mk VI tanks. Technical Manual TM-E 30-451: Handbook on German Military Forces. United States War Department. USGPO, Washington, D.C. 15 March 1945. II-64.

30 *NWAf,* 409, and fn. 19: FO, *10th Panzer Div.,* 9 Feb 43, and supplement, 12 Feb 43, in *21st Panzer Division, KTB Anlagen, Band 9.*

31 Ibid., and fn. 20: (1) FO, *21st Panzer Div.,* Nr. 102/43, 12 Feb 43, in *21st Panzer Div. KTB, Anlagen, Band 9.* (2) *Gefechtsbericht ueber die Kampfhandlungen im Abschnitt Faid uam 13.–18. II.43* (Combat Report on the Fighting in the Attack on Faïd 13–18 February 43) (cited hereafter as *Gefechtsbericht Faid*), in *Fifth Panzer Army, Anlage zum Kriegstagebuch IV A* (cited hereafter as *KTB, Anlagen, Band IV A*), *1.–26.II.43, Anlage 117.*

32 Ibid., and fn. 21: (I) *Panzer Army Africa, KTB, Band 2, 10 Feb 43*. (2) MS # D-124, *Beitrag zum Vorstoss ueber Gafsa gegen den Kasserine-Pass* (Paper on the Advance from Gafsa against the Kasserine Pass) (*Generalleutnant* Freiherr Kurt von Liebenstein).

33 Ibid., and n. 22: (1) Rpt, *German-Italian Panzer Army* to *Comando Supremo*, 16 Feb 43, in *Panzer Army Africa, Anlagenband 9, Anlage 1081 / 4*. The Gafsa operation by Rommel's *DAK* was termed *Unternehmen* Morgenluft (transl., code name Morning Air). (2) FO, *Panzer Army Africa*, Nr. 1, in *Panzer Army Africa, KTB, Anlagen, Band 8, Anlage 1028 / 1*.

Chapter 16

1 *NWAf,* 411; *AAD,* 336; "The Battle of Sidi bou Zid," n.d., Paul McD. Robinett Papers, Library of Congress, box 6; Waters, John Knight, Senior Officers Oral History Program, 193 ("*My error*").

2 *NWAf,* 411.

3 Ibid.

4 For example, the pincer movement around the Soviet forces behind Kiev; by the end of September 1941 the claws of the encircling movement had caught 520,000 Russian soldiers.

5 *NWAf,* 408, 412; *AAD,* 339–43; Hudel and Robinett, "The Tank Battle at Sidi bou Zid," in "Kasserine Pass Battles," n.d., vol. I, part 1, U.S. Army Center for Military History; James Lucas, *Panzer Army Africa*. San Rafael, CA: Presidio, 1977, 165; After Action Report, CCA Narrative of Events box 14767; *Tätigkeitsbericht, 10th Panzer Div.,* 14–22 Feb 1943, NARA RG 319, Office of the Chief of Military History, box 225; Ankrum, *Dogfaces,* 186 ("*Krupp Iron Works*"); *Kriegstagebuch, 21st Panzer Div.,* 14–23 Feb 1943, in "Kasserine Pass Battles," vol. I, part 2, U.S. Army Center for Military History ("*of fifty-two Shermans*"); Hudel and Robinett, supra.

6 Drake, *Factual Account,* 16.

7 *See* Ch. 15, Note 1 above.

8 *NWAf,* 411–12.

9 Drake, *Factual Account,* 16.

10 *AAD,* 343–4; Robert K. Waters, Senior Officer Oral History Program, U.S. Army Military Institute, 203–22; 596 ("*There must be something*"); After Action report, 2nd Bn, 168th Inf Regt, Feb 1943, IGSMM; "Kasserine Pass Battles," n.d., vol. I, part 1, U.S. Army Center for Military History; Blumenson, *Kasserine Pass,* 164–5.

11 Blumenson, "Kasserine Pass, 30 January – 22 February 1943." Chapter 8, *America's First Battles, 1776–196.,* 248.

12 *NWAf,* 412.

13 Ibid., and n. 27: Ltr, LTC Henry P. Ward to Colonel Charles E. Hart, 16 Feb 43, in 17th FA Regimental Hist.

14 Ibid., 412–13.

15 *AAD,* 339–43; Hudel and Robinett, supra; Lucas, *Panzer Army Africa,* 165; After Action Report, CCA Narrative of Events box 14767; *Tätigkeitsbericht, 10th Panzer Div.,* 14–22.

16 Drake, *Factual Account,* 17; *AAD,* 345–6.

17 Martin Blumenson. "The Agony and the Glory", *Infantry Magazine,* Vols 57–8, July–August 1967, 47. Online at: https://books.google.com/books/download/Infantry.pdf?id=bLjAK1jMt-FQC&hl=en&capid=AFLRE72FsFZfD4fDj5qWT-yf7ejFYJsyiIwtAkdPNuEO7Y8gdb2paOy-bjw8ZDfP-imqfXoul90bmhMlerertpWE4gKbtYd7irw&continue=https://books.google.com/books/download/Infantry.pdf%3Fid%3DbLjAK1jMtFQC%26output%3Dpdf%26hl%3Den (hereinafter cited as "Blumenson, 'The Agony and the Glory'").

18 *AAD,* 345; CCA Narrative of Events box 14767 ("*Drake soon recognized*").

19 Drake, *Factual Account,* 17; *AAD,* 345–6.

20 *AAD*, 344.

21 Drake, *Factual Account*, 17–18; *AAD*, 344–5.

22 Drake, *Factual Account*, 17–18; *AAD*, 344–5; Blumenson, "The Agony and the Glory," 49.

23 Drake, *Factual Account*, 17–18; *AAD*, 344–5.

24 *NWAf*, 413, and n. 29: (1) *21st Panzer Div, KTB*, 14 Feb 43. (2) Memo. Col Drake for G-2 WD, 14 May [19]45, subject: Account of l68th Inf Opns 24 Dec 42 – 17 Feb 43. DRB AGO.

25 Ibid.

26 Ibid., 413.

27 *AAD*, 346; chronology, Eisenhower Papers, 956; Truscott, 155–6 ("*There was no reason*").

28 *AAD*, 345; Edgar P. Moschel, statement in "168th Inf Regt. Narrative of Action," n.d., IGSMM; Davis, Jr., Franklin M. "The Battle of Kasserine Pass," *American Legion*, Apr. 1965, 22 ("*It seems like*"); After action report accounts by Gerald C. Line, Thomas D. Drake, Harry P. Hoffman, in "Kasserine Pass Battles," vol. I, part 1, U.S. Army Center for Military History; Hougen, 51–3.

29 A photographic copy of Drake's handwritten message is set out in Hougen, at 52.

30 Ryder Papers, box 1, Letter, Thomas D. Drake to Charles W. Ryder, Oct. 4, 1944; Blumenson, "The Agony and the Glory," 49; *NWAf*, 413; *AAD*, 345–6; After Action Report, 3rd Bn, 168th Inf. Regt, Feb. 8–20, 1943, IGSMM; "Brief Statement of Lt. Col. John H. van Vliet, Jr.," in "168th Inf Regt Narrative of Action," IGSMM (see Appendix A, Documents, Document 6); After action report account, Marvin E. Williams, 3rd Bn, 168th Inf, "Kasserine Pass Battles," vol. I, part 1, U.S. Army Center for Military History; Blumenson, *Kasserine Pass*, 145.

31 *NWAf*, 413, and n. 30: Report by Gen Welvert, in *DMC Jnl*, 14 Feb 43.

32 Ibid., and fn. 31: Entries 303, 307, 309, 334, 335, and 353, in II Corps G-3 Jnl, 14 Feb 43; 168th Inf AAR, 12 Nov 42 – 15 May 43.

33 Ibid. 414, and n. 33: (1) Based on after action reports of CCA 1st Armed Div, 168th Inf, 3d Bn 1st Armd Regt, 1st Bn 6th Armd Inf, and Co A 70lst TD Bn. (2) M. Sgt. Clarence W. Coley, A Day With the 1st Armored Division, 6 Jul 51, in Howe, *1st Armored*, 150–3. (3) Info supplied by Gen McQuillin, 13 Jan 51. OCMH.

34 *AAD*, 346; David W. Hazen, "Role of the Field Artillery in the Battle of Kasserine Pass," Master's thesis, U.S. Army Command and Staff College, 1973, 42, 48–54; William R. Betson, "Sidi bou Zid—A Case History of Failure," *Armor*, Nov.–Dec. 1982, 38; message, D. D. Eisenhower to GCM, Feb. 15, 1943, in Eisenhower Papers, Vol. 5, 956; After action report, 60th Inf Regt. (9ID), Feb. 1943, NARA RG 407, E 427, box 7535.

35 *NWAf*, 415–16, and fn. 35: *Gefechtsbericht Faïd.*

36 Ibid., 416–17.

37 Ibid., 415 and fn. 34: (1) Report by Col Hains, 12 Mar 43, and Report by Col Hightower, 1 Jul 46, in 1st Armored Div Hist Records. (2) *10th Panzer Div*, Ic, *Taetigkeitsbericht*, 14 Feb 43, lists the following Allied losses: 71 prisoners, 40 tanks, 7 armored personnel carriers, 15 self-propelled mounts, 1 anti-tank gun, 9 machine guns, 1 prime mover, 4 trucks, and 18 other vehicles. (3) The initial estimate of Combat Command A's losses in personnel after the fights at Sidi bou Zid and Sbeïtla on 14 and 15 February were 62 officers and 1,536 enlisted men killed, wounded, or missing in action (see Msg, G-3 1st Armd Div to G-3 II Corps, 0745, 16 Feb 43, Entry 116 in II Corps G-3 Jnl). Of these, 573 were 1st Armored Division troops (see 1st Armd Div G- 3 Jnl, 14 Feb 43). The balance was largely troops of 168IR.

38 *AAD*, 342–3, 349; After action report, "Operations of 3rd Bn, 1st Armored Regt," Feb 14, 1943, NARA RG 407, E 427, box 14916; Harold V. Boyle, Associated Press, account of "Texas," *Cavalry Journal*, March–April 1943, 12; Howe, *1st Armored*, 150–3; Louis V. Hightower, DSC Citation, NARA RG 492, NATOUSA General Orders; Blumenson, *Kasserine Pass*, 141–2; Charles J. Hoy, "Reconnaissance Lessons from Tunisia," *Cavalry Journal*, Nov.–Dec., 1943, 16–19 ("*A battlefield*

bromide"); Ben Crosby, oral history, March 1951, G. F. Howe, Sidney Matthews Papers, MHI ("*badly used up*"); Edgar P. Moschel, statement in "168th Inf Regt. Narrative of Action," n.d., IGSMM.

39   *NWAf,* 417, and fn. 36: (1) *DMC Jnl,* 14 Feb 43. (2) Phone Convs, Fredendall to Ward, 1250 and 1305, 14 Feb 43, Entries 318 and 330; Phone Conv, Anderson to Fredendall, 1300, 14 Feb, Entry 329; Radio, Adv First Army to II Corps, 14 Feb 43, Entry 346. II Corps G-3 Jnl.

40   Ibid.

41   Ibid., 418, and fn. 39: Msg, II Corps to CG 1st Armd Div, 2010, 14 Feb 43, Entry 369, in II Corps G-3 Jnl.

42   *AAD,* 349–50; Letter, Robinett to H. Gardiner, Dec 26, 1967, Paul McD. Robinett Papers, G. C. Marshall Library, box 5, folder 21 ("*mood of benighted denial*").

43   *NWAf,* 418, and fn. 40: (1) *XIX Corps Jnl,* 14 Feb 43. (2) 19th Engr Regt (C). Hist Records, Oct 42 – Jan 44; and fn. 41: Msg 0-409, Adv CP First Army to II Corps, 14 Feb 43. AFHQ CofS Cable Log, 96; *AAD,* 349–50.

44   *AAD,* 349–50.

45   *AAD,* 349–50; First Army to II Corps, Feb 14, 1943, 2010 hrs, NARA RG 331, AFHQ micro, AFHQ G-3 Forward, R-100-D, 319.1 ("*As regards action*"); George F. Hoffman and Donn A. Starry, eds., *Camp Colt to Desert Storm: The History of U.S. Armored Forces.* Lexington, KY: University Press of Kentucky, 1999, 151; O. Ward diary, Feb 15, 1943, Oliver Ward Papers, MHI; Paul McDonald Robinett, *Armor Command.* Washington, D.C.: McGregor & Werner, 1958, 163 ("*saluted and smiled*") (hereinafter cited as Robinett, *Armor Command*).

46   See Bruce Catton, *A Stillness at Appomattox,* New York: Doubleday, 1953, 211. Catton wrote of Meade's ineptness in July 1864 in handling the assaults on the rebel defenses in front of Petersburg: "[Meade's] angry complaint on the fourth day, that since he had found it impossible to co-ordinate attacks each commander should go ahead and do the best he could on his own hook, went far to merit the comment it got from General [Horatio] Wright—that the different attacks had been ordered '*without brains and without generalship.*'" *A Stillness at Appomattox,* 211, n. 16 (citing Dana, Charles A., *Recollections of the Civil War,* New York, 1898, 227). The same could well be said of the counterattack at Sidi Bou Zid ordered by the Allied generals on February 15, 1943.

47   *NWAf,* 418–19, and fn. 42: Msg CG II Corps to CO 1st Armd Div, 1120, 15 Feb 43. Entry 17, in II Corps G-3 Jnl; and fn. 43: Original in CCC 1st Armd Div Opns Jnl, Feb 43.

48   Ibid., 419, and fn. 44: Msg, Lt Col Hamilton H. Howze to CCC, 1st Armd Div, 1350, 15 Feb 43, and Phone Conf, Cols Williams, Hamlett, and Arnold, 1900, 14 Feb 43, in II Corps G-3 Jnl.

49   Ibid., and fn. 45: See II Corps G-3 Jnl, 1420, 15 Feb 43, Entry 28.

50   *AAD,* 350–1.

51   *AAD,* 350–1; Edwin H. Burba, "Battle of Sidi bou Zid," *Field Artillery Journal,* Sept. 1943, 643; "The Attack on Sidi bou Zid," 2nd Bn, 1st Armored Regt, "By officers of the battalion while POWs," n.d., James D. Alger Collection, USMA Archives; "Record of Events," 2nd Bn appendix to After Action Report, 1st Armored Regt, North African campaign, Nov 8, 1942 – May 8, 1943, NARA RG 407, E427, box 14916.

52   *NWAf,* 419.

53   *NWAf,* 419–21; *AAD,* 351; "Record of Events," 2nd Bn appendix to After Action Report, 1st Armored Regt, North African campaign, Nov 8, 1942 – May 8, 1943, NARA RG 407, E427, box 14916; Howze, Hamilton, "The Battle of Sidi bou Zid," lecture, MHI; Howe, *1st Armored,* 159; war diary, *10th Pz. Div.,* Feb 15, 1943, "Kasserine Pass Battles," Vol. I, part 2, U.S. Army Center for Military History; "G-3 Journal," and message traffic, 1st AD, Feb 15, 1943, NARA RG 407, E 427, box 14767 ("*Tanks now approaching*" and "*Keep your eyes peeled*").

54   *NWAf,* 420, and fn. 48: Msg, CG, 1st Armored Div to CCC, 1422, 15 Feb 43, in CCC Jnl.

55   Ernie Pyle, Radio broadcast, March 2, 1942, The Tunisian Front. *Reporting World War II: Part One: American Journalism 1938–1944.* New York: Literary Classics of the United States, Inc. 1995, 545. (Hereinafter cited as *Reporting WWII Pt. One.*).

56   *NWAf,* 420.

57   Ibid., and fn. 46: CCC, 1st Armored Div Jnl, 15 Feb 43.

58   Ibid., and fn. 47: (I) *Gefechtsbericht Faid,* IS Feb 43. (2) George F. Howe interview with Col Hains, 26 Apr 51.

59   Ernie Pyle, Scripps Howard wire copy, March 3, 1943, The Tunisian Front. *Reporting WWII Pt. One,* 547–8.

60   *AAD,* 351; Rame, *Road to Tunis,* 247–8 ("*Within a matter of minutes*"); Ernie Pyle, *Here is Your War.* New York: Henry Holt, 1943, 170 ("*Brown geysers*") (hereinafter cited as Pyle, *Here is Your War*).

61   *NWAf,* 421.

62   Ibid., 420–1.

63   *NWAf,* 421; *AAD,* 352.

64   *NWAf,* 421, *AAD,* 352.

65   *AAD,* 352.

66   *NWAf,* 421.

67   *AAD,* 352; "Record of Events," 2nd Bn appendix to After action report, 1st Armored Regt, North African campaign, Nov. 8, 1942 – May 8, 1943, NARA RG 407, E427, box 14916 ("*None returned*").

68   *NWAf,* 421, and fn. 49: (1) CCC 1st Armored Div Journal, 15 Feb 43. (2) *10th Panzer Div,* Ic, *Taetigkeitsbericht,* 15 Feb 43. (3) Ltr, Col Drake to Gen Ward, 15 Jan 51. OCMH. (4) G. Howe interview with Col Hains, 26 Apr 51. (5) Rpt by Lt Col James D. Alger, The Attack on Sidi Bou Zid by the 2nd Battalion, 1st Armored Regiment, 15 Feb 43. In private possession.

69   Ibid., 421–2, and fn. 50: (1) Msg, CO, CCC to G-3 1st Armored Div, 1348, 16 Feb 43, in CCC, 1st Armored Div Jnl. (2) *10th Panzer Div,* Ic, *Taetigkeitsbericht,* 15 Feb 43. (3) The estimate of U.S. losses at 0325, 16 February, by G-3, 1st Armored Division, was 46 medium and 2 light tanks, 130 vehicles, and 9 self-propelled 105mm guns. II Corps G-3 Jnl, 16 Feb 43; Entries 76 and 87. (4) See sketch map, Howe, *1st Armored Division,* 164.

70   *NWAf,* 415; *AAD,* 352–3; Howe, *1st Armored Division,* 163–5.

71   *NWAf,* 422, and fn. 52: (1) Lt Col James D. Alger, The Attack on Sidi Bou Zid by the 2nd Battalion, 1st Armored Regiment, 15 Feb 43. MS, in private possession. (2) *10th Panzer Div,* Ic, *Taetigkeitsbericht,* 15 Feb 43.

Chapter 17

1   *NWAf,* 423, and fn. 1: Msg 0-420, Anderson to Eisenhower, 15 Feb 43. AFHQ CofS Cable Log, 100.

2   Ibid., 423, and fn. 2: Dir, CG, First Army to CG, II Corps, 1700, 15 Feb 43, Entry 121, in II Corps G-3 Jnl.

3   Ibid., 424, and fn. 3: Msg 254, Truscott to Eisenhower, 16 Feb 43, reporting views of Maj Gen Sir Richard L. McCreery, CofS designate of 18 Army Gp. AFHQ CofS Cable Log.

4   Ibid., 422, and fn. 51: Phone Conversation, Gen Ward with Col Akers, 2220, 15 Feb 43, Entry 65, in II Corps G-3 Jnl.

5   *NWAf,* 424; *AAD,* 353–4; *Des Moines Sunday Register,* July 18, 1943, 1; After Action Report, 2nd Bn, 168th Inf Regt, Feb 3–19, 1943, "Kasserine Pass Battles," vol. I, part 1, U.S. Army Center for Military History; Austin, *Birth of an Army,* 87 ("*message okay*").

6   *NWAf*, 424; *AAD*, 353–4; *Des Moines Sunday Register*, July 18, 1943, 1; After Action Report, 2nd
     Bn, 168th Inf Regt, Feb 3–19, 1943, "Kasserine Pass Battles," vol. I, part 1, U.S. Army Center for
     Military History; After Action Report, 2nd Bn, 168th Inf Regt, Feb 15–16, 1943, Iowa GSMM,
     (*"at 10:30 p.m.* and *"so close"*); Norland Norgaard, AP dispatch in *Red Oak Express*, Feb 22, 1943,
     1; Hougen; Eugene. L. Daniels, DSC Citation, NATOUSA General Order 66, July 30, 1943,
     NARA RG 492.

7   *NWAf*, 424; *AAD*, 354; *Des Moines Sunday Register*, July 18, 1943, 1; After Action Report, 2nd
     Bn, 168th Inf Regt, Feb 3–19, 1943, "Kasserine Pass Battles," vol. I, part 1, U.S. Army Center
     for Military History.

8   *NWAf*, 424., and fn. 4: (1) CCC 1st Armored Div Jnl, 16 Feb 43. (2) *10th Panzer Div.* Ic.
     Taetigkeitsbericht, 16 Feb 43.

9   Truscott, 157–8, 52–3.

10   Blumenson, "The Agony and the Glory," 50.

11   Drake, *Factual Account*, 18–19 and Incl. 1, Brief Statement of van Vliet (see Appendix A,
     Documents, Document 6); Blumenson, "The Agony and the Glory," 50; *AAD*, 354–5; After
     Action Report account, Marvin E. Williams, 3rd Bn. 168th Inf., "Kasserine Pass Battles," vol. I,
     part 1, U.S. Army Center for Military History; Ryder Papers, box 1, Letter, Thomas D. Drake
     to Charles W. Ryder, Oct. 4, 1944.

12   Drake, *Factual Account*, 19; *AAD*, 354.

13   Drake, *Factual Account*, 20.

14   Drake, *Factual Account*, Brief Statement of Lt. Col. John H. Van Vliet, Jr.; *AAD*. 355.

15   Blumenson, "The Agony and the Glory," 50.

16   Ibid.

17   Ibid.

18   Drake, *Factual Account*, 20–1; *AAD*, 355.

19   Drake, *Factual Account*, 21; Drake, *Factual Account*, Inclosure 1, Van Vliet Statement, 1; Blumenson,
     "The Agony and the Glory," 49, 50.

20   Drake, *Factual Account*, 21.

21   *AAD*, 355.

22   Drake, *Factual Account*, 21–2.

23   *AAD*, 354–7; After Action Report, Harry Hoffman, 3rd Bn, 168th Inf Regt, IGSMM; Ann Larson,
     ed., "The History and Contribution to American Democracy of Volunteer 'Citizen Soldiers' of
     Southwest Iowa, 1930–1945," 1981. National Endowment of the Humanities, 57–8, 61–3,
     66–7; After action report, 3rd Bn, 168th Inf Regt, Feb 16–17, 1943, IGSMM; Bill Roth, "The
     Longest Days of a G.I.," n.d., IGSMM (*"We marched"* and *"Whenever the moon"*); R. Atkinson
     interviews of Clifton J. Warner and of Ross W. Cline, Oct. 19, 1993 (*"Dawn caught them"*).

24   *AAD*, 356.

25   Blumenson, "The Agony and the Glory," 50–1.

26   Blumenson, "The Agony and the Glory," 50–1; *AAD*, 356.

27   Drake, *Factual Account*, 21–2 (*"gained the desired ground"*); Blumenson, "The Agony and the
     Glory," 50–1; *AAD*, 356.

28   Drake, *Factual Account*, 21–2 and Incl. 1: Brief Statement of van Vliet; Blumenson, "The Agony
     and the Glory," 51 (*"compliment your command"*); *NWAf*, 424 and fn. 5: (1) Report of Activities
     of the 168th Infantry in the Sidi Bou Zid Area, 14–17 February 1943, 27 Feb 43, by four officers
     who escaped, in 168th Inf Hist, Jan – Feb 43. (2) Memo, Col Drake for G-2 WD 14 May 1945,
     sub: Account of 168th Inf Opns 22 Dec 42 – 17 Feb 43. DRB AGO; *AAD*, 354–7.

29   Drake, *Factual Account*, 22–3 (see Appendix A, Documents, Document 6); *AAD*, 354–7; After
     Action Report, Marvin E. Williams, 3rd Bn, 168th Inf, "Kasserine Pass Battles," vol. I, part 1,

U.S. Army Center for Military History; Ryder Papers, box 1, Letter, Thomas D. Drake to Charles W. Ryder, Oct 4, 1944 (see Appendix A, Documents, Document 6); *Tätigkeitsbericht, 10th Panzer Div.*, Feb 16, 1943, NARA RG 319, Office of the Chief of Military History, box 225; After action report, "168th Inf Regiment Narrative of Action," IGSMM; Blumenson, *Kasserine Pass*, 196, 199; *Kriegstagebuch, 21st Panzer Div.*, Feb 17, 1943, "Kasserine Pass Battles," vol. I, part 2, U.S. Army Center for Military History; After action report accounts, G.C. Line, T.D. Drake, "Kasserine Pass Battles," vol. I, part 1, U.S. Army Center for Military History; "Brief statement of Lt. Col. John H. Van Vliet, Jr.," appended as Inclusion 1 to Drake, Factual Account; After Action Report, Harry Hoffman, 3rd Bn, 168th Inf Regt, IGSMM; Ann Larson, ed., "The History and Contribution to American Democracy of Volunteer 'Citizen Soldiers' of Southwest Iowa, 1930–1945," 1981. National Endowment of the Humanities, 57–8, 61–3, 66–7; William Walling Luttrell, "A Personal Account of the Experiences as a German Prisoner of War, typescript, n.d., IGSMM; letter, Gerald C. Cline to wife, March 2, 1943, IGSMM, #1999.25.2.

30 Blumenson, "The Agony and the Glory," 52.

31 Drake, *Factual Account*, 23–5 and Incl. 1: Brief Statement of van Vliet.

Chapter 18

1 *NWAf,* 424–5.

2 *NWAf,* 425–6; *AAD,* 357; "Signal Communication in the North Africa Campaigns," 1945, Historical Section, Special Activities Branch, Office of the Chief Signal Officer, "Tactical Communication in World War II, Part 1," MHI, 166 (*"unbelievably low"*); Philipsborn report to Robinett, CCB, 1st AD, Feb 16, 1943, NARA RG 407, E427; Howe, G.F., "American Signal Intelligence in Northwest Africa and Western Europe," 1980, U.S. Cryptologic History, series IV, WWII, vol. I, NARA RG 457, NSA files, SRH 391, box 114, 29–30; war diary (*Kriegstagebuch*), *Panzer Armee Afrika,* Feb 16, 1943, "Kasserine Pass Battles," vol. I, part 2 (mislabeled "Fifth Panzer Army"), U.S. Army Center for Military History; Playfair, *The Destruction of the Axis Forces in Africa,* 273, 292.

3 *NWAf,* 425 and fn. 8: (1) *Fifth Panzer Army,* KTB IV, 15, 16 Feb 43. (2) *Gefechtsbericht Faïd.*

4 Ibid., 426–7, and fn. 11: (1) *Panzer Army Africa, Kriegstagebuch, Band 2,* 17 Feb 43. (2) Rommel, *Krieg ohne Hass,* 352–3. (3) *Panzer Army Africa, KTB, Anlagenband 9 Anlage 1095*; and fn. 12: Msg, *Fifth Panzer Army,* von Arnim to *Comando Supremo,* 1935 hrs, 17 Feb 43, *Fifth Panzer Army, Ia, Kriegstagebuch, Anlagen, Geh. und Geh. Kdo. Sachen (Afrika), Band 2,* 281, and fn. 13: *Panzer Army Africa, KTB, Band 2,* 18 Feb 43 and Rpt, *DAK* to *Panzer Army Africa,* 18 Feb 43, in *KTB, Anlagenband 9, Anlage 1102/2.*

5 *NWAf,* 427–8.

6 Ibid., 428, and fn. 11: (1) Info supplied by Cabinet Office, London. (2) II Corps AAR, 2 May 43.

7 Ibid.

8 *NWAf,* 432; *AAD,* 362; Scott McCurtain, oral history, March 1976, Russell A. Gugeler, Orlando Ward Papers, MHI; diary, Feb 16, 1943, Orlando Ward Papers, MHI; Russell A. Gugeler, typescript, Unpublished biography of Orlando Ward, n.d., Orlando Ward Papers, MHI, X-85; CCA, "Narrative of Events from 23 January 1943 to 26 Feb.," NARA RG 407, E 427, 601-CCA-0.3, box 14825; Ben Crosby, oral history, March 1951, George F. Howe, Sidney Matthews Papers, MHI.

9 *NWAf,* 430 and fn. 15: Phone Conversation, Gen Ward with Col Akers, 16 Feb 43, Entry 109, in II Corps G-3 Jnl.

10 Ibid., and fn. 16: 1st Armored Div G-3 Jnl, 431 and fn. 21: (1) CCC 1st Armored Div S-3 Jnl, 16 Feb 43. (2) 6th Armored Inf AAR, 2 Sep 43; CCA 1st Armored Div AAR, 23 Jan – 26 Feb 43, 33–4.

11 Ibid., 430–1.

12 Ibid., 432.

13 Ibid.

14 Ibid., and fn. 23: (1) *21st Panzer Div, KTB*, 17 Feb 43. (2) CCC 1st Armored Div Jnl, 16–17 Feb 43. (3) CCB, 1st Armored Div AAR, 1 Mar 43.

15 *NWAf*, 432; *AAD*, 362–3; phone memos, Feb 16–17, 1943, Lucian K. Truscott Papers, George C. Marshall Library, box 9; L. K. Truscott, Jr., *Command Missions*, New York: E. P. Dutton, 1954, 159–62; Blumenson, *Kasserine Pass*, 191; Paul M. Robinett, "Comments on *Kasserine Pass* by Martin Blumenson," P. M. Robinett papers, MHI, 7; II Corps Provost Marshal journal, Feb 19, 1943, NARA RG 402, E 427, box 3126.

16 *NWAf*, 432–3, and fn. 24: See *NWAf*, 417–18. Stark's force included the 3rd Battalion, 26th Infantry, the 1st Ranger Battalion, the 175th Field Artillery Battalion (detached from 34ID), E & C Squadrons, British Derbyshire Yeomanry, French units of the Constantine Division, and, beginning February 8th, the 1st Battalion, 168th Infantry (detached from 34ID), held in Fériana as II Corps reserve. (1) Constantine Division Journal. (2) 168th Inf Hist. (3) 175th FA Bn. War Diary. (4) 1st Armored Div G-3 Jnl; *AAD*, 363–4; *Kriegstagebuch, 21st Panzer Div.*, Feb 16–17, 1943, "Kasserine Pass Battles," vol. I, part 2, U.S. Army Center for Military History; Howe, *1st Armored Division*, 172–3; war diary, *10th Panzer Div.*, Feb 17, 1943, "Kasserine Pass Battles," vol. I., part 2, U.S. Army Center for Military History.

17 Ibid., 434, and fn. 28: (1) *Gefechtsbericht Faïd*, 16–17 Feb 43. (2) *21st Panzer Div, KTB*, 16–17 Feb 43.

18 Ibid., 435, and fn. 30: (1) CCC, 1st Armored Div Journal, 17 Feb 43. (2) 6th Armored Inf AAR, 23 Jan – 26 Feb 43. (3) Howe Interview with Lt Col Jacob Shapiro (Ret.) (then CO, Co A, 13th Armored Regt), 7 Dec 51. (4) *21st Panzer Division, KTB*, 17 Feb 43.

19 *AAD*, 365.

20 Ibid.

21 *NWAf*, 434–6; *AAD*, 365–6; Robinett, *Armor Command*, 167–75; Howe, *1st Armored Division*, 175–9; CCB log, Feb. 17, 1943, NARA RG 407, E 427, 601-CCB-0.3, box 14825.

22 Ibid., 433, and fn. 25: (1) CCC, 1st Armored Div Jnl, 16–17 Feb 43. (2) Ltr, Col Hightower to Col Howze, 1 Jul 46. In private possession. (3) G. Howe Interviews with Col Hains, 26 Apr 51, and Col Crosby, 19 Mar 51. (4) Msg R-255, Truscott to Rooks for Eisenhower, 17 Feb 43. Copy in AFHQ CofS Cable Log, Ill. (5) Msg 0436, Adv First Army to II Corps, V Corps, and XIX Corps. Same file, 112, (6) DMC Jnl, 17 Feb 43.

23 Truscott, 162–3.

24 Truscott, 164.

25 *NWAf*, 434–6; *AAD*, 365–6; Robinett, *Armor Command*, 167–75; Howe, *1st Armored Division*, 175–9; CCB log, Feb. 17, 1943, NARA RG 407, E 427, 601-CCB-0.3, box 14825.

26 *AAD*, 366.

27 Ernie Pyle, Scripps Howard wire copy, March 3, 1942, The Tunisian Front. Reporting WWII Pt. One, 537("*You need feel*"); James Tobin, *Ernie Pyle's War*. Lawrence, KS: University Press of Kansas, 1997, 82 (hereinafter cited as Tobin, *Ernie Pyle's War*).

28 *AAD*, 366.

29 *NWAf*, 433, and fn. 26: (I) II Corps G-3 J nl and Msg file, (2) Msg 261, Truscott to Rooks, 17 Feb 43. Copy in AFHQ CofS Cable Log, 116.

Chapter 19

1   Ibid., 438 and fn. 1: (1) *Panzer Army Africa*, KTB, Band 2, 17, 18 Feb 43. (2) Rpt, *German-Italian Panzer Army* to *OB SÜD* (Kesselring), 17 Feb 43, in *Panzer Army Africa, KTB, Anlagenband 9, Anlage 1099/3*. (3) *Fifth Panzer Army, KTB IV*, 17, 18 Feb 43. (4) *Gefechtsbericht Faïd*, 17, 18 Feb 43.

2   Ibid., 438., and fn. 2: *Panzer Army Africa*, KTB, Band 2, 17 Feb 43.

3   Ibid., and fn. 3: (1) Msg, *German-Italian Panzer Army*, Rommel to *Comando Supremo* and *OB SÜD*, 1420, 18 Feb 43, in *Panzer Army Africa, KTB, Anlagenband 9, Anlage 1107*. (2) *Panzer Army Africa, KTB, Band 2*, 18 Feb 43.

4   Ibid., and fn. 4: (1) See *NWAf* 426–7. (2) [Foreign Military Studies] MS # C-07S (Kesselring). (3) [Foreign Military Studies] MS # D-309 (Deichmann).

5   Ibid., 439–40 and fn. 5: Radio, Kesselring to Rommel and von Arnim, 1630 18 Feb 43 in *Panzer Army Africa, KTB, Anlagenband 9, Anlage 1108*, and *Fifth Panzer Army, KTB, Anlagen, g. Kdos. (Chefsachen)*, 16.I-26.II.43, *Tunisien, Anlage 23/43*.

6   Ibid., 441–2, and fn. 13: (1) Minutes of confs between Kesselring, von Arnim, and others, 19 and 20 Feb 43, in *Fifth Panzer Army, KTB IV*, (2) [Foreign Military Studies] MS #C-075 (Kesselring). (3) [Foreign Military Studies] MS #T-3-P II (Kesselring), Pt. 2.

7   *NWAf.*, 440; *AAD*, 359–60; War diary, *Panzer Army Afrika*, Feb. 18, 1943, "Kasserine Pass Battles," vol. I, part 2, U.S. Army Center for Military History; Irving, *Trail of the Fox*, 270; Arnim, "Recollections of Tunisia," Foreign Military Studies, C-098, 55; minutes of conference with Kesselring, Arnim *et al.*, war diary, *10th Panzer Div.*, Feb. 15, 1943, "Kasserine Pass Battles," vol. I, part 2, U.S. Army Center for Military History; war diary, *Panzer Army Africa*, Feb. 18, 19, 1943, "Kasserine Pass Battles," vol. I, part 2, U.S. Army Center for Military History (*Kesselring dithered*).

8   *NWAf*, 440, and fn. 6: Radio, Rommel to *Comando Supremo*, 2230, 18 Feb 43, in *Panzer Army Africa, KTB, Anlagenband 9, Anlage 1109*.

9   Ibid., 440, and fn. 7: (1) Msg, *Comando Supremo* to Rommel and von Arnim, 2115, 18 Feb 43, in *Panzer Army Africa, KTB, Anlagenband 9, Anlage 1113/1*. (2) Msg, OB SÜD (Kesselring), *O Qu* [headquarters] to *Panzer Army Rommel*, 2030, 18 Feb 43, *ibid., Anlage 1113/2*. and fn. 8: citing Rommel, *Krieg ohne Hass*, 353–4.

10 *NWAf*, 440; *AAD*, 359–60; Liddell Hart, *The Rommel Papers*, 400, 402 ("*appalling and unbelievable*"); war diary, *Panzer Army Afrika*, Feb. 18, 1943; Irving, *Trail of the Fox*, 270; Arnim, "Recollections of Tunisia," Foreign Military Studies, C-098, 55; minutes of conference with Kesselring, Arnim *et al.*, war diary, *10th Panzer Div.*, Feb. 15, 1943, "Kasserine Pass Battles," vol. I, part 2, U.S. Army Center for Military History; war diary, *Panzer Army Afrika*, Feb. 18, 19, 1943, vol. I, part 2, U.S. Army Center for Military History.

11 *NWAf*, 441.

12 *NWAf*, 441, and fn. 9: Telephone orders, Rommel to Lt Col Stolbeck. *DAK*, Lt Col Pomptow, *Fifth Panzer Army*, and *Div Centauro*, all 19 Feb 43, in *Panzer Army Africa KTB, Anlagenband 9, Anlagen 1114/1,2,3,4* and *1121/1,2,3* and *1122/1*. The operation was named *STURMFLUT*.

13 Ibid., and fn. 10: *Panzer Army Africa, KTB, Anlagenband 9, Anlagen 1123, 1124, 1125*.

14 Ibid., 436, and fn. 33: (1) *Fifth Panzer Army, KTB IV*, 17 Feb 43. (2) *Gefechtsbericht Faïd*. (3) *10th Panzer Div*, Ic, *Taetigkeitsbericht*, 17 Feb 43, (4) XIX Corps *Journal de Marche*, 16–18 Feb 43.

15 Regimental History, 135IR (Musel)), IGSMM PDF file gs_4102.pdf, 38 of 103.

16 *NWAf*, 437 and fn. 34: Info supplied by Cabinet Office, London.

17 Ibid., 443 and fn. 14: (1) 133rd and 135th Inf Histories, 1943. (2) Info supplied by Cabinet Office, London. (3) XIX Corps Jnl, 17–19 Feb 43; and fn. 15: Info supplied by Cabinet Office,

London. Dunphie's command included Headquarters, 26th Armoured Brigade; the 2nd Battalion, Lothians; 10th Battalion, Royal Buffs (not at full strength); 17th/21st Lancers (not at full strength); Squadron A, 56th Reconnaissance Regiment; engineers and smaller artillery and anti-tank units.

18 Ibid., and fn. 16: Msg L-1, Liaison Officer First Army (Boye) to FAIRFIELD (Truscott) and FREEDOM (AFHQ, Eisenhower), 20 Feb 43. AFHQ CofS Cable Log.

19 Ibid., 452–3.

20 Ibid., 453.

21 *AAD*, 378.

22 *NWAf*, 459, and fn. 1. (1) Info supplied by Cabinet Office, London. (2) 135th Inf Hist, 1943. (3) 18th Inf AAR and Jnl, 16 Feb – 9 Mar 43. (4) Nigel Nicholson and Patrick Forbes. *The Grenadier Guards in the War of 1939–1945*, in two volumes. Aldershot.: Gale and Polden, vol. II, 281–2. (5) G. Howe interview with Brig Gen Benjamin F. Caffey, Jr., 21 Feb 50. (6) *21st Panzer Div*, KTB, 19–20 Feb 43.

23 Ibid., 453, and fn. 29: (1) *21st Panzer Div, KTB, I.I.-31.III.43,* 19 Feb 43. (2) 133rd Inf Hist. 7 Jun 43, and, in particular, AT Co 133rd Inf Hist, Jan – Jun 43. (3) Howe interview with Brig Gen Benjamin F. Caffey, Jr., 21 Feb 43. (4) *Journal de Marche de la Brigade Legere Mecanique* (Light Armored Brigade), 19 Feb 43. Photostat in OCMH [See NARA Record Group 319, Office of the Chief of Military History].

24 *NWAf*, 452–3; *AAD*, 377–8; war diary, *10th Panzer Div.*, Feb. 19, 1943, "Kasserine Pass Battles," vol. I, part 2, U.S. Army Center for Military History; Benjamin Caffey, oral history, Feb. 1950, G.F. Howe, Stanley T. Matthews Papers, U.S. Military History Institute; "18th Infantry, Draft Regimental Wartime History," Stanhope Mason Collection, McCormick Research Center, First Division Museum, Cantigny, Illinois; Camp, T. L., ed., "Tankers in Tunisia," 1943, Ft. Knox, KY. Armored Replacement Training Center, 23 ("*taking shoe boxes*"); "The Fragrance of Spring Was Heavy in the Air," account of 185 FA Bn, *Trail Tales*, Boone County (Iowa) Historical Society, No. 35, 1979, 37; Vernon Hohenberger, "Retracing My Footsteps in World War II," typescript, n.d., IGSMM, 37; "The Tunisian Campaign, 34th Division," IGSMM, 5.

25 *NWAf*, 459, and fn. 2: (1) *21st Panzer Div, KTB*, 19–21 Feb 43. (2) *Opns Order No.6*, 20 Feb 43, ibid., *Anlagenband 9.*

26 *135IR History (Breit))*, Phase III, 19–21; Blumenson, *Kasserine Pass*, 261.

27 *135IR History (Breit))*, Phase III, 19–21.

28 War diary, *Panzer Army Africa*, Feb. 30, 1943, vol. I, part 2, U.S. Army Center for Military History, 159.

Chapter 20

1 *NWAf*, 348, 446 ("crudely corrugated"); *AAD*, p. 366.

2 *NWAf*, 446.

3 *AAD*, 367.

4 *AAD*, 367–8.

5 *NWAf*, 447; Blumenson, *Kasserine Pass*, 257.

6 *AAD*, 369; History of the 26th Infantry, 8/14–16 ("*Pull a Stonewall Jackson*"); letter, Stark to O. Ward, Jan. 28, 1951, Oliver Ward Papers, U.S. Army Military Institute.

7 *NWAf*, 453.

8 Ibid., 453, and fn. 30: (1) *DAK, KTB*, 19 Feb 43. (2) *Panzer Army Africa, KTB 2*, 19–20 Feb 43.

9 *NWAf*, 451–2; *AAD*, 370–1; "Historical Record of the 19th Engineer Regiment," Oct. 1942 – Oct. 1943, NARA RG 407, E 427, box 19248; After Action Report, 2nd Bn, 19th Engineers, NARA

RG 407, E 427, box 19248; Hans von Luck, *Panzer Commander*, New York, Praeger, 1989, 113; war diary, *[Deutsche] Afrika Corps*, Feb. 19, 1943, "Kasserine Pass Battles," vol. 1, part 2; Franklin M. Davis, Jr., "The Battle of Kasserine Pass," *American Legion Magazine* (April 1965), 22; History of the 26th Infantry, 8/19; John Ellis, *On the Front Lines*, London: John Wiley, 1991, 89 (*Nebelwerfer*); II Corps Provost Marshal journal, report from William A. Seitz, Co. A, 26th Inf, n.d., NARA RG 407, E 427, box 3126 (Arab brigands).

10   *NWAf,* 457

11   *NWAf,* 454–5; *AAD*, 371–2 History of the 26th Infantry, 8/22–25; Blumenson, *Kasserine Pass*, 249–52, 255 (*"casualties among infantrymen"*); "Historical Record of the 19th Engineer Regiment," Oct. 1942 – Oct. 1943, NARA RG 407, E 427, box 19248; After action report, 2nd Bn, 19th Engineers, NARA RG 407, E 427, box 19248.

Chapter 21

1   *NWAf,* 458, and fn. 38: (1) CCB, 1st Armored Div AAR, 1 Mar 43. (2) Info supplied to G. Howe by Brigadier Dunphie, Sep. 1951.

2   Ibid., 457–8.

3   Ibid., 458, and fn. 37: Msgs, CG II Corps to Col Stark, Brig Dunphie, and Gen Robinett, 20 Feb 43, Entries 419, 420, and 421, in II Corps G-3 Jnl.

4   Ibid.

5   Ibid., and fn. 3: (1) Erwin Rommel, *Krieg ohne Hass*, 355ff. (2) [Foreign Military Studies] MS # T-3-P II (Kesselring), Pt. 2. (3) [Foreign Military Studies] MS # C-066 (Kesselring).

6   Ibid., 461 and fn. 4: (1) CCB, 1st Armored Div AAR, 1 Mar 43. ... (4) II Corps AAR, 3 May 43. (5) Rpt by Lt Col John T. Honeycutt, 21 Feb 43, Entry 164, in II Corps G-3 Jnl.

7   Ibid., 463 and fn. 7: (1) 1st Inf Div G-3 Opns Rpt, 15 Jan – 8 Apr 43, Annex 6. (2) Memo with Ltr, Col Crawford to George Howe, 27 June 51. (3) Robinett, "Among the First," MS, 412–13. (4) Battle Report, 3rd Bn 16th Inf to CO 16th Inf, 8 Mar 43, in 1st Inf Div AAR. (5) CCB, 1st Armored Div S-3 Jn1, 22 Feb 43.

8   Ibid., 461–2, and fn. 5: Rommel, *Krieg ohne Hass*, 360.

9   Ibid., 458, 460, 461, 462, and fn. 6: (1) *DAK*, KTB, 21 Feb 43. (2) Msg, *German Italian Panzer Army* to *DAK*, 21 Feb 43, in *Panzer Army Africa, KTB, Anlagenband 9, Anlage 1151/3.* (3) Msg, *German Italian Panzer Army* to *580th Rcn Bn*, 21 Feb 43, ibid., *Anlage 1151/4*, 463–4; *AAD*, 379–80; Stanhope Mason and F. W. Gibb, oral history, April 26, 1951, G. F. Howe, Sidney Matthews Papers, MHI; Hazen, David W. "Role of the Field Artillery in the Battle of Kasserine Pass," Master's thesis, U.S. Army Command and Staff College, 1973, 104; Robinett, *Armor Command*, 181, 183; Howe, *1st Armored Division*, 191; "Combat Command B, Operations Report, Bahiret Foussana Valley, 20–25 February, 1943," "Kasserine Pass Battles," vol. I, part 2, U.S. Army Center for Military History; II Corps, "report of operations," May 2, 1943, "Kasserine Pass Battles," vol. I, part 2, U.S. Army Center for Military History; Macksey, *Crucible of Power*, 166.

10 *NWAf,* 463–4; *AAD*, 380–1; Paul McD. Robinett, "The Axis Offensive in Central Tunisia, Feb. 1943," lecture, Library of Congress Manuscript Division; Robinett, *Armor Command*, 185, 187; Paul McD. Robinett, "Comments on *Kasserine* Pass by Martin Blumenson," Paul McD. Robinett Papers, U.S. Military History Institute, 13; Blumenson, *Kasserine Pass*, 279.

11 *NWAf,* 463–4; *AAD*, 380–1; Clift Andrus, notes on Omar Bradley's *A Soldier's Story*, n.d., Cantigny, IL: McCormick Research Center, First Division Museum, (*"An artilleryman's dream"*); Clift Andrus biographical file, compiled by Albert H. Smith, MHI (*"most skillful and practical"*); "Combat Command B, Operations Report, Bahiret Foussana Valley, 20–25 February, 1943," "Kasserine Pass Battles," vol. I, part 2, U.S. Army Center for Military History (*"A single battalion"*).

12 *NWAf,* 464, and fn. 10: *DAK KTB,* 22 Feb 43.

13 *NWAf,* 463–4, and fn.9: *DAK, KTB,* 22 Feb 43 *AAD,* 380–1.

14 War diary, *Panzer Army Africa,* Feb. 18, 19, 1943, "Kasserine Pass Battles," vol. I, part 2, U.S. Army Center for Military History, 103–4, 162, 165.

15 *NWAf,* 458, and fn. 39: (1) Msg, Maj W. B. Chase to Adv CP First Army, Entry 359, in II Corps G-3 Jnl. (2) Robinett, "Among the First," MS. In private possession. (3) Info supplied by Cabinet Office, London; *AAD,* 382–3; Charles Messenger, *The Tunisian Campaign.* Shepperton: Ian Allan, 1982, 54 (hereinafter cited as "Messenger, *The Tunisian Campaign*"); Irving, *Trail of the Fox,* 274; intelligence report, "Re the advance of the *10th Panzer Division* through the Faïd Pass to Thala," Feb. 25, 1943, NARA RG 319, Office of the Chief of Military History, box 225; memorandum, S. L. Irwin to P. M. Robinett, June 23, 1949, NARA RG 319, Office of the Chief of Military History, box 229 (*"usual story"*); Nigel Nicholson, *Alex: The Life of Field Marshal Earl Alexander of Tunis.* New York: Atheneum, 1973, 176 (*"He's right behind us"*).

16 *NWAf,* 465.

17 *NWAf,* 465; *AAD* 383–4.

18 *NWAf,* 465 and fn. 11. (1) Rommel, *Krieg ohne Hass,* 359. (2) Info supplied to G. Howe by Cabinet Office, London; *AAD,* 383–4.

19 *NWAf,* 465–6; *AAD,* 382–4; Dunphie memorandum, forwarded to G. F. Howe from Cabinet Office historical section, Sep. 11, 1951, NARA RG 319, Office of the Chief of Military History, box 229 (*inter alia, "tank fight in the dark"*); Gregory Blaxland, *Alexander's Generals.* London: William Kimber, 1979, 163 (hereinafter cited as "Blaxland"), ffrench Blake, 17th/21st Lancers, 119; "D.G.A." "With Tanks to Tunis." *Blackwood's* (U.K. magazine, June 1945) 399 passim (*inter alia, "two thousand yards"*); Macksey, *Crucible of Power,* 169; *Tätigkeitsbericht, 10th Panzer Div.,* Feb. 21, 1943, NARA RG 319, Office of the Chief of Military History, box 225; Heller and Stofft, eds., *America's First Battles, 1776–1965,* 259; Blumenson, *Kasserine Pass,* 270–5.

20 *NWAf,* 467 and fn. 14. (1) Msgs, 22 Feb 43, Entries 145, 147, and 152, in II Corps G-3 Jnl (2) Info supplied by Cabinet Office, London. (3) *10th Panzer Div,* Ic, *Taetigkeitsbericht,* 22 Feb 43.

21 Ibid., 470–1

22 *NWAf,* 466.

23 *AAD,* 385–7; Dunphie memorandum, forwarded to G. F. Howe from Cabinet Office historical section, Sep. 11, 1951, NARA RG 319, Office of the Chief of Military History, box 229 (*"Irwin himself"*); memorandum, S. L. Irwin to P. M. Robinett, June 23, 1949, NARA RG 319, Office of the Chief of Military History, box 229 (*"extremely critical"*); Stafford Irwin, oral history, January, 1950, G. F. Howe, Sidney Matthews Papers, MHI; After Action Report, "Thala Engagement, 21–24 Feb. 1943," 9th ID Artillery, n.d., NARA RG 407; E 427, box 7424; After Action Report, 60th FA, n.d., NARA RG 407, E 427, box 7471; Blumenson, *Kasserine Pass,* 275.

24 Ibid., 472–3

25 Charles Whiting, *Disaster at Kasserine.* London: Secker & Warburg Ltd., 1984. Republished by Leo Cooper, an imprint of Pen & Sword Books, Ltd. Barnsley, S. Yorkshire, UK, 2003, 176–8; Brian J. Murray. "Facing the Fox," *America in World War II* (April 2006 issue), 28–35; NWAF, 473, G. Howe interview of Ernest Harmon, September 15, 1952.

26 *NWAf,* 466, and fn. 12: (1) G. Howe Interview with Major General Stafford LeRoy Irwin, 25 Jan 1950. (2) 60th Inf Regt Hist, 1943, 1–5. (3) Division Artillery Report, Thala Engagement, in 9th Div AAR. (4) AFHQ G-3 Rpts 100–7.

27 Ibid., 466, and fn. 13. 13th Armored Regt Operations Jnl, 0845, 22 Feb 43.

28 *AAD,* 385–7; Stafford Irwin, oral history, January 1950, G. F. Howe, Sidney Matthews Papers, MHI; After Action Report, "Thala Engagement, 21–24 Feb. 1943," 9th ID Artillery, n.d., NARA RG 407; E 427, box 7424; After Action Report, 60th FA, n.d., NARA RG 407, E 427, box 7471.

29 *NWAf,* 469, and fn. 21: Daily Report for 22 Feb 43, *Fifth Panzer Army* to *Panzer Army Africa,* 1005, 23 Feb 43, in *Panzer Army Africa, KTB, Anlagenband 9, Anlage 1159.*
30 Ibid., and fn. 22: *Panzer Army Africa,* KTB 2, 22 Feb 43.
31 Ibid., ("The field marshal had shot"); *NWAf,* 470 and fn. 23: (1) Daily Rpt for 22 Feb 43, *German-Italian Panzer Army,* 0030, 23 Feb 43, in *Panzer Army Africa, KTB, Anlagenband 9, Anlage 1163.* (2) [Foreign Military Studies] MS # C-066 (Kesselring). (3) Radio, *Comando Supremo,* Ambrosio to Rommel and others, 2310, 22 Feb 43, translated in *Panzer Army Africa, KTB, Anlagenband 9, Anlage 1162.*
32 Ibid., 467 and fn. 15.
33 Ibid., and fn. 16: Compilation of sorties from *KTB, Fliko, Ic,* in *10th Panzer Div, Ic, TB Anlagen, 29.XI.42-J5, III.43.*
34 Ibid., and fn. 17: *10th Panzer Div, Ic, Taetigkeitsbericht,* 22 Feb 43.
35 *AAD,* 385–7; Liddell Hart, *The Rommel Papers,* 406–7; A. Kesselring, "The Events in Tunisia," 1949, Foreign Military Studies, #D-066; MHI, 5–10; After Action Report, *Panzer Army Africa,* Feb. 22, 1943, NARA RG 319, Office of the Chief of Military History, box 225; A. Kesselring, "The War in the Mediterranean, Part II, The Fighting in Tunisia and Tripolitania," Foreign Military Studies, MHI, #T-3, P1, 38; "Narrative of Events, Thala Engagement, 21–24 Feb. 1943," 9th ID artillery, March 4, 1943, "Kasserine Pass Battles," vol. I, part 1, U.S. Army Center for Military History; A. Kesselring, "Final Commentaries on the Campaign in North Africa," Foreign Military Studies, #C-075, U.S. Army Military Institute, appendix, 14; After Action Report, *Panzer Army Africa,* Feb. 22, 1943, NARA RG 319, Office of the Chief of Military History, box 225 ("*The enemy follows only hesitantly*").
36 *NWAf,* 470–1, fn. 28: Compilation of sorties, *KTB, Fliko, Ie,* in *10th Panzer Div, Ie, TB Anlagen,* 29.XI.42-15.III.43.
37 *AAD,* 387; D. D. Eisenhower to Fredendall, Feb. 22, 1943, Eisenhower Papers, 980; DDE, 145 ("*perfectly safe*"); "American Signal Intelligence in Northwest Africa," U.S. Cryptologic History, series IV, vol. 1, NARA RG 457, NSA files, SRH 391, box 114, 29–30; Blumenson, *Kasserine Pass,* 282.
38 AAD, 387–9; Truscott, 170–2; After Action Report, "The Tunisian Campaign, 34th Division," [Dec. 13, 1943, NARA RG 407, E 427, 334-0.3]; 5; E. Harmon, oral history, Sep. 1952, G. F. Howe, Sidney Matthews Papers, MHI; Harmon, Ernest, with Milton MacKaye and William Ross MacKaye, *Combat Commander,* Englewood Cliffs, NJ: Prentice-Hall, 1970; 50, 111–16 (hereinafter cited as "Harmon"); "Report of General Harmon on taking command of II Corps as deputy," n.d., L.K. Truscott Jr. Papers, G. C. Marshall Library, box 9.
39 *NWAf,* 474 and fn. 35: (1) II Corps AAR, 2 May 43. (2) CCB, 1st Armored Div. AAR, 20–25 Feb 43. (3) Info supplied to G. Howe by Cabinet Office, London. (4) Memo by Gen. Ward, in 1st Armored Div. Hist Records, Vol. II. (5) Ward, Personal Diary, 22–25 Feb 43. In private possession. (6) Robinett, "Among the First," Mss., 430–2.

Chapter 22

1 *AAD,* 389–90.
2 Ibid., 395–8; articles in *Red Oak* (Iowa) *Express, Villisca* (Iowa) *Review, Clarinda* (Iowa) *Herald Journal, Council Bluffs Nonpareil,* February – April, 1943; Larson: *Volunteers,* 43; "War Hits Red Oak" *Life,* May 3, 1943, 26 (see https://books.google.com/books?id=500EAAAAMBAJ&print-sec=frontcover&source=gbs_ge_summary_r&cad=0#v=onepage&q&f=false)
3 *NWAf,* 478.
4 Ibid.

5   *AAD*, 390.
6   Truscott, 537–8.
7   DDE, 146.
8   *AAD*, 391.
9   Fussell, *Wartime*, 1–2.
10 *NWAf*, 478.
11 Ibid., 478–9, and fn. 46: In *Krieg ohne Haas*, 357, Rommel wrote of the defense at Djebel el Hamra and the western Foussana Bahiret valley: "*Die Amerikaner hatten sich vorzüglich geschlagen.*" [Tr. "The Americans had fought well [or 'excellently']."]
12 Ibid., 479 and see fn. 47: See [Foreign Military Studies] MS # C-075 (Kesselring) and [Foreign Military Studies] MS # D-309 (Deichmann).
13 *AAD*, 377.
14 Ibid., 391–2.
15 *NWAf*, 479.
16 Ibid., 479–81 and fn. 48: These observations are derived from several sources: (1) Msg 2771, Eisenhower to Marshall, 24 Feb 43, CinC AF Diary. (2) Interview, 1st Lt H. F. Hillenmeyer with Maj Gen Omar Bradley. OPD 381 Africa Sec 3, Case 96. (3) Observer's Rpt, Lt Col Boyd Hubbard, Jr., via Brig Gen John E. Hull to Gen Arnold, 19 Apr 43. OPD 381 Africa Sec 3, Case 97. (4) Ltr, Eisenhower to Handy, 20 Mar 43. OPD Exec 3, Item 1a.
17 *AAD*, 398.

Chapter 23

1   *NWAf*, 475 and fn. 36: (1) Alexander, *The African Campaign*, 870. (2) Radio, *Comando Supremo*, Ambrosio to Rommel and von Arnim, 1530, 23 Feb 43, in *Panzer Army Africa, KTB, Anlagenband 9, Anlage 1172*; see *NWAf*, 485, 509–19.
2   Ibid., 475.
3   Ibid., 485.
4   Ibid., and fn. 1: Alexander, *The African Campaign*.
5   Ibid., and fn. 2: (1) Note of War Room Mtg, 22 Jan 43, AFHQ G-3 Ops 58/2.1, Micro Job 10C. Reel 1880, (2) AFHQ Opn Memo 30 (rev.). 18 Feb 43. (3) Dir, 17 Feb 43. printed in Alexander, *The African Campaign*, App. B, 885–6.
6   Ibid., 486 and fn. 3: (1) 18 Army Gp Staff Appointments List, 27 Feb 43 and Mar 43. AFHQ Micro Job 10A, Reel 6C. (2) History of Allied Force Headquarters and Headquarters NATOUSA, December 1942 – December 1943, Pt. II, 110–16, 324–6. DRB AGO. (3) Memo, G-3 AFHQ for CofS AFHQ, 30 Jan 43, sub: Army Gp Hq. AFHQ Micro Job 10A, Reel 6C. (4) Alexander, *The African Campaign*. (5) Interviews, Field Marshal Alexander with Sidney Mathews, 10–15 Jan 49. In private possession.
7   Ibid., 486–7. The chain of command was in the form shown at *NWAf*, 749 [Chart 2 – Allied Command Relationships in the Mediterranean, March 1943.]
8   Ibid., 487.
9   Ibid., 489, and fn. 7: (1) DDE, 147. (2) CinC AF Diary, 20 Feb 43, Bk. V, A-236. (3) Msg 1977, FREEDOM to TROOPERS, 20 Feb 43; Msg 65014, TROOPERS to FREEDOM, 20 Feb 43. ETOUSA Incoming and Outgoing Cables, Kansas City Records Ctr.
10 *AAD*, 399–400; E. A. Mockler-Ferryman, typescript, n.d., Liddell Hart Center for Military Archives, King's College, London, 129–35 (*First to go*); Robinett, "The Axis Offensive in Central Tunisia, Feb. 1943," lecture ("*professional graveyard*").
11 See Ch. 7, Note 84, supra.

12 *AAD*, 399–400; Butcher diary, DDE Presidential Library, A-250 (*"voicing regret"*); D. D. Eisenhower to Fredendall, Feb. 20 and March 2, 1943, Eisenhower Papers, 969, 1002; Benjamin S. Persons, *Relieved of Command*. Manhattan, KS: Sunflower University Press, 1997, 2; Harmon, 50, 120 (*"no damned good"*); Ernest Harmon, oral history, G. F. Howe, Sidney Matthews Papers, MHI (*"common, low"*); Martin Blumenson, ed., *The Patton Papers, 1940–1945*. New York: Da Capo Press, 1996, 177 (*"coward"*), 181; Truscott, 173; Alexander, oral history, Sidney Matthews Papers, MHI; Omar N. Bradley, *A Soldier's Story*. New York: Henry Holt, 1951, 42 (hereinafter cited as "Bradley, *Soldier's Story*"); Eisenhower to Marshall, March 3 and 4, 1943, Eisenhower Papers, 1006–7; W.B. Smith, oral history, May 12, 1947, G.F. Howe, Sidney Matthews Papers, MHI (*"a good colonel"*).

13 *NWAf*, 487.

14 *NWAf*, 487 and fn. 5: (1) Interviews, Alexander by Sidney Mathews, 10–15 Jan 49. (2) CinC AF Diary, 1–5 Mar 43. (3) Msg 4267, Eisenhower to Marshall, 4 Mar 43: Msg 4580, Eisenhower to Marshall, 5 Mar 43: Msg 3471, Marshall to Eisenhower, 8 Mar 43. Smith Papers. (4) Gen Ward, Personal Diary, 1–5 Mar 43. In private possession; Bradley, *Soldier's Story*, 41–8.

15 *NWAf*, 488–9, and fn. 6: CinC AF Diary, 7 Mar 43, Bk. V, 270–1.

16 Bradley, *Soldier's Story*, 43 (*"with sirens shrieking"*), 44.

17 *AAD*, 402.

18 Martin Blumenson, *Patton: The Man Behind the Legend, 1885–1945*. New York: William Morrow, 1985, 183 (hereinafter cited as Blumenson, *Patton*) (*"Determined and energetic"*).

19 *NWAf*, 488–9, and fn. 6: CinC AF Diary, 7 Mar 43, Bk. V, 270–1.*AAD*, 400–3; D. D. Eisenhower to G. C. Marshall, March 11, 1943, Eisenhower Papers, 1022; memo, D. D. Eisenhower to G. S. Patton, Jr., Eisenhower Papers, 1010; memo to AFHQ chief engineer, March 9, 1943, NARA, AFHQ micro, R-90-F (*"morale improved"*); letters, Theodore Roosevelt, Jr. to Eleanor, March 2, 6, 11, and 20, 1943, Theodore Roosevelt, Jr. Papers, Library of Congress, box 9.

Chapter 24

1 *NWAf*, 490.

2 Ibid., and fn. 9: (1) First Army Opn Instruc 19, 24 Feb 43. DRB AGO. (2) First Army Sitrep 123, 28 Feb 43; 18 Army Group Cositrep 7, 26 Feb 43. AFHQ CofS Cable Log. (3) DMC Jnl, 28 Feb 43. (4) By 17 March, French XIX Corps had a strength which approximated 53,800, including British units in the corps troops. See 18 A Group SD 1, 17 Mar 43. AFHQ Joint Rearmament Committee 370/001, and also in AFHQ G-3 (Ops) 37/13, Micro Job 10C, Reel 157F.

3 Ibid., 490.

4 Jack K. Johnson. "The Last Man's Club of Battery B." (article) ALLIES (newsletter), Spring 2010, Volume XVIII, No. 2. Military Historical Society of Minnesota, 4, fn. 3.

5 Fussell, *Wartime*, Chapter 7: *Chickenshit, an Anatomy*, 83 ("The literature of chickenshit is extensive, and not surprisingly, since so many authors-to-be were, in the services, precisely the types that are chickenshit's eternal targets, bright Jewish boys like Norman Mailer and Joseph Heller, or intelligent sarcastic kids from good colleges, like Kingsley Amis… One of the first American novels about the war, Robert Lowry's *Casualty* (1946) is about little but chickenshit, and its appearance the moment the war was over suggests the propellant of deep anger.").

6 *NWAf*, 492, and fn. 11: Bradley, *Soldier's Story*, 44–5.

7 In War Department parlance, an MOS identified an Army job which comprised one or more related duties and responsibilities normally requiring special knowledge and skills acquired through civilian training and experience supplemented by military training and experience, or military training and experience only. The War Department's table of MOSs for infantry weapons included:

...

1. Gunnery and Gunnery Control.

a. Light and Heavy Weapons (including organizational maintenance),

511 Armorer.

604 Light Machine Gunner.

605 Heavy Machine Gunner.

607 Light Mortar Crewman.

745 Rifleman.

746 Automatic Rifleman.

812 Heavy Weapons Crewman.

1607 Heavy Mortar Crewman.

1812 Light Weapons NCO

...

United States War Department Technical Manual TM12–427. *Military Occupational Classification of Enlisted Personnel.* Washington, D.C., 1945, 9.

8   Robert R. Palmer, *et al. U.S. Army in World War II: The Procurement and Training of Ground Combat Troops.* Washington, D.C.: Department of the Army, 1948, 170 ("*soldiers were viewed*"), 175, 181–3 ("*as one would buy*"); *AAD*, 403–4; Marvin A. Kreidberg and Merton G. Henry. *History of Military Mobilization in the United States Army, 1775–1945.* Washington, D.C.: Department of the Army, 1955, 647; letter, J. L. Devers to L. J. McNair, Feb. 4, 1944, NARA RG 165, Director of Plans and Ops, corr., box 1230; Ernest Harmon, "Notes on Combat Experience During the Tunisian and African Campaigns," in "Kasserine Pass Battles," vol. II, part 3, U.S. Army Center for Military History; report, Walton H. Walker, June 29, 1943, NARA 165, E 418, box 1229; "Activities of the G-1 Section During the Tunisian Campaign," 34th Infantry Division, no date, IGSMM; memo, from 5th Replacement Bn to II Corps, Apr. 12, 1943, NARA RG 492, MTO, special staff, box 1043; report #42, March 13, 1943, NARA RG 337, Observer Reports, box 52.

9   Hans Pols. "War Neurosis, Adjustment Problems in Veterans, and an Ill Nation: The Disciplinary Project of American Psychiatry during and after World War II." Source: Osiris, Second Series, Vol. 22, The Self as Project: Politics and the Human Sciences (2007), 72–92. Published by: The University of Chicago Press on behalf of The History of Science Society. JSTOR Stable URL: http://www.jstor.org/stable/40206990.

10 *AAD*, 404–6; Russell Hill, *Desert Conquest.* New York: Knopf, 1943, 235 ("*a bit windy*"); Roy R. Grinker and John P. Siegel. *War Neuroses in North Africa.* U.S. Army, 1943, 14–15, 31, 38, 59, 63, 71, 232–4 [Roy R. Grinker and John P. Spiegel, War Neuroses (Philadelphia, 1945). First published in 1943 as Roy Grinker and John P. Spiegel, War Neuroses in North Africa: The Tunisian Campaign (New York: Josiah Macy, Jr. Foundation for the Air Surgeon, Army Air Forces), (1943); see also: Grinker, Roy R., Lt. Col., M.C., USA and John P. Spiegel, Maj., M.C., USA. *War Neuroses.* Philadelphia: The Blakiston Company, Inc., 1982] (hereinafter cited as "Grinker, *War Neuroses*"); Eisenhower to Patton, April 12, 1943, NARA RG 94, II Corps, box 3161 ("*increasing number*").

11 Ernie Pyle, Scripps Howard wire copy, March 3, 1942, The Tunisian Front. Reporting WWII: Part One, 548 (emphasis supplied).

12 *AAD*, 404–6; Donald Vining, ed. *American Diaries of World War II.* New York: Pepys Press, 1982, 53; Grinker, *War Neuroses*, 59, 63, 71, 232–4; Albert E. Cowdrey, *Fighting for Life: American Military Medicine in World War II.* New York. Free Press, 1994, 137–44; "Casualties, Wounded, and Wounds, 1946–7," G-3 Section, Army Field Forces, NARA RG 337, file 704, series 10, box 46; Paul Wanke, "American Military Psychiatry and Its Role Among Ground Forces in World War II." *Journal of Military History* 63, no. 1. 127–46; Michael D. Doubler, *Closing With the*

Enemy. Lawrence, KS: University Press of Kansas, 1994, 243–4 (hereinafter cited as "Doubler, *Closing With the Enemy*").

13   *AAD*, 404–6; Philip G. Cochran, oral history, USAF Historical Research Center, 106 ("*Am I becoming uncourageous?*").

14   *AAD*, 404–6.

15   Ernie Pyle, Scripps Howard wire copy, April 22, 1943, Northern Tunisia. Reporting WWII Pt. One, 549.

16   Ernie Pyle, Scripps Howard wire copy, February 9, 1943, "A Forward Airdrome in French North Africa." Reporting WWII Pt. One, 530–1 ("*animates them*"); *AAD*, 461–2; Pyle, *Here is Your War*, 106 ("*they lost*"), 241–2; "Report on Operation 15 March – 10 Apr. 1943, II Corps, Combined Arms Research Library, Fort Leavenworth, Kansas, N-2652A ("*nearly six thousand casualties*"); G-2 summary #7, Apr. 19, 1943, II Corps, NARA RG 407, E427, box 7334.

Chapter 25

1   Col. Randy A. Smith, "The Technologically Hollow Force of the 21st Century." *Air Force Journal of Logistics*, Vol. 23, No. 2, Summer 1999, 10.

2   United States War Department. FM 7-30 Infantry Field Manual: Supply and Evacuation: The Infantry Regiment; Service Company and Medical Detachment. USGPO Washington, D.C., 1944, 3.

3   *AAD*, 413.

4   *NWAf*, 495, and fn. 17: (1) Hist of AFHQ and NATOUSA, Pt. II., 240–5 (2) General Eisenhower's directive as theater commander is Message ZRH—2624, AGWAR to FREEDOM, 20 February 1943. OPD Msg Center File.

5   Ibid., 495–6.

6   Ibid., 496, and fn. 20: U.S. II Corps was under First Army until 2400, 8 Mar 42, thereafter under 18 Army Group. Information supplied to G. Howe by the British Cabinet Office, London.

7   Ibid., 496–7.

8   Ibid., 498, and fn, 22: Trans Sec EBS NATOUSA, 22 Feb – 30 Apr 43, 7–8. Office of the Chief of Transportation ("OCT") HB.

9   Ibid., and fn. 23: citing report of Maj Arthur G. Siegle, OCT, 9 Apr 43.

10 Ibid., and fn. 24: (1) Memo, Brig Gen Carl R. Gray, Jr., for Deputy Chief of Trans NATOUSA, 1 May 43, cited in H. H. Dunham, U.S. Army Transportation and the Conquest of North Africa, 1942–1943, History Unit, OCT, Jan 45, 208. (2) Joseph Bykofsky and Harold Larson. *United States Army in World War II: The Technical Services. The Transportation Corps: Operation Overseas.* Washington, D.C. Center for Military History, U.S. Army, 1990. (hereinafter cited as Bykofsky, *The Transportation Corps*).

11 Ibid., and fn. 25: Memo, Lt Col Edwin C. Greiner for Brig Gen Robert H. Wylie, 3 Feb 43, sub: Cargo for UGS 5-A: Memo, Gen Wylie for Gen Styer, 25 Feb 43, sub: Cargo shipped on UGS 5 1/2 OCT HB.

12 Initially called the Services of Supply, the name of the command was changed to Army Service Forces by War Department General Orders 14, 12 March 1943. It is best known by this designation, which was used from 1943 to 1946. John D. Millett, Ph.D. *United States Army in World War II: The Army Service Forces: The Organization and Role of the Army Service Forces.* Washington, D.C.: United States Army, Center for Military History, 1987 [1954] (hereinafter cited as *Army Service Forces*), 1, fn. 1.

13 *Army Service Forces*, 63–4, fn 19: Log, Somervell's Party, 24–29 Jan 43, Hq ASF, Casablanca Conf, 1943 (Jan – Feb); Min of conf at Hotel St. George, 25 Jan 43, Hq ASF, North African

Theater; Richard M. Leighton and Robert Coakley, *United States Army in World War II, Global Logistics and Strategy, 1940–1943*, Center of Military History, United States Army. Washington, D.C. (1995) (hereinafter cited as *Global Logistics 1940–43*), 51 (1) Ltr. Eisenhower to Handy, 7 Dec 42, Item 1, Exec 5. (2) Min, 57th–58th mtgs CCS, 15–16 Jan 43. (3) Min cited n. 48(2).

14 *Army Service Forces*, 63–4; *Global Logistics* 1940–43, 475, and fn. 52 (1) Min cited n. 48(2). (2) Diary, 4 Dec 42, 27 Jan 43 entries, and passim, cited n. 21(7). (3) Msg 7428, AGWAR to Styer [from Somervell, signed Eisenhower], 26 Jan 43, Hist Mat, Mediterranean Campaigns folder, Plng Div ASF. (4) See Table 14.

15 *Global Logistics 1940–43*, 475, and fn. 53: Msg, CofS SOS to Somervell, 29 Jan 43, copy in History of the Planning Division, ASF, App. 4A, OCMH.

16 *Global Logistics 1940–43*, 475; Army Service Forces, 64, and fn. 41: Msgs, 26, 29 Jan 43, Hq ASF. See also DDE, 148–9.

17 *AAD*, 413–14.

18 *NWAf*, 498, and fn. 26: (1) Trans Sec EBS NATOUSA Hist Records. 22 Feb – 30 Apr 43, 12. (2) H.H. Dunham, *U.S. Army Transportation and the Conquest of North Africa. 1942–1943.* Hist Unit OCT, Jan 45, 263, 266, 268.

19 Ibid., 398–9, and fn. 27: Dunham, *U.S. Army Transportation and the Conquest of North Africa. 1942–1943.* History Unit, OCT, Jan 45, 269; and fn. 28: in March, 146,000 tons were discharged in Moroccan ports and 220,000 tons in Oran, Arzew, and Mostaganem. Chiefly by reshipment, 91,000 tons came into Philippeville.

20 Bykofsky, *The Transportation Corps*, 148; *Global Logistics* 1940–1943, 485; *AAD*, 413–14; Martin van Creveld, *Supplying War*, Cambridge: Cambridge University Press, 1977, 201 (*Rommel famously observed*); 601st Ordnance Battalion, unit history, MHI; Logistical History of NATOUSA/MTOUSA, n.d., NARA RG 407, AG WWII Operations Reports, 95-AL1-4, box 203; quartermaster memo, n.d., NARA RG 319, OCMH, box 225; John Ellis, *Brute Force: Allied Strategy and Tactics in the Second World War*, New York: Viking, 1990, 298 (*II Corps lost more armor*); "Signal Communications in the North African Campaigns," from "Tactical Communications in World War II," part I, Historical Section, Chief Signal Officer, U.S. Army Military Institute, 120 (*500 miles*); Andrew T. McNamara, Quartermaster Activities of II Corps. Fort Lee, VA: U.S. Army, 1955, 60 (new shoes), 70; Logistical History of NATOUSA/MTOUSA, n.d., NARA RG 407, AG WWII Operations Reports, 95-AL1-4, box 203, 82.

21 *Global Logistics 1940–43*, 477–8.

22 *AAD*, 414–15; Ellis, *Brute Force*, 525 (*overwhelms them*); Donald Davison, "Aviation Engineers in the Battle of Tunisia," Orlando, FL: Army Air Forces School of Applied Tactics, 1943, MHI, 12; Alfred M. Beck, *et al. The Corps of Engineers: The War Against Germany. US Army in World War II*. Washington, D.C.: U.S. Army Center for Military History, 1985, 90.

23 Ibid., 415–16 ("pioneered modern military logistics;" "alarms from Africa grew shrill"); Matthew Cooper. *The German Army 1939–1945*. Lanham, MD: Scarborough House, 1980, 262–3 ("wanted to be stronger than mere facts").

Chapter 26

1 *NWAf*, 501–2, and fn. 4: These tanks had just arrived at Tunis for shipment to *21st Panzer Division. Fifth Panzer Army*, *KTB*, 24 Feb 43.

2 Ibid., 502.

3 Ibid., 505–6.

4 Ibid., 507, and fn 10: (1) Info supplied by Cabinet Office, London. (2) XIX Corps Jnl, 28 Feb – 1 Mar 43. (3) *Fifth Panzer Army*, *KTB IV* and *V*, 26 Feb – 4 Mar 43.

5 Ibid., 508 and fn. 12: (1) *Fifth Panzer Army, KTB IV* and *V*, 26 Feb – 2 Mar 43. (2) [Foreign Military Studies] MS # T-3 (Nehring *et al.*), Vol. 3a, Pt. II, Ch. II I. (3) Info supplied by Cabinet Office, London.

6 Ibid., and fn. 14: (1) Radio, Lang to Weber, 0935, 1 Mar 43, in *334th InfDiv, KTB 1, Anlagenband IV*. (2) *Fifth Panzer Army, KTB V*, 1 Mar 43.

7 Ibid., and fn. 15: Conf, von Arnim with Gause, Chief of Staff, *Army Group Africa*, at Sfax, 6 Mar 43, in *Fifth Panzer Army, KTB V*, 6 Mar 43.

8 Ibid.

9 Regimental History, 135IR (Musel), IGSMM PDF file gs_4102.pdf, 39 of 103.

10 Maj Roland Anderson. *Operations of 135th Infantry, 34th Division, in the vicinity of Fonduk (sic) el Okbi, North Africa, 26 March – 11 April 1943 (Tunisian Campaign)*, (MS, 1947). Donovan Research Library, U.S. Army Command and Staff College, Fort Leavenworth, Kansas, 10 (hereinafter cited as Anderson, *Opns. 135th Inf. Fondouk*). (One of 135th Infantry Regiment's supply officers, Roland Anderson, wrote the monograph about the operations of the Regiment at Fondouk as part of his work in the Advanced Infantry Officers Course at The Infantry School, Fort Benning, Georgia, during 1947–1948. The supporting units were the 125th FA Bn., a platoon of anti-aircraft guns from the 107th AAA Bn., a company of the 751st Tank Destroyer Battalion, a platoon from 813th Tank Destroyer Battalion, the 34th Cavalry Reconnaissance Troop, and 4 squads of 'pioneers' and demolition personnel from 109th Engineers. *The Story of the 34th Infantry Division, Louisiana to Pisa*, Book I, 11; Anderson, *Opns. 135th Inf. Fondouk*, 10.

11 *Story of the 34th Infantry Division, Louisiana to Pisa* Book I, 11; *NWAf*, 509, and fn. 17: (2) The German troops holding this sector were part of *Gruppe Fullriede*, a provisional unit, which had replaced the *47th Grenadier Regiment* when the latter was pulled out and moved north in support of Arnim's offensive of 26 February. The Germans claimed to have destroyed two American tanks and several vehicles. See *Fifth Panzer Army, KTB V*, 5 Mar. 43.

12 *Story of the 34th Infantry Division, Louisiana to Pisa* Book I, 11–12; Anderson, *Opns. 135th Inf. Fondouk*, 11.

13 *NWAf*, 519–20, and fn. 36: (1) Louis P. Lochner, ed. and transl., *The Goebbels Diaries, 1942–1943*. New York: Doubleday, 1948, 352, 369. (2) [Foreign Military Studies] MS # C-065a (Greiner), 10 Mar 43. (3) Telegrams, von Arnim to Rommel, 0345, 10 Mar, 1045, 10 Mar, 0455, 14 Mar, 1620, 13 Mar 43, and Ltr, Rommel to von Arnim, 12 Mar 43, in EAP 21-a-14/7.

Chapter 27

1 Ibid., 547–8.

2 *Story of the 34th Infantry Division, Louisiana to Pisa* Book I, 12–13; Anderson, *Opns. 135th Inf. Fondouk*, 12.

3 *NWAf*, 564–5.

4 Ibid., 577.

5 Ibid., 578–9 and fn. 1: 18 A Gp Opn Instruc 9, 25 Mar 43. AFHQ Micro Job10A, Reel 6C; and fn. 2: The staff of the 34th Division was as follows: commanding general, General Ryder; assistant division commander, General Benjamin F. Caffey; chief of staff, Col. Norman E. Hendrickson; G-1, Lt. Col. Thomas L. Gaines; G-2, Lt. Col. Hubert Demarais; G-3, Lt. Col. Robert B. Neely; G-4, Lt. Col. Walter W. Wendt; artillery, Brig. Gen. Albert C. Stanford; and fn. 3 (1) Memo, CG 34th Inf Div for CG II Corps, 25 Mar 43, sub: Opn Plan, with copy of outline plan annexed, Entry 321, in II Corps G-3 Jnl. (2) G. Howe interview with Gen Ryder, 21 Feb 1950.

6   Ibid., 579, and fn. 4: Northwest of Pichon, the French XIX Corps (*Divisions Mathenet* and *Welvert*—also known as the *Constantine Division*) were to push across the Ousseltia valley at this time.

7   *AAD*, 468; "G-2 Report on Tunisian Campaign," June 12, 1943, 34th ID, IGSMM; Gustav. von Vaerst, "Operations of the Fifth Panzer Army in Tunisia." n.d. U.S. Army European Command, Foreign Military Studies, D-001, MHI, 18; Hans J. T. von Arnim, "Recollections of Tunisia." Transl. Janet E. Dewey. U.S. Army European Command, Foreign Military Studies, C-098, 91.

8   Anderson, *Opns. 135th Inf. Fondouk*, 13.

9   *NWAf*, 580–1, and fn. 6: (1) *999th Africa Division, KTB, Anlagenband 2 Einsatz TUNIS*, 26.III.-12.V.43, and maps in *Anlagenband 3*. (2) AFHQ G-2 Rpts, 8–9 Apr 43. (3) Daily Sitrep, 26 Mar 43, in *Fifth Panzer Army, KTB, Anlagenband V A, Anlage 117 A. 2*.

10   Hougen, 59.

11   See Appendix A, Documents, Document 7, Ryder Letter to Officers of 34th Infantry Division re Offensive Spirit, March 11, 1943.

12   *AAD*, 469–70; Ryder, Charles, Oral history, Feb. 21, 1950, Sidney Matthews Papers, MHI ("*go out in that area*"); "The Tunisian Campaign, 34th ID, Dec. 13, 1943, NARA RG 407, E 427, 334-0.3; Ryder Papers, box 2, Ryder personal 201 file, msg. "to all officers of the 34th Div., 11 March 1943," ("*creeping paralysis*"); Clem Miller, *Some Things You Never Forget*. Superior, WI: Savage Press, 1996. 109 (hereinafter cited as Miller, *Some Things*); Davies, *To the Last Man*, 103–7; Hougen, 59–60; After Action Report, 109th Medical Battalion, n.d., in "109th Medical Battalion Publications," IGSMM.

13   *Story of the 34th Infantry Division, Louisiana to Pisa*, 14.

14   Anderson, *Opns. 135th Inf. Fondouk*, 13.

15   *NWAf*, 579–80, and fn. 5: (1) 135th Inf Hist, Sec. IV, 9–11. (2) 133rd Inf Hist, 7 Jun 43, Incl I, 11–13, and Incl 2, 4–5. (3) Geographical Sec Gen Staff Map 4225, Sheet 70 (1:50,000). (4) G. Howe Interview with Col. Ward, 30 Nov. 1950; Anderson, *Opns. 135th Inf. Fondouk*, 12.

16   *Story of the 34th Infantry Division, Louisiana to Pisa*, 14.

17   *NWAf*, 581, and fn. 7: 34th Div FO 34, 26 Mar 43.

18   Anderson, *Opns. 135th Inf. Fondouk*, 13.

19   *NWAf*, 581.

20   *Story of the 34th Infantry Division, Louisiana to Pisa*, 14.

21   Ibid.

22   *135th Inf. Rgt. History (Breit, IGSMM)*, (hereinafter cited as *135IR History (Breit)*), Phase IV, 1–2; Anderson, *Opns. 135th Inf. Fondouk*, 13.

23   *NWAf*, 581.

24   *135IR History (Breit)*, Phase IV, 1–2.

25   *AAD*, 470.

26   See, Regimental History, 135IR (Musel), IGSMM PDF file gs_4102.pdf, 49 of 103.

27   *NWAf*, 581.

28   Ibid., 581, and fn. 8: (1) 135th Inf Hist, Sec. IV, 9–11. (2) 168th Inf Hist, 12 Nov 42 to 15 May 43, 38–9. (3) G. Howe Interview with Col Ward, 30 Nov 1950. (4) Memo, Col Ward for Gen. Ward, 22 Jan 51. OCMH.

29   *135IR History (Breit)*, Phase IV, 1–2; Regimental History, 135IR (Musel), IGSMM PDF file gs_4102.pdf, 41 of 103.

30   *AAD*, 470.

31   Ibid.

32   *NWAf*, 582.

33 Ibid., and fn. 9: (2) 751st Tank Bn (M) AAR, 30 Apr 43. The force consisted of Company C, 751st Tank Battalion; Company A, 813th Tank Destroyer Battalion; one motorized company of the 109th Combat Engineers.

34 *Story of the 34th Infantry Division*, Book I, 14–15; *135IR History (Breit)*, Phase IV, 2.

35 *NWAf*, 582, and fn. 12: (1) 34th Inf Div G-3 Periodic Reports 48, 31 Mar 43, and 49, 1 Apr 43. (2) 168th Inf Hist, 12 Nov 42 – 15 May 43, reported casualties as follows: killed, 17; wounded, 108; missing, 178.

36 *Story of the 34th Infantry Division, Louisiana to Pisa* Book I, 15; *135IR History (Breit)*, Phase IV, 2.

37 *NWAf*, 582 and fn. 10: (1) G. Howe Interview with Gen. Benjamin F. Caffey, 21 Feb 1950. (2) Ltr., Lt Col Donald C. Landon to G. Howe, 17 June 51; and fn. 11: *999th Africa Division, KTB, Anlagenband 2, Einsatz TUNIS 26.III.-12.V.43, Rpt Nr. 4* (Capt Retzlaff), *Sec. III*.

38 *Story of the 34th Infantry Division, Louisiana to Pisa* Book I, 14–15.

39 Arnold N. Brandt, "The Operations of the 1st Battalion, 135th Infantry Regiment at Hills 609 and 531," Ft. Benning, Georgia, Infantry School, 1948, 11 (hereinafter cited as "Brandt").

40 *NWAf*, 582; *Story of the 34th Infantry Division, Louisiana to Pisa*, 15.

Chapter 28

1 *AAD*, 470; Walter Nehring, Foreign Military Studies, MS T-3, vol. 3a, United States Army Military History Institute; Macksey, *Crucible of Power*, 149–53.

2 *NWAf*, 582–3, and fn. 13: Rpt, Brig Sugden to G-3 AFHQ, 7 Apr 43, sub: Conv between Sugden and Gen McCreery, 6 Apr; Memo, Col James F. Torrence, Jr., for G-3 AFHQ, 3 Apr 43. AFHQ G-3 Ops, Micro Job 10A, Reel 6C.

3 Anderson, *Operations 135th Inf. Fondouk*, 18–19.

4 *Story of the 34th Infantry Division, Louisiana to Pisa* Book I, 15.

5 In addition to its organic artillery and service units, the British 6th Armoured Division was constituted as follows during the Second Battle of Fondouk:

26th Armoured Brigade:
16th/5th Lancers
17th/21st Lancers
2nd Lothians and Border Horse
10th Battalion, Rifle Brigade (Prince Consort's Own)

1st Guards Brigade:
3rd Battalion, Grenadier Guards
2nd Battalion, Coldstream Guards
3rd Battalion, Welsh Guards

6 *NWAf*, 583, and fn. 14: Some German officers who took part in the operation later stated to their Allied captors that a maximum effort at Fondouk el Aouareb and by Eighth Army north of Sfax could have shortened the war in Tunisia by one month. [Foreign Military Studies] MS. # T-3 (Nehring *et al.*), Vol. 3a.

7 Ibid., and fn. 15: For former objective, see Colonel Torrence's Memo of 3 April based on 2 April conference with General McCreery and Brigadier Holmes; for the latter, Brigadier Sugden's report of 7 April after talking with McCreery. Both cited in endnote 2 above.

8   Craven, V., 5–6.

9   Ibid., 26.

10   Ibid.

11   Ibid., 25.

12   Ibid., 24–5.

13   Ibid., 7. See Craven, V., Map D, which shows what CPT Craven recalled to be the position of I Company, and of 133IR, in the second attack on Dj El Haouareb.

14   *NWAf,* 583, and fn. 16:(1) General Crocker visited the area for ground reconnaissance presumably on 1 April, Msg, 18 A Gp to II Corps, 1826, 31 Mar 43, Entry 159, in II Corps G-3 Jnl.

15   Ibid., and fn. 16: (2) G. Howe Interview with Gen Ryder, 21 Feb 1950.

16   Ibid., 583.

17   Ibid., 585.

18   *See* Shelby Foote, *The Civil War: A Narrative: Fredericksburg to Meridian.* New York: Random House, 1963, 528–31.

19   *NWAf,* 583–5; *AAD,* 471–2; "The Tunisian Campaign, 34th ID," Dec. 13, 1943, NARA RG 407, E427, 334-0.3; Ryder, Charles, Oral History, Sidney Matthews Papers, MHI; Caffey, Benjamin, Oral History, Feb. 1950, Sidney Matthews Papers, MHI (Ryder's plan); Playfair, *The Destruction of the Axis Forces in Africa,* 377–80; Harold G. Bull, Oral History, Sep. 21, 1950, Sidney Matthews Papers, MHI; Louis-Marie Koeltz, "Memo on meeting held on April 6, 1943 at the command post of General Ryder," 1950, NARA RG 319, Office of the Chief of Military History, box 225; Robinett, *Armor Command,* 126; Gen. Harold R. L. G. Alexander, Oral History, Sidney Matthews Papers, MHI; letter, J. T. Crocker, Sep. 8, 1950, and memo, Gordon H. A. MacMillan, n.d., in memo, H. B. Latham, Cabinet Office Historical Section, to G. F. Howe, Sept. 25, 1950, NARA RG 319, Office of the Chief of Military History, box 229.

20   *NWAf,* 586 and fn. 20: (1) G. Howe interviews with Gens Ryder and Bull, 21 Sept 1950. (2) Lieutenant General Koeltz, *Note établié de memoire sur la reunion tenue le 6 avril 1943 au P. C. du General Ryder,* 1950, NARA RG 319, Office of the Chief of Military History, box 225.

21   *AAD,* 471–2.

22   *NWAf,* 585–6.

23   Ibid., 585, and fn. 19: The then prevailing methods of tactical bombing support required that the troops remain west of a bomb line 2,000 yards, more than 1.1 miles, from the target. But the required safe distance substantially reduced the ability of the advancing troops to take advantage of the effect of the bombing on an entrenched enemy.

24   Ibid.

25   Ibid., and fn. 17: Br. IX Corps's Operations Order 2, 1100, 6 Apr 43, in 34th Div G-3 Journal.

26   Ibid., and fn. 18: (1) G. Howe Interviews with Generals Ryder, Caffey, and Bull, 21 Feb 1950. (2) Statement by Lt Gen Sir Gordon MacMillan, 4 Sep. 1950, based on his diary. OCMH. (3) Lieutenant General Koeltz, *Note établié de memoire sur la reunion tenue le 6 avril 1943 au P. C. du General Ryder,* J 950, NARA RG 319, Office of the Chief of Military History, box 225. (4) Info supplied by Cabinet Office, London. (5) 9 Corps Opn Order 2, 6 Apr 43. in 34th Div G-3 Journal.

27   *AAD,* 472; "The Tunisian Campaign, 34th ID," Dec. 13, 1943, NARA RG 407, 334-0.3.

28   *NWAf,* 586, and fn. 21: (1) 34th Div FO 30, 0830, 7 Apr 43, and amendments, 1130, 7 Apr 43. (2) G-S Msg File and Jnl, 34th Inf Div, 1–8 Apr 43; 133rd Regt Jnl, Apr   May 43. (3) Statement by Gen MacMillan, 4 Sep 50. 0CMH.

29   Ibid.

30   Ibid., and fn. 22: 34th Div FO 30, 0830, 7 Apr 43, with amendments, 2350, 7 Apr 43.

31 Craven, V., 7–8.

32 *AAD*, 472; citing JAG, 34th ID, "Historical Report on Activities,' June 30, 1943, IGSMM; "Chaplain's Report on the Tunisian Campaign," 34th ID, n.d., NARA RG 407, E 427, box 9417; Alexander to D. D. Eisenhower, Apr. 7, 1943, Alexander files, DDE Presidential Library, box 3, folder 8 ("*reasonably confident*"); Carlo D'Este, *Bitter Victory: The Battle for Sicily, July–August 1943*. New York: Harper-Perennial, 1992, 62 ("*soft, green*"); Robert Ward, Oral History, Nov. 30, 1950, G. F. Howe, Sidney Matthews papers, U.S. Army Military Institute ("*no one was saying*"); C. B. Hansen, draft of Omar N. Bradley's *A Soldier's Story*, U.S. Military Institute, 3/60-6 ("*brittle and axiomatic*"); Charles W. Ryder, Oral History, Feb. 21, 1950, Sidney Matthews papers, MHI ("*wished to win*").

33 Craven, V., 8–9.

34 Ibid., 9.

35 *AAD*, 472–3; see Craven, V., 6, 9–19; Ankrum: *Dogfaces*, 243, 250; Austin, *Birth of an Army*, 114; Bailey, *Through Hell*, 90; "D.G.A." "With Tanks to Tunis." *Blackwood's* (U.K. magazine, June 1945) 399.

36 *NWAf*, 587.

37 Survey of U.S. Army Uniforms, Weapons and Accoutrements, US Army Center of Military History: https://www.history.army.mil/html/museums/uniforms/survey_uwa.pdf

38 *AAD*, 473.

39 *Story of the 34th Infantry Division, Louisiana to Pisa* Book I, 15; *135IR History (Breit)*, Phase IV, 3; *A Partial History of 135IR (Rudolf)*, Landings at Oran, 9.

40 Craven, V., 10.

41 Ibid., 11.

42 *NWAf*, 586–7; *AAD*, 473; Milo L. Green and Paul S. Gauthier, *eds. Brickbats from F Company*. Corning, IA: Gauthier Publishing, 1982, 154 (hereinafter cited as Green, *Brickbats*); letter, Ray C. Fountain, *Des Moines Tribune*, Aug. 5, 1943, IGSMM; "Proposed Mission Against Fondouk Gap, Tunisia, On April 7, 1943," Air University Library, NARA RG 319, Office of the Chief of Military History, box 228; Richard G. Davis, *Carl A. Spaatz and the Air War in Europe*. Washington, D.C.: Center for Air Force History, 1993, 207.

43 *NWAf*, 587, and fn. 23: (1) 34th Div FO 30 with amendments. (2) Msgs, 8 Apr 43, in 34th Div G-3 Journal; (3) Interviews with Col Ward, 30 Nov. 1950. (4) Memo, Col Ward for Gen Ward, 22 Jan. 1951. OCMH. (5) Interviews with Gens Ryder and Caffey, 21 Feb. 1950; *Story of the 34th Infantry Division, Louisiana to Pisa* Book I, 15; *135IR History (Breit)*, Phase IV, 3; *A Partial History of 135IR (Rudolf)*, Landings at Oran, 9; Regimental History, 135IR (Musel)), IGSMM PDF file gs_4102.pdf, 42 of 103; Anderson, *Opns. 135th Inf. Fondouk*; Craven, V., 10–19.

44 *NWAf*, 587; Regimental History, 135IR (Musel)), IGSMM PDF file gs_4102.pdf, 42 of 103.

45 Craven, V., 12

46 Ibid., 13

47 Ibid., 13–14.

48 Jim Hook, Chambersburg Public Opinion, February 28, 2018. Richard Lohrens. "Days from age 98, WWII veteran is of two minds about war." https://www.publicopiniononline.com/story/news/2018/02/28/days-age-98-wwii-veteran-two-minds-war/383337002/.

49 Craven, V., 14–15.

50 Ibid., 15–16.

51 *NWAf*, 587 and fn. 24; Brandt, 11: Craven, V., 13–17.

52 *NWAf*, 581; *AAD*, 473; log, Co C, 1st Bn, 133rd Infantry Regt, IGSMM ("*A wave of flying dust*"); Miller, *Some Things*, 111 ("*a pea on plate*"); Anderson, *Opns. 135th Inf. Fondouk*; Bailey,

Through Hell, 90 ("*we continued*"); letter, Robert P. Miller to G. F. Howe, Jan. 14, 1951, NARA RG 319, Office of the Chief of Military History, box 229; Robert Moore, Oral History, Nov. 30, 1950, G. F. Howe, Sidney Mathews papers, MHI; R. Atkinson interview, Paul Calder, Nov. 8, 1999; Ankrum, *Dogfaces*, 238 ("*the mere raising*").

53 *NWAf*, 581; *AAD*, 473; letter, Robert P. Miller to G. F. Howe, Jan. 14, 1951, NARA RG 319, Office of the Chief of Military History, box 229; Craven, V., 10–19 ("*did little more*"); Robert Moore, Oral History, Nov. 30, 1950, G. F. Howe, Sidney Mathews papers, MHI.

54 Regimental History, 135IR (Musel), IGSMM PDF file gs_4102, 42–3 of 103.

55 Ibid.

56 Ibid.

57 Regimental History, 135IR (Musel), IGSMM PDF file gs_4102, 42–3 of 103; *NWAf*, 587–8.

58 *NWAf*, 587–8 and fn. 25: Info supplied by Cabinet Office, London.

59 Ibid., 588 and fn. 26: Issued as 9 Corps Operation Order 3, at 2050, 8 April 1943, supplied by Cabinet Office, London.

60 Ibid., 589 and fn. 30: *Gefechtsbericht, 3rd Co* to *334th Reconnaissance Battalion* for 9 and 10 Apr 43, dtd 11 Apr 43, and *Gefechtsbericht, 334th Reconnaissance Battalion* to *Kampfgruppe Fullriede*, 11 Apr 43, in *Fifth Panzer Army KTB mit Anlagen vom 11.IV.-21.IV.43.*

61 Ibid., 590.

62 Craven, V., 16.

63 Ibid, 16–17.

64 Ibid., 17–19.

65 Ibid., 19.

66 Craven, V., 19–20.

67 Ibid.

68 *135IR History (Rudolf)*, Landings at Oran, 9 [The Second Fondouk]; Regimental History, 135IR (Musel), IGSMM PDF file gs_4102, 42–3 of 103.

69 Private Robert Booker was from Callaway, Custer County, Nebraska and served with Company B, 1st Battalion, 133rd Infantry Regiment, 34th Infantry Division. Booker's CMOH citation reads: "For conspicuous gallantry and intrepidity at the risk of life above and beyond the call of duty in action. On 9 April 1943 in the vicinity of Fondouk, Tunisia, Pvt. Booker, while engaged in action against the enemy, carried a light machine gun and a box of ammunition over 200 yards of open ground. He continued to advance despite the fact that two enemy machine guns and several mortars were using him as an individual target. Although enemy artillery also began to register on him, upon reaching his objective he immediately commenced firing. After being wounded he silenced one enemy machine gun and was beginning to fire at the other when he received a second mortal wound. With his last remaining strength he encouraged the members of his squad and directed their fire. Pvt. Booker acted without regard for his own safety. His initiative and courage against insurmountable odds are an example of the highest standard of self-sacrifice and fidelity to duty." See https://valor.militarytimes.com/hero/2730. Sadly, Robert's brother Glenn I. Booker was killed in action on Saipan a year later, two months after the posthumous award of the Medal of Honor to Robert.

70 *AAD*, 474–5; RA RG 407, e 427, box 9549; letter, Donald C. Landon to G. F. Howe, Jan. 17, 1951, NARA RG 319, Office of the Chief of Military History, box 228; Richard F. Wilkinson, typescript, n.d., in After Action Report, Co C, 1st Bn, 133rd Inf Regt., IGSMM ("*brew tea*").

71 *NWAf*, 588, fn. 27.

72 Ibid., and fn. 28: (1) See *NWAf*, 587, n. 24 cited at endnote 903 above; (2) Msgs in 168th Inf Miscellaneous File, April 1943. (3) Letter, Col Landon to G. Howe, 17 Jan. 1951.

73 Craven, V., 20–2.

74 *NWAf*, 588.

75 *AAD*, 474; After Action Report, letter, 1st Guards Brigade, Apr. 21, 1943, Public Record Office, Kew, England, War Office 175/186; L. F. Ellis, *Welsh Guards at War*. Aldershot: Gale and Polden, 1946, 114–21; Blaxland, 221.

76 *NWAf*, 588; *AAD*, 474.

77 *NWAf*, 588. and fn. 29: (1) Statement by Gen MacMillan, 4 Sep 50, OCMH. (2) Info supplied by Cabinet Office, London. (3) G. Howe interview with Col Ward, 30 Nov 50. (4) 34th Div G-3 Journal, 1430, 9 Apr 43. (5) *Fifth Panzer Army, KTB V*, 9 Apr 43.

78 Ibid., 590.

79 *AAD*, 474–5; Alexander, "The African Campaign," 877–9; French Blake, 17th/21st Lancers, 133 ("*we shall all*").

80 *AAD*, 474–5.

81 *NWAf*, 590.

82 *AAD*, 475; C. N. Barclay, *History of the 16th/5th The Queen's Royal Lancers*. Aldershot: Gale and Polden, 1963, 88–91; *Gefechtsbericht, 3rd Co [German], 334th Mobile Bn*, NARA RG 319, Office of the Chief of Military History, box 225; Anderson, *Opns. 135th Inf. Fondouk*; After Action Report, 16th/5th Lancers, Apr. 9–10, 1943, Public Records Office, Kew, England, U.K., War Office 175/291; Bailey, *Through Hell*, 96 ("*as smooth and white*").

83 *NWAf*, 589.

84 Ibid., 590, and fn. 30: 9 Corps Opn Order 4, 2252, 9 Apr 43, supplied by Cabinet Office, London.

85 Ibid.

86 Craven, V., 22–3.

87 *NWAf*, 589–90.

88 *Story of the 34th Infantry Division, Louisiana to Pisa* Book I, 16. Lt. Col. John Miller would distinguish himself in future battles in North Africa. He was later a technical advisor about the Army Ground Forces, 34th Inf. Div. for William Wellman's 1945 movie "The Story of GI Joe" based on the writings of Ernie Pyle and starring Burgess Meredith as the esteemed war reporter and Robert Mitchum as a veteran officer. Pyle also advised on the film; he was killed by Japanese fire on Ie Jima on April 18, 1945, after the film was completed.

89 See *NWAf*, 540–1.

90 *NWAf*, 590, and fn. 32: *Kriegstagebuch V, Fifth Panzer Army*, 1625, 9 Apr 43.

91 Ibid., and fn. 33: (1) See n. 447 (*NWAf*, 589, n. 30) above. (2) *Fifth Panzer Army, KTB V*, 10 Apr 43. (3) *Army Group Africa, KTB*, 10–11 Apr 43.

92 *NWAf*, 588–90; *AAD*, 475; *Kriegstagebuch V, Fifth Panzer Army*, Apr. 9, 1943, NARA RG 319, Office of the Chief of Military History, box 226; Playfair, *The Destruction of the Axis Forces in Africa*, 382; Philip Jordan, *Jordan's Tunis Diary*. London: Collins, 1943, 226.

93 Ibid., 588–90.

94 Ibid., 591, and fn. 36: (1) Info supplied by Cabinet Office, London. (2) Patton Diary, 10 Apr 43. (3) 168th Inf Hist, 11 Nov 42 – 15 May 43, 43.

95 *NWAf*, 591, fn. 35, item (3).

96 *NWAf*, 591–2; *AAD*, 476.

97 *AAD*, 476–7.

Chapter 29

1 *NWAf*, 590; *AAD*, 477.

2 *AAD*, 477–8; J. T. Crocker, Sept. 8, 1950, and memo, Gordon H. A. MacMillan, n.d. ("*all commanders*"), both in memo, H. B. Latham, Cabinet Office Historical Section, to G. F. Howe,

Sep. 25, 1950, NARA RG 319, Office of the Chief of Military History, box 229; Bull, Harold R., oral history, Sep. 21, 1950, Sidney Matthews papers, MHI; *Time*, Apr. 19, 1943, 28; Richard Wilson, "The Gallant Fight of the 34th Division," 1943, *Des Moines Register and Tribune*; Charles Wertebaker, account of Fondouk, *Time*, May 24, 1943; Bailey, *Through Hell*, 100; E. N. Harmon to H. G. Bull, Apr. 1943, Harmon Papers, U.S. Army Military Institute; Butcher diary, DDE Presidential Library, PP-pres, box 166, A 306, 307, 308, 313 ("*whale tracks*").

3   *NWAf*, 599, and fn. 1: Ltr, CinC, AF to CG 18 A Gp, 23 Mar 43. Copy in OPD Exec 8, Bk. 8, Tab 53.

4   Ibid., and fn. 2: Queries, CinC AF to CG 18 A Gp, in FRCOS to 18 A Gp, No. 1044, 2 Apr 43; Ltr, CinC AF to CofS, 29 Mar 43. Copies in OPD Exec 8, Bk. 8, Tab 53.

5   *Story of the 34th Infantry Division, Louisiana to Pisa* Book I, 16; *DDE*, 151; *NWAf*. 591, and fn. 35: G. Howe Interviews with Gens Ryder and Caffey, 21 Feb 1950.

6   *Story of the 34th Infantry Division, Louisiana to Pisa* Book I, 17.

7   Brandt, 10–11.

8   *135IR History (Breit)*, Phase IV, 5–6.

9   Craven, V., 23.

10   *NWAf.*, 599–600.

11   *AAD*, 481–2, citing: C. S. Sugden, 18 Army Group, to AFHQ G-3, Apr. 7, 1943, NARA, AFHQ micro, R-6-C ("*present low state*"); Morton Yarmon, "The Administrative and Logistical History of the ETO: IV, TORCH and the ETO," March 1946, Historical Division, U.S. Army Forces, ETO, U.S. Army Center for Military History, 8.31 AA v. 4, 97 ("*467,000 troops*"); G. S. Patton to Alexander, Apr. 11 and 12, 1943, G. S. Patton papers, Library of Congress, box 32; Omar N. Bradley and Clay Blair, *A General's Life*. New York: Simon & Schuster, 1983, 150 ("*take them*") (hereinafter cited as Bradley, *General's Life*).

12   *NWAf*, 599–600.

13   *AAD*, 481–2; G. S. Patton to Alexander, Apr. 11 and 12, 1943, G. S. Patton papers, Library of Congress, box 32; Bradley, *General's Life*, 150.

14   *135IR History (Breit)*, Phase IV, 6–8.

15   *AAD*, 478.

16   *NWAf*, 592.

17   *AAD*, 478–9; Curtiss, Mina ed. *Letters Home*. Boston: Little, Brown, 1944, 61 ("*We have found*").

Chapter 30

1   *NWAf*, 595.

2   Ibid., 592.

3   Ibid., 595, 597.

4   Ibid., 600–1, and fn. 4: First Army Opn Instruction 37, 19 Apr 43, copy in II Corps AAR, 15 May 43.

5   The order of battle for British First Army and U.S. II Corps was as follows:

U.S. II Corps
1st Armored Division (less 1st Armored Regiment)
1st Infantry Division
9th Infantry Division
34th Infantry Division (less 2nd Battalion, 133rd Infantry)
Corps Franc d'Afrique (three battalions)

British V Corps
1st Infantry Division
4th Infantry Division
78th Infantry Division
25th Tank Brigade (less 51st Royal Tank Regiment)
British IX Corps
1st Armoured Division
6th Armoured Division
46th Infantry Division
51st Royal Tank Regiment

French XIX Corps
Moroccan Division
Algiers Division
Oran Division
Tank Battalion (Valentines and Renault Somuas)
18th King's Dragoon Guards.

6 Ibid., 603.
7 Ibid., 604
8 *AAD*, 480–1.
9 Carl Sandburg, *Abraham Lincoln: The Prairie Years, and The War Years*. One Volume Edition. New York: Harcourt, Brace & World, 1954, 668.
10 Pyle, *Here is Your War*, 247 ("*dead weary*").
11 *AAD*, 480–1, citing "Operations of II Corps, Northern Tunisia, 23 Apr. – 9 May," NARA RG 407, E 427, box 3113; letter, Raymond Dreyer, May 18, 1943, in *Fenton* (Iowa) *Reporter*, July 1, 1943, Mina Curtiss Collection, Yale University Library, Archives and Manuscripts; Meyer, "Strategy and Logistical History: Mediterranean Theater of Operations," n.d., vol. I, U.S. Army Center for Military History, X-16; Chester B. Hansen diary, April 1943, CMH; *To Bizerte With II Corps: 23 April – 13 May 1943*, first printed by the Historical Division, War Department, for the American Forces in Action series, 1943, reprinted by the U.S. Army Center for Military History, CMH Publ. 100–6, 1989, 4–9 (hereinafter cited as CMH, *To Bizerte*) ("*To Béja*"); Playfair, *The Destruction of the Axis Forces in Africa*, 398; Alexander memo, Apr. 21, 1943, NARA AFHQ micro, R-6-C.
12 *NWAf*, 604.
13 See *NWAf*, 605, Map 20.
14 *NWAf*, 604–5.
15 Ibid., 607, and fn. 17: 34th Div FO 34, 1700, 20 Apr 43, and Annex A (March table).
16 *135IR History (Breit)*, Phase IV, 8.
17 *Story of the 34th Infantry Division, Louisiana to Pisa* Book I, 17.
18 *NWAf*, 608, and fn. 20: (1) II Corps AAR, 15 May 43. (2) Msg, 18 Army Group to FREEDOM, 19 Apr 43. AFHQ CofS Cable Log. (3) Col. William B. Kean relieved General Hugh Gaffey as chief of staff, and Col. Robert A. Hewitt resumed his functions as G-3 as Colonel Lambert took command of Combat Command A, 1st Armored Division, in place of General McQuillin; see "BEJA. (TUNISIE) DURANT LA DEUXIEME GUERRE MONDIALE" https://archive.org/stream/Beja.tunisieDurantLaDeuxiemeGuerreMondiale/guerre_djvu.txt.
19 *NWAf*, 608, and fn. 21: (1) II Corps G-3 Journal, 19–20 Apr. 1943. (2) Bradley, *A Soldier's Story*, 75.

20 *AAD*, 482–6; George S. Patton, *War As I Knew It*. Boston: Houghton Mifflin, 1995, introduction by R. Atkinson, xi (*"fighting general"*); Martin Blumenson, ed. *The Patton Papers, 1940–1945*. New York: Da Capo Press, 1996, 221; Bradley, *General's Life*, 25, 35, 50, 58, 159; A. J. Liebling, *Mollie & Other Pieces*. New York: Schocken, 1989, 89 (*"least dressed up"*; *"with map unfurled"*); Bradley, *Soldier's Story*, 29; Fletcher Pratt, *Eleven Generals: Studies in American Command*. New York: William Sloane, 1949, 300, 314; D. D. Eisenhower to Bradley, Apr. 16, 1943.

21 *AAD*, 486; Eisenhower Papers, 1093; Bradley, *A General's Life*, 155; Ralph Martin, *The G.I. War, 1941–1945*. Boston: Little, Brown, 1967, 57 (*"hunting wild goats"*); Chester B. Hansen, diary, April 1943, MHI, 5/60A (*"djebel hopping"*); "Operations of II Corps, Northern Tunisia, 23 Apr.–9 May," NARA RG 407, E 427, box 3113.

22 *NWAf*, 613.

23 Ibid., 614.

24 Ibid., 613–14, 627.

25 Ibid., 614.

26 Ibid., 609.

27 Ibid.

28 Ibid., 609–10, and fn. 2: 2 (1) *Gefechtsbericht der Division Hermann Goering fuer die Zeit v.16. IV.-l. V.43, 1. Teil*, dated 5 May 43 in Folder CRS No. 77513/4. (2) Daily Rpt, *Army Group Africa, Ic* to *OB SÜD*, 21 Apr 43, in *OBS/Fuehr Abt Ie, Heeresgruppe Afrika*, 43 (cited hereafter as *Army Group Africa, Rpts*). (3) Morning Rpt, 22 Apr 43, ibid. (4) Noon Rpt, *OB SÜD* to *OKH/GenStdH/ Op Abt*, 21 Apr 43, and G-2 Rpt, *Comando Supremo* to *OKH/GenStdH/Op Abt*, 21 Apr 43, both in *OKH/GenStdH/Op Abt, Meldungen des Ob Süd v. 1.111.30.1V,43, Band 11*.

29 Ibid., 610–11, and fn. 5: Djebel Bou Keurnine (396), about three miles east-northeast of Sebkret el Kourzia, was named "Camelback Mountain" for its characteristic silhouette. (1) Second Intermediate and Daily Rpt, *Army Group Africa* to *OKH/GenStdH/Op Abt*, 24 Apr 43, in *Army Group Africa*, sitreps (2) MS # T-3 (Nehring *et al.*) Vol. 3a.

30 Ibid., 613; *AAD*, 499; Butcher, 292 (*"3,500 casualties"*).

31 Ibid., 611, and fn. 6: Rpt, *Army Group Africa, Ic*, to *OB SÜD*, 26 Apr 43, in *OKH/GenStH/Op Abt, Meldungen des Ob Süd v. 1.III.-30.IV.43, Band II*; and fn. 7: Daily Rpt, *Army Group Africa* to *OKH/GenStH/Op Abt*, 26 Apr 43, in *Army Group Africa*, Sitreps.

32 Ibid., and fn. 8: The *10th Panzer* and *15th Panzer Divisions* were down to approximately one half of one unit of consumption, limiting their operations to a radius of about thirty miles. The remaining armored units and the two armies were reduced to one quarter of a unit of consumption. At the prevailing rate of ammunition expenditure the army group estimated its ability to sustain operations as follows: for small arms, three days; for light artillery, five to six days; for medium artillery, three days; for heavy artillery, one to two days; and for anti-tank units, four days. Rations were sufficient for at least another week. Daily Rpts, *Army Group Africa* to *OKH/GenStdH/Op Abt*, 23–25 Apr 43, in *Army Group Africa*, Sitreps.

Chapter 31

1 *AAD*, 499.

2 *NWAf*, 626.

3 Frasher, 6–10.

4 *NWAf*, 620.

5 Tobin, *Ernie Pyle's War*, 95 (*"long slow line"*).

6 *NWAf*, 621–3; *AAD*, 500.

7 CMH, *To Bizerte*, 12.

8 *NWAf*, 622.

9 Ibid., 624–5.

10 Ibid., 624, and fn 31: 6th Armored Inf AAR, 2 Sep 43.

11 Maj Ross P. Frasher. "Operations of the 2nd Battalion, 168th Infantry, 34th Infantry Division, at Iill 473, Djebel El Hara, Northwest of Sidi Nsir, Tunisia, 26–28 April 1943" (Tunisia Campaign), Ms. The Infantry School, Fort Benning Ga. 1949–1950, 5–6. [Digital Collections, WWII Student Paper Collection, Donovan Research Library, Ft. Benning Ga.] http://www.benning.army.mil/library/content/Virtual/Donovanpapers/wwii/STUP2/FrasherRossP.%20MAJ.pdf (hereinafter cited as Frasher).

12 *NWAf*, 624, and fn. 30: (1) Msg, 2240, 23 Apr 43, Entry 77, in 1st Div G-3 Jnl. (2) 168th Inf FO 14, 24 Apr 43. (3) 1st Div G-3 Operations Report, 24 Apr 43. (4) Msg, 24 Apr 43, Entry 44, in II Corps G-3 Journal.

13 *Story of the 34th Infantry Division, Louisiana to Pisa* Book I, 17.

14 Ibid., 17–19.

15 *NWAf*, 621.

16 Frasher, 10; CMH, *To Bizerte*, 14.

17 *NWAf*, 625.

18 *NWAf*, 625, and fn. 33: (1) 1st Bn, 6th Armored Inf Diary, 1942–43. (2) 6th Armored Inf Hist, 21–11 May 43, 14 May 43. (3) 6th Armored Inf AAR, 2 Sep 43. (4) 1st Armored Div AAR, 2 May 43.

19 Frasher, 6–10.

20 Major General Ward was relieved of his command on April 1st by Patton; Major General Harmon assumed command of 1AD. *See AAD*, 451.

21 *NWAf*, 627, and fn. 39: For the Axis decision to pull back, see Daily Rpt, *Army Group Africa to OKH/GenStdH/Op Abt*, 24 Apr 43, in *Army Group Africa*, Sitreps.

22 Frasher, 6–10.

23 *NWAf*, 626–7, and fn. 38: (1) Msgs, 26 Apr 43, Entries 13, 14, 19, 22, 29, 47,49, and 50, and Overlay, Entries 52 and 53, in 1st Div G-3 Jnl. (2) 1st Div G-3 Opns Rpt, 27 Apr 43.

24 Bradley, *Soldier's Story*, 84.

25 Ibid., 85.

26 *Story of the 34th Infantry Division, Louisiana to Pisa* Book I, 19, 20; *135IR History (Breit)*, Phase IV, 9; *AAD*, 503–4.

27 *Story of the 34th Infantry Division, Louisiana to Pisa* Book I, 19, 20; *135IR History (Breit)*, Phase IV, 9; *AAD*, 503–4; Anderson, *Operations in North West Africa*; Alexander, *The African Campaign*, ("*the best German troops*").

28 *Story of the 34th Infantry Division, Louisiana to Pisa* Book I, 19.

29 *NWAf*, 628, and fn. 1: (1) 168th Inf Hist, 1943. (2) 168th Inf FO 15, 26 Apr 43. (3) Maj Ross P. Thrasher (*sic*, should read Frasher), Operations of the 2nd Battalion, 168th Infantry, at Hill 473 (Djebel el Hara), 26–28 Apr 43, MS. The Infantry School, Fort Benning, GA, 1949–50.

30 Ibid.

31 Bradley, *Soldier's Story*, 85.

32 *AAD*, 506; Benjamin Caffey, Oral history, Sidney Matthews papers, MHI; letter, Robert P. Miller to G. F. Howe, Jan. 14., 1951, NARA RG 319, Office of the Chief of Military History, box 225.

33 Bradley, *Soldier's Story*, 85 ("*Get me that hill*").

34 *NWAf*, 628–9 and fn. 3: (1) Geog Sec Gen Staff Map 4225 (Tunisia), 1: 50,000, Sheets 11, 12. (2) Aerial and ground photos by Lt Col John C. Hatlem (USAF). OCMH. (emphasis supplied)

35 Ibid., 630, and fn. 4: (1) Report of Activity of 1st Battalion, 135th Infantry, Vicinity of Hill 531, dated 10 May 43, in 3rd Bn 16th Inf AAR. (2) Ltr, Col Robert P. Miller to G. Howe, 14 Jan 1951, with incls. (3) Ltr, Brig Gen George A. Taylor (Ret.) to G. Howe, 22 Nov and 20 Dec 1950. (4) Ltr, Col Landon to G. Howe, 27 Jan 51.

36 A Partial History of 135IR (Rudolf), 9–12 [Hill 609]; *135IR History (Breit)*, Phase IV, 9–15; Regimental History, 135IR (Musel), IGSMM PDF file gs_4102, 43–4 of 103 [Vicinity of Hill 609].

37 *NWAf*, 631, and fn. 5: (1) G. Howe Interview with Col Ward, 30 Nov 50. (2) Ltr, Col Miller to G. Howe 14 Jan 51, with incls. (3) G. Howe Interview with Gen Caffey, 21 Feb 50. (4) 34th Div FO 35, 26 Apr 43, and FO 36, 27 Apr 43.

38 Bradley, *A Soldier's Story*, 85.

39 Brandt, 12–13.

40 Brandt, 13–14.

41 Brandt, 14.

42 *AAD*, 506; Brandt. 14–16; Charles Ryder, Oral history, Sidney Matthews papers, MHI.

43 Brandt, 16.

44 *NWAf*, 628, fn. 2.

45 *AAD*, 506; Berens, *Citizen Soldier*, 62; Bailey, *Through Hell*, 106; Green, *Brickbats*, 120–4 ("*For the love of heaven*" and "*crouched gray shapes*"); Pyle, *Here is Your War*, 254 ("*rocks wrapped*"); Bolstad, *Dear Folks*, 140 ("*we lay there waiting dawn*").

Chapter 32

1 A Partial History of 135IR (Rudolf), 9–12 [Hill 609]; *135IR History (Breit)*, Phase IV, 9–15; Regimental History, 135IR (Musel), IGSMM PDF file gs_4102, 43–4 of 103 [Vicinity of Hill 609].

2 A Partial History of 135IR (Rudolf), 9–12 [Hill 609]; *135IR History (Breit)*, Phase IV, 9–15; Regimental History, 135IR (Musel), IGSMM PDF file gs_4102, 43–4 of 103 [Vicinity of Hill 609].

3 Brandt, 14–15.

4 A Partial History of 135IR (Rudolf), 9–12 [Hill 609]; *135IR History (Breit)*, Phase IV, 11–12; Regimental History, 135IR (Musel), IGSMM PDF file gs_4102, 43–4 of 103 [Vicinity of Hill 609].

5 *NWAf*, 631–2.

6 Regimental History, 135IR (Musel), IGSMM PDF file gs_4102, 43–4 of 103 [Vicinity of Hill 609]; *135IR History (Breit)*, Phase IV, 12.

7 *NWAf*, 626.

8 Frasher, 10.

9 Ibid., 10–11.

10 Ibid., 11–12.

11 Ibid., 12–14.

12 Ibid., 15–16.

13 Ibid., 16–17.

14 Ibid., 17–18.

15 Ibid., 18–19.

16 Ibid., 19–20.

17 Ibid., 20–1.

18 Ibid., 21–2.

19 CMH, *To Bizerte*, 18.

20 Ibid., 22–3.

21 Regimental History, 135IR (Musel), IGSMM PDF file gs_4102, 44 of 103 [Vicinity of Hill 609]; A Partial History of 135IR (Rudolf), 9–12 [Hill 609].

22 Brandt, 15.

23 *AAD*, 504; Bradley, *Soldier's Story*, 86–7; Bradley, *General's Life*, 157 ("*in over his head*"); CMH, *To Bizerte*, 16; Chester B. Hansen Diary, May 1, 1943, MHI; "G-3 Report, Tunis Operations," 1st ID, Apr. 28–30, 1943, NARA RG 407, E 427, box 5759.

24 Bradley, *Soldier's Story*, 86.

25 *NWAf*, 631–2.

26 Frasher, 22–3.

27 A Partial History of 135IR (Rudolf), 9–12 [Hill 609]; see https://valor.militarytimes.com/hero/22170 and https://valor.defense.gov/Portals/24/Documents/ServiceCross/ArmyDSC-WWII.pdf, 57.

28 *135IR History (Breit)*, Phase IV, 13.

29 Regimental History, 135IR (Musel), IGSMM PDF file gs_4102, 44 of 103 [Vicinity of Hill 609]; A Partial History of 135IR (Rudolf), 9–12 [Hill 609].

30 *135IR History (Breit)*, Phase IV, 12–13; Regimental History, 135IR (Musel), IGSMM PDF file gs_4102, 44 of 103 [Vicinity of Hill 609].

31 *AAD*, 506–7; *NWAf*, 631–2.

32 *NWAf*, 631; *AAD*, 506–7; CMH, *To Bizerte*, 18–21; "Operations Following the Battle of Fondouk," 1st Bn, 133rd Inf Regt, Apr. 30, 1943, IGSMM; Ankrum, *Dogfaces*, 22–34; Mickey C. Smith and Dennis Worthen, "Soldiers on the Production Line," *Pharmacy in History*, 1995, 183.

33 *NWAf*, 631–2, and fn. 5: (1) G. Howe Interview with Col Ward, 30 Nov 50. (2) Ltr, Col Miller to G. Howe 14 Jan 51, with incls. (3) G. Howe Interview with Gen Benjamin F. Caffey, 21 Feb 50. (4) 34th Div FO 35, 26 Apr 43, and FO 36, 27 Apr 43.

34 Ibid., 632, and fn. 8: Msgs, 28 Apr 43, Entries 13, 14, and 83, in 1st Div G-3 Jnl.

35 *AAD*, 507; T. Allen, "A Factual Summary of the Combat Operations of the 1st Infantry Division," 28, Terry de la Mesa Allen papers, MHI ("*unshirted hell*"); Curtis, Donald McB, *The Song of the Fighting First*. Self-published, 1988 ("*Hill 606*").

36 *NWAf*, 631–2 and fn.6: (1) Msg, Cpt Fanning (CO Co. C 135th Inf) to Bn Comdr, 1125, 28 Apr 43, Incl. 4 to Ltr, Col Miller to G. Howe, 14 Jan 51. (2) Ltr, Col Landon to G. Howe, 27 Jan 51. (3) Msgs, 0700, 28 Apr 43, Entries 11–13, and 0930, 28 Apr 43, Entry 23, in 1st Div G-3 Jnl.

37 *NWAf*, 632, and fn. 7: (1) See II Corps plans as arranged between General Bradley and Generals Allen and Ryder, and recorded next morning in Entry 231, 28 Apr 43, in II Corps G-3 Jnl. (2) Bradley, *A Soldier's Story*, 85–7.

38 Brandt, 16–17.

39 *NWAf*, 633 and fn 9: 135th Inf Hist, Sec. IV, Pts. e, f.; A Partial History of 135IR (Rudolf), 9–12 [Hill 609].

40 Brandt, 17.

41 *NWAf*, 633.

42 *AAD*, 507; Drew Middleton, *Our Share of Night*. New York: Viking, 1946, 275 ("*wheat at Gettysburg*"); "The Tunisian Campaign, 34th Div.," Dec. 1943, IGSMM; "Report of Action on Hill 609, 135th Inf Regt.," June 30, 1943, IGSMM; Leslie W. Bailey, "An Infantry Battalion in Attack," IGSMM.

43 *AAD*, 507.

44 A Partial History of 135IR (Rudolf), 9–12 [Hill 609]; Regimental History, 135IR (Musel), IGSMM PDF file gs_4102, 45 of 103 [Vicinity of Hill 609]; *135IR History (Breit)*, Phase IV, 15.

45 *AAD*, 507; "The Tunisian Campaign, 34th Div.," Dec. 1943, IGSMM; "Report of Action on Hill 609, 135th Inf Regt.," June 30, 1943, IGSMM; Leslie W. Bailey, "An Infantry Battalion in Attack," IGSMM; Robert Ward, Oral history, Nov. 30, 1950, G. F. Howe, Sidney Matthews papers, MHI; Franklyn A. Johnson, *One More Hill*. New York: Funk & Wagnalls, 1949, 65 ("*erupting volcano*"); Bolstad, *Dear Folks*, 138–40; Miller, *Some Things*, 123–4.

46 A Partial History of 135IR (Rudolf), 9–12 [Hill 609]; Regimental History, 135IR (Musel), IGSMM PDF file gs_4102, 45 of 103 [Vicinity of Hill 609]; *135IR History (Breit)*, Phase IV, 15.

47 *135IR History (Breit)*, Phase IV, 17–18; Regimental History, 135IR (Musel), IGSMM PDF file gs_4102, 45 of 103 [Vicinity of Hill 609].

48 *NWAf*, 633 and fn 10: (1) G. Howe interview with Col Ward, 30 Nov 50. (2) 135th Inf Hist, 18 Oct 42 – 15 May 43, 12–13. (3) Brandt, 17–18.

49 Ibid., and fn. 11: Half of the wounded (781) had been evacuated. Strength of II Corps remained 95, 194. II Corps Weekly Rpt, 30 Apr 43, copy in II Corps G-4 Journal.

50 Ibid., 634 and fn. 13: (1) Msgs, 29 Apr 43, Entries 30, 31, 36, and 41 in 1st Div G-3 Journal. (2) Letter, Maj John A. Lauten (then S-2, 16th Inf) to Gen Taylor, 28 Dec 50. Copy in Office of the Chief of Military History. (3) Army Croup Africa, Sitreps, 28–29 Apr 43.

51 Bradley, *A Soldier's Story*, 87.

52 *NWAf*, 634.

53 Bradley, *A Soldier's Story*, 154.

54 Ernie Pyle, *Brave Men*. New York: Henry Holt, 1944, 214.

55 *AAD*, 508–9; Maraist, Col. Robert V., and Hains, Col. Peter C. III, transcript, "Conference on North Africa Operations," Fort Knox, KY, 16 June 1943, Sidney Matthews papers, MHI ("*no one*").

56 Bradley, *A Soldier's Story*, 87.

57 *NWAf*, 634. and fn 14: (1) 34th Div FO 37, 2000, 29 Apr 43. (2) Memo, CPT Gwin for CO 3rd Bn 1st Armored Regt, 14 May 43, sub: Opns of Co I while attached to 34th Div near Sidi Nsir 30 Apr – 4 May 43, in 3rd Bn 1st Armored Regt AAR.

58 Ibid., 634–5, and fn. 15: Opns Overlay for CT 16 Attack, 29 Apr 43, Entry 41, in 1st Inf Div G-3 Jnl.

59 Brandt, 18; *AAD*, 508.

Chapter 33

1 Regimental History, 135IR (Musel), IGSMM PDF file gs_4102, 45 of 103 [Vicinity of Hill 609]; A Partial History of 135IR (Rudolf), 9–12 [Hill 609]; *NWAf*, 634–5.

2 *135IR History (Breit)*, Phase IV, 17–19.

3 *NWAf*, 635.

4 *Story of the 34th Infantry Division, Louisiana to Pisa* Book I, 20.

5 Bradley, *A Soldier's Story*, 87.

6 *AAD*, 509.

7 *NWAf*, 635.

8 *135IR History (Breit)*, Phase IV, 17–19.

9 A Partial History of 135IR (Rudolf), 9–12 [Hill 609]; *135IR History (Breit)*, Phase IV, 17–19.

10 Brandt, 19–20.

11 Ibid., 19.
12 Ibid., 20.
13 Ibid., 20–1.
14 *NWAf,* 635–6.
15 Brandt, 20–2.
16 Ibid., 22.
17 Ibid., 22–3.
18 Ibid., 23.
19 Ibid., 23–4.
20 Ibid., 24–5.
21 A Partial History of 135IR (Rudolf), 9–12 [Hill 609]; Regimental History, 135IR (Musel), IGSMM PDF file gs_4102, 45 of 103 [Vicinity of Hill 609].
22 Brandt, 25.
23 Ibid., 25.
24 *NWAf,* 635–6, and fn. 16: (1) Brandt, 18–22; (2) Ltr, Col Miller to G. Howe, 14 Jan 51, with incls. (3) 135th Inf Hist, Sec IV.
25 A Partial History of 135IR (Rudolf), 9–12 [Hill 609].
26 A Partial History of 135IR (Rudolf), 9–12 [Hill 609].
27 Brandt, 25–6.
28 *NWAf,* 635–6.
29 Ibid., 637, and fn. 19: (1) 135th Inf Hist, Sec. IV, 13. (2) 1st Bn133rd Inf AAR in 34th Div Opns Rpt, 11 Dec 42 – 15 July 43; see 135IR (Musel), IGSMM PDF file gs_4102, 45–6 of 103 [Vicinity of Hill 609].
30 *Story of the 34th Infantry Division, Louisiana to Pisa* Book I, 20–2.
31 *AAD,* 508–9.
32 *Story of the 34th Infantry Division, Louisiana to Pisa* Book I, 22; Regimental History, 135IR (Musel), IGSMM PDF file gs_4102, 45–6 of 103 [Vicinity of Hill 609].
33 Brandt, 26.
34 *NWAf,* 637–8, and fn. 20: (1) 168th Inf Hist, 1943, 46–7. (2) 135th Inf Hist, Sec. IV; A Partial History of 135IR (Rudolf), 9–12 [Hill 609].
35 *AAD,* 508–9; Ankrum, *Dogfaces,* 274 (*"God bless all of you"*); 276 (*"Tell my mother"*); B. A. Dickson, Oral history, Sidney Matthews papers, U.S. Army Military History; Bradley, *Soldier's Story,* 87; After Action Report, "Operations of this Company While on Detached Service," Co I, 1st Armored Regiment, May 14, 1943, possession of Roger Cirillo; After Action Report, "Operations Following the Battle of Fondouk," 1st Bn, 133rd Inf Regt, June 30, 1943, IGSMM; Hougen, 69–70; Larson, *Volunteers,* 84–6.
36 *Story of the 34th Infantry Division, Louisiana to Pisa* Book I, 22; Regimental History, 135IR (Musel), IGSMM PDF file gs_4102, 45–6 of 103 [Vicinity of Hill 609].
37 Ibid., 638.
38 *AAD,* 509; "Dennis Frederick Neal, Soldier," typescript, n.d., IGSMM, 68 (*"literally covered"*); "German Tanks Trapped," *Times* (London), May 5, 1943 (*"thick as currants in cake"*); Pyle, *Here is Your War,* 259 (*"Those who went"*).
39 *AAD,* 509–10; "The Tunisian Campaign, 34th Division," Dec. 1943, IGSMM; Marshall, Malcolm, *Proud Americans.* Self-published, 1994, 96 (*"shoes hanging"*); log, 16th Inf., Beja-Mateur Campaign," May 1, 1943 (*"no prisoners will be taken"*).
40 *AAD,* 509; log, "16th Inf., Beja-Mateur Campaign," May 1, 1943 (*"Jerries approach"* and *"A panorama"*); Robert R. Moore quoted in *Villisca* (Iowa) *Review,* n.d., Iowa GSMM (*"killed by such treachery"*); Robert R. Moore, "Tunisian Stand," typescript, Oct. 1943, NARA RG 319, Office

of the Chief of Military History, box 103; "The Tunisian Campaign, 34th Division," Dec. 1943, IGSMM; Brandt, 25–6; Ankrum, *Dogfaces*, 282; Bradley, *Soldier's Story*, 94 ("*few prisoners*").

41 *Story of the 34th Infantry Division, Louisiana to Pisa* Book I, 22.

42 *NWAf*, 641.

43 *NWAf*, 640–1; *AAD*, 510, citing "German Tanks Trapped," *Times* (London), May 5, 1943 ("*at our feet*"); Chester B. Hansen Diary, May 1, 1943, MHI; After Action Report, "Report of Operations, 23 Apr. – 9 May," 1st AD, NARA RG 407, E 427, box 14767; Charles J. Hoy, "The Last Days in Tunisia," *Cavalry Journal*, Jan. – Feb. 1944, 8; CMH, *To Bizerte*, 36.

44 *NWAf*, 639, and fn. 23 (1) 1st Div G-3 Jnl, 1 May 43. (2) 135th Inf Hist, Sec. IV, 14. (3) 6th Armored Inf Hist, 14 May 43; 6th Armored Inf AAR, 2 Sep 43. (4) 1st Armored Div AAR, 3 May 43.

45 Ibid., 641 and fn. 30: Msg, 0610, 3 May 43, Entry 9, 1st Inf Div, G-3 Jnl.

46 *Story of the 34th Infantry Division, Louisiana to Pisa* Book I, 22.

Chapter 34

1 Brandt, 26–7.

2 A Partial History of 135IR (Rudolf), 9–12 [Hill 609]; 135IR History (Breit)), Phase IV, 26–7; Regimental History, 135IR (Musel), IGSMM PDF file gs_4102, 46–7 of 103 [Vicinity of Hill 609].

3 Bradley, *A Soldier's Story*, 87.

4 *NWAf*, 652 and fn. 15: (1) 1st Armd Div AAR, 2 May 43. … (3) Casualties in II Corps in the week ending 6 May were: killed 112, wounded 870, missing 432, evacuated 798. Strength was 94,202. Prisoners taken were 1,344. Rpt, AG II Corps to 18 A Gp, 8 May 43, in II Corps G-4 Jnl.

5 Ibid., 652–3.

6 Ibid., 658.

7 Ibid., and fn. 27: 168th Inf Hist, 12 Nov 42 – 15 May 43, 47–54.

8 Ibid., 653, 658.

9 *NWAf*, 650, 653; *AAD*, 517–18; Col. Benjamin A. Dickson, "G-2 Journal," MHI, 64; After Action Report, "Operations of 18th Inf in Mateur Sector," n.d., includes 1st, 2nd and 3rd Bn reports, NARA RG 407, E 427, box 5937; "18th Regiment, Draft Regimental Wartime History," Stanhope Mason Collection, McCormick Research Center, First Division Museum, Cantigny, Illinois; Allen, "A Factual Summary of the Combat Operations of the 1st ID," Terry de la Mesa Allen Papers, U.S. Army Military Institute; "G-3 Report, Tunis Operation." 1st ID, May 5–6, 1943, NARA RG 407, E 427, box 5759; H. R. Knickerbocker *et al.*, *Danger Forward: The Story of the First Division in World War II*. Atlanta, GA: Albert Love Enterprises, 1947, 80.

10 *AAD*, 520–1; letter, C. P. Eastburn to OCMH, June 6, 1947, NARA RG 319, OCMH, box 103; *a dead city*: interrogation report, Anatole Cordonier, chief naval engineer, Bizerte, by 9th ID, May 7, 1943, NARA RG 407, E 427, box 7334; Pyle, *Here is Your War*, 281 ("*Bizerte was*"); Henry Gerard Phillips, *Sedjenane: The Pay-off Battle*. Penn Valley, CA, self-published, 1993, 133.

11 *NWAf*, 658–9.

12 Ibid., 661, and fn. 33: (1) 168th Inf Hist, 12 Nov 42 – 15 May 43, 54–5. (2) 133rd Inf Hist, 1943, IV, 14.

13 *NWAf*, 645–9; *AAD*, 513–15; Blaxland, 252; "Report of Participation of the Allied Air Force in the North Africa Campaign, Apr. 11 – May 14, 1943," n.d., NARA RG 319, 2-3.7 BA, box

103; Francis Tuker, *Approach to Battle*. London: Cassell, 1963, 367 (hereinafter cited as Tuker, *Approach to Battle*); Anderson, *Operations in North West Africa*; *Kriegstagebuch V, Fifth Panzer Army*, May 6, 1943, NARA RG 319, Office of the Chief of Military History, box 226.

14 *AAD*, 521–3; Dudley Clarke, *The Eleventh at War*. London: Michael Joseph, 1952, 299–300; Playfair, *The Destruction of the Axis Forces in Africa.*, 452.

15 *NWAf*, 661, and fn. 35: (1) *Army Group Africa*, Sitreps, 8 and 9 May 43. (2) [Foreign Military Studies] MS # D-001 (von Vaerst).

16 Ibid., 662, and fn. 36: *Army Group Africa*, Sitreps, 9 May 43.

17 *NWAf*, 662, and fn. 37: (1) Msg, 9 May 43, Entry 12, in II Corps G-3 Jnl. (2) II Corps AAR, 10 Sep 43. (3) *Fifth Panzer Army* was out of communication with *Army Group Africa*. Morning Report, 1015/8 May 43, in *Army Group Africa*, Sitreps; Bradley, *Soldier's Story*, 97.

18 *AAD*, 523; Harmon, 138; John A. Parris, Jr., and Ned Russell, with Leo Disher and Phil Ault, *Springboard to Berlin*. New York: Thomas Y. Crowell, 1943, 346 (hereinafter cited as Parris and Russell, *Springboard*); Pyle, *Here is Your War*, 277.

19 *NWAf*, 662, and fn. 38:(1) Msg, 9 May 43, Entry 24, in II Corps G-3 Jnl. (2) Msg 39, II Corps to FREEDOM, 9 May, AFHQ CofS Cable Log, 64. (3) Bradley, *Soldier's Story*, 97–9.

20 Bradley, *Soldier's Story*, 97.

21 *NWAf*, 662, and fn. 39: (1) Msg, 9 May 43, Entry 56, in II Corps G-3 Jnl. (2) II Corps AAR, 10 Sep 43. (3) Msg, FREEDOM to USFOR, 10 May 43, NAF 218. (4) 1st Armored Div AAR, 2 May 43.

22 *NWAf*, 662; *AAD*, 527; C. B. Hansen, draft of Omar N. Bradley's *A Soldier's Story*, U.S. Military Institute, 5/104.

23 A Partial History of 135IR (Rudolf), 9–12 [Hill 609]; 135IR History (Breit), Phase IV, 27; Regimental History, 135IR (Musel), IGSMM PDF file gs_4102, 47 of 103 [Vicinity of Hill 609].

24 *NWAf*, 661, and fn. 32: (1) 1st Armored Div AAR, 2 May 43. (2) 1st Armored Regt AAR, 10 Jul 43. (3) 3rd Bn 13th Armored Regt Hist, 1942–43.

25 Ibid., and fn. 34: Msg, 10 May 43, Entry 78, in II Corps G-3 Jnl.

26 A Partial History of 135IR (Rudolf), 9–12 [Hill 609]; *135IR History (Breit)*, Phase IV, 27.

Chapter 35

1 *NWAf*, 662; *AAD*, 527; John Mayo, Oral history, Army Service Experience Questionnaire, 1987, 1st AR, U.S. Army Military Institute; film, "At the Front in North Africa with the U.S. Army," Dec. 1942, NARA RG 111, Office of the Chief Signal Officer, #1001; Pyle, *Here is Your War*, 273 (*"Germans were everywhere"*); letter, Raymond Dreyer, *Fenton* (Iowa) *Reporter*, Nov. 4, 1943, Mina Curtiss Collection, Yale University Library, Manuscripts and Archives; D. D. Eisenhower to G. C. Marshall, May 5, 1943, Eisenhower Papers, 1114 (*"the Axis cannot"*), 1146n; memos, MTOUSA, May 1943, NARA RG 492, Records of the Office of the Commanding General, box 56; memo, B. M. Strawbridge to W. B. Smith, July 1943, MTOUSA, NARA RG 492, Office of the Commanding General, box 332; Playfair, *The Destruction of the Axis Forces in Africa*, 445–6; Hansen, C. B., draft of Omar N. Bradley's *A Soldier's Story*, U.S. Military Institute, 5/104.

2 *AAD*, 527–8; Playfair, *The Destruction of the Axis Forces in Africa*, 624–5 (Kindle ed.); Parris and Russell, *Springboard*, 357.

3 *AAD*, 528–9; von Arnim, Hans J. T., "Recollections of Tunisia." Transl., Janet E. Dewey, 1951. U.S. Army European Command. Foreign Military Studies, C-098, 113–15; Playfair, *The Destruction of the Axis Forces in Africa*, 623–4 (Kindle ed.); Tuker, *Approach to Battle*, 374–8; DDE, 157.

4 Rt. Hon. Sir Winston S. Churchill, *The Second World War*. Vol. IV: *The Hinge of Fate*. Boston: Houghton Mifflin, 1950, 780 (hereinafter cited as Churchill, *The Hinge of Fate*); *AAD*, 529.

5 *AAD*, 523; CMH, *To Bizerte With II Corps*, 51–2; "Operations of II Corps, Northern Tunisia, 23 Apr. – 9 may, 1943," NARA RG 407, E 427, box 3113; Bradley, *General's Life*, 159.

6 *NWAf*, 675; *AAD*, 536; Playfair, *Destruction of the Axis Forces in Africa*, 460.

7 *AAD*, 537; Blaxland, 265; Messenger, *The Tunisian Campaign*, 120; Playfair, *Destruction of the Axis Forces in Africa*, 460; Von Arnim, Hans J. T. "Recollections of Tunisia." Transl. Janet E. Dewey. U.S. Army European Command, Foreign Military Studies, C-098, MHI, 115; Siegfried Westphal, *The German Army in the West*. London: Cassell, 1951, 124; Volkmar Kuhn, *German Paratroops in World War II*. Transl. H. A. and A. J. Barker. London: Ian Allan, 1978, 179; Roger Parkinson, *A Day's March Nearer Home*. New York: David McKay, 1974, 104.

8 *AAD*, 530–1; Signal Corps footage, NARA film, ADC-1113 and ADC-2407; Bailey, *Through Hell*, 119; letter, Joe Farley, n.d., Mina Curtiss Collection, Yale University Library, Archives and Manuscripts (*"too damned hot"*); Butcher, 312; Moorehead, *The End in Africa*, 65; Hougen, 74–5; diary, George S. Patton, Library of Congress, box 2, folder 13 (*"lack of pride"*); Harmon, *Combat Commander*, 141; Davies, *To the Last Man*, 110–11.

9 Bradley, *Soldier's Story*, 100.

10 Ibid., 87.

11 Churchill, *The Hinge of Fate*, 780.

12 *AAD*, 537; Doubler, *Closing With the Enemy*, 13; Norman Gelb, *Desperate Venture*. New York: William Morrow, 1992, 320 (hereinafter cited as Gelb, *Desperate Venture*); "The Administrative and Logistical History of the ETO," Vol. 4, March 1946, Historical Division, U.S. Army Forces, ETO, U.S. Army Center for Military History, 124 (*"high grade stock"*).

13 *AAD*, 538–9; Gelb, *Desperate Venture*, 319, 320 (*"walking around"*); Bryant, *Turn of the Tide*, 419; Walter Warlimont. "High Level Decisions—Tunisian Campaign." Transl. Janet E. Dewey, 1951. U.S. Army European Command. Foreign Military Studies, C 092a, 277–8; Churchill, *The Hinge of Fate*, 778, 779; "An Interview with General Field Marshal Albert Kesselring," May 1946, *World War II German Military Studies*, vol. 3, ETHIN 72, MHI (*"It was in Tunisia"*); Albert Kesselring, *The Memoirs of Field-Marshal Kesselring*. London: Greenhill, 1997, 157; Michael Howard, *Grand Strategy*. Vol. IV, August 1942 – September 1943. London: Her Majesty's Stationery Office, 1972, 337, 338 (*"milk and rice"*), 355.

14 *AAD*, 537–8; Truscott, 192; Eric Larrabee, *Commander in Chief*. New York: Touchstone, 1987, 436 (*"a place to be lousy"*); Richard Wilson, "The Gallant Fight of the 34th Division in the North African Campaign," 1943, *Des Moines Register and Tribune*, IGSMM (*"There are three things"*); Drew Middleton, "We'll Take 'Em Apart and Then Get Home," *New York Times Magazine*, July 1943, 8 (*"grudge fight"*).

15 Stewart, Red Bull Division Training, 8.

16 *AAD*, 534–5; Miller, *Some Things*, 126; "History of the 168th Infantry," IGSMM; Fussell, *Wartime*, 139 (*"When you figure"*); letter, Joe Spring, *PM*, n.d., in Mina Curtiss Collection, Yale University Library, Archives and Manuscripts (*"Dame Rumor"*); Lee B. Kennett, *G.I.: The American Soldier in World War II*. New York: Scribner's, 1987, 136–7; "Dennis Frederick Neal, Soldier," typescript, n.d., Iowa GSMM, 68 (*"There are many rumors"* and *"Ol' General Ryder's"*).

17 *AAD*, 538–9; letter, Stephen Dinning, *Des Moines Register and Tribune*, March 21, 1943, Mina Curtiss Collection, Yale University Library, Manuscripts and Archives (*"There's nothing over here"*); letter, n.d., submitted by James D. Buckley, Mina Curtiss Collection, Yale University Library, Manuscripts and Archives (*"we didn't know"*); letter, Ray Salisbury to sister, July 6, 1943, in Annette Tapert, ed., *Lines of Battle*. New York: Times Books, 1987; letter, anonymous, Apr. 1943, *Minneapolis Tribune*, Mina Curtiss Collection, Yale University Library, Manuscripts and Archives (*"We all feel"*).

18 *AAD*, 540–1; Fraser, *Alanbrooke*, 336; Roger Barry Fosdick, "A Call to Arms: The American Enlisted Soldier in World War II," Ph.D. diss., 1985, Claremont Graduate School, 22 ("*war is a burden*"); Peter R. Mansoor, *The GI Offensive in* Europe. Lawrence, KS: University Press of Kansas, 1999, 85; Craven, W., *Torch to Pointblank*, 50.

19 Cable, Prime Minister to General Eisenhower (Algiers), May 14th, 1943, in Churchill, *The Hinge of Fate*, 777–8.

Appendix B

1 The following discussion is based on Virgil Ney, "Evolution of the U.S. Army Division 1939–1968." Typescript, Technical Operations, Inc., Fort Belvoir, VA, 1969 (hereinafter cited as Ney, *Evolution*).

2 Ibid., citing F. Weigley, *History of the United States Army*. The Macmillan Company, New York, 1967, 461.

3 Ibid., citing F. Weigley, *History of the United States Army*. The Macmillan Company, New York, 1967, 461–2.

4 See Kent Roberts Greenfield *et al.*, *The United States Army in World War II: Organization of Ground Combat Troops*. Washington, D.C. United States Army Center for Military History, 1987, 11–12, 54, 271–80, 283–4, 291, 322 (hereinafter cited as *Ground Combat Troops*).

5 Ibid., citing L. Naisawald, *The US Infantry Division, Changing Concepts in Organization 1900–1939*, The John Hopkins University, Operations Research Office, ORO-S-239, Silver Spring, Maryland, 7 March 1952, 35–6.

6 Ibid., 37–8, citing Bruce Jacobs, *Soldiers – The Fighting Divisions of the Regular Army*. New York: W. W. Norton and Company, Inc., 1958.

7 Ibid., 38, citing *Army Lineage Book, Vol II, Infantry*. United States Department of the Army, Office of the Chief of Military History, Washington, D.C. 1953, 47–8.

Glossary

1 *Ground Combat Troops*, 302.

Index